# Epistemology of Language

# Epistemology of Language

*Edited by*

ALEX BARBER

OXFORD
UNIVERSITY PRESS

# OXFORD
## UNIVERSITY PRESS

Great Clarendon Street, Oxford OX2 6DP

Oxford University Press is a department of the University of Oxford.
It furthers the University's objective of excellence in research, scholarship,
and education by publishing worldwide in

Oxford New York

Auckland Bangkok Buenos Aires Cape Town Chennai
Dar es Salaam Delhi Hong Kong Istanbul Karachi Kolkata
Kuala Lumpur Madrid Melbourne Mexico City Mumbai Nairobi
São Paulo Shanghai Taipei Tokyo Toronto

Oxford is a registered trade mark of Oxford University Press
in the UK and in certain other countries

Published in the United States
by Oxford University Press Inc., New York

British Library Cataloguing in Publication Data
Data available

Library of Congress Cataloging in Publication Data
Data available

ISBN 0-19-925057-x
ISBN 0-19-925058-8 (Pbk.)

10 9 8 7 6 5 4 3 2 1

Printed in Great Britain
on acid-free paper by
T. J. International Ltd., Padstow, Cornwall

# Acknowledgements

Many of the contributions to this collection developed out of papers presented to a conference hosted by the Department of Philosophy at the University of Sheffield, 10–13 July 2000. Without a Major Conference Award from the Arts and Humanities Research Board, as well as grants from the Mind Association and the Analysis Trust, that conference would not have been possible. The Sheffield Department of Philosophy itself provided welcome administrative support as well as further funding. Thanks are also due to other participants at that conference, and in particular to commentators, for their roles in the transformations many of the talks have since undergone. Peter Momtchiloff, Philosophy Editor at Oxford University Press, has provided invaluable advice and support as the collection has taken shape.

A.B.

*London, January 2003*

# Contents

## Part Three: Linguistic Externalism

## Part Four: Epistemology through Language

# Contributors

**Professor Louise M. Antony,** Department of Philosophy, Ohio State University, Ohio, USA.

**Dr Alex Barber,** Department of Philosophy, The Open University, UK.

**Dr Jessica Brown,** Department of Philosophy, University of Bristol, UK.

**Professor Michael Devitt,** Philosophy Program, The Graduate Center, City University of New York, New York, USA.

**Professor Reinaldo Elugardo,** Department of Philosophy, University of Oklahoma, Oklahoma, USA.

**Dr Elizabeth Fricker,** Magdalen College, University of Oxford, UK.

**Professor James Higginbotham,** School of Philosophy, University of Southern California, California, USA.

**Dr Stephen Laurence,** Department of Philosophy, University of Sheffield, UK.

**Professor Peter Ludlow,** Department of Linguistics and Department of Philosophy, University of Michigan, Ann Arbor, Michigan, USA.

**Professor Robert J. Matthews,** Department of Philosophy, Rutgers University, New Brunswick, New Jersey, USA.

**Dr Alexander Miller,** Department of Philosophy, Macquarie University, Sydney, Australia.

**Professor Paul M. Pietroski,** Department of Linguistics and Department of Philosophy, University of Maryland at College Park, Maryland, USA.

**Professor Georges Rey,** Department of Philosophy, University of Maryland at College Park, Maryland, USA.

**Professor Stephen Schiffer,** Department of Philosophy, New York University, New York, USA.

**Professor Gabriel Segal,** Department of Philosophy, King's College London, UK.

**Professor Robert J. Stainton,** Department of Philosophy, Carleton University, Ottawa, Canada

# CHAPTER I

# Introduction

*Alex Barber*

Because it has no established usage, the phrase 'epistemology of language' can suggest any of a number of different agendas. But speaking broadly, there seem to be two levels at which epistemology bears on language.

First there is what might be called 'the discipline level'. We need to make decisions on how to investigate the phenomena of language. How to describe these phenomena? What questions are worth asking of them? What avenues of enquiry are most likely to bear fruit? What methodologies are best suited to these investigations, now or in the foreseeable future? These are epistemological decisions in roughly the sense that any decisions in the philosophy of science are epistemological, the scientific discipline in this case being linguistics.[1]

Second there is what might be called 'the language-user level'. We are speakers and understanders of language ourselves, able to communicate, to be expressive, and to reason using language. An interest in how such achievements are humanly possible is epistemological in the same sense that an interest in, say, our capacity to come to know facts about the physical objects around us through perception is epistemological.

Epistemology of language is characterized by epistemic concerns that recur across a broad range of areas other than language. Through reflection on these concerns in a specifically linguistic context we can hope to learn as much about knowledge as about language. At the language-user

Thanks to Jonathan Knowles, Ben Shaer, and individual authors, particularly Rob Stainton, for valuable comments on earlier drafts of this introduction. Responsibility for any errors remains my own.

[1] Whether a scientific approach to language is appropriate is itself a question many would wish to pitch at the discipline level. I shall speak indiscriminately of the philosophy of language and linguistics except where it is obvious from the context that I am talking of distinct traditions.

level this is borne out—to take just one example—by changes in thinking about unconscious and innate knowledge, changes that have sprung from work that has had linguistic knowledge at its heart. And these changes at the language-user level have taken place only because of parallel developments at the discipline level: attributions of innate knowledge of language are called for only if one accepts the poverty-of-the-stimulus methodology that is standardly used to motivate them.[2] More generally, those contributions to the philosophy of science that have come with the progress of the cognitive sciences, including linguistics as a paradigm case, bear witness to ongoing interaction between language and epistemology at the discipline level. Another example of such interaction is also a pressing methodological consideration: do appeals to intuitions, and the associated method of thought experimentation (e.g. concerning reference and meaning), have a place alongside more orthodox experimental methods, and if so what place is that?

The sixteen contributors to this volume engage with a variety of quesitons, posed at both levels. Some have chosen to work towards settling disagreements that have been in place for decades or more, disagreements that are as critical now as they have ever been. Others take the epistemology of language into newer areas that are likely to define the field in years to come. Each chapter can be read and understood in isolation, but in this introduction I outline the authors' ambitions and the context in which their contributions are made. I have divided the papers into four sections: 'Knowledge in Linguistics'; 'Understanding'; 'Linguistic Externalism'; and 'Epistemology through Language'.

## 1 Knowledge in Linguistics

The two levels of epistemology of language just distinguished are welded together in the claims, associated with the work of Noam Chomsky and others,[3] that:

---

[2] Laurence and Margolis (2001) provide an opinionated survey of debates over poverty-of-the-stimulus argumentation. I return to the topic of unconscious knowledge below in connection with Searle (1990).

[3] See e.g. Chomsky (1986), 4.3 for (i) and ch. 1 for (ii). Chomsky's most developed statement and discussion of the ground and implications of these two claims—including cer-

(i) ordinary language users possess structures of knowledge, reasonably so called, of a complex system of rules or principles of language,

and that

(ii) the core part of a scientific ('naturalistic') approach to the study of language should consist of an attempt to render this knowledge explicit.

The proposal is not that ordinary speakers are like professional linguists in the manner in which they *arrive at* or *deploy* this knowledge. But linguistic theories, on this conception of linguistics, are nevertheless to be understood as the explicit statement of certain aspects of the *content* of knowledge states possessed by ordinary speakers. The papers in Part One are all concerned with this conceptualist understanding of linguistics, as it has come to be known.[4] Debate over conceptualism in this sense has turned on what kind of knowledge linguistic knowledge is, if indeed it is any kind of knowledge, and on what goals might be proper to linguistics other than or in addition to that of rendering explicit the content of states of linguistic knowledge.

Conceptualism often serves as the default conception many linguists have of the project they are engaged in. Particularly among syntacticians and semanticists, the answer to the question 'What are your theories theories *of*?' is that they are being put forward as explicit statements of knowledge possessed by individual speakers, knowledge that by hypothesis plays some pivotal role in these individuals' overt capacity to use language in the way they do. Conceptualism is now also fairly widespread among those whose background is primarily in the philosophy of language.

But conceptualism is far from achieving hegemony. This can be put down in part to the vociferousness of its sceptics. Some of these sceptics are unwill-

tain qualifications to my raw statement of them—can be found in the essays in Chomsky (2000). There are several collections that, unlike the present one, are dedicated specifically to the assessment of Chomsky's contributions to philosophy and linguistics: Harman (1974); George (1989*b*); Kasher (1991); Antony and Hornstein (2003); and McGilvray (forthcoming). Radford (1997) gives an introduction to the technicalities of Chomskian syntax from the minimalist perspective favoured at least since Chomsky (1995*b*).

[4] The label is not an entirely happy one since the knowledge is held by many 'conceptualists' to be non-conceptual, non-intentional, and subdoxastic. But it has had wide currency since being introduced by Jerrold Katz (in Katz 1990 and elsewhere), so I shall stick with it throughout this introduction.

ing to accept that ordinary speakers have knowledge of the kind standardly attributed to them by linguists; others are happy with this in principle, but do not think that explicating this knowledge is what linguists have or should have as their primary concern. ('Scepticism' is thus a doubly appropriate term here since it can operate at both the language-user level and the discipline level.) Equally significant is the persistence of disagreements within the conceptualist camp concerning what *kind* of knowledge is being imputed to speakers, with some holding back from calling the relevant psychological state 'knowledge' at all, preferring to talk of representation or cognition.[5]

The schismatic character of the conceptualist church originates in the variety of objections to the unadorned statement of conceptualism I provided above. Each objection gives rise to different responses and qualifications. Objections can be distinguished according to whether they threaten (i) or just (ii). The first three papers of Part One are concerned with objections to (ii) alone, the final two with objections to (i) (and hence (ii)).[6] I shall consider them in this order.

Those who deny that linguistics is or should be concerned to reveal the knowledge states of ordinary speakers normally have some non-conceptualist understanding of the goals of linguistics ready to hand as an alternative. One such alternative is Platonism, named as such and defended by Jerrold J. Katz. Katz takes the main objective of linguistics to be the description of languages, thought of as abstract entities akin to the abstract structures of mathematics. The task of describing the partial cognitive grasp we have of these objects falls, not to linguistics, but to *psycho*linguistics. Linguistics is not

---

[5] A spectrum of positions have been adopted. Knowles (2000) argues for treating the relation as one of straightforward knowledge-that. Dwyer and Pietroski (1996) argue it is belief but not knowledge. Chomsky (1980), 91, claims that it is more like knowledge than belief. Others hold that it is neither knowledge nor belief but something we can construct from scratch (see in particular a long-running debate from Wright's criticism (1986b) of Evans (1981), the replies in Davies (1987), Peacocke (1986), Davies (1989), and Peacocke (1989), with useful complementary discussion and criticism in George (1989a), Miller (1997), and Antony (1997). Some constructions of the relation between linguistic theories (especially semantic ones) and speakers are, however, not conceptualist at all but more or less instrumentalist: Foster (1976); Sainsbury (1980); Fricker (1983); and, again, Wright (1986b) (on which see Antony 1997).

[6] Some authors, e.g. Devitt and Sterelny (1987), reject (i) on certain readings, but hold that even if these objections fail there are independent reasons for rejecting (ii).

even an empirical discipline. To assume otherwise would be akin to claiming that mathematics could be studied using the methods of psychology.[7]

Conceptualists have replied that our interest in these abstract objects resides wholly in the fact that they are abstractions from the minds of individual speakers. What other point could there be to studying them? Unlike mathematical facts, which are distinct from our knowledge of those facts, 'pure' linguistic facts seem to be pointless abstracta. This charge is borne out, they add, by the observation that what Katz calls 'linguistics' bears little relation to what goes on in linguistics departments, which seem to practise what he calls 'psycholinguistics'.[8]

The first two contributions in Part One were written a few years earlier than the others in this collection and have been revised to appear in print here for the first time. Both seek to apply morals drawn from elsewhere in the philosophy of science to the specific case of linguistics, with a view to defending conceptualism against Scott Soames (Chapter 2) and against Michael Devitt and Kim Sterelny (Chapter 3).

Soames differs from Katz in holding that linguistics is an empirical discipline; yet like Katz he argues that linguistics does (or should) aim to describe the properties of languages or expressions, properties that are to a degree independent of facts about individual speakers: 'there are linguistics facts that are non-psychological in nature', with semantic properties in particular being dependent on 'extra-psychological notions'.[9] Moreover, there are 'psychological facts [about linguistic competence] that are non-linguistic', having to do with speed or order of processing and the like. From this he concludes that linguistics—the attempt to uncover these linguistic facts— is an enterprise conceptually distinct from anything that can be called a

---

[7] Katz (1990; 1996). Apart from conceptualism and Platonism, Katz gives the label 'nominalism' to those performance-fixated conceptions of the goal of linguistics that are widely regarded as having preceded the cognitive revolution, as criticized in, for example, Chomsky (1959).

[8] See Fodor (1981) and George (1996). Devitt and Sterelny (1989) agree with the criticism (pp. 515–16) but not with the inference to conceptualism.

[9] Soames (1984), 163. Soames seems to have in mind the thought that an individual can be mistaken about the correctness conditions on utterances in her or his language, conditions that are determined by facts about the community and/or by facts about the physical world. An earlier and briefer criticism of Soames (1984) than that provided by Antony in ch. 2 below can be found in Chomsky (1986), 34–6. Both Soames and Katz are criticized in Higginbotham (1983). For Soames on Katz, see Soames (1991).

branch of psychology. Linguistic theories are nevertheless empirical, since although they 'abstract away from potential differences in the internal representations and computational routines of various mental systems', they do so 'in order to concentrate on the structure of the common output they all produce', a structure that can only be revealed empirically.

Louise M. Antony (Chapter 2) accuses Soames of applying to linguistics standards that are manifestly inappropriate when applied in other scientific domains. At first glance, she says, Soames appears to be guilty of trying to specify a priori what kinds of evidence can bear on linguistics, and inferring from this specification that linguistics is only about facts belonging to the domains that are evidentially relevant to it. If that were his point, he would be overlooking the fact that evidence is holistic: there is potential for discoveries in one discipline to bear evidentially on puzzles in some apparently unrelated field. She concedes that Soames is not making *this* mistake. But he is, she says, relying on a related claim: that one can distinguish between evidence that bears on a discipline in such a way as to define the ambitions of that discipline, and other evidence that, though it bears on the discipline, does so in a non-constitutive way. The example that gives her contribution its title is designed to show up the error of this way of thinking.

Michael Devitt and Kim Sterelny regard language as a human product, but not one that is a 'characteristic of the human mind'. Although (*contra* Katz) linguistics will be an empirical discipline, it will not be so because the facts of linguistics are a proper subclass of the facts of psychology. But (*contra* Soames) their main argument for this conclusion does not turn on an a priori claim about what the facts are that linguists must uncover, where these turn out to be distinct from the facts of psycholinguistics. Rather, it develops from a kind of discipline-sized principle of charity: 'The best reason that we can expect to find for thinking that linguistics is about *x* rather than *y* is that the considerations and evidence that have guided the construction of linguistic theory justify our thinking that the theory is *true* about *x* but not *y*.'[10] By this criterion, they continue, linguists cannot be taken at their word

---

[10] Devitt and Sterelny (1989), 498–9. See also Devitt and Sterelny (1987), ch. 8, and other articles cited by Laurence (in ch. 3 below). Related discussion can be found in Wiggins (1997) and Millikan (2003), both of whom argue that the notion of a language that is more than an abstraction from the mind/brain of an individual speaker has a place beyond folk linguistics.

when they say they are concerned with uncovering innate structures that underpin our competence. Devitt and Sterelny instead attribute to linguists an ambition to identify the syntactic and semantic properties of 'symbols', which are 'parts of the physical world'. These properties are the ones by virtue of which symbols are able to 'have their roles in our lives', most notably their communicative role. Linguistics will be an empirical discipline with psychological aspects, but not a wholly psychological discipline.

According to Stephen Laurence (Chapter 3), the criterion Devitt and Sterelny appeal to is flawed. As a *reductio*, Laurence applies the criterion to the practice of developing what actually *is* intended to be a psycholinguistic theory (a theory backed up by claims about reaction times). Once again, the result is that the theories arrived at would not count as a branch of psychology. Laurence concludes that to accept the criterion would be to endorse bad philosophy of science, since it is a criterion that yields absurd results when applied in other contexts.[11]

In Chapter 4 Michael Devitt develops the alternative theory of the aims of linguistics outlined in his earlier work with Sterelny and summarized above. Drawing analogies between linguistic competence and the competence of chess players, logic machines, and dancing bees, Devitt defends the thought that there is a linguistic reality that is distinct from any psychological reality in speakers. Anticipating various charges that have been levelled against similar-sounding views, he insists that this linguistic reality does not collapse into facts about performance; and though the structure of this reality is characterized by rules, these need not be represented, or otherwise present, in the mind of speakers. At most we can say that the competence of speakers to speak a language must 'respect' the rules of that language. He also claims to be going beyond Katz (1990) and Soames (1984) in arguing not only for the conceptual distinctness of linguistic facts from psychological facts, but also for our having a legitimate theoretical interest in uncovering these linguistic facts.

Turn now to objections to clause (i) of the conceptualist stance. Most objections to this clause turn on the supposed implausibility of the claim that ordinary speakers know the axioms, rules, and theorems of linguistic

---

[11] Laurence (this volume), sect. 4. In sect. 5 he rejects other forms of arguments against conceptualism, including others he attributes to Devitt and Sterelny.

theories. They also tend to share a common form, asserting the existence of some feature $F$ such that both:

(a)  $F$ is an essential feature of knowledge,

and

(b)  $F$ is missing from the relation—the putative 'knowledge' relation—that ordinary speakers bear to the linguistic theories purportedly applicable to them.

Any true-making substituend for '$F$' in (a) and (b) will mean that conceptualism, at face value, must be rejected.

To illustrate, take the ascription of knowledge of the c(onstituent)-command condition on polarity expressions:[12]

A polarity expression must be c-commanded by an affective constituent.

(Constituent X c-commands constituent Y iff X and Y are distinct, neither dominates the other, and X is immediately dominated by a constituent that dominates Y.) If we are free to suppose that adult speakers know this and certain other principles, innately or otherwise, then we are in a position to explain why they distinguish between (1) and (2), with the second being deemed unacceptable (conventionally indicated with an asterisk):

(1)  The fact that he has resigned won't change anything.
(2)  *The fact that he hasn't resigned will change anything.[13]

In (2), *hasn't* is an affective constituent that, in contrast to *won't* in (1), fails to c-command the polarity expression *anything*. But acceptance of this explanation requires that there be no feature $F$ such that the relation borne by ordinary speakers to the c-command condition lacks $F$ whereas

[12]  Radford (1997), 3.9, introduces the theory behind this condition using the example in the main text.

[13]  Strictly, what is unavailable is a non-free-choice reading of (2). There are acceptable 'free choice' readings of the same string that require stressing 'anything' or adding, say, 'you care to mention'. Compare the different readings obtained according to whether 'any' is stressed in 'I don't want any house'.

knowledge requires *F*. Many regard as absurd the supposition that ordinary speakers know the c-command condition.

John Searle, for instance, charges that the kind of knowledge attributed to ordinary speakers by linguists is not available to consciousness and so is not genuinely knowledge.[14] More recently, Dean Pettit has suggested that knowledge must be possessed of a species of epistemic warrant that is missing from the cognitive relation ordinary speakers bear to linguistic theories.[15] Other candidates for *F*, properties essential to knowledge but missing from ordinary speakers' linguistic competence, include: verbalizability,[16] conceptuality and rational integration,[17] objectivity,[18] and propositionality.[19]

[14] Searle (1990); see also Dummett (1981) and the reply in Chomsky (1986). A slightly different set of challenges turns on the topic of knowledge of the content of one's own mind ('self-knowledge'), particularly the properties of the expressions of one's idiolect—see Higginbotham (1998*b*) and Smith (1998).

[15] Pettit (2002); see also Nagel (1969). Chomsky talks explicitly of knowledge that is unjustified in Chomsky (1976) and (1980).

[16] Quine (1970) objects to a lack of evidence for attributions of non-verbalizable knowledge. He has been widely criticized for inferring from this (alleged) lack of evidence to the incoherence of such attributions. For more on this debate, as well as the notion of an 'extensionally equivalent set of rules' that lies at its heart, see Laurence (this volume); Stich (1971; 1972); Chomsky and Katz (1974); Root (1974); George (1986); Neale (1987); as well as, in a more conciliatory mood, Quine (1975).

[17] The concepts that a speaker allegedly lacks—making it inappropriate for us to attribute knowledge to them—can include concepts invoked only by language theorists, such as the concept *c-command* or *satisfaction by an infinite sequence* (Campbell 1982), as well as concepts expressed by words that the speaker can use despite only 'partially grasping' their 'full meaning', e.g. 'carburettor' (see Higginbotham 1989*b*: sect. 3, and the papers in pt. 3 of this collection for discussion). What lacking a concept in either category may be taken to consist in is itself relatively open. It could be the failure of the putative knowledge to integrate with the rest of their rational system through a failure to be 'inferentially promiscuous'; or it may be simply that it lacks the marks of intentionality in Bentano's sense, such as substitution failure or lack of existential import. For discussion relating to one or other of these forms of the objection see Cooper (1973); Evans (1981); Stich (1983); Higginbotham (1989*a*); Stainton (1996); Barber (1997; 1998); Higginbotham (1998*a*); and Knowles (2000).

[18] George (1990), Higginbotham (1991), and Barber (2001) offer different attempts to deal with the concern that, if what we know is constituted out of our knowing it, the knowledge will lack objectivity. There is also a large literature coming at the problem of objectivity via the topics of scepticism and rule-following, often using Wittgenstein's discussion in *Philosophical Investigations* and/or Kripke (1982) as a springboard. See Forbes (1984); Chomsky (1986), 223–43; Wright (1989); and references in the useful survey

[*See p. 10 for n. 18 cont. and n. 19.*]

One approach conceptualists could take or have taken to these objections is to deny that the relevant *F* is missing from our relation to our language; another is to deny that *F* is an essential feature of knowledge. Sometimes making careful distinctions means that both forms of response can be taken at once. Regarding the need for knowledge to be consciously available, for example, one could distinguish between access consciousness and phenomenal consciousness. Knowledge is consciously accessible if it plays a role in the subject's wider cognitive life; linguistic knowledge *is* available to the subject in this sense, as can be seen precisely from the role it plays in linguistic behaviour. And we may lack phenomenal consciousness of our linguistic knowledge, but this form of consciousness is not essential to the explanatory potential of knowledge attributions, and so can be regarded as an inessential feature of knowledge.[20]

Conceptualists have also responded by refusing to enter into discussions of what is or is not essential to knowledge in the traditional philosophical sense of the term, or even in its ordinary usage. Such a discussion, they imply, would quickly degenerate into a pointless verbal dispute. What matters when thinking about features listed as candidates for *F* is not that they are essential to knowledge as conceived of by the folk or by René Descartes, but whether they are explanatorily essential. The refusal to get bogged down in merely verbal disputes is crystallized in the popular move, initiated by Chomsky, of abandoning the word 'knowledge' in favour of some surrogate, to be thought of as a term of art, such as 'tacit knowledge', 'competence', 'cognizing', 'representation', or even simply 'R'.[21]

discussions by Hale (1997) and Miller (1998), ch. 5. Wiggins (1997) cites the possibility of error as a reason to reject Chomsky's (1995a) claims about linguistic knowledge.

[19] Several critics of conceptualism (e.g. Harman 1968) have compared the attribution of tacit knowledge of linguistic principles unflatteringly to the attribution of knowledge of the principles of mechanics in the explanation of cycle-riding. The moral of the analogy is that linguistic principles describe what speakers know *how* to do, not something they know propositionally ('knowledge that').

[20] See Block's reply to Searle (1990) in the same volume, rounded out in Block (1995).

[21] See Chomsky (1980) and (1986), 267–8. Cognizing is stipulated to be the same as knowledge but stripped of those features that stand in the way of using knowledge attributions in psychological explanations in cognitive science. (Chomsky is also keen to add that, although science is not bound to ordinary usage, as it happens ordinary usage of 'knowing' is often closer to that of 'cognizing' than it is to traditional philosophical definitions.) Searle (1990) objects to the practice in cognitive science of (as he sees it)

This terminological manœuvre has its place but hardly eliminates the importance of reflecting on the character of the corresponding relatum. After all, at the very least we are presupposing attributions of cognizing to be explanatory, and for this to be the case there must be some explanatory framework within which the attribution is embedded—one cannot simply stipulate one's way to an explanation.[22] To what extent does letting go of the *word* 'knowledge' (or equally, the word 'belief') signal an abandonment of the associated explanatory framework, intentional explanation?

Georges Rey takes up this question in Chapter 5, where he attempts to identify the explanatory framework at work in linguistics. The default framework, he says, is standard computationalism, according to which semantically evaluable entities—mental representations—are felicitously transformed in computational processes, something that is possible because these same entities have causal properties in addition to their semantic ones. Rey is highly sympathetic to this computationalist framework, and argues that this is the framework within which linguistics must operate if it is to operate at all. Given this, he is puzzled by anti-intentionalist claims made by Chomsky (especially in Chomsky 2000) that, Rey believes, sit uneasily with the appeal to computationist explanation.

Rey notes that at the heart of linguistics are appeals to intentional terms such as 'representation', e.g. as embedded within the context: 'level of . . .'. Rey is interested in whether linguists' use of this and other terms, either in their practice or in their reflections on that practice, fit with the role representations are supposed to play within computationalist explanation as it is normally understood. Some of the remarks made by Chomsky, for example, can seem to be at odds with this role: ' "representation" is not to

---

defining one's way to successful explanations by coining a special notion, cognizing, that is just like knowledge save that is lacks any of knowledge's troublesome features; appealing to inference to the best explanation in order to give this notion legitimacy widens the diameter without removing the circularity. See Matthews (1991) for discussion of inference to the best explanation in this context. Philosophical discussion of tacit knowledge in cognitive science more generally can be found in Fodor (1968), Graves *et al.* (1973), and Crimmins (1992), as well as the literature cited parenthetically in n. 5 above.

[22] To say this is not to say that one should actually stop doing linguistics until one has understood the nature of the explanation, as Searle (1990) seems to be suggesting (see previous note). As Fodor (1981) remarks, one often comes to understand why an explanatory strategy is legitimate long after one has taken it to be such.

be understood relationally, as "representation of" '.[23] Chomsky repeatedly rejects the relevance to naturalistic enquiry of intentional phenomena: 'intentional phenomena relate to people and what they do as viewed from the standpoint of human interests and unreflective thought, and thus will not (so viewed) fall within naturalist theory, which seeks to set such factors aside'.[24] Chomsky has offered his own interpretation of his apparent appeals to intentionality in other places, saying that they are merely inessential expository devices. Rey, after seeking but failing to reconcile this hostitlity to intentionality with the need to adopt the computationalist framework, concludes that we should charitably overlook Chomsky's anti-intentionalism and take at least some of his uses of intentionalist discourse at face value.

The final chapter of this section serves as a bridge to Part Two, which focuses on specifically *semantic* knowledge. Robert Matthews (Chapter 6) examines the adequacy of conceptualism in linguistics, focusing on refuting an argument advanced by Jerry Fodor and Stephen Schiffer to the effect that, whatever the truth about syntactic knowledge, attributions of knowledge of truth-conditional semantic theories are unnecessary and empirically unmotivated.[25]

In *Remnants of Meaning* (1987) Schiffer introduced the character of Harvey, who comes to know the meaning of utterances not by deploying knowledge of a semantic theory, but by virtue of possessing a mechanism in his head that takes sentences of Mentalese into other sentences of Mentalese. For example, it might take

JEAN JUST UTTERED, 'LA NEIGE EST NOIR'

into

JEAN JUST SAID THAT SNOW IS BLACK

(where an upper-case English expression is to be understood as referring to the Mentalese expression with the same content as the English one). To effect this translation, there is no need to suppose that Har-

---

[23] Chomsky (1995a), 53. I offer an interpretation of this particular claim in Barber (2001). [24] Chomsky (2000), 22.

[25] Fodor (1976) and Schiffer (1987). For similar claims see Soames (1985) and (1989). The Harvey example, introduced immediately below in the text, is discussed by Fricker (this volume) and Lepore (1997).

vey actually knows the axioms of a semantic theory, or even the relevant theorems of such a theory (its 'T-sentences'). The point of the example is that ordinary speakers could be just like Harvey in terms of what is going on in their heads, and so also just like him in not knowing the axioms or theorems of a semantic theory. Schiffer suggests that, for all the empirical evidence we have available to us, this is not only possible but likely.

Matthews rejects this conclusion by rejecting the assumption that someone like Harvey should be described as failing to know a semantic theory. Under its most plausible reconstruction within the computationalist framework, the knowledge relation is *precisely* one that Harvey could be said to bear to a semantic theory: a semantic theory provides a specification-in-intension of the function computed by the mechanism attributed to Harvey, which takes Mentalese expressions into Mentalese expressions. To this extent, Harvey's cognition certainly 'involves' a semantic theory. Matthews takes it to be an open empirical question whether Harvey knows a semantic theory, specifically its axioms, in some stronger sense than simply being able to effect the pairing of utterances with meanings/truth conditions specified by the theory.

## 2 Understanding

Part One concerns the status of linguistics as a discipline, and the adequacy of conceptualism. Rightly or wrongly, the content and category of the linguistic theory that is ostensibly known/represented/cognized are often treated as irrelevant to this debate. Part Two focuses more specifically on semantic theories and their status. Two questions dominate: whether semantic theories that attribute extensional properties such as reference, satisfaction, or truth conditions to expressions can or should be married to the conceptualist perspective; and what to make of the connection between knowledge of meaning and linguistic understanding.

On the first question, there is an interesting symmetry between Chomsky's approach to linguistics and Donald Davidson's philosophy of language. Chomsky, we have seen, treats theories in linguistics as objects of ordinary-speaker knowledge; but he has long been sceptical of the agenda, popular among philosophers of language in the analytic tradition, of seeking to provide truth-conditional semantics for natural languages. Since 1967 Davidson has been a consistent advocate of this latter agenda; yet he has equally consistently abstained from treating these theories as objects of actual knowledge.[26] What they agree on is the claim that it is unwise to assume that truth theories are objects of knowledge.

A move that has become popular in recent years is to fuse these two perspectives—to psychologize Davidson and extensionalize Chomsky. Those who take this approach regard extensional theories as objects of knowledge, knowledge that partially accounts for our capacity to under-stand one another through language. The case for this fusion is simple enough: only if we were possessed of such knowledge could we have cer-tain of the linguistic abilities that we do.

One ability we have is a capacity to intuit the difference between valid and invalid arguments, a difference that seems to turn on the semantic structure of the sentences out of which arguments are composed. Our sensitivity to this structure depends, by hypothesis, on our having somehow internalized the clauses of the relevant semantic theory.[27]

Another ability is the capacity to assign truth conditions to utterances in a systematic and accurate way. By supposing that a speaker has knowledge of semantic clauses for the component expressions of an uttered sentence and for grammatical concatenation, and then by granting her an ability or disposition to carry out appropriate derivations, we can begin to see how she could arrive at an appreciation of the truth condition of the utterance. That phonological and syntactic knowledge alone fails to come close to providing what is needed for understanding is obvious. In the following passage, from the novel *The Corrections* by Jonathan Franzen, a boy is not allowed from the family table until he has eaten his rutabaga and liver:

'Dad means for you to sit there till you eat that. Finish it up now. Then your whole evening's free. . . . Noun adjective,' his mother said, 'contraction possessive noun. Conjunction conjunction stressed pronoun counterfactual verb pronoun I'd just

---

[26] See Chomsky (2000), throughout; and Davidson (1967; 1990). Though Davidson is sceptical of the value of embedding truth theories inside psychological operators, he is not wholly explicit on the reasons for this reluctance. Soames (1956), esp. sect. 3, criticizes the argument in the main text. Peacocke (1986) incorporates a reply to Soames (1985), with Soames responding in the same volume; see also Soames (1989); (1992), 25.

[27] Structural validity is the cornerstone in Evans (1976), part of an early attempt to psychologize Davidson (see Evans 1981 and the subsequent literature cited in n. 5 above).

gobble that up and temporal adverb pronoun conditional auxiliary infinite—'
Peculiar how unconstrained he felt to understand the words that were spoken to
him. Peculiar his sense of freedom from even that minimal burden of decoding
spoken English. (Franzen 2002: 261–2)

To explain why this is not how it is for us, what is needed, over and above tacit
knowledge of phrase-structure rules, is tacit knowledge of a compositional
truth theory. That, at least, is what many have claimed.[28]

At one time persuaded of the value of grafting Davidsonian semantics
onto Chomskian syntax, Paul M. Pietroski (Chapter 7) is now sceptical
of the value of extensional semantics. Pietroski is willing to grant that
speakers have a certain kind of thin semantic knowledge, sufficient to
explain a far more limited range of semantic phenomena. Consider the
various contrasts within the following list (where a common subscript
index requires the words to be assigned a common referent, a distinct index
signifies a distinct referent, and an asterisk indicates the unacceptability of
the string so interpreted):

(3) Rachel$_i$ knew she$_i$ would laugh.
(4) Rachel$_i$ knew she$_j$ would laugh.
(5) She$_i$ knew Rachel$_j$ would laugh.
(6) *She$_i$ knew Rachel$_i$ would laugh.
(7) Rachel$_i$ laughed at her$_j$.
(8) *Rachel$_i$ laughed at her$_i$.
(9) Rachel$_i$ laughed at herself$_i$.
(10) *Rachel$_i$ laughed at herself$_j$.
(11) She$_i$ knew Rachel$_j$ would laugh at herself$_j$.
(12) *She$_i$ knew Rachel$_j$ would laugh at herself$_i$.

The pattern of acceptability judgements associated with the different inter-

[28] Larson and Segal (1995) draw together and develop various strands of the Chom-
sky/Davidson programme. See also Higginbotham (1985; 1986; 1988; 1992) and Laurence
(1996). Davidson's work takes the syntax of the first-order predicate calculus as its foundation and adds to it as necessary. But once truth theories come to be regarded as embedded
within the mind of a particular speaker, this presupposition is unmotivated. Within the
new framework, work on sorting out traditional problems of opacity, reference failure,
the logical form of adverbs, and so forth is undertaken on the understanding that it must
ultimately gel with a syntax that is more likely to be Chomskian than Fregean.

pretations of these strings can be accounted for by supposing that we all know the c-command condition on binding:[29]

> A bound constituent must be c-commanded by an appropriate antecedent,

that *herself* is a reflexive anaphor and so must take its reference from ('be bound by') an antecedent expression by which it is c-commanded (9–12), and that the pronouns *her* and *she* either need not or must not pick up their referential properties in this way (3–8). Another 'thin' semantic phenomenon is our capacity to distinguish readings of structurally ambiguous strings such as (13):

(13) Visiting relatives can be tedious.

This capacity to disambiguate can be understood to reside in our possessing the knowledge that leaves us the option of parsing in either of two ways. Finally, there are certain judgements we make about necessary connections, inferences that seem to be analytic and/or a priori, that could be rooted in the lexicon. The inference from (14) to (15) may serve as an example:

(14) John knows that he will survive.
(15) John will survive.[30]

But such 'thin' semantic knowledge[31] falls a long way short of allowing the knower to interpret the sentences as a whole. For this, one must know what 'laugh at' means, what 'visiting' means, and so forth, where this is equivalent to appreciating how the appearance of these expressions within any given sentence contributes to the truth conditions of that sentence. Or so many have assumed.

Pietroski challenges the assumption, using as a springboard the scepticism Chomsky and others have voiced about extensional semantics as a contribution to any properly scientific study of language.[32] His argument

---

[29] See Radford (1997), 3.9, and Chomsky (1995b), 1.4.2 (co-author Richard Larson).

[30] See Jackendoff (1990) for discussion of the interpretation of this kind of phenomenon.

[31] 'Fat syntax' would perhaps be a better label, but it has been used already by Stich (1991) in a different context.

[32] The others include Hornstein (1987; 1988; 1989; 1995) and McGilvray (1998). For discussion and further references see Ludlow (2003).

distils down to the complaint that truth conditions are an 'interaction effect', the motley product of many different factors. This means not only that judgements about truth conditions cannot be systematized in a compositional theory, but also that it is not worth our trying to systematize them in this way. He accepts that there can be systematicity in semantics; but he denies that we should interpret '1' (or 'T') in systematic semantic theorems:

(16) ... is 1 iff ...

as 'true'. It might just as well be left as it is. Systematicity gets you a theory of 1-conditions; things only get messy in the move from 1-conditions to truth conditions.

The idea can be made vivid using an example found in Chomsky (1986: 44). He notes various cases of what we might pre-theoretically label as 'referential dependency', such as the contrasting adequacies of (17), (18), and (19):

(17) John$_i$ thinks that he$_i$ is intelligent.
(18) He$_j$ thinks that John$_i$ is intelligent.
(19) *He$_i$ thinks that John$_i$ is intelligent.

These can be explained using binding principles seen already in connection with (3)–(12), in particular the rule that a pronoun must not be bound by an item that c-commands it. But exactly the same phenomenon seems to appear even when the relevant noun phrases fail to refer:

(20) Joe Public$_i$ thinks that he$_i$ is intelligent.
(21) *He$_i$ thinks that Joe Public$_i$ is intelligent.
(22) The average man$_i$ thinks that he$_i$ is intelligent.
(23) *He$_i$ thinks that the average man$_i$ is intelligent.

This suggests we should not describe the phenomenon as being about reference after all. To this example we might add that of Bob Dole, an unpopular Republican candidate for the US presidency in 1996. Dole was fond of referring to himself in the third person: 'Bob Dole won't raise taxes', and so forth. Disrespectful commentators were given to violating the binding principles needed to rule out (19) by uttering sentences like (24):

(24) (?) No one wants Bob Dole$_i$ to win; even he$_i$ doesn't want Bob Dole$_i$ to win.

Odd though it is, all names and pronouns in (24) *are* used to refer to the same person. Troublesome cases (20)–(24) and others like them can be sidelined by dropping the assumption that the term 'refers' in 'co-refers' is to be taken as full-blown reference in the pre-theoretic sense, something that people do in acts of communication in all its complexity, not a property of expressions as such. 'Co-referring' could instead be interpreted as 'co-indexed', where indexing has *something* to do with reference, but not necessarily something that we can (or should want to) spell out in detail.

Instead of resting at the level of thin 'quasisemantics' and talking of the 'r-relation' instead of the 'reference relation' (Chomsky 1986: 44; 1995*b*: 1.4.2), one could attempt to hold on to a face-value interpretation of 'refers' by confronting these and other examples using technical solutions that, as tends to happen, invoke ever more elaborate hidden syntactic machinery.[33] Pietroski prefers to conclude that, since semantics is whatever our best theory of semantics is about, and our best (most progressive) theory of semantics is not about extensional properties but about their thinner counterparts, the extensional approach should be dropped for the white elephant it is.[34]

An ongoing debate about richness of syntax serves to link Pietroski's paper with the next contribution, from Reinaldo Elugardo and Robert M. Stainton (Chapter 8). When someone utters (25):

(25) I haven't had breakfast,

[33] Positing hidden syntax to deal with supposedly semantic problems is remarkably widespread among philosophers of language, often worryingly so: for example, to cope with the problem of deference to what is in fact gibberish Récanati (1997) suggests that we silently quantify over languages; and Forbes (1997) posits hidden logophors in replying to the problem of apparent opacity in the absence of any opaque operators (see Saul 1997 and Barber 2000).

[34] Two interesting points for discussion here are, first, the extent to which this last argument relies on the principle found in Devitt and Sterelny (1989) and criticized by Laurence in this volume (see pp. 6–7 above); and second, how Pietroski's position compares with that of Wilson and Sperber (2002), who also argue for a downgrading of the theoretical interest of truth conditions in favour of relevance conditions, though their concern is that truth conditions are *insufficiently* sensitive to the context of use.

we do not default to the interpretation that at no point since the dawn of time has the utterer had breakfast. But this distinction is not marked in the overt syntax. So either we should give up the attempt to tie this feature of the default interpretation of the sentence to its syntax, or we should posit hidden syntax.[35] If the latter option is tempting, it becomes less plausible as a strategy the more endemic the problem is seen to be.

(26) I opened three tins of beans.

(26) is, by default, interpreted as being true when and only when the utterer opened exactly (or at least) three tins, but rarely as being true just in case she opened *at most* three tins. Yet there are contexts when an at-most interpretation would be appropriate. Should we posit hidden syntax to explain this? Where is this syntax? In the language module? Is it innately specified?[36] Assuming that answers to these questions are not forthcoming, and that this is a reason to worry, we might be tempted—in keeping with the proposal by Pietroski—to shield the syntax from some proportion of the myriad of factors that enter into determining truth conditions, treating the process whereby the jump from syntax to truth conditions is achieved as having one or more of the following features: not part of the language module; pragmatic not semantic; *ad hoc*; unsystematic; unworthy of our seeking to systematize it.

The connection to Elugardo and Stainton's chapter is that the surface incompleteness of (25) and (26) can be treated as of a kind with the more radical surface-incompleteness phenomenon they address: non-sentential assertion. To borrow an example of theirs, when Andrew walks into a room uttering:

(27) From France

while wiggling a box of cigarettes in his raised hand, we are happy to regard his utterance as true or false according to whether the box of cigarettes is

---

[35] Thus one might argue that the present-perfect tense form means the sentence is referring to an 'extended now', so that it is encoded in the sentence that it is true only if a past event of having breakfast and the utterance itself both occur within this extended now.

[36] For discussion see Stanley (2000); Borg (forthcoming); Cappelen and Lepore (forthcoming).

from France. Yet there is no sentence to interpret. Or at least there is no sentence on the surface, and there are good reasons for not positing hidden but determinate syntax such as:

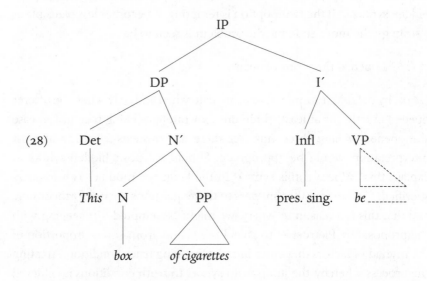

(28)

to combine with (27) so as to deliver up a complete interpretable sentence.[37] So the task of getting from the uttered fragment of language to the proposition expressed cannot be fully captured in a compositional truth theory, since compositional truth theories operate on syntax and there is no more than a subsentential fragment of syntax available in this case.

Elugardo and Stainton address the following question (among others): if the proposition expressed by (27) is not arrived at through the interpretation of a partially hidden sentence, how is it arrived at? They outline the options before plumping for a particular answer on more or less empirical grounds. Drawing on recent work on visual cognition they suggest that the uttered subsentential language fragment combines with descriptive and indexical referring terms of Mentalese to yield a fully propositional formula of Mentalese whose content is the proposition expressed by the utterance. The principles at work to make this happen felicitously will be pragmatic rather than semantic. If their solution is adequate for these radically incomplete,

---

[37] The case against the 'elliptical sentence' view is summarized by Elugardo and Stainton in the present volume, but see also Stainton (2000).

non-sentential cases, it would seem to carry over to the incompleteness apparently endemic even in the utterance of whole sentences.

In what became known as the 'modesty' debate that took place in the 1970s and 1980s, Michael Dummett and John McDowell disagreed over how far semanticists owe an explanation of what knowledge by a native speaker of English of the semantic propositions expressed in (29) and (30) must 'consist in' if its attribution is to deliver an account of understanding:[38]

(29) 'Snow' refers in English to snow.
(30) 'Snow is white' is true in English iff snow is white.

Dummett claimed that modesty in the elaboration of what knowledge of reference or of truth conditions consists in turns semantic knowledge into something trivial, something a non-competent speaker could learn in a book without having the faintest understanding of 'snow'. What is to prevent my being said to know that 'snow' refers to snow merely upon reading the letters s-n-o-w in a book and so realizing that such a word exists? To answer this we need a 'full-blooded' account of what knowledge of reference conditions consists in. Against this McDowell claimed that, in an account of linguistic understanding, nothing need be added beyond the modest claim that semantic clauses express what is known.

The debate in that context had to do with Dummett's rejection of global realism (on which see further Alexander Miller's contribution in Chapter 15), but it is a debate that takes place upstream of that controversy. Even though they each keep away from the metaphysical debates that once drove the interest in the question, the authors of the next three chapters are all concerned with how knowledge of semantic clauses relates to linguistic understanding.

Stephen Schiffer (Chapter 9) begins to address the question of what it is to know the meaning of an expression by noticing some difficulties facing what, approached naively, are initially attractive answers. One of these answers is that to know the meaning of an expression *e* is to have the propositional knowledge that *e* means that such-and-such. Another is that it is to be possessed of a certain knowledge-how. A succession of modifications

[38] Dummett (1975), 101–2, 108; (1976); McDowell (1980); and McDowell (1987) plus Dummett's reply in the same volume. Higginbotham (1989*b*), sect. 3, defends a position that resembles McDowell's in its modesty.

in response to the shortcomings of these and other proposals leads him to the opinion that for someone to know what an expression means in a given language is for her to be in a state that plays a certain role—called the *knowledge-of-meaning role*—in the information processing that takes one from a perception of the utterance of a sentence containing the expression to knowledge of what was said in that utterance.

This raises the question of what processing role the knowledge-of-meaning role for an expression, complex or primitive, might be. Roughly speaking, Schiffer holds that it is an information-processing state that directly or indirectly represents the expression as linked with what Schiffer calls its *character\**, which, again roughly speaking, is Schiffer's replacement for David Kaplan's notion of character (Kaplan 1989). Along the way, Schiffer also argues that, while expressions do indeed have meaning, there may not be any *things* that are the meanings of expressions.

Chapters 10 and 11 turn from the understanding of expressions to the understanding of utterances. They also trade in notions that, for all their importance in traditional epistemology, tend to be confined to the background in discussions in the philosophy of the cognitive sciences, if they figure at all. In Chapter 10 Elizabeth Fricker is concerned with justification; in the following chapter I am concerned with the objectivity of knowledge.

Fricker's focus on justification may appear beside the point, a traditional philosopher's misplaced concern with an explanatorily inessential feature of knowledge which is of no interest to theoretical linguists. But a broader perspective ought to dispel this impression. Epistemologists have always striven to understand how the various possible routes to knowledge— perception, memory, a priori knowledge, inference, and so forth—could deliver opinions to which we are epistemically entitled. One such (putative) route to knowledge is testimony. Much of the literature on testimony turns on the nature of trust, expertise, and authority of sources, on whether we should attach credence to reports of miracles, defer to scientists in public policy, and so forth. But a comprehensive theory of testimony will need also to include an account of how we come to understand the utterances we are called on to trust. From this perspective, a concern with justification lies at the core of the topic of linguistic knowledge. Our capacity to communicate with one another is an astonishing epistemic achievement, every bit as startling as, say, our capacity to perceive other features of the world around us. (Indeed, allowing us to communicate is just one among several respects in which possessing a language is to our epistemic advantage.) Leaving justification out of the picture on the grounds that it is inessential to the explanation of linguistic competence misses something crucial: that we have an epistemic right to our linguistic judgements is one part of what we are trying *to explain*.

One could adopt a reliabilist line on the nature of this justification, insisting that all the epistemic entitlement we need is provided by our minds' reliably tracking the truth (regarding what our interlocutors are saying, for example, or regarding what the normal state of I-languages among salient adult speakers is). But simple reliabilism must face up to well-known difficulties that even most epistemological externalists recognize.[39] Fricker's application of this dialectic to the linguistic domain is therefore welcome, as is her attempt to develop a notion of understanding that respects these broader lessons.

Fricker defends a view that treats understanding an utterance as the exercise of a quasi-perceptual capacity. Like Schiffer in the previous paper, she notes that merely knowing what a person has said is insufficient for understanding what that person has said. (For example, A may know through an interpreter what B has said, and yet fail to understand what she has said.) What explains this deficit, she proposes, is that understanding must come through a characteristic form of experience, grounded in a reliable mechanism for the achievement of representations of the content and force of an utterance. But though reliability has a role to play, the key component of her account of understanding is a theory that has explicit affinities with the claim made by John McDowell that moral competence is a quasi-perceptual capacity.[40]

In the final contribution to Part Two (Chapter 11), I seek to establish both the need for and the availability of an intention-based account of the truth conditions of utterances. The need is driven by another consideration at the heart of traditional epistemology: objectivity of subject matter. A belief or an

---

[39] See e.g. Conee and Feldman (1998).

[40] McDowell (1985); McDowell himself proposes to think of understanding as a kind of perception in McDowell (1977), 165–9, and McDowell (1980). Hunter (1998) reaches a similar conclusion and also stresses the relevance to understanding of justification, as does Lepore (1983).

instance of knowledge is objective only if the condition for its correctness is independent of the fact of our holding that belief or possessing that knowledge. Resignation to the non-objectivity of our linguistic knowledge is not an option, since the subjectivity of our linguistic knowledge is hardly compatible with its manifest usefulness in understanding what others have said. Objectivity may seem to call for a realm of semantic facts that is so constituted as to be independent of the mental states of individual speakers: we are wrong when we depart from the norms governing some salient linguistic community. Against this conclusion I argue that for semantic knowledge to be objective—for it to possess the requisite independence of subject matter—we must treat the truth conditions of utterances as inherited from the intention out of which those utterances are performed (and not from expression meaning of a kind that floats free from each utterer's intentions).[41]

I then defend an account of the form of the relevant intentions. The intention on the part of the utterer that determines the truth condition of a given utterance is the intention to be recognized as performing an action with that truth condition. The notion of 'recognition' requires some chiselling before this suggestion becomes plausible. And it turns out that once this chiselling is finished, recognizing is equivalent to understanding. This fact connects my paper to the two preceding ones, since all three of us have as a subconcern the existence of a distinction, alluded to above, between knowledge of meaning on the one hand, and understanding on the other. Schiffer, Fricker, and myself all agree that there is a distinction to be drawn but differ, superficially at least, in where we locate the source of this difference.[42]

## 3 Linguistic Externalism

The papers in Part Three are concerned with linguistic externalism, central to over three decades of debate in the analytic philosophical tradition. Externalism is a multifaceted topic, relevant in more than one way to episte-

---

[41] This much is argued for in Barber (2001) and merely summarized in the present paper. Other discussions of objectivity are cited in n. 18 above.

[42] For more discussion of the topic of understanding and knowledge of meaning, see Dummett (1975; 1976); Peacocke (1976); Campbell (1982); Heck (1995); and Hunter (1998).

mology of language. One way of trying to frame the discussion is in terms of the $F$-schema introduced above in Section 1. Critics of conceptualism have often sought to find features that are essential to knowledge but missing from the relation we supposedly bear to linguistic theories. Is there a troublesome feature that can be generated out of externalist intuitions?[43]

Consider the thought that the extension of our term 'water' is $H_2O$, in part because of facts about our environment (specifically, that the stuff we happen to refer to when using the term has, to a close approximation, $H_2O$ as its chemical composition). This does not seem to be compatible with treating the extensional properties of our terms as a function of our knowledge states. After all, for a speaker to know that the extension of 'water' is $H_2O$ is for her to know a lot more than we would normally feel entitled to attribute to her on the basis of her linguistic competence.

It is true that many people today could be said to know the chemical composition of water. But what about those who lived before Cavendish and others showed, in the late eighteenth century, that water had a compound structure? Did these people's use of the term have a different extension? Intuitively not. Did they in fact know that they were referring to $H_2O$? Again intuitively not. Should we attribute to them only the weaker knowledge that 'water' refers to water? Maybe, but this attribution appears to suffer from being in one way or other unfit for our purpose, too modest to account for speakers' capacity to avoid speaking about superficially indistinguishable colourless liquids every time they use the term 'water'. Perhaps we can make a distinction between reference and a technical notion, semantic value, where it is knowledge of the latter that determines extension. But this is a promissory note until we are told more about what knowing the semantic value of a term amounts to.

Alternatively, we could leave the *content* of pre-1770 semantic knowledge untouched but regard it as a special *kind* of knowledge. But this does not seem a promising strategy for conceptualists to adopt either. Such knowledge would be very different from the tacit knowledge we ostensibly

---

[43] The two classic statements of content externalism are Putnam (1975) and Burge (1979). Moreover, Burge (1989) argues that semantics can be 'a social phenomenon' without this fact jeopardizing the conceptualist position that 'the study of language is a part of individual psychology' (p. 174). Larson and Segal (1995), ch. 13, provide a useful introduction to the topic of how externalism relates to conceptualism. See also Dummett (1991), ch. 4; Lycan (1986); and Peacocke (1994).

have of, say, the c-command condition on polarity items. Tacit knowledge plays a role in our cognitive processes, even if it does so unconsciously. The special knowledge pre-1770 speakers of English had of the semantic relation between 'water' and $H_2O$ was not only unconscious, it played no cognitive role at all. This is in considerable tension with the individualist aspirations that typically lie behind conceptualist thinking. Linguistics is no longer a branch of individualist psychology if it must consider an individual's physical and social environment before it can identify the content of the theory supposedly known by speakers.

These reflections hint at a potential substituend—'being internal'—for '$F$' in the schema. But the incompatibility (if there is one) between externalism and conceptualism arises more naturally, not through the isolation of an objection to fit that schema, but as a challenge to conceptualists to formulate a policy towards the externalist intuition that 'meaning ain't in the head', a policy of either reconciliation or rejection.

Chomsky's attitude towards twin-earth thought experiments is dismissive.[44] He describes the intuitions allegedly mined from the entertainment of these scenarios as folk intuitions with no more than sociological interest, belonging to 'ethnoscience', specifically to the study of folk linguistics, where the folk in this case are late twentieth-century analytic philosophers. This is apparent, he suggests, in the way our intuitions about reference are contextually determined, and only occasionally accord with the essentialism that ties reference to chemical composition. We can be interested in externalist intuitions about reference as part of a sociological investigation, but we would be mistaken to subscribe to them ourselves in the expectation that doing so will contribute to a natural science of language.

Those wishing to defend conceptualism in the extensional sphere cannot simply replicate Chomsky's dismissal of externalist thought experiments, which is part and parcel of his rejection of extensionalist semantics in its entirety. The three discussions that make up Part Three of the present book help us to understand the options available to those who wish to reconcile externalism with the reality of semantic knowledge, narrowing down the possibilities in some areas and opening them up in others, often in unexpected ways.

---

[44] Chomsky (2000), ch. 5. For discussion of whether thought experiments have any role to play in sciences other than linguistics see Gendler (1998).

Probably the most unexpected is contained in Chapter 12, by Peter Ludlow. He discusses externalism with regard to a linguistic property other than semantic content, asking whether it might not be worth regarding the *logical form* of an utterance as sensitive to facts about the physical environment.[45] To the extent that differences in logical form can affect content, this carries implications for content externalism. But advocates of content externalism usually take content to be directly dependent on external circumstances, unmediated by any difference in logical form; logical form is tacitly assumed to remain unchanged. So Ludlow's proposition that a difference in the extra-cranial world can affect the logical form of an expression is a radical one.

Defending his 1905 account of the logical form of quantified noun phrases, Russell pronounced that a philosophical theory could be assessed according to how many problems it solved without generating new ones of its own. The same can be said for the proposal that logical form has the potential to vary according to external factors. Ludlow considers possible applications of the idea, the most striking of which deals with the capacity of proper names to be used meaningfully in the absence of any referent. The so-called problem of non-referring singular terms[46] has proven to be one of the most intractable in semantics. And most philosophies of mind face a clearly related conundrum: how it is possible for us to think about objects that do not exist. It is not often that a wholly new perspective emerges in this area. Ludlow is well aware that his suggestion risks creating more difficulties than it disposes of, and his conjecture should be taken in that spirit. But here, in brief, is how externalism about logical form could help.

Suppose that, were they to have a Russellian logical form, utterances involving *non-referring* proper names would present no semantic problem.

[45] Differing conceptions of logical form can be found in a recent collection of essays edited by Preyer and Peter (2002). The possibility of externalism about logical form raises the possibility that still other properties could depend on the speaker's environment. Chomsky (2000), 129, 177, lampoons talk of semantic value by introducing a parallel notion, phonetic value, noting its lack of theoretical value, and asking his reader to explain the relevant difference between the two notions. In the light of Ludlow's example, it would be interesting to reflect on whether phonetic form could ever usefully be regarded as an externalist notion, and if not why not.

[46] My hesitancy in accepting the label has to do with a preference for the view that it is *people* who refer, using language to do so. By this score, all singular terms are non-referring. I ignore this consideration in what follows.

Uses (in this world, now) of (31) and (32) would both be false, for a common reason: the emptiness of the domain of an existential quantifier belonging to the utterance's logical form.[47]

(31) The king of France is bald.
(32) Santa Claus is bald.

Suppose, moreover, that there are Kripkean reasons against assigning utterances containing *referring* proper names a logical form that treats them as disguised definite descriptions.[48] Granting these two suppositions, what is to stop us assigning the complex Russellian logical form to utterances containing non-referring proper names, and a simple non-Russellian logical form to utterances containing proper names that successfully refer? This would require treating logical form as externally determined, sensitive to the existence of a denotation. But it would also clear up a lot of difficulties.

Awkward questions come thick and fast, as Ludlow is willing to acknowledge. They turn mostly on the consequence that we could be *radically* ignorant of the logical form of our utterances. There is an already familiar sense in which we cannot know the logical form of our utterances in the traditional, Cartesian sense of 'know': logical form on any conception is unconscious, embedded at a level deep within our thought or our brains. That is why it takes a Russell or an entire empirical discipline to reveal it. But the lack of knowledge countenanced under Ludlow's envisaged solution is of an altogether different order: facts about logical form would depend on facts fixed outside the head. Limits to our powers of introspection could never account for our failure to know whether there was ever a real Moses.

One of the more bizarre apparent consequences of externalism about logical form is that whether an inference is valid would not always be something we can realistically know, since validity can depend on logical form and we can be radically ignorant of facts that determine logical form. Indeed, validity threatens to depend on contingent matters of fact. Ludlow raises these questions before asking to what extent they are simply special cases of the widely recognized tension between self-knowledge and exter-

---

[47] There are various ways of fleshing out the basic idea in Russell (1905), with the theory that quantified noun phrases refer to generalized quantifiers having widest currency today (see Neale 1990; Larson and Segal 1995).

[48] Kripke (1980); see also Soames (1998).

nalism about content (which is not to diminish their critical significance), or whether externalism about logical form gives rise to wholly new worries.[49]

Gabriel Segal's contribution is orthodox in its concern with content rather than logical form, but is no less provocative than Ludlow's. He offers an argument for an internalist position that is radically holistic in the following sense: no term—e.g. 'tiger'—can have the same content for different individuals if there is a sentence—e.g. 'Tigers are indigenous to Africa'—over which they disagree.

The argument works only for a certain species of content—*cognitive* content—that satisfies the following 'Fregean' principle of discrimination: two terms in an individual's idiolect will differ in such content whenever substitution of one for the other in an extensional context would lead that individual to withdraw assent. But he points out at the beginning of the paper that such fine-grained content is needed for us to make sense of equally fine-grained differences in behaviour. Lois Lane does not touch up her make-up when she hears 'Clark Kent is coming to lunch'; yet she does when she hears 'Superman is coming to lunch'. Explaining this difference requires assigning different content to her terms.[50]

Segal is persuaded by his own argument that cognitive content is radically holistic, but acknowledges the difficulties holism brings in its wake. For this reason, the paper can be thought of as throwing down a challenge to anyone who is persuaded—like Segal himself—by the arguments for the existence of cognitive content.

One consequence of holism that is particularly relevant to the present volume is its apparent incompatibility with our knowing the meaning of the expressions in our language. If nothing else, this would seem to threaten the conceptualist stance on semantic theory that Segal also happens to favour. The threat arises as follows. We do not suppose that the meanings of our words change every time we undergo a change of belief. Yet if holism is right, our meanings, like our beliefs, are in continual flux. Does this mean we do not know what our words mean? Segal carefully isolates some different senses in which we can and cannot be said to be ignorant of meaning—

---

[49] For work on the tensions between self-knowledge, a priori knowledge, and regular (content) externalism see McKinsey (1991); Brown (1995); and the essays in Ludlow and Martin (1998).

[50] Braun (2001) criticizes this argument.

alleging that these differences have been glossed over by Burge (1988) and others—and evaluates their relative importance.

Jessica Brown (Chapter 14) takes issue with Segal's starting point: the need to hypothesize a species of content satisfying the Fregean criterion of content individuation, as opposed to working entirely and solely with a social externalist notion wherein contents are partly individuated by the practices of a linguistic community. Indeed, the main burden of her paper is to argue against those who, like Tyler Burge, try to combine social externalism with a Fregean notion of content.

Brown's main argument against the wisdom of adopting a Fregean notion of content if you are an externalist is that externalism is committed to sameness of content being potentially opaque, something that undermines the main motivating argument for adopting the Fregean notion. Sameness of content is potentially opaque if it is possible for someone not to realize that two of her terms express the same concept. That social externalists are committed to this is fairly clear: I could fail to realize that 'guillemot' and 'murre' both refer to the same species of auk, yet they have the same content according to social externalists, because their content is tied to the identical use to which British and Canadian experts (respectively) put the terms. And granting this opacity undermines the classic Fregean argument for sense. The failure of Lois Lane to put together the respective contents of 'Superman' and 'Clark Kent' in inference and in behaviour can be put down to her ignorance of their sameness of content, rather than to an actual difference in content.

## 4 Epistemology through Language

Most discussion of linguistic knowledge in Parts One to Three focuses in one way or another on the nature of the relation holding between speakers / hearers and their language. The two papers in Part Four travel beyond this agenda, asking what reflecting on our epistemic relation to language can tell us about other topics in philosophy, specifically in epistemology.

Philosophy of language was once burdened with the task of dissolving the traditional philosophical problems by showing how they resulted from confusion about language. Most philosophers today would concur that this was harmful to philosophy; most philosophers of language would add that

it was especially harmful to the philosophy of language. Bad linguistic solutions to genuine philosophical concerns often depend on questionable
claims about language. Because language is a challenging and interesting
enough phenomenon in its own right, the strategy of approaching philosophical problems through language as a matter of routine is showing few
signs of a renaissance.[51]

This is quite compatible with the practice of carrying over lessons learnt
in thinking about language to other domains, and indeed of seeking out
linguistic solutions to a philosophical problem where specific reasons exist
for thinking this is an appropriate strategy. The papers reviewed so far are
replete with instances of lessons of the first kind; the two papers in this
section are concerned with more direct attempts to draw epistemological
conclusions from independently plausible linguistic claims.[52]

In Chapter 15 Alexander Miller examines one of several arguments against
semantic realism that have been developed by Michael Dummett and others,
reviewing the current state of the debate before offering his own reasons
for rejecting the argument.[53]

Semantic realism is committed to the view that understanding statements
consists in knowing or 'grasping' their truth conditions, where truth, here,
is to be thought of as potentially evidence-transcendent. The acquisition

[51] Gellner (1959) was an early opponent of the ordinary-language movement. Grice's
1967 lectures 'Logic and Conversation' (in Grice 1989, esp. essay 2, pp. 22–40) were a
landmark for their contribution to our understanding of the difference between semantics
and pragmatics, and to the analysis of the notion of meaning. This fact sometimes
overshadows its originally intended purpose, which was to undermine the use of ordinary
language as a beacon with which to approach various philosophical problems.

[52] Three papers illustrate the potential and variety of applications for epistemology
of lessons drawn from linguistic theory: Davidson (2001) argues that there are limits
to sceptical possibilities that spring from the possibility of interpretation; Dwyer (1999)
applies poverty-of-the-stimulus reasoning to the case of moral knowledge, outlining a
kind of principles-and-parameters moral psychology that explicitly parallels the linguistic
case. And Botterell (forthcoming) follows Stainton (1998) in rejecting Russell's principle
of acquaintance—crudely, that one can think about something only if one is in some way
directly acquainted with it—because of its incompatibility with non-sentential uses (see
ch. 8 of the present volume) of quantified noun phrases.

[53] Other arguments against semantic realism include the manifestation argument
(which Miller discusses and responds to in this chapter since it is pertinent to his rejection
of the acquisition argument) and the normativity argument. See the introduction to
Wright (1986a) for an overview.

argument against semantic realism turns on the alleged impossibility of our ever being able to acquire understanding of this kind, at least for those fragments of language that can be used to make evidence-transcendent claims. The alleged problem is that acquiring an understanding of language involves being trained in its correct usage, and we cannot be subjected to such training for evidence-transcendent portions of language since we cannot possibly be exposed to definitively correct usage. (Rejection of semantic realism would be compatible with continuing to think of understanding in terms of grasp of truth conditions; but the relevant notion of truth would need to be epistemically constrained.)

A tempting reply to this argument is that the training needed to provide us with an understanding of our language could take place using statements that are subject to confirmation or disconfirmation. With that understanding in place, nothing stands in the way of making claims that, though not subject to confirmation or disconfirmation, are still comprehensible in the realist's sense: our understanding of these statements consists in appreciating what conditions must be met for the statements to be true, even if we can never in fact tell whether these conditions are met. Miller considers the virtues of this and related responses, as well as several variants of the acquisition argument, before rejecting it even in a far weaker form than it was originally intended to have.

It is not immediately clear what to make of the relation between an assumption at the heart of the acquisition argument, that language comprehension is a rational achievement, and the contrasting view that language acquisition consists, not in a rational process of hypothesis formation and confirmation or disconfirmation, but in the largely unreflective maturation of an innately specified language module, triggered and to some extent shaped by a particular linguistic environment. The 'data' in this environment, looked at rationalistically, underdetermine the adult languages of every actual speaker. Since we *in fact* acquire understanding in circumstances that would not enable a rational investigator to do so, why assume that acquisition must, *in principle*, be rationalistically viable?[54]

While this consideration may serve to undermine the acquisition argu-

---

[54] Antony (1997) uses this Chomskian claim about language acquisition to argue for the irrelevance of rationally reconstructing linguistic competence after the fashion of Foster (1976) or Wright (1986b).

ment, it is not obvious that it does so. For one thing, poverty-of-the-stimulus arguments are more plausible in the theory of the acquisition of syntax (or 'thin' semantics in the sense of Section 1, above) than they are for extensional semantics. There is a healthy debate on the extent to which the range of concepts available to us is innately specified, but the implications of this for the acquisition of semantic knowledge are by no means settled.[55] Second, to the extent that innate knowledge is acquired by a species, it may well be possible to replay the acquisition argument at a species level rather that at the level of an individual organism.

James Higginbotham's contribution (Chapter 16) has more positive claims to make about the way reflection on language can yield epistemological conclusions. He is interested in so-called *de se* knowledge (roughly: 'knowledge of self') and in judgements that are immune to error through misidentification, though his claims about the logical form of gerundive complements and related constructions will be of interest in their own right.[56]

*De se* knowledge, if there is such a thing, is that category of knowledge manifest in the contrast between these two scenarios:

> A is watching a police raid taking place live on television; he believes (correctly as it happens) that he himself is the person shown sitting on a sofa inside the targeted house.

> B is watching a police raid taking place live on television; he does not believe (what is in fact the case) that he himself is the person shown sitting on a sofa inside the targeted house.

Higginbotham is interested in the ways in which the contrast between A's and B's predicaments can be marked in our language, in a variety of ways:

(33) (*a*) A expects that he will be arrested (true).

    (*b*) B expects that he will be arrested (true under at least one reading).

(34) (*a*) A expects that he himself will be arrested (true).

---

[55] See Cowie (1999) and the extensive reaction, for example.

[56] Contemporary discussion of these and related topics begins with Castañeda (1966) and Shoemaker (1968), usefully collected along with later work in Brook and DeVidi (2001).

(b) B expects that he himself will be arrested (false under all readings).

(35) (a) A expects himself to be arrested (true).

(b) B expects himself to be arrested (false under all readings).

(36) (a) A expects PRO[57] to be arrested (true).

(b) B expects PRO to be arrested (false under all readings).

What allows (33b) to be read in such a way as to tolerate B's relative ignorance, when no such reading is available for (34b), (35b), or (36b)? Higginbotham argues that the emphatic reflexive, the reflexive, and PRO respectively receive a special first-personal interpretation, an interpretation that is only optionally available in (33b).

Being immune to error through misidentification is a property of states such as my being in pain. I may wonder whether it is pain rather than repressed pleasure that I am feeling; but I cannot wonder whether it is really *me* who is feeling the supposed pain. This phenomenon has preoccupied epistemologists at least since Sydney Shoemaker coined the contagious phrase 'immunity to error through misidentification' in 1968; before him it provoked Wittgenstein into claiming, characteristically, that only confusion about language would lead a person into thinking that some especially robust evidence lies behind the knowledge we have of our mental states.[58] Higginbotham is hardly committed to Wittgenstein's view that philosophy occurs only when 'language goes on holiday'; but he does think that linguistic considerations can shed considerable light on this phenomenon.

Higginbotham claims that what underlies immunity to error through misidentification is a peculiar feature of perceptual states: when someone is in them (in pain, say), what she is in is the state of thinking that the subject of these very states is in them (i.e. in pain). This understanding of what underlies immunity to error through misidentification receives support in the way it gels with Higginbotham's account of what distinguishes (33) from (34)–(36). The key is his observation of a curious fact about gerundive complements. PRO constructions can be used to give voice to attitudes

---

[57] PRO = the understood subject, with no phonetic realization.

[58] Wittgenstein (1958), sect. 304, writing about our knowledge of pain, says of pain sensation that 'it is not a *something*, but not a *nothing* either! The conclusion was only that a nothing would serve just as well as a something about which nothing could be said. We have only rejected the grammar which tries to force itself on us here.'

that are immune to error through misidentification in certain gerundive complements, even though the parallel use of reflexives fails to do so—still less the parallel use of a simple pronoun. This is manifest in the fact that (38) seems to follow validly from (37), even though (39), like (40), does not.

(37) I remember someone saying that John should finish his thesis by July; my colleagues assure me that I was the one who said it.

(38) I remember my saying John should finish his thesis by July.

(39) I remember me myself saying John should finish his thesis by July.

(40) I remember PRO saying John should finish his thesis by July.

Higginbotham is led to suspect that 'the problems of the *de se*, immunity to error through misidentification, and the rest, call for a solution in terms of logical form', and makes a number of claims about logical form with this design in mind.

In this introduction I have glossed over the fact that contributors diverge from one another as much in methodologies and ambitions as they do over specific theses about language. Sometimes this divergence is explicit in a claim about how to do effective science; sometimes it is implicit in the use of a reasoning style that departs in some respect from the commonly acknowledged norms of naturalistic enquiry. Epistemology of language is unlikely ever to become a tightly circumscribed field of study. Much of this discrepancy can be put down to differences between traditions and disciplines. But another factor is that epistemological issues are always tangled up with ontological ones. How knowledge of language is possible is bound to turn on what the *object* of knowledge is, yet there is a paucity of agreement on what expressions are, what languages are, and what it is for them to have the properties they do. An optimal ontology is probably more readily available for the epistemology of language than it is for the epistemology of either morality or mathematics, also characteristically human domains. But if this is so, it does not show up in anything that could be called a consensus on ontology in the chapters that follow.

Despite all this, themes that recur throughout the present volume add to the integrity already implicit in works listed in the References below. Irrespective of whether one agrees with their conclusions, the contributors reshape and advance the field here dubbed 'epistemology of language' by addressing issues that are absolutely basic in linguistics, in philosophy of language, and in epistemology.

## REFERENCES

ALMOG, J., PERRY, J., and WETTSTEIN, H., eds. (1989), *Themes from Kaplan* (Oxford: Oxford University Press).

ANTONY, L. M. (1997), 'Meaning and Semantic Knowledge', *Proceedings of the Aristotelian Society*, suppl. 71: 177–209.

—— and HORNSTEIN, N., eds. (2003), *Chomsky and his Critics* (New York: Blackwell).

BARBER, A. (1997), 'Deflated Concepts: A Reply to Stainton', *Crítica*, 29: 83–105.

—— (1998), 'The Pleonasticity of Talk about Concepts', *Philosophical Studies*, 89: 53–86.

—— (2000), 'A Pragmatic Treatment of Simple Sentences', *Analysis*, 60: 300–8.

—— (2001), 'Idiolectal Error', *Mind and Language*, 16: 263–83.

BLOCK, N., ed. (1981), *Readings in the Philosophy of Psychology* vol. ii (Cambridge, Mass.: Harvard University Press).

—— (1995), 'On a Confusion about a Function of Consciousness', *Behavioral and Brain Sciences*, 18: 227–87.

BORG, E. (forthcoming), 'Saying What You Mean: Unarticulated Constituents and Communication', in Stainton and Elugardo (forthcoming).

BOTTERELL, A. (forthcoming), 'Knowledge by Acquaintance and Meaning in Isolation', in Stainton and Elugardo (forthcoming).

BRAUN, D. (2001), 'Russellianism and Explanation', *Philosophical Perspectives*, 15: 253–89.

BROOK, A., and DEVIDI, R. C., eds. (2001), *Self-Reference and Self-Awareness* (Amsterdam, Philadelphia: John Benjamins).

BROWN, J. (1995), 'The Incompatibility of Anti-Individualism and Privileged Access', *Analysis*, 55: 149–56.

BURGE, T. (1979), 'Individualism and the Mental', *Midwest Studies in Philosophy*, 4: 73–121.

—— (1988) 'Individualism and Self-Knowledge', *Journal of Philosophy*, 85: 649–663.

—— (1989), 'Wherein is Language Social?', in George (1989b), 175–91.

CAMPBELL, J. (1982), 'Knowledge and Understanding', *Philosophical Quarterly*, 32: 17–34.

CAPPELEN, H., and LEPORE, E. (forthcoming), 'Radical and Moderate Pragmatics: Does Meaning Determine Truth Conditions?', in Szabo (forthcoming).

CASTAÑEDA, H. N. (1966), '"He": A Study in the Logic of Self-Consciousness', *Ratio*, 8: 130–57.

CAUMAN, L. S., ed. (1983), *How Many Questions? Essays in Honor of Sidney Morgenbesser* (Indianapolis: Hackett).

CHOMSKY, N. (1959), 'A Review of B. F. Skinner's *Verbal Behavior*', *Language*, 35: 26–58.

—— (1976), *Reflections on Language* (London: Temple Smith).

—— (1980), *Rules and Representations* (New York: Columbia University Press).

—— (1986), *Knowledge of Language: Its Nature, Origin, and Use* (New York: Praeger).

—— (1995a), 'Language and Nature', *Mind*, 104: 1–61.

—— (1995b), *The Minimalist Program* (Cambridge, Mass.: MIT Press).

—— (2000), *New Horizons in the Study of Language and Mind* (Cambridge: Cambridge University Press).

—— and KATZ, J. J. (1974), 'What the Linguist is Talking About', *Journal of Philosophy*, 71: 347–67.

CONEE, E. and FELDMAN, R. (1998), 'The Generality Problem for Reliabilism', *Philosophical Studies*, 89: 1–29.

COOPER, D. E. (1973), 'Grammar and the Possession of Concepts', *Proceedings of the Philosophy of Education Society of Great Britain*, 7: 204–22.

COWIE, F. (1999), *What's Within? Nativism Reconsidered* (New York: Oxford University Press).

CRIMMINS, M. (1992), 'Tacitness and Virtual Beliefs', *Mind and Language*, 7: 240–63.

DAVIDSON, D. (1967), 'Truth and Meaning', *Synthese*, 17: 304–23.

—— (1990), 'The Structure and Content of Truth', *Journal of Philosophy*, 87: 279–328.

—— (2001), 'A Coherence Theory of Truth and Knowledge (with Afterthoughts)', in id., *Subjective, Intersubjective, Objective* (Oxford: Oxford University Press), 137–58.

DAVIES, M. (1987), 'Tacit Knowledge and Semantic Theory: Can a Five Per Cent Difference Matter?', *Mind*, 96: 441–62.

—— (1989), 'Connectionism, Modularity, and Tacit Knowledge', *British Journal for the Philosophy of Science*, 40: 541–55.

DEVITT, M., and STERELNY, K. (1987), *Language and Reality: An Introduction to the Philosophy of Language* (Cambridge, Mass.: MIT Press).

—— —— (1989), 'Linguistics: What's Wrong with "The Right View"', in Tomberlin (1989), 497–531.

DUMMETT, M. A. E. (1975), 'What is a Theory of Meaning?', in Guttenplan (1975), 97–138.

—— (1976), 'What is a Theory of Meaning (II)?', in Evans and McDowell (1976), 67–137.

—— (1981), 'Objections to Chomsky', London Review of Books, 3–16 Sept.

—— (1991), The Logical Basis of Metaphysics (Cambridge: Harvard University Press).

DWYER, S. (1999), 'Moral Competence', in Murasugi and Stainton (1999), 167–90.

—— and PIETROSKI, P. M. (1996), 'Believing in Language', Philosophy of Science, 63: 338–73.

EVANS, G. (1976), 'Semantic Structure and Logical Form', in Evans and McDowell (1976), 199–222.

—— (1981), 'Semantic Theory and Tacit Knowledge', in Holtzman and Leich (1981), 118–37.

—— and McDOWELL, J., eds. (1976), Truth and Meaning: Essays in Semantics (Oxford: Clarendon Press).

FODOR, J. A. (1968), 'The Appeal to Tacit Knowledge in Psychological Explanation', Journal of Philosophy, 65: 627–40.

—— (1976), The Language of Thought (Hassocks: Harvester Press).

—— (1981), 'Some Notes on What Linguistics is About', in Block (1981), 197–201.

FORBES, G. (1984), 'Scepticism and Semantic Knowledge', Proceedings of the Aristotelian Society, 84: 223–40.

—— (1997), 'How Much Substitutivity?', Analysis, 57: 109–13.

FOSTER, J. A. (1976), 'Meaning and Truth Theory', in Evans and McDowell (1976), 1–32.

FRANZEN, J. (2002), The Corrections (New York: Picador).

FRICKER, E. (1983), 'Semantic Structure and Speakers' Understanding', Proceedings of the Aristotelian Society, 83: 49–66.

GARFIELD, J. L., ed. (1987), Modularity in Knowledge Representation and Natural Language Understanding (Cambridge, Mass.: MIT Press).

GELLNER, E. (1959), Words and Things: An Examination of, and an Attack on, Linguistic Philosophy (London: Gollancz).

GENDLER, T. S. (1998), 'Galileo and the Indispensability of Scientific Thought Experiment', British Journal for the Philosophy of Science, 49: 397–424.

GEORGE, A. (1986), 'Whence and Whither the Debate between Quine and Chomsky', Journal of Philosophy, 83: 489–99.

—— (1989a), 'How Not to Become Confused about Linguistics', in George (1989b), 90–110.

—— ed. (1989b), *Reflections on Chomsky* (Oxford: Basil Blackwell).

—— (1990), 'Whose Language is it Anyway? Some Notes on Idiolects', *Philosophical Quarterly*, 40: 275–98.

—— (1996), 'Katz Astray', *Mind and Language*, 11: 295–305.

GRAVES, C., et al. (1973), 'Tacit Knowledge', *Journal of Philosophy*, 70: 318–30.

GRICE, P. (1989), *Studies in the Way of Words* (Cambridge, Mass.: Harvard University Press).

GUNDERSON, K., ed. (1975), *Language, Mind, and Knowledge* (Minneapolis: University of Minnesota Press).

GUTTENPLAN, S. (1975), *Mind and Language* (Oxford: Oxford University Press).

HALE, R. (1997), 'Rule-Following, Objectivity and Meaning', in Wright and Hale (1997), 369–96.

HARMAN, G. (1968), 'Psychological Aspects of the Theory of Syntax', *Journal of Philosophy*, 64: 75–87.

—— (1974), *On Noam Chomsky: Critical Essays* (Garden City, NY: Anchor Press).

HECK R. G. (1995), 'The Sense of Communication', *Mind*, 104: 79–106.

HIGGINBOTHAM, J. (1983), 'Is Grammar Psychological?', in Cauman (1983), 170–9.

—— (1985), 'On Semantics', *Linguistic Inquiry*, 16: 547–93.

—— (1986), 'Linguistic Theory and Davidson's Program in Semantics', in Lepore (1986), 29–49.

—— (1988), 'Is Semantics Necessary?', *Proceedings of the Aristotelian Society*, 88: 219–41.

—— (1989a), 'Elucidations of Meaning', *Linguistics and Philosophy*, 12: 465–517.

—— (1989b), 'Knowledge of Reference', in George (1989b), 153–74.

—— (1991), 'Remarks on the Metaphysics of Linguistics', *Linguistics and Philosophy*, 14: 555–66.

—— (1992), 'Truth and Understanding', *Philosophical Studies*, 65: 3–16.

—— (1998a), 'Conceptual Competence', in Villanueva (1998), 149–62.

—— (1998b), 'On Knowing One's Own Language', in Wright, Smith, and MacDonald (1998), 429–41.

HOLTZMAN, S., and LEICH, C. M., eds. (1981), *Wittgenstein: To Follow a Rule* (London: Routledge and Kegan Paul).

HONDERICH, T., ed. (1985), *Morality and Objectivity* (London: Routledge and Kegan Paul).

HOOK, S., ed. (1969), *Language and Philosophy: A Symposium* (New York: New York University Press).

HORNSTEIN, N. (1987), 'Levels of Meaning', in Garfield (1987), 133–50.

—— (1988), 'The Heartbreak of Semantics', *Mind and Language*, 3: 9–27.

HORNSTEIN, N. (1989), 'Meaning and the Mental: The Problem of Semantics after Chomsky', in George (1989b), 23–40.

—— (1995), 'Putting Truth into Universal Grammar', *Linguistics and Philosophy*, 18: 381–400.

HUNTER, D. (1998), 'Understanding and Belief', *Philosophy and Phenomenological Research*, 58: 559–80.

JACKENDOFF, R. (1990), *Semantic Structures* (Cambridge, Mass.: MIT Press).

KAPLAN, D. (1989), 'Demonstratives: An Essay on the Semantics, Logic, Metaphysics, and Epistemology of Demonstratives and Other Indexicals', in Almog, Perry, and Wettstein (1989), 481–563.

KASHER, A., ed. (1991), *The Chomskyan Turn* (Oxford: Basil Blackwell).

KATZ, J. J., ed. (1985), *The Philosophy of Linguistics* (Oxford: Oxford University Press).

—— (1990), *The Metaphysics of Meaning* (Cambridge, Mass.: MIT Press).

—— (1996), 'The Unfinished Chomskyan Revolution', *Mind and Language*, 11: 270–94.

KNOWLES, J. (2000), 'Knowledge of Grammar as a Propositional Attitude', *Philosophical Psychology*, 13: 325–53.

KRIPKE, S. A. (1980), *Naming and Necessity* (Cambridge, Mass.: Harvard University Press).

—— (1982), *Wittgenstein on Rules and Private Languages* (Oxford: Basil Blackwell).

LARSON, R. K., and SEGAL, G. (1995), *Knowledge of Meaning: An Introduction to Semantics* (Cambridge, Mass.: MIT Press).

LAURENCE, S. (1996), 'A Chomskian Alternative to Convention-Based Semantics', *Mind*, 105: 269–301.

—— and MARGOLIS, E. (2001), 'The Poverty of the Stimulus Argument', *British Journal for the Philosophy of Science*, 52: 217–76.

LEPORE, E. (1983), 'The Concept of Meaning and its Role in Understanding Language', *Dialectica*, 37: 133–39.

—— ed. (1986), *Truth and Interpretation: Perspectives on the Philosophy of Donald Davidson* (Cambridge, Mass.: Basil Blackwell).

—— (1997), 'Conditions on Understanding Language', *Proceedings of the Aristotelian Society*, 97: 41–60.

LOEWER, B., and REY, G., eds. (1991), *Meaning in Mind: Fodor and his Critics* (Cambridge: Blackwell).

LUDLOW, P. (2003), 'Referential Semantics for I-Languages?', in Antony and Hornstein (2003), 140–61.

—— and MARTIN, N., eds. (1998), *Externalism and Self Knowledge* (Stanford, Calif.: CSLI Publications).

LYCAN, W. G. (1986), 'Semantics and Methodological Solipsism', in Lepore (1986), 245–61.

MATTHEWS, R. J. (1991), 'Psychological Reality of Grammars', in Kasher (1991), 182–99.

McDOWELL, J. (1977), 'On the Sense and Reference of a Proper Name', *Mind*, 86: 159–85.

—— (1980), 'Meaning, Communication, and Knowledge', in Van Straaten (1980), 117–39.

—— (1985), 'Values and Secondary Qualities', in Honderich (1985), 110–29.

—— (1987), 'In Defence of Modesty', in Taylor (1987), 59–80.

McGILVRAY, J. (1998), 'Meanings are Syntactically Individuated and Found in the Head', *Mind and Language*, 13: 225–80.

—— ed. (forthcoming), *A Companion to Chomsky* (Cambridge: Cambridge University Press).

McKINSEY, M. (1991), 'Anti-Individualism and Privileged Access', *Analysis*, 51: 9–16.

MILLER, A. (1997), 'Tacit Knowledge', in Wright and Hale (1997), 146–74.

—— (1998), *Philosophy of Language* (London: UCL Press, and Montreal: McGill-Queens University Press).

MILLIKAN, R. G. (2003), 'In Defense of Public Language', in Antony and Hornstein (2003), 215–35.

MURASUGI, K., and STAINTON, R. J., eds. (1999), *Philosophy and Linguistics* (Boulder: Westview Press).

NAGEL, T. (1969), 'Linguistics and Epistemology', in Hook (1969), 171–82; repr. in Harman (1974).

NEALE, S. (1987), 'Meaning, Grammar, and Indeterminacy', *Dialectica*, 41: 301–19.

—— (1990), *Descriptions* (Cambridge, Mass.: MIT Press).

PEACOCKE, C. (1976), 'Truth Definitions and Actual Languages', in Evans and McDowell (1976), 162–88.

—— (1986), 'Explanation in Computational Psychology: Language, Perception and Level 1.5', *Mind and Language*, 1: 101–23.

—— (1989), 'When is a Grammar Psychologically Real?', in George (1989b), 111–30.

—— (1994), 'Content, Computation and Externalism', *Mind and Language*, 9: 303–35.

PETTIT, D. (2002), 'Why Knowledge of Language is Unnecessary for Understanding Language', *Mind*, 111: 519–50.

PREYER, G., and PETER, G. (2002), *Logical Form and Language* (Oxford: Oxford University Press).

PUTNAM, H. (1975), 'The Meaning of "Meaning"', in Gunderson (1975), 131–93.

QUINE, W. V. (1970), 'Methodological Reflections on Current Linguistic Theory', *Synthese*, 21: 386–98.

—— (1975), 'Mind and Verbal Dispositions', in Guttenplan (1975), 83–95.

RADFORD, A. (1997), *Syntactic Theory and the Structure of English: A Minimalist Approach* (Cambridge: Cambridge University Press).

RÉCANATI, F. (1997), 'Can We Believe What We Do Not Understand?', *Mind and Language*, 12: 84–100.

ROOT, M. D. (1974), 'Quine's Methodological Reflections', *Metaphilosophy*, 5: 36–50.

RUSSELL, B. (1905), 'On Denoting', *Mind*, 14: 479–93.

SAINSBURY, R. M. (1980), 'Understanding and Theories of Meaning', *Proceedings of the Aristotelian Society*, 80: 127–44.

SAUL, J. M. (1997), 'Substitution and Simple Sentences', *Analysis*, 57: 102–8.

SCHIFFER, S. (1987), *Remnants of Meaning* (Cambridge, Mass.: MIT Press).

SEARLE, J. R. (1990), 'Consciousness, Explanatory Inversion, and Cognitive Science', *Behavioral and Brain Sciences*, 13: 585–96.

SHOEMAKER, S. S. (1968), 'Self-Reference and Self-Awareness', *Journal of Philosophy*, 65: 555–67.

SMITH, B. (1998), 'On Knowing One's Own Language', in Wright, Smith, and MacDonald (1998), 391–428.

SOAMES, S. (1984), 'Linguistics and Psychology', *Linguistics and Philosophy*, 7: 155–80.

—— (1985), 'Semantics and Psychology', in Katz (1985), 204–26.

—— (1989), 'Semantics and Semantic Competence', in Tomberlin (1989), 575–96.

—— (1991), 'The Necessity Argument', *Linguistics and Philosophy*, 14: 575–80.

—— (1992), 'Truth, Meaning, and Understanding', *Philosophical Studies*, 65: 17–35.

—— (1998), 'The Modal Argument: Wide Scope and Rigidified Descriptions', *Noûs*, 32: 1–22.

STAINTON, R. J. (1996), 'The Deflation of Belief Contents', *Crítica*, 28: 63–82.

—— (1998), 'Quantifier Phrases, Meaningfulness "in Isolation", and Ellipsis', *Linguistics and Philosophy*, 21: 311–40.

—— (2000), 'The Meaning of "Sentences"', *Noûs*, 34: 441–54.

—— and ELUGARDO, R., eds. (forthcoming), *Ellipsis and Non-Sentential Speech* (Dordrecht: Kluwer Academic Press).

STANLEY, J. (2000), 'Context and Logical Form', *Linguistics and Philosophy*, 23: 391–434.

STICH, S. (1991), 'Narrow Content Meets Fat Syntax', in Lower and Rey (1991), 239–54.

—— (1971), 'What Every Speaker Knows', *Philosophical Review*, 80: 476–96.

—— (1972), 'Grammar, Psychology, and Indeterminacy', *Journal of Philosophy*, 69: 799–818.

—— (1983), *From Folk Psychology to Cognitive Science: The Case against Belief* (Cambridge: MIT Press).

SZABO, Z., ed. (forthcoming), *Semantics vs. Pragmatics* (Oxford: Oxford University Press).

TAYLOR, B., ed. (1987), *Michael Dummett: Contributions to Philosophy* (Dordrecht: Nijhoff).

TOMBERLIN, J. E., ed. (1989), *Philosophy of Mind and Action Theory* (Philosophical Perspectives, 3; Atascadero: Ridgeview).

VAN STRAATEN, Z., ed. (1980), *Philosophical Subjects: Essays Presented to P. F. Strawson* (Oxford: Clarendon Press).

VILLANUEVA, E., ed. (1998), *Concepts* (Philosophical Issues, 9; Atascadero: Ridgeview).

WIGGINS, D. (1997), 'Languages as Social Objects', *Philosophy*, 72: 499–524.

WILSON, D., and SPERBER, D. (2002), 'Truthfulness and Relevance', *Mind*, 111: 583–632.

WITTGENSTEIN, L. (1958), *Philosophical Investigations*, ed. and trans. G. E. M. Anscombe, 2nd edn. (Oxford: Blackwell).

WRIGHT, C. (1986a), *Realism, Meaning, and Truth* (Oxford: Oxford University Press).

—— (1986b), 'Theories of Meaning and Speakers' Knowledge', in Wright (1986a), 204–38.

—— (1989), 'Wittgenstein's Rule-Following Considerations and the Central Project of Theoretical Linguistics', in George (1989), 233–64.

—— and HALE, B., eds. (1997), *A Companion to the Philosophy of Language* (Oxford: Basil Blackwell).

—— SMITH, B., and MACDONALD, C., eds. (1998), *Knowing Our Own Minds: Essays on Self-Knowledge* (Oxford: Oxford University Press).

# PART ONE

## Knowledge in Linguistics

CHAPTER 2

# Rabbit-Pots and Supernovas: On the Relevance of Psychological Data to Linguistic Theory

*Louise M. Antony*

A number of philosophers remonstrate against the 'psychologizing' of linguistics: in particular, Jerrold Katz (Katz 1984), Scott Soames (Soames 1984), and Michael Devitt and Kim Sterelny (Devitt and Sterelny 1987; 1989). All of them have argued against the view, due to Chomsky, that linguistics ought properly to be conceived as a branch of psychology. On the Chomskian model, linguistic theories aim at describing the internalized grammars of native speakers of particular languages, in a way that reveals universal principles of grammatical structure natively present in all human beings. Katz, Soames, and Devitt and Sterelny all contend that this conception is based on a conflation of two theoretical domains—an abstract domain of linguis-

An initial draft of this paper was written while I was an Andrew W. Mellon Fellow at the National Humanities Center. I would like to thank both the Mellon Foundation and the Center for their generous support. I would also like to thank David Auerbach, Norbert Hornstein, Harold Levin, Joe Levine, Ed Martin, David Sanford, Geoff Sayre-McCord, and Amy Weinberg for their help in thinking through the issues in this paper. Earlier versions were presented at the 1991 meeting of the Society for Philosophy and Psychology (with comments from Scott Soames) and at the University of North Carolina at Chapel Hill, and the University of Massachusetts at Amherst. I thank everyone involved in those discussions, and especially Professor Soames, for their stimulating questions and comments. Permission to include a photograph of the Mimbres pot was was kindly provided by the Frederick R. Weisman Art Museum at the University of Minnesota.

tic structure, and a psychological domain of *knowledge* of that structure. The result of this conflation, they all argue, is a linguistics inappropriately constrained by psychological data. In what follows, I shall refer to the sort of linguistics deplored by these philosophers as 'psychologized linguistics', and I shall call the alternative, which they endorse, 'pure linguistics'.[1]

The arguments of the critics of psychologized linguistics fall into roughly two categories: 'conceptual' arguments, intended to show that the psychologizing of linguistics amounts to a change in theoretical domain, and thus to a 'change of subject'; and empirical arguments, which purport to show that the kinds of appeal made to psychological data by proponents of psychologized linguistics have yielded results that are empirically inadequate by uncontroversial theoretical standards. Both kinds of argument need answering, but in this paper I am going to focus on a representative argument of the first type, developed by Soames. An analysis of his discussion as to whether psychology and linguistics are (in Soames's terms) 'conceptually distinct' will reveal that advocates of pure and psychologized linguistics are divided by deep metatheoretical disagreements about the objectives of linguistic theory, which in turn are based in deep disagreements about the nature and purpose of empirical enquiry in general.

Indulge me in a rehearsal of some recent history. Pre-Chomskian linguistics was a largely descriptive field of enquiry. Linguists like Bloomfield and Harris aimed primarily at the systematization of facts about human languages; the metatheory for this endeavour was thoroughly instrumentalist, so that the only accepted empirical constraint on linguistic theories was the observational adequacy of their predictions.[2] Chomsky's alternative was a linguistics constrained by an explanatory, rather than a descriptive, goal:

---

[1] It should be noted that there is substantial disagreement among the critics of psychologized linguistics about the nature and proper methodology of pure linguistics. In particular, there is no consensus among the critics about whether linguistics should be regarded as an empirical discipline. Soames believes that it is an empirical discipline, concerned with the analysis of an empirical phenomenon. Katz, on the other hand, contends that languages are abstract objects, and that linguistics as a science is therefore on a par with mathematics. My arguments in this paper are mainly addressed to Soames, and thus they presume that linguistics is an empirical science. Although Katz makes arguments very similar to those of Soames that I am about to discuss, his arguments will be less vulnerable to my criticisms than Soames's, precisely because Katz is unwilling to treat linguistics as an empirical science.

[2] This is uncontroversial, even among advocates of pure linguistics. See Katz (1985b).

figure out how human children master their languages in the conditions in which they do.[3]

Chomsky's revision of the theoretical objectives of linguistics is acknowledged to have resulted in a wholesale transformation of the field. But it is important to see exactly how and why this transformation was effected. Chomsky's different understanding of the goals of linguistic theory did not automatically entail a psychologizing of the field, nor the abandonment of a descriptive, instrumentalist take on linguistic theory. What transformed linguistics was not the question Chomsky asked, but rather the way he answered it.

The going line on language acquisition in the time of structuralism had been behaviourist: language learning was simply an aspect of general learning, and thus, by current theories, a matter of behavioural conditioning. This line, had it worked, would have justified treating linguistics in just the way the structuralists had treated it, as a systematic description of the distributional patterns of sounds and ink-marks.

But Chomsky had compelling arguments for the empirical inadequacy of the behaviourist account of language acquisition (Chomsky 1959). The alternative he advocated involved the rehabilitation of two dishonoured philosophical views, mentalism and nativism. Chomsky argued, first, that language acquisition was essentially a computational process by which a child constructed a grammar for her language, and second, that the child's ability to construct an adequate grammar on the basis of the data available to her depended upon the existence of powerful native constraints on the set of hypotheses she could entertain.

It is this explanatory goal—that of accounting for acquisition—that seems to me to have been lost in much of the criticism of psychologized linguistics. The critics seem to feel that the Chomskian turn has resulted in a change

[3] See Chomsky (1977). It is admittedly a bit anachronistic to suggest that Chomsky's motivations for abandoning structuralism were identical to the justifications he would now give for the generative approach. Katz points out that Chomsky originally defended structuralism's positivistic ontology and methodology, and began to have doubts only as a result of his inability to get a minimally adequate grammar for Hebrew working within structuralist constraints. But the fact that Chomsky's reconstrual of the ontology of linguistics was motivated by a need for more abstractness in the grammar than structuralism allowed does not mean that abstractness *per se* is a virtue, as Katz's discussion sometimes suggests.

of subject matter for linguistics, or even that it has led to the demise of an entire area of study—that what used to be the science of *language* has been replaced by a specialization within the science of the mind. My picture of the development of linguistics is rather one of the refinement of the theoretical goals of the science of language—a movement from a relatively young and unconstrained descriptive project to a mature science devoted to the explanation of central linguistic phenomena, and creative in finding empirical purchase for its theoretical claims. In what follows, I shall try to show how Soames's neglect of the explanatory impetus behind the Chomskian revolution has distorted his general views on how the domain of a theoretical field is determined.

## 1  The 'Conceptual Distinctness' of Linguistics and Psychology

As Soames characterizes it, his goal is to demonstrate that linguistics and psychology are 'conceptually distinct', which is to say that 'they are concerned with different domains, make different claims, and are established by different means' (Soames 1984: 155). Soames's argument for this segregation of linguistics from psychology is essentially a priori, and proceeds from the observation that the subject matter of the two fields is ostensibly different. Specifically, Soames contends that a neutral, pre-theoretic survey of the domain of linguistic theory is enough to establish that linguistics is distinct from 'psychological theories of the mental states and processes underlying language acquisition and mastery' (Soames 1984: 156).

Now on the face of it, such a strategy seems flawed in its very conception—one simply cannot derive substantive conclusions about the methodology and database of an empirical field of study just from a characterization of the field's domain. The reason is that a specification of the phenomena of interest—no matter how accurate or well motivated—cannot by itself tell us what kinds of evidence we may need to appeal to in constructing an *account* of those phenomena. This can only be determined empirically, because in science, a discipline's methods and databases depend upon the empirical connections in which its subject phenomena participate, some of which may be known, and some of which are yet to be discovered. Knowing what a language is does not equip us to say what facts about the world we shall need to exploit in order to account for the linguistic phenomena that interest us.

Verification is holistic: a suitable chain of inference could bring any fact to bear on any empirical issue.[4] It is thus impossible to rule out anything as a potential source of data for an empirical theory. We do not know a priori where evidence about languages may be found because we do not know a priori what empirical connections languages participate in, nor can we fully anticipate the ways clever experimenters and theorists may contrive to exploit those connections, once discovered, to generate testable predictions.

It is standard and valorous scientific practice to achieve testability for a particular hypothesis by conjoining it in a creative way with well-confirmed theories in other domains. This is a particularly prudent practice in areas where it is impractical, for one reason or another, to obtain 'direct' evidence. Particle physics, evolutionary biology, and cognitive psychology are, in this respect, all in the same boat. In any of these fields, researchers would be hamstrung if they were to follow (what appears to be) Soames's advice, viz. mind your own business.

But surely Soames agrees with all of this—that verification is holistic, and that empirical disciplines borrow readily from other empirical disciplines. So why does he think that linguistics is any different? Why does he think that a psychologistic linguist's appeal to psychological data is any different from an evolutionary biologist's appeal to geological data? Why does he think that a linguist who talks about memory limitations or order of acquisition has literally *changed the subject*?

To answer these questions, let us look at his argument in detail. Here is my reconstruction of the central line in 'Linguistics and Psychology' (Soames 1984):

(1) Linguistics is the science of language.

Therefore,

(2) Linguistics ought to be constrained only by facts that are directly relevant to the linguistically significant properties of sentences.

(3) Facts about the psychological states and processes underlying linguis-

---

[4] Jerry Fodor emphasizes this point in Fodor (1985).

tic behaviour are not directly relevant to the linguistically significant properties of sentences.

Therefore,

(4) Facts about the psychological states and processes underlying linguistic behaviour should not constrain linguistic theory.

Therefore,

(5) Linguistic theories are conceptually distinct from psychological theories. QED.

The crucial step in this argument, it seems to me, is the move from (1) to (2), and this move turns on the notions of 'linguistic significance' and 'direct relevance'.[5] We thus need to see, first, what Soames takes to be the criterion of 'linguistic significance', and second, what evidential relation he has in mind when he speaks of data that either are or are not 'directly relevant' to a given body of fact.

Let us start with 'linguistic significance'. Not just any criterion will do here—what Soames needs is a criterion of linguistic significance that is both intuitively plausible and non-trivial, *and* at the same time substantive enough to rule out certain kinds of things without begging the crucial question. And in fact, Soames thinks that he has such a criterion: he says that the linguistically significant properties of linguistic phenomena are those properties of utterance and inscription types that are *essential* to the individuation of the language to which they belong—those 'characteristics which define languages and serve to identify or distinguish them'. More precisely, the linguistically significant properties and relations holding of and among sentence types are those which 'constitute individually sufficient and disjunctively necessary conditions for individuating the languages (or dialects) of different speakers' (Soames 1984: 159).

Thus, a property of a sentence type counts as linguistically significant if and only if a difference with respect to that property would be enough to make us count two sets of sentence types as distinct languages. Soames cites the following as examples of linguistically significant properties and relations: grammaticality, ambiguity, synonymy, entailment, analyticity, and

---

[5] These are Soames's terms: see Soames (1984), 159.

contradiction; and the following as examples of non-linguistically significant properties and relations: degree of ease with which a construction can be processed, and relative time at which a construction is acquired. He offers the following thought-experiment in defence of this categorization (this is a close paraphrase):

Imagine two linguistic communities, the Xers and the Yers, and suppose that we wish to discover whether the language spoken by the Xers is different from or the same as the language spoken by the Yers. If we were to discover that there was a certain class of sentences which the Xers accepted as grammatical, but which the Yers rejected, we would conclude that the X-language was indeed distinct from the Y-language (similarly for variation in judgements about synonymy, entailment, and ambiguity).

But now suppose that there were no differences between Xers' and Yers' judgements regarding grammaticality, synonymy, entailment, or ambiguity, but that there were systematic differences between the Xers and Yers of the following sorts, concerning classes of constructions A and B: (i) Xers acquired As before Bs, while Yers acquired Bs before As; or (ii) Xers process As faster than Bs, but Yers process Bs faster than As; or (iii) Xers make characteristically more errors with respect to As than Yers make. If these were the nature of the differences between the linguistic behaviour of Xers and Yers, then we would *not* conclude that the X-language was different from the Y-language. (Soames 1984: 159)

One thing to notice right away is that Soames is advocating an *a prioristic* methodology for discovering the essential properties of something he regards as an *empirical* phenomenon: he maintains that we can identify the linguistically significant properties by consulting our intuitions about the kinds of difference two bodies of linguistic phenomena would need to display in order for us to judge them to be distinct languages. This strategy should cause eyebrows to rise—we know this method would not serve us well in discerning the essential properties of water. The reason it would not is that in advance of any *theory* about water, we do not know which of its superficial characteristics reflect essential properties and which are mere accidents: does water *have* to be colourless, or is there (genuinely) blue water somewhere? The process of answering this question is inseparable from the process of finding out what water *is*, and either answer to the first question must be tentative, pending further progress on the second.

But these misgivings concern Soames's method for identifying the linguistically significant properties of linguistic phenomena, and have nothing to do with the *criterion* of linguistic significance itself. Let us therefore suppose that, by whatever means, Soames has correctly isolated the properties of languages that satisfy that criterion—let us suppose that grammaticality etc. are the properties that are genuinely individuative of languages. Will it then follow that linguistics need only account for data that are 'directly relevant' to the attribution of those properties and relations?

Here is where things get really interesting (in my opinion). I said earlier that the holistic character of verification entails that one cannot tell *a priori* what data might be relevant to a given field of enquiry, and thus that no *a priori* considerations could show that psychological data are irrelevant to linguistic theorizing. But Soames is not claiming *that*—he does not say that psychological data are *always* or *necessarily* irrelevant to linguistic theorizing. What he in fact says is that '*once the linguistically significant facts have been accounted for*, there is no need for the theory to be concerned with psycholinguistic data . . .' (Soames 1984: 160, my emphasis). The qualification is crucial—while Soames readily concedes that 'data which are not themselves linguistically significant often provide evidence for attributions of properties and relations which are', he still avers that: 'even when [such data] bear on [attributions of linguistically significant properties], they need not be predicted by linguistic theories, so long as the theories correctly account for all linguistically significant facts' (Soames 1984: 160). He thus acknowledges that linguistically insignificant data can be relevant to the construction of theories of the facts that interest us, but stigmatizes their contribution, saying that 'the relevance of such psycholinguistic data to theories in linguistics is limited to this indirect role' (Soames 1984: 160).

It is not immediately clear what Soames has in mind—how can data 'bear on' theories without constraining them? Surely data 'bear on' a theory when the occurrence of those data is entailed by the theory in conjunction with background assumptions, or when those data can be conjoined with the theory to achieve greater explanatory or predictive power. In any such case, the theory would seem to be 'constrained' by the data at least to the following extent: a theory that predicts or conforms to data that 'bear on' it in one of the above senses is to be preferred, *ceteris paribus*, to one that does not.

What Soames's remarks suggest is that he thinks that there are, in general, 'direct' and 'indirect' ways in which data can support theory, and that only data that bear 'directly' are ones that the theory must answer to—for the rest, the theory's ability to predict them is gratuitous. I presume that he is not here making tacit appeal to a discredited observation/theory distinction (observations providing 'direct' support, and theoretically mediated inferences providing only 'indirect' support). Rather, he seems to be alluding to some measure of *topical* distance. The idea, perhaps, is that bits of information very far removed from the domain in question may, by some convoluted inferential route, provide evidence for some hypothesis concerning that domain, without theorizing about the domain becoming constrained to predict every bit of such potentially useful information.

## 2 The Lesson of the Rabbit-Pots

If this is what Soames has in mind, then here is a case that may serve to illustrate: the story begins seventy years ago, when an archaeological team from the University of Minnesota discovered a cache of over 800 ceramic pieces at Indian ruins near Silver City, New Mexico. About 200 of the pieces were 'narrative' bowls, some with drawings depicting activities like hunting and fishing, others illustrating stories or chronicling events.

Many of the pieces, including a particular bowl of special interest, were decorated with stylized drawings of a rabbit. These 'rabbit-pots' were especially interesting to Dr R. Robert Robbins, an astronomer at the University of Texas at Austin, and his associate, Dr Russell B. Westmoreland, an archaeologist. Robbins and Westmoreland contend that these pots have *astronomical* significance. It seems that when the Mimbres Indians (the potters) looked at the moon, they saw on its surface not the image of a man, as many North Americans see, but rather that of a rabbit, so that the drawings of rabbits found on the pots were either depictions of, or symbolic references to, the moon.

Now the bowl that Robbins and Westmoreland found particularly interesting (Figure 2.1) differed from the other rabbit-pots in the following detail: just below the moon-rabbit's back foot there is a small, filled-in circle surrounded by twenty-three radiating lines. Robbins and Westmoreland are convinced that this 'sunburst' is in fact a record of the Mimbres tribe's observation of the supernova that created the Crab Nebula. Astronomers

FIG. 2.1. Mimbres Painted Bowl

Collection Frederick R. Weisman Art Museum at the University of Minnesota,
Minneapolis. Transfer, Anthropology Department, University of Minnesota

had previously dated the occurrence of the supernova from documents
left by astrologers to the emperor of China, which told of the sudden appearance of a bright object in the sky on 5 July 1054, visible in daylight for
twenty-three days. Carbon dating indicates that the Mimbres rabbit-pot was
produced in the middle of the eleventh century, placing it at the time of the
supernova, and the number of rays extending from the object at the rabbit's
foot—twenty-three [I'm not making this up!]—corresponds to the number of days the supernova was visible, according to the Chinese documents.
Dr Robbins says of the pot that it is 'the most certain record of the supernova
that has ever been discovered outside China and Japan' (Wilford 1990).

Now perhaps this is the sort of situation Soames has in mind: it seems
not unreasonable to describe this case as one in which a certain bit of
evidence bears on, but does not constrain, a hypothesis. After all, one might
contend, it is fine and good if archaeology turns up some pots depicting an
astronomical occurrence—they certainly can be marshalled in support of

a theory that asserts such an occurrence. But at the same time, we would not want to insist that a theory of astronomy *must* make predictions about ancient pots—that is just not astronomy's job. A theory that thoroughly explained celestial phenomena, but was utterly silent on the subject of eleventh-century American pottery, would be quite satisfactory.

There is something that seems right here—we do not in fact expect theories to be able to predict every single datum that might conceivably bear on their truth or falsity, and yet there are other data that we regard as absolutely central, data that must be accounted for by any adequate theory of that domain. But this innocent observation must not mislead us—there is nothing here that is going to help Soames establish that linguistic theories are constrained only by linguistically significant data.

Notice that although drawings on eleventh-century pots do not 'constrain' astronomical theories in one sense, there is another sense of 'constrain' in which they do. On the one hand, I doubt that anyone would want to make it a condition of adequacy for a theory of celestial phenomena that it can account for rabbit-pots, whereas most people would be willing to say in advance that an astronomical theory ought to have something to say about the orbit of the moon. But on the other hand, the rabbit-pots do constrain astronomical theories in the sense that is relevant to the debate about linguistics: other things beings equal, we shall prefer the astronomical theory that *can* account for the rabbit-pots over the one that *cannot*. Even more to the point, a *dispute* about the astronomical facts could in principle be decided by appeal to the rabbit-pots: if theory $T_1$ says that a supernova *did* occur in the eleventh century, and theory $T_2$ says that it did not, then the discovery of the rabbit-pots counts in favour of $T_1$.

Now of course, two astronomical theories are not likely to disagree just on the occurrence of a supernova. Supernovas are a big-time, gauche kind of thing, and tend to leave traces of themselves all over the place, so it is very unlikely that the whole matter would boil down to there being or not being rabbit-pots. But the idea that astronomy can be indifferent to the existence or non-existence of such things is, I think, a kind of perceptual illusion—we boggle at the sheer number of mediating assumptions necessary to take us from the hypothesis that the supernova occurred to the prediction that rabbit-pots will be found. The feeling that astronomy should not be expected to account for whatever archaeologists happen to dig up stems partly from our inability to imagine—in advance of its happening—a route that takes us from supernovas to rabbit-pots.

## 3  The A Posteriori Nature of Nomological Connections

But maybe this is a misdiagnosis—maybe our reaction to the rabbit-pots case is not simply due to the fact that there is a long inferential chain from data to theory. Maybe the reason the rabbit-pot evidence seems to bear only 'indirectly' on astronomical theory is rather that the connection between the evidence—some old pottery with pictures on it—and the hypothesis—that a certain star became a supernova at a particular time—seems to be *utterly* contingent. There seems to be no *lawlike* connection between the two: it is perfectly consistent with the laws of astronomy generally, and the laws governing supernovas in particular, that human beings never even existed, much less that any of them ever set out to record heavenly events on clay pots.[6] The connection between supernovas and rabbit-pots would appear to differ in this regard from the connection between, for example, the phases of the moon and the timing of the tides, since the latter are nomologically tied to the central phenomena of the theory's domain. But this is not going to do Soames any good either. Let us quickly recap. Soames wants to argue, ultimately, that linguistics and psychology are 'conceptually distinct', by which he means that they 'are concerned with different domains, make different claims, and are established by different means' (Soames 1984: 155). He intends to show this by showing that there is a body of evidence to which psychology must answer, but towards which linguistics can be indifferent. The reason why linguistics is not constrained to explain or predict this evidence is supposed to be that such evidence is not *directly relevant* to *linguistically significant* properties of sentence types. We have been assuming,

[6] Actually, I am not sure that this point should be conceded. I am sympathetic to the view that whenever one event explains another, there is some sort of nomological connection between the two. Suppose that instead of finding rabbit-pots, archaeologists had uncovered pages of incredibly detailed photographs. I imagine that people would not feel that the connection was quite as contingent in this case, but there is no essential difference between this and the case of the pots. Or, at any rate, so I am prepared to argue. But it would take me too far afield to make this argument, and I do not want to rest anything on it.

with Soames, that we have an adequate criterion of linguistic significance, and that we have in fact identified several properties and relations that satisfy this criterion. The issue we have been exploring is whether or not there is any acceptable interpretation of 'direct relevance' that will yield the conclusion Soames is after.

The current suggestion is that the only data that are 'directly relevant' to the linguistically significant properties are data that derive from phenomena that are *nomologically connected* to the linguistically significant phenomena. But now we can see at a glance two reasons why such a suggestion will be of no help to Soames: first, on this interpretation of 'direct relevance', it is going to come out false that theories are only constrained by data that are directly relevant to the 'significant' phenomena in that domain; and secondly, we shall not be able, in any case, to *tell* which data will or will not be directly relevant to the theoretically significant properties just by looking at them. The game is over once it is conceded that *we cannot know in advance which phenomena are nomologically connected to which other phenomena.*

We can make both points at once by considering the case of palaeontology, the study of ancient things. Palaeontologists wish, among other things, to achieve the correct biological classification of the animal fossils they discover. Now while the notion of 'species' is somewhat controversial, we probably have a good enough consensus on what makes two organisms conspecific to be able to effect at least a partial division of properties according to their 'palaeontological significance'. Let us, at any rate, for the sake of clarity, presume the notion of 'biological' as opposed to 'taxonomic' species (Futuyma 1986: 219), according to which two individual organisms are assigned to distinct species only if they belong to populations that are reproductively isolated from each other. On this view of species, morphological differences between two animals are neither necessary nor sufficient for assigning them to different species.

Applying Soames's criterion to the field of palaeontology, then, we might argue that phylogenetic history is 'palaeontologically significant', but that geographical location and morphological similarity are not. That is, if two organisms share the appropriate aspects of phylogenetic history, we would count them as conspecifics, whether or not they are (or were) found in different parts of the world, and whether or not they display what otherwise might appear to be significant morphological differences. Neither location nor morphology *per se* can serve to individuate species; location and morphology must *bear on* phylogenetic history in order to do that. (Take, for example, human beings: because of our relatively recent descent from common ancestors, and because of the lack of effective reproductive isolators between human populations, we are all people counted as members of the same species, wherever we live, and whatever we look like.)

Now of these two palaeontologically insignificant properties, it could be argued that one is, and that one is not, *nomologically* connected to phylogenetic history.[7] Geographical placement is a largely contingent affair—although there are some lawful constraints on the kinds of genotype that will lead to viable fertile offspring in various environments, limiting the *de facto* geographical range of certain genomes, a good deal about where an animal ends up living is a matter of chance, and some organisms that evolve in one location need only a trick of fate to turn up and flourish in a different one. Thus, on the current interpretation, facts about geographical placement will not be 'directly relevant' to palaeontologically significant properties.

Suppose it so—does it follow that palaeontology is not constrained by facts about the geographical distribution of animal kinds? Clearly not. It is on precisely such facts that palaeontologists must rely in the early stages of phylogenetic theorizing: the physical location of a fossil might well provide crucial evidence about the phylogenetically significant properties.[8] As a result, the finding of a fossil at the 'wrong' place might easily count against assigning it to the species suggested by its morphology.

The reason that the location of the find can be evidence for the species of the fossil it discloses is that there is an *empirically regular* connection between the area in which something lived and the kind of thing it is. Even if not a law, it may be a *fact*, and a discoverable one, that certain animals will never be found at certain geological depths or in the company of certain other kinds of animal or in particular geographical locations. And even though

[7] Remember that I am allowing the possibility of making such a division sensible only for the sake of argument. Rejecting such a division only strengthens my case against Soames.

[8] Conversely, palaeontological findings can occasion changes in geological theory, as happened when discrepancies between the order of fossil placement in a geological formation and the order predicted by the extant fossil record prompted (or supported) a theory of geological folding. See Kitcher (1982).

these accidental facts about the distribution of species in time and space are not conceptually criterial for being a member of a particular species, they may none the less *predict* species membership quite reliably, *just because of the way the world happened to be.*

Analogously, a systematic difference in the order of acquisition of two sets of syntactic constructions might well predict deep underlying grammatical differences in the languages of two speaker groups, despite the contingency of the connection between order of acquisition *per se* and linguistically significant properties. It could happen that, in the absence of complete grammatical descriptions of the languages from which two fragments are available, information about the order in which certain constructions are acquired could be used reliably to predict the existence of hitherto unremarked differences in the 'linguistically significant' properties of the language.

This possibility seems especially salient if one keeps firmly in mind the fact that the grammars of humanly natural languages *are* acquirable, under conditions of casual learning. If two groups of speakers showed *systematic* differences in the order of acquisition of certain constructions, that fact would itself require explanation. One possible explanation would be a significant difference in the linguistic environments of the two different speaker groups during the relevant stage of development. But the existence of such differences would itself undercut the view that the two groups were speaking the same language—that is, that the languages of the two groups were identical with respect to the linguistically significant properties.

More moderately, and more realistically, it could be that differences in acquisition corresponding to differences in linguistic environment served to signal the early stages of the kind of grammatical reanalysis involved in linguistic change. David Lightfoot points out that while parents and children usually share linguistic environments, there are circumstances in which the environments of a later generation can come to differ from those in which the members of the parent generation acquired their language, to such an extent that the children develop a different grammar from their parents'. Lightfoot believes that something of this sort might explain the switch from SOV word order in Old English to the SVO order that is present in modern English (Lightfoot 1982: 149–58).

There are, Lightfoot observes, factors that cause languages with SOV order to 'leak' sentences with surface SVO order: for example, (1) perceptual and memory limitations that make 'heavy' centre-embeddings difficult to process will sometimes cause displacement of sentential NPs in object place to post-verb position, and (2) stylistic innovations for rhetorical effect often have the form of 'violations' of normal word order. If such forms become sufficiently common, there may be enough SVO sentences in a language learner's environment to trigger a grammar that has SVO as an underlying phrase-structure rule—yielding a reanalysis of the language spoken by the adults.

Such a reanalysis could have been evidenced by changes in the manner of acquisition (although this is not the evidence that Lightfoot in fact appeals to). While 'the language' of both parent and child would contain both SOV and SVO surface structures, it is most likely that the parent would not have produced SVO sentences until after or at about the time that he or she was beginning to produce sentential complements. On the other hand, we would expect that the child, for whom SVO order is the default, would produce sentences displaying that order *initially*, even before displaying any competence with respect to sentential NPs.[9]

The alert reader will notice that the above example does not really meet specifications: it is not an example of acquisitional data prompting revisions in the theory of grammar—on the contrary, it is a case in which acquisitional differences are posited in order to account for already known grammatical differences. But this situation is hard to avoid—the fact is that linguists are

[9] This example serves to make a couple of other points. First, it illustrates the role that processing information—in this case, independently confirmed claims about memory limitations and perceptual capabilities—can play in the development of an elegant grammatical analysis—in this case, explaining the occurrence of SVO sentences in a language that otherwise appears to be SOV. Second, the case serves to raise doubts about the perspicuity of the notion of 'language' itself: does Soames have any clear intuitions about whether or not the parent and child languages should be counted the same? If the grammatical analyses are correct, then they differ in grammatical (and hence linguistically significant) properties. But by the same token, the parental and child languages are perfectly mutually intelligible, and may even be very close in output, differing extensionally only to the degree that might be expected in the corpuses of two different speakers with different rhetorical styles. From a Chomskian perspective, the question of whether we have one or two languages is utterly without interest, since from that perspective we are interested in what the internalized grammar is, and in what it reveals about universal cognitive structure. From Soames's perspective, it is a question of central importance that must receive a principled answer.

rarely, if ever, faced with a situation like that of Soames's imaginary linguist, in which they possess refined data about acquisition and processing, but at the same time have so small and fragmentary a corpus that there is serious doubt about whether two bits of text or speech should be counted as part of the same language or not.

None the less, despite its disanalogy with Soames's thought-experiment, the above case still serves to make the needed point, viz. that facts that are only contingently linked to the linguistically significant properties of a language can still constrain theorizing in that domain. Thus, either the notion of 'direct relevance' of data has no interesting bearing on questions about the relevance of a particular body of data to a particular theoretical domain, or we ought to reject the principle that only data with properties lawfully connected to linguistically significant properties are 'directly relevant' to linguistic theorizing. That said, I would like to conclude by pointing out that even if we were to accept this principle, we would not obtain the conclusion that Soames wants.

If we were to accept the principle, then the whole issue about the relevance of psychological data to linguistic theory would turn on the facts about what actual nomological connections exist. Two things immediately follow that undercut Soames's position: first, because it cannot be determined a priori that two phenomena are *not* lawfully connected, no conclusions can be drawn about the relation between psychological data and linguistic phenomena without looking at the facts, and at currently available theories. Second, when one *does* look at the facts, and at currently available theories, it begins to look *very* likely that there are connections between psychological phenomena and linguistic phenomena that are every bit as lawful as the connection between genotype and morphology.

Imagine someone arguing in the following way: genotype is not palaeontologically significant because if two organisms were found to have the same genotype, but morphologies so different that they could not interbreed, we would not count them as members of the same species. The proper response to such an argument, I take it, is to say that if such a case were ever found, it would disprove a great deal of biological theory, but that we can therefore have the same degree of confidence that such a scenario will never come to pass as we have in the relevant portions of biological theory. That is, our reasons for thinking that no case of this sort will be forthcoming are precisely our reasons for thinking that a particular *account* of morphological variation is true—namely, the account that posits a lawlike connection between genotype and aspects of the phenotype.

Thus, it is no good for Soames to point to the *logical* possibility that two speakers could produce utterances conforming to exactly the same grammar, while differing non-trivially with respect to acquisition or processing. The thought-experiment should not yield results. Until we know what nomological connections there may be between the psychological facts and the linguistic facts, we are not in a position to say what factors can *in fact* vary independently of what other factors, and the mere logical point that the description of the case is coherent is quite irrelevant to the matter of what data can be brought to bear on what theories.

## 4 Connecting Psychology and Linguistics

What are the connections, then, between processing and acquisitional facts, on the one hand, and linguistic facts on the other? The first thing that must be noted is that Soames tends to caricature the ways in which psychologistic linguists actually do make use of psychological data. Soames seems to suggest, for example, that a psychologistic linguist is saddled with the view that *any* difference in the details of processing or acquisition must be theoretically relevant, so that the psychologistic linguist is not allowed any freedom to idealize. Soames does not burden the abstract linguist with what would seem to be the corresponding principle—that *any* difference between two speakers with respect to the linguistically significant properties is enough to count their languages as distinct.[10]

But in fact, linguists of a Chomskian bent have always emphasized the dangers of trying to derive quick predictions about production or comprehension—'performance'—from descriptions of grammatical knowledge—'competence'. They have, furthermore, emphasized the importance of keeping an open mind about the classification of phenomena, abjuring a priori rulings about whether a fact is syntactic or semantic or pragmatic, or

---

[10] Soames gives us no indication, for example, of how we are supposed to tell whether a sentence like 'He's a good man, Moe is' is to be counted as part of English or not, given that people who regard themselves as English-speakers are divided on its grammaticality. Is one disagreement enough? Are some speakers simply *wrong* in their grammaticality judgements? Which ones? More on this below.

something to be accounted for by the grammar or by a theory of perception or attention or memory. In sum, Chomskians have a very complicated story to tell about how processing and acquisitional data bear on theories of grammar.

Having registered that caveat, we still have to show that theorizing in this vein vindicates the claim that there are nomological connections between psychological properties and linguistic ones. I shall comment here only on the relevance of facts about acquisition. Lydia White, although generally very cautious about the applicability of acquisitional data to issues in theory of syntax, has none the less offered several examples of ways in which grammatical facts may be linked to, and thus generate predictions about, acquisitional facts (White 1981: 257–69). I shall conclude with a brief summary of one of these examples.

It is well known that children are not provided with much in the way of *negative* data—parents and care-givers tend not to correct utterances that are ungrammatical from the adult point of view, and on the few occasions when they do issue corrections, the children pay little attention. This raises the question of how children do eventually come to learn of certain forms that they are ungrammatical. They cannot be relying on trial and error, because they cannot count on being told when they are in error. And obviously they cannot infer from the mere non-occurrence of the form in the primary linguistic data that it is ungrammatical, since there are an infinite number of grammatical forms that they will not see (or have not yet seen). This is one facet of the poverty-of-the-stimulus argument: how do kids acquire rules that proscribe certain forms?

Consider the proposed transformation of Dative Movement. This is supposed to move an NP that is the object of the preposition 'to' into indirect object position. Dative Movement, applied to:

(1) We sent the book to George.

yields:

(2) We sent George the book.

If such a rule were part of the grammar, and if the child had to infer it from positive instances, then how would a child, on hearing a sentence like:

(3) We reported the accident to the police,

ever learn that:

(4) *We reported the police the accident.[11]

is ungrammatical?

This situation has suggested to some linguists that it should be a constraint on the kinds of rule that can compose a humanly natural grammar that they be acquirable on the basis of positive evidence alone. C. L. Baker, for example, proposes what he calls an 'inductive requirement' on grammars: 'If a linguist proposes a grammar G for some language, then G meets the "inductive requirement" if it is accompanied by a set of hypotheses about human cognitive capacities from which G can be deduced, given primary linguistic data' (Baker 1979, cited in White 1981: 267). Baker proposes a different analysis of data (1)–(4) that satisfies the inductive requirement. He argues that the grammar base-generates dative constructions (V NP NP) alongside sentences with prepositional phrases (V NP PP), and that verbs are subcategorized for either or both constructions. The child's task is considerably simplified—she simply waits for positive evidence that a particular verb allows the dative construction before producing a sentence with that verb in that context.

I note in passing another interesting feature of this example: Baker's hypothesis effectively involves a reassignment of a phenomenon from the category 'grammatical' to the category 'lexical'. Now if we reflect on the fact that, whatever else is true of languages, human children have to acquire them, we should find this sort of move a very good one. Given that children are not built to acquire specific languages, but rather need to be able to pick up the local lingo, would it not be extremely sensible for nature to have worked it out so that *grammar* was more or less universal, and only the *lexicon* showed local variation? We know that languages vary with respect to the words that compose them, and so we know that children *have* to cope with variety of that sort. Wouldn't it be a good deal if *all* linguistic variety could somehow be shown to consist in or derive from the lexical variety?

---

[11] The * symbol before a construction is the conventional way, among transformational linguists, of indicating that native speakers judge the sentence to be unacceptable.

This is indeed the sort of thinking that has been informing a good deal of syntactic theory in the last decade and a half.

Moral: linguistics is hard. It is considerably more than a semester's work to figure out the grammar of a language—even of one's own idiolect. Linguists, like all other scientists, are going to take whatever help they can get. The fact that languages are things that human beings can and do acquire under certain circumstances, and things that human beings can understand and use, given the cognitive resources at our disposal, is, evidentially speaking, of *huge* importance. On pain of being laughed at, philosophers should stop trying to tell linguists to ignore it.

# REFERENCES

BAKER, C. L. (1979), 'Syntactic Theory and the Projection Problem', *Linguistic Inquiry*, 10: 533–82.

BEVER, T., CARROLL, J. M., and MILLER, L. A., eds. (1984), *Talking Minds: The Study of Language in Cognitive Science* (Cambridge, Mass.: MIT Press).

CHOMSKY, N. (1959), 'Review of Skinner's *Verbal Behavior*', *Language*, 35: 26–58.

—— (1977), *Reflections on Language* (New York: Pantheon Books).

DEVITT, M., and STERELNY, K. (1987), *Language and Reality* (Cambridge, Mass.: Bradford Books).

—— —— (1989), 'Linguistics: What's Wrong With "The Right View"', in Tomberlin (1989), 497–531.

FODOR, J. (1985), 'Some Notes on What Linguistics is About', in Katz (1985a), 146–60.

FUTUYMA, D. (1986), *Evolutionary Biology* 2nd edn. (Sunderland, Mass.: Sinauer Associates).

HORNSTEIN, N., and LIGHTFOOT, D., eds. (1981), *Explanation in Linguistics: The Logical Problem of Language Acquisition* (London: Longman Linguistics Library).

KATZ, J. J. (1984), 'An Outline of Platonist Grammar', in Bever, Carroll, and Miller (1984), 1–33.

—— ed. (1985a), *The Philosophy of Linguistics* (Oxford: Oxford University Press, 1985).

—— (1985b), 'Introduction', in Katz (1985a), 1–16.

KITCHER, P. (1982), *Abusing Science: The Case against Creationism* (Cambridge, Mass.: MIT Press).

LIGHTFOOT, D. (1982), 'How Languages Change', in id., *The Language Lottery* (Cambridge, Mass.: Bradford Books), 147–70.

SOAMES, S. (1984), 'Linguistics and Psychology', *Linguistics and Philosophy*, 7: 155–79.

TOMBERLIN, J. E., ed. (1989), *Philosophy of Mind and Action Theory* (Philosophical Perspectives, 3; Atascadero: Ridgeview).

WHITE, L. (1981). 'The Responsibility of Grammatical Theory to Acquisitional Data', in Hornstein and Lightfoot (1981), 257–69.

WILFORD, J. N. (1990), 'Explosion of 1054 Seen in Indian Bowl', *The New York Times*, 19 June 1990.

# CHAPTER 3

# Is Linguistics a Branch of Psychology?

*Stephen Laurence*

## 1 Introduction

According to Noam Chomsky's well-known and influential account, linguistics is properly conceived of as a branch of cognitive psychology. Linguistics studies one aspect of the mind, namely our 'competence' or knowledge of the natural language we speak. This view is widely endorsed by linguists, but has encountered considerable and sustained resistance among philosophers. Though the issue has been much debated, it seems far from settled. It would certainly be interesting if it could be shown, for example, that the Chomskian approach was fundamentally in error (perhaps embodying some deep confusion), or that linguistics could not be thought of as a scientific discipline, or that some different conception of linguistics was manifestly superior. However, the kinds of considerations philosophers have raised do not in fact show anything of this sort. Nearly all of the arguments purporting to raise particular problems for linguistics generalize in fairly immediate ways to other sciences. But, whereas the arguments may initially seem plausible when directed particularly against linguistics, I think that it becomes clear when they are considered in the light of these other sciences that they are based on rather dubious general principles. Accordingly, my strategy will in large part be to draw analogies to other sciences, and see how the arguments directed against linguistics play out there.

This is a revised version of a 1995 manuscript, adapted for inclusion in this volume. I would like to thank Alex Barber, Jane Grimshaw, Eric Margolis, and Stephen Stich for their helpful comments. I would also like to thank the AHRB.

In my view, a broadly Chomskian account of linguistics is the default hypothesis, for reasons having to do with the explanatory power that this interpretation confers on linguistic theory (as I explain in Section 2). I briefly sketch out some alternatives to the Chomskian account in Section 3. In the remainder of the chapter, I examine two of the main arguments that have been directed against the Chomskian account to see whether they offer good grounds for abandoning this default hypothesis in favour of one of the rival views.[1] Section 4 is devoted to what I call the *Methodological Argument* and Section 5 is concerned with what I call the *Martian Argument*. Versions of both arguments have been put forward by a number of different authors. I argue that these arguments do not provide us with any good reason for abandoning the Chomskian account and that the continued resistance the Chomskian view faces is not justified.

## 2 The Chomskian Account of Linguistics

According to Chomsky, linguistics is a 'branch of cognitive psychology' (1972: 1). He writes, 'I would like to think of linguistics as that part of psychology that focuses its attention on one specific cognitive domain and one faculty of mind, the language faculty' (1980: 4); or again, that 'the theory of language is simply that part of human psychology that is concerned with one particular "mental organ," human language' (1975: 36).

This psychological interpretation of linguistics naturally breaks down into two components, corresponding to the dual focus of linguistics on Universal Grammar and on the grammars of particular languages. Universal Grammar is essentially a theory of the knowledge embedded in the language-acquisition mechanism. According to recent linguistics, this knowledge is embodied in the system of parameters. And language acquisition is basically a matter of setting the parameters of that language, these being 'set' by 'triggering' information in the corpus that the child is exposed to. For each general way that languages can differ from one another, there corresponds a parameter. Having set all the parameters, a child will have

[1] Other arguments against the Chomskian view have been discussed in more detail elsewhere. See e.g. Chomsky (1975; 1980; 1986); J. A. Fodor (1981); Laurence (1993); Antony (this volume); Matthews (this volume); and references in Barber (introduction to this volume).

learnt all the syntactic principles governing the language. Theories of particular languages' grammars are theories of the knowledge which results from this process, embodied in the acquired set of principles determined by the parameter settings. Chomsky interchangeably describes one's having this knowledge base as one's having acquired a 'competence', or one's having 'internalized' the grammar of the language, or as one's knowing the grammar of the language or internally representing the grammar of the language. And according to Chomsky, this knowledge base plays a central and essential role in language processing.

The Chomskian account ties the interpretation of linguistic theory to our psychological mechanisms for language acquisition and processing. The account thereby allows linguistics to contribute to the explanations of these abilities and increases the explanatory power of linguistic theory. At the same time, it opens the possibility of bringing a large number of alternative sources of data to bear on linguistic theory. I think that this is the main reason why most linguists adopt a Chomskian account of linguistics. It gives linguistic properties a central role in the explanation of the two chief language-related explananda—language processing and language acquisition—and it is supported by and explains a wide range of empirical data, including data concerning language change, language breakdown, processing errors, and the course of language development.

It will be useful for what follows to have a bit more detailed sense of the explanatory power of the Chomskian account. On the Chomskian view, linguistic properties play a crucial role in normal language acquisition and processing. They play this role in virtue of being identified with features of representational structures essentially involved in the exercise of these capacities. Accordingly, linguistic properties will play a substantial role in our explanations of patterns in utterances and commonalities among languages through their role in the mechanisms underlying the exercise of these capacities. Similarly, linguistic properties, through their role in these mechanisms, will play a vital role in explaining a whole host of results of psycholinguistic experiments concerning reaction times, priming effects, cognitive illusions, and the like, as well many ordinary phenomena concerning speech errors, processing errors, and the like. Given the Chomskian account, linguistic theory plays an important role in explaining these various phenomena, and at the same time the phenomena can be seen to provide new sources of evidence for linguistic theory.

Furthermore, taking the population of adult native speakers of a given language as a sort of core group, we may view more peripheral members of the linguistic community as deviating in different systematic ways in their linguistic capacities and behaviour from the capacities and behaviour of the core members.[2] The explanatory power of the Chomskian account is further displayed in its ability to extend to various peripheral groups, including young children still in the process of language acquisition, aphasiacs, and various others whose mastery of the target language is imperfect. Linguistic theory is proving increasingly useful in categorizing and making sense of data from neurological studies, developmental studies, studies of the historical course of language change, and many other data.[3] The Chomskian account will explain the various systematic deviations in linguistic behaviour and capacities of these groups from 'normal' speakers in terms of systematic differences in the representational base which subserves the relevant capacities (or operations defined over these representations), and which on the Chomskian account is tied to the interpretation of linguistic theories and properties themselves. And again, in each case, while linguistic theory explains the phenomena in these domains, the domains provide new sources of evidence for the Chomskian account.[4]

Much of the research I have alluded to is still in its early stages, but the results are quite suggestive. A brief discussion of a couple of examples will help make the attractions of the Chomskian account a bit more concrete. Consider, for example, an experiment by Swinney, Ford, Bresnan, and Frauenfelder (1988; reported in J. D. Fodor 1991) providing evidence for the existence of traces. Their experiment, using the cross-modal prim-

---

[2] If we replace the assumption that there is such a thing as a 'normal' speaker with the more plausible assumption that each speaker speaks her own idiolect, we derive further explanatory potential in describing each of the variable idiolects within the framework of a particular linguistic theory.

[3] It is really a question of *producing* these data. The data which linguistic theory, on a Chomskian interpretation, 'makes sense of' simply would not be available otherwise (see Chomsky 1992).

[4] And of course the explanatory power of the Chomskian account might be yet further increased through the study of priming effects, cognitive illusions, speech errors, processing errors, and the like, in peripheral groups.

ing paradigm, tested for the existence of traces by looking for priming effects of words semantically related to the moved noun phrase at the trace position. Sentences like (1) were presented orally, and semantically related lexical items and controls were presented visually on a computer screen at selected intervals (see Figure 3.1).

The policeman saw the boy$_i$ that the crowd at the party accused t$_i$ of the crime.

FIG. 3.1. Cross-Modal Priming Experiment

(1)  The policeman saw the boy$_i$ that$_i$ the crowd at the
     party accused t$_i$ of the crime.
     |      |           |
     1      2           3

So, as the subjects heard this sentence through their headphones, lexical items appeared on the computer screen at the times indicated by numerals. Subjects were given a lexical decision task in one experiment (that is, they were asked to decide whether the word on the screen was a word or not) and a naming task in another (that is, they were asked to read the word on the screen aloud). In both experiments Swinney *et al.* found a significant priming effect (that is, the reaction—deciding whether it is a word, or naming the lexical item—was faster) in positions 2 and 3 for lexical items semantically related to 'boy' (e.g. 'girl'), but not at position 1. At position 1, but not 2 or 3, lexical items semantically related to 'crowd' (e.g. 'group') showed a priming effect.

How does such an experiment support the Chomskian account? Since there is no significant priming effect for 'boy' at position 1, but there is at 2 and 3, we cannot simply explain the outcome in terms of a priming effect from the overt occurrence of 'boy', since this effect has evidently 'worn off' by position 1. We can make sense of the data, however, on the assumption that the internalized grammar is one that incorporates traces and, in particular, posits the existence of a trace of the NP 'the boy' as the object of the verb 'accused'. This trace will explain the renewed priming effect. Grammars that are in some sense extensionally equivalent to such grammars, but do not incorporate traces or posit this particular trace in this location, will face a prima facie difficulty explaining these data.[5] What is more, it is only on the Chomskian account that such data can be used to determine which linguistic theory is correct and it is only on the Chomskian account that linguistic theory will have the added explanatory power involved in explaining such data.

Turning to a much older piece of data, Fodor, Bever, and Garrett in a series of early experiments discovered that subjects, when asked to determine the temporal location of 'clicks' made during the oral presentation of sentences, tended to displace these clicks to major phrasal boundaries (see Fodor, Bever, and Garrett, 1974). Again, such data can be made sense of on the assumption that the internalized grammar is one that assigns phrasal boundaries, in a way consistent with the data from these experiments. And grammars that are in some sense extensionally equivalent to such grammars, but do not make comparable assignments of phrasal boundaries will face a prima facie difficulty explaining these data. And again, it is only on the Chomskian account that such data can be used to determine which linguistic theory is correct and it is only on the Chomskian account that linguistic theory will have the added explanatory power involved in explaining such data.

Much the same point can be made by considering data from cases involving more 'peripheral' members of the linguistic community. Yosef Grodzinsky (1990), analysing behavioural data concerning the phenomenon of 'agrammaticism', suggests an analysis of this phenomenon in terms

---

[5] Of course a Chomskian account of linguistic theory can be correct even if current linguistic theory is not. But evidence for the psychological reality of a particular grammar is *ipso facto* evidence for the psychological reality of some grammar, and therefore, in the context of the argument here, evidence for the Chomskian account of linguistic theory.

of the Principles and Parameters theory. In particular, he suggests that the peculiar pattern of behaviour associated with this aphasia can be accounted for by supposing that patients suffering from it delete traces at S-structure, and assign theta roles using a default heuristic. If these data held up, and could be extended, they would offer strong support for grammars incorporating the basic features Grodzinsky claims are manipulated in this aphasia.

Parameters, in addition to their roles in explaining cross-linguistic variation and the fact of language acquisition, may plausibly also be invoked in the explanation of the *course* of language acquisition and development. Lightfoot (1991) discusses several cases of historical changes in languages, attributing them to the effects of changes of parameter settings. Regarding the course of language acquisition, one much-discussed hypothesis (due to Hyams 1986) attributes early subjectless sentences in English to the fact that the default setting of a parameter is to allow a 'phonologically null' (i.e. unpronounced) element called 'pro'. The details are not essential for my purposes here. Hyams's idea, which she uses to explain various data concerning language acquisition, is that whereas adult English does not allow pro, children learning English use pro for a time, until the parameter is reset (see Rizzi 1992 for discussion). The crucial point here is that, as above, these various phenomena all get *explained* largely in terms of linguistic properties through their roles in language-processing and acquisition mechanisms. These few examples illustrate the explanatory power of the Chomskian account. In each case, on the Chomskian account and given a particular linguistic theory, we can explain the data—importantly, all extensionally equivalent grammars will not be equally illuminating of the data.[6] And in each case, we can only bring the data to bear on our choice of grammar under the assumption that the Chomskian account is correct.

Much of this research (like that in much of psychology in general) is still in the early stages, and undoubtedly further refinements of research methods, and more powerful future methods, will necessitate theoretical changes. But this is only natural and to be expected. The Chomskian account of the nature of linguistics is not tied to any particular linguistic theory, and certainly does not require the truth of current linguistic theory in any detail. In fact, quite to the contrary, changes in current linguistic theory occasioned by present

---

[6] This will be important in connection with some of the alternative accounts of linguistics discussed below.

and future results of this sort will rather serve to support the Chomskian picture. Thus, the Chomskian interpretation both gives linguistic theory vast explanatory power and gives us a very large base of potential sources of confirmation (or disconfirmation) for linguistic theories. In my view such considerations as these not only make the Chomskian account the default hypothesis, but also provide considerable grounds for supposing that it is actually the right account.

## 3 A Look at the Alternatives

Before getting into the objections that have been raised against the Chomskian account, it will be useful to have a brief look at some of the alternatives to that view that have been proposed. Often enough much the same argument is presented by different authors, but the argument takes on a slightly different shape depending on the background perspective of the author in question. And, of course, ultimately we will need to evaluate the strength of the Chomskian view relative to its rivals.

One of the earliest philosophical alternatives to the Chomskian interpretation of linguistics was suggested by Stephen Stich in a series of papers in the early 1970s. According to Stich, linguistic theory is best thought of as a theory of our capacity for linguistic intuition. An integral part of the methodology of linguistic theory involves the production of linguistic intuitions—of grammaticality, synonymy, ambiguity, and the like—these constituting the bulk of the data informing our linguistic theories. Stich argued (largely on the grounds that this interpretation was the most charitable one, giving linguistic theory the best chance of being *true*—see below) that linguistic theory should be thought of as a theory of this psychological capacity of ours to generate such linguistic intuitions (1972: 142–5; 1975: 94–5).[7]

A rather different interpretation has been offered by Jerrold Katz in a series of publications (see e.g. Katz 1977; 1981; 1985b; Katz and Postal 1991; also Langedeon and Postal 1985). The view which emerges from these

---

[7] Note, however, that Stich treats this capacity as analogous to a perceptual capacity. It delivers knowledge in the form of linguistic intuitions when presented with given sentences and is equally well described by a host of extensionally equivalent grammars, none being internally represented (see esp. Stich 1971: 494–6).

publications, which Katz has called 'Realism' or 'Platonism' (I shall use the latter, less ambiguous, term), is that linguistic theory is a theory of a particular sort of abstract object, languages. In this, linguistics is analogous to mathematics and other formal disciplines.

Jerry Fodor in an interesting and influential article 'Some Notes on What Linguistics is About' (1981) lumps together the positions of Katz and Stich under the heading 'the Wrong View', which he characterizes as a sort of instrumentalism. It may be that from a methodological point of view Stich and Katz should be thought of as instrumentalists,[8] but from a metaphysical point of view neither seems to fit the bill. Stich and Katz both believe that there is an independent object of linguistic enquiry, and differ about the character of this domain.

Interestingly though, two more recent critics of 'the Right View' (Fodor's name for the Chomskian position) seem far closer to the description Fodor gives of the Wrong View. In 'Language and Languages' David Lewis says that he can find no way to 'make objective sense of the assertion that a grammar G is used by a population P whereas another grammar G′ which generates the same language as G, is not' (1983: 177). Scott Soames (1984) does not explicitly say that there is no objective basis for linguistic claims, but does say that what makes a grammar correct is simply the fact that it provides (one of) the simplest overall account(s) of a specific set of data.

Finally, there is the position of Michael Devitt and Kim Sterelny (1987; 1989), put forward in their popular philosophy-of-language textbook *Language and Reality* and in a follow up paper 'Linguistics: What's Wrong with "the Right View"'. Taking up the terms of the debate that Fodor sets out, Devitt and Sterelny claim to be offering an alternative to both the Right View and the Wrong View. According to Devitt and Sterelny, linguistics is a 'theory of symbols' as opposed to a theory of competence. However, they do not say much about what symbols have their linguistic properties in virtue of, stating merely that such properties are most likely complexes of psychological and environmental factors and drawing an analogy with the properties of being a pawn, or being worth a dollar. Thus it is not clear what

---

[8] Fodor's charges are best seen as challenging methodological assumptions of anti-Chomskians, in my view. As such they will be relevant to what I take to be the two main arguments to be offered against the Chomskian, the Methodological Argument and the Martian Argument (see below).

their view really amounts to or even if they are in fact offering *an alternative* to the Chomskian view, as they claim (see below).

From such various positions as these, over the years, there have been quite a number of criticisms of the Chomskian view. It is not possible, nor would it be particularly beneficial, to consider all of them here. Instead, I focus on two arguments which recur in one form or another throughout the literature, which I call, respectively, the 'Methodological Argument' and the 'Martian Argument'. Both have broader methodological implications, and my main interest will be in these broader implications.

## 4 The Methodological Argument

The Methodological Argument originates with Stich. As Stich presents it, the basic idea is that, given the methods of linguistic theory, we should not adopt a Chomskian interpretation of linguistics, because on such an interpretation, linguistics is most likely false (Stich 1972; 1975). The burden of Stich's argument, then, is establishing that current linguistic methods are rather unlikely to uncover psychologically real grammars (or UG). It is worth noting at the outset that the argument, so formulated, looks to be inferring a metaphysical conclusion (that linguistic theory is *not about* language competence) from epistemological premises (that on the basis of current linguistic methods, we could not come to *know* or *determine* or be *justified* in believing facts about what is responsible for our capacity to process language).

Refining Stich's principle, Devitt and Sterelny (1989) state a general methodological principle for determining the subject matter of linguistics:

*Devitt and Sterelny's Methodological Principle*

[T]he best reason that we can expect to find for thinking that linguistics is about *x* rather than *y* is that the considerations and evidence that have guided the construction of linguistic theory justify our thinking that the theory is *true* about *x* but not *y*. (1989: 498–9)

Though Devitt and Sterelny do not say so, we may assume that this principle is intended to be an instance of a more general methodological principle for determining the subject matter of a science, since the principle would not be worth much if it applied only to linguistics.

Why, then, is linguistics most likely false if it is interpreted as a theory of competence? For Devitt and Sterelny, as for Stich, the principal reason stems from the fact that there exist many alternative grammars which are extensionally equivalent to any given grammar: the same set of acceptable strings can be generated by many different formal systems. This is unquestionably true. However, Devitt and Sterelny (following Stich) assert that this provides us with an argument that the grammar, G, of current linguistic theory has no more claim to psychological reality than any of a whole host of extensionally equivalent grammars. In particular they claim that 'the evidence and considerations that have guided transformational grammarians provide insufficient reason for thinking that it *is* G [rather than some extensionally equivalent grammar, G']', that is psychologically real (Devitt and Sterelny, 1989: 504).[9]

Devitt and Sterelny offer four points in support of their claim that the evidence and considerations which have guided linguists do not justify us in taking G to be psychologically real. The four are closely related to claims made by Stich.

The first point, made by both Stich and Devitt and Sterelny, concerns the fact that the primary evidence offered in favour of a particular grammar such as G is evidence concerning linguistic intuitions. Such evidence, they argue, provides at best indirect evidence about what is or is not psychologically real. As Devitt and Sterelny say, 'there is no basis in this evidence that the speaker has internalized G rather than the meaning-equivalent G''' (1989: 505).[10]

Second, following Stich, Devitt and Sterelny argue that considerations of simplicity and elegance of G over G' do not provide a basis for taking G to be psychologically real. As Devitt and Sterelny put it, such considerations of simplicity and elegance are 'psychologically irrelevant' (1989: 507). There is no reason to suppose that the brain uses the formally most simple and ele-

[9] I should note, however, that Devitt and Sterelny hold that '*some* aspects of G are psychologically real, in particular those aspects that go into determining meaning' (1989: 504). Stich, in the papers under discussion, is rather sceptical about the coherence of the notion of mental representation, and thus of the availability of a robust sense of 'psychological reality' for grammars.

[10] The idea of a 'meaning-equivalent' grammar is never fully explained by Devitt and Sterelny. The rough idea is that two grammars are meaning-equivalent if the differences between them do not affect the meanings assigned to utterances.

gant grammar. In fact, there is reason to suppose that from an evolutionary or a neurobiological point of view, the formally most simple and elegant grammar is *less likely* to be the one actually used by the speaker.[11] Therefore, we are not justified in believing G rather than G' to be psychologically real on grounds of simplicity.

The third point concerns evidence drawn from research and experiments on language acquisition. Study of UG offers a constraint on particular grammars because grammars might be rejected by theorists if they serve to complicate UG unecessarily. The simplicity and elegance of particular grammars must be balanced against the simplicity and elegance of the general theory, UG. However, as Devitt and Sterelny point out, if the arguments above are sound they will carry over to the case of UG. If the considerations of simplicity and elegance are 'psychologically irrelevant' (1989: 507), then given that there are indefinitely many extensionally equivalent grammars, there will likewise be indefinitely many extensionally equivalent theories of UG and, so the argument goes, no way to choose between them.

Stich develops the point in a slightly different way. He imagines a logical space defined by the class of all extensionally equivalent grammars for all natural languages, and notes that there will be many ways to build theories of UG which develop different commonalities among these. The initial choices we make in theorizing about grammars for particular grammars and the initial commonalities we emphasize start us off in some particular corner of this logical space. But we are there, Stich argues, only by reason of historical accident. We might have started elsewhere, and arrived at different particular grammars and a different account of UG. Nothing but historical accident sets our theories apart.

Finally, Devitt and Sterelny consider evidence from studies of language processing: 'evidence about reaction times, the types of errors we make, the relative ease of understanding sentences, the order in which sentences are learned, and so on' (1989: 508). They suggest that in principle such evidence could settle a claim of psychological reality, but that in practice the evidence has failed to support currently popular linguistic theories. As they put it:

We need to show that the deep structure, intermediate structures, surface structure, and the rules of G, have all been internalized. It is generally agreed that there

[11] Devitt and Sterelny credit Stephen Jay Gould (1983), David Lewis, and Robert Berwick and Amy Weinberg (1984).

is little evidence of this. There are problems even finding the transformationalist's levels and rules at all, let alone the particular details specified by G. (1989: 509)

Stich, writing earlier, notes that such evidence, though potentially relevant, is not presented by linguists. And at one point he suggests that evidence concerning brain structure is available and renders evidence from linguistic intuitions for the psychological reality of grammars otiose (1975: 99–100).

In sum, Stich and Devitt and Sterelny argue that the sorts of evidence and considerations in these four categories do not justify us in taking G, essentially current linguistic theory, to be psychologically real. But then, if we adopt the Chomskian view, we are not justified in believing that current linguistic theory is likely to be *true*. By Stich's general methodological principle, then, linguistics is not about competence as the Chomskian would have it. And the same is true for Devitt and Sterelny's general Methodological Principle, provided there is an alternative interpretation on which linguistic theory *is* likely to be true (which Devitt and Sterelny claim to provide).

What should we make of this argument? In my view, the trouble with the Methodological Argument goes right to its core: the methodological principles of Stich and Devitt and Sterelny are false. I think that even if we grant that much of the evidence that linguists appeal to is in a sense 'indirect', that simplicity and elegance are not guides to psychological reality, and finally that what direct evidence there is has tended not to support current theory in detail, this does not give us reason enough to suppose that linguistics is not a theory of competence.[12] This becomes clear when we consider theory construction in psychology, for much the same case that has been made against attributing psychological reality to linguistic theory can be made, for example, against attributing psychological reality to the constructs of *psycholinguistics*.

Contemporary psycholinguistic theory generally divides the task of language comprehension into a number of component processes. One of these components is the process of recovering the syntactic structure of a given sentence. And one much-discussed hypothesis concerning this process is that it is governed by the principle of Minimal Attachment. The hypoth-

---

[12] As should be clear from the discussion in sect. 1 above, however, it is not at all clear to me that we should accept any of these points either.

esis has been advocated by Lyn Frazier and others. Frazier characterizes Minimal Attachment as follows:

*Minimal Attachment*

Attach each new item into the current phrase marker postulating only as many syntactic phrase nodes as is required by the grammar. (1987: 520)

A significant component of the evidence adduced in favour of this principle and the model of language processing incorporating it comes from linguistic intuitions. Consider, for example, the classic sentence (2):

(2) The horse raced past the barn fell.

which is very difficult to process. The structure of (2) is something like (3):[13]

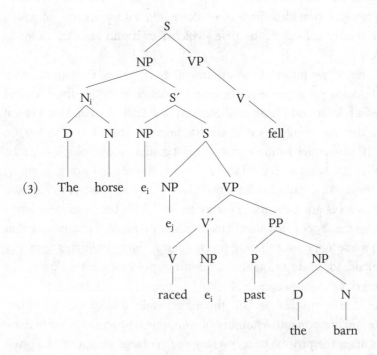

---

[13] Arguments for Minimal Attachment clearly interact with particular accounts of syntactic structure, and alternative accounts of structure may well affect the arguments for Minimal Attachment (as is briefly noted below). However, since I am not concerned to argue for or against Minimal Attachment, the structure in the text will suffice.

The sentence says that a certain horse, namely the one that was raced past the barn, happened to fall. Though the sentence is grammatical on this reading, this is not how the sentence is typically read. The dominant reading of the sentence assigns it a structure on which the sentence is *ungrammatical*. This structure is something like (4):

(4)

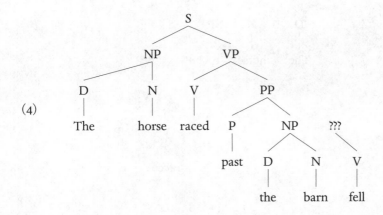

where the initial segment 'the horse raced past the barn' means that a certain horse went racing past a certain barn. The sentence provides evidence for a model of language processing incorporating the principle of Minimal Attachment since attaching 'raced' as in (4) rather than as in (3) is less costly in terms of the number of nodes, and thus is the attachment predicted by Minimal Attachment. The important point to notice is that when 'raced' is added to the tree, more new nodes need to be added in (3) than in (4). To see this, notice that we start with (5), and when we add 'raced' in building (3) we get (6), whereas when we add 'raced' in building (4) we get (7). Since (7) requires that fewer new nodes be added to (5) than (6) requires (to say the least), it is the reading predicted by Minimal Attachment.

(5)

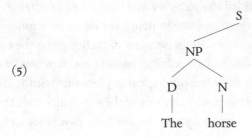

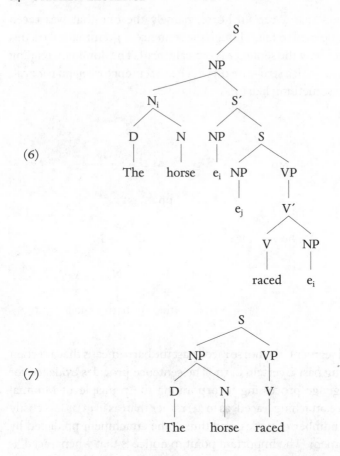

(6)

(7)

Now although a model of language processing incorporating the principle of Minimal Attachment explains these intuitive data, there are many alternative models of language processing which also explain the data. Indeed, given any computational model of parsing, we might generate indefinitely many alternative models, simply by adding in a computationally superfluous step or two. Provided the steps we add have an equal effect on minimal assignments and non-minimal assignments, the alternative models so generated will all be compatible with these same data. But given the existence of indefinitely many alternative possible parsing mechanisms, we might argue, by analogy with the Methodological Argument, that the intuitive evidence adduced does not justify any one of these theories over the others. Furthermore, if formal simplicity and elegance are 'psychologically irrelevant', they cannot help us narrow the field.

Of course, there is also more direct evidence in the form of reaction time experiments and the like (see e.g. Frazier 1987; Rayner, Carlson, and Frazier 1983; Ferreira and Clifton 1986). And it is true that psychologists in general stay closer to chronometric data than purely intuitive data. However, continuing with the analogy to the Methodological Argument, we might argue further that though reaction-time experiments and the like might in principle decide between the competing alternative parsing models, most of the relevant experiments have not been done and the evidence we do have is at best equivocal—certainly no model of language processing is supported in detail. There are many theories in the field and they are undergoing a constant process of revision. And certainly, Minimal Attachment has significant difficulties facing it. To cite just one sort of problem for the theory, Edward Gibson (1991) notes that the interpretation of experiments favouring Minimal Attachment may rely on controversial assumptions about phrase structure that may not be independently justified. Indeed, it seems that in general most of the difficulties Devitt and Sterelny allege in the case of linguistics are inherited by a linguistically based psycholinguistics, simply in virtue of the fact that such theories in psycholinguistics will be informed and inspired by the theories in linguistics.

So what are we to make of all this? If we are not justified in accepting as psychologically real theories which tend not to be supported in detail by 'direct' psychological evidence, then perhaps we should conclude that we are not, by and large, justified in accepting current psycholinguistic theories. Perhaps. But we most definitely should *not* conclude that by and large current psycholinguistic theories *are not theories of psychological capacities*. But this, of course, is *exactly* the conclusion the analogue of the Methodological Argument would urge on us. The argument in psychology would be just as it was in linguistics: since current theories are not justified by these sorts of evidence, we should not, given their general methodological principle, consider these theories to be *about the psychological domain*, since so construing them makes them probably false. Clearly something has gone wrong. Certainly, constructing a theory of the mind should not be *easy*, but neither should it be conceptually impossible. What has gone wrong, I think, is that the Methodological Argument's central principle, the Methodological Principle, is false. This principle should be rejected.

Returning to linguistics, it seems clear that the problem is that the Methodological Principle essentially conflates the issue of the likely truth of current theory with the issue of the subject matter of that theory. Of course much of current theory—in linguistics as in almost any science—is likely to be false. A cursory glance at the history of science will demonstrate that. And of course current theories in newly developing sciences such as linguistics are especially vulnerable. But equally clearly, *this should not deprive these sciences of their natural subject matters*. It is perhaps true that crucial evidence has not yet been brought to bear. And it is further true that current theory is likely to be lacking in various ways and inaccurate in detail. But the reason why crucial evidence has not been brought to bear is that science is not easy. Theories in linguistics are still developing in what look to be very productive ways, and neurological and psycholinguistic evidence, though growing, is constrained by limitations of experimental paradigms, testing methods— and crucially, the paucity of well-defined theoretical alternatives to test among.[14] Neurological and psycholinguistic evidence is not independent of linguistic theory. Indeed, linguistic theory can be seen as directly responsible for such evidence, since we can only make sense of (and therefore only have access to) the data because of the theory. And again, though current linguistic theory is likely to be inaccurate in many ways, what choice do we have in seeking out psychologically real grammars but to go with those judged best using whatever data we have available at any given time? And certainly, theorists should adopt as their working hypothesis the simplest, most elegant one available. What else are they to begin with—the least simple hypothesis? Similarly, the fact that in constructing psycholinguistic models of processing and acquisition we naturally (and unavoidably) make many assumptions about our general cognitive architecture, other cognitive mechanisms, the brain, computation, and mental representation, among other things, makes our models only as good as those assumptions. These sorts of considerations apply to *any* scientific theory, though. Linguistics, being a relatively new science, is just more vulnerable. The fact that a theory of competence is tied to further theory or that, given the current state of evidence, it is not likely to be accurate in detail should not, however, make it any less a theory of competence.[15]

---

[14] This last point is one that Chomsky has frequently emphasized.

[15] Robert Cummins, illustrating a different point, discusses a possible explanation for molecular bonding, where atoms are held together in molecules by 'hook-and-eyes' (1983:

I have not offered any alternative interpretation on which psycholinguistic theory is likely to be true, as Devitt and Sterelny's Methodological Principle requires. So before turning to the Martian Argument, I should make a few brief points about this.

First, it is not difficult to come up with alternative accounts of what psycholinguistics might be about by looking for them closer to the actual data that have been used thus far in psycholinguistic theorizing. One possibility is that psycholinguistics is simply an account of the intuitive data which it has attempted to account for, or of some posited psychological faculty responsible for such data. Alternatively, we might take it to be about some realm of abstracta isomorphic to the theory. Arguably, these alternatives are more likely to be true, given the considerations that have largely guided psycholinguistic theorizing. However, they should not make what otherwise *seems* to be a theory directed at explaining language processing fail to be about this subject matter at all.

Second, we should also note that Devitt and Sterelny do not really have an alternative conception of linguistics to offer. They create the appearance of offering an alternative conception of linguistics by drawing a contrast between 'symbols' and 'competence'. As they note in a different context, however, the natural Chomskian reply is that 'the Right View's failure to mention symbols is excusable because the theory of symbols is completely derivative from the theory of competence' (1989: 521). This may not be Chomsky's own view, but someone with broadly Chomskian sympathies might well argue as follows:

In a sense it is true that linguistics *is* about symbols. However, the important properties of these symbols—the properties in virtue of which symbols have their linguistic properties—are properties pertaining to our linguistic competence, and perhaps aspects of how these symbols are processed in language comprehension and production. So it is clearer to say that linguistics is about competence, since it is only because native speakers internally represent the grammar of their language that symbols have the linguistic properties they do. Thus, although linguistics could be said to be about symbols, it is, in the first instance, about

8–9). This theory, by current lights, seems to be a false theory of molecular bonding: we do not think molecules are held together in this fashion. But it does seem to be *a theory of molecular bonding*, none the less. The Methodological Principle seems to rule out the possibility of such false, or poorly justified, accounts as even being *about* their purported subject matter.

competence. The linguistic properties of symbols are completely derivative from properties concerning competence.

The important issue is not over whether linguistics is about symbols, but rather over the nature of the facts which determine the linguistic properties of symbols. Here the Chomskian has a more or less concrete suggestion. Devitt and Sterelny say only that these properties are clearly not intrinsic properties of the symbols, but rather involve some combination of 'psychological facts, and facts about the natural environment' (1989: 516–17). However, this does not even serve to *distinguish* their position from the Chomskian's, who also holds that linguistic properties are not intrinsic properties of symbols, and that they involve some combination of psychological facts and environmental facts. Thus the apparent stark contrast between their view of linguistics as 'the theory of symbols' and the Chomskian's, according to which linguistics is 'the theory of competence', amounts to no more than an issue about which properties of the environment, and local psychological agents, symbols inherit their linguistic properties from. And Devitt and Sterelny offer no definite suggestion concerning this issue (see 1989: 517). The only suggestion that they make that may serve to distinguish their position from the Chomskian one consists in a somewhat vague analogy to properties in other 'social sciences':

Like all social sciences, [linguistics] seems to be immediately dependent on psychological facts and facts about the natural environment. The nature of this sort of dependency is complex and hard to describe. . . . Consider some examples of this sort of dependency. What makes a physical object a pawn or a dollar? What makes a physical event a vote or unlawful? Nothing intrinsic to the objects and events in question; rather, it is the psychological states, within certain environments, of people involved with such objects and events. Exactly what states, what involvement, and what environment, is hard to say. (1989: 517)

One might imagine that what Devitt and Sterelny have in mind here is some complex of propositional attitudes concerning the purposes or intentions of inventors or users of objects (such as chess pieces) or which otherwise establish the legitimacy of certain practices (voting, law). The idea would then be that linguistic objects, properties, relations, and so on can be treated similarly.

It is not clear that there is any definite suggestion here at all. None the less, to the extent that there is a discernible position, it seems that the view faces serious difficulties. I will mention only one problem here. It stems from the fact that linguistic properties are hierarchically structured and do not typically have direct physical realizations—linguistic properties do not typically attach to physical properties directly, but rather do so only by way of further layers of linguistic properties. So, for example, morpho-syntactic properties attach to phonological strings as opposed to mere sequences of sound. Even the sound properties in language are abstract, not directly 'there' in the physical realization of language. Similarly, to the extent that there is 'movement' involved in the analysis of sentence structure (or multiple layers of structure), these features of sentences will not be present in the physical realization of language. These 'layers' of linguistic properties pose a difficulty for Devitt and Sterelny because they seem to require layers of propositional-attitude complexes of a very implausible sort: for example, attitude complexes to establish the existence of the phonological properties of a string, which could then figure in attitude complexes to establish morphological properties of a string, which could then figure in . . . and so on. To get an alternative along the general lines alluded to by Devitt and Sterelny, it seems that a very complex (and as yet wholly unspecified) account would seem to be necessary. And we have no reason to believe that intricate complexes of attitudes of this general sort exist.[16]

Finally, it is perhaps worth noting that, given their Methodological Principle, linguistic theory for Devitt and Sterelny would probably be a theory of our 'folk' theory of linguistics, not a theory of symbols at all. In order to explain how linguistic intuitions could count as evidence for linguistics, Devitt and Sterelny draw an analogy with our physical intuitions and biological intuitions and suggest that our linguistic intuitions might be generated by a 'folk linguistics', just as our physical intuitions and biological intuitions

---

[16] At the same time, we should bear in mind that regardless of what one says about the nature of linguistic properties, an account of language processing is still needed, and any remotely plausible model is going to be built around representations of the sort articulated by working linguists. The result is that whether we call the knowledge base involved in language processing 'the language', as Chomskians would, or whether we think of language as some sort of public phenomenon, as Devitt and Sterelny suggest, we are going to be committed to the existence of the knowledge base that Chomskians take linguistic theory to be about. Given this, though, there is no need for the complex attitude-based alternative Devitt and Sterelny allude to.

are perhaps guided by folk theories of physics and biology. In particular, they say:

Just as physical intuitions, biological intuitions, and economic intuitions can be produced by central-processor responses to the appropriate phenomena, so also can linguistic intuitions. These linguistic phenomena are not to be discovered by looking inward at our own competence but by looking outward at the social role that symbols play in our lives. When linguists do this now, they do not start from scratch. People have been thinking about these matters for millennia. The result of this central-processor activity is folk, or otherwise primitive, theory or opinion: the linguistic wisdom of the ages. The wisdom will be a good, albeit fallible and incomplete, guide to the nature of linguistic symbols. (1989: 522)

But if linguistic intuitions are simply a reflection of folk linguistics, why should they count as evidence for linguistic reality? When we are looking for evidence regarding the constitution of the physical or biological world we do not consult folk theories, we investigate the physical or biological domain directly. Furthermore, given the track record of folk theories, we can probably conclude that folk linguistics, if it exists, is a false theory. Investigations of folk physics have revealed that our naive (folk physics) intuitions about a wide range of physical phenomena, and their apparent theoretical basis, turn out to be radically mistaken (see e.g. McCloskey 1983). Indeed, the 'evidence' of intuition about physical reality seems far more a reflection of our folk theory than of physical reality. It is not at all clear, then, why in the case of language the evidence of folk linguistics should justify our belief in any theory constructed on its basis regarding linguistic reality. Thus, linguistics seems unlikely to be true construed as a theory of linguistic reality if the predominant source of evidence for the theory really is, as Devitt and Sterelny suggest, linguistic intuition, and such intuitions derive from our folk theory of linguistics. However, as Stich (1972) suggested in much the same context, if we take grammars to be part of the story about how our capacity for making folk-linguistic judgements works, it seems we are far more likely to have the theory come out true—after all, the evidence from intuitions is, by hypothesis, much more directly related to this capacity than it is to 'linguistic reality'. But, then, according to Devitt's and Sterelny's own Methodological Principle, we should interpret linguistics to be about $x$ rather than $y$ if 'the considerations and evidence that have guided the construction of linguistic theory justify our thinking that the theory is *true* about *x* but not *y*' (1989: 498–9). Since they claim that the predominant type of evidence for linguistics comes in the form of linguistic intuitions, and these considerations are more likely to justify our thinking that linguistics is a true theory of our capacity for folk linguistics than a true theory of 'linguistic reality', it seems that Devitt and Sterelny's own Methodological Principle suggests that linguistic theory should be taken to be a theory *about our folk theory of linguistics, not some independent 'linguistic reality'*.

## 5 The Martian Argument

We may now turn to what I call the Martian Argument. The argument is very simple. Basically, the argument is just that since different speakers of English, for example, *could* have different grammars, the linguistic properties of English cannot be determined by the nature of the internalized grammar. Devitt and Sterelny put it as follows:

According to the transformationalists, English competence consists in internalizing a grammar. They go further: all English speakers have internalized near enough the one grammar; competence has a uniform structure across the linguistic community. Even if this is so, it is not necessarily so. Many other grammars could agree on the meaning-relevant structures they assign to the sentences of English. Suppose that Martians became competent in English by internalizing one of these other grammars. The theory of Martian competence would have to be different from the theory of ours. Yet the theory of symbols would be the same, for it would still be English that they spoke. Returning to Earth, it would not matter a jot to the theory of symbols if competence among actual English speakers was entirely idiosyncratic. (1989: 514)

Versions of this argument can also be found in, among other places, Soames (1984), Katz (1977), and Lewis (1983).

I must say that I find the prevalence of this argument quite puzzling. As far as I can see, the argument owes whatever plausibility it has to the fact that linguistics is not yet a well established science. The argument itself merely begs the question against the Chomskian account. Thus, the Chomskian might respond that the language that the Martians speak, despite sounding an awful lot like English, *is not English*. It is after all an open empirical question what constitutes a language, to be settled in part by empirical research and in part by general theoretical considerations. Presumably the general theoretical considerations tie the nature of a kind like 'natural language' or 'English' to various explanatory goals. We can see the Chomskian to be taking the goal of explaining the fact that humans acquire and process natural language as among the central explanatory goals of linguistics. Whatever properties languages have which account for our ability to acquire and use them will thus characterize the nature of languages and linguistic properties. But, according to Chomskians, what is really essential about language, what accounts for our ability to acquire and use language, is something about *us*—namely, the psychological capacities and representational resources we have underlying these abilities.

Certainly the Chomskian must grant that it is logically possible, perhaps nomologically possible (and, for all we know, even actual), that there are beings with a different competence that otherwise resemble English-speakers as much as you like. But this is just as the philosopher of chemistry must grant that it is logically possible, perhaps nomologically possible (and, for all we know, even actual), that there exists a substance which is not $H_2O$, but otherwise resembles water (in appearance and behaviour) as much as you like. The logical possibility of such a substance, however, should not require the philosopher of chemistry to hold that water is not (identical to) $H_2O$.[17]

It is logically possible that there exists a substance that resembles water as much as you like, just as the language the Martian speaks resembles English. But in both cases it is an open theoretical question whether the nature of the kind in question must take this logical possibility into account. Similarly, it is logically possible that there be a substance that obeys all the same laws that water obeys (apart from those which presuppose that water $=H_2O$) just as it is logically possible that there be something that obeys all the laws governing, for example, a sentence of English (apart from those which presuppose that the language is determined by competence). But again it is an open theoretical question whether the nature of the kind in question must take this logical possibility into account.

---

[17] Much the same argument could be made for other natural kinds, including those whose nature is broadly functional—such as species kinds, for example—where the crucial functional properties turn out to be non-superficial ones.

Given any substantive independent account of the nature of a kind, it is not hard to come up with a logically possible 'counter-example' of the sort the Martian Argument offers. Ned Block (1990) describes a logically possible being that encodes plausible continuations to all possible English conversations, and in 'conversing' with you, chooses a plausible continuation at random, given as input the initial segment of the conversation to that point. Such a being is likely to be a 'counter-example' to any reasonable psychologically based account of the nature of linguistic kinds (including, for example, Devitt and Sterelny's account).[18] This example is a more sophisticated version of the age-old example of parrots which mimic English. Is the parrot, mimicking an English-speaker—or the valley echoing your voice, or the tape recorder replaying your voice, or the computerized telephone operator or machine at the supermarket checkout counter that 'tells' you the prices of your groceries—are these things speaking English? Is the system that Block imagines?

Presumably these sorts of cases are not enough to rule out every substantive account of linguistic properties. What, then, should we say about them? In the case of the valley, or the parrot, or the tape recorder I assume that we want to say something like: 'We should rule these cases out because they do not involve full command of the language.' As Chomsky says, they lack the 'creative aspect of language use': they do not have the capacity for potentially infinite use of language in an innovative way that is free from stimulus control, and yet coherent and appropriate to context. But why should this be relevant? Essentially, we are appealing to theoretical considerations about what aspects of speech are theoretically important. We are deciding *on theoretical grounds* that despite the fact that these things produce 'utterances' that seem to be English sentences, they are not in fact speakers of English. Some of the other cases introduce further complications.[19]

---

[18] As noted above, it is not clear that Devitt and Sterelny actually offer an alternative substantive account, despite their claims to the contrary. The sketchy remarks they do make suggest that they perhaps have in mind an account based in a set of beliefs, intentions, and other attitudes, in which case the Block example would presumably be a 'counter-example' to their view inasmuch as the Martian case is a 'counter-example' to Chomsky's.

[19] In the Block case we may actually have a system which satisfies Chomsky's criteria for having the creative aspect of language use. It will regularly produce novel 'utterances' (and has a boundless capacity for doing so), they will be appropriate to context and

The main point I want to make here, though, is that we must use theoretical considerations of some sort to rule out these potential 'counter-examples'.[20] Why should systems that lack the creative aspect of language use not be counted speakers of natural languages if they produce 'utterances' phenomenologically indistinguishable from utterances of mine? Why should beings of the sort Block imagines not be counted as speakers of natural languages? Broadly theoretical considerations must be brought to bear. But if such considerations can be brought to bear in these cases they can in principle be brought to bear against the imagined Martians as well. And in that case as in these we might decide that the imagined beings just do not speak English rather than reject the account of the nature of linguistic properties which such creatures are allegedly a counter-example to.[21]

Given that it is a theoretical issue, the question is what sorts of theoretical consideration should be brought to bear? Arguably, exactly the sorts of consideration that have been offered in favour of the Chomskian view: considerations pertaining to the explanatory power of the theory. Given that the central explanatory roles of linguistic kinds are in explaining our ability to use language (language processing) and our ability to acquire the ability to speak a language (language acquisition), the sorts of possible evidence discussed in connection with the Chomskian view above seem directly relevant to the evaluation of which grammar is the correct theory of a given language. Taking into account data pertaining to language processing, change, breakdown, and acquisition provides us with a rich and diverse source of potentially confirming or refuting evidence for linguistic theories. And such data, being directly tied in with the central explanatory roles of linguistic kinds, seem directly relevant to the evaluation of linguistic theories.

In Section 2 above I tried to illustrate the explanatory power of linguistic theory on the Chomskian account, suggesting that there was actually a fair

coherent, and they seem as free from stimulus control as our own utterances are (since in neither case is a particular response determined by the stimulus alone).

[20] Of course, in any of these cases we might accept that the system *really is* an English-speaker. Block's being might be taken to speak English. The parrot or the tape recorder or the valley might be taken to speak English as well. See below for further discussion.

[21] J. A. Fodor (1981) argues in much the same way against the claim that there is no way to decide between grammars which are equally simple on 'linguistic grounds' alone (see esp. pp. 153–4).

amount of data which could be used to support various aspects of current linguistic theory given the Chomskian account. It is important to bear in mind, however, that it is not really necessary for our present purposes to establish that any of these data will stand up to further empirical scrutiny. The point here is a conceptual one. The burden of the Martian Argument is not to show that the sorts of evidence discussed above will not *in fact* be substantiated. The point is rather to question whether *in principle* such data are even *relevant* to the evaluation of linguistic theories. Thus, for the purposes of this discussion, we can take the evidence discussed above as given. In fact, we can suppose that some particular linguistic theory is corroborated in full detail along the lines suggested above. The point, then, is that the Chomskian account, in allowing such data to be relevant to the choice between linguistic theories, and construing linguistic kinds as intimately tied to the nature of language processing and acquisition, greatly increases the range of evidence that can be brought to bear in evaluating linguistic theories and confers enormous explanatory power on linguistic theory. And it does these things in ways that are very natural given that language processing and acquisition are perhaps *the* central linguistic explananda. So the Chomskian interpretation provides us with a satisfying account of what theoretical considerations might be brought to bear in determining whether or not a parrot, a tape recorder, or a Martian is in fact an English-speaker.

The main reply to considerations of this sort by opponents of the Chomskian account is that this account makes linguistic theory *insufficiently general*. This sort of reply is offered by philosophers attempting to provide alternative substantive accounts and those offering more or less instrumentalist accounts, where any number of grammars turn out to be 'equally true' of a given speaker, provided they are in some sense extensionally equivalent (and on some views equally simple or elegant).[22] These philosophers believe that it is a problem for the Chomskian account that it does not take Martians and human English-speakers to speak the same language. There

[22] Among the non-substantive alternatives, I count Lewis (1983), Soames (1984), and perhaps Katz (1977). I should note that to the extent that these authors are being non-realist, it is not part of a general anti-realism with regard to all science. In each case the claim is that there is something special about linguistics which makes it the case that many alternative accounts are all 'equally true', in a sense that would not apply to alternative physical or biological theories.

are a number of points to consider in developing and responding to this argument.

The first is that it is not at all clear why we should stop here in the argument. Why stop with *Martians*? Why not extend the generality to cover, for example, beings of the sort Block imagines? Or parrots? Or valleys? Notice that we would then be including objects that do not make use of *any* internalized grammar. Of course we *could* say that all of these things *do* speak the same language, that normal human English-speakers, Martians, Block's beings, even parrots and valleys, are all equally well described by the whole host of 'extensionally equivalent' grammars that are said to describe our linguistic abilities. The problem with this move, I think, is that it robs linguistic theory of explanatory power. In seeking 'greater generality' we actually *lose* explanatory power.

Suppose that the data from acquisition, processing, and breakdown patterns continue to corroborate a particular grammar as the grammar internally represented in human English-speakers (and likewise for human French-speakers, German-speakers, Hindi-speakers, and so on), along the lines discussed in Section 2. Under the Chomskian account such data can be brought to bear in determining the correct grammars for the languages spoken by these various groups, and linguistic kinds will play an important role in explaining language acquisition, processing, and breakdown in these groups. As noted above, this is not true of all the extensionally equivalent grammars. Presumably most of these grammars will be completely unilluminating when it comes to describing and explaining these data from acquisition, breakdown, processing, etc.

But then I think we have to ask what exactly *the point* is of construing linguistic kinds in the way these opponents of the Chomskian view suggest. What is *the point* of construing linguistic kinds so that they apply equally to normal human English-speakers, Martians, Block's beings, even parrots and valleys? Now it seems *possible* to me that a conception of linguistic properties which construes linguistic kinds so that they apply equally to normal human English-speakers, Martians, Block's beings, even parrots and valleys, should be in some way valuable from an explanatory point of view. But at the same time, it is far from *obvious* that such a conception is in fact required.

What might defenders of the Martian Argument suppose needs to be explained? One possibility is that they simply feel that what look like the same phenomena from a superficial behavioural point of view must receive the same explanation, and the Chomskian account precludes this. Another possibility is that they might point to the possibility of 'communication' between human speakers of English and Martians. The second suggestion is perhaps more interesting, so let us look at it first.

Presumably the implicit argument here is that the ability of human speakers of English and Martians to 'communicate' with each other should be explained in terms of linguistic properties, and that linguistic properties construed along Chomskian lines are either unable to explain such 'communication' or cannot provide as good an explanation of such 'communication' as rival accounts can. I see no reason why this argument should be accepted, since it seems clear that there is in fact an explanation of all of this in Chomskian terms. The Martian language, like English, can be characterized relative to the linguistic competence of its speakers—in this case the grammar that the Martians have internalized. Communicative exchanges between human speakers of English and Martians would then be thought of (charitably) as essentially unintentional translations from one language to the other (or less charitably as involving relatively harmless systematic misinterpretations of each other's speech).

It is not at all clear that the defender of the Martian Argument can provide even an equally good explanation here, much less a better one. It will take some work to see why this is so. The details of the alternative explanation will vary somewhat depending on which alternative account we adopt. But the various alternatives would all presumably claim that there was a whole class of explanations (corresponding to the class of extensionally equivalent grammars describing the common language). These explanations will differ from the Chomskian one in that they will not get bogged down in 'irrelevant processing details' and therefore, perhaps, allow for some simpler, more general characterization of the linguistic properties involved in the communicative exchange. Supposing that this is true, what I want to call into question is whether this 'simplicity' and 'generality' should be thought of as a virtue. The considerations here are essentially the same as those involved in the question put aside earlier, of whether there is good reason to suppose that what look like the same phenomena from a superficial behavioural point of view must receive the same explanation. To put these issues in perspective, I think that it is once again valuable to consider the case of other sciences, such as chemistry or genetics/molecular biology.

Imagine someone making the analogue of the Martian Argument in chemistry or genetics/molecular biology, and charging that those who want to identify water with $H_2O$, or identify the things responsible for transmitting given traits in a population with chains of polynucleotides of a certain sort, were illegitimately limiting chemistry or genetics in taking these kinds to be insufficiently general. After all, the advocate of the Martian Argument analogy might go on, these reductionists would be excluding certain logically possible[23] substances which resemble water in appearance and behaviour as much as you like, or obey the same laws of trait transmission as genes do, and yet are distinct from $H_2O$ or the proposed polynucleotide basis for the trait transmitter. Surely the response in this case would be that we *might* use the more general kinds, but what is *the point*, given that the 'more restricted' kinds the reductionist advocates vastly increase the explanatory power of the kinds and link these kinds to new and powerful sources of evidence? I am arguing that the same should be said in the case of linguistics.

Now suppose that our Martians look just like humans do, and to all appearances, are able to mate with humans in the normal way, and produce what seem to be normal human children. But suppose it turns out that in fact Martians have no DNA, and so do not transmit their traits to offspring in the same way that we do. Perhaps instead their cells contain a much more complex mechanism for controlling development, which when it interacts with a normal human sex cell 'reads' the genetic information off from this cell, and alters its development-controlling mechanism appropriately. Perhaps half the offspring produced in this way turn out to have human mechanisms of trait transmission and half have Martian ones. The details are unimportant since presumably there are a great many logically possible mechanisms which might do the job and whose superficial behaviour might resemble that of the human genetic system as much as you like. *The question then is whether such logical possibilities require us to give up our belief that genes are chains of polynucleotides of a certain sort as an insufficiently general account of the nature of genes.*

[23] Advocates of the Martian Argument do not want to rest their argument on the empirical claim that such beings as Martians in fact exist, only on the fact that such beings are *possible*.

I think it is clear that they should not. But just as the defender of the Martian Argument asked 'But how are we to explain human/Martian communication?', the defender of the analogue of the Martian Argument might ask 'But how are we to explain human/Martian procreation?' Following the logic of the linguistic case we should presumably look for a (perhaps simpler) more general explanation in terms of 'genetic properties' *without regard for biochemical reality*. I think it is clear, however, that this would result in massive loss of explanatory power. The explanations gain much of their explanatory power by their link to the underlying biochemical properties. But this, of course, is just as it is in the case of the Chomskian account of linguistic properties which ties their nature directly to the nature of our abilities to acquire and process language.

I think it is also clear that the natural way we would go about explaining human/Martian procreation under the imagined circumstances would be in terms of the interaction of different kinds of 'trait transmitters'. Despite the superficial behavioural appearances, humans and Martians (in the imagined circumstances) have fundamentally different trait-transmission properties. Not only does this not preclude an explanation in terms of properties linked to particular sorts of 'processing' mechanisms, but such an explanation, in bringing out the real complexity of human/Martian procreation (not to mention the increased explanatory power of the kinds, and the wider evidentiary basis allowed), is actually preferable. Exactly the same considerations seem to apply to the Chomskian account of linguistic kinds.

The moral, I think, is that we do not want to leave the kinds of a science open to any logically possible 'counter-example' of the sort raised by the Martian Argument. The analogies to chemistry and biology make it clear that we cannot just assume that more generality—especially generality over various merely possible sorts of entities—is necessarily a good thing. There is a real danger of draining the explanatory power of kinds by trying to get them to explain too much. As the examples from chemistry and biology make clear, we often want our understanding of the nature of a kind to explain relatively specific properties associated with the kind, not just properties of the greatest generality.

Perhaps some future science of language or communication will be interested in more general properties than properties connected to our ability to process and acquire natural languages. Perhaps the science will be interested only in semantic properties of utterances and cover us, and Martians, and many other sorts of being. Perhaps. But I see no reason to let the nature of natural-language linguistic properties turn on this possibility. The kinds in linguistics, like the kinds in other sciences, can legitimately exclude, on essentially theoretical grounds, certain objects that might pre-theoretically be taken to be instances of those kinds, thereby increasing the explanatory power of linguistic theory in the ways suggested above. And assuming that the data concerning language processing, acquisition, and breakdown continue to be systematically describable on the assumption of an internal representation of particular grammars, I think it would be perverse to ignore these rich sources of evidence and to deny linguistic theory the generality and explanatory power involved here.

## 6 Conclusion

My argument for the Chomskian account of linguistics comes down to this. Because of the great explanatory power the Chomskian account offers linguistic theory in explaining a vast range of phenomena from language acquisition, processing, breakdown, and historical change, in terms of lin-guistic kinds (and the correlative prospect of extending the base of evidence for linguistic theory), the Chomskian account should be our default hy-pothesis concerning the nature of linguistic kinds. These considerations provide us with a powerful prima facie reason for accepting the Chomskian account. Of course, prima facie reasons are not conclusive reasons, and the Chomskian account may yet be dislodged. The data may not work out in the end. Perhaps we will eventually conclude that, contrary to our present expectations, *no grammar at all* is in fact internally represented. We will just have to wait and see about this. The question then becomes whether there are any powerful theoretical or conceptual (or further empirical) reasons for rejecting the Chomskian account in favour of one of its rivals. Here I have considered two influential arguments that have been raised against the Chomskian account, and I have argued that neither poses any real dif-ficulty for the Chomskian account. Moreover, as the last section makes clear, apart from the question of whether there are effective arguments against the Chomskian view, the alternatives to that view themselves face serious empirical and methodological difficulties. The main issue facing the alternatives is that they all serve to reduce the usefulness of linguistics by restricting its explanatory power. They restrict the explanatory power of linguistics by putting indefinitely many extensionally equivalent grammars essentially on equal footing, though the vast majority of these grammars will not be psychologically real. At the moment, then, there is every reason to believe that linguistics *is*, as Chomsky claims, a branch of psychology.

## Appendix

Scott Soames (1984) presents a curious blend of the Methodological and Martian Arguments that is worth considering briefly. Soames wants to argue that:

(i) There is a theoretically sound, empirically significant conception of linguistics in which its subject matter is the structure of natural language, considered in abstraction from the cognitive mechanisms causally responsible for language acquisition and mastery.

(ii) This conception of linguistics fits the ways in which practising linguists formulate, defend, and criticize their theories better than the received view does. (1984: 157)

Soames characterizes the domain of enquiry for linguistics by means of a set of 'leading questions'. He then argues that this domain of enquiry is conceptually distinct and empirically divergent from the study of psychological reality. In arguing for empirical divergence, Soames is in effect arguing that further evidence from neurology or psycholinguistics will not end up supporting current linguistic theory as a theory of what is psychologically real. In arguing for conceptual distinctness, he is in effect arguing that this evidence is not relevant, given his characterization of the autonomous domain of linguistics in terms of the 'leading questions' (and his interpretation of them).

'Leading questions' are central questions which work in a given field attempts to answer. According to Soames, among the leading questions of linguistics we find (Q1)–(Q3).

(Q1) In what ways are . . . alike and in what ways do they differ from one another? Instances are obtained by filling in the blank with a list or description of some (or all) natural languages.

(Q2) What (if anything) distinguishes natural languages from . . .? Instances are obtained by filling in the blank with a description of some set of artificial languages—e.g. 'finite state languages'—or animal communication systems—e.g. 'bee language'.

(Q3) In what ways have (has) . . . changed and in what ways have (has) . . . remained the same? Here, instances are obtained by filling in both blanks by the same description, or list, of one or more natural languages. (1984: 158)

In answering questions of this sort, Soames suggests, we will appeal to our pre-theoretic sense of what constitutes a linguistically significant property or relation, and this in turn will tell us that considerations such as (8)–(10) are not *directly relevant* to determining whether or not two groups, the Xs and the Ys, speak the same language or different languages:

(3) Xs process sentences of type A faster than they process sentences of type B; whereas Ys process Bs faster than As.

(4) Xs make fewer mistakes comprehending As than they do comprehending Bs, whereas Ys make fewer mistakes with Bs than As.

(5) Xs learn A-constructions as children before they learn B-constructions, whereas Ys learn them in reverse order. (1984: 159, original numbering)

Of course if such evidence is excluded, we may well end up with a number of equally simple and elegant theories, and these may well diverge from whatever grammar, if any, is psychologically real. It is hard to see, though, why such evidence should not be relevant, harder still to see how we could rule it irrelevant a priori.[24] An answer to any of the leading questions may well appeal to linguistic properties of any sort. If utterances have linguistic properties in virtue of facts concerning our capacities for language processing and acquisition, as the Chomskian holds, then evidence of the sort cited in (6)–(8) is quite relevant. Background assumptions about the nature of linguistic properties are thus being used to exclude these as relevant data.

Again it is useful to consider an analogy to another science. A Soamesian geneticist might argue as follows.[25] The domain of enquiry for the science of genetics is given by a set of leading questions:

---

[24] I see no issue here between a piece of evidence's being relevant and its being *directly relevant*. Provided it is relevant evidence, I do not care whether or not it is *directly relevant* evidence. For a forceful statement of the view that what counts as relevant evidence is determined a posteriori, see J. A. Fodor (1981), 150–2.

[25] J. A. Fodor (1981) uses this argument against 'the Wrong View' (using the example of astronomy). As noted above, Soames and Lewis (both writing after Fodor's article) seem especially clear instances of the Wrong View.

(Q4) In what ways are . . . alike and in what ways do they differ from one another? Instances are obtained by filling in the blank with a list or description of some, or all, types of organism.

(Q5) What (if anything) distinguishes naturally replicating organisms from . . .? Instances are obtained by filling in the blank with a description of some set of artificial systems—e.g. self-duplicating programs—or non-organic natural systems of property transmission—e.g. in chemical reactions.

(Q6) In what ways have (has) . . . changed and in what ways have (has) . . . remained the same? Here, instances are obtained by filling in both blanks by the same description, or list, of one or more type of organism.

Appealing to our pre-theoretic sense of what constitutes a genetically significant property or relation tells us that while data from cross breeding are '*directly* relevant,' considerations such as (6)–(8) are not '*directly*' relevant' to determining whether or not two groups, the Xs and the Ys, are both members of the same type of organism, or members of different types:

(6) Xs reproduce faster in situations of type A than situations of type B; whereas Ys reproduce faster in situations of type B than type A.

(7) Xs produce fewer mutations in situations of type A than they do in situations of type B, whereas Ys produce fewer mutations in situations of type B than type A.

(8) Xs exhibit trait A before they exhibit trait B, whereas Ys acquire these traits in reverse order.

The issue, as J. A. Fodor (1981) makes clear, is that one cannot specify a priori what counts as evidence in a science, and to all appearances (3)–(5), as (6)–(8), are relevant to the sciences of languages and genetics. If leading questions do set the domain for sciences, they do not thereby determine what counts as relevant evidence.[26] The main conclusion here is the same as that of the Martian Argument: one does not determine the subject matter of linguistics on the basis of pre-theoretic intuitions about whether or not two populations are or are not

[26] Enough has been said now about Soames's view. I should add for completeness, however, that the argument for empirical divergence builds on the alleged conceptual distinctness. Noting the multitude of extensionally equivalent grammars, Soames argues that the best theory from the point of view of psychology will not be the best theory from the point of view of linguistics, since the two theories will have to answer to different sets of data, each appropriate to their domain as characterized by a set of leading questions. This argument can never get off the ground, though, if Soames does not have an argument for restricting the base of evidence for linguistics, as I have argued he does not.

speaking the same language—rather this is an issue that gets settled only by doing linguistic theory.

# REFERENCES

BERWICK, R., and WEINBERG, A. (1984), *The Grammatical Basis of Linguistic Performance: Language Use and Acquisition* (Cambridge, Mass.: MIT Press).

BLOCK, N., ed. (1981), *Readings in Philosophy of Psychology*, vol. ii (Cambridge, Mass.: Harvard University Press).

—— (1990), 'The Computer Model of the Mind', in Osherson and Smith (1990), 247–89.

CHOMSKY, N. (1972), *Language and Mind*. Enlarged Edition (New York: Harcourt Brace Jovanovich).

—— (1975), *Reflections on Language* (New York: Pantheon Books and Random House).

—— (1980), *Rules and Representations* (New York: Columbia University Press).

—— (1986), *Knowledge of Language: Its Nature, Origin, and Use* (New York: Praeger Publishers).

—— (1992), 'Explaining Language Use', *Philosophical Topics*, 20: 205–31.

COHEN, D., and WIRTH, J., eds. (1975), *Testing Linguistic Hypotheses* (Washington: John Wiley and Sons).

CUMMINS, R. (1983), *The Nature of Psychological Explanation* (Cambridge, Mass.: MIT Press).

DEVITT, M., and STERELNY. K. (1987), *Language and Reality* (Cambridge, Mass.: MIT Press).

—— —— (1989), 'Linguistics: What's Wrong With the "Right View"', in Tomberlin (1989), 497–531.

FERREIRA, F., and CLIFTON, C. (1986), 'The Independence of Syntactic Processing', *Journal of Memory and Language*, 25: 348–68.

FODOR, J. A. (1981), 'Some Notes on What Linguistics is About', in Block (1981), 197–207.

—— BEVER, T., and GARRETT, M. (1974), *The Psychology of Language* (New York: McGraw-Hill).

FODOR, J. D. (1991), 'Sentence Processing and the Mental Grammar', in Sells, Shieber, and Wasow (1991), 83–113.

FRAZIER, L. (1987), 'Syntactic Processing: Evidence From Dutch', *Natural Language and Linguistic Theory*, 5: 519–59.

GENTNER, D., and STEVENS, A., eds. (1983), *Mental Models* (Hillsdale, NJ: LEA).

GIBSON, E. (1991), 'A Computational Theory of Human Linguistic Processing: Memory Limitations and Processing Breakdown' (diss. Ph.D., Carnegie Mellon University).

GOULD, S. J. (1983), *The Panda's Thumb* (Harmondsworth: Penguin).

GRODZINSKY, Y. (1990), *Theoretical Perspectives on Language Deficits* (Cambridge, Mass.: MIT Press).

HYAMS, N. (1986), *Language Acquisition and the Theory of Parameters* (Dordrecht: D. Reidel).

KATZ, J. J. (1977), 'The Real Status of Semantic Representations', in Block (1981), 253–75.

—— (1981), *Language and Other Abstract Objects* (Totowa, NJ: Rowman and Littlefield).

—— ed. (1985a), *The Philosophy of Linguistics* (New York: Oxford University Press).

—— (1985b), 'An Outline of a Platonist Grammar', in Katz (1985a), 172–203.

—— and POSTAL, P. (1991), 'Realism vs. Conceptualism in Linguistics', *Linguistics and Philosophy*, 14: 515–54.

LANGEDEON, D., and POSTAL, P. (1985), 'Sets and Sentences', in Katz (1985a), 227–48.

LAURENCE, S. (1993), 'Naturalism and Language' (diss. Ph.D., Rutgers University).

LEWIS, D. (1983), 'Languages and Language', in id., *Philosophical Papers*, vol. i (Oxford: Oxford University Press), 163–88.

LIGHTFOOT, D. (1991), *How to Set Parameters* (Cambridge, Mass.: MIT Press).

McCLOSKEY, M. (1983), 'Naive Theories of Motion', in Gentner and Stevens (1983), 299–324.

OSHERSON, D., and SMITH, E., eds. (1990), *Thinking* (Cambridge, Mass.: MIT Press).

RAYNER, K., CARLSON, M., and FRAZIER, L. (1983), 'The Interaction of Syntax and Semantics during Sentence Processing: Eye Movements in the Analysis of Semantically Biased Sentences', *Journal of Verbal Learning and Verbal Behavior*, 22: 358–74.

RIZZI, L. (1992), 'Early Null Subjects and Root Null Subjects' (unpublished manuscript).

SELLS, P., SHIEBER, S. M., and WASOW, T., eds. (1991), *Foundational Issues in Natural Language Processing* (Cambridge, Mass.: MIT Press).

SOAMES, S. (1984), 'Linguistics and Psychology', *Linguistics and Philosophy*, 7: 155–79.

STICH, S. (1971), 'What Every Speaker Knows', *Philosophical Review*, 80: 476–96.

STICH, S. (1972), 'Grammar, Psychology and Indeterminacy', in Katz (1985a), 126–45.

—— (1975), 'Competence and Indeterminacy', in Cohen and Wirth (1975), 93–109.

SWINNEY, D., FORD, M., BRESNAN, J., and FRAUENFELDER, U. (1988), 'Coreference Assignment during Sentence Processing' (unpublished manuscript).

TOMBERLIN, J., ed. (1989), *Philosophy of Mind and Action Theory* (Philosophical Perspectives, 3; Atascadero: Ridgeview).

# CHAPTER 4

# Linguistics is Not Psychology

*Michael Devitt*

## 1 Chomsky's View

The wonderfully successful research programme in linguistics initiated and sustained by Noam Chomsky starts from the assumption that a person competent in a language *knows* that language. The programme then defines the linguistic tasks in terms of this knowledge. Thus, at the beginning of a book called, appropriately enough, *Knowledge of Language* (1986), Chomsky claims that 'the three basic questions that arise' in the study of language are:

(i)   What constitutes knowledge of language?
(ii)  How is knowledge of language acquired?
(iii) How is knowledge of language put to use? (Chomsky 1986: 3)

In general, talk of 'knowledge' is very loose. This has led to some initial difficulty in interpreting (i)–(iii). However, there is a natural interpretation which takes Chomsky pretty much at his word.[1] On this interpretation, his answer to question (i) urges that competent speakers of a language

This paper is drawn from a book in progress, *Ignorance of Language*. It is similar to a paper delivered under that title at the Epistemology of Language conference in June 2000. The first version of the paper was delivered at King's College London in March 1997. Later versions were delivered at many universities. I am indebted to these audiences for comments. I also benefited from discussions in a seminar given by Stephen Crain, Juan Uriagereka, and myself in Fall 1997 at the University of Maryland. Most of all I am indebted to Georges Rey for many discussions of the topic over the last few years. Finally, my thanks to Gurpreet Rattan, Sara Bernal, and Philip Robbins for comments on the penultimate version.

[1] See esp. Chomsky (1986), 263–73, which includes the following: 'Knowledge of language involves (perhaps entails) standard examples of propositional knowledge' (p. 265);

have propositional knowledge of its rules.[2] This knowledge underlies the speakers' intuitive judgements about the syntax of expressions.

The key point concerning the rules of the language is that speakers stand in *a propositional attitude to representations of these rules*, albeit an unconscious or tacit one. Chomsky puts the point with characteristic firmness: 'there can be little doubt that knowing a language involves internal representation of a generative procedure' (1991*a*: 9; see also 1980*b*: 9). The term 'know' is mostly used for the propositional attitude in question but, when the chips are down, Chomsky is prepared to settle for the technical term 'cognize' (1980*a*: 69–70). The representations that are cognized are in a special faculty of the mind, 'the language faculty'. I shall call this the Representational Thesis.

The key point concerning the intuitions about particular syntactic matters is the strongly Cartesian view that speakers *derive their intuitive judgements from their representations of rules* by some process that is both causal and rational. The intuitions are, we might say, 'the voice of competence'. So, *simply* in virtue of being competent, speakers have propositional knowledge of syntactic facts; their competence gives them 'privileged access' to this reality. Because of this, these intuitions provide the main evidence about the nature of the rules.[3] This is not to say that the intuitions are infallible: performance error can lead to mistakes (Chomsky 1986: 36). Still, apart from this 'noise', intuitions reflect the underlying representations of the rules of the language.

To be competent in a language is to be able to produce and understand the expressions of that language. According to Chomsky, on our natural

'it is proper to say that a person knows that R, where R is a rule of his or her grammar' (p. 268).

[2] Recent versions of generative grammar talk of 'principles', not rules. These principles are overarching rules and their difference from what were previously called 'rules' is unimportant to my discussion (as I think Chomsky would agree: 1986: 243–4).

[3] Thus: 'It seems reasonably clear, both in principle and in many specific cases, how unconscious knowledge issues in conscious knowledge . . . it follows by computations similar to straight deduction' (Chomsky 1986: 270); 'we cognize the system of mentally-represented rules from which [linguistic] facts follow' (Chomsky 1980*b*: 9; the facts are expressed in intuitive judgments); 'We can use intuitions to confirm grammars because grammars are internally represented and actually contribute to the etiology of the speaker/hearer's intuititve judgments' (J. A. Fodor 1981: 200–1); 'Our ability to make linguistic judgments clearly follows from our knowing the languages that we know' (Larson and Segal 1995: 10; see also Baker 1995: 20).

interpretation, this competence involves representations of the rules of the language. So those representations determine what expressions the speaker produces and understands. According to the point about intuitions, those representations also determine what the speaker says *about* those expressions in her intuitive judgements.

On our interpretation, task (i) for a language comes down to the study of the system of rules that is the object of the speaker's knowledge. Chomsky calls this object an 'I-language'. Since the speaker's knowledge about this I-language constitutes her competence, task (i) is, in effect, the study of that competence. In attempting this task, the linguist produces a 'grammar', which is a theory of the I-language. That theory, hard-won by the linguist, is precisely what the speaker tacitly knows. Task (ii) is concerned with how the speaker acquires her competence. How much of her knowledge of the language is innate and how much learnt from experience? Task (iii) is concerned with the role played by this competence in performance. What role does her knowledge of the language play in understanding and producing expressions of the language?

So what, according to Chomsky, *is* a language? What is the reality that is the concern of a grammar? A language is a system of rules represented in the language faculty. Those represented rules are the reality that a grammar is theorizing about.

Chomsky is naturally interpreted as urging the Representational Thesis because doing so takes his talk of 'knowing that', 'propositional attitudes', and 'representation' at face value. The thesis is the core of what Jerry Fodor (1981) calls 'the Right View' of what a grammar is about. The thesis is certainly widespread among linguists.[4] Still, the interpretation of Chomsky may not be right. And many sympathetic to his research programme think the thesis is obviously mistaken (as I have discovered when proposing it as an interpretation).[5]

So, suppose that the interpretation is wrong. What then is Chomsky's view of the reality of a language? A language is a system of rules *embodied somehow* in the mind without being represented (just as, say, arithmetical

---

[4] '[M]y linguist friends tell me that learning how to talk a first language requires quite a lot of learning that the language has the grammar that it does' (J. A. Fodor 1998: 125).

[5] On this and other problems of interpretation, see Rey (2003) and his contribution to the present volume.

rules are embodied in a simple mechanical calculator without being represented). Those embodied rules are the reality that a grammar is theorizing about.

It can be seen that, according to Chomsky, the reality of a language is in the mind, whether as represented rules or as otherwise embodied rules: the reality is psychological. He has persuaded many others of this. As Robert Matthews says: 'It is a measure of the depth of the conceptual revolution wrought by Noam Chomsky in linguistics that few linguists would quarrel with his notion that theoretical linguistics is a subfield of psychology' (1991: 182).[6] So it is not surprising that Chomsky is irritated by the oft-raised question: 'Are the rules described by a grammar "psychologically real"?' (see e.g. 1980a: 189–201). He points out that a grammar is a scientific theory and so should be treated just like any other scientific theory. And a scientific theory should be treated realistically, for the alternative of treating it instrumentally has surely been discredited. This yields a very fast argument for the psychological reality of the rules decribed by the grammar. We have good, though not of course conclusive, evidence for a grammar's truth and so we have good evidence for the reality it concerns. And, in Chomsky's view, that reality is psychological.

Yet, on the face of it, this view of linguistics seems implausible. In any case, Kim Sterelny and I (1987; 1989) have argued against it. Jerry Katz (1981; 1984) and Scott Soames (1984) have argued independently along similar lines.[7] Our point seems simple, even rather obvious. Chomsky (1986: 34–6; 1991b: 31; 1995: 33–4) has responded to it briefly and dismissively. Louise Antony (2003) has responded critically to Soames in a 1991 talk that is now published in this volume. Stephen Laurence (2003) has mounted a lengthy attack in this volume.[8] Some people stopped talking to us. Beyond this, there is no evidence that our arguments have had any effect.

My aim in this paper is to argue the matter somewhat differently and,

---

[6] Some do quarrel, however: 'We make no claims, naturally enough, that our grammatical theory is *eo ipso* a psychological theory' (Gazdar *et al.* 1985: 5).

[7] See also related views in Cummins and Harnish (1980), Stabler (1983), and George (1989b).

[8] I had written this paper before receiving Laurence's. I have made several responses to his paper in the notes.

I hope, better.[9] I claim that there is something other than psychological reality for a grammar to be true of: it can be true of a *linguistic* reality.[10] One might think that this claim was uncontroversial and yet Chomsky and others seem to resist it. So I shall start by arguing for the claim carefully with the help of three quite general distinctions. I shall then argue that it is plausible to think that the grammar is indeed more or less true of that linguistic reality. Furthermore, this reality is worthy of theoretical study in its own right, whatever the case may be with psychological reality. The grammar might *also* be true of a psychological reality, of course, but to show that it is requires an explicitly *psychological* assumption. I think, but will not attempt to argue here, that it is hard to establish a psychological assumption that will do the trick. In particular, I think that there is no evidence for the Representational Thesis. If this is right, the very fast argument that we have good evidence for the psychological reality of linguistic rules because psychological reality is what grammars are about is revealed as not only fast but dirty.

How important is all this? What hangs on it? One indubitable triumph of 'generative grammar' does *not* hang on it: the extraordinary progress in providing explicit statements of the linguistic rules with the aim of deriving complete structural descriptions of all the possible sentences of a language. So I suspect that the vast majority of the day-to-day work of linguists and psycholinguists in Chomsky's research programme does not hang on it. However, the view does have great importance for the issue of the psychological reality of a language. If the view is right, the research programme is revealing a lot about language but, contrary to advertisements, rather little about the place of language in the mind (beyond the idea that, whatever that place, it may be largely innate).[11] So I think that the extent to which the rules of the language are in the mind is a fairly open question.

A person's I-language, according to Chomsky, supervenes on intrinsic properties of the person's brain: it is, as philosophers would say, 'narrow'

[9] The earlier argument now seems to me to have many errors. A preview of the present argument is to be found in Devitt and Sterelny (1999), ch. 8.

[10] Earlier (Devitt 1981: 92–5) I argued an analogous point against philosophers who identify semantics with the explanation of linguistic competence or understanding.

[11] Cowie (1998) takes a sceptical view of the innateness claim.

and individualistic. It does not involve language-world connections and so does not involve semantics proper. In effect, an I-language has only syntactic properties, in a broad sense of the term. This restriction reflects Chomsky's doubts about the scientific study of reference.[12] I do not share these doubts and so think that the object of study should not be an I-language but rather something 'wide', a 'wide-I(ed)-language': the study should include the referential properties which, together with syntactic properties, determine the truth-referential meanings of expressions. But this difference of opinion is largely beside the present issue and so, for the sake of argument, I shall go along with Chomsky's restriction to an I-language and to syntax.

## 2 Competence vs. Outputs

A competence is a competence to produce a certain sort of output/product; or it is a competence to process a certain sort of input; or it is both.

### Distinction 1

Distinguish the theory of a competence from the theory of its outputs/ products or inputs.

For convenience, I shall focus on competences to produce certain sorts of outputs.

I shall draw the distinction first with a simple example, distant from the concerns of linguistics: the competence of a blacksmith and the horseshoes he produces. Horseshoes are obvious parts of the physical world. A study of them will quickly conclude that they are made of iron, have a certain shape, have holes for nails, and so on. The blacksmith's competence is some state of his mind or body that plays the central role in explaining his behaviour in producing horseshoes. Goodness knows what a study of it would conclude. The key point is that the 'theory' of the horseshoes is one thing, the theory of the competence another, because horseshoes are very different from the competence to produce them. Of course, given the causal relation between the competence and the horseshoes it produces, we can expect a theory of the one to bear on a theory of the other. But manifestly this does not make the two theories the same.

---

[12] Related doubts are expressed in Pietroski (this volume).

With an eye to two important features of constructing a grammar, we note that there are two respects in which a theory of the outputs of a competence is not simply about the *actual* outputs of that competence. First, there can be performance errors in the exercise of a competence. Thus sometimes what a blacksmith produces is not a good horseshoe. The theory is only concerned with the nature of the outputs of a competence when it performs as it should; the theory idealizes by abstracting from error. Second, the theory is concerned with any *possible* output of the competence (when working well). Thus, the theory of horseshoes is concerned not only with the actual outputs of competent blacksmiths but with any of an indefinitely large number of outputs that they might produce.

The discussion to follow provides several other illustrations of Distinction 1.

## 3 Structure Rules vs. Processing Rules

The theory of a competence explains what it is about an object that makes it competent. Part of the explanation must be that the object embodies rules that govern the process of producing the appropriate output when the competence is exercised. Call these rules 'processing rules'. Sometimes the *outputs* of a competence are also rule-governed, but in a different way: their natures are constituted by their place in a 'structure' defined by a system of rules. Call these rules 'structure rules'.

> *Distinction 2*
> Distinguish the structure rules governing the outputs of a competence from the processing rules governing the exercise of the competence.

In characterizing the output of the blacksmith we shall not appeal to rules, but in characterizing other outputs we shall. Thus, consider the output of a chess player: chess moves. The characterization of chess moves must appeal to a rather elaborate system of rules: a bishop may only move diagonally; the king may only move one square; no piece except a knight may move through an occupied square; and so on. Chess moves are rule-governed in that something counts as a chess move at all only if it has a place in the structure defined by the rules of chess. Something counts as a particular chess move in virtue of the particular rules that govern it, in virtue of its particular place in the structure. (This was an insight of the structuralists, of course.) A 'theory' of the nature of chess describes these structure rules.[13] In doing so it describes constraints on the appropriate output of a chess player. A chess player should only make moves that have a place in the system the structure rules describe. That is, a chess player should make only legal moves. The structure rules *may* also be among the rules governing the psychological process by which she produces chess moves. They may be among the processing rules activated in the exercise of her chess competence. However, this is not necessary and may be unlikely. In figuring out a move, the player may not actually go through processes like that of inferring '*x* moves diagonally' from '*x* is a bishop'. In any case, the key point is that *being a structure rule*—a rule governing outputs—is a very different property from *being a processing rule*, a rule governing the psychological production of outputs.

A nice example of this distinction is provided by the distinction between the *formation* and *transformation* rules of a formal logic (the latter are not to be confused with the very different transformation rules of grammar). The *formation* rules are structure rules characterizing the *wff*s (well-formed formulae) of the system: nothing counts as a *wff* unless it accords with those rules. In this way, *wff*s are rule-governed. Each *wff* has its particular syntactic structure in virtue of the particular formation rules that govern it, in virtue of its particular place in the structure defined by the system of rules. The *transformation* rules are processing rules governing the move from one *wff* to another; they govern a process of valid derivation (if the rules are good). Nothing is both a formation and a transformation rule.

Think of the formal logic as embodied in a 'logic machine'. The machine takes *wff*s as inputs, processes them according to the transformation rules, yielding *wff*s as outputs (so it embodies a proof procedure). The outputs of this machine are all in accord with the formation rules, but those rules are not the ones that govern the process of producing them.

Bees provide another good example of the distinction between structure rules and processing rules. A bee returning from a distant food source produces a 'waggle dance' on the vertical face of the honeycomb. The positioning of this dance and its pattern indicate the direction and distance

---

[13] An *interesting* theory of chess will describe good strategies, of course. But that is a different matter.

of the food source. These dances form a very effective symbol system governed by a surprising set of structure rules. It is the task of a theory of the dance symbols to describe these structure rules. Scientists completed this task some time ago. In contrast, the processing rules by which the bee performs this rather remarkable feat remain a mystery.[14]

Here is a description of one of the structure rules of the bee's dance:

> To convey the direction of a food source, the bee varies the angle the waggling run makes with an imaginary line running straight up and down . . . If you draw a line connecting the beehive and the food source, and another line connecting the hive and the spot on the horizon just beneath the sun, the angle formed by the two lines is the same as the angle of the waggling run to the imaginary vertical line. (Frank 1997: 82)

How *might* the bee manage this? To start with it must 'remember where the food source is' when it gets back to the hive. How? Two popular ideas are that the bee uses variations in Earth's magnetic field or in the polarization of the sun's light. A wilder idea is that the bee is sensitive to quantum fields (Frank 1997: 84). Whatever the truth of this matter, the real mystery remains: what process does the bee go through to turn this memory into an appropriate dance, a dance governed by the structure rule? We should not rush to the judgement that the structure rule itself must govern this unknown process. It may be the *wrong sort* of rule to play this role. Nature faced the design problem of adapting the pre-existing structures of an insect to produce (and respond to) the message of the bee's dance. We have no reason to suppose a priori that nature solved this problem by making the bee go through the structure rule 'calculation'. Indeed, it is not at all clear that the bee could plausibly be seen as performing this calculation: can the bee even manage the necessary representations of the food source, of the spot on the horizon, and of the angles?

With an eye to important features of grammar construction, we have noted, first, that our theory of outputs idealizes by abstracting from performance errors. So we are not concerned with the chess player's moves when he is drunk, with any 'noise' produced by the logic machine, or with the

[14] 'Scientists have known of the bee's dance for more than 70 years, and they have assembled a remarkably complete dictionary of its terms, but one fundamental question has stubbornly remained unanswered: How do they do it?' (Frank 1997: 80).

bee's dance when it is shaken off course. We have noted, second, that we are concerned not only with any actual output but with any possible output. So we are concerned with any of an indefinitely large number of *wff*s that the logic machine might produce and of dances that the bee might perform.[15] We now note, third, that we also abstract from properties of the outputs that are irrelevant to our concerns. For example, consider a collection of logic machines each embodying the same formal logic. One machine may produce a 'written' *wff* in one script, another in another script; one may produce a fast high-pitched spoken *wff*, another a slow low-pitched one. We might be interested in these differences and so distinguish these *wff*s and the competences that produce them. But we might well not be. We may be simply interested in the rule-governed syntactic structures of the *wff*s, structures shared by the outputs of all these machines. So in our theorizing we abstract from these differences.

Still with an eye to important features of grammar construction, we note, fourth, that although our theory is of the idealized output we can use it to make distinctions among the non-ideal. Moves that are not chess moves, formulae that are not well-formed, and manœuvres that are not proper bee dances can differ in their *degree* of failure. For they can differ in the sort and number of structure rules of chess, *wff*s, and bee dances that they fail, respectively, to satisfy.

## 4 Respecting Structure Rules

Although processing rules need not include any of the structure rules, they must, I shall say, 'respect' them.

> *Distinction 3*
>
> Distinguish the respecting of structure rules by processing rules from the inclusion of structure rules among processing rules.

[15] This talk may appear to commit theories of outputs to the existence of unactualized possibilia, but the talk can be, and in my view should be, a mere manner of speaking. It is a convenient way of capturing the fact that these theories, like all interesting ones, are lawlike. Strictly speaking, the theories quantify only over actual entities but the theories are, in some sense, necessary. So the talk captures the modal fact that if something *were* a *wff*, a chess move, a *wff*, a bee's dance, or whatever, then it *would have* the properties specified by the appropriate theory of outputs. (How are we to explain modal facts? I do not know but, *pace* David Lewis, surely not in terms of unactualized possibilia.)

I have mentioned that there is a causal relation between a competence and its output. There is also a 'constitutive' relation. This arises from the fact that the *very nature* of the competence is to produce its outputs: producing them is what makes it the competence it is. Thus, the blacksmith's competence is (partly) the ability to produce horseshoes; the chess player's, to produce chess moves, things governed by the structure rules of chess; the logic machine's, to produce *wff*s, things governed by the formation rules; the bee's, to produce dances, things governed by the dance rules. So a theory of the outputs of a competence is automatically, to that extent, a contribution to the theory of the competence, for it tells us about the outputs the production of which is definitive of the competence. And we can say that a competence and its processing rules must 'respect' the nature of the appropriate output in that, performance errors aside, the processing rules must produce outputs that have that nature. Where we have to appeal to structure rules to characterize that nature, as we do with the outputs of the chess player, the logic machine, and the bee, these structure rules must be respected by the processing rules. Thus, whether or not the chess player actually goes through a process of inferring '*x* moves diagonally' from '*x* is a bishop', whatever processes she does go through must respect the structure rule that a bishop moves diagonally; any moves she makes must be in accord with that rule. And even if I am right in suggesting that the processing rules governing the bee's dancing cannot plausibly be seen as including the previously described structure rule for the direction of the food source, the processing rules must respect that structure rule in that they produce dances that are governed by it.

On the strength of the fact that these structure rules must be thus respected, it may be appropriate to say that the competent object behaves *as if* those rules were embodied in the object, but it is surely not appropriate to say *solely* on those grounds that the rules *are* embodied in it. The respecting might, of course, be the *result* of the rules being embodied; for example, the rules might also be processing rules. But the respecting alone does not require that the rules be actually realized in the speaker; for example, it does not require that they be processing rules. For there may be many other possible ways that a competence might respect the rules. So the claim that a competence and its processing rules respect the structure rules is the minimal claim on the internal-reality issue. In a sense, this claim tells us little about the competence because it tells us nothing about *the way in which* the competence respects the structure rules. Still, we should not minimize the minimal claim. We know something quite substantial about a bee when we know that there is something-we-know-not-what within the bee that respects the structure rules of its dance. And were the respected rules richer and more complicated than those of the bee's dance, we would know something more substantial.

It follows from the minimal claim that a theory of a competence must posit processing rules that respect the structure rules of the outputs. Similarly, a theory of the outputs must posit structure rules that are respected by the competence and its processing rules. Let us capture this by saying that both theories must meet the 'Respect Constraint'.

I have remarked that a theory of the outputs of a competence must be a contribution to the theory of the competence. I think that we should go further: it seems plausible to think that the theory of a competence must *begin* with a theory of its outputs. A competence is a competence to produce certain outputs. How could we make any significant progress studying the nature of a competence until we knew a good deal about the outputs that it is supposed to produce? How could we start trying to solve the mystery of the bee's competence to dance until we knew the previously described structure rule for the direction of the food source? In brief, the theory of outputs has a certain epistemic and explanatory priority over the theory of competence.

## 5 Application to Linguistics

I shall now apply this discussion to linguistics, arguing that we should see grammars as primarily theories of linguistic reality, not psychological reality. In the discussion I have had an eye to certain important features of grammar construction. This was in anticipation of a certain objection to the view of linguistics I am urging. The objection is that this view cannot be right because it cannot account for those features. We shall see that it can and does.

Observing Distinction 1, we distinguish the theory of a speaker's competence in a language, a psychological state, from the theory of the outputs of that competence, sentences in the language. The construction of the former theory is Chomsky's task (i). The construction of the latter theory is a *different* task, one that I wish to promote. What can we say about it?

Like the theory of the outputs of the blacksmith, chess player, logic machine, and bee, the theory of the outputs of linguistic competence is not concerned simply with the actual outputs. It abstracts from performance error to consider outputs when the competence is working well. Thus we account for the first important feature of grammar construction. And our theory of outputs is concerned with any of an indefinitely large number of these idealized outputs that the competence might produce, with any possible output.[16] Thus we account for a second important feature. Like the theory of the outputs of the logic machine, our theory can abstract also from a range of properties of the outputs—for example, form of script and pitch of sound—focusing simply on the syntactic properties that we are interested in. Thus we account for a third important feature. The outputs of a linguistic competence, physical linguistic symbols, are governed by a system of rules, just like the outputs of the chess player, the logic machine, and the bee. Something counts as a sentence only if it has a place in the linguistic structure defined by these structure rules. Something counts as a particular sentence, has its particular syntactic structure, in virtue of the particular structure rules that govern it, in virtue of its particular place in the linguistic structure. Like the theory of the idealized outputs of the chess player, logic machine, and bee, our theory can be used to make distinctions among the non-ideal. Strings that are not sentences can differ in their *degree* of failure. For they can differ in the sort and number of linguistic structure rules that they fail to satisfy. Thus we account for a fourth important feature.

Observing Distinction 2, we distinguish these structure rules from processing rules involved in the exercise of linguistic competence. These two sorts of rules have very different roles. The processing rules produce sentences of the language in the exercise of linguistic competence. It is because those sentences are governed by the structure rules that they are indeed sentences of the language. It may be possible that a structure rule will also be a processing rule, but it is not necessary that it be.

---

[16] And, as with the earlier theories (n. 15), such talk need not be construed as a commitment to unactualized possibilia but rather as a way of capturing the fact that the linguistic theory is lawlike. So if something *were* a sentence, a wh-question, a passive, or whatever, it *would have* the properties specified for such items by the theory.

Finally, observing Distinction 3, we note that although the structure rules governing sentences may not be among the processing rules that govern the exercise of linguistic competence, they must be respected by the competence and its processing rules: performance errors aside, the outputs of the process must be sentences of the language and hence must be governed by the rules of the language. For, it is the very nature of the competence to produce such sentences. The claim that the structure rules of the language must be respected by the competence and its processing rules is the minimal claim on the issue of the psychological reality of language. In this sense, at least, we might say that the grammar describes 'what the competent speaker knows'. And on the strength of this minimal claim we might say that the speaker behaves *as if* those linguistic structure rules were psychologically real in her, *as if* she embodied them. But it is surely not appropriate to say *solely* on the strength of that minimal claim that those rules *are* psychologically real in her, *are* embodied, for the claim does not require that the rules be actually realized in her. In a sense, the claim tells us little about linguistic competence because it tells us nothing about *the way in which* the competence respects the linguistic rules. Still, we do know something substantial about a person when we know that there is something-we-know-not-what within her that respects the rich and complicated structure rules of a certain natural language.

Both a theory of a person's linguistic competence, of her knowledge of her language, and a theory of her linguistic outputs must meet the Respect Constraint. A theory of the competence must posit a psychological state that respects the rules governing the linguistic outputs. And a theory of the linguistic outputs must posit rules that are respected by the competence and its processing rules.

On my view, a language is composed of the outputs of a linguistic competence, symbols that are governed by a system of linguistic structure rules. That is the reality of a language. And the task we have been contemplating, and that I wish to promote, is the study of the nature of this reality. This is not Chomsky's task (i), the study of the nature of the competence itself. Indeed, at first sight the contemplated study may seem to be alien to Chomsky's enterprise. It may even seem to smack of studying an 'E-language', of which Chomsky takes a dim view: 'the concept [of an E-language] appears to play no role in the theory of language' (1986: 26); an E-language has 'no corresponding real-world object' (1986: 27). But I rather doubt that the outputs of linguistic competence fit Chomsky's description of an E-language. According to him, an E-language is 'externalized . . . in the sense that the construct is understood independently of the properties of the mind/brain' (1986: 20). An E-language for Chomsky seems to be essentially Platonic. The outputs I have identified, physical sentence tokens governed by a system of linguistic rules, are certainly not divorced from the mind/brain since they are the symbolic outputs of the mind/brain. In studying them our *object* of study is not the mind/brain, of course, but it is likely to turn out that their properties are largely *determined* by the mind/brain. Finally, the theory of them is as much concerned with real-world objects as the theories of horseshoes, chess moves, bees' dances, and *wff*s. It is often convenient to talk of the objects posited by these theories as if they were *types* not tokens, abstract Platonic objects, but this need be nothing more than a manner of speaking: when the chips are down the objects are parts of the spatio-temporal physical world.

Here I part company with Jerrold Katz (1981; 1984; 1996). He also favours a linguistic task that is quite different from Chomsky's task (i), but the one he favours is the study of a system of Platonic objects. For him talk of sentence *types* is not a mere manner of speaking but essential to the task. He calls Chomsky's view 'conceptualism' and my sort of view 'nominalism'. He takes nominalism to have been refuted by Chomsky's criticisms of Bloomfieldian structuralism. Yet, so far as I can see, these criticisms are not of the *nominalism* of the structuralists but rather of their *taxonomic methodology*, a methodology in the spirit of positivism. According to Chomsky, this methodology imposed 'arbitrary and unwarranted' limitations on linguistics: it insisted on defining 'lower levels' before 'higher levels'; it was inductive instead of explanatory (abductive); its epistemology was localist instead of Quinean holist. Indeed, despite the explicit nominalism of the structuralists, Chomsky is prepared to take the structuralists as implicitly concerned with the psychological reality of language and hence not really nominalist at all (Chomsky 1975: 30–6).[17] Yet he still thinks his methodological criticisms stand. In any case, Chomsky's methodological criticisms

---

[17] In taking this line, Chomsky follows a common and effective pattern in realist philosophy of science: arguing that scientists who claim to be instrumentalists follow practices that are implicitly realist.

can be and, in my view, should be embraced by the nominalist. In particular, we should not demand that the linguistic properties of tokens be reduced to 'brute-physical' intrinsic properties of the tokens. The linguistic properties that concern us are 'high-level' relational properties.[18]

There are likely to be lingering doubts about my contemplated task. One doubt is about how the domain of study is to be determined: how do we select the tokens to be studied from all the other behavioural outputs of speakers? And the answer is: In the way science usually determines domains. That is, guided by folk linguistics, we start with an intuitive idea of the domain of grammatical tokens to be studied. We do not include many items that seem 'unacceptable' to speakers. As our linguistics goes scientific, we modify our view of the domain, accepting some strings that we had thought ungrammatical because they were, say, too hard to parse or 'meaningless'. We may even reject some strings previously thought to be grammatical. Linguistics, like other sciences, largely determines its own domain.

Another doubt arises out of attitudes to Bloomfieldian linguistics. From the generative perspective, the Bloomfieldian approach often appeared to be somewhat superficial and instrumentalist, concerned merely with describing regularities in the corpus of observed utterances rather than with the language's underlying generalizations. The generative focus on the psychological reality of language is seen as the way to avoid this instrumentalism and be a realist about linguistic theory.[19] So there may be doubts about

---

[18] Katz has another objection to nominalism: grammars are about an infinite number of sentences but there cannot be an infinite number of tokens. If there is a problem for my sort of nominalism, it lies in its apparent commitment to non-actual possible sentences, a problem that would arise even if we were dealing with a finite language (e.g. English with a limit of one million words to a sentence). The only significance of any apparent commitment to an infinite number of sentences is that it would *guarantee* that some were non-actual. But talk of there *being* non-actual possible outputs of a competence can be a mere manner of speaking (nn. 15 and 16). So too can talk of there *being* an infinite number of such outputs. The truth behind the talk of the non-actual can be simply that the grammar is lawlike. And the truth behind the talk of the infinite can be simply that there is no limit to the number of different sentence tokens that might be governed by the rules the grammar describes.

[19] For example, consider the following quotes and the text that surrounds them: 'On other grounds, it is difficult to explain why investigators continually found it necessary to revise and modify their procedures in the light of results that were, in some unexplained

how my contemplated task can be realist about language. But, as I have emphasized, the study of linguistic tokens is not concerned only with actually observed tokens: like any other scientific theory, it is modal, concerned with any possible token. And the approach should indeed be realist, concerned with the underlying generalizations of the language. Linking language to the mind is important, of course—and I do plenty of it—but it does not require that we collapse the contemplated task into task (i). And the link to the mind is not needed for realism. We should be realist in linguistics as everywhere else in science,[20] as Chomsky has frequently insisted. But we can be realist in linguistics without taking the grammar to be true of psychological reality, but rather taking it to be true of linguistic reality: all being well, linguistic symbols really do have the properties ascribed to them by the grammar; some really are c-commanded, some really are coreferential, and so on.

Here is a more disturbing doubt. I have talked of studying the nature of a sentence token, a nature that we reach by abstracting from properties that are irrelevant to our concerns. But what are these concerns? *What is our theoretical interest in the token?* It would not be enough to argue for what Soames (1984) calls the 'conceptual distinctness' of this task from the study of competence. We have to show that the task is worthwhile. I suspect that the presupposition, often the conviction, that there is no such worthwhile task is the main reason for thinking that the linguistic task is Chomsky's (i). The view is that we need to take the task to be about competence for it to be worthwhile.[21]

Here are four reasons for thinking that my contemplated task is worthwhile. First, it must be worthwhile *if Chomsky's task (i) is.*[22] For, although we have distinguished the two tasks, we have also related them in a way that makes completing the contemplated task *necessary* for completing task (i).

sense, "unacceptable" though in no way inconsistent with the corpus of data' (Chomsky 1975: 36); 'we are interested in linguistic analyses primarily insofar as they may be claimed to represent the knowledge speaker-hearers have of the structure of their language' (J. A. Fodor, Bever, and Garrett 1974: 40); 'The shift of focus from language itself to the native speaker's knowledge of language is the major feature of the Chomskian tradition' (Haegeman 1994: 7).

[20] See Devitt (1997). I often do missionary work for realism.

[21] See Laurence (2003), sect. 5, for a vigorous argument to that effect.

[22] I owe this reason to Roblin Meeks.

For, the nature of the speaker's competence studied by task (i) *involves* the nature of the symbols studied by the contemplated task: those symbols are what the competence produces. Indeed, the contemplated task has a certain epistemic and explanatory priority over task (i). How could we make any significant progress studying the nature of competence in a language unless we already knew a good deal about that language? Just as explaining the bee's dances is a prerequisite for discovering how the bee manages to produce those dances, so also explaining the syntax of sentences is a prerequisite for explaining how speakers manage to produce those sentences.

A second reason for thinking that my contemplated task is worthwhile is that analogous ones are. This may not seem so obvious with the horseshoe, chess, and the logic machine, but it is surely obvious with the bee's dance. A serious researcher spent years 'cracking the code' of this dance, working out how it indicates the direction and distance of the food source. And his findings were certainly interesting to scientists.[23] The study of human language must surely be more worthwhile and interesting than the study of the bee's.

A third reason for thinking the task worthwhile would be that substantial and interesting theories are fulfilling the task. In the next section I shall argue that generative grammars are such theories.

The fourth and most important reason starts from the intuition that our concern with sentence tokens, as with bees' dances, is with their *meanings*. This is a widely held view[24] but it is unsatisfactorily vague. I have argued elsewhere that we should be concerned with the properties of sentence tokens that enable them to play certain striking roles in our lives, including the role of informing us about reality; these are the 'meanings' of tokens (1996: 2.3–2.8). Analogously, the properties of bees' dances that concern us are the ones that enable them to play their role of indicating food sources. Sentence tokens have their meanings partly in virtue of their syntactic

---

[23] 'Von Frisch's *Dance Language and Orientation of Bees* was some four decades in the making. By the time his papers on the bee dance were collected and published in 1965, there was scarcely an entomologist in the world who hadn't been both intrigued and frustrated by his findings. Intrigued because the phenomenon Von Frisch described was so startlingly complex; frustrated because no one had a clue as to how bees managed the trick' (Frank 1997: 82).

[24] Randy Harris calls the definition of linguistics as 'the study of the links between sound and meaning' 'one that virtually all linguists would agree to' (1993: 5).

properties and partly in virtue of the meanings of their words. So, accepting the restriction to syntax for the sake of argument, the nature of the sentence token that we need to explain is made up of the syntactic properties in virtue of which the token can play those striking roles.

Our first reason seemed to make our theoretical interest in the contemplated task dependent on our theoretical interest in Chomsky's task (i). On the basis of our fourth reason, I shall soon argue for the opposite dependency (Section 7.4).

Much more needs to be said about the theoretical interest of studying linguistic symbols than I can attempt to say here. I think that this interest does indeed arise out of our interest in the mind, in particular from our interest in thoughts and their role in explaining behaviour (1996: 2.5).[25] But, once again, this does not make our study psychological: in particular, it does not turn it into task (i), the study of competence.

Is my contemplated task appropriately characterized as nominalistic? It takes all the objects that linguistics is about to be concrete tokens, and so to that extent it is nominalistic. Where it stands ultimately on the nominalism issue depends, of course, on what we make of its ascription of meaning *properties* to those objects. However, it seems unlikely that the nominalist would have any *special* difficulty paraphrasing away this property talk. My contemplated task for linguistics is likely to be as nominalistic as tasks in physics, biology, or economics.

# 6 The Contemplated Task and the Linguistic Enterprise

Whether or not this study of the outputs of competence is the study of an E-language in Chomsky's sense, and whatever the case about the psychological reality of languages, I want to argue that there is nothing alien to the linguist's enterprise in the contemplated task.

First, these actual and possible idealized outputs, governed by a system

---

[25] It is this theoretical interest that is likely to make a grammarian of English as concerned with the outputs of Laurence's Martians as with our own outputs. And it will prevent her concern from spreading to the outputs of parrots, tape recorders, and the like (Devitt and Sterelny 1999: 145), a spread that Laurence argues is a likely consequence of not taking the Chomskian view (2003: sect. 5).

of rules and fitting into a structure, *are* what we would normally call a language. Indeed, wherever there is a linguistic competence there *has* to be such a language, for the language is what the competence produces: the language is what the speaker is competent *in*; it is definitive of the nature of the competence.

Second, we note that Chomsky himself often describes his task in ways that suggest it is the one we have been contemplating. For example, consider the following from the early pages of *Syntactic Structures*: 'The fundamental aim in the linguistic analysis of a language L is to separate the *grammatical* sequences which are sentences of L from the *ungrammatical* sequences which are not sentences of L and to study the structure of the grammatical sequences' (1957: 13; see also 1980a: 222).

Third, prima facie, a great deal of the work that linguists do, day by day, in constructing a grammar is studying a language in the nominalistic sense I have described.[26] Work on phrase structure, case theory, anaphora, and so on, talk of 'nouns', 'verb phrases', 'c-command', and so on, all appear to be concerned, quite straightforwardly, with *the properties of expressions* in a language, symbols that are the outputs of a competence. This work and talk seems to be concerned with items like the very words on this page. And, we have already noted, four important features of grammar construction are also part of the contemplated study: the idealization of outputs; concern with all possible outputs; abstraction from irrelevant properties; the making of distinctions among the non-ideal.

Fourth, the linguistic evidence adduced for a grammar bears directly on a theory of the language in my sense; evidence about which strings of words are grammatical; about the ambiguity of certain sentences; about statement forms and question forms; about the synonymy of sentences that are superficially different; about the difference between sentences that are superficially similar; and so on.

Objection: 'But this so-called "linguistic" evidence is largely the intuitions of the native speaker. These arise from her underlying competence. So the evidence bears directly on task (i), not your task.' Now it is indeed true that if the speaker's knowledge of her language consists in her representation of its rules and if her intuitions are derived from those representations by a

---

[26] Or in Katz's Platonic sense, which can be taken as simply a convenient manner of speaking of language in my sense (sect. 5).

causal and rational process, then those intuitions are direct evidence for task (i) because they are direct evidence of what rules are represented. I would argue that this view of the intuitions is mistaken; that the intuitions are theory-laden opinions resulting from ordinary empirical investigation, just like any intuitions.[27] But, whatever the truth of this matter, the main point now is that the intuitions are direct evidence about language in my sense, provided that we have good reason to think that they are accurate. It does not matter to this point whether we think that they are accurate because they are derived from representations of the rules or for some other reason. If they are accurate they are evidence about language because language is what they are about: they are about the grammaticality, ambiguity, etc. of linguistic *symbols or expressions*. So if the intuitions are indeed derived from a representation of linguistic rules, then they will be direct evidence for *both* task (i) and my contemplated task. If, on the other hand, as I think, they are not so derived but are none the less generally accurate, then they will still be direct evidence for my task even if only indirect evidence for task (i).

Fifth, the *psycholinguistic* evidence about language perception and acquisition, offered to support the view that a grammar is psychologically real,

[27] Devitt (1996), 2.10–2.11; Devitt and Sterelny (1999), 8.6. Laurence (2003) goes badly astray in responding to our earlier discussion of linguistic intuitions (1989: 520–3). The central thesis of our paper is that linguistic theory is about the properties of linguistic symbols. Yet Laurence argues that our view of linguistic intuitions, together with what he calls our 'Methodological Principle' for deciding what linguistics is about, should yield the view that linguistics is really about the folk theory of linguistics (above, pp. 89–91). This is presumably intended as some sort of *reductio* of our position. The main problem with his argument is that the view of intuitions he attributes to us is clearly not one we hold. He attributes the view that these intuitions constitute the 'predominant' evidence for a linguistic theory. Yet, in discussing the evidence we never single out the intuitions as predominant. Quite the contrary. We single out *the linguistic symbols we produce and react to* as the main evidence. And we say twice that 'strictly speaking' these symbols, not our intuitions about them, are the evidence (pp. 520, 523). Aside from this puzzling misrepresentation, it is surely obvious that Laurence's argument is a misapplication of our Methodological Principle. The argument's conclusion that linguistic theory is about folk linguistics is, in effect, the instrumentalist view that the theory's task is simply to capture folk intuitions. J. A. Fodor calls this view 'the Wrong View'. We set it aside at the beginning of our paper (p. 498) before even introducing the Methodological Principle. And later, when we discuss realism and instrumentalism as general approaches to science, we endorse realism in no uncertain terms: 'Sydney realism is the most virulent known strain' (p. 511). The Methodological Principle is a principle for choosing among *realistically construed* theories and so could not possibly yield an instrumentalist conclusion.

bears directly on a theory of the language in my sense. Thus, concerning perception, evidence that speakers are sensitive to a proposed syntactic property in parsing an expression is evidence that the expression really has that property, for it is evidence that their competence respects the structure rules that determine that property. The right theory of a language must ascribe rules to the language that competent speakers of the language respect: the Respect Constraint. In this way, the psycholinguistic evidence bears directly on our theory of the linguistic reality.[28] And, concerning acquisition, evidence about nature and nurture showing that a language with a certain structure could not be learnt by a person is direct evidence against any theory that ascribes such a structure to a language that has been learnt by the person.[29]

In the light of responses to a related point that Soames made about evidence (1984), I should guard against possible misunderstandings.

(a) I am making the empirical claim that, as a matter of fact, the linguistic and psycholinguistic evidence bears directly on a theory of language in my nominalistic sense (whatever its bearing on anything else). This sort of claim about the bearing of evidence on a theory is a familiar part of science and ordinary life. The claim is *not* an attempt to impose a priori restrictions on the domain of evidence relevant to Chomsky's task (i) or to my contemplated task (cf. J. A. Fodor 1981: 199–200; Chomsky 1986: 34–6; 1995: 33–4; Antony 2003; Laurence 2003: 101–4). I go along with the Duhem–Quine thesis which allows, roughly, that anything might be

---

[28] Cf. 'A parser which is well-attuned to the competence grammar can be a source of information about the properties of the grammar' (J. D. Fodor 1989: 174). My point is that the parser *has* to be a source of information for the grammar because it has to be sufficiently well attuned to assign the right syntactic structures, performance errors aside. Of course, on the received assumption that the grammar is psychologically real and applied in parsing, evidence about parsing will obviously be seen as bearing on the grammar; see e.g. Chomsky (1980a), 200–1; Berwick and Weinberg (1984), 35. My point is that the evidence bears on the grammar even without the assumption.

[29] Laurence (2003: sect. 5) names one of my earlier arguments (Devitt and Sterelny 1989: 514) 'the Martian Argument' and takes it 'to question whether in *principle* [psycholinguistic] data are even *relevant* to the evaluation of linguistic theories' (above, p. 95). I doubt that I ever questioned this but I obviously do not question it now. One of the two advantages that Laurence claims for the Chomskian view of linguistics over its rivals is that it brings psycholinguistic data to bear on linguistic theory. The Chomskian view does not have this advantage over the view I am urging.

evidence for anything. But it is clearly not a consequence of that thesis that a piece of evidence bears with equal directness on all theories. It is not a consequence, for example, that the experience of green grass bears equally on the theory that grass is green and the theory that echidnas have spikes.

(b) I am not claiming that the linguistic evidence mentioned in my fourth point *is* irrelevant to task (i). Indeed, since the processing rules of linguistic competence must respect the structure rules, any direct evidence about the structure rules must to that extent bear on task (i). For the same reason, the psycholinguistic evidence mentioned in my fifth point must also bear on task (i) to that extent. Of course, we hope that this evidence will bear on task (i) to a much greater extent, throwing light on *the way in which* competence respects the structure rules. However, I would argue that the psycholinguistic evidence now available does not in fact throw much light on this matter and gives no support to the view that competence respects the structure rules by representing them. So it gives no support to the Representational Thesis.[30]

In brief, my evidential point is simply that evidence that has played a big role in linguistic and psycholinguistic theorizing bears directly on the task that I have distinguished from Chomsky's task (i), whether or not that evidence, or any other evidence, bears on task (i). And my general point

---

[30] The second of the two advantages that Laurence (2003) claims for the Chomskian view of linguistics over its rivals is that it confers *explanatory power* on linguistic theory, in particular the power to explain language use and acquisition. (1) On the view I am urging, the power of a linguistic theory is to be found primarily in its explanation of the properties of linguistic tokens. (2) Still, the theory does contribute to the explanation of language use and acquisition because competence must respect the linguistic rules ascribed by the theory. So use and acquisition phenomena that would be predictable if those rules were the ones respected—for example, the phenomena Laurence describes (sect. 2)—are indeed partly explained by a theory that ascribes those rules. (3) Of course, the theory would make a greater contribution to the explanation of use and acquisition were it the case that competence respected the linguistic rules by representing them. I have just doubted that there is psycholinguistic evidence to support this thesis (or even the more modest thesis that competence respects the rules by embodying them without representing them). But the point to be made in response to Laurence is: if the psycholinguistic evidence were ultimately to support the thesis, thus expanding the explanatory power of linguistic theory, this expansion would not count against the view of linguistics I am urging. Rather, the expansion would be welcomed as an explanatory bonus: the theory not only explains language, it plays a larger role in the explanation of language use and acquisition than we had any reason to expect.

is that linguists appear to be studying, partly at least, a language in my nominalistic sense.

Sixth and finally, the appearance that linguists are studying language in this sense is just what we should expect *given Chomsky's assumption (on the natural interpretation) that the competence that is the concern of task (i) is knowledge of the language, involving the representation of its rules; i.e. given 'the Representational Thesis'* (Section 1). For, *the language that would be thus known and represented would be the very same language that is the output of the competence.* Chomsky assumes that competence consists in knowledge about the I-language. The point I am emphasizing is that this very I-language is, indeed *must be*, at the appropriate level of abstraction, the output of that very competence. So, *given Chomsky's assumption*, task (i) requires just the same study as we have been contemplating. So it is no surprise to find Chomsky moving straight from an account of the task like the one quoted to the following version of task (i):

> The problem for the linguist . . . is to determine . . . the underlying system of rules that has been mastered by the speaker-hearer . . . Hence, in a technical sense, linguistic theory is mentalistic, since it is concerned with discovering a mental reality underlying actual behavior. (1965: 4)

*Given the assumption of the Representational Thesis*, task (i) and the contemplated task are much the same.[31] At one and the same time we study the symbolic system that is the output of the competence and the competence itself which is a representation of that very system.

If this is so, the contemplated task is not open to objection from Chomsky. Given his assumption, it is a task that must be performed in performing his task (i). The contemplated task acknowledges the link between competence and language but differs from task (i) in being neutral about the precise psychological nature of that competence.

Not only must Chomsky accept the contemplated task, we should all accept it. A competence is a competence to do something. So whenever there is a competence to investigate there is also a product of that competence to investigate. When the output is a language, it should go without saying

---

[31] A similar assumption yields a similar conflation in some philosophers of language; hence Michael Dummett's slogan 'a theory of meaning is a theory of understanding' (1975: 99).

that its investigation is theoretically interesting. Still, we can say why it is and I have started to do so in the last section.

## 7 Four Methodological Points

If this discussion is right, it has a great deal of methodological significance. I have pointed out (Section 1) that Chomsky is irritated by the issue of the psychological reality of language. For him the only issue here is the truth of the grammar: if the grammar is true then of course it is true of psychological reality because that is what the grammar is about.

### 7.1 *First methodological point*

There is something theoretically interesting for a grammar to be true about other than the internal reality of speakers, just as there is something theoretically interesting for a theory of chess moves, *wff*s, or bees' dances to be true about other than the internal reality of chess players, logic machines, or bees. The grammar might be true about a symbolic system, a *linguistic* reality. The claim that 'the language has no objective existence apart from its mental representation' is false (Chomsky 1972: 169). So we can take the grammar realistically without taking it to be true of *psychological* reality. Furthermore, given the weight of evidence adduced for a grammar, it is plausible that it *is* (more or less) true of linguistic reality.

### 7.2 *Second methodological point*

The view that a grammar has any more to do with psychological reality than the amount allowed by the minimal claim requires a powerful psychological assumption about competence, if not Chomsky's assumption then one of similar strength. Without such an assumption, the grammar simply concerns a language system. This system is the output of something psychological but it remains to be argued that it is itself psychological.

Of course, this does nothing to show that the grammar is *not* true of the psychological reality, that the rules of the language are *not* actually realized in the speaker. The point is that whether the grammar is true of psychological reality is a *further* question to its being true of the linguistic reality. Settling that further question depends on settling the truth of a powerful psychological assumption. *The psychological reality of language is not something 'you get for nothing' with the truth of the grammar.* I fuss about this because I think it is hard to find evidence for a psychological assumption that will do the trick.[32]

## 7.3 Third methodological point

According to the Respect Constraint, a theory of competence in a language must posit processing rules for perception and production that respect the structure rules of the language. And the grammar must posit structure rules that are respected by the competence and its processing rules. So, the Respect Constraint makes the justification of the grammar partly dependent on the justification of the theory of competence, and vice versa. Beyond that, however, *the grammar and the theory of competence are independent of each other.* So there should be no a priori demand that an acceptable grammar must meet some further constraint concerning psychological reality, e.g. what Robert Berwick and Amy Weinberg call 'transparency' (1984: 38). And a grammar should not be dismissed—as, for example, transformational grammars were by Joan Bresnan and Ronald Kaplan (1982)—for failing to meet such further constraints. A grammar that attributes rules that are respected by users of the language may be a perfectly adequate theory of the language however little it can be incorporated into a model of language use. Nor, in setting out to examine psychological reality, should we look to the grammar for any insights beyond those arising from the Respect Constraint. So far as the grammar is concerned, 'the psychological cards can fall where they may', subject only to the Respect Constraint. Similarly, the theory of the bee's dance, including the previously described theory of how the dance indicates the direction of the food source (Section 3), provides no help to the theory of the bee's competence to dance beyond that arising from the fact that the competence must respect the rules of the dance.

This bears on a popular criticism of the claim that a grammar's rules are

---

[32] In Devitt and Sterelny (1989) my case for the thesis that a grammar is about linguistic reality rested heavily on the view that it was very likely not true of psychological reality. This is what Laurence (2003: sect. 4) criticizes as 'the Methodological Argument'. I am still doubtful that the grammar is true of psychological reality but my present case for the thesis does not rest on that doubt.

psychologically real.[33] The criticism is that we lack evidence as to *which* grammar's rules are psychologically real: 'If we can come up with one grammar for a language, we can come up with many which, though they posit different syntactic rules, are equivalent in their explanation of meaning: they are equally able to capture all the syntactically determined facts about meaning. We need psycholinguistic evidence to show which grammar's rules are in fact playing the role in linguistic processing, evidence we do not have.' This criticism is not quite right. We need evidence that the rules of *any* grammar are processing rules. These rules may simply be the *wrong sort of rules* to be processing rules, just as the rules of the bee's dance very likely are, and the rules of the logic machine's language certainly are. Suppose, as seems quite likely, that the human language capacity is an adaptation. Then nature faced the problem of designing this capacity out of pre-existing structures in our ancestors. We should not think, in advance of empirical discovery, that nature solved this problem by making humans go through processes governed by linguistic rules. We should not suppose a priori that a correct account of the linguistic reality will describe the psychological reality. A grammar may have nothing more to do with psychological reality than comes from its meeting the Respect Constraint.

So it was a mistake to assume that psycholinguistic evidence would decide which of many meaning-equivalent grammars was true of psychological reality: perhaps none of them are. But something interesting remains of the criticism: we need psycholinguistic evidence to decide which of many meaning-equivalent grammars are true of *linguistic* reality. For, we need the psycholinguistic evidence to tell us which grammar meets the Respect Constraint, which one posits rules that are respected by the competence and its processing rules. The syntactic properties determined by rules that are respected are the ones that linguistic tokens really have.

## 7.4 *Fourth methodological point*

We have noted (Section 5) that a grammar as a theory of a language has a certain epistemic and explanatory priority over a theory of the psychological reality underlying language. We cannot make any significant progress studying competence in a language until we know a good deal about that

---

[33] Devitt and Sterelny (1989) is an example. The criticism is related to what Laurence (2003: sect. 5) calls 'the Martian Argument'.

language. So it is appropriate that, from the start, much of the work in generative grammar has been directly concerned more with the linguistic than with the psychological reality.[34]

I think that we can go further. Our *theoretical interest* in explaining competence in a language surely starts from our theoretical interest in that language. Think of the bee once more. Were it not for our interest in the nature of the bee's dance, we would never have become interested in the state that manages to produce that dance: it is because that state produces something so theoretically interesting that the state itself is so theoretically interesting. I think that the same goes for the state that produces language. If so our theoretical interest in a language is prior to our interest in its psychological reality.

Earlier (Section 5) I suggested that our theoretical interest in language arises from our interest in thoughts. I said almost nothing to support this suggestion but suppose that it is right. Now put it together with what I have just claimed. We have the following 'direction of theoretical interest': from thoughts to language to linguistic competence. This order of interest does not, of course, undermine the relative independence of the theories of these three realities.

## 8 Interesting Psychological Matters

I trust, then, that it is obvious that I am *not* suggesting that the psychological reality underlying language is unworthy of study. Indeed, the theoretical interest in a language leads immediately to an interest in two matters psychological. (i) It is not enough to know that there is something-we-know-not-what within a speaker that respects the rules of her language, any more than it is enough to know that there is something-we-know-not-what within a bee that respects the rules of the bee's dance. We would like to go beyond these minimal claims to discover the ways in which the competence of the speaker, and the competence of the bee, respect these rules.[35] But,

---

[34] Cf. 'many generativists assert that they aim to account for how children master their native languages, but the vast majority of their analyses do not contribute to that aim' (Hornstein and Lightfoot 1981: 7); 'it is possible, and arguably proper, for a linguist (*qua* linguist) to ignore matters of psychology. But it is hardly possible for a psycholinguist to ignore language' (Gazdar *et al.* 1985: 5).

[35] Hence the frustration of entomologists mentioned in n. 23.

in studying these matters, to emphasize my third methodological point, it is a mistake to insist on finding or even to expect to find, embodied in the organism, processing rules that are also structure rules of its outputs. The processing rules and structure rules have very different jobs to do. We should keep a totally open mind about how the organism manages to respect the structure rules.

(ii) The language a person is competent in has one structure and not another. We should like to know *why* the person speaks such a language, why the something-we-know-not-what that she embodies respects the structure rules of that language and not other structure rules.[36] The bee's competence to dance is surely innate. To what extent is this also true of a person's linguistic competence and to what extent is that competence the result of the person's environment?

Our interest in language will surely also lead us in the end to an interest in a very different psychological matter. (iii) It is impossible to give deep explanations of linguistic reality without appeal to the psychological: very likely, psychological facts together with environmental facts determine linguistic facts. So in the end we shall need to study the psychological in order to explain the linguistic. But in the beginning we do not. Syntactic investigations of *being c-commanded*, *being doubly embedded*, and the like, the sort of investigations that linguists do every day, are not psychological. Even when, in the end, we have to appeal to psychology to explain in virtue of what tokens have these properties, the object of our study remains linguistic. Analogously, a study of the property of the bee's dance that indicates the direction of the food source is not a study of the bee's 'psychology' even if the explanation of in virtue of what the dance has that property appeals to inner states of the bee. A linguistic symbol, like a bee's dance or a horseshoe, really has its properties whatever the explanation of its having them. The symbol objectively exists with its properties 'apart from its mental representation'.[37]

---

[36] Cf. 'we want to know why there are these social regularities and not others, or why we consider these abstract mathematical structures and not others. Surely the facts might be otherwise' (Chomsky 1980c: 57).

[37] At one point Laurence suggests that 'someone with broadly Chomskian sympathies' might accept that 'linguistics *is* about symbols' and yet still maintain that 'it is, in the first instance, about competence'. She can do this because: 'the important properties of these symbols—the properties in virtue of which symbols have their linguistic properties—are

## 9 Conclusion

Linguistics has something worthwhile to study apart from the psychological reality of speakers: it can study a linguistic reality. This reality is in fact being studied by linguists in grammar construction. The study of this linguistic reality has a certain priority over the study of psychological reality.

The truth of a grammar for a language leaves the question of the psychological reality of the language open. To close the question we need to look for other evidence, especially to psycholinguistic evidence about language production, perception, and acquisition. I think that this evidence will leave the Representational Thesis unsupported and implausible. And it will make it hard to choose among a range of other positions on the question of psychological reality.

## REFERENCES

ANTONY, L. (2003), 'Rabbit-Pots and Supernovas: On the Relevance of Psychological Data to Linguistic Theory' (this volume).

—— and HORNSTEIN, N., eds. (2003), *Chomsky and his Critics* (New York: Blackwell).

BAKER, C. L. (1995), *English Syntax*, 2nd edn. (Cambridge, Mass.: MIT Press; 1st edn. 1989).

BERWICK, R. C., and WEINBERG, A. S. (1984), *The Grammatical Basis of Linguistic Performance: Language Use and Acquisition* (Cambridge, Mass.: MIT Press).

properties pertaining to our linguistic competence, and perhaps aspects of how these symbols are processed in language comprehension and production. . . . The important issue is not over whether linguistics is about symbols but over the nature of the facts which determine the linguistic properties of symbols' (above, pp. 87–8). There are two errors here. The first is to think that because symbols have their properties in virtue of certain facts then the theory of symbols is about those facts. If this were generalized, then every theory—economic, psychological, biological, etc.—would be about physical facts because physical facts ultimately determine everything. A special science does not lose its own domain because that domain supervenes on another. The second error is to assume that the determining facts for linguistic properties are facts about linguistic competence rather than other psychological facts and environmental facts. I do not know of any evidence for this assumption and it seems to me almost certainly false (Devitt and Sterelny 1999: chs. 7–8).

BEVER, T. G., CARROLL, J. M., and MILLER, L. A., eds. (1984), *Talking Minds: The Study of Language in Cognitive Science* (Cambridge, Mass.: MIT Press).

BLOCK, N., ed. (1981), *Readings in the Philosophy of Psychology*, vol. ii (Cambridge, Mass.: Harvard University Press).

BRESNAN, JOAN, ed. (1982), *The Mental Representation of Grammatical Relations* (Cambridge, Mass.: MIT Press).

—— and KAPLAN, R. (1982), 'Introduction: Grammars as Mental Representations of Language', in Bresnan (1982), pp. xvii–lii.

CHOMSKY, N. (1957), *Syntactic Structures* (The Hague: Mouton & Co.).

—— (1965), *Aspects of the Theory of Syntax* (Cambridge, Mass.: MIT Press).

—— (1972), *Language and Mind* (New York: Harcourt Brace Jovanovich).

—— (1975), *The Logical Structure of Linguistic Theory* (New York: Plenum Press).

—— (1980a), *Rules and Representations* (New York: Columbia University Press).

—— (1980b), 'Rules and Representations', *Behavioral and Brain Sciences*, 3: 1–14.

—— (1980c), 'Author's Response' to peer commentary on 1980b, *Behavioral and Brain Sciences*, 3: 42–58.

—— (1986), *Knowledge of Language: Its Nature, Origin, and Use* (New York: Praeger Publishers).

—— (1991a), 'Linguistics and Adjacent Fields: A Personal View', in Kasher (1991), 3–25.

—— (1991b), 'Linguistics and Cognitive Science: Problems and Mysteries', in Kasher (1991), 26–53.

—— (1995), 'Language and Nature', *Mind*, 104: 1–61.

COWIE, F. (1998), *What's Within: Nativism Reconsidered* (New York: Oxford University Press).

CUMMINS, R., and HARNISH, R. M. (1980), 'The Language Faculty and the Interpretation of Linguistics', *Behavioral and Brain Sciences*, 3: 18–19.

DEVITT, M. (1981), *Designation* (New York: Columbia University Press).

—— (1996), *Coming to Our Senses* (Cambridge: Cambridge University Press).

—— (1997), *Realism and Truth*, 2nd edn. with new afterword (Princeton: Princeton University Press).

—— and STERELNY, K. (1987), *Language and Reality: An Introduction to the Philosophy of Language* (Cambridge, Mass.: MIT Press).

—— —— (1989), 'What's Wrong with "the Right View"', in Tomberlin (1989), 497–531.

—— —— (1999), *Language and Reality: An Introduction to the Philosophy of Language*, 2nd edn. (Cambridge, Mass.: MIT Press).

DUMMETT, M. (1975), 'What is a Theory of Meaning?', in Guttenplan (1975), 97–138.

FODOR, J. A. (1981), 'Introduction: Some Notes on What Linguistics is Talking About', in Block (1981), 197–207.

—— (1998), *Concepts: Where Cognitive Science Went Wrong* (Oxford: Clarendon Press).

—— BEVER, T. G., and GARRETT, M. F. (1974), *The Psychology of Language: An Introduction to Psycholinguistics and Generative Grammar* (New York: McGraw-Hill).

FODOR, J. D. (1989), 'Empty Categories in Sentence Processing', *Language and Cognitive Processes*, 4: 155–209.

FRANK, A. (1997), 'Quantum Honey Bees', *Discover* (November), 80–7.

GAZDAR, G., KLEIN, E., PULLUM, G., and SAG, I. (1985), *Generalized Phrase Structure Grammar* (Oxford: Basil Blackwell).

GEORGE, A., ed. (1989a), *Reflections on Chomsky* (Oxford: Basil Blackwell).

—— (1989b), 'How Not to Become Confused about Linguistics', in George (1989a), 90–110.

GUTTENPLAN, S. (1975), *Mind and Language* (Oxford: Oxford University Press).

HAEGEMAN, L. (1994), *Introduction to Government and Binding Theory*, 2nd edn. (Oxford: Blackwell; 1st edn. 1991).

HARRIS, R. A. (1993), *The Linguistics Wars* (New York: Oxford University Press).

HORNSTEIN, N., and LIGHTFOOT, D. (1981), 'Preface', in eid. (eds.), *Explanation in Linguistics: The Logical Problem of Language Acquisition* (London: Longman), 7–8.

KASHER, A., ed. (1991), *The Chomskyan Turn* (Oxford: Blackwell).

KATZ, J. J. (1981), *Language and Other Abstract Objects* (Totowa, NJ: Rowman and Littlefield).

—— (1984), 'An Outline of a Platonist Grammar', in Bever, Carroll, and Miller (1984), 17–48.

—— (1996), 'The Unfinished Chomskyan Revolution', *Mind and Language*, 11: 270–94.

LARSON, R., and SEGAL, G. (1995), *Knowledge of Meaning: An Introduction to Semantic Theory* (Cambridge, Mass.: MIT Press).

LAURENCE, S. (2003), 'Is Linguistics a Branch of Psychology?' (this volume).

MATTHEWS, R. J. (1991), 'The Psychological Reality of Grammars', in Kasher (1991), 182–99.

REY, G. (2003), 'Chomsky, Intentionality and a CRTT', in Antony and Hornstein (2003), 105–39.

SOAMES, S. (1984), 'Linguistics and Psychology', *Linguistics and Philosophy*, 7: 155–79.

STABLER, E. P. (1983), 'How are Grammars Represented?', *Behavioral and Brain Sciences*, 6: 391–402.

TOMBERLIN, J. E., ed. (1989), *Philosophy of Mind and Action Theory* (Philosophical Perspectives, 3; Atascadero: Ridgeview).

# CHAPTER 5

# *Intentional Content and a Chomskian Linguistics*

*Georges Rey*

Chomsky often presents his account of grammatical competence in what would appear to be the terms of a 'computational representational theory of thought' (CRTT), but it is not clear that what he intends involves either *computations* or *representations* in the sense in which most other theorists use those terms. Specifically, he has recently insisted that ' "representation" is not to be understood relationally, as "representation of" ', and that, indeed, the latter sort of intentional idiom has no place in any serious science.

In an earlier paper I set out what I take to be the tensions produced by these views. Chomsky has since replied, and in this paper I reply to his reply (knowledge of my earlier paper will not be presupposed). After summarizing CRTT and sorting out a few distinctions regarding 'represent' (Sections 1 and 2), I proceed in Section 3 to set out passages in which Chomsky appears to endorse intentionalisms (Section 3.1), and then other passages in which

This paper pursues some issues that I originally set out in Rey (2003), written in 1998, to which Professor Chomsky replied in the same volume. To avoid asking the reader to consult my previous article, I have included its main points here (consequently with a slight overlap in passages), along with further developments occasioned by numerous talks with linguists and philosophers since then, particularly Louise Antony, Dan Blair, Sylvain Bromberger, Michael Devitt, Janet Fodor, Jerry Fodor, Wolfram Hinzen, Andreas Kemmerling, Betsy Klipple, Jim McGilvray, Ignatius Mattingly, Paul Pietroski, Neil Smith, Juan Uriagereka, and Deirdre Wilson, to all of whom I am very grateful for their help and patience. I have also benefited from an extended e-mail exchange with Professor Chomsky on the topics, as well as from audience reaction at the Sheffield Epistemology of Language conference in July 2000, Queen's and McGill Universities (Canada) in October 2001, Regensburg University (Germany), the École Normale Supérieure (Paris) in November 2001, and at the annual Canadian Philosophical Association meeting, Toronto, in May 2002.

he seems to reject them (Section 3.2). In Section 4 I consider Chomsky's (2003) reply: his appeal to different senses of 'represent' (Section 4.1), and his dismissal of his intentionalisms as merely 'informal motivation' (Section 4.2) that has no place in the technical linguistic theory itself (Section 4.3). The different senses are irrelevant to the patent reliance on intentionalisms in a number of technical works.

In Section 5 I consider what is driving Chomsky to his anti-intentionalism: an erroneous conviction that all intentionalism is committed to an exaggerated form of content externalism (Section 5.1); a mistaken understanding of the 'mind-dependence' of linguistic phenomena (Section 5.2); persistent use/mention confusions in the explication of his theory (Section 5.3); and a related confusion, the 'intention/ representation' confusion, generated by a misunderstanding of the claim that certain phenomena are 'in the mind' or head (Section 5.4).

Although a non-intentionalist reading of these latter phrases is conceivable, in Section 6 I present two important reasons for resisting it at least in linguistics: (1) phonetic explanation requires phonetic features to be phenomena produced in the oral cavity, and (2) the 'computations' (or 'derivations') of the various linguistic categories and features that are the heart of the theory need to be defined over local, physical properties, and the usual linguistic features cannot in general be expected to be properties of this sort. Consequently, in order for these categories and features to figure in the computations, they must be *represented* by formal objects of one sort or another, and it is at that point that intentionality must play a role in the theory. Indeed, I shall conclude that the most natural way to understand Chomskian linguistics is in fact as being about the *intentional contents* of those computations' representations—a consequence that is actually quite close to the ways in which linguists, and even Chomsky himself, seem spontaneously to understand the enterprise, when they are not reflecting philosophically upon it.

## 1 The Problem

Mental representation is all the rage these days—as it has been most days, except during the dark days of behaviourism. But for all its perennial and new-found popularity, it remains an oddly baffling notion. What makes some state of a person's mind or brain a representation?[1] What makes it a representation of one thing rather than another, of, say (just to give some indication of the range of cases that need to be considered): Julius Caesar, the number three, quarks, the edge of a surface, a colour, a noun, an NP, a round square, or the Greek god Zeus? To use the (unfortunate) terminology from medieval philosophy: what provides a representation with its 'intentionality', or 'aboutness', and its specific 'content', or the 'thing' it is about? The Austrian philosopher Franz Brentano (1874) awakened modern interest in the topic, calling attention to its many logical oddities: as the above examples show, one can bear the representation 'relation' to 'things', like Zeus, that do not exist (see Section 2.2 below). He concluded that intentionality was the distinctive property of the mental that rendered it 'irreducible' to the physical, a conclusion that many resist, but someone has yet to refute.

It is important to distinguish the question as it might be raised about something we *deliberately produce*—say, a painting, an utterance, or an inscription in a book—from the question as it raised about our thoughts and intentions in the first place. In the first kind of case we have a clue about what to begin to say: it presumably has something to do with the mental states that were responsible for the production, and perhaps the mental states of others who may have been responsible for conventions involved in that production. These are cases of what has come to be called 'derived intentionality'. They are presumably derived from cases of 'original intentionality', or the intentionality of those very mental states of the producer, or of her conventional cohorts. The question that bothers many philosophers is where this original intentionality comes from, and, more particularly, where precisely it is needed in any serious scientific theories of the world.

One might have thought that linguistics would have a great deal to say about this issue. However, it appears that linguists seem everywhere

---

[1] Some terminological conveniences: I shall use 'representation' as the most generic term for anything (pictures, diagrams, words, mental states) that has intentional properties (i.e. is 'about' something, 'real' or 'unreal'). I shall also use 'thought' generically for any intentional mental state, e.g. any 'propositional attitude' like believe, know, or 'cognize' (whether or not it involves a full 'proposition'); and I shall use 'intentionalist' for anything that is committed to a serious appeal to intentionality (since the word 'intentional' has quite enough uses already).

to presuppose the notion without any effort to explain it. To be sure, many linguists have a lot to say about 'the meaning of natural-language expressions', but this is invariably along the lines of some form of derived intentionality: they tend to assume that *minds* have representations—e.g. of time, place, objects, events, things, people, as well as of nouns, verbs, traces, tree structures, and sentences—and on the basis of *these representations* try to account for the specific intentional properties of natural language, e.g. why 'killing' is about an action, why plurals need second-order logic, or why in 'John hopes Bill likes himself', 'himself' cannot refer to John.

As a matter of sociological fact, it has largely been philosophers who have addressed the question of original intentionality. Not that they have met with a great deal of success. There are some interesting suggestions,[2] but I think few would pretend that they are anywhere near adequate. If it is in fact a real property in the world, it is one where our grasp of it far exceeds our understanding: children cotton on to it (e.g. in distinguishing a bear from a picture of a bear) with astonishing ease, and people deploy it with bewildering insouciance, 'anthropomorphizing' animals, their 'subconscious minds', and (in the case of religion) sometimes the universe as a whole, with only the vaguest ideas of what would legitimize such ideas. One step towards getting a better understanding of intentionality would be to get a clearer idea about how it plays a role in some good account of something that itself needs explaining. And that is the question on which I want to focus here. A particular instance of that question is: *what precisely is the role that representation, or original intentionality, plays in current linguistic theory, specifically in Chomskian theories of syntax, or (as he prefers to think of the matter) of the human language acquisition device (the 'LAD')?*

I pick Chomskian linguistics for three reasons: (1) it strikes me and many others as affording a surprisingly deep and empirically informed theory of a significant feature of the human mind; (2) it is one in which quite strong and sometimes quite startling claims have been made about (apparently) the representational capacities of even very young children, creatures about whom it can seem quite surprising to suppose that they represent some of the highly abstract categories—and maybe even the

---

[2] In Rey (2003), sect. IV, I sketched some relevant ones, e.g. proposals of Dretske (1988), Peacocke (1992), and J. A. Fodor (1990; 1998), and I discuss them at greater length in Rey (1997), ch. 9.

rules—of a Chomskian grammar; and (3) Chomsky himself has written copiously about the significance of his theory of acquisition for a general theory about the mind. Indeed, I think it is safe to say that he has produced—or resuscitated from the Rationalist tradition—some of the most interesting proposals about the structure of the mind that are presently available, and he has done so with extraordinary energy and insight, often in reply to fierce opposition.

The only trouble is that it turns out to be extremely difficult to say precisely what those proposals are. As I noted at the start, Chomsky often presents his account of grammatical competence in what would appear to be the terms of a CRTT, and one would have thought that he had in mind here the widespread view that thinking processes consist in computational processes that take place in a person's brain with respect to representations that are betokened there, on the now familiar model of processes in actual computers (see e.g. J. A. Fodor 1975). Many recent passages in his work, however, seem to suggest otherwise. Indeed, it is not clear that Chomsky's understanding of a 'computational representational' theory really involves either *computations* or *representations* in the sense in which most other theorists use those terms. In many places both he and many other linguists claim that the notion of 'computation' is only the abstract notion that one finds in, for example, proof theory in mathematics, where one can indeed speak of 'the computation of a certain function' without any commitment to this computation being actually executed in space and time (see Section 6 below). And, more importantly for the issues I want to discuss, there are other passages where he insists that '"representation" is not to be understood relationally, as "representation of"' (2000: 159).

## 2 Causal/Computational Representational Theories of Thought (CRTTs)

CRTTs can be regarded as proposals to treat thought processes as causal/computational processes defined over representations that are encoded in our nervous systems on the model of processes in a computer.[3] Various propositional attitudes, whether they be *know*, *believe*, *think*, or *cognize*,

---

[3] See J. A. Fodor (1975) for the classic statement of the idea. I include 'causal' in the

are to be distinguished by the different causal relations they bear to those representations as they are processed in the brain's cognitive architecture. In this way CRTT promises to provide the 'mechanism' many have sought to link mental and physical phenomena, providing a mentalistic explanation of rational—as well as of much non-rational—behaviour.

As things stand, CRTT is not so much a theory as a research programme, a little like Boyle's postulation of 'atoms' as constituents of chemical phenomena, before there was any clear idea of what the precise character of those atoms might be. It leads us to ask interesting and often empirically testable questions about, for example, the precise character of the medium of representation—its expressive power, the kind of information it needs to represent, whether it consists of sentence-like structures or of 'mental images' and 'models'—as well as about the character of the computations defined over or between those representations—whether they are serial, parallel, sometimes 'connectionist' or 'dynamic', to what extent they are modularized or 'encapsulated' from one another. Discovering the subtle principles and algorithms by which we understand the world and adjust our behaviour to it is, of course, not something to be expected in our grand-children's lifetimes, if ever.[4] But CRTT does seem to be the only serious framework in which these questions can be posed.[5]

Most work within the CRTT programme focuses on the computational aspects of the processes. There has been some, but by no means equal, progress in understanding the notion of representation. Even though many computations can be *specified* and studied without appeal to content, content

characterization of CRTT since (1) this is an important, if often a regrettably implicit, feature of any application of Turing's original idea to actual physical systems, and (2) it is important to allow that some processes might involve causal relations among representations that might not be appropriately regarded as computational (e.g. brute associations). I discuss these and other issues surrounding CRTT in Rey (1997) and (2002).

[4] See J. A. Fodor (1983) and (2001) for expressions of pessimism in this regard, as well as Chomsky (1975c: 156–7; 1980a: 250–2). Nothing in the present discussion turns on whether that pessimism is correct.

[5] For excellent surveys of recent CRTT-driven research in a variety of domains, see the four volumes of Osherson (1995–8), especially the many articles on language acquisition and processing in vol. i; by Nakayama, He, and Shimojo, and by Biederman on vision research in vol. ii; by Shafir and Tversky on decision-making in vol. iii; by Gallistel on animal navigation, and by Sternberg and by Dosher on object and face recognition in vol. iv.

is arguably *presupposed* by computational theories of mental processes: in vision, representations of, for example, edges and surfaces; in decision-making, of options, losses, and gains; in parsing, of nouns and verbs. Or so it would appear—as we shall see, Chomsky sometimes claims otherwise.

It will be important in assessing Chomsky's remarks to appreciate just how modest the claims of a CRTT need be. In particular, a CRTT itself makes no claims about the character of a *linguo*semantics (Section 2.1), nor even about whether intentional content involves relations to phenomena in the external world (Section 2.2).[6] It is one thing for CRTT to require *some* theory of representational content; quite another actually to provide one.

## 2.1 *Psycho- vs. linguo-semantics*

Questions about representation arise in very different ways with regard to the meaning or content of *mental* representations—a 'psychosemantics'— vs. the meaning or content (or 'semantics') of natural language—a 'linguosemantics' (cf. Chomsky 2000: 165). Natural-language expressions may, for example, be subject to a variety of constraints different from those of mental representations generally (cf. Chomsky 1993: 34–5). A particular way in which the two may differ is that with regard to natural language it is plausible to claim that it is not *words* but *people* that refer (Chomsky 2000: 36–52). This is less plausible in the case of CRTT, since it is not at all obvious that its expressions are 'used' by people in the way that they use natural-language expressions: people do not obviously 'use' components of their mental states intending to refer to cats in the way that they might use the English word 'cats' to do so. Arguably, a person has a thought about a cat merely because she stands in a certain computational relation to a term in her internal code that means *cat*. More to the point, a newborn child may represent, say, nouns or [+aspiration] in her psychosemantics without there being a natural-language equivalent to that word remotely available to her.

## 2.2 *A crucial ambiguity about intentional idioms*

Intentional expressions ('belief', 'thought', 'representation') are 'about' or 'of' things. But they can standardly be about, or of, two different kinds of

[6] By 'external world', I shall throughout mean (the less euphonious) 'extra-cranial world'.

'things', depending on the existential assumptions of the user. For example, in a number of places Chomsky describes recent work in vision theory in which 'tachistoscopic presentations . . . caused the subject to see a rotating cube, though there was no such thing in the environment' (1995: 52); '[internal] representations are postulated entities, to be understood in the manner of the mental image of a rotating cube, whether it be the result of . . . a real rotating cube . . . or imagined' (2000: 159–60). Such usage of 'see' and 'represent(ation)' can be contrasted with usages where this would certainly be puzzling ('This is a representation of Mozart's nephew, although there is no such person'). Without trying to give a theory about this difference in use, I shall call the use of ⌜represent(ation of) $x$⌝ and related uses of nouns and verbs, where we can easily *deny* the existence of $x$, '*purely* intentional uses'; the others, 'existential uses'.[7] Of course, sometimes we may want to leave it open whether or not the $x$ exists ('Let "John Doe" represent the guy we're looking for'), although if we learnt that the $x$ actually does exist, it might then be a (delicate) open question whether we would still be using 'represent' purely intentionally, or would then switch to the existential (real existence has, as it were, a way of grabbing our intentions). For present purposes, I shall assume that 'represent' can be used even when the object turns out to exist, even though the definition of (intentional) content will be in terms of cases when it does not, as follows:

> An (intentional) content is *however we are to understand* x *when we use the idiom* ⌜*represent(ation of)* x⌝ *purely intentionally.*

That is:

> An (intentional) content is *however we are to understand* x *when we use the idiom* ⌜*represent(ation of)* x, *but there is no* x⌝.

---

[7] '$x$' here is a metalinguistic variable, sanctioned by the corner-quotes. I would have phrased the issue in a more natural way (e.g. '. . . where we deny the existence of the thing represented'), except for (1) the maddening ambiguity of *that* way of speaking, and (2) Chomsky's persistent complaint (see e.g. 2000: 41) that philosophers crucially presuppose some 'mystical' relation of 'reference' that they nowhere explain. Indeed, to avoid contaminating the present discussion with any such presuppositions that Chomsky might find unacceptable, I draw the distinction in a way that is *based on his very own words* (a fact that he unfortunately disregards in his 2003 reply to Rey 2003: see sects. 4.1 and 5.1 below).

For example, a content is however we are to understand 'a rotating cube' when we read 'representations of a rotating cube, though there is no rotating cube'. If it is important (as it sometimes, but not always, will be) to distinguish an intentional content from the actual object whose existence in a purely intentional use is being denied, I shall place the words for that content in curly brackets. Thus, *a rotating cube* is one thing, *the content,* {*rotating cube*} quite another (for one thing, the latter can exist when the former does not).

A reason for being careful in distinguishing the purely intentional from the existential uses of intentional terms is the almost universal appeal of (what has come to be called) the 'McX' response to the ancient 'riddle of non-being' ('How can you deny that Pegasus exists, since your denial talks about him, and so he had better exist to be talked about?'—see Quine 1953: 1–2). As any teacher of that riddle will attest, a standard response is 'McX's' (in Quine's fable): 'Pegasus is an idea in one's mind.' It is to avoid suggestions such as that there really are winged horses in one's head that I think one needs to resort to the purely intentional usage that will concern me here.[8]

This provisional definition relies on the purposefully vague 'however we are to understand $x$' in order to be as neutral as possible about any *serious theory about what contents might be*, i.e. about precisely *how* we are to understand purely intentional uses. *All I want to achieve by this definition is to call attention to the fact that a theorist who relies on idioms like 'representation of* x *although there is no* x' is ipso facto *committed to some theory of representational contents*—roughly speaking, the 'values' of '$x$' in such expressions. These contents *might* involve idiosyncratic entities of some sort, e.g. 'ideas', 'concepts', 'intensions', or perhaps other 'Platonic entities' (as in Katz 1981); or they could be constructions from (perhaps) more familiar materials: functions from possible worlds to extensions (Lewis 1972);

---

[8] There is a further verbal complication that needs to be noted so as to be set aside: it would be tempting to say 'so a purely intentional use of "representation of $x$", for lack of any $x$, is really about an intentional content'. This could, however, invite a confusion about, as it were, a person's focus of attention: someone thinking about Zeus and his philandering ways certainly would not take herself to be thinking about the philandering ways of an intentional content. Speaking more carefully, we should instead say something like: when $x$ is a purely intentional content, *a person is standing in the thinking relation to* {$x$}; but this does not entail she is *thinking about* {$x$}. Even in a purely intentional usage, 'thinking about $x$' is one thing; 'thinking about {$x$}' quite another.

properties with which states of mind/brain lawfully covary (Dretske 1988: J. A. Fodor 1990); the causal chain linking someone to a phenomenon (Devitt 1996); the 'causal/computational' role a representation plays in some system (Block 1986; Peacocke 1992); or *files* associated with an expression (Kamp 1981; Heim 1982; Récanati 1993).

But, putting aside these bold conjectures, intentional contents in the weak way that I am understanding them might even be regarded as mere labels, a *façon de parler*, a way of *classifying* representations, along lines suggested by Goodman (1949): a representation of Zeus is simply a representation that is grouped for some reason or other with other representations that we also say to be 'of Zeus', or 'Zeus representations' (e.g. sculptures, pictures, descriptions, tall tales). The crucial question then, of course, would be how to understand the principles of such classification—what makes something an ⌜*x*-represent(ation of)⌝ even though there is no *x*⌝. If one were not a nominalist averse to properties, one might even go on to say that intentional contents are the properties of representations by virtue of which they are to be grouped in these ways. Particularly when combined with the idea of files, I myself rather like this latter way of thinking about the matter, but I am under no illusion that we understand enough about intentionality to opt for it, or to suppose that such purely ontological claims address the really hard question, the only question I mean to raise here: *what are the principles for sorting representations in ways that capture this purely intentional (or even existential) usage of them?*

## 2.3 Representation of 'properties' or 'features'

The above ambiguity between intentional and existential uses of 'represent' is especially hard to sort out when the complement is a 'feature' or 'property'—and this for the unsurprising reason that the ontological commitments of people who talk about features and properties are often wholly obscure. For example, many assume that a property may exist but be *uninstantiated*. Some (but fewer) assume that a property may exist and even be uninstantiable (e.g. the property *round and square*). And this may be because they assume that there is a property for every predicate and/or concept people employ. In keeping with the above neutrality about the nature of content, I shall avoid also making any such metaphysical assumption (why

should the real properties in the world happen to conform to our thought?).
Thus, in accordance with the above purely intentional usage, it will also
be possible to say 'This is a representation of the feature [+aspirated], even
though no such feature exists outside the head.'

## 3 Chomsky's Ambivalence about Intentionality[9]

### 3.1 *Pro-intentionalism*

Chomsky has very often couched his theory expressly in intentionalist
terms, indeed, in terms of a CRTT (see e.g. 1969: 155–6; 1977: 3–6; 1980a:
54; 1986: 239; 1993: 40, 52; 1994: 153–4; 1995b: 225–35). Perhaps the earliest
such passage is in *Aspects of the Theory of Syntax* (1965), in which he wrote
(throughout the quotations I cite, I italicize what seem to me to be crucially
intentionalist words and phrases):

(ATS) A child who is capable of language learning must have:

  (i) a technique for *representing* input signals;
 (ii) a way of *representing* the structural information *about* these signals;
(iii) some initial delimitation of a class of possible *hypotheses about* language
      structure;
(iv) a method for determining what each such hypothesis *implies* with respect
      to each sentence;
 (v) a method for selecting one of the (presumably, infinitely many) *hypotheses*
      that are allowed by (iii) and are *compatible with* the given primary linguistic
      data. (Chomsky 1965: 30)

What is striking about this passage is just how extremely intentionalist
it is. The child is presumed to be deriving, for example, 'what each such
hypothesis implies' much as a scientist might derive predictions about ob-
servables from her own theoretical proposals. 'Implies' and 'compatible
with' standardly apply to items with *truth-valuable* content.

It is worth noting that this is no passing remark. Thus, in the introduction
(1975a) to the 1975 publication of *The Logical Structure of Linguistic Theory*

---

[9] I summarize here the bulk of the discussion of Rey (2003), citing some passages that
are included there, but also many further ones. It is worth calling attention to the sheer
multitude of passages in which Chomsky sets out his views in intentionalist terms, since
they all need to be considered in the light of his dismissal of them (to be discussed in
sect. 4.2 below) as 'informal motivation'.

(1975*a*, 1st edn. 1953; hereafter *LSLT*) he is even more explicit about the child as theorist:

> The construction of a grammar . . . by a linguist is in some respects analogous to the acquisition of language by a child . . . The child constructs *a mental representation of the grammar of the language* ... The child must also select among the grammars compatible with the data. (*LSLT* 11)

Indeed:

> The language learner (analogously the linguist) approaches the problem of language acquisition (grammar *construction*) with a *schematism* that *determines* in advance the general properties of human language and the general properties of the grammars that might be constructed to *account for* linguistic phenomena . . . Hypotheses [in linguistics] aim to characterize *the schematism that the mind imposes in examining the data of sense and acquiring knowledge on the basis of evidence produced by such an examination and analysis.* . . . In my personal view, the general intellectual interest of the work in generative grammar lies primarily in its contribution to the understanding of these issues. (*LSLT* 12–13)

In Chomsky (1980*a*) he makes his commitments here even more vivid by claiming that we 'cognize the grammar that constitutes the current state of our language faculty and the rules of this system as well as the principles that govern their operation', where 'cognizing has the structure and character of knowledge but may be and in interesting cases is inaccessible to consciousness' (1980*a*: 69–70; see also 1986: 265). What is particularly striking is the analogy he then proceeds to draw between our cognizing the principles of grammar and a missile that

> incorporates an explicit theory of the motions of the heavenly bodies and information about its position and velocity and that *carries out measurements and computations using its internalized theory to adjust its course as it proceeds.* . . . In [this] case . . . inquiry might lead us to attribute to the missile something like a 'mental state' . . . postulating a system which involves the cognizing of certain principles and computation involving those principles and certain representations. (Chomsky 1980*a*: 102)

One way to appreciate just how intentionalist such a missile would have to be is to imagine that the 'internalized theory' and information about its position are actually *false*, leading the machine systematically (i.e. predictably) astray. In such a case, we would be forced to ascribe to it a *(mis-)representation* of that world and those data. Indeed, we would even have to ascribe to it *intentional content* in exactly the sense I defined above (Section 2.2), for it might well, for example, 'represent a planet that does not exist'.

## 3.2 Anti-intentionalism

In surprising contrast to these passages,[10] Chomsky has in the last ten years had pretty harsh things to say about CRTT and intentionality:

Computer models are often invoked to show that we have robust, hard-headed instances of the kind: psychology then studies software problems. That is a dubious move. Artifacts pose all kinds of questions that do not arise in the case of natural objects. Whether some object is a key or a table or a computer depends upon designer's intent, standard use, mode of interpretation, and so on. The same considerations arise when we ask whether the device is malfunctioning, following a rule, etc. There is no natural kind of normal case . . . Such questions do not arise in the study of organic molecules, the wings of chickens, the language faculty, or other natural objects. (Chomsky 2000: 105; see also 1994: 154)

Indeed:

We can be reasonably confident that 'mentalistic talk' will find no place in attempts to describe and explain the world. . . . The notion 'common store of thoughts' has no empirical status, and is unlikely to gain one even if the science of the future discovers a reason, unknown today, to postulate entities that resemble 'what we think (believe, hope, expect, want, etc.)'. (Chomsky 1996: 45–7; see also 1993*b*: 18; 1994: 165–6)

More generally, intentional phenomena relate to people and what they do as viewed from the standpoint of human interests and unreflective thought, and thus will not (so viewed) fall within naturalistic theory, which seeks to set such factors aside. Like falling bodies, or the heavens, or liquids, a 'particular intentional phenomenon' may be associated with some amorphous region in a highly intricate and shifting space of human interests and concerns. But these are not appropriate concepts for naturalistic inquiry. . . . If 'cognitive science' is taken to be concerned with intentional attribution, it may turn out to be an interesting pursuit (as literature is), but is not likely to provide explanatory theory or to be integrated into the natural sciences. (Chomsky 2000: 22–3)

[10] In Rey (2003) I call attention to many more: e.g. (1969: 155–6; 1977: 3–6; 1980*a*: 54; 1986: 239; 1993*b*: 40, 52; 1994: 153–4; 1995*b*: 225–35).

One has, of course, heard much of this before. Skinner, Quine, Rorty, and the Churchlands have spent much of their careers inveighing about the 'emptiness of a science of intention' (Quine 1960: 221). But it has not gone unnoticed that they really offer no serious substantive theory in its place: Skinner's and Quine's radical behaviourism was at best a promissory note that serious psychology no longer honours; and the replacement of an intentionalist psychology by neurophysiology envisaged by Rorty and the Churchlands is no more plausible than the replacement of computer science by electrical engineering, or economics by quantum mechanics. If Chomsky has some further proposal along these lines, it would be well worth his spelling it out clearly—and in a way that is free of the apparently intentionalist expressions he persistently employs.

## 4 Chomsky's Reply

### 4.1 *Different senses of 'represent'?*

How are we to reconcile these anti-intentionalist remarks with the former apparently intentionalist ones? In his reply to Rey (2003), in which I first presented this conflict, Chomsky tries to distinguish a number of uses of 'represent', some of which are not intentional. Thus, he claims that the faculty of language is an example of a variety of 'internal . . . computational systems' that

> are often called '(internal) representations,' in approximately the sense in which *the computational system* involved in insect navigation or bird song is said to be 'internally represented,' all at the psychological level; this seems to be the sense Rey has in mind when he speaks of 'specific representations' that have 'contents.' The search for unification [of psychology with neuroscience] is guided by the expectation that corresponding in some manner to such psychological entities there are *physiological configurations, also said to be internally represented*. (Chomsky 2003: 276)

I myself am unacquainted with these senses of 'represent'. I would have thought the right words here would have been, respectively, 'implement' and 'instantiate', but certainly neither of these is what I had in mind, which is rather the sense that he immediately goes on to consider:

To take an example virtually at random, recent studies show that if the optic nerve of an animal is 'rewired' to connect to the auditory pathway early in life, 'the auditory cortex gradually takes on a representation that is normally found in the visual cortex' (Weng 2001); the 'representation' is some internal structure R, which is used when the 'rewired' animal performs 'vision tasks with the auditory cortex.' In such performance, R enters into *complicated relations with things in the outside world*, but it does not 'represent' them in anything like the sense in which a photograph of a landscape is said to represent the landscape (not that that notion is trivial).

Uncontroversially, the internal representations PHON(E) are like R in this respect. Features of PHON(E) can be plausibly construed as *instructions for articulatory gestures* (Halle 1983), but the external manifestation of these varies widely depending on intricate circumstances. I think the same general picture is appropriate for problems of meaning and use, apparently a significant distinction between animal communication and human language. (Chomsky 2003: 276)

It is hard to see how Weng's specific usage here is an 'example' of either the representation of *a computational system*, or of any *physiological configuration*. Indeed, Chomsky himself does not actually read it as though it were, since he immediately proceeds to cite Weng's further description of the animal performing 'vision tasks with the auditory cortex'. So 'representation' *at this point* is an issue about *tasks*, not about implementation or instantiation. In fact, unlike computational systems or physical configurations, which Chomsky explicitly regards as 'internal', 'tasks' are apparently to be identified by 'complicated relations with things in the outside world', in the way that phonetic representations 'can be plausibly construed as instructions for articulatory gestures'. But, if such 'task'-related 'instructions' are what is involved in identifying something as a 'representation', then, I submit, we *are* employing 'represent' in precisely the sense that has been the concern of my discussions: the sense of 'represent' in which, for example, an 'instruction' to flap one's tongue must represent, *inter alia*, one's tongue.

It is revealing that Chomsky is anxious that this sense not be mistaken for 'the sense in which a photograph of a landscape . . . represent[s] the landscape'. He is perfectly right that photographs do not ordinarily represent in the way instructions do, since photographs ordinarily represent specific spatio-temporal phenomena (e.g. scenes, objects, events) that *caused* them in a very specific way (a way that is, indeed, not trivially specifiable), whereas instructions involve no such commitment: for lack of Zeus, you cannot have a photograph of him; but someone lacking a tongue could still issue an instruction to flap one. We might contrast these two senses as follows:

*Aetiological representation*
x aetiologically represents y iff there actually exists a y that entered into the production of a token of x in the appropriate way (the details of which are left to another time).

*Purely intentional representation*
x purely intentionally represents y iff it makes sense to say 'x represents y, even though there may be no y.'

That is to say, instructions (unlike photographs) involve precisely the kind of representation that can have *purely intentional content* precisely along the lines in which I (provisionally) defined this latter notion in Section 2.2 above (and in 2003: 128 n. 3).[11] Chomsky cannot seriously complain that these notions are some 'unexplained' (2003: 286) *addition* to his discussion, since, as I have gone out of my way to ensure, these (provisional) characterizations are based upon *his very own explicit understanding of his own uses of 'represent' and other intentionalisms*, not only in the passage we have just discussed, but in earlier passages in which he quite explicitly explains how he understands the term:

. . . studies of determination of structure from motion used tachistoscopic presentations that caused the subject to see a rotating cube, though there was no such thing in the environment; 'see,' here, is used in its normal sense, not as an achievement verb. . . . We need not ponder what is represented, seeking some objective construction from sounds to things. The representations are postulated entities, to be understood in the manner of a mental image of a rotating cube, whether it be the result of tachistoscopic presentations of a real rotating cube or stimulation of the retina in some other way; or imagined, for that matter. (Chomsky 2000: 159–60)[12]

[11] Along the lines I mentioned in sect. 2.2, I shall understand 'x purely intentionally represents y' to be usable also in cases where 'y exists' turns out in fact to be true—it is just not defined in terms of such cases.

[12] Shortly before this passage, Chomsky also writes: 'In ordinary usage, person X refers to Y by expression E under circumstances C, so the relation [of reference] is at least tetradic; and Y need not be a real object in the world or regarded that way by X' (2000: 150). But this, for him, is 'ordinary usage', not the use of 'represent' that he claims is

Note that *none of the other senses of 'represent' that we have set out from his discussion can be read in this way*: it would not make much sense to say that something implemented or instantiated a programme or configuration that did not exist. Since purely intentional representation is both my concern and—despite his denials—is patently the concern of Chomsky in the above passage and elsewhere, I shall dispense with the qualification and understand 'represent' in just this way (which is how I think the word is standardly used anyway).[13]

Purely intentional representation does, however, have a role to play in computational discussions. When Jerry Fodor (1975) famously claimed 'no computation without representation', it was pretty clearly intentional representation he had in mind. In the case of, say, a Turing machine that computes arithmetic, it arises when we try to express the relation between the specific numerals the machine uses and the *numbers* ($\neq$ *numerals*) that the numerals stand for, or represent. Thus '2' represents the number two in standard decimal notation; '10' represents it in binary. (Why *purely intentional* representation? Well, the represented number may not exist, as it would not were some machine to produce an expression with the content {7/0}). Or, to take Chomsky's own example (1980a: 69–70, 102–3, quoted above, Section 3.1), a computer might be programmed to represent the contents of 'an explicit theory of the motions of the heavenly bodies and information about its position and velocity'—even when that theory were false and the postulated heavenly bodies did not exist.

Of course, in the case of standard computers, what certain states, e.g. some specific arrangement of flip-flops in a register, do or do not represent

intended in theories of vision and language. (Nevertheless, it is hard to resist wondering how he understands the relation to be 'tetradic' in cases where Y is not a real object. Is Y in such cases an intentional content?)

[13] Chomsky does use 'represent' in still another way, defining, in *LSLT*, a non-intentional relation Δ, 'read "represents," defined on the strings of the system [of phones]. This holds between *Sentence* and *NP^VP*, and between *Sentence* and *John^came^home*, between *NP* and *my^friend*, etc.' (*LSLT* 69); that is, Δ is essentially a composition relation holding between a string of symbols and all its theoretical subsegments. There is no suggestion of intentionality in this usage, which, however, also seems entirely neologistic. As he notes in his (2003: 278), this usage is quite distinct from another also discussed in *LSLT*, that is supposed to capture the relation between the phonetic primitives of the system and the 'utterance tokens represented by them' (*LSLT* 159). This relation does seem patently intentional (I shall return to it in sect. 4.3 below).

is almost entirely determined by the stipulations of their artificer: these are largely cases of 'derived intentionality', like the intentionality of the words on a page (see Section 1 above). Those of us who think that the mental processes of naturally occurring systems like ourselves are best understood computationally will correspondingly think that there is some naturalistic account of the requisite 'original intentionality' that does not depend upon any artificer's stipulations. Such an account would certainly seem to be required in the case of, say, Gallistel's (1990) computational theory of insect navigation, which would hope to explain, for example, a desert ant's movements by adverting to computations (e.g. a vector algebra) over intentional representations of, *inter alia*, the area around its home burrow, even in cases in which there is no burrow, but the animal has merely been led to think there is—which is why, *pace* Chomsky (2003: 277), a 'photo-landscape', aetiological representation will not in fact suffice.[14]

It is worth noticing that intentional representation does gives rise to a second, I think rather more natural, reading of Chomsky's initial claim in the above passage, that '*the computational system* involved in insect navigation or bird song is said to be "internally represented"'. *A system of computations itself* could be intentionally represented in precisely the same way that numbers, burrows, or songs can be. It is, of course, this possibility that is key to Turing's splendid idea of a *Universal Turing Machine*, or a machine that computes what any Turing Machine itself would compute, which it can do only if the latter Turing Machines are represented on its tape.

So far as I understand it, Gallistel's theory of the desert ant requires only that the ant represent things like its home burrow, and the distance and time of a particular trip away from it; there is no need for it to represent *the system of vector algebra* itself. That system is, at best, merely implemented somehow in the ant's nervous system. In the case of Chomsky's ascription of UG to a child, it is not at all clear that this involves the intentional representation of *the linguistic principles themselves*—in addition to the representation of the specific categories, e.g. NP, VP, and the like, over which those principles range (see e.g. Stabler 1983; Devitt, this volume). Settling the issue probably involves establishing fairly subtle facts about language use and/or acquisition, e.g. whether there is some stage at which some computation has either

---

[14] I hasten to add that I do not pretend to have a theory of intentionality myself, or think that any of those presently on offer are nearly adequate.

to keep track of the application of a principle, or to apply some metric to the selection of one principle over another (as was the explicit doctrine of Chomsky, 1965: 30—see Section 3.1 above). Both here and in my earlier paper I have wanted to remain neutral about this issue, addressing only the logically prior question of where and why representation was needed for any part of linguistic theory at all.

### 4.2 Informal motivation?

Actually, in his reply Chomsky himself seems to regard *all* talk of representation as 'informal' in any of the senses he considers (2003: 276; see also pp. 278–9). Specifically, he claims that whatever use he makes of intentionalistic idioms does not seriously commit his actual theory to any sort of intentionality (p. 281). He has similarly dismissed Burge's intentionalistic reading of the work of Marr:

Talk about organs or organisms 'solving problems,' or being adapted to their functions, is to be understood . . . as metaphoric shorthand. . . . It is, correspondingly, a misreading of informal talk to conclude that Marr's theory of vision attributes 'intentional states that represent objective, physical properties' because 'there is no other way to treat the visual system as solving the problem that the theory sees it as solving' (Burge 1986, pp. 28–9). The theory itself has no place for the concepts that enter into the informal presentation, intended for general motivation. (Chomsky 2000: 161)

Thus, an immunologist might speak of the immune system 'solving problems', or a physicist about light rays 'seeking the shortest path'.[15] These sound intentionalistic, but it would be silly to insist that the theories are genuinely so, since they can be easily stated without such claims.

But then the question we need to ask is whether Chomsky's theory can in fact be stated without the intentionalisms that he and other linguists persistently employ. It is by no means obvious that they can. Consider again the passages I cited in Section 3.1 above, especially the well-known, explicit

---

[15] Chomsky made these comparisons to immunology and physics in correspondence. In his (2003: 279), he makes instead a comparison to Lorenz's use of intentionalisms in describing imprinting in a duckling. Unfortunately, this latter case is as controversial as the case of linguistics—imprinting arguably involves some sort of representation of the object the duckling is thereby disposed to 'follow around', even if that representation probably does not involve 'the proposition that the first thing it sees is its mother'.

model of hypothesis-testing set out at Chomsky (1965: 30) that we saw reiterated so vividly ten years later in the introduction to *LSLT* (1975*b*). It is hard to believe that, at least in presenting these quite detailed proposals, Chomsky regarded them as *literally false*, as false as an immunologist's claim that the immune system is 'solving problems'.[16] What of his striking and original claims about children innately 'representing' and 'cognizing' the principles of universal grammar? What about the distinction between the cognizing and non-cognizing missiles? What about his assimilation of his views to the 'innate ideas' of the Rationalists?

Now it is true that, with the development of the 'Principles and Parameters' model around 1980, Chomsky began to reject the specific model of hypothesis confirmation that he had set out in 1965, replacing it with a 'triggering' model in which there need be no 'rational' relation between the input a child receives and the grammar she eventually acquires (see 1980*a*: 136 and 2003: 279).[17] Someone might suppose that, where there is no rationality, there need be no intentionality. Quite apart from the implausibility of that supposition,[18] there is the fact that intentionalisms linger in Chomsky's statement of this alternative model. Thus, he writes:

under [the] concept of learning as 'abduction' or 'self-design', the question whether language is learned or grows will depend upon whether the mind equipped with universal grammar presents a set of grammars as hypotheses to

[16] As Chomsky well knows, unlike the intentionalistic metaphors of the physicist or immunologist, his own can be and regularly are interpreted quite literally. Jim Higginbotham opened his comments on the version of the present paper delivered at Sheffield with the remark that 'linguists have been for some time in bad faith with regard to the issue of intentionality'. Renouncing the literal interpretation of so much of one's earlier writings in this way might well serve as a case in point.

[17] Chomsky (2003) sometimes insists that he never did propose a hypothesis-confirmation model. It is awfully hard to read the passage at Chomsky (1965: 30), cited in sect. 3.1 above, and especially the discussion that follows it, in any other way; but, fine: so perhaps there was merely a change in the *appearances* of the model. For the record, it bears mentioning that efforts actually to implement a triggering model along the lines Chomsky sketches have apparently not met with great success; see J. D. Fodor (1998: 343–4).

[18] I argue at length against this supposition in Rey (2002), citing the myriad ways in which intentional states are implicated in myriad non-rational relations, as when, for example, people laugh at jokes, weep at bad news, dance with glee, and evince startled responses at the unexpected (all reactions that, despite their non-rationality, are dependent crucially on the *content* of an antecedent state).

be selected on the basis of data and an evaluation metric, or whether the steady state grammar arises in another way—for example, by virtue of a hierarchy of accessibility . . . and *a process of selection of the most accessible grammar compatible with given data*. (Chomsky 1980a: 136)

But 'compatibility' is presumably 'logical compatibility', and this can arise only with respect to truth-valuable phenomena: for example, the steady-state grammar must not generate structural descriptions of object-language expressions that are contradicted by the structural descriptions assigned to heard utterances. The difference from the earlier model concerns only whether, in the face of various compatibilities and incompatibilities with the data, the *selection* of the grammar is by some rational evaluation metric, or merely by some non-rational ordering that makes certain grammars more accessible than others.

In a commentary on this latter proposal, Robert Matthews (1980) wonders whether Chomsky is committed to 'the assumption that an adequate theory of language acquisition would employ the intentional idiom of knowledge, belief, intention and the like', and raises the question whether the abandonment of the hypothesis-testing model 'should not be construed as an abandonment of the intentional idiom itself' (p. 26). Ironically enough, Chomsky in his reply *there* explicitly *resists* this suggestion, claiming (quotations from the Matthews text):[19]

We agree that, *at some level*, much of what is called 'learning' . . . should be characterized in a 'non-intentional, presumably physiological vocabulary . . .' But I do not see that this amounts to abandoning a 'rationalist' account of language acquisition in which 'the various processes . . . are defined over . . . contents [of a state]', and innate structure 'is characterized intentionally in terms of both the *content* of a state and the learner's *relation* to that content' (say, cognizing). (Chomsky 1980b: 47)

But perhaps, incredibly, passages such as these are also mere 'metaphoric shorthand' and 'informal motivation', and not part of the theory proper.

---

[19] For the record, Chomsky claimed in correspondence that he understands the whole of this (1980b) reply to Matthews to be 'perfectly explicit in rejecting the intentional interpretation'. It is some measure of the difficulty of understanding Chomsky's position on intentionality that none of the half dozen colleagues I have asked have been able to read it in this way (see also n. 22 below).

## 4.3 *Technical theory*

The basic logical structure of the theory proper is possibly best set out in the impressively formal *LSLT*. Here it is hard to take much to be informal or merely metaphoric. As I mentioned in note 13, Chomsky does introduce a relation, $\Delta$, which he calls 'represent', but it is essentially a composition relation holding between a string and its parts, and so does not involve any intentionality—or, at least, not until one reaches the *terminal* strings, which have no parts:

There is a set of *terminal* strings that are the 'last' in the ordering, in the sense that they bear the relation $\Delta$ to no string. These terminal strings correspond (in a loose way) to strings of words and morphemes. (*LSLT* 69)

The way may be 'loose', but a few pages earlier the condition is laid down that

The grammar must indicate the structure of each utterance on each of [the levels **Pm, M, W, C, P, T**]. To accomplish this end, we construct on each level **L**, certain elements that we call '**L**-markers' and we construct a mapping called '$M^L$' that assigns these **L**-markers to utterances. *The L-marker assigned to an utterance gives the complete information as to the structure of this utterance on level **L**.* (*LSLT* 66)

Indeed, the lowest level is spelt out quite unambiguously in just such terms:

The characterization of the linguistically significant levels is much simplified if we introduce a lowest level of representation *whose elements are given a physical description by means of the mapping M on this level.* We thus establish a phonetic alphabet **Pn** as the lowest level of representation. *The primes of **Pn** are phonetic symbols* . . . For any given language $:^{Pn}$ will be a set of strings whose membership is largely determined by higher-level constructions. $M^{Pn}$ will *associate these strings with specific utterances by providing a physical description of phones.* . . . [It] gives a specification of strings in **Pn** in terms of certain physical properties associated with the alphabet **Pn**. . . . *Each such string is essentially a phonetic description of some utterance, recorded or unrecorded, grammatical or ungrammatical.* (*LSLT* 158–9)

Here there is not even a pretence of avoiding intentionality. In the case of the terminal phonological primes, not only can we ask what they are 'about', we are explicitly told. Despite its being paraphrased as 'represent', the relation $\Delta$ is quite beside the point. It is $M^{Pn}$ that is patently the function that tells us the phone that each phonetic prime represents. And, as the end of the last quote makes clear (but in any case an interest in infinite generativity would require), all these intentionalist usages are *purely* intentional in the sense of Sections 1 and 4.1 above: we may say that, for example, 'a string represents some utterance, though the utterance was never produced'.

In his reply, Chomsky actually does claim that *LSLT* appeals to some kind of 'external', intentionalist use of 'represent'. However:

the external one is only mentioned. It is the topic of articulatory and acoustic phonetics, which study how the features of PHON(E) enter into performance (problems (B1)). The broader goal is to reveal the ways in which the I-language (there called 'grammar') 'provides a basis for a description of how, in fact, language is used and understood'. (2003: 277)

As I shall emphasize in Section 5.1, this may actually be a stronger claim than Chomsky needs, since arguably linguistics could get by with a 'narrower', 'internalist' notion of content. But, putting that issue aside, what is puzzling about this remark is why he does not regard this intentionalist use of 'represent' as part and parcel of his theory. It certainly appears to be so in the passages of *LSLT* that I have just quoted. Indeed, it seems essential to specifying the strings of phones that are the domain of the rest of the theory.[20] It may well be that linguistic theory cannot tell us very much about *what the sensori-motor systems do* with the information the language system provides; but it may still be perfectly crucial to specifying just *what that information is*.

One could, of course, *abstract* the purely 'computational' (e.g. '$\Delta$') portions of the theory from such information and the function $M^{\mathrm{Pn}}$. One can, after all, *abstract from* (i.e. disregard) phenomena in any way one chooses. Sometimes this is theoretically useful, as when physics abstracts from matters of taste. A number of philosophers (e.g. Stich 1983) have suggested that cognitive psychology in general should be confined to the characterization of internal formal computations, abstracted from their semantic properties. Whether or not this is plausible for psychology as a whole, it is patently not

---

[20] Arguably, analogous issues about intentionality would arise even more patently with regard to whatever primes would be involved at the interface between syntax and the 'conceptual-intentional' system—e.g. primes representing features such as [+agent], [+animate]—an issue that does not arise in *LSLT*, but has become crucial in more recent discussions (e.g. Chomsky 1995b; 2000: 10–14, quoted below).

the way in which a Chomskian theory is in fact presented; and, I submit, it is doubtful that the theory *could* be presented in this way.

In the first place, it is unclear that it could do so and still take seriously the standard sort of evidence that is adduced for it, viz. speakers' (intentionalistically specified) *verdicts* about the acceptability of phonetic strings. How could any of this be data or evidence for a theory if the theory does not at least purport to explain it? Condensation trails in cloud-chamber photographs provide evidence of particle interactions only because physical theory offers an explanation of why those interactions give rise to those trails. *Perhaps some of the linkages to evidence are not strictly part of some specific 'technical' theory being considered: but that does not mean that the truth of the theory does not depend upon those linkages being available,* the 'informal motivational' claims being *true.* If the relation of linguistic theory to speakers' utterances and judgements is really as mysterious, 'barely glimpsed' an issue as Chomsky suggests, then it is hard to see why the LAD has anything whatsoever to do with utterances and judgements, or why the latter should be taken as any sort of serious evidence of its structure.

But, more importantly, a Chomskian theory is standardly understood as not about any spatio-temporal computations taking place in anyone's nervous system, much less about the character of the specific symbolic system over which such computations would have to be defined (e.g. whether it is binary, decimal, alphanumeric, or—most likely—some other notation). The theory is not about *the notation* the brain might use, but about *the categories and relationships any such notation would be required to capture.* The categories of the theory are, for example, *nouns, verbs, NPs, VPs,* not *expressions* like 'noun', 'verb', 'NP', or 'VP'. (Moreover, surely Chomsky does not want to concern himself with the ways in which representations in the brain are *spelt,* much less commit himself to the claim that all human minds/brains are actually *spelt* the same.) Even the meticulous formalism of *LSLT* only indicates the formalism *schematically,* the letters he uses (e.g. 'Pı' . . . 'Pn') standing for *whatever representations play the specific role he indicates* (in the case of 'P', . . ., 'Pn' , the phonemic primitives of the system). Although any *particular symbols* could, of course, be individuated without regard to their interpretation, that some symbol is a *phonemic primitive,* or an *NP-, VP-,* or *IP-symbol,* requires that we be able to identify the role the symbols play, not only internally in a system, but also at the interfaces, and not only for a single human at a time, but for all humans across time—otherwise, how could the principles of grammar be regarded as 'universal'? But to specify those roles just *is* to provide a theory of the content of the symbols that play them.

In yet another important, technical work—*The Sound Pattern of English* with Morris Halle—not only are phonetic and phonological representations employed throughout the theory, but the question 'What exactly is a phonetic representation?' is explicitly raised in a separate section. It is answered thus:

A phonetic *representation has the form of a two-dimensional matrix* in which rows *stand for* particular phonetic features; the columns *stand for* the consecutive segments of the utterance generated; and the *entries in the matrix determine the status of each segment with respect to the features*. In a full phonetic representation, an entry might *represent the degree of intensity* with which a given feature is present in a particular segment. (Chomsky and Halle 1968: 5)

Lest these matrices be regarded as being there merely for the linguist, Chomsky and Halle 'propose further that such representations are mentally constructed by the speaker and the hearer and underlie their actual performance in speaking and "understanding" ' (p. 14). Indeed, a subsequent section is devoted to the question of psychological reality:

We do not doubt that the stress contours and other phonetic facts . . . constitute some sort of perceptual reality for those who know the language in question. In fact we are suggesting a principled explanation for this conclusion. A person who knows the language should 'hear' the predicted phonetic shapes . . . We take for granted, then, that *phonetic representations describe a perceptual reality*. (Chomsky and Halle 1968: 25)

In any case, a robust intentionalist idiom seems to be precisely what linguists employ throughout their technical work. In a recent, standard text, for example, Kenstowicz (1994) discusses how 'English speakers conceptualize the phonological information comprising the lexical units of their language in two different ways', using a 'phonetic representation [which] indicates how the word is actualized in speech—the instructions sent to the vocal apparatus to articulate the sounds and acoustic properties that are isolated in order to decode the speech signal', and a 'phonological representation [which] is called into play when speakers have occasion to represent the word in spelling' and 'is essentially the form in which the lexical item is stored in memory' (p. 7). Note here that we have *two different representations* of the same lexical units, which clearly implies the reality of such representations as *distinct* from what they represent, an issue that will become crucial in the next section.

Perhaps a Chomskian theory and its explanatory deployment can be restated in a way that does not involve such patently intentional notions. However, it is noteworthy that no one, least of all Chomsky, has even tried to present the theory in that way. Until someone does, it is hard to take seriously the claim that the intentional idioms play only an informal, expository role.[21]

It is worth noting again that, in the reply to Matthews in which the issue of intentionality is explicitly addressed, Chomsky himself happily allows that 'if the intentional idiom is appropriate . . . for the state attained, it is also appropriate for the initial state and the transition to the state attained, on grounds of the (assumed) success of a theory of language acquisition in these terms' (1980b: 47).[22] So, whether or not the intentionalisms are strictly speaking part of the theory, it would certainly appear that Chomsky regards them as *true*. And it is the commitment to the *truth* of the intentionalistic claims that is crucial to the general issue of intentionality, not merely whether some theoretic treatment might conveniently ignore or abstract from that truth.

Why, then, does Chomsky so strenuously resist the perfectly straight-forward, literal reading of his and other linguists' words? What is really at issue for him here? In the next section I want to consider some of the things that might be leading him to resist intentionalism, before turning in the last section to consider positive reasons why it nevertheless should be embraced.

[21] A different way of avoiding intentionality would be to allow that the objects of the theory are linguistic features, but that these features are not *represented* in the brain, but actually *instantiated* in it. I shall consider this strategy in sects. 5.2–5.4 below.

[22] Along the lines of n. 19 above, Chomsky claimed in correspondence that he intended this conditional as a *reductio* of the antecedent. But this seems clearly incompatible not only with the tenor of the rest of the reply, but also with the claims of the original (1980a), according to which 'we cognize the grammar that constitutes the current state of our language faculty' (p. 69; see sect. 3.1 above).

## 5 Bad Reasons to Resist Intentionalism

I think there are a number of different sources of Chomsky's resistance to intentionalism. Some of them, I suspect, are purely historical and sociological;[23] but others involve a loose chain of reasoning involving mixtures of insights and confusions that have, I think, tempted people in many areas of cognitive science. The reasoning begins with the presumption that intentionalism is committed to representations being of *mind-independent objective phenomena*, and then, observing that linguistic phenomena are mind-dependent, concludes that *linguistics can make do with the representations in the mind/brain alone*, with no need of their having any intentional content. It will take a little effort to separate the confusions from the insights here.

### 5.1 *Exaggerations of externalism*

Semantic Externalism is the view that propositional attitude states of individual organisms cannot be understood in isolation from the historical, biological, or social environments those organisms inhabit (see e.g. Burge 1986). Internalist approaches, to which Chomsky feels himself committed, deny this, and argue that the mental states they study entirely 'supervene' only on the organism's brain. Chomsky is understandably wary of Externalist approaches, since they often rely on claims about E(xternal)-languages, such as 'English' or 'French', which he has reasonably argued are an inappropriate focus of linguistic theory. He regards them as superficial sociological phenomena, whereas linguistic theory is concerned with 'I(nternal)-language', or the specific idiolectic grammar on which an individual's LAD has settled. And he is also reasonably sceptical of many externalists' reliance on a word relation of 'reference' that he believes is not sufficiently clear to bear any theoretical weight.

That being said, it is important to notice ways in which Externalism is, however, *not* committed either to claims about E-language or to any

---

[23] I especially have in mind the atmosphere of extreme scepticism about meaning and mind that hung heavily over philosophy and linguistics in Chomsky's formative years, especially in the work of his teacher, Nelson Goodman. Another source may be an understandable scepticism about specific programmes for a referential *linguo*-semantics that have been influential for the past several decades, e.g. in the work of Montague and his followers. Since these sources are only indirectly related to the present issues, I leave their exploration to a later time.

particularly strong claims about reference. For example, Burge's (1986) discussion of Marr's work on vision, which we have seen particularly exercises
Chomsky, concerns not natural language, but simply how to understand
Marr's own theoretical apparatus, arguing that it presupposes the operation of the visual system in a normal environment. Whatever the merits
of his argument, it certainly does not rely on anything like the very strong
commitments about reference with which Chomsky burdens it. Specifically,
although Burge does indeed claim that 'our perceptual experience represents or is about objects, properties and relations that are *objective*' (Burge
1986: 125, quoted at Chomsky 2000: 159), this is not a view that is supposed
to exclude imaginings, hallucinations, or other non-veridical perceptions.
It is a view about the *content* of a state, not its accuracy, or the availability
of the objective features, on any particular occasion. So it is no objection
to it that there might be representations of a rotating cube but no cube in
the experimental setup (Chomsky 1995a: 52; 2000: 159–60; cf. Section 4.2
above). It would be enough that there simply *have been*, or simply *could be*,
cubes (or at least their features, such as edges and surfaces) in the normal
environment of the subject. Certainly it does not follow from the mere lack
of a cube on a particular occasion that 'there is no meaningful question
about the "content" of the internal representations of a person seeing a
cube under the [tachistoscopically induced] conditions of the experiments'
(Chomsky 1995a: 52). As I have emphasized by my definition of 'intentional
content' (Section 2.2), Chomsky himself is committed to those representations having content: precisely the content he himself identifies, viz. [a
rotating cube]. *Note, again, that it is these very idioms, such as 'representation of a
rotating cube though there is none', that are constitutive of the notion of intentional
content on which I am insisting.*

However, as I have also been anxious to emphasize in my deliberately
unspecific definition, this notion of intentional content is not committed
to any specific theory of it. Specifically, it is not committed to Externalism. Although it is true that externalist theories have been all the rage in
philosophy since Putnam (1975), there are plenty of proposals regarding
so-called 'narrow content', or content individuated without reference to
the environment (see e.g. White 1982; J. A. Fodor 1987; Segal 2000; Rey
1998).[24]

---

[24] In the light of our discussion, and particularly of his dismissal of narrow content at

But, lastly, even if Externalism were correct, its consequences for linguistics would be quite minimal. It might well be that correctly characterizing a computational system in the brain as processing language depends crucially upon its environment being one in which languages are in fact spoken and heard. All that would follow is that, were the same computational system to occur in a different environment, its states would no longer be correctly characterizable as linguistic. But Chomsky should hardly disagree with this: as we saw (Section 4.1; 'Reply': 276), he approvingly cites Weng's observations that the same system subserving vision could subserve audition and consequently represent different features. Indeed, the LAD itself might be 'embedded in performance systems that use it for locomotion' (Chomsky 2000: 27). Linguists reasonably presume that the system they are investigating is in fact used for language. Although this presumption is indeed partly about facts external to the individual, this does not make that research any the less internal: identification of ethnic groups inside the United States may make reference to the origins outside of it; but research on those groups could still be entirely confined to their relations within it.

## 5.2 Misplaced mind-dependence

Externalism could seem to be incompatible with a different aspect that emerges in recent linguistic theory, the evident mind-dependence of linguistic phenomena. For example, immediately following one of the passages about the psychological reality of phonetic representation that I set out above, Chomsky and Halle go on to note

that there is nothing to suggest that these phonetic representations also describe a physical or acoustic reality in any detail. For example, there is little reason to suppose that the perceived stress contour must represent [*sic*] some physical property of the utterance in a point-by-point fashion . . . In fact there is no evidence from experimental phonetics to suggest that these contours are actually present

(2003), 279, it is interesting that Chomsky complains that 'any such thing as I-meaning ("semantic representations," "narrow content") even exists is now commonly denied', and goes on 'tentatively [to] assume that postulation of I-sound and I-meaning [i.e. narrow content] is legitimate' (2000: 170), indeed, to endorse them in the rest of the chapter. Apparently he is not always quite the opponent of intentionalism that he has made himself out to be.

as physical properties of utterances in anything like the detail with which they are perceived. (Chomsky and Halle 1968: 25)

And, of course, if this is true of phonetic phenomena, how much more will they be true of the further linguistic phenomena that they compose, e.g. nouns, verbs, NPs, IPs, etc.

These observations might lead a very hard-line physicalist to suppose that such phenomena do not actually exist in the external world, which would appear to tolerate only physically delineable phenomena. Chomsky sometimes seems to draw just such a conclusion:[25]

Suppose we postulate that corresponding to an element 'a' of phonetic form there is an external object '*a' that 'a' selects as its *phonetic value*; thus, the element [ba] in Jones's I-language picks out some entity *[ba], 'shared' with Smith if there is a counterpart in his I-language. Communication could then be described in terms of such (partially) shared entities, which are easy enough to construct: take '*a' to be the singleton set {a}, or {3, a}; or, if one wants a more realistic feel, some construct based on motions of molecules. With sufficient heroism, one could defend such a view, though no one does, because it's clear we are just spinning wheels. (Chomsky 2000: 129)

An expression E of [language] L is a pair ⟨PHON, SEM⟩, *where PHON(E) is the information relevant to the sound of E* and SEM(E) to its meaning. PHON and SEM are constructed by computational operations on lexical items. . . . PHON(E) and SEM(E) are elements at the 'phonetic level' and 'semantic levels' respectively; they are phonetic and semantic 'representations.' The terms have their technical sense; there is nothing 'represented' in the sense of representative theories of ideas, for example. (Chomsky 2000: 173)

An expression E has no existence apart from its properties at the interface levels, PHON(E) and SEM(E), if these exist. (Chomsky 2000: 175)

(I shall return to these puzzling passages in Section 5.3.) In any case, a denial

---

[25] But not always, since he often seems to think there *is* a relation between the phonetic primitives of the internal computational system and *some* kind of phenomena produced outside the cranium, as in the passages of *LSLT* (pp. 66, 158–9) quoted above. Chomsky even writes in his 'Reply': 'The study of language use tries to find out how Jones with I-language L proceeds to produce and interpret sounds and tell us about the book he read' (2003: 276); 'One may also, if one likes, say that elements of I-language "represent" sounds and things, having in mind problems (B1) and (B2), but this third usage merely points to problems to be investigated and should not be misinterpreted as a substantive proposal' (2003: 277).

of externality to linguistic phenomena is certainly the conclusion that James McGilvray draws on Chomsky's behalf:[26]

One must recognize that what goes from one person's mouth to another person's ears in the form of an event that could be called a 'signal' is just a set of compressions and decompressions in the air between them. Not even a sound 'goes across', much less a linguistic sound or meaning. Ordinary sounds like buzzings, linguistic sounds described by phonetics, and linguistic meanings are *in people's heads, and only there.* They are not to be found between people . . . [Chomsky's] primary aim is to emphasize that no one wants to place *sounds* outside linguistic items; there are no serious proposals for doing so. . . . It is far simpler to assume that the sound (the relevant kind of 'knowledge') is in the lexical item and hence the language faculty to begin with, and that the computation that leads to an expression simply takes it into account. Not surprisingly, no one proposes moving sounds 'outside'. The stakes are too high. (McGilvray 2000: 165–7)

Despite the high stakes, I shall argue in Section 6 that there actually are a number of good reasons to suppose that sounds are indeed outside—well, at least our crania. But, to make room for those reasons, it is important to note that the fact of mind-dependence does not require that they are not. It may well be that a linguistic feature is not a *localizable, physical* feature of a sound, but can only be *identified* by reference to the human perceptual and articulatory apparatus.[27] It does not follow that they are

---

[26] McGilvray actually goes so far as to say: 'Chomsky is a *constructivist*. This stems from his internalism and nativism and amounts to the idea that the things and the "world" of common sense understanding, and, in a different way, of science are in large measure products of our minds. As Chomsky says in an interview that appears in *Language and Politics*, "You could say that the structure of our experience and our understanding of experience is a reflection of the nature of our minds, and that we can't get to what the world really is. . . .' Common sense understanding is anthropocentric and serves our interests. The sciences try to be objective, but they and, in a different way, the phenomena they deal with are human constructs or artifacts, made by us in order to understand. In this respect, their worlds are still products of our minds' (McGilvray 2000: 5–6). Apart from the quoted interview remark, it is hard to find Chomsky actually committing himself to such extreme 'constructivism'. The closest I have found is a passing endorsement of 'naming as a kind of "world-making," in something like Nelson Goodman's sense' (2000: 181), which is followed by expressions of sympathy with various forms of 17th-/ 18th-cent. idealism, according to which 'The world as known *is* the world of ideas', which Chomsky (2000: 182) quotes approvingly from Yolton's (1984) account of that period.

[27] See Kenstowicz (1994), 184–5, for an excellent summary of research on the issue.

not *perfectly real phenomena in extra-cranial space and time*. Tables, chairs, cities, nations, perhaps even mountains, rivers, and molehills, may well have identity conditions that also depend very heavily upon human thought and perception. But that does not make them any the less physical objects occupying the space/time positions they seem to occupy. They may just be physically weird, highly gerrymandered parts of that space and time. This would be true, for example, on any number of *dispositional analyses* of what it is to be a table, a chair, a mountain, or a molehill. The point is familiar from discussions of colour since Locke: red surfaces may have nothing physical in common *save the fact that under some suitably idealized circumstances they would be judged to look red by some selected set of human beings*.[28] *Mutatis mutandis* for tables, chairs, mountains and molehills, London and the river Nile—and phones, phonemes, and most phonetic, syntactic, and semantic features. At least it remains an open question whether such phenomena exist outside our crania, not settled merely by the observation that they are not physically definable.[29]

## 5.3 *Use/mention equivocations*

Another source of Chomsky's opposition to intentionalisms is his conviction that he can avoid them, relying merely on the internal representations alone. In reply to my claim that they are needed, he writes:[30] 'The theory of I-language attributes such features as [+voice] to the mind/brain. The I-language generates expressions E constructed from these elementary features; E is accessed by [the Sensori-Motor system] and used to carry out articulatory gestures' (Chomsky 2003: 277). So there appears to be no need

[28] J. A. Fodor (1998), ch. 7, makes precisely such dispositions a crucial part of his account of concepts.

[29] One could take a harder line on mind-dependent phenomena. Perhaps once speakers learnt just how arbitrary and gerrymandered the physical reality corresponding to a phonetic feature was, they would no longer regard it as a real thing in the world; and perhaps that is a good reason for thinking that words or features, as speakers conceive them, do not exist in the external world. It still does not follow that they should be identified with phenomena in the mind/brain instead. The error here verges on the 'McX' mistake noted earlier (sect. 2.2): the fact that Pegasus is not a real item in the external world does not mean that *he* is an 'idea in the mind'—or some sort of structure in our brains.

[30] He is replying here to an earlier version of the present paper, portions of which he had by e-mail.

of intentionalisms—until one wonders how features such as [+voice] are rightly attributed to the *mind/brain*. One would have thought—one expects phoneticians to think (see Section 6)—that they are features of *sounds,* or some kind of event in the oral cavity. If the sounds are not *there,* they—much less the feature of being voiced—surely are not in the *brain* either. Why does Chomsky think otherwise?

What smooths the way for relocating phonetic features from the mouth to the brain is an equivocation between use and mention that runs throughout both Chomsky's and many other linguists' work. This is the distinction between, respectively, saying that *dogs* have four legs and no letters, but that *the word 'dogs'* has four letters and no legs. What greater difference could there be than that between a word and what it represents?[31] What is insidious about this equivocation is that it can begin quite harmlessly—and then, unmonitored, lead to the most extravagant philosophical confusions (Quine regarded it as 'original sin' in philosophy).

Thus, consider its innocuous introduction in *LSLT*. Within a page of setting out the primes of **Pn** as phonetic *symbols* that will be mapped by $M^{Pn}$ to 'physical descriptions of phones', Chomsky proposes a convenient convention: 'We will henceforth apply the term "phones" to symbols of **Pn,** as well as to utterance tokens represented by them' (*LSLT* 159). This actually just makes explicit a relaxing of use/mention conventions that was in fact in force already (see *LSLT* 106), and continues to the present day. Consider, for a recent example, the way in which Chomsky talks about 'features' in discussing the general strategy of Minimalism:

The language involves three kinds of elements:

- (i) the properties of sound and meaning, called 'features';
- (ii) the items that are assembled from these properties, called 'lexical items'; and
- (iii) the complex expressions constructed from these 'atomic' units.

It follows that *the computational system that generates expressions has two basic*

---

[31] Or, a little more carefully, between noun-phrases and the purported phenomena to which those phrases can, by particular people on particular occasions, be used to 'refer' (where this word is used in the intentional sense, i.e. the sense in which one can say '*x* refers to *y*, although there is no *y*'; cf. sects. 2.1, 4.1 above, as well as Chomsky's similar rendition, 2000: 150, quoted in n. 13 above). I shall abbreviate this cumbersome wording by simply talking about 'words referring'.

*operations: one assembles features into lexical items, the second forms larger syntactic objects out of those already constructed . . .*

Legibility conditions impose a three-way division among the features assembled into lexical items:

1. semantic features, interpreted at the semantic interface;
2. phonetic features, interpreted at the phonetic interface; and
3. features that are not interpreted at either interface.

In a perfectly designed language, *each feature would be semantic or phonetic, not merely a device to create a position or to facilitate computation.* (Chomsky 2000: 10–14)

'Feature' here equivocates between referring to a property of an expression, contributing to its meaning or pronunciation, and referring to something that refers to (or can be interpreted as) that property. Combining the latter three conditions with clause (i) in the former proposal about the elements of language, we could conclude that the properties of sound and meaning, called 'features', are interpreted at the semantic and phonetic interfaces—as the properties of sound and meaning that partially constitute language; that is, the features are interpreted as themselves. It is unclear how such self-referential features would present informative constraints at either interface. In any case, such usage fits ill with the suggestion that 'features of PHON(E) can be plausibly construed as *instructions for articulatory gestures*' which Chomsky cited approvingly from Halle (1983) (see Section 4.1 above). On this view, the feature [+voice], rather than being the *consequence* of certain articulatory gestures, would actually be their *cause*.

Of course, one might protest that this way of talking is simply a convenience, common in mathematics, where sorting out use and mention is notoriously tedious.[32] And innocuous and welcome convenience it is, so long as it is not used to buttress controversial theses. Although this way of speaking may have been conceived in a deliberate finessing of mention and use, it is striking how it seems to have become a substantial part of what Chomsky regards as 'internalist':

The computational procedure maps an array of lexical choices into a pair of symbolic objects, phonetic form and LF. . . . *The elements of these symbolic objects can be called 'phonetic' and 'semantic' features, but we should bear in mind that all of*

---

[32] I am told that Richard Cartwright once quipped that the way you could distinguish a philosopher from a logician is that only the philosopher cares about use vs. mention.

*this is pure syntax and completely internalist. It is the study of mental representations and computations, much like the inquiry into how the image of a cube rotating in space is determined from retinal stimulations, or imagined.* We may take the semantic features S of an expression E to be its *meaning* and the phonetic features P to be its *sound*; E *means* S in something like the sense of the corresponding English word, and E *sounds* P in a similar sense, S and P providing the relevant information for the performance systems. (Chomsky 2000: 125)

Here, as in the convention introduced in *LSLT*, for example, 'phonetic features' are understood both as *properties of sounds* and as *'symbolic objects'*, or *'mental representations'*, and the study of the latter is like the study of *imagined rotating cubes* (which are therefore also syntactic objects?). Similarly, in the passage Chomsky (2000: 173), quoted towards the end of the previous section, 'PHON(E)' and 'SEM(E)' are used *both* for 'information' and for its 'representations' over which the computations range, the convenience of identifying the two (however puzzling that may be) being that it allows us to dispense with the view that a representation stands for an 'idea'—i.e., presumably, an intentional content.[33]

## 5.4 *Intention/representation confusions*

The passage regarding PHON(E) and SEM(E) at Chomsky (2000: 173) raises a further complication, something of an interaction between these use/mention equivocations and the earlier exaggerations of Externalism. One might, after all, wonder what happens to the use/mention confusion in the case of an expression '*x*' about which we might say, *per* Sections 2.2 and 4.2:

'A rotating cube' represents a rotating cube, but there is no such cube.

The non-existence of the represented phenomenon might lead one to suppose that there is no longer a possibility of confusing use and mention, since

---

[33] Perhaps not, since the passage bears a footnote in which it is explained that 'PHON(E) (and hence markers at all levels) could be taken to "represent" utterances in a similar way. Since utterances are associated with states of speakers, the predication could be construed as holding of these, the course taken by Bromberger and Halle (1996), discussing phonological levels in terms of intentions of speakers (understood as supervening on brain states)' (2000: 203–4 n. 8). But how, then, is this latter not an example of the 'representative theory of ideas'?

there is no real object whose properties could be confused with those of the respective representation; so conflating use and mention in the ways that Chomsky does is of no consequence.

But this would obviously be an error. Consider Pegasus: he is supposed to have wings, but from the fact that there is no Pegasus, it does not follow that the word 'Pegasus' has wings; nor even that the 'idea of Pegasus' does: ideas themselves may be many things—good, bad, silly, bold—but they do not have wings. Similarly, the expression 'a rotating cube' is not cubical. But what, then, in such cases would be being confused with what?

There is, of course, a long tradition, extending back to the Middle Ages, that claims that existing 'in thought' is a way or 'mode' in which an otherwise actual, spatio-temporal object may exist, or perhaps 'subsist'; that, anyway, such 'intentional objects' or 'intentional inexistences' as Pegasus need to be postulated for the purposes of psychology as much as quarks need to be postulated for physics. And perhaps this is what Chomsky has in mind when he speaks of linguistic representations as '*postulated entities*, to be understood in the manner of a mental image of a rotating cube' (2000: 160).[34] It would be true, then, that 'we need not ponder what is represented, seeking some objective construction from sounds to things', since there need only be these entities 'in the mind', with nothing that they themselves need be 'of'. But, notoriously, such postulations seem puzzling and extravagant: what on earth could be their relation to the brain? Does a mental image of a cube actually *rotate—in the brain*? Does a phonetic feature in the brain actually *sound* a certain way? Or are there unhearable sounds? Are linguistic features actually *moved* in the brain in the way that Chomskian theories routinely claim? Could the hypothalamus perchance block a feature's movement? It is hard to believe that Chomsky would want to risk burdening his theory with these sorts of commitments, especially given the serious possibility of an independently intelligible alternative: CRTT easily claims that all such features are merely *coded*, i.e. *represented*, by arbitrary bits of the brain, and these certainly need not themselves either *rotate* or *move* in order to

[34] Conceivably he picked it up from Descartes, whose Rationalism he admires, and who seems to have held just such a view, claiming that the same objects that exist in the world in the 'formal mode' exist in our minds in the 'material mode' (see Kemmerling 1996 for useful discussion). The view can be traced back to Aquinas, who probably got it from Aristotle.

represent rotation or reassignment of location in a syntactic tree (I shall return to this point in Section 6).

In any case, identifying even non-worldly features with representations themselves would seem to be a close cousin to the use/mention confusion, what might be called the 'intention/representation' confusion: we confuse properties of *the intended object*[35] with properties of its representation; or, more generally, properties specified in the intentional content of a representation with properties of the representation itself. This confusion is especially inviting in psychological cases: thus, from the fact that many people have experiences of, say, rotating images of cubes, psychologists have sometimes supposed that there must be an image actually rotating in the head. But that does not follow. All that follows is that there is a representation in the head with the intentional content, e.g. [image of a rotating cube].[36] The confusion is abetted by the seemingly harmless phrases 'in the mind' and 'in the head'—as in 'The image isn't in the external world, it's in your mind/head'. But here it is crucial to distinguish 'in your mind' meaning '*part of the intentional content of something in your mind*' and meaning 'in a *place*: your mind' (which, as every materialist knows, is in—if not identical to—your brain). Failure to observe this distinction can lead to pointless perplexities about how an image could be rotating in a brain.[37]

The confusion can be even more enticing when the intentional content

---

[35] Usually 'intentional object', but I prefer 'intended' (cf. 'purported') since there is less temptation to think that such objects are genuine *objects*, inviting the extravagances mentioned in the previous paragraph. (I think one should also resist the tempting identification of such objects with *possible* objects, as in e.g. Lycan 1987. Some of us, after all, share The White Queen's penchant of thinking of a dozen impossible things before breakfast.)

[36] Of course, there could be other, better reasons for thinking there are imagistic representations in the brain, e.g. response-time phenomena (see Kosslyn 1980). However, the bad reasons are seldom distinguished from the better ones.

[37] Equivocation of 'in your head' between reference to intentional content and reference to an actual place can invite the idea that 'intentional objects' exist in a special 'internal' realm of the mind, in which there are 'postulated entities, to be understood in the manner of a mental image of a rotating cube'. It is to avoid this reification that I prefer 'intended object' (cf. n. 31). A better metaphor than that of an object in a special place might be something like a *file* associated with a word, which provides, *inter alia*, information about what properties the referent of the word *would* have, in the event that there is one. Thus, 'Pegasus has wings' tells us that the file for 'Pegasus' includes the claim that he has wings.

concerns linguistic items, i.e. representations themselves. Thus, as we observed above (Section 5.2), someone might be tempted to infer that, because
linguistic phenomena are not *physically delineable*, they therefore do not exist
in the external physical world; but now, since representations *do* plausibly
exist in the head, it can seem natural to identify the linguistic phenomena
instead with those very representations, precisely as we have seen Chomsky is inclined to do. But, on reflection, it hardly seems more plausible than
identifying the mental image of a rotating cube with *its* representation, or
Pegasus—the horse, or even the idea we have of him—with *his*: are we to
wonder 'how fast' a linguistic feature 'moves', or what happens when a
bit of brain gets in the way? In any case, since, as we already noted (Section 4.3), the same lexical item can have two different representations, by
the transitivity of identity, this entails that the item cannot be *identical* to
those representations without those representations being, contrary to the
theory, identical to each other.

## 6 Why Linguistics Needs Intentional Contents

> Results of computations have content.
> (Bromberger and Halle 1992: 215)

So there are these many bad reasons for resisting intentionalism and trying
to get by with internal representations alone. Are there any good reasons for
embracing it? Why insist that speakers are deploying representations with
contents such as {'bell'}, {[+cons]}, {NP}, {[+past tense]}, or {[+animate]},
as opposed to merely the features themselves? Why clutter up the notation
with still more brackets? Well, one might equally ask, why clutter up the
mind/brain with all the corresponding features? Putting aside issues of
notation and ontology, there are two important reasons that, together,
argue for intentional content in linguistics:

(1) Phonetic features such as [+voice] or [−continuant] enter into im-
    portant *brute physical laws and explanations about the oral cavity and the
    articulatory system* in ways that make them patently not features of
    anything inside the brain.

(2) In so far as phonetic and other linguistic features are the *objects of
    computations*, they must be represented within the brain.

(1) not only coheres with common sense, but seems essential to phonentic theory, which regularly regards phones and their features as being produced by the articulatory system. This is not just sloppy talk. Consider standard 'impossible articulations', e.g. velar trills and flaps, bilabial and labiodental lateral fricatives, voiced glottal plosives, as indicated in the standard chart of the phonetic alphabet (see e.g. Malmkjaer 1991: 222). At least some of these—e.g. velar flaps and trills—are surely so because they are *physically* impossible: the velum cannot flap. A little more subtly, physical/physiological facts seem to play a crucial explanatory role in the character of human phonetics. Kenstowicz (1994) observes, for example, that nasal fricatives do not occur because 'so much airflow is diverted to the nasal cavity that not enough remains to generate the turbulence required of a fricative' (p. 16); and that consonantal constructions tend to occur in languages where the resonances of the front and back oral cavity reinforce one another (p. 180). Given the abundance of explanations of this sort, it is crucial that we understand such phonetic phenomena as flaps and trills as *phenomena produced in the oral cavity*. But if they are produced there, they surely are *not also produced inside the brain or language system*: presumably nothing flaps or trills *there*.

So what is produced in the brain? Well, something that must bear some systematic relation to the phenomena in the oral cavity; and, moreover, something that (at least in generative theories like Chomsky's) had better be able to figure in 'computations'. Now, it is perhaps not clear just what Chomsky means by 'computation', but when Alan Turing provided his famous characterization of computation in terms of Turing Machines, he quite sensibly did not make such things as NPs or VPs the primitive symbols on the tapes, or postulate a machine that operated by detecting features like [+voice], [−continuant]—much less [+past tense], [+agent], or [+goal]. And this is in part because of the very difficulties that Chomsky and Halle (1968) stressed, of treating such phenomena as *physical* phenomena, not to mention *local* ones (see Section 5.2 above). *Given that such linguistic phenomena are not local, physical features of the acoustic signal, there would be no reason to think that a machine could be built that was sensitive to whether such features were instantiated on the tape.*[38] What Turing did was to put on his 'tapes' *formal symbols* that have some *local and physically detectable* features, e.g. 'o's and '1's that could

---

[38] Note that the issue here needs to be distinguished from the issue of 'formal features that are accessible in the course of the computation and others that are not' (Chomsky

be individuated by their physical shape (or, in your modern computer, by electro-magnetic properties), so that it would be perfectly clear that a mere machine could respond to their presence and proceed accordingly.[39] Indeed, getting a machine to detect standard linguistic categories would very likely require—another computer!, i.e. some procedure for proceeding from the detection of local, physical properties to the linguistic categories.[40] *Mutatis mutandis* for 'derivations': at least as they are understood in proof theory, they, too, are operations on *formally specified* objects, strings of, typically, *letters of an alphabet*. Indeed, it is no accident that in *LSLT* Chomsky defines his 'primes' as '*letters*':

A linguistic level is a system **L** in which we construct unidimensional representations of utterances. Thus, a level has a certain fixed and finite 'alphabet' of elements which we will call its 'primes.' Given two primes of **L** we can form a new element of **L** by an operation called 'concatenation', symbolized by the arch, ^. . . . Concatenation is essentially the process of spelling, where primes are taken as letters. (*LSLT* 105)[41]

Strings of letters are precisely what derivations derive.

1995*b*: 230). I take Chomsky's use of the latter phrase to be about features that are part of the computations of the grammar prior to spell-out.

[39] Strictly speaking, of course, Turing Machines are *abstract* mathematical objects that may be 'implemented' in any number of ways. Indeed, operations specified at the fairly abstract level of standard linguistics discussions may be implemented by any number of different ('real-time') algorithms at lower levels, which may in turn be run in real time on actual machines in any of a vast multitude of ways. My point is that, *however computations are to be implemented in real time, it is crucial to Turing's proposal that these abstract devices be specified in a way that permits local physical, 'mechanical' realizations.* Issues of intentionality consequently arise when a system is sensitive to (a wide range of) non-local or non-physical properties. This point seems to me implicit in Chomsky (1965), 58; it surfaces in Pylyshyn (1984) and in J. A. Fodor (1986); and I try to improve on the latter formulation in Rey (1997), sect. 4.3.

[40] For present purposes, I leave aside discussion of non-Chomskian approaches to phonology, e.g. 'optimality theory' (see Prince and Smolensky forthcoming), which are conceivably realizable on non-computational 'radical connectionist' machines.

[41] What is a 'letter'? Well, Chomsky (*LSLT* 107 n. 4) explicitly cites Quine's treatment of logical syntax at Quine (1965), ch. 7, which emphasizes in its opening paragraph that 'all [its] characterizations are *formal*, in that they speak only of the typographical constitution of the expressions in question and do not refer to the meanings of those expressions' (p. 283), this being a necessary condition for specifying 'the quite mechanically recognizable properties of being a formula, matrix, tautology or axiom' (p. 291).

To emphasize a point treated in passing above (Section 5.3): if one regards linguistic phenomena as straightforward phenomena in the mind/brain as we saw Chomsky apparently wants to do, one might well wonder what it would *be* to perform an operation, such as 'concatenate' or, more recently, 'move', on such phenomena *themselves*. Are we to understand such operations as literally *concatenating, merging*, or *moving* these very features *in the mind/brain*? Perhaps; but surely linguistic theory should not be *committed* to any such literal interpretation. Linguists may talk about concatenating and moving features, and there is usually no harm in it, any more than there is harm in mathematicians talking about 'computations on numbers'. But, *if it matters, numbers* are not strictly what are involved in mathematical computations; rather, it is *numerals*, i.e. *representations* of numbers (which is why there can be perfectly well-defined but *non-computable* functions). Or, consider again the cognizing missile 'that incorporates an explicit theory of the motions of the heavenly bodies . . . and that carries out measurements and computations using its internalized theory to adjust its course' (1980a: 103; see Section 3.1 above): surely the only way such a missile could 'incorporate a theory' and carry out computations with it is by *representing* it. Otherwise, how on earth does the thing work? What other kind of 'incorporation' is there?

Similarly then: when 'two phones are concatenated', or 'a feature is moved', surely what this should be taken to mean is merely that:

> *A representation that assigns a feature to one location is revised or replaced by a representation that assigns it to a different one,*

rather in the way the moves of a possible chess game could be described as '1. P–K4, P–K4, 2. P–Q4, P×P . . .', or an address book might indicate that someone has moved by changing the person's address entry.[42] At any rate,

---

[42] The point here can get particularly confusing when the intentional contents are themselves syntactic *strings*, as in *LSLT*, since *concatenation* is then involved *both* as a *represented* operation on the *object*-language items *within* that content and, perhaps, as a *real* operation on the actual *meta*linguistic representations in the mind/brain *of* that content. Even more confusingly, one might even use the real operation to represent the result of performing the represented operation on represented items: for example, one might actually concatenate 'a' with 'b', creating 'ab', to represent the content {'aˆb'}. I think this may be what led Chomsky in *LSLT* (p. 69) to read 'Δ' as 'represent' (see sect. 4.2 above), since in this sort of case the very structure of the representation could indeed

this is a literally intelligible suggestion (and, along the lines of CRTT, an independently plausible one), in a way that talk of *moving features themselves* is not—at least not until someone says something further about just what other sorts of 'computations' or 'derivations' are on offer.[43] If Chomsky does have some further, non-Turing conception of a *computational process* in mind, it would be great to hear all about it. But until we do, it is certainly reasonable to go with the only general theory of such processes anyone has ever developed, one, again, that seems to afford the promise of an answer to the question of how any physical system, biological or otherwise, could be sensitive to the range of non-local or non-physical properties mentioned in linguistics.

In short: we need the phones in the mouth to explain their physical characteristics; we need their representations in the brain to explain their computational/derivational ones. The very different roles these items play in their respective domains bar them from being the same items in both cases. Yet they are obviously intimately related. Representation seems to be the only way we have of thinking of that relation, at least for the nonce. It brings together the way phones and other linguistic phenomena can cause speech *perceptions* and acquisition, be the *intended result* of speech *acts*, and generally be integrated into the rest of a person's cognitive life, giving rise, for example, to the very 'linguistic intuitions' on which so much of linguistic

be regarded as 'providing the information used by the sensorimotor apparatus and other systems of language use' (2000: 173). It also may be yet another source of the temptation to collapse the distinction between a linguistic feature and a representation of it that I discussed in sect. 4.2 above.

[43] When pressed about this issue, some linguists have replied to me that Chomsky has a 'different notion of computation in mind'. Juan Uriagereka has suggested, for example, that what Chomsky intends is more along the lines of computational models in biology. This will not do. So far as I am aware, 'computational models' in biology consist in *modelling* some biological process by a computational one. For example, one might model processes of natural selection, as in, e.g. Dawkins (1996), 30–72. But this is simply the *theoretical biologist's tool*; it is *not* claimed that those computations and codings are themselves 'biologically real' in the sense that the species (or the individuals, or their DNA) are *themselves* doing computations. As Dawkins notes: 'The fact that a fly is more valuable to an empty spider than to a full one needs no imported computation' (p. 68). One needs to distinguish *a computational model of a process* from *a model of a computational process*. The latter does not follow from the former. One can computationally model almost *any* physical process (e.g. even a 'non-cognizing missile'); but this surely does not entail that all such physical processes are *computational* (like those in a 'cognizing' one).

theory rests. And since, as Chomsky likes to stress, these representations can and do regularly occur in the *absence* of the phones or other represented phenomena, the linguistic use of 'representation' is *purely intentional* (in the sense of Sections 2.2 and 4.1 above). Consequently, linguistic theory would seem to be about the *purely intentional content* of a speaker/hearer's representations of linguistic phenomena, QED.

Despite his avowed anti-intentionalism, this conclusion is really not any different from how Chomsky himself often spontaneously characterizes the subject matter of linguistics, both early and late: for example, as various computational procedures defined over representations classified according to 'the complete information as to the structure of [an] utterance' (*LSLT* 159), e.g. 'the information used by the sensori-motor apparatus and other systems of language use' (2000: 173). For what else is 'information' other than intentional content, i.e. what is 'represented' by a 'description of some utterance, recorded or unrecorded' (*LSLT* 159)? Linguistic theory is in this respect no different from theories of vision, like Marr's (1982), which also (at its 'computational' level) characterize the performance of the system 'as a mapping of one kind on *information* to another' (Marr 1982: 24), and so might speak of such things as the 'mental image of a rotating cube, even when there is no cube'—i.e. of a mental representation having {rotating cube} as its content. Indeed, it is quite like the theory Chomsky credits to his cognizing missile, which would certainly have to assign to the missile *representations with the contents* of 'an explicit theory of the heavenly bodies' (even if the theory were completely false).[44] And, of course, intentionalism here permits Kenstowicz's (1994) observation (see Section 4.3 above) that the '*same* lexical item' can have '*different* internal representations'.

Why, then, do linguists not use my curly brackets, or some other indication of the merely intentional status of the entities they study? *Because it does not matter one whit for the vast majority of their work. It only matters when someone like Chomsky goes out of his way to deny that intentionality does in fact play any serious role in the theory.* So long as such gauntlets are not

---

[44] Indeed, I suspect the moral here is quite general, and that disregard of it pervades many of the claims about 'mental imagery' and 'mental models' of reasoning and discourse, which too often are presented as claims about the structure of mental *representation*, when in fact they are simply claims about the structure of *the representation's intentional content*. But this is a topic for another day.

being hurled onto the table, working linguists should no more bother with noting these intentional contents as such than working mathematicians should bother noting when they are talking about numbers vs. numerals, or working logicians should always keep use/mention straight. But in fact ordinary English seems to provide a perfectly good idiom for talking about intentional contents: the very intentional idioms we use, which allow us to speak of representations of things that may not exist. That is: the very abundant intentionalist talk that I have quoted from both Chomsky and other linguists is just fine as it is. All I am resisting is Chomsky's recent refusal to take this talk at face value.[45]

# REFERENCES

ANTONY, L., and HORNSTEIN, N., eds. (2003), *Chomsky and his Critics* (Oxford: Blackwell).

BLOCK, N. (1986), 'Advertisement for a Semantics for Psychology', in French, Euhling, and Wettstein (1986), 615–78.

BRENTANO, F. (1874), *Psychology from an Empirical Standpoint*, trans. by A. Rancurello, D. Terrell, and L. McAlister (London: Routledge and Kegan Paul, 1973).

BROMBERGER, S., ed. (1992), *On What We Know We Don't Know* (Chicago: University of Chicago Press).

—— and HALLE, M. (1989), 'Why Phonology Is Different', *Linguistic Inquiry*, 20: 51–70.

—— —— (1992), 'The Ontology of Phonology', in Bromberger (1992), 209–28.

—— —— (1996), 'The Content of Phonological Signs' (manuscript, MIT).

BURGE, T. (1986), 'Individualism and Psychology', *Philosophical Review*, 95: 3–46.

CHOMSKY, N. (1965), *Aspects of the Theory of Syntax* (Cambridge, Mass.: MIT Press).

—— (1969), Comments on Harman's Reply, in Hook (1969), 152–60.

---

[45] Which is not to say there might not be any number of further reasons to think that some specific categories, rules, principles are not represented. I take it that recent discussions of more purely 'derivationalist' approaches within the minimalist programme want to dispense with *certain levels* of representation (see Uriagereka 1998: 159–60, 583); and, of course, there have been ongoing controversies about whether grammatical *rules and principles* need to be explicitly represented (see Stabler 1983; Devitt, this volume). I have been concerned here only with the ways in which the issue of representation and intentional content begin to be raised *in any way* within linguistic theory.

CHOMSKY, N. (1972), *Language and Mind* (New York: Harcourt, Brace and World).

—— (1975*a*), *The Logical Structure of Linguistic Theory* (New York: Plenum Press).

—— (1975*b*), introduction to Chomsky (1975*a*).

—— (1975*c*), *Reflections on Language* (New York: Pantheon).

—— (1977), *Essays on Form and Interpretation* (Amsterdam: Elsevier North-Holland).

—— (1980*a*), *Rules and Representations* (New York: Columbia University Press).

—— (1980*b*), Précis of *Rules and Representations* with Replies to commentators, *Behavioral and Brain Sciences*, 3: 1–61.

—— (1981), *Lectures on Government and Binding* (Dordrecht: Foris).

—— (1986), *Knowledge of Language* (New York: Praeger).

—— (1993), *Language and Thought* (London: Moyer Bell).

—— (1994), entry on (and by) 'Chomsky', in *Blackwell's Companion to Philosophy* (Oxford: Blackwell), 153–67.

—— (1995*a*), 'Language and Nature', *Mind*, 104: 1–61.

—— (1995*b*), *The Minimalist Program* (Cambridge, Mass.: MIT Press).

—— (1996), *Powers and Prospects* (Boston; South End Press).

—— (2000), *New Horizons in the Study of Language* (Cambridge: Cambridge University Press).

—— (2003): 'Reply to Rey', in Antony and Hornstein (2003), 274–87.

—— and HALLE, M. (1968), *The Sound Pattern of English* (New York: Harper and Row).

DAVIDSON, D., and HARMAN, G., eds., *Semantics of Natural Language* (Boston: Reidel).

DAWKINS, R. (1996), *Climbing Mount Improbable* (New York: W. W. Norton & Co.).

DEVITT, M. (1996), *Coming to Our Senses* (Cambridge: Cambridge University Press).

DRETSKE, F. (1988), *Explaining Behavior: Reasons in a World of Causes* (Cambridge, Mass.: MIT Press).

FODOR, J. A. (1975), *The Language of Thought* (New York: Crowell).

—— (1983), *Modularity of Mind* (Cambridge, Mass.: MIT Press).

—— (1986), 'Why Paramecia Don't Have Mental States', *Midwest Studies in Philosophy*, 10: 3–24.

—— (1987), *Psychosemantics* (Cambridge, Mass.: MIT Press).

—— (1990), *A Theory of Content and Other Essays* (Cambridge, Mass.: MIT Press).

—— (1998), *Concepts: Where Cognitive Science Went Wrong* (Cambridge, Mass.: MIT Press).

—— (2001), *The Mind Doesn't Work That Way* (Cambridge, Mass.: MIT Press).

FODOR, J. D. (1998), 'Parsing to Learn', *Journal of Psycholinguistic Research*, 27: 339–74.

FRENCH, P., EUHLING, T., and WETTSTEIN, H., eds. (1986), *Studies in the Philosophy of Mind* (Midwest Studies in Philosophy, 10; Minneapolis: University of Minnesota Press).

GALLISTEL, C. (1990), *The Organization of Learning* (Cambridge, Mass.: MIT Press).

GILLET, C., and LOEWER, B., eds. (2002), *Physicalism and its Discontents* (Cambridge: Cambridge University Press).

GOODMAN, N. (1949), 'On Likeness of Meaning', *Analysis*, 10: 1–7.

GROENENDIJK, J., JANSSEN, T., and STOKHOF, M., eds. (1981), *Formal Methods in the Study of Language* (Amsterdam: Mathematical Centre Tracts).

HALLE, M. (1983), 'On Distinctive Features and their Articulatory Implementation', *Natural Language and Linguistic Theory*, 1: 91–105.

HEIM, I. (1982), 'The Semantics of Definite and Indefinite Noun Phrases' (diss. Ph.D., University of Massachusetts, Amherst).

HOOK, S., ed. (1969), *Language and Philosophy* (New York: New York University Press).

KAMP, H. (1981), 'A Theory of Truth and Semantic Representation', in Groenendijk, Janssen, and Stokhof (1981), 277–322.

KATZ, J. J. (1981), *Language and Other Abstract Objects* (Totowa, NJ: Rowman and Littlefield).

KEMMERLING, A. (1996), *Ideen des Ichs: Studien zu Descartes' Philosophie* (Frankfurt a.M.: Suhrkamp).

KENSTOWICZ, M. (1994), *Phonology in Generative Grammar* (Cambridge, Mass.: Blackwell).

KOSSLYN, S. (1980), *Image and Mind* (Cambridge, Mass.: Harvard University Press).

LEWIS, D. (1972), 'General Semantics', in Davidson and Harman (1972), 169–218.

LYCAN, W. (1987), *Consciousness* (Cambridge, Mass.: MIT Press).

McGILVRAY, J. (2000), *Chomsky: Language, Mind and Politics* (Oxford: Blackwell).

MALMKJAER, K. (1991), *The Linguistics Encyclopedia* (London: Routledege).

MARR, D. (1982), *Vision* (Cambridge, Mass.: MIT Press).

MATTHEWS, R. (1980), 'Language Learning *versus* Grammar Growth', *Behavioral and Brain Sciences*, 3: 25–6.

OSHERSON, D. (1995–8), *An Invitation to Cognitive Science* (4 vols.; Cambridge, Mass.: MIT Press).

PEACOCKE, C. (1992), *A Study of Concepts* (Cambridge, Mass.: MIT Press).

PRINCE, A., and SMOLENSKY, P. (forthcoming), *Optimality Theory: Constraint Interaction in Generative Grammar* (Cambridge, Mass.: MIT Press).

PUTNAM, H. (1975), 'The Meaning of "Meaning"', in *Philosophical Papers*, ii. *Mind, Language and Reality* (Cambridge: Cambridge University Press), 215–71.

PYLYSHYN, Z. (1984), *Computation and Cognition: Toward a Foundation for Cognitive Science* (Cambridge, Mass.: MIT Press).

QUINE, W. (1965), *Mathematical Logic*, rev. edn. (Cambridge, Mass.: Harvard University Press; 1st edn. 1940).

—— (1953), *From a Logical Point of View and Other Essays* (New York: Harper and Row).

—— (1960), *Word and Object* (Cambridge, Mass.: MIT Press).

RÉCANATI, F. (1993), *Direct Reference: From Language to Thought* (Oxford: Blackwell).

REY, G. (1997), *Contemporary Philosophy of Mind: A Contentiously Classical Approach* (Oxford: Blackwell).

—— (1998), 'A Narrow Representational Account of Qualitative Experience', in Tomberlin (1998), 435–57.

—— (2002), 'Physicalism and Psychology: A Plea for a Substantive Philosophy of Mind', in Gillet and Loewer (2002), 99–128.

—— (2003), 'Chomsky, Intentionality and a CRTT', in Antony and Hornstein (2003), 105–39.

SEGAL, G. (2000), *A Thin Book about Narrow Content* (Cambridge, Mass.: MIT Press).

STABLER, E. (1983), 'How are Grammars Represented?', *Behavioral and Brain Sciences*, 3: 291–421.

STICH, S. (1983), *From Folk Psychology to Cognitive Science* (Cambridge, Mass.: MIT Press).

TOMBERLIN, J., ed. (1998), *Language, Mind and Ontology* (Philosophical Perspectives, 12; Atascadero: Ridgeview).

URIAGEREKA, J. (1998), *Rhyme and Reason* (Cambridge, Mass.: MIT Press).

WENG, J., McCLELLAND, J., PENTLAND, A., SPORNS, O., STOCKMAN, I., SUR, M., and THELAN, E. (2001), 'Autonomous Mental Development by Robots and Animals', *Science*, 291: 599–600.

WHITE, S. (1982), 'Partial Character and the Language of Thought', *Pacific Philosophical Quarterly*, 63: 347–65.

YOLTON, J. (1994), *Perceptual Acquaintance* (Minneapolis: University of Minnesota Press).

# CHAPTER 6

# Does Linguistic Competence Require Knowledge of Language?

*Robert J. Matthews*

## 1 Introduction

Among the most basic tenets of modern linguistic theory are the claims that competence in speaking and understanding a natural language requires knowledge of that language, that such knowledge is propositional in nature, and that it is the task of linguistic theory to characterize this propositional knowledge. More than a few philosophers have challenged these three tenets. They argue either that what linguists call 'knowledge' of language does not deserve the name, or if it does, then ordinary speakers do not have it, or if they do have it, then they do not use it, or if they do use it, then it is not propositional, or if it is propositional and speakers do use it, then at least such knowledge is not what linguistic theory in fact characterizes. So in one way or another, linguists are mistaken in their basic supposition that linguistic competence requires knowledge of language of a sort that a linguistic theory might characterize.

The ongoing debate over this basic supposition would be of little theoretical interest to philosophers of language or linguists if the issue were simply whether what linguists call 'knowledge' of language fits some definition of the term currently favoured by epistemologists. For clearly such 'knowledge' differs from many other informational states that are commonly so labelled. For example, most speakers do not have conscious access to the rules and principles that they are said by linguists to know. Nor, in most

This paper has benefited from the comments and criticisms of a number of people, most notably Alex Barber, Michael Devitt, Frances Egan, Kent Johnson, and Paul Pietroski.

cases, is their knowledge of language inferentially involved with any conscious knowledge of speakers, except perhaps such knowledge of language,
e.g. of meaning or of syntactic acceptability, as knowledge of these postulated rules and principles is intended to explain. Nor do most speakers
appear to possess the concepts that such knowledge would presumably
require. It is for such reasons as these that Noam Chomsky has long been
willing to concede to critics the notion of 'knowing' a language in favour of
'cognizing' a language, where the latter is understood as an informational
state, specifically a propositional attitude, that is stripped of just those features that render contentious claims by linguists to the effect that speakers
know the rules and principles postulated by linguistic theory.

But terminological issues aside, there remain at least two substantive
questions that deserve careful examination. First, there is the question of
the truth (or at least, plausibility) of the supposition that language understanding *requires* 'knowledge' of language of a sort that a linguistic theory
might characterize. Second, there is the question of the role, if any, that a
causal account of language understanding would attribute to such 'knowledge'. In this paper I examine both of these questions, focusing primarily
on semantics. I shall argue that an influential argument by Stephen Schiffer
(1987; 1995) and Jerry Fodor (1990) fails to establish what it claims to establish, namely, that language understanding does not require knowledge
of a semantic theory for the language understood. I shall also suggest a
computational construal of the semantic knowledge that a semantic theory
might characterize, one which attributes to such knowledge a specific causal
role in language understanding. The proposed construal will, I hope, raise
doubts as to whether it is really possible that ordinary speakers might be
ignorant of language, viz. might lack knowledge of a semantic theory, and
yet none the less be competent in their use of language.

## 2 Linguistic Competence Requires Knowledge of Language: The Received View

Linguists often defend the supposition that linguistic competence requires
knowledge of language by offering the following account, which I shall dub
the 'Received View', of the presumed causal role of such knowledge in exercises of linguistic competence: knowing a language is a matter of knowing

the system of rules and principles that is the grammar for that language. To have such knowledge is to have an explicit internal representation of these rules and principles, which speakers use in the course of language production and understanding.[1] On the Received View, linguistic theory does not provide a model of language use; however, models of language use, it is assumed, will incorporate these explicit representations of the rules and principles that are constitutive of a speaker's linguistic competence.[2] The details of how these knowledge representations are incorporated, as a basic component, in a processing model are never spelt out, but clearly it is envisaged that such representations will figure causally in language processing (see e.g. Fodor 1981). Proponents of the Received View often describe the causal processes that allegedly make use of these knowledge representations in computational terms: they speak of mental computations involving grammatical rules and principles and of the role of these computations in the aetiology of linguistic behaviour.

The Received View provides support for the supposition that linguistic competence requires knowledge of language of a sort that linguistic theory might characterize by sketching an empirical account of language processing according to which explicit representations of such knowledge play a causal role in language processing. But the Received View is vulnerable to a number of well-known criticisms, any of which might undercut any support for this supposition that the view might provide.

Early criticisms of the Received View focused on the claim that speakers *know* the rules and principles of the grammar of their language. Critics conceded that speakers know certain facts about their language, e.g. that *Boy over fence jumped* is ungrammatical (or at least unacceptable), that the proper names in *John shaved John* cannot corefer, that *It's raining* is true if

---

[1] Cf. Chomsky (1980), 201: 'The systems of rules and principles that we assume have, in some manner, been internally represented by the speaker who knows a language . . . enable the speaker, in principle, to understand an arbitrary sentence and to produce a sentence expressing this thought.'

[2] Cf. Chomsky (1965), 9: 'A generative grammar is not a model for a speaker or hearer. It attempts to characterize in the most neutral possible terms the knowledge of the language that provides the basis for actual use of language by a speaker-hearer. . . . No doubt, a reasonable model of language use will incorporate, as a basic component, the generative grammar that expresses the speaker-hearer's knowledge of the language; but this generative grammar does not, in itself, prescribe the functioning of a perceptual model of speech production.'

and only if it is raining, and so on. But they denied that speakers know certain linguistic rules and principles that entail these facts, and for rather predictable reasons, e.g. that such rules and principles are not accessible to consciousness, that speakers lack the relevant concepts, and so on. Proponents of the Received View responded by conceding in effect that speakers did not know the rules and principles of the grammar in the full-blooded sense of that term. Speakers, they admitted, had only 'tacit knowledge' of the rules and principles. Or, as Chomsky would put it, they only 'cognized' them. In effect, proponents conceded that speakers' grasp of the rules and principles was subdoxastic. But they nevertheless insisted that what these speakers grasped was a propositional content, so that what they had initially described as 'knowing' the rules and principles of their language still turned out to be a matter of having a propositional attitude towards those rules and principles, and hence such 'knowledge' could, like other propositional attitudes, be causally efficacious in the production of behaviour.

The argument for the claim that speakers tacitly know (or cognize) the rules and principles of their language is perhaps most explicit in the early paper of Graves *et al.* (1973). This argument held that intentional explananda demanded for their explanation intentional explanantia, so that only another propositional attitude could explain (in Hempel's deductive-nomological sense of that term) such uncontroversial knowledge of language as even critics of the Received View were willing to concede. The argument is, as Egan (1995) has argued, clearly unsound, entailing as it does the impossibility of intertheoretic, reductive explanations, but it none the less offered proponents of the Received View what they needed for their account of the causal role of knowledge of language in language production and understanding, namely, a justification for assuming that knowing a language was a matter of having a propositional attitude towards the grammar of that language. By preserving this assumption, proponents were able to preserve the intentional explanations that they favoured—a kind of explanation that might be dubbed 'explanation by intentional attribution'.

But there was still a problem. Arguably, such explanations might be able to explain, in the nomological-deductive sense of that term, the uncontentious knowledge of language that virtually all parties to the debate were prepared to concede to speakers—viz. the knowledge expressed by speakers' intuitions. But it was unclear whether such explanations were genuinely causal, and hence whether appeals to speakers' knowledge of language, tacit or otherwise, could find any place in a causal account of language production and understanding, and thereby give substance to the claim that linguistic competence requires knowledge (or tacit knowledge) of the rules and principles of language. What was needed was a causal construal of the relevant propositional attitudes that established their causal bona fides. Proponents of the Received View such as Evans (1981), Davies (1987), Peacocke (1986, 1989), and Larson and Segal (1995) attempted to provide a causal construal of tacitly knowing a semantic theory for one's language. The worries that their proposed construals were intended to address have nothing in particular to do with the fact that tacit knowledge of language is subdoxastic; similar worries would also arise for someone prepared to argue that knowing a language was a matter of knowing such a theory, in the full-blooded sense of that term (whatever that is). Nor do the worries have anything in particular to do with semantics. The same worries could also have been raised about tacitly knowing the rules and principles of syntax or phonology.

Proponents of the Received View offered two different sorts of causal construal of tacitly knowing a semantic theory: one dispositional, the other representationalist.[3] Dispositional construals, such as the one proposed by Evans (1981), held that to tacitly know a semantic theory is to tacitly know the theory's axioms, where to tacitly know such an axiom is at least to have a disposition to understand utterances containing the term mentioned in the axiom in accordance with the truth conditions assigned by the axiom (in conjunction with the other axioms of the theory). Moreover, tacit knowledge, as Evans construes it, requires that every axiom have a causal counterpart that underpins the aforementioned disposition to understand utterances in the way that the semantic theory's T-sentences specify. The proposed construal thus presumes that the axioms' causal counterparts will compose causally in a way parallel to the way that the corresponding axioms compose inferentially, yielding for every sentence of the language a disposition to understand the sentence as having the meaning or the truth conditions specified by the semantic theory.

The problem is that there is as yet no reason to suppose that the causal counterparts associated with the axioms will so compose. And even if they did, which arguably they could be made to do over very simple domains,

---

[3] For a useful discussion, see Barber (2002).

there is, as Wright (1986) argues, no reason to suppose that the semantic axioms, as opposed to their causal counterparts, are doing any real work here in explaining linguistic competence. The semantic theory looks to be idle.

Representationalist construals, such as that proposed by Peacocke (1986; 1989), are arguably more plausible. They propose to associate with every tacitly known axiom of semantic theory an explicit mental representation of that axiom. In effect, these construals are simply a particular application of Fodor's so-called Representational Theory of Mind, according to which having a certain attitude to a proposition is just a matter of bearing a certain computational relation to a mental representation that expresses that proposition. The postulated mental representations of semantic axioms are said to be consulted in the course of the computational processing that eventuates in the production or understanding of utterances. The computational operations that are defined over these representations are postulated to be inferential, so that language processing turns out to be a species of theorem-proving that effects a pairing of utterances in a natural language with a mental representation of their contents.

Proposed representationalist construals of tacit knowledge of semantic theory do not appear vulnerable to the objections raised against dispositional construals. The mentally represented axioms will compose in just the manner that the semantic theory demands, thus imputing to language understanding just the compositionality that the semantic theory imputes to the language being understood. Nor are such construals vulnerable to Wright's objection that the axioms are explanatorily otiose, for mentally represented tokens of the axioms themselves are assumed to be causally implicated in language processing. Nevertheless, there is, as critics were quick to point out, a price to be paid. On the one hand, representationalist construals assume that natural-language semantics is compositional, an assumption that has been sharply criticized by Schiffer (1987) and others. On the other hand, such construals assume without empirical justification that speakers' tacit knowledge of language is explicitly represented, something that may well not be the case, especially if, as connectionists would have it, human computational architecture is non-classical (in the sense of not being what Newell (1980) termed a 'physical symbol system'). Failure of natural language to have a compositional semantics would be deadly to the proposed construal, while failure of the axioms to be explicitly represented would leave representationalists without any account of how knowledge of language, tacit or otherwise, specifically knowledge of the axioms of semantic theory, is causally efficacious in language processing.

## 3  Can Competent Speakers be Ignorant of Language?

The Received View offers an account of linguistic competence according to which knowledge of language, or at least tacit knowledge of language, is a central causal component in exercises of linguistic competence. But even leaving aside any problems with the account, it does not establish that language understanding actually *requires* such knowledge. Several philosophers, notably Michael Devitt, Jerry Fodor, and Stephen Schiffer, have seized on just this point, arguing that it is possible that linguistically competent speakers have no knowledge whatever of their language, or at least no knowledge of the semantics of their language. Devitt (2000) argues the general claim that speakers can be linguistically competent yet completely ignorant of language, at least ignorant of the rules and principles that linguistic theory attributes to speakers. Fodor (1990) and Schiffer (1987; 1995) argue that speakers can be linguistically competent yet not know a semantic theory for their language. Devitt's arguments are grounded in his conviction that linguistic theory is not about what many linguists take it to be about, namely, the linguistic competence of speakers, but is rather about the products of such competence. The arguments of Fodor and Schiffer, on the other hand, are grounded in a conception of language understanding which, they believe, does not require knowledge of semantic theory. I shall focus on the latter arguments, though some of what I have to say by way of criticism of these arguments will bear on Devitt's argument as well.

The claim that speakers can be linguistically competent yet lack knowledge of semantic theory is, strictly speaking, consistent with the empirical account of language processing offered by proponents of the Received View. The latter claims that knowledge of language, specifically knowledge of a semantic theory of a language, is, as a matter of empirical fact, a crucial causal constituent of linguistic competence, whereas the former claims simply that such knowledge is not necessary for such competence. Fodor and Schiffer's argument in support of this claim is simply that rather than using

his knowledge of semantic theory to determine what a speaker said in uttering a sentence, a hearer—'Harvey', as Schiffer dubs him—might instead
rely on a 'translation manual' that maps whatever the speaker is heard to
say into knowledge of what that speaker said. As Schiffer puts it:

It's at least *possible* that we're built like Harvey and arrive at our knowledge of
what was said via processing that uses not an internally represented compositional semantics but rather an internally represented *translation manual* that
correlates sentences of one's public language with content-equivalent mental
representations.

. . . For all we know, language processing—the processing that takes us from
perceptions of utterances to knowledge of what propositional speech acts were
performed in those utterances—works in Harvey's wholly syntactic way. (Schiffer
1995: 2–3)

Or as Fodor puts it in his review of Schiffer (1987):

It is very widely assumed, among cognitive scientists at least, that semantics
is *a level of linguistic description*, just like syntax or phonology; specifically, that
the same sorts of arguments that suggest that speaker-hearers have to know the
syntax of their language also suggest that they have to know its semantics. . . . But
in fact this is all wrong. . . . It's entirely natural to run a computational story about
the attitudes together with a translation story about language comprehension;
and there's no reason to doubt, so far at least, that the sort of translation that's
required is an exhaustively syntactic operation. That you know the semantics of
your language *does not follow* from the fact that you can understand the indefinitely
many sentences of your language; it doesn't follow even by argument to the best
explanation. . . .

There is, in short, a way of developing the computational picture in philosophy
of mind that suggests much the same moral as recent 'externalist' speculations
in philosophy of language: Syntax is about what's in your head, but semantics is
about how your head is connected to the world. Syntax is part of the story about
the mental representation of sentences, but semantics isn't. (Fodor 1990: 187)

Whether hearers do *in fact* rely on such a wholly syntactic procedure is not
at issue here. Schiffer's and Fodor's claim is that hearers *could* rely on such
a procedure, and given that they could, language understanding does not,
as many have assumed, require knowledge of a semantic theory.

Proponents of the Received View are unlikely to be at all moved by these
speculations. Even if Fodor and Schiffer are right that language understand-

ing does not require knowledge of a semantic theory, if such knowledge is, as a matter of empirical fact, a crucial causal constituent of linguistic competence, then claims both for the role of such knowledge in language understanding and for the psychological import of semantic theory will have been vindicated. It will be of little consequence that knowledge of semantic theory *might* have been irrelevant, if in point of fact it is not. If Fodor and Schiffer are going to make the case against the claim that knowledge of semantic theory plays a role in language understanding, then they are going to have to make a case for the stronger claim that semantic knowledge, specifically knowledge of semantic theory, is *in fact* not used in the course of language processing. But, so far as I can see, they offer no argument or, more pertinently, no empirical evidence for this stronger claim. Certainly they do not have a candidate translation theory, which, one would have thought, is precisely what they need.

In his defence of the counter-claim that there must be, as he puts it, 'some sort of epistemic/psychological/doxastic relationship towards semantic information that stands between the heard utterance and the acquired belief about what is said', Lepore (1997: 54) takes Fodor and Schiffer to be arguing for the stronger, empirical claim that hearers do not in fact make use of semantic knowledge. He describes them as offering 'an *account* [my emphasis] of language understanding that *excludes* metalinguistic (semantic) knowledge, and therefore knowledge of semantic *theory*' (p. 41), as denying that 'knowledge (or any other kind of epistemic/doxastic/psychological attitude) about the semantics of one's spoken language is causally relevant' (p. 42). Now, there is textual support for Lepore's imputing to both Fodor and Schiffer the stronger claim that knowledge of semantic theory in fact plays no causal role in language understanding. But none of the arguments that Fodor and Schiffer adduce actually bears on this stronger claim; rather their arguments bear only on the weaker claim, which is fully compatible with the empirical claim that Lepore and many other semanticists want to defend. So let us consider Schiffer's argument, which Fodor endorses, for the weaker of the two claims, namely, that language understanding *might* not require semantic knowledge.

Schiffer, we have seen, argues that what learners acquire when they acquire a natural language is the productive capacity to map what is heard onto what is said, where the capacity so acquired is a capacity the exercise of which does not require recourse to knowledge of a semantic theory. Rather the mapping of what is heard onto what is said might, as he puts it, be effected 'in a wholly syntactic way'. If Schiffer is right, then competent speakers might in fact know that the utterance *It's raining* means that it is raining (or, is true if and only if it is raining), but nevertheless not rely on such knowledge in language understanding. Such knowledge as speakers have might very well be a product of the envisaged translation procedure rather than a causal constituent of it.

Let us consider just how this imagined translation procedure is supposed to work. A speaker utters the English sentence *It's raining*, and I, a competent speaker of English who hears this utterance, form the belief that this speaker said that it is raining. How am I able to perform this feat? According to Schiffer, it is because I have acquired (and am able to compute) a recursive function, call it $f$, that takes as arguments mental representations of the contents of my beliefs as to what words or sentences I heard uttered and delivers as values mental representations that will be for me the contents of beliefs as to what the speaker said in uttering what I believe him to have uttered.

More expansively, Schiffer imagines the procedure to work as follows: when I hear someone utter a sentence of English, say *It's raining*, my perceptual mechanisms grind a bit and then drop a mental sentence with the content ⟨he said, 'It's raining'⟩ into what language-of-thought theorists picturesquely call my 'belief box'. The translation module in my head, the one for English that computes $f$, takes this mental sentence as its argument and delivers back to my belief box a second mental sentence, viz. one with the content ⟨the speaker said that it is raining⟩, which is the value of the function for that argument.[4] (Schiffer sometimes describes the function as returning a mental sentence with a more complex content, viz. with the content ⟨the speaker said that it is raining, and consequently the speaker's utterance is true just in case it is raining⟩, in which case the speaker comes to have a belief not only about what was said but also about the truth conditions of the utterance.)

---

[4] Or as Schiffer elsewhere puts it, 'Harvey works in the following way. His internally represented translation manual determines a function that maps each English sentence onto its Mentalese synonym, and he is so "programmed" that when he has an auditory perception of an utterance of a, then straight-away there enters his belief box the Mentalese translation of "The speaker in uttering 'a' said that a"' (1993: 244).

Schiffer and Fodor claim that the computations performed by the imagined translation module that implements *f could be* wholly syntactic and not at all semantic. But on what basis do they conclude this? Schiffer, for his part, rests his conclusion on the possibility, or at least the conceivability, of what he assumes would be a wholly syntactic translation procedure, viz. one that implements the recursive function *f*. (Schiffer, it should be noted, does not attempt to prove that there exists such a function; rather he simply stipulates its existence.) Fodor, on the other hand, seemingly rests his conclusion on the claim that the computations in question could *not* possibly be semantic. What Fodor says (1990: 187), we recall, is this: 'Syntax is about what's in your head, but semantics is about how your head is connected to the rest of the world. Syntax is part of the story about the mental representation of sentences, but semantics isn't.' The reasoning here *seems* to be that knowledge of a semantic theory could not possibly play a causal role in language understanding because such knowledge is not about what is in your head. But if this is Fodor's argument, it is a very curious argument indeed. For we have all sorts of knowledge that is not about what is in our heads, and yet such knowledge routinely plays a causal role in all sorts of transactions with the world. Why should language understanding be any different? And doubly so for Fodor, given that for him, the representations of semantic knowledge would still be in one's head, irrespective of their content, and hence would be capable of being causally efficacious.

Perhaps what Fodor has in mind here is a somewhat different argument, viz. one to the effect that semantics could not play a causal role in language understanding since the computations in question, like all computations, are sensitive only to the formal, i.e. 'syntactic', properties of the mental representations over which computations are defined. But surely this argument cannot be correct either, since by this criterion, all computations of any sort, including those, for example, in the visual system that compute three-dimensional structure from motion, would turn out to be syntactic, since by definition all computations are purely formal operations. Computational processes may be purely formal (and in this sense 'syntactic'), but they can nevertheless be computations of all sorts of different functions, over all sorts of different domains (including semantic ones). No one need doubt that if semantic knowledge is causally efficacious in language understanding, then it is so in virtue of the formal, i.e. 'syntactic', properties of the mental representations of this knowledge, without thereby having to conclude that such knowledge cannot therefore be semantic, i.e. cannot be knowledge of a semantic theory.

Fodor's remark about how syntax is about what is in your head, whereas semantics is not, as well as his remark in the earlier, longer quotation about how semantics is not a level of linguistic description, raises an interesting question: what is to prevent an extension of Schiffer's Harvey argument to *syntactic* knowledge? In other words, why would there not be a similar argument to the effect that language understanding does not require knowledge of a syntactic theory either? Language understanding, it is widely assumed, involves the recovery and representation for later use of the syntactic structural descriptions associated with the uttered sentence (or phrase). Such recovery and representation, it is widely assumed, requires knowledge of a syntactic theory. So let us imagine, following Schiffer's story for semantics, that upon hearing an utterance of some English sentence $S$, Harvey drops a Mentalese sentence having the content $\langle S$ has associated syntactic structural descriptions $\langle d_1, d_2, \ldots \rangle\rangle$ into his belief box. Now why does Harvey need any knowledge of English syntax to do this? Why could he not simply compute a recursive function, call it $f^*$, that takes a Mentalese sentence to the effect that the speaker uttered a certain sentence as its argument and returns a Mentalese sentence having the content just described as its value? As far as I can see, if Harvey can do it in the case of semantics, then for all Schiffer has said, Harvey ought also to be able to do it for syntax. The two cases seem perfectly analogous.

Now perhaps Schiffer and Fodor would argue that the two cases are not analogous, that Harvey could not do the same sort of thing in the case of syntax, because *by stipulation* Harvey works in a 'wholly syntactic way'. But this response will not do, because for all that we have been told, it may rest on the equivocation noted above between 'syntactic' understood as meaning having to do with the syntax of the natural language being understood, and 'syntactic' understood as meaning purely formal. Harvey may work in a wholly syntactic way, i.e. in a purely formal way; indeed he had better work in this way if his mental processes are, as Schiffer assumes, computational. But nothing so far requires that in so working Harvey must know, much less make use of, the syntax of the natural language (say, English) whose sentences he translates into Mentalese. The stipulated translation function

$f$, it will be recalled, maps a Mentalese sentence that expresses a belief about what English sentence a speaker uttered into a Mentalese sentence that expresses a belief about what that speaker said. But nothing in Schiffer's story presumes any knowledge of the *syntax* of the translated language. Harvey may work in a wholly syntactic, i.e. formal, way, but nothing requires that in so working Harvey must use the syntax of the natural language that he parses. If he can none the less be said to know that syntax, it is only in virtue of his being able to compute the stipulated parsing function $f^*$ that maps a Mentalese sentence that expresses a belief about what sentence a speaker uttered into a Mentalese sentence that expresses a belief about that sentence's associated structural descriptions.

So it would seem that *if* Schiffer is right that Harvey could do without knowledge of semantics, then, for all Schiffer has said, Harvey should be able to do equally well without knowledge of syntax. So there would seem to be nothing special about knowledge of semantics that would set it apart from knowledge of syntax. But let us return to Schiffer's account of the semantics case; we shall come back to the syntax case shortly.

Schiffer stipulates that Harvey works 'in a wholly syntactic way', which he explains by saying that members of the sequence of tokened occurrences of mental formulae that would realize Harvey's comprehension process do not, as he puts it, 'presuppose', 'appeal to', or 'have access to' to a compositional semantics. Schiffer does not explain what it would be for a comprehension process to presuppose, appeal to, or have access to a compositional semantics. But the idea seems to be that if the comprehension process did, then the axioms and T-sentences of the semantic theory for the language in question would figure in the processing in much the way that they do in the formal deductive derivation of a T-sentence and, furthermore, the intermediate products of such a derivation would be explicitly represented as members of the sequence of token formulae that he assumes would realize the comprehension process. Schiffer says this about the account that a compositional semantic theorist (a 'CS theorist', for short) would give of some speaker, Harvey, coming to understand an utterance of another speaker, Carmen:

The CS theorist is evidently constrained to say that some of these formulae [in the sequence that realizes Harvey's comprehension process] represent segments of Carmen's utterance as having certain semantic values, and that, on the basis of this, and in accordance with a certain compositional semantics . . ., some formulae later in the comprehension sequence represents Carmen's entire sound sequence as having a certain semantic value. (Schiffer 1987: 195)

It is unclear why Schiffer thinks that a CS theorist should be constrained to say anything of the sort. Perhaps Schiffer supposes that in the absence of such formulae, there would be *no* reason to construe the comprehension process as 'semantics-involving' (or at least 'CS-involving'). The idea might be that such processes must have certain distinguishing features if they are to count as semantics-involving, and what Schiffer is offering here is a proposal as to the requisite nature of these features.

This much seems right: what makes a certain causal process the type of computational process that it is, e.g. semantic or syntactic, has to do with the computational interpretation that it is imposed on that process, in particular, on what is taken to be the proper computational description of its inputs and outputs, its intermediate products, if any, and its elementary computational operations. Of course, physical processes are not amenable to just any computational interpretation. The interpretation has to be reasonable, appropriate, theoretically illuminating, or sometimes just plain useful; otherwise, there would be a fortune to be made selling small rocks as hand calculators.[5] But if this is right, then to be wholly syntactic (in the linguistics sense of this term) or to be semantics-involving, the language-comprehension process, whatever that process turns out to be, must be reasonably (appropriately, illuminatingly, etc.) interpretable in those terms.

Thus, to be semantics-involving, a process must be reasonably interpretable in semantic terms. It is not obvious that to be so interpretable a process would, as Schiffer assumes, have to be prominently marked by formulae that can be interpreted as specifying the semantic values of subsentential expressions or entire sentences. It is not obvious, for example, that a semantics-involving process that pairs the English sentence *Bill jumped over the fence* with its Mentalese equivalent would have to include, within the sequence of formulae that Schiffer imagines would mediate this pairing, a formula that is interpretable as specifying the semantic value for *Bill*, viz. the formula '$SAT(x, Bill)$ iff $x = Bill$'. It might be enough that the semantic theory provides the pairing of inputs and outputs. In particular, simply

---

[5] I am thinking here of arguments by Putnam, Searle, and others to the effect that under a suitable interpretation, any object can compute any computable function.

computing Schiffer's translation function $f$ might be enough. That is to say, it might be enough for the imagined process to be semantics-involving that the stipulated function $f$ effects a pairing between utterances and mental sentences that express the content of what the speaker said (e.g. that Bill jumped over the fence), and also the fact that the utterance has the truth conditions that it does (viz. that it is true iff Bill jumped over the fence). That would be, after all, a good deal of semantically interpretable behaviour upon which to base an interpretation of the function $f$ as semantics-involving.

We can see this, I think, if we consider once again the proposed extension of Schiffer's Harvey argument to syntax. We can certainly imagine learning that there is in us a computational process which, by computing some function $f^*$, effects just the pairing of sentences with their structural descriptions specified by a syntactic theory for English. But would we conclude from this that the computed function was *not* syntax-involving? No, more likely we would conclude that describing this computational process in this way, viz. as computing the function $f^*$, is simply an alternative description of the computational implementation of a syntactic theory for English, even if it turned out that the computation of this function did not involve the computation of the intermediate products of the associated formal syntactic derivation. After all, what other explanation is there for the fact that this function's inputs and outputs can be interpreted as effecting a pairing of sentences with their structural descriptions? And what would be the point of refusing to characterize this function as syntax-involving, of refusing to count the process that computes this function as an implementation of the speaker's syntactic knowledge? Certainly natural-language parsers are *routinely* described as implementations of one or another syntactic theory, despite the fact that they do *not* incorporate an explicit representation of a grammar of the sort made available by the theory or even have as intermediate products representations that correspond to lines in a syntactic derivation of the structural descriptions using the rules and principles of the grammar.[6] The syntactic and semantic cases strike me as being both on a par.

Now, the point of trying to get clear on just what would count as a wholly syntactic process of language comprehension as opposed to one that is semantics-involving is to put us in the position of being able to ask

---

[6] For discussion see Matthews (1991) and Berwick and Weinberg (1984).

whether the so-called translation procedure that Schiffer imagines Harvey instantiating is, as Schiffer supposes, clearly *not* semantics-involving. For if it is not clearly such, then Schiffer will have failed to make a case for even the weaker claim that linguistic competence does not require semantic knowledge. But this, I want to argue, is precisely the situation. It seems to me that one can plausibly argue that the stipulated translation function $f$ that Schiffer describes as mapping heard utterances into beliefs about what is said is semantics-involving, specifically it effects the mapping specified by a semantic theory, and hence it is a computational implementation of the speaker's knowledge of a semantic theory.

Schiffer's argument for the possibility of a wholly syntactic process of language comprehension involves the stipulation (1987: 196) that there is a recursive function $f$ that is definable in terms of formal features of the expressions in its domain and range, without reference to any semantic features. But this stipulation is simply question-begging given that the function can be plausibly interpreted as computing a semantics-involving function, viz. the function specified by a semantic theory, under the quite standard assumption that such theories characterize a speaker's semantic knowledge. On this assumption, a semantic theory *minimally* specifies what a speaker knows about the pairing of utterances in his language with their meanings or truth conditions. It does this by means of the M-sentences or T-sentences which are its theoretically significant theorems (conditional, of course, on a particular assignment of referents to any terms of variable reference and on a contextual disambiguation of any syntactic or lexical ambiguities). Consider the postulated recursive function $f$. It is said to effect a pairing of representations of belief contents, specifically of contents of beliefs about what was uttered and contents of beliefs about what was said (conditional, as Schiffer himself points out, on a particular assignment of referents to any terms of variable reference and on a contextual disambiguation of any syntactic or lexical ambiguities). But where, then, is the difference that makes a difference that would preclude taking this function as semantics-involving in virtue of the fact that it computes the pairing specified by the semantic theory? The values of $f$ for the arbitrary utterances that are the function's arguments give the meaning or truth conditions of those utterances no less than do the M-sentences or T-sentences of the semantic theory. The values of this function do this because the mental representations that are these values, like their counterpart in M-sentences and T-sentences, are used rather than mentioned; moreover, they are used in a way that ensures that they give the meaning or truth conditions of utterances. It is this that explains why Schiffer himself can describe the function as returning not only a representation of the content of what the hearer believes about what the speaker said, e.g. that Carmen said that some snow is purple, but also a representation of the content of another of the hearer's beliefs, viz. that 'thus what she said, and so her utterance, is true just in case some snow is purple' (1987: 194).

If, as I am arguing, the function $f$ can be reasonably construed as effecting the pairing specified by the M-sentences or T-sentences of the semantic theory, this may not establish that the function *is* semantics-involving. But it does undercut the confident assertion that it is not. And it does therefore undercut the argument that Schiffer offers for the conclusion that linguistic competence does not require semantic knowledge, since it undermines the claim that the imagined translation procedure does not presuppose, appeal to, or have access to semantic knowledge. Schiffer's stipulation that there exists a function $f$ that computes the pairing without recourse to a semantic theory turns out to be question-begging. There is considerable room for argument regarding whether the postulated function is indeed semantics-involving, and if it is, whether the involvement is sufficient, and of the right sort, to establish that language understanding requires semantic knowledge of the sort that a semantic theory might characterize. There are obviously a number of other issues that will bear on this issue, e.g. whether, as Schiffer assumes, the language-comprehension process is realized by a sequence of token formulae that begins with a formula that represents what is heard and ends with one that represents what is said, whether the postulated function could be acquired on the basis of a learner's access to data, given plausible assumptions about the initial state of the learner, and so on. But when we start to consider all these issues, the debate quickly begins to look very much like an *empirical* dispute about which of two largely unspecified empirical theories of language comprehension is correct, which suggests that we would do well to let any discussion of possible models of language comprehension be governed by usual standards of empirical plausibility and evidence. In such an event, it seems to me that a case can be made for the claim that linguistic competence does in fact require semantic knowledge of the sort that a semantic theory might characterize, even if it turns out that language understanding is semantics-involving in nothing like the way that the Received View imagines. Semantics involvement does not obviously require the explicit representation of a semantic theory, any more than syntax involvement requires the explicit representation of syntactic theory. Arguably, to be semantics-involving it is enough that the semantic theory can be reasonably construed as providing an abstract characterization of language-understanding processes.[7]

## 4 What Speakers Know When They Know a Semantic Theory

Semanticists such as Higginbotham (1988; 1995), Larson and Segal (1995), and Lepore (1997) claim that competent speakers of a language know a semantic theory for that language, by which they presumably mean that competent speakers know both the axioms of the theory and the T-sentences (or M-sentences) that are its theorems. Schiffer and Fodor, we have seen, do not challenge this knowledge claim but instead challenge the weaker claim that such knowledge is required for language understanding. Having offered reasons for doubting that their challenge is successful, I want now to discuss briefly the knowledge claim itself. It seems to me that a reasonably strong case can be made for the claim that speakers know the T-sentences (or M-sentences) of a semantic theory, though perhaps only a weaker case for the claim that they know its axioms.

I base this conclusion on what I take to be the reasonable criterion that speakers know the information that they are said to know if they can be shown to possess this information and furthermore use it in language understanding. If speakers can satisfy this criterion, then I see little point in denying that they know it. The epistemic/doxastic standards for knowledge are remarkably flexible, varying widely from one domain to another depending on the specific explanatory purposes to which knowledge claims in a given domain are likely to be put. Given the explanatory purposes to which such claims in linguistics and psycholinguistics are typically put, there would seem to be little theoretical point in insisting that speakers do not really know the information that they are said to know, if they both

---

[7] For further discussion see Matthews (1991).

possess and use it. The explanations in which these knowledge claims figure rarely trade on the epistemic/doxastic features of the claimed knowledge that critics typically find disqualifying. It is irrelevant that speakers may not be aware of their possession and use of this information, that they may be unable to call it to consciousness, or that they may not be able to make use of this information except in language processing.

The case for the claim that competent speakers know the T-sentences that a semantic theory associates with sentences of their language rests on three premises: first, that what competent speakers acquire, when they acquire a language, is the productive capacity to produce and understand novel utterances in their language; and second, that the capacity to understand such utterances is, as Fodor and Schiffer would have it, the capacity to form correct beliefs about what the utterer said in uttering what he did. In effect, competent speakers acquire the capacity to effect a pairing of heard utterances with correct beliefs about what was said. But, and here is the third premiss, to acquire such a capacity is just to come to know the pairing that is specified by the set of T-sentences (or M-sentences) that are the theorems of a semantic theory for the language. The set of T-sentences specifies the pairing, inasmuch as the T-sentence that the semantic theory associates with the utterance of an arbitrary sentence specifies what the utterer said in uttering that sentence by specifying the utterance's truth conditions. Put another way, the competent speaker is one who upon hearing an utterance comes to believe that the utterer said what in fact he said, and the T-sentence that the semantic theory associates with the utterance specifies what in fact the utterer said, by giving the utterance's truth conditions (or its meaning).

So competent speakers know the set of T-sentences that a semantic theory associates with sentences of their language in the sense that they know the pairing of heard utterances and beliefs about what is said that these T-sentences specify. Of course, they do not know the pairing in the sense that they know it extensionally; rather they presumably know it in the sense that they know a function, i.e. can compute a function, that maps heard utterances to beliefs about what is said (conditional, as we said above, on a particular assignment of referents to any terms of variable reference and on a contextual disambiguation of any syntactic or lexical ambiguities). The semantic theory provides what Chomsky (1980: 82) describes as a specification *in intension* of that function.

An objection comes immediately to mind. It might be objected that knowing the pairing specified by the set of T-sentences in the sense of knowing or being able to compute a function that effects the specified pairing is not the same as knowing the T-sentences themselves. In the former case, the objection goes, one knows (in the sense explained above), for example, that the utterance 'It's raining' is paired with the belief that the utterer said that it is raining, whereas in the latter case, one knows, correspondingly, that 'It's raining' is true if and only if it is raining. Clearly, the objection continues, knowing the pairing is knowledge of a different sort from knowing the T-sentences—a matter of knowing-how rather than knowing-that, as philosophers of the 1950s and 1960s might have put it.

This objection does not strike me as at all persuasive. Intuitively, there certainly does seem to be a clear difference between knowing (in the sense explained) the pairing specified by the T-sentences and knowing the T-sentences themselves. But whether there are any substantive differences between these sorts of knowledge claims can be assessed only within the theoretical context in which they are made. And within the theoretical context of linguistics and psycholinguistics, there are, I would argue, no substantive differences. Knowing the T-sentences, no less than knowing the pairing that the T-sentences specify, is a matter of knowing how utterance types are paired with their contents—in one case, the content of the belief about what is said, in the other case, the content of the sentence used on the right-hand side of the T-sentence. But these two contents are one and the same. This is required by the fact that a competent speaker is one who, for every utterance in his language, comes to believe that what the utterer said is what the T-sentence associated with the utterance by the semantic theory for that language states to be its truth conditions.

The common-sense intuition that knowing the pairing specified by the T-sentences must be different, perhaps different in kind, from knowing the T-sentences is perhaps reinforced by the widely held representationalist assumption, embodied explicitly in what I earlier called the Received View, that propositional knowledge must, for computational purposes, be explicitly represented. For if such knowledge must be explicitly represented, then it is going to be different from knowing the pairing specified by the T-sentences, which, I have explained, is a matter of being able to compute a function of a particular sort. But arguably the assumption here is mistaken. Ascriptions of linguistic knowledge to speakers are decidedly neutral as regards their computational, not to mention their neurophysiological, implementation. To say, for example, that speakers know that all languages satisfy a c-command condition on binding, viz. that a bound constituent must be c-commanded by an appropriate antecedent, is not to say anything at all about how this condition is computationally implemented. The condition might be explicitly represented, with this explicit representation then consulted in the course of parsing to ensure its satisfaction, or the condition might equally well be implemented procedurally, without its ever being explicitly represented anywhere in the speaker.[8]

Nor does the hoary distinction between knowing-that and knowing-how find a foothold in the present context, inasmuch as claims to linguistic knowledge are explicitly construed by virtually all computational psycholinguists as a characterization of a particular linguistic capacity or ability of speakers, specifically the capacity or ability to effect a certain pairing, i.e. to compute a certain function. There is not in this context the conceptual space between knowing-that and knowing-how that this distinction requires for its application. Knowledge claims are construed here, as they are construed elsewhere in computational psychology, as abstract characterizations of computational processes—abstract in the sense that they abstract away from implementation details.[9] They tell us what a computational device does, viz. what function it computes, e.g. a pairing of heard utterances with beliefs about what is said, but they provide no information as to how this is accomplished.

But what about the claim that competent speakers know the specific axioms postulated by a particular semantic theory? Certainly the fact that speakers know, in the sense explained, the T-sentences that are the theorems of a semantic theory provides some measure of indirect empirical support for the claim. But such support is clearly not decisive. At least it is not decisive if the claim that speakers know the axioms is intended to be, as surely it is, a stronger claim than simply that speakers know the T-sentences that are the theorems. For different semantic theories, with different sets of axioms, could in principle at least have as theorems the very same set of

---

[8] For discussion see Berwick and Weinberg (1984) and Matthews (1991).

[9] See e.g. Newell (1981).

T-sentences. One would like to have independent empirical support for the claim that speakers know the axioms.

Three sorts of empirical evidence might provide support for the stronger claim that speakers know specific axioms of the semantic theory. First, there might be evidence from longitudinal-acquisition studies suggesting that changes in speakers' capacity for language comprehension could be explained in terms of the sequential acquisition of new axioms. Evidence along these lines is surely available for lexical axioms. A second sort of empirical evidence might be found in language comprehension. Consider the case in which a speaker utters an incomplete sentence, perhaps in response to a *wh*-question, e.g. 'Whom did you see?'—'Jones', or 'The man with the red shoes.' Perhaps in understanding such utterances the hearer uses only those axioms of the semantic theory required to assign a semantic value to the uttered word or phrase. If this were so, then the hearer's ability to understand such utterances would provide empirical support for the claim that speakers know these particular axioms every bit as strong as for the claim that speakers know the T-sentences. Of course, it is not obvious that in such cases the hearer uses only these axioms. In understanding such utterances, what the competent speaker comes to believe is presumably a complete thought, e.g. that the utterer said that he had seen Jones, or that he had seen the man with the red shoes. One sceptical of the claim that speakers know the specific axioms of a semantic theory might argue that the pairing that the hearer makes in understanding such utterances is not between the utterance of the name 'Jones' (or the noun phrase 'the man with the red shoes') and whatever the relevant axioms give as their semantic values. Rather the pairing is between the utterance of a complete sentence for which the utterance 'Jones' was elliptical and the belief that the speaker said whatever would have been said by an utterance of the complete sentence. So long as such a construal cannot be ruled out, these sorts of case do not provide evidence that speakers know the axioms of the semantic theory that is not already available in the evidence that establishes that speakers know the T-sentences that are their theorems.[10] An added problem here is that we do not have a plausible candidate, other than beliefs about what is said, with which to pair these utterances. If we are to make a case in these terms for the claim that speakers

---

[10] Elugardo and Stainton (this volume) argue that such construal can be ruled out on linguistic grounds.

know specific axioms, then we are going to need a plausible proposal regarding the kinds of psychological state with which the utterances of incomplete sentences of various sorts are to be paired. It is not too hard to imagine a story for the lexical axioms, where speakers might be said to bear certain psychological relations to the entity or property that is the semantic value of the lexical item mentioned in the axiom, but it is less clear how the story might go for phrasal axioms. People do not, typically, go around uttering and thinking about bare syntactic structures such as '[NP]^[VP]', after all.

A third sort of empirical support for the claim that speakers know specific axioms of the semantic theory is one to which Chomskians would naturally incline, if they were not for independent reasons dismissive of semantics.[11] Suppose that a speaker's assignment of truth conditions to heard utterances could be accurately captured using either of two extensionally equivalent, but inconsistent, semantic theories, call them $T_1$ and $T_2$. (Never mind that linguists rarely, if ever, find themselves in such an enviable situation.) Which semantic theory should we attribute to this speaker? A theory of universal grammar (UG) might help here. Suppose that on any empirically plausible theory of UG, $T_2$ is not an accessible parameterization of UG, i.e. $T_2$ is not accessible given the speaker's access to the primary linguistic data on the basis of which that speaker learns his or her language, but $T_1$ is such an accessible parameterization. The theory of UG would provide empirical support for $T_1$ over $T_2$, and hence for knowledge of the axioms of $T_1$.

One might hope to find a further sort of empirical support in proposed computational models of language understanding. The idea here is that perhaps the computational implementation of the semantic knowledge that enables speakers to pair utterances in their language with beliefs as to what was said by means of those utterances will turn out to be sufficiently transparent to enable an assignment of individual axioms to specific computational operations and/or data structures, presumably on the basis of an isomorphism of computational processes in the model and formal derivational structure in the theory. In such an event, the claim that speakers know the axioms would presumably inherit whatever empirical support the implementing computational model enjoys. The Received View, we saw, envisages just such a transparency of implementation, imagining that the computational processes will have a proof-theoretic character that apes

---

[11]  I owe this to Alex Barber.

the formal structure of a derivation. But as attractive as this possibility may be, the prospects of having such an implementation are not good. Certainly the computational implementation of syntactic knowledge has turned out to be considerably less transparent than proponents of so-called Derivational Theories of Complexity had hoped (cf. Berwick and Weinberg 1984). The computational processes that implement the syntactic rules and principles of a grammar typically cannot, because of architectural and resource constraints, be partitioned in a way that permits such a tidy isomorphism. At best these models have succeeded in achieving what might be described as an *explanatory* transparency, by which I mean that it is possible to explain in computational terms why the syntactic rules and principles correctly characterize the linguistic competence of the parser to assign correct structural descriptions to sentences (cf. Matthews 1991). The growing sophistication of connectionist parsers also does not bode well for the prospects of such computational support.

But even if a proposed model of language understanding exhibited a sig-nificant degree of explanatory transparency *vis-à-vis* the semantic theory, and furthermore the model enjoyed a considerable measure of empirical support, it is not clear that this would go very far in convincing sceptics that speakers know the axioms of the theory. They might continue to in-sist that speakers could be said to know the axioms only if they could be said to possess and use these axioms in the sense that there existed distinct computational operations and structures that could be said to im-plement each of the specific axioms directly. It is not clear what more can be said to dissuade such sceptics, except perhaps to point out that their reductionist criterion for knowing the axioms of a semantic theory will undercut proposed computational models of virtually all cognitive com-petences, since in virtually none of these models do the knowledge-level characterizations of these competences find so transparent an implemen-tation.[12]

## 5 Some Concluding Remarks

My rebuttal of Schiffer's and Fodor's argument that semantic knowledge is not necessary for language understanding, that a competent speaker might

[12] For discussion, again see Newell (1981).

be ignorant of the knowledge characterized by a semantic theory, presumes that semantic theory can effect a pairing between utterances and belief about what is said, or between utterances and truth conditions. But some semanticists, e.g., Pietroski (this volume), have recently argued that it is naive to suppose, as semanticists traditionally have, that a semantic theory will have M-sentences or T-sentences as theorems. These semanticists argue that M-sentences and T-sentences are more likely to be the result of the interaction of a number of competences, of which knowledge of semantic theory is only one, so that whatever such knowledge contributes to language understanding, it is not a competence for pairing utterances with meanings or truth conditions. It does not specify the pairing of utterances with meaning/truth conditions that competent speakers are able to effect. At most, they argue, it might specify the pairing of an utterance with something that might be termed 'intrinsic' meaning, which when combined with context and world knowledge might eventuate in meaning or truth conditions as traditionally conceived.

Whatever the merits of this speculation, and there are, I think, reasons to give it credence, it does not blunt the force of the criticisms that I have raised against Schiffer and Fodor, because it goes no way towards establishing what Schiffer and Fodor need to establish, namely, that the processes that map utterances into meaning or truth conditions are not semantics-involving. For suppose, as Pietroski suggests, that the semantic theory specifies a pairing of utterances with 'intrinsic meanings', and it is these which, when paired with context, world knowledge, and so on, eventuate in a representation of the utterance's meaning or truth conditions. That there exists, as Schiffer and Fodor imagine, a recursive function that maps utterances into meaning or truth conditions in a wholly formal way hardly shows that the mapping is not semantics-involving, if, as we are supposing, one step in the mapping, the pairing of utterances with intrinsic meanings, is specified by the semantic theory.

# REFERENCES

BARBER, A. (2002), 'Semantic Theory and Causal-Explanatory Structure' (The Open University, unpublished manuscript).

BERWICK, R., and WEINBERG, A. (1984), *The Grammatical Basis of Linguistic Performance* (Cambridge. Mass.: MIT Press).

BLOCK, N., ed. (1981), *Readings in Philosophy of Psychology*, vol. ii (Cambridge., Mass.: Harvard University Press).

CHOMSKY, N. (1965), *Aspects of the Theory of Syntax* (Cambridge, Mass.: MIT Press).

—— (1980), *Rules and Representations* (New York: Columbia University Press).

DAVIES, M. (1987), 'Tacit Knowledge and Semantic Theory: Can a Five Percent Difference Matter?', *Mind*, 96: 441–62.

DEVITT, M. (2000), 'Ignorance of Language', unpublished paper presented to the Epistemology of Language conference, Sheffield, UK, July 2000.

EGAN, F. (1995), 'Computation and Content', *Philosophical Review*, 104: 18–203.

EVANS, G. (1981), 'Reply: Semantic Theory and Tacit Knowledge', in Holtzmann and Leich (1981), 118–37.

FODOR, J. A. (1981), 'Some Notes on What Linguistics is About', in Block (1981), 197–207.

—— (1990), 'Review of Stephen Schiffer's *Remnants of Meaning*', in id., *A Theory of Content and Other Essays* (Cambridge, Mass.: MIT Press), 177–91.

GEORGE, A., ed. (1989), *Reflections on Chomsky* (Oxford: Blackwell).

GRAVES, C., KATZ, J. J., NISHIYAMA, Y., SOAMES, S., STECKER, R., and TOVEY, T. (1973) 'Tacit Knowledge', *Journal of Philosophy*, 70: 318–30.

HIGGINBOTHAM, J. (1988), 'Is Semantics Necessary?', *Proceedings of the Aristotelian Society*, 87: 219–41.

—— (1995), 'The Place of Natural Language', in Leonardi and Santamobrogio (1995), 113–39.

HOLTZMANN, S., and LEICH, C., eds. (1981), *Wittgenstein: To Follow a Rule* (London: Routledge & Kegan Paul).

KASHER, A., ed. (1991), *The Chomskyan Turn* (London: Basil Blackwell).

LARSON, R., and SEGAL, G. (1995), *Knowledge of Meaning* (Cambridge, Mass.: MIT Press).

LEONARDI, P., and SANTAMABROGIO, M., eds. (1995), *On Quine* (Cambridge: Cambridge University Press).

LEPORE, E. (1997), 'Conditions on Understanding Language', *Proceedings of the Aristotelian Society*, 19: 41–60.

MATTHEWS, R. (1991), 'Psychological Reality of Grammars', in Kasher (1991), 182–99.

NEWELL, A. (1980), 'Physical Symbol Systems', *Cognitive Science*, 4: 135–83.

—— (1981), 'The Knowledge-Level', *AI Magazine* (Summer), 1–20.

PEACOCKE, C. (1986), 'Explanation in Computational Psychology: Language, Perception, and Level 1.5', *Mind and Language*, 1: 101–23.

—— (1989), 'When Is a Grammar Psychologically Real?', in George (1989), 111–30.

SCHIFFER, S. (1987), *Remnants of Meaning* (Cambridge, Mass.: MIT Press).

—— (1993), 'Actual-Language Relations', *Philosophical Perspectives*, 7: 231–58.

—— (1995), 'Lepore on the Epistemology of Language Understanding', presented at the Symposium on Epistemology of Language Understanding, APA (Pacific Division), San Francisco (unpublished).

WRIGHT, C. (1986), 'Theories of Meaning and Speaker's Knowledge', in id., *Realism, Meaning, and Truth* (London: Blackwell), 204–38.

# PART TWO

Understanding

# CHAPTER 7

# *The Character of Natural Language Semantics*

*Paul M. Pietroski*

I had heard it said that Chomsky's conception of language is at odds with the truth-conditional programme in semantics. Some of my friends said it so often that the point—or at least a point—finally sank in.[1]

My aim in this paper is to describe and motivate what I take to be Chomsky's (2000) conception of semantics, with emphasis on his scepticism about more traditional approaches. But the goal is not exegetical. It is to advance a view, whose attractions are considerable, that often gets ignored.

## 1 Overview

Let me start by simply presenting the main claims. In Section 2 I go through them again more slowly, with examples and arguments. This will, I hope, compensate for the stark initial statement of some ideas that may initially seem odd.

This paper is a written descendant of an informal talk at the Epistemology of Language conference; especially in sects. 3 and 5, the informality remains. I am indebted, for illuminating discussions of context dependence, to Jerry Fodor, Jason Stanley, Zoltan Szabo, and especially Ernie Lepore. Thanks also to: Noam Chomsky, Susan Dwyer, Jim Higginbotham, Gabe Segal, Peter Ludlow, Georges Rey, Rob Stainton, Alex Barber, and the helpful group he brought together in Sheffield.

[1] Let me acknowledge, at the outset, Jim McGilvray and Norbert Hornstein. Much of what I say was prompted and shaped by many conversations with them. McGilvray (1998; 1999) and Hornstein (1984) provide a helpful context for Chomsky's (2000) remarks. See also Stainton (forthcoming).

### 1.1 *Truth conditions as (intractable) interaction effects*

We should be sceptical of the idea that a theory of meaning for a natural language will have theorems that specify the *truth* conditions of all the declarative sentences of that language. The successes in semantics suggest that the theoretical action lies elsewhere; semantics is concerned with 'internalist' features of linguistic expressions, rather than truth *per se*. The fact that (an utterance of) a sentence has a certain truth condition is typically an *interaction effect* whose determinants include (1) intrinsic properties of the sentence that we can isolate and theorize about, and (2) a host of facts less amenable to theorizing, like facts about how 'reasonable' speakers would *use* the sentence. If this is correct—if our best semantic theories turn out to be theories of linguistic features that do not determine truth conditions—and meaning is what our best semantic theories are theories of, then the meaning of a sentence does not determine its truth condition. Sentences, as products of (largely innate and modular) language systems, have truth conditions only by virtue of their relation to other cognitive systems and the environments in which the sentences are used. But sentences have their *meanings* by virtue of more local facts concerning the psychology (and hence biology) of language users. So a semantics that makes the right theoretical cuts will not *itself* associate sentences with truth conditions.[2]

There is, of course, a familiar sense in which the meanings of natural sentences—i.e. sentences of a natural language—fail to determine truth conditions: sentences with indexicals or demonstratives do not *have* truth conditions apart from potential contexts of use. But let truth conditions be sensitive to context. A theory of meaning will still not have theorems that specify truth conditions. Indexicals and demonstratives have intrinsic

---

[2] Semanticists need to see past truth conditions, much as physicists need to see past 'noisy' surface phenomena. This is not to deny that the ordinary term 'meaning' is used in different ways. But I am concerned with meaning as a theoretical notion—meaning in so far as we can have a theory of it. I am inclined to equate this with (what) meaning (really is), though one can introduce the explicitly technical term 'meaning*'. In the end, we probably need to think of meaning* as layered, perhaps along the lines of a Marr-style theory of vision that posits primal, 2-D, and 2½-D sketches; see Marr (1982). But for the most part, I focus below on (at best) primal aspects of meaning*, leaving open the possibility that other aspects of meaning* are (partly) tractable in ways not yet understood; though like Chomsky, I suspect that all theoretically tractable aspects of meaning* will turn out to be internalistic.

features that introduce a theoretically tractable kind of context sensitivity; see Kaplan (1989) and the discussion below. Truth conditions, however, depend on less tractable features of communicative situations. Indeed, while meaning is compositional, truth conditions may not be. We can hope to specify the 'semantic character' of a sentence in terms of a function from Kaplan-style contexts to *something* that is determined compositionally. But a theory of meaning need not associate sentences with anything that (given the world) determines their truth or falsity; and there is no empirical warrant for claiming that sentential meanings are functions from communicative situations to truth values. Correlatively, natural-language semantics should not be viewed as an attempt to formulate Tarski-style characterizations of truth for natural languages.

From this perspective, semantics is not the study of symbol-to-world relations, or of recursively characterized sets of abstract propositions to which sentences are semantically related. Semantics, like syntax and phonology, is an internalist enterprise concerned with linguistic expressions and the minds that generate them. This is clearly not Davidson's (1984) programme, though significant aspects of that programme can be preserved.[3] The proposal will be anathema to anyone who thinks that psychologistic conceptions of semantics are misguided, like psychologistic conceptions of logic, because semantic facts are *normative* in a way that facts concerning (the nature and organization of) human brains are not. But even if logical truths are mind-independent, semantic truths may not be.

We gesture at certain facts by: saying what sentences mean; noting the compellingness of certain inferences; contrasting the ambiguity of certain strings of words with the non-ambiguity of others; observing the kinds of referential (in)dependence exhibited by quantifiers, names, and pronouns; etc. (For a useful review, see Larson and Segal 1995.) There is no reason to believe that these facts, pre-theoretically regarded as semantic, are inexplicable in Chomskian terms. On the contrary, the available evidence tells against 'logicist' conceptions of semantics according to which sentences have meanings only by virtue of being 'regimentable' into sentences of a *Begriffsschrift*—a language designed for conducting 'ideal inference'. Thus, we should be sceptical of the idea that expressions of natural language have

---

[3] See Pietroski (1994) for discussion of Davidson (1986), who makes some relevant concessions. But the emphasis on *truth*-theoretic semantics remains, if uneasily.

Fregean *Bedeutungen*, which reflect the truth-conditional contributions of expressions in a *Begriffsschrift*.

Drawing on Davidson (1967) and/or Montague (1970), however, one might adopt the following bold hypothesis: the apparatus used to stipulate a semantics for a formal language—truth values, entities in a canonical domain, and functions from such entities to truth values—can be used to provide a correct semantics for natural languages (without first associating natural sentences with sentences of a *Begriffsschrift*). Indeed, this idea has become so familiar that Frege (1892) and Tarski (1944) can seem quaint for warning us against it. We name and describe things around us; and modulo cases that can seem peripheral—involving, for example, referential failure or vagueness—our sentences are true or false (as used in particular situations). So why not say that a natural sentence, minus its referential devices, is semantically associated with a mapping from entities we can denote to truth values? We can then try to characterize semantic compositionality in Fregean terms. Whether or not this hypothesis is fruitful, one might think the framework assumptions are relatively innocuous. So it is important to distinguish various claims concerning the utility of Fregean tools for the study of natural language.

## 1.2 *Preserving the structure of truth theories*

A modest view is that the *structure* of a Fregean semantics, shorn of any presumptions about actual interpretation, can be applied to natural languages. A stronger view is that this structure shows how the *truth* conditions of natural sentences are *compositionally determined*.[4] I endorse the former.

---

[4] Consider the following quote from Montague (1970): 'Like Donald Davidson I regard the construction of a theory of truth—or rather, of the more general notion of truth under an arbitrary interpretation—as the basic goal of serious syntax and semantics; and the developments emanating from the Massachusetts Institute of Technology offer little promise towards that end' (p. 188 in the reprint). This may correctly report the goal some semanticists have had, the importance they have assigned to it, and the relevance of Chomskian linguistics to that goal. But it is hardly obvious that truth is a special case of truth-in-a-model (see Lepore 1983); and the remark about syntax shows the risk of making pronouncements about the basic goal of 'serious' work in an active domain of enquiry. Those who seek a Tarski-style characterization of English may well end up with non-psychologistic conceptions of syntax and semantics. But this makes a mystery of many (quite robust) linguistic intuitions that speakers report and many psycholinguistic

There are, no doubt, various semantic types. Sentences, quantifiers, and verbs have importantly different semantic properties. One can encode this fact by positing several kinds of *valuations*, and associating expressions of different semantic types with valuations of different kinds. One can also encode facts about the meanings of particular words by associating each word with a particular valuation. But it hardly follows that expressions denote their valuations. The valuation of an expression is a reflection of that expression's theoretically important semantic properties. We *discover* which properties are important, and how they are related to the truth conditions of sentences. Maybe sentences have truth values as valuations, and the valuation of a name is what one refers to by using the name; and maybe not. Frege defined 'Bedeutung' so that the *Bedeutung* of a (formal) sentence is its truth value, and the *Bedeutung* of an expression $X$ reflects $X$'s contribution to the truth conditions of sentences in which $X$ can appear. This technical notion proved useful for the study of valid inference. Whether it has further utility for the study of natural language remains to be seen.

It has, however, been fruitful to posit valuations that satisfy the following constraints: (1) the valuation of a complex expression is determined by the valuations of its constituents, given the expression's grammatical structure; (2) there are exactly two possible valuations for declarative sentences; and (3) every analytic sentence has the same valuation.[5] Semantic typologies of this kind have shed considerable light on the compositionality of meaning. And it is a matter of indifference how we *label* valuations. We can call the two sentential valuations '1/0', 'on/off', or 't/f'. But if we say that a sentence $\Sigma$ has the valuation 1 iff $\Sigma$ is true, we make an immodest claim that requires further evidence. Sentences are *apt for use as* devices for expressing

studies of young children; see Crain and Pietroski (2000) for a review. But even setting this aside, it is worth pausing to ask, as Chomsky (2000) does, why a non-psychologistic phonology would be absurd; why few of us would say that a sentence has its sound and syntax only by virtue of being 'regimentable' into a sentence of a suitable formal language; and what *evidence* suggests that semantics is different in this respect.

[5] Condition (3) ensures that 'If Pat ran, then Pat ran' and 'If Fido barked and Fido is Rex, then Rex barked' have the same valuation. But 'valuation' is not a good translation of 'Bedeutung'. Neither is 'referent'; users of a sentence typically do not refer to its truth value. (Names for the same object have the same *Bedeutung*, since inferences of the form 'Fa & a = b; so Fb' are valid. But 'Bedeutung' is not *defined* so that the *Bedeutung* of a name is its intuitive 'referent'.)

truth-evaluable claims, since there are exactly two sentential valuations. There may also be domains, like arithmetic, in which the relation between sentential valuations and truth values is transparent; but this is a poor basis for generalization. The relation between sentential valuations and truth values may be theoretically intractable in other domains.

If the valuation of a natural sentence is not its truth value, then theories of meaning for natural languages should not associate sentences with (functions from contexts to) truth values. Similarly, the valuation of 'Aristotle' does not have to be a dead philosopher. There is nothing surprising about this: 'valuation', like 'electron', is a theoretical term; and there is no empirical reason for supposing that the theoretically important semantic properties of a name determine what users of the name refer to when using it. People refer to things, words do not. The meanings of words may constrain without determining what people can refer to by using words. (This will be an important theme.) In order to formalize a semantic theory, one might inscribe axioms like the following: Valuation('Aristotle') = Aristotle. But such notation is potentially confusing, since semantic axioms need not be viewed as claims about how natural expressions are related to things like ancient Greeks. A semanticist might use 'Aristotle' *in her metalanguage* to represent a valuation, where this valuation is unlikely to *be* a person who died long before any English was ever spoken, in an attempt to gesture at semantically relevant properties of the object-language name. So one need not view the axiom as a formalization of the claim that the name 'Aristotle' refers to (or denotes) a certain dead guy.[6]

With these caveats in place, let us grant that a semantic theory for a natural language *L* will (conditionally, and relative to Kaplan contexts) associate each declarative sentence of *L* with a sentential valuation via (1) axioms that assign valuations to semantically primitive expressions of *L*, and (2) rules for deriving consequences from these axioms.[7] Let us also

---

[6] Thus, it might be better to say: Valuation('Aristotle') = Aristotle*, leaving it open whether Aristotle* is (the late) Aristotle himself or some (yet to be defined) theoretical construct that reflects the important semantic properties of the name 'Aristotle'. If names are 'pure tags' with *no* further semantic content, then perhaps Aristotle himself is a good choice for the valuation of 'Aristotle'. But while I agree that names are rigid designators, and not disguised descriptions (see Kripke 1980), this hardly shows that names have no semantic content.

[7] Suppressing context relativization, the theory will have theorems of the form 'Valu-

assume that natural languages contain primitive terms that are apt for use as devices for referring to things, and that such terms have entities (in some domain or other) as valuations. Then we can advance various hypotheses about the semantic types of other subsentential expressions. Perhaps the valuations of predicates are functions from entities to $1/0$; the valuations of quantifiers are functions from the valuations of predicates to $1/0$; etc. For now, we need not dwell on whether these particular proposals are correct; cf. Pietroski (2002; forthcoming). The point is simply that the structure of standard typologies is independent of the further claim that a sentence is true iff it has the valuation $1$.

Still, even if semanticists neither can nor must specify the truth conditions of object-language sentences, one might think that a name surely bears *some* semantic relation to its bearer. If so, one can always stipulate that the name–bearer relation is semantic. But recall that Kripke (1980) denied offering any *theory* of how 'Aristotle' is connected to Aristotle; and despite considerable literature on this topic, no one has shown that names *do* bear any interesting and theoretically tractable relation to their bearers. As Kripke noted, highlighting the relevance of causal chains does not amount to a theory. We can let go of the idea that 'Aristotle' *must* bear some semantic relation to Aristotle—and that a 'real' theory of meaning will provide an account of that relation—if we think of semantics as an internalist enterprise concerned with aspects of human psychology that determine

---

ation($\Sigma$) = $1$ iff $\sigma$' for each sentence $\Sigma$ of $L$, where '$\sigma$' is a sentence of the metalanguage. But there is no reason to expect such theorems to be homophonically disquotational. The left side of a meaning-specifying theorem will involve a *structural* description of the object-language sentence, while the right side will typically involve semantic analysis. Actual theorems look more like

Valuation($[_S[_{NP}$ Pat$][_{VP}[_V$ ran$][_{Adv}$ quickly$]]]$) = $1$ iff
$\exists$e[Agent(e, Pat) & Ran(e) & Quick(e)]

than

Valuation('Pat ran quickly') = $1$ iff Pat ran quickly.

But even if one resists analysis, one cannot derive instances of '*p*' *is true iff p* from an honest theory. Try deriving '*Pat ran*' *is true iff Pat ran*, as opposed to something more like

$[[_{argument}$ Pat$][_{predicate}$ ran$]]$ is true iff Ran(Pat).

One can add the premises that $[[_{argument}$ Pat$][_{predicate}$ ran$]]$ is true iff 'Pat ran' is true, and that Ran(Pat) iff Pat ran. But even if these biconditionals are correct, they do not seem to be semantic truths of English.

certain intrinsic features of linguistic expressions. Similarly, we can let go of the idea that a predicate *must* bear some semantic relation to a certain set of things. Which is a good thing, as we shall see, since the evidence suggests that predicates do not have classical extensions. (I shall soon return to this last point.)

One might reply that speakers of English *tacitly believe* that 'Aristotle' is used to refer to Aristotle; that 'dog' is used as a predicate that applies to dogs; etc. So perhaps we should retain axioms like 'Valuation("Aristotle") = Aristotle' without reinterpreting their right-hand sides. Perhaps we should construe such axioms as hypotheses about what speakers tacitly believe—or to use an explicitly technical term, what speakers *t-believe*, leaving it open whether t-belief is a species of belief. The idea is that: speakers understand sentences by virtue of bearing some psychological relation to axioms (and rules that license the derivation of theorems) which determine the truth conditions of those sentences; and sentences mean what they do because of how speakers understand them. Of course, one wants to hear more about what it is to t-believe semantic axioms. But there are proposals; and if the truth-theoretic axioms can be provided, one might well think that speakers bear some psychological relation to them. This neo-Davidsonian view is inspired by the idea that syntax and semantics are continuous enterprises with a shared goal of characterizing aspects of human psychology; see Higginbotham (1985; 1986), Larson and Segal (1995).[8] So this is a big step in Chomsky's direction. But a tension remains.

Imagine a neo-neo-Davidsonian who grants that speakers t-believe theories whose theorems assign sentential valuations to sentences, but not that all and only true (uses of) sentences have the valuation 1. If this weaker hypothesis explains the relevant facts equally well, it undercuts the bolder claim that speakers t-believe *truth* theories; and according to the neo-

---

[8] I used to endorse this conception of semantics wholeheartedly, and still extol its many virtues; see Pietroski (2000d). Someone can believe that 'Aristotle' bears a certain relation to a certain thing, whether or not the name and thing are so related. So semantic axioms, construed as psychological reports, could be correct even if natural expressions do not really have valuations at all. One might argue that facts about speaker psychology determine the linguistic facts: if speakers of English tacitly believe that Valuation('Aristotle') = Aristotle, then Valuation('Aristotle') = Aristotle. But that would not show that semantics is really concerned with the relation between words and things; one would need an externalist gloss of the relevant psychological states.

neo-Davidsonian, facts surrounding the compositionality of meaning—the meat and potatoes of semantic theorizing—are explained equally well by the weaker hypothesis. The neo-Davidsonian will say that other semantic facts (e.g. the putative fact that 'dog' applies to dogs) remain unaccounted for. But even if such facts can be described and explained in theoretically interesting ways, it does not follow that such facts (in conjunction with a psychologically realized compositional system) determine the truth conditions of sentences. For the respects in which neo-Davidsonians go beyond neo-neo-Davidsonians may concern aspects of speaker-psychology (and/or the external world) that are not directly relevant to understanding. That is, even if speakers of English t-believe that 'dog' applies to dogs, they may not draw on this metalinguistic belief in understanding sentences with the word 'dog' (in the way speakers of English typically understand such sentences). And without independent reason for thinking that speakers t-believe *truth* theories, the neo-Davidsonian needs to argue that *understanding* involves deployment of the metalinguistic t-beliefs in question.

Moreover, even if speakers have the metalinguistic t-beliefs, appeals to such t-beliefs may label theoretically intractable aspects of cognition. Perhaps in speaking of t-beliefs, the neo-Davidsonian is actually referring to a hotchpotch of psychological states that are not unified in any theoretically interesting way. (It would not be surprising if understanding speech involved some such hotchpotch.) If the theoretically tractable semantic facts concern *certain* aspects of speaker psychology, but speakers t-believe truth-theoretic axioms in part via *other* aspects of their psychology, then neo-Davidsonian semantics is an idealization in need of refinement. Or put another way, theorists who use terms like 'truth' may mischaracterize (at least much of) what speakers t-believe *qua* speakers, since notions like 'truth' may be ill-suited to characterizing the mental states that underly linguistic competence. The needed refinements of the neo-Davidsonian programme, as currently practised, may be relatively minor. But the shift in perspective may well affect future developments if appeals to *truth* fail to cut nature at its semantic joints.

One last qualification before concluding this polemical introduction. Humans often try to make their linguistic behaviour conform (in certain respects) to that of other speakers—at least when successful communication matters and others show no sign of modifying their usage. A child may strive to make it the case that: her use of 'dog' conforms, in various ways, to adult usage; and adults can correctly say, with regard to her, 'When she says "dog" she means what we do.' Similarly, adult speakers often hold themselves to external linguistic standards, which are often presupposed in ordinary meaning ascriptions. But it does not follow that *valuations* should reflect these aspects of our linguistic practice. Many humans try to modify their 'accent' by way of conforming to certain (external, social) standards; but it does not follow that phonologists should employ a typology designed to reflect these standards. There are, however, some delicate issues here. Understanding may involve deployment of *some* mental states whose contents are (in some theoretically interesting sense) externalist. We must also leave open the possibility that 'linguistic competence' is like 'jade': a term we apply to things that are importantly similar yet (in a deeper sense) different. Even if current semantic theories mix internalist apples and externalist oranges, theorists may want to discuss both. I shall briefly touch on these matters in the final section.

## 2 Function and Context

Let us try all that again, this time starting with some sentences.

### 2.1 *Composing meanings or composing truth conditions*

Chomsky (1977) discusses

(1) Unicycles have wheels,

which seems to be true. But (1) is not true iff each normal (operational, unvandalized) unicycle has wheels. The truth of (1) does not ensure the truth of

(2) Jim's unicycle has wheels,

even given that Jim owns a normal unicycle. Indeed, (1) is true even though no unicycle has wheels—and 'some unicycle has wheels' is false. By contrast, consider:

(3) Cars have wheels.

(4) Jim's car has wheels.

An utterance of (3) seems to imply that each normal car has wheels. If Jim's car is normal, (4) is true. And it is hard to see how a semantic theory could assign the right truth conditions to (3)–(4), without assigning the wrong truth conditions to (1)–(2).

If 'has wheels' applies only to things with wheels, the truth-conditional semanticist needs to explain why (1) still comes out true. For in that case, one cannot say that 'Φs have wheels' is true iff every normal Φ has wheels—or that 'Φs have wheels' is true iff $\{x : \text{is a } \Phi\}$ bears the right generic relation to $\{x : x \text{ has wheels}\}$. If 'has wheels' applies to all wheeled things, including unicycles, we need to be told why (2) is false—and why (4) is false if Jim's futuristic car has only one wheel. If 'has wheels' applies in some contexts to anything with at least one wheel, but applies in other contexts only to things with more than one wheel, we need to hear how *that* works.[9] One might reply that 'have wheels' and 'has wheels' are semantically distinct predicates, with the former applying to all wheeled things (maybe counting some *species* as wheeled) while the latter applies only to things with wheels. But 'I have wheels' would be false if uttered by a unicycle yet true if uttered by a car; similarly, 'I have eyes' would be false if uttered by a Cyclops yet true if uttered by a (normal) human. One can say that 'have eyes' is ambiguous: sometimes it means 'has eyes', which applies to an individual $x$ only if $x$ has eyes (counting a plurality of Cyclopes as an individual that has eyes, to accommodate 'We have eyes'); but in generic sentences like (1), 'have wheels' can only apply to wheeled things (or perhaps wheeled species). One begins to wonder, though, if this is a theory of meaning or just a stipulation of the facts.

Moreover, Chomsky provides other examples that extend the point. While the truth of:

---

[9] There also seems to be a truth-conditional difference between 'No unicycles have wheels' and 'No cars have wheels'; the latter is clearly false, but I think the former is true. Even if it is analytic that each unicycle has one wheel, that will not help. Why is (1) not a contradiction? If one insists that (1) is false *strictly speaking*, then 'true *strictly speaking*' becomes a technical term; and we shall have no reason to think that a sentence is true iff it is true *strictly speaking*. Of course, this is not to deny that interesting things can be (and have been) said about the compositional semantics of generic sentences; see e.g. Carlson and Pelletier (1995); Koslicki (1999).

(5) Beavers are mammals

requires that *all* beavers be mammals,

(6) Beavers build dams

requires only that *typical* beavers (in the wild, with suitable resources, free to express their beaverish nature) build dams. Correlatively, (6) does not have the same truth condition as the passive

(7) Dams are built by beavers,

which falsely implies that typical dams are built by beavers. But (8) is true, relative to a context,

(8) Beavers built this dam,

if and only if (9) is true relative to that context:

(9) This dam was built by beavers.

This suggests that the truth conditions of plural sentences—which involve quantification, including quantification over events (see Schein 1993)— exhibit interesting *but not obviously compositional* effects. While the facts are clear, and non-arbitrary, they may not be fully systematic. Consider

(10) Poems are written by fools like me.
(11) Mountains are climbed by fools like me.

The truth of (10) requires that all poems be written by fools, but the truth of (11) does not require that all mountains be climbed by fools. In each case, the truth condition can be specified roughly as follows: all the NOUNs that are VERBed are VERBed by fools like the speaker. Since all poems are written (or at least created intentionally), but not all mountains are climbed, there is a truth-conditional difference. Correspondingly, there is a significant difference between 'write' and 'climb'. But the challenge is to show how the *truth* conditions for (10)–(11) are compositionally determined without getting the truth conditions for (5)–(9) wrong. Note, for example, that

(12) Dams that are built are built by beavers

is logically weaker than (7), even though both sentences are actually false.

Of course, particular examples are open to dispatch by clever theorists; and one can always say that the examples are complex in ways that have not yet been understood. But given the available evidence, which includes many examples like (1)–(12),

> even a principle of compositionality is suspect. Global properties of the sentence, which may be quite involved, seem to play a role. We cannot simply assign a meaning to the subject and a meaning to the predicate (or to a sentence form with a variable standing for the subject), and then combine the two. Rather, the meaning assigned to each phrase depends on the form of the phrase with which it is paired. (Chomsky 1977: 31)

Chomsky does not state the composition principle he has in mind. But consider the following view:

> If $\Sigma$ is a sentence formed by combining a singular term $\alpha$ with a predicate $\Phi$, then $\Sigma$ is true iff the *valuation* of $\Sigma$ is the truth value *true*; and the valuation of $\Sigma$ is the value of (the function that is) the valuation of $\Phi$ given the valuation of $\alpha$ as argument. Or more briefly, letting '$\| \dots \|$' stand for 'the valuation of . . .', $\Sigma$ is true iff $\|\Sigma\| = $ *true*; and $\|\alpha{}^{\smallfrown}\Phi\| = \|\Phi\|(\|\alpha\|)$.

The idea is simple and familiar. Names are associated with entities in some canonical domain; predicates are associated with functions from such entities to truth values; and the result of combining a name with a (unary) predicate is a sentence that is true iff the relevant function maps the relevant entity onto the valuation *true*. A sentence like

(13)  Aristotle was Greek

is said to be true iff $\|$'was Greek'$\|(\|$'Aristotle'$\|) = $*true*. Thus, $\|$'Aristotle'$\|$ is said to be Aristotle. And the valuation of 'was Greek' is said to be the smallest function F from entities $x$ in a specified domain to truth values, such that $F(x) = $*true* if $x$ was Greek and *false* otherwise. Or more briefly, $\|$'was Greek'$\| = [\lambda x : x \in D_e$ . *true* if $x$ was Greek and *false* otherwise]; or briefer still, $\|$'was Greek'$\| = [\lambda x$ . *true* iff $x$ was Greek]. On this view, (13) is true iff $[\lambda x$ . *true* iff $x$ was Greek](Aristotle) $= $*true*.[10]

---

[10]  I urge a different view in Pietroski (2000b; 2002; forthcoming). But let this pass

While this can seem almost trivial, it is not. If we say that a sentence is true iff it has the valuation *true*, it is tendentious that sentential valuations are compositionally determined; if we say that sentential valuations are compositionally determined, it is tendentious that sentential valuations are truth values. Similar remarks apply to subsentential valuations. Consider the predicate 'has wheels'. One might think that specifying its valuation is simple: [$\lambda x$ . *true* iff $x$ has wheels]. But which function is this? Is it a function whose extension includes only objects with more than one wheel; or is it a function whose extension includes some objects—like unicycles—with just one wheel? Merely surrounding the English predicate 'has wheels' with formal notation does not answer this question. Without an answer, we do not know what the theory says about the difficulty posed by (1); and a theory should not paper over the difficulties it faces. One can depart from strict homophony, and say either that $\|$ 'has wheels' $\|$ =[$\lambda x$ . *true* iff $x$ has at least one wheel], or that $\|$ 'has wheels' $\|$ =[$\lambda x$ . *true* iff $x$ has at least two wheels]. But either way, difficulty awaits. Similar remarks apply to other examples of the general point illustrated with (1)–(12): while there is presumably some complex semantic property of a sentence that is determined by its parts and syntax, *truth* conditions may not be similarly compositional.

## 2.2 *Lexical meanings and composition*

Chomsky (1995*a*; 2000) returns to this theme, often with examples like

(14) This book weighs about a pound. It is available in bookstores every-where.

Each sentence in (14) can be true. Speakers can use 'book' to make remarks about certain concrete particulars, or to make remarks about 'things' like *Sense and Sensibility*; and while certain copies of Austen's book may weigh about a pound, *Sense and Sensibility* does not. Moreover, it seems that a single use of 'book' can serve as the basis for both kinds of remarks. So

for now. Sentences with indexical/demonstrative/quantificational subjects can be accommodated, in the usual way, by relativization to Kaplan-contexts (or sequences), and associating quantifiers (like 'every beaver') with functions from functions to truth values; although sentences with quantificational subjects have the form $[D^\wedge N]_i{}^\wedge[t_i{}^\wedge\Phi]$, where '$t_i$' is a bound trace of a raised quantifier (composed of a determiner and a noun), and where $\|[D^\wedge N]_i{}^\wedge[t_i{}^\wedge\Phi]\| = \|[D^\wedge N]_i\|(\|[t_i{}^\wedge\Phi]\|)$.

what is the valuation of 'book'? It is no answer to say that $\|$ 'book' $\| =$ [$\lambda x$ . *true* iff $x$ is a book]. Does the relevant extension include things like *Sense and Sensibility*; concrete copies; things of both kinds; or entities that somehow have the properties of both authorial works and copies? There is no empirical reason to expect a determinate answer. While there are facts concerning the meaning of 'book', those facts need not determine a book function from entities to truth values; and speakers' judgements/usage provide no evidence of such a function.

Similar issues arise with respect to verbs. My wife and I once visited a Swiss campsite in which sentence (15) was prominently displayed:

(15) The bathhouse will be cleaned at 10 a.m.

At 10 a.m. a maintenance team duly began to wash down the *outside* of the bathhouse. In fact, the inside was also rendered immaculate; but suppose that only the outer walls had been affected at 10 a.m. Would (15) have been true? If the answer is unclear, it is equally unclear which function corresponds to the hybrid English/Formalese expression '[$\lambda x$ . *true* iff $x$ was cleaned at 10 a.m. (on 1 July . . .)]'. Would the imagined bathhouse be mapped to *true*? To answer in a way that determines truth conditions for (15), we also have to be clear about which function is described with '[$\lambda x$ . *true* iff $x$ is a bathhouse]'. So let us stipulate that the relevant extension consists of objects with interiors—containers, as opposed to their surfaces— and that such objects are in the extension of 'cleaned' only if their interiors are made tidy. (Whereas such objects are in the extension of 'painted' if only their exteriors are covered with paint.) Then (15) is false in the imagined scenario. But on this view, (15) is effectively synonymous with

(16) The inside of the bathhouse will be cleaned at 10 a.m.

And that seems wrong, since (16) cannot *ever* be true if only the outside walls are cleaned.

Moreover, the proposal about the extension of 'cleaned' needs revision, assuming that

(17) Norbert cleaned the globe in his office

can be true in a situation where Norbert wiped the surface of his globe, without dusting its interior—unless '[$\lambda x$ . *true* iff $x$ is a globe]' describes a function that maps the relevant globe-like surface in Norbert's office onto *true* (while mapping the relevant container onto *false*). But that would complicate the treatment of

(18) The volume of this globe is greater than the volume of my bowling ball.[11]

In reply, it will be said that the valuations of predicates are context-sensitive, like the valuations of indexicals/demonstratives. I return to this suggestion presently. But let us at least consider another possibility: invented expressions like '[$\lambda x$ . *true* iff $x$ is a book]' and '[$\lambda x$ . *true* iff $x$ was cleaned]' fail to specify functions, despite the formalistic paraphernalia.

While '[$\lambda x$ . *true* iff $x$ is a prime number]' specifies a function, it is a hypothesis that 'book' is relevantly like 'prime number'. Lambdas do not guarantee function descriptions, just as curly brackets do not guarantee set descriptions. Consider '$\{x : x$ is not an element of itself$\}$'. Like Sainsbury (1990), I think that '$\{x : x$ is bald$\}$' fails to specify a set, since sets have determinate extensions. There is the set of primes less than 1,000, but there is no *set* of bald things. At best, there is the set of bald$_1$ things, the set

---

[11] In stressing this kind of point, Chomsky (2000) occasionally comes close to saying that London does not exist, on the basis of examples like 'He wants to move London up the Thames, but its elected officials are opposed'. But of course, Chomsky believes in cities (pers. comm.). I construe any remarks suggesting the contrary (if read in isolation) as dramatic reports of the following thought: since it is not analytic that London exists, the most a semanticist should say is that London is the valuation of 'London' if London exists; if London is the valuation of 'London', then there is some entity $x$ such that $x$ is movable *and* $x$ has elected officials; but the actual world contains no such entity. The last premiss is tendentious, but not implausible: the movable—and hence spatio-temporal—things have no elected officials; and the 'things' with elected officials—political units—do not move. (Unless we are playing fast and loose with 'move' and 'has', in just the ways that are illicit if one is trying to specify functions.) And is the semantics of natural language so demanding that the truth of ordinary claims about London *requires* a potentially exotic metaphysics? In the absence of an independent reason for an affirmative answer, one might simply deny that (the real city) London is the valuation of 'London'; where one can reject this conception of natural-language semantics, while granting that speakers can and do refer to London. That said, Chomsky (*qua* scientist, if not *qua* political critic) has nominalistic tendencies, which may bear on how he would resolve the puzzles that attend sentences of the form '—— does (not) exist'; see McGilvray (1999; forthcoming) for illuminating discussion. But one can reject nominalism while still insisting that semanticists who take the valuations of names to be mind-independent things need to say more about the posited valuations.

of bald$_2$ things, and so on; where in each case, 'bald$_n$' is some precisified variant of 'bald'; cf. Williamson (1994). Moreover, precisifications are hard to come by: '$\{x : x$ has fewer than 1,000 hairs$\}$' does not specify a set, since it can be indeterminate whether something that clearly has 999 hairs *has* one more.[12] Since almost all natural-language predicates are vague, in my view, this makes it hard even to *say* which function is alleged to be the valuation of a given predicate.

This is often viewed as a pernickety point that does not really challenge the idea that the valuations of natural-language predicates are functions. I find this attitude baffling. The available evidence suggests that natural predicates are not semantically associated with the kinds of 'boundaries' that are essential to functions/sets; see Sainsbury (1990). Arguments to the contrary are *paradoxes*. Still, it is widely held that the phenomenon of vagueness is—and given certain logical considerations, *must* be—a kind of illusion: natural predicates really have valuations that can be characterized with sharp predicates (perhaps with the aid of context relativization and/or techniques like supervaluation); it just seems otherwise for epistemic reasons of one sort or another. I shall not press scepticism about this, since the Chomskian point illustrated by (14)–(18) does not concern vagueness of the usual sort.[13] But it is worth pausing to distinguish two claims about the related phenomena of *standard-shifting*. For this highlights the important distinction between Kaplan-style relativization to contexts and much vaguer relativizations to conversational situations.

---

[12]  Perhaps the hair has dislodged, but remains on the head, for the moment. And even if this situation does not arise, it might; and 'bald' can appear in modal claims.

[13]  As McGee and McLaughlin (1995) rightly note, you need an assumption to get claims about the object language to follow from reasoning in the metalanguage. And many proposals about how to avoid the paradoxes look (to me) more like proposals about how we ought to use sharp predicates than plausible hypotheses about the valuations of natural predicates; see Williamson (1994). One can, however, formulate a truth-conditional semantics without the usual function-talk by employing axioms like 'Valuation($x$, bald) iff $x$ is bald'; the idea is that a predicate has many valuations (instead of a single function as its valuation). See Larson and Segal (1995). Among the benefits of this notational scheme is that one can use 'bald' to say (with just the right degree of vagueness) which things are valuations of 'bald'.

## 2.3 *Varieties of context dependence*

Consider the following thesis:

(*) The predicate 'bald' applies to an individual in a given situation iff the individual counts as bald given the standards operative in that situation.

This could be a modest claim whose point is simply to note that an individual can count as bald for *some but not all* conversational purposes. There is no single all-purpose standard for what counts as bald; as we often say, it depends on the context. This is the case for many predicates, if only because standards for precision vary across conversations. Whether a certain person counts as six feet tall may depend on whether inches, or fractions of millimetres, are what matter.[14]

One might, however, intend (*) as the bolder claim that 'bald' is a context-sensitive term (like 'I', 'here', and 'now') whose valuation is relativized to Kaplan-style contexts (henceforth, K-contexts). Since the valuation of 'I' cannot be any particular individual, semanticists say that 'I' has a valuation only relative to a context K. The valuation of 'I' relative to K is the speaker of K; or more briefly, $\|\,'I'\,\|_K =$ speaker(K). Similarly, $\|\,'here'\,\|_K =$ place(K); $\|\,'now'\,\|_K =$ time(K); etc. Correlatively, we can say that a K-context just *is* an ordered *n*-tuple of elements $\langle \alpha, \beta, \gamma, \ldots \rangle$ that correspond to the context-sensitive terms in sentences; a K-context will be interpretatively relevant to a given *use* of 'I' only if the speaker is speaker(K); and similarly for other indexical terms. One can speculatively extend this model to predicates like 'bald' by suggesting that K-contexts include a baldness-standard parameter, **s,** which ranges over positive integers; s(K) would be a certain number (of hairs) relevant in K. Then one can say that $\|\,'bald'\,\|_K = [\lambda x\,.\,true$ iff there are fewer than s(K) hairs on $x$'s head]. Perhaps there is also a cleaning-standard parameter **s´**, ranging over functions from entities to parts of those entities,

---

[14] Travis (1985) seems to think this tells against compositional semantics; but cf. Cappellen and Lepore (forthcoming), and see n. 2 on the possibility of 'layered' meanings*, which may be what Austinian observations suggest. Correspondingly, one might reject the idea that axioms like 'Valuation(x, *bald*) iff x is bald'—see the previous note—are formulated in a 'canonical conversational situation' with the intention of specifying a 'canonical standard' for 'bald'. If there is no canonical standard, the axiom can still state that 'bald' has certain semantic properties.

such that $\|\,'\text{cleaned}'\,\|_K = [\lambda x \,.\, true$ iff $[\mathbf{s}'(K)](x)$ was made tidy]. But prima facie, these suggestions are implausible. One needs reasons for positing context-sensitive terms (and slots in K-contexts), thereby increasing the complexity of a semantic theory; and the increased complexity will be staggering if any significant portion of the Chomsky–Austin–Wittgenstein-inspired examples are dealt with by treating ordinary predicates as relevantly like indexicals.[15]

Let me stress, however, that the point of the examples is not to present paradoxes that call for resolution. The illustrated features of words 'do not indicate that people have contradictory or otherwise perplexing beliefs. There is no temptation to draw any such conclusion, if we *drop the empirical assumption that words pick out things, apart from particular usages, which they constrain in highly intricate ways*' (Chomsky 1995a: 23; emphasis added). Examples like (1)–(18) do not reveal paradoxical semantic facts. The troublemaker is a certain theoretical assumption that we can and should do without.[16] But this is *not*—I repeat, *not*—a recommendation that we abandon attempts to construct compositional semantic theories.

On the contrary, it is a recommendation that we abandon a certain conception of meaning (and its relation to truth) that threatens to frustrate our semantic theorizing. As Evans (1981) noted, in response to rather dif-

---

[15] Suppose that each demonstrative element in a sentence is associated with some index, as in 'That₁ is better than that₂.' Then one can say that the valuation of a demonstrative $\Delta_i$ relative to a context K is the $i$th object demonstrated in K (the object demonstrated in the act of demonstration associated with $\Delta_i$): $\|\Delta_i\|_K = K_i$. And one can say that K-contexts are ordered $n$-tuples of the form $\langle \alpha, \beta, \gamma, \ldots, 1, 2, 3, \ldots \rangle$, where Greek letters represent 'indexical slots' and arabic numerals indicate demonstrative slots. (See Larson and Segal 1995.) The proposal considered in the text would involve K-contexts of the form $\langle \alpha, \beta, \gamma, \ldots, 1, 2, 3, \ldots \mathbf{s}, \mathbf{s}', \mathbf{s}'', \ldots \rangle$. This is bad enough, since most predicates will require at least one 'floating standard' parameter. But think of all the other ways in which context bears on truth. Stanley and Szabo (2000) posit a covert domain-restriction parameter for every nominal expression. And so on. Phrase markers (and K-contexts) as currently conceived would represent only the tiniest fraction of sentential meanings. Perhaps this is the case. (Maybe most matter is 'dark', and most meaning is covert.) But one wants to see the arguments for this view, as opposed to arguments that other ways of showing how meaning can determine truth conditions are worse. See Hornstein (1986) for related discussion.

[16] Similarly, perhaps, for 'the average philosopher publishes 2.7 papers, and he is overpaid' or 'The average philosopher disguises his contempt of the average man'; cf. Higginbotham (1993).

ferent Wittgenstein-inspired criticisms of the Davidsonian programme, we have learnt a great deal about the compositionality of meaning by applying Fregean tools to the study of natural language. Only 'intellectual Luddites' would dismiss the whole project 'without a detailed consideration of its findings, and an alternative account of the enterprise' (p. 326). So let me stress that Chomsky is not opposing semantics. He is proposing, in the spirit of technological progress, a certain revision of traditional semantic machinery. But I sympathize with those who find it hard to get their head around the idea that sentences have meanings that do not fix their truth conditions. So at the risk of tedium, I propose to say this all yet again, emphasizing—as Chomsky (2000) does—some concerns that will occur to philosophers.

## 3 Once More, with Dialogue

PHIL. As I was saying yesterday, since the meaning of a sentence determines its truth-conditions . . .

LING. That's false. *Truth* conditions are context-sensitive in a way that meanings aren't.

PHIL. OK, if you want to be precise: for each context, the meaning of a sentence $\Sigma$ determines a truth-condition for $\Sigma$ relative to that context. So . . .

LING. That's either vacuous or very implausible. If 'context' is a label for all the factors relevant to the truth of $\Sigma$, apart from the meaning of $\Sigma$, your claim is trivial: meaning plus everything else relevant to truth determines truth. If by 'context' you mean a sequence of possible assignments for any indexicals and demonstratives in $\Sigma$, at least your claim is substantive: the meaning of $\Sigma$ determines its truth condition relative to a K-context. But why believe this, given all the apparent counter-examples?

PHIL. You never let me get on with an argument. Before my first premiss is out, you say 'trivial or false'. But you haven't offered an objection. You've described a research programme: specify the context-sensitive aspects of meaning and describe contexts in a suitably detailed way.

LING. In other words, you're positing a *lot* of indexicality. Why?

PHIL. Because the meaning of a sentence determines its truth conditions (relative to a context).

LING. Is there independent evidence for the required indices? And if not, what does that tell you?

PHIL. Not yet. And it tells me that there are *hidden* indices.

LING. Are there also hidden leprechauns? Let's at least distinguish two senses of 'hidden'. An index (or indexed element) might be *covert*, but still part of the sentence—like the trace in 'Whom$_i$ did Bill see $t_i$?'

A different idea is that sentences have Meanings, aspects of which are contextually determined but not indicated by any parts of sentences. This is to posit *agrammatical* indices. Thus, one might speak of $K^+$-contexts that include more parameters than K-contexts, which reflect the grammatical indices of sentences. So are the 'hidden' indices you posit supposed to be covert or agrammatical?[17]

PHIL. Yes.

LING. You know, some of us have to work for a living.

PHIL. Truth be told, *sentences* don't excite me. I'm more interested in what we express with sentences—viz. Propositions; and they may have contextually determined elements that sentences don't.

LING. Sentences don't excite me either. I'm more interested in the minds of sentence users. But the question is whether sentential meanings, which manifest minds, have the kinds of agrammatical constituents that you're so glibly countenancing.

PHIL. One can express doubts about particular proposals. But as Russell (*et al.*) showed, the meaning of a sentence $\Sigma$ typically has a structure that differs considerably from the grammatical structure of $\Sigma$.

LING. No one has shown that. If you think the syntax of 'the king is bald' is $\{[_{subj}$the king$][_{pred}$is bald$]\}$, and you represent the meaning with '$\exists x\{King(x)\ \&\ \forall y[King(y)\rightarrow y=x]\ \&\ Bald(x)\}$', you might be misled. But a more plausible syntax is:

$$\{[_{DPi}\ [_D\ the][_N\ king]]\{t_i\ [_{VP}\ is\ bald]\}\}$$

with the determiner phrase binding a covert trace; and we can encode Russell's hypothesis, using restricted quantifiers, with 'the$(x)$ : King$(x)$ [Bald$(x)$]'. Similar remarks apply to other examples, including those that

---

[17] For representative views see Stanley (2002) and Bach (1994), respectively.

led Frege to think that Propositions/Thoughts have agrammatical structures. So where is the fabled divergence?[18]

PHIL. If surface form sometimes differs from grammatical form because
sentences have covert elements, that's fine; and particular examples may
have been misdiagnosed. But the general point remains. Meanings/
Propositions may have structure that sentences don't. By the way, do
you really think there is evidence *independent of semantic intuitions* for
covert traces?

LING. Will you admit that if I provide lots of independent evidence for
traces, you have to provide at least some independent evidence for your
hidden indices? Consider 'Who$_i$ do you think t$_i$ will win?', and . . .

PHIL. The general point remains. Meanings/Propositions may have structure that sentences don't.

LING. And there may be leprechauns. You're saying that meaning determines truth conditions, despite the apparent counter-examples, because
(1) sentences are littered with covert indexicals that we can't detect given
current technology; and/or (2) a sentence $\Sigma$ has its Meaning by virtue
of its association with something that has more context-sensitive constituents than $\Sigma$. But appeals to covert sentential elements are always
prima facie implausible; that's why we need *arguments* for traces. And
since facts about quantifiers (names, pronouns, referential dependence,
etc.) don't establish the existence of agrammatical 'logical' structures,
what's the evidence for agrammatical indices—and yours in particular?[19]

PHIL. Our intuitions about the truth conditions of sentences, coupled with
the banality that the meaning of a sentence determines its truth conditions (relative to a context).

LING. I don't see how we could have reliable intuitions about the truth

---

[18] See Neale (1990; 1993); Higginbotham and May (1981); Barwise and Cooper (1981).

[19] One might think that propositional-attitude reports motivate appeals to hidden indexicals of the sort discussed (but rejected) by Schiffer (1992). See Pietroski (1994; 2000a)
for a '(c)overt indexical' view, according to which complementizers (which may or may
not be overt) are semantically associated with Fregean senses. This is a variation on 'Interpreted Logical Form' views; see Larson and Ludlow (1993); Segal (1989); Higginbotham
(1986); Harman (1972). A more ambitious style of argument starts with certain assumptions about logical possibility and its relation to meaning; see Wittgenstein (1921); Lewis
(1986). But one can imagine denying the assumptions; see Pietroski (2000a) for related
discussion.

conditions of sentences (or Propositions) on your view. But in any case, your 'banality' leads to implausible claims.

PHIL. I don't understand your resistance to the idea. If you're willing to posit meanings, why *not* suppose they determine truth conditions? Isn't that what meanings are supposed to do?

LING. I don't think meanings are supposed to *do* anything. I'm not *positing* meanings (*qua* theorist). I just think there are semantic facts that call for explanation; sentences have meanings, and we want to know more about this. But why think the meanings of sentences, which we discern so rapidly and effortlessly, determine truth conditions (relative to parameters statable in advance in terms of K-contexts)?

Whether a sentence counts as true in a conversational situation typically depends on a host of factors—including various 'saliences' and the judgements reasonable speakers would make about their listeners. Even Davidson (1986) admitted that we can't describe all these factors in any theoretically interesting way; but then, following Quine, he proceeded to unparalleled depths of triviality by . . .

PHIL. Let's leave Quine and Davidson out of it. You can be very hard on them. I'll grant that contexts are complex—maybe even too complex for us to *fully* characterize. But my thesis concerns the relation of meaning to truth, not our ability to characterize that relation in detail.

LING. Did you just use 'context' as a label for all factors relevant to truth, apart from meaning?

PHIL. No. My claim is that while $K^{(+)}$-contexts are complex, the semantic character of a sentence (which is what theories of meaning ought to specify) is a function from $K^{(+)}$-contexts (i.e. ordered $n$-tuples of possible valuations corresponding to the context-sensitive aspects of sentential meanings) to truth conditions (i.e. conditional assignments of *truth* values). Without an alternative conception of how meaning is related to truth, I'll posit the hidden indices required.

LING. So let's try to develop an alternative conception of how meaning is related to truth.

PHIL. This is your show.

LING. Fair enough. Here's the alternative: the fact that a sentence has a certain truth condition, as used in a certain conversational situation, is a massive *interaction effect*. The meaning of the sentence is a *contributing factor* that we can try to isolate and theorize about. But facts about the truth conditions of sentences don't constitute the target explananda in semantics, any more than facts about thermometers constitute the target explananda in chemistry.

PHIL. I'm lost. We *shouldn't* be trying to explain why (utterances of) sentences have the truth conditions they do?

LING. It depends what you mean by 'explain'. If explanations need to have rigorous deductive structures, as in real science, forget about explaining why (utterances of) sentences have the truth conditions they do—or why a given leaf followed exactly *that* trajectory. We occasionally formulate rigorous explanations of stable *phenomena*, which are typically unobservable and discovered only by long bouts of enquiry, but not the idiosyncratic interaction effects that we typically observe; see Bogen and Woodward (1988). A more relaxed conception of explanation might allow for combinations of a genuine semantic theory with some common-sense remarks that connect the theory with certain facts about communicative situations. But allowing for 'explanations' of this sort doesn't give you a *theory* that explains the particular facts, at least not in any interesting sense of 'theory'.

PHIL. Then all the intuitions linguists cite are surely interaction effects. So why all the fuss about them?

LING. Because facts about speakers' judgements can, like facts about thermometers, be evidence for hypotheses. But we know that judgements about sentences depend on things besides grammaticality and truth. So in syntax, we distinguish the *acceptability* of a word-string from more theoretical properties, like *grammaticality*. And in semantics, we already distinguish *felicity* conditions from *truth* conditions. Similarly, I claim, truth conditions often depend on a lot of things that count as 'noise' from the perspective of a (compositional) theory of meaning.

PHIL. Then why pick on truth? Why don't you say that grammaticality is an interaction effect?

LING. I do. There is no useful notion of well-formedness for natural languages. We can speak of (un)grammatical word-strings and (il)licit phrase markers; but we shouldn't insist that a theory of *syntax*, which is really a theory about some portion of the mind-brain, must itself deliver explanations for why a given string of words either does or doesn't consititute a 'well-formed' expression. Similarly, we shouldn't insist that a theory of *meaning* deliver explanations for why certain sentences have certain truth conditions. Syntax bears on grammaticality (and acceptability); semantics bears on truth (and felicity). But semantics, like syntax, deals with *systematic and intrinsic* features of sentences. These features *constrain* truth conditions (by constraining how sentences can be used); but they don't *determine* truth conditions, which depend on many factors, including unsystematic and extrinsic properties of sentences. In short, meaning doesn't determine truth conditions, because meaning isn't even a symbol–world relation. The meaning of a sentence is an intrinsic property of that sentence.

PHIL. That can't be right. As Putnam and Burge have shown, . . .

LING. Please, spare me your Twin Earth intuitions. They don't show that a *theoretical* notion of meaning has to be externalist. If 'meaning' is a kind-term, meanings are intrinsic properties of sentences. (Thoughts, construed as Fregean senses, *may* be another matter.)

PHIL. But it's a Moorean fact that meaning is a symbol–world relation. You really must read Lewis (1972) on what a theory of *meaning* needs to do.

LING. Oh, I read it. If you're taking it to be *definitional* that meaning determines truth conditions, you're lapsing back into triviality. If a 'Lewisian theory of meaning' tells one how to connect expressions with (things in the world and) *truth* conditions, good luck providing a Lewisian theory of meaning for any natural language. And why think there is one to provide?

PHIL. But why adopt your internalist conception of semantics? What's the evidence for that?

LING. Let's look at various textbook results that show us where attempts at semantic theorizing have actually been successful. In my view, they *all* concern intrinsic features of sentences. Consider standard accounts of quantifiers, anaphora, relative clauses, causatives, adverbs, . . .

PHIL. Let's not, at least not before lunch. Even if you're right, that may reflect the (short) history of semantics. Tell me why we shouldn't expect theories that specify truth conditions.

LING. Consider examples like 'Unicycles have wheels', which counts as true even though no unicycle has wheels. How can its truth condition be compositionally determined? Facts about usage constrain theories of meaning. But we don't need—or want—a massively parameterized semantic theory. If we try to represent the truth conditions of our sentences as used, we'll lose the distinction between representations of sentential meanings and representations of the facts that sentence users gesture at by using sentences.

PHIL. Exactly! There is no analytic distinction, as Quine taught us. So 'there is no boundary between knowing a language and knowing our way around in the world' (Davidson 1986: 446).

LING. Rubbish. The positivistic theses Quine criticized were, no doubt, objectionable. Maybe he was even right about the following conditional: *if* you take semantic facts to be normative facts about the inferences we ought to make, you will be led to reject any analytic/synthetic distinction (and perhaps the notion of meaning itself). But then Modus Tollens is the appropriate inference.[20]

PHIL. You *can't* distinguish semantic facts from the other facts we report with our sentences.

LING. Is that an empirical claim, or a threat to call the enquiry police? What's the argument that sentences like 'If you boiled the soup, the soup boiled'—'If someone persuaded you to sing, you intended to sing', 'If Pat thinks that Chris likes himself, Pat thinks that Chris likes Chris', etc.—are not analytic? Why should we deny that such examples differ, in semantically interesting ways, from 'If you boiled the soup, the mean molecular energy of the soup rose'?

PHIL. You're going to make a speech, aren't you?

LING. Various fomulations of the analytic/synthetic distinction may be untenable; and analytic truths won't do the *epistemic* work that some philosophers have wanted them to do. But how does that even begin to warrant the claim that 'there is no boundary between knowing a language and knowing our way around in the world'? Maybe our ordinary notion of *truth* is connected with epistemic notions, in a way that makes Davidson's remark defensible; and likewise for meaning *if* meaning is related to truth

---

[20] Similarly, *if* semantic facts are abstractions from the usage of ideal scientists trying to report the facts. There are related issues concerning the degree to which meanings are *innately* determined; see McGilvray (1998; 1999), Crain and Pietroski (2000). But no sane person denies that experience matters. The questions concern the constraints imposed by biology on the kinds of cognitive state human beings normally come to have under the pressure of normal linguistic experience—and the degree to which scientific discourse involves *invention* of symbol systems not governed by these constraints.

in the way you (and he) suggest. But that's what we were arguing about. You can hardly assume all this just on the alleged strength of the idea that meaning determines truth conditions. If that little slogan encodes the whole Quine–Davidson world-view, then we need to see some evidence *before* adopting the slogan. Let's follow empiricist advice, and see what actual enquiry suggests.

## 4  What's Next

So what *is* a (natural-language) semanticist supposed to do if we abandon the project of recursively specifying the truth conditions of natural sentences?

### 4.1  *The interesting explananda remain*

There remains the non-trivial project of finding a semantic typology, with an associated theory whose theorems assign valuations to expressions, that helps explain the range of facts that semanticists discuss. But valuation assignments have to be motivated by the facts they purportedly explain. One can't just 'observe' that the theory assigns the right truth conditions and declare it materially adequate. For this reason, one cannot tell in advance what *form* a correct theory of meaning will take, or which facts such a theory will explain. The details will be revealed, if at all, only through enquiry. We cannot know a priori what a semantic theory should look like any more than pre-Newtonian theorists could have known what the right theory of celestial mechanics would look like. (Anyone who insisted that a theory of planetary motion had to be about *planetary motion*, or that talk of tides and falling bodies was just a distraction, got the theory he deserved; see Antony, this volume.) It may once have seemed clear that a semantic theory should associate each object-language sentence with a meaning-giving specification of its truth conditions. But that was a proposal, which we can refine, about how to study meaning.

Moreover, it bears emphasis that the target explananda in semantics go well beyond the facts cited when we disquotationally report what particular sentences mean. The sentence 'Deflationists miss the point' has a certain meaning; and we want a compositional semantics to reveal how the parts (and structure) of the sentence conspire to produce that meaning. But this is the tip of an explanatory iceberg. Semanticists try, often with some success, to help explain why speakers find inferences like the following impeccable: 'Pat boiled the soup at noon, so Pat boiled the soup'; 'Pat boiled the soup, so the soup boiled'; 'Every kid swam, so every tall kid swam' (cf. 'Most kids swam, so most tall kids swam'); 'Every kid is a kid who swam, so every kid swam'; etc.[21] We also want to explain various semantic contrasts. Why is the position occupied by 'Fido' semantically opaque in 'I heard that Fido barked', but not in 'Fido barked' or 'I heard Fido bark'? Facts concerning ambiguity are familiar, but facts concerning non-ambiguity are just as important. Why can speakers of English not use 'Was the child who lost kept crying?' to ask whether the child who was lost kept crying? One of Chomsky's most famous examples still bears repeating: 'John is eager to please' means (roughly) that John is eager that he please someone *and not* that John is eager for someone to please him; 'John is easy to please' means (roughly) that it is easy for someone to please John *and not* that it is easy for John to please someone. Or more mundanely, 'Brutus stabbed Caesar' has no reading on which Brutus is the stabee and Caesar is the stabber. Why?

Semantics textbooks are loaded with descriptions and partial explanations of such facts. Unsurprisingly, the explanations involve both hypotheses about the structures of sentences and how various aspects of structure are related to meaning. For example, 'John is easy to please' involves covert elements as indicated in [John$_i$ is easy [_to please $e_i$]]; while the logically possible structure [John$_i$ is easy [$e_i$ to please _]] is unavailable in natural language. But 'eager' differs from 'easy'; the former cannot take a pleonastic subject. (Consider what 'It is eager to please John' means.) This constrains the possible structures of English: [John$_i$ is eager [$e_i$ to please _]] is fine, while [John$_i$ is eager [_to please $e_i$]] is not. Similarly, given constraints on extractions from relative clauses, natural languages do not include expressions like {Was$_i$ [[the child who $e_i$ lost][kept crying]]}; but {Was$_i$ [[the child who lost][$e_i$ kept crying]]} is fine. These structural facts help explain the semantic facts, given certain assumptions about the interpretation of unvoiced elements—and the background assumption that meaning is compositional. (If the meaning of the whole is not determined by the meanings of the parts,

---

[21] This last inference pattern holds for all natural-language determiners, though we can easily invent determiners for which it does not. While 'only' is not a determiner, it illustrates the point: only boys are boys who swam; but it hardly follows that only boys swam. See Larson and Segal (1995) for discussion.

and the way the parts are structured, why does [_to please $e_i$] *not* have the meaning of [$e_i$ to please _] or the meaning of 'bark'? Similarly, when semanticists account for the compellingness of inferences—even simple ones like 'Pat ran, so someone ran'—compositionality is assumed.)

I stress this point, in part because some philosophers fail to give it due weight when making claims about meaning.[22] More importantly in the present context, it bears emphasis that specifying *truth* conditions was never the only semantic project in town. And in my view, the explanations remain equally good if we replace occurrences of '*true*' in current semantic theories with occurrences of '1'—with compensating adjustments elsewhere—and eschew the assumption that a sentence $\Sigma$ is true (as used in a given context) iff the $\Sigma$ has the valuation 1 (relative to that context). One can retain the structural aspects of our theories, which are typically the aspects that do the explanatory work, without the illusion that we are *also* explaining why (utterances of) sentences have the truth conditions they do. Perhaps there will be some cases in which such revision leads us to think that a putative explanation is really no explanation at all, as opposed to a more modest explanation of a more modest fact. But if so, better to see our theories for what they are. (For analogous discussion in the context of vision theory, see Egan 1992; 2003.)

Trading in truth values (and entities referred to) for different valuations does not change the basic questions. We still want to know, for any given

---

[22] Cf. Schiffer (1987). Or consider Horwich's (1998) claim that 'Dogs bark' means what it does simply because: 'dogs' means *dogs*; 'bark' means *bark*; and the relevant syntax means what it does. This may account for the extremely 'thin' fact that the sentence means what it does; and in a correspondingly thin sense, Horwich may be right that one can account for the *mere* compositionality of meaning without further semantic machinery, like a Davidsonian truth theory (or a neo-Davidsonian valuationist theory). But whatever the merits of deflating truth—see Horwich (1990)—a deflationary account of meaning leaves the facts that semanticists really care about completely unexplained. It does no good to say that the syntax of 'ran slowly' makes the semantic contribution it makes: our best theories of meaning reveal *which semantic contribution this is* in a way that sheds light on inferences that speakers recognize as impeccable. (By and large, the semantic correlate of syntactic adjunction is conjunctive—as opposed to disjunctive. But you need to *say* that in your semantic theory, if you want to explain the semantic relation between 'red box' and 'box'.) It is no *explanation* of opacity to say that the parts of 'heard that Fido barked', together with how they are arranged, give the verb-phrase a meaning that differs from that of 'heard Fido bark'. And so on. See Pietroski (2000c) for extended discussion.

sentence: what is its structure; what does it mean; and how is the former related to the latter? Or in the psychologized mode, which structures and meanings (if any) do speakers unconsciously assign to utterances? When the answers start to stabilize—and *phenomena* emerge—we can ask more general questions: why do human languages exhibit *these* structures, meanings, and structure–meaning relations; why do humans assign *these* structures and meanings, as opposed to others? At any given time, these big questions are translated into more manageable ones in the usual ways (see e.g. Chomsky 1980; 1986; 1995b). But so far as I can tell, the issues that animate current research in semantics are orthogonal to the question of whether *truth* values are really the valuations of sentences.

To take a much-discussed example, one can ask whether syntactically binary predicates like 'stab' should be associated with: binary functions— from the valuations of singular terms like 'Caesar' to functions from the valuations of singular terms like 'Brutus' to sentential valuations, as in Montague (1970); ternary functions—with an additional 'event position' as in Davidson (1967); or unary functions from eventish to sentential valuations, as in Parsons (1990) and Schein (1993). Regardless of what sentential valuations are, one can ask whether 'stabbed' is *apt for use as* an event sortal, a binary-function expression, a ternary-function expression, or something else entirely. Similarly, one can ask whether adverb phrases like 'with a knife' are apt for use as event sortals (which can be conjoined with other event sortals) or as expressions for creating a complex function expression of the same type as the relevant verb. The possible answers have empirical consequences, including consequences for how syntax contributes to meaning, which we can test and evaluate. Natural-language semantics is a field rich with such questions if we will just ask them. Questions about the truth conditions of sentences were good questions to ask; they got the field going. But now it is going.[23]

[23] This is, admittedly, too quick. One wants to see how semantics is done, starting with basic facts about predicates and quantifiers, without the standard truth-theoretic assumptions. But this is not the place to pursue the detailed project; see Pietroski (forthcoming) for an attempt to deliver some goods. With regard to 'Unicycles have wheels', one hypothesis would be that it has the valuation 1 iff each (typical) valuation of 'unicycle' is a valuation of 'have wheels'. It seems unlikely that any valuation of 'unicycle' will be a valuation of 'have wheels', since no unicycle has wheels. On this view, a true sentence has the valuation 0. If this is correct, the truth of the sentence has something to do with our

Some (neo-)Davidsonian projects will seem less urgent from the present perspective. Consider the fact that 'The book is red' can be true, as used in a given context, even though the universe contains more than one book. If a semantic theory does not *have* to explain this fact by positing a (covert or agramamtical) domain-restriction parameter, we might not posit one until there is evidence for a corresponding index. Such evidence may be forthcoming. But there is no pressure to devote research energy to finding an index, if the fact about truth conditions is not a theoretically interesting fact. If a fact challenges an important aspect of our best semantic theories, we need to deal with that; but if it is just one fact among many, we can ignore it. Of course, one cannot tell in advance which facts are theoretically interesting. Perhaps the really interesting questions will emerge by trying to save the idea that meaning determines truth conditions relative to a K-context. But as I read Chomsky, he is urging us to adopt a different view of what is important (and what to ignore). In any case, we can question the assumption that facts about truth conditions are *ipso facto* of theoretical interest to semanticists. Maybe our time is better spent elsewhere. Physicists do not spend their time determining the trajectories of particular leaves.

## 4.2 *Room for knowledge of reference*

Still, when a speaker of English understands

(19) Brutus killed Caesar,

she seems to grasp *more* than that (*a*) the constituent words belong to certain semantic types, and (*b*) the sentence exhibits a certain 'valuational structure'. Someone who knew only that 'killed' is a binary predicate, and that 'Brutus' and 'Caesar' are referential devices, would not know the specific meaning of (19)—i.e. that it means that Brutus killed Caesar, as opposed to (say) that Antony saw Cleopatra. A neo-neo-Davidsonian can say there is more to meaning than meets the eye; 'Killed(Brutus, Caesar)' may reflect an over-simple view about the semantic structure of (19). Consider the following alternative:

(20) $\exists e\{\text{Agent}(e, \text{Brutus}) \ \& \ \exists f[\text{Die}(f) \ \& \ R(e, f)] \ \& \ \text{Theme}(e, \text{Caesar})\}$

tendency to use 'have wheels' instead of 'are wheeled', despite the 'mismatch' between the truth conditions and the (compositionally determined) valuation conditions.

where 'R' stands for some relation that holds between eventish valuations. Still, this does not explain how speakers distinguish the meaning of (19) from that of 'Bob felled Chris.' No matter how rich the intrinsic features of sentences are, they come to an end. There is a sense in which we don't know what

(21) All mimsy were the borogoves

means. And one might think that a semantic theory should be (*inter alia*) a theory of what (21) lacks; see Higginbotham (1989).

A radical line is to deny this outright; see McGilvray (1998; 1999). Perhaps a semantic theory does not have to explain the (alleged) difference between the interpretable and uninterpretable aspects of (21). Perhaps the difference between 'mimsy' and 'flimsy' is like the difference between the name of your best friend and a name you have never heard before; and it is not obvious that a semantic theory has to account for *that* kind of felt difference. Or perhaps 'borogove' is like 'quark'—a word that physicists use to talk of charming things, but which is effectively meaningless for ordinary speakers. There is, no doubt, a difference between knowing that 'flimsy' applies to flimsy things and that 'mimsy' applies to mimsy things. Speakers of English not only know that something counts as flimsy (in a conversational situation) iff it is flimsy (by the standards operative in that situation), they know—or at least have an idea of—what counts as flimsy (at least in many situations). But not so for 'mimsy'. How this bears on linguistic understanding is a hard and potentially interesting question.

Consider just one of the potentially confounding factors. To what degree are intuitions about (21) affected by the (perhaps dim) recognition that *there is nothing to know* about what counts as mimsy? How relevant is Kripke's (1980) discussion of unicorns? Suppose I utter

(22) All bimsy were the chimeras,

thinking that 'bimsy' is the word for Hume's missing shade of blue. Is (22) importantly different from (21); or does (22) also lack a meaning in a way that a semantic theory should illuminate? If we drop the idea that semantics *must* connect sentences with truth conditions and things we refer to, lots of things need rethinking. On the other hand, we should leave room for the following thought: speakers have certain t-beliefs with externalistic (broad) contents; this will help explain certain facts about linguistic understanding; and so a theory of meaning will be externalist at least to this extent.[24]

It might be useful to distinguish facts speakers t-believe by virtue of *having a language faculty* from other facts speakers t-believe by virtue of *being a language user in some environment*. Speakers may t-believe that 'dog' is true of dogs; and perhaps this bears on how speakers understand sentences with the word 'dog'—say because understanding a sentence (as used in a conversational situation **c**) involves being able (somehow) to figure out its truth conditions (in **c**). Understanding may involve two or more kinds of cognition, and correspondingly related but different theoretical notions of meaning. If there are interesting things to say about what speakers t-believe, even where we specify what they t-believe by using notions like truth, let us hope we discover this. But let us not assume, without evidence, what there is to discover. This will not be concessive enough for a certain kind of theorist who will say (rightly) that the facts concerning a speaker's language faculty include facts that reflect her linguistic experience, *and* (more tendentiously) that at least some of these facts are properly characterized (for theoretical purposes) in terms of an externalist/normative notion of truth. Someone should sort out, in a clear and systematic way, what the available evidence suggests on this score. But a Chomsky-style internalism is at least worthy of serious consideration. Indeed, it may provide the best overall account of what a theory of meaning is a theory of.

## 5 Afterthought

PHIL. I've decided to adopt the Language of Thought hypothesis.

LING. Pardon?

PHIL. The structure of a Proposition differs from the structure of the public

[24] Whether this is a view supported by evidence, or a dispensable way of talking, is a topic for another day. At the conference it was rightly noted that a strongly internalist conception of semantics would (given familiar and not implausible views about rationality) threaten the idea that acquiring a language is a *rational* achievement. But however initially attractive this idea may be—especially if one wants to view linguistics as continuous with Intentional Psychology (see Higginbotham 1989; Rey, this volume)—it is not a datum. Facts about what children try to do leave the issue unsettled (see the last paragraph of sect. 1), as do facts about their 'errors' (see Crain and Pietroski 2000). See Dwyer and Pietroski (1996) for an approach to t-belief compatible with an internalist semantics.

sentence used to express it, because (tokens of) public sentences have their meanings by virtue of their causal relations to mental sentences, which contain indices not present in the public sentences. What you called a $K^+$-context is really just a K-context. But the sentences that matter for semantics are those of Mentalese; see Fodor (1987) for elaboration and better dialogues.

LING. It's very late. So I'll grant that when a person hears an utterance $u$ of her language, $u$ typically causes a tokening of some Mentalese sentence that is germane to how the person interprets $u$.

PHIL. Not just *some* Mentalese sentence, but one that differs in semantically important ways from the public (though perhaps idiolectical) sentence that $u$ is a token of.

LING. Fine. When I hear you speak, certain expressions are generated via my language faculty. And those expressions might be transformed, in any number of ways, in the process of figuring out what you said.

PHIL. Not transformed. Public sentences get *transduced* into sentences of a completely different language. Mentalese sentences don't merely encode speaker meanings, they're the only sentences that *have* meanings. For unlike the expressions generated by your language faculty, sentences of Mentalese have compositionally determined (characteristic functions from K-contexts to) truth conditions.

LING. Why suppose that unicycle-type examples won't apply, *mutatis mutandis*, to Mentalese?

PHIL. It's an empirical hypothesis that they won't. Do you have evidence to the contrary?

LING. No. But neither do I have evidence against the claim that Mentalese wards off leprechauns. What's your reason for thinking that Mentalese is as different from English as you suggest? We're not worried about phonology here. And for all we know, which is very little, the grammar of (my idiolect of) Mentalese is identical to the grammar of (my idiolect of) English—or some other language that differs from English only in the trivial ways that Japanese differs from English.[25]

---

[25] This leaves open the possibility that when you say 'The book is blue', my language faculty generates a token of $\{[_{DPi}\,[_D\,the][_N\,book]][t_i\,[_{VP}\,is\,blue]]\}$, which then triggers further processing that results in a token of $\{[t_i[_{Adj}\,blue]]\,[_{DPi}\,[_D\,that][_N\,book\,by\,Russell]]\}$. *If* we go on to identify the truth conditions of the first token with those of the latter,

PHIL. Mentalese isn't English or any other language of the sort that people speak. We probably share Mentalese with chimps—maybe even rats.

LING. I knew it would come back to rats and chimps. But when I *say* 'Tigers are nigh' you are far more likely to have the thought that tigers are nigh than the semantically unrelated thought that fish swim. (See Fodor 1983.) Doesn't this suggest—at least a little—that the English sentence has a semantic character that at least constrains translation into Mentalese?

PHIL. It's not translation; it's transduction, the sort of thing the vision system does to light. The speed of the process makes it seem as though the sentence has a meaning of its own, but it doesn't.

LING. And what makes it transduction as opposed to translation?[26]

PHIL. The fact that Mentalese sentences have genuine meanings—functions from K-contexts to truth conditions—while English sentences don't. And we need genuine meanings for Intentional Psychology.

LING. Let's not get into Intentional Psychology. Tell me why English sentences *don't* have meanings?

PHIL. Because meanings, which determine truth conditions, are what Mentalese sentences have.

LING. I thought meanings were what theories of meaning were theories of. Is all the work that appears to be about the semantic character of English really a proto-semantics for Mentalese?

PHIL. At best.

LING. So we can try to characterize the semantically relevant aspects of English—i.e. the aspects in virtue of which it approximates Mentalese? And we can occasionally succeed?

PHIL. If I deny it, you'll go on and on about quantifiers and anaphora.

LING. So we can have (partial) theories of how the languages we speak approximate some Ideal Language for which a truth-conditional semantics can be given. But we mustn't say that English actually *has* a semantics,

---

say because we think English-as-Mentalese is what matters for purposes of assigning truth conditions to utterances, then we might adopt the following view: there *is* a truth-conditional semantics for English; but when we utter an English sentence, the utterance typically has the truth conditions of some *other* English sentence (relative to the context in question).

[26] Bob Matthews effectively challenges this distinction—cf. Schiffer (1987); Fodor (1998)—in his contribution to this volume.

because it's analytic that only expressions in an Ideal Language can have Meanings?

PHIL. Nice try. But no, it's not analytic. And I didn't hypothesize Mentalese as a regulative ideal.

LING. So it's an empirical hypothesis that (1) Mentalese is effectively a *Begriffsschrift* and (2) the semantic facts are facts about Mentalese, as opposed to the languages we speak.

PHIL. That's the idea. Meaning is really a topic for philosophical psychology, not linguistics.

LING. And you have results to back up this claim? A truth-conditional semantics for Mentalese?

PHIL. Not yet. But how else could we have *thoughts* with determinate truth conditions?

LING. Let's try to walk upright before running a marathon. At least for now, the way to study meaning is by supposing that our publicly available sentences have meanings—and then trying to say how various features of sentences contribute to sentential meanings. But we shouldn't assume that English has a *truth*-conditional semantics, since that would distort the semantic facts; about that, we seem to agree.

PHIL. Yes, but when the facts are in, we'll see that the real bearers of meanings are Mentalese sentences.

LING. Fine. Call me when those facts are in. But what shall we do tomorrow?

# REFERENCES

ALMOG, J., PERRY, J., and WETTSTEIN, H., eds. (1989), *Themes from Kaplan* (New York: Oxford University Press).

ANTONY, L., and HORNSTEIN, N., eds. (2003), *Chomsky and his Critics* (Oxford: Blackwell).

BACH, K. (1994), 'Conversational Implicature'. *Mind and Language*, 9: 124–62.

BARWISE, J., and COOPER, R. (1981), 'Generalized Quantifiers and Natural Language', *Linguistics and Philosophy*, 4: 159–219.

BOGEN, J., and WOODWARD, J. (1988), 'Saving the Phenomena', *Philosophical Review*, 97: 303–52.

CAPPELLEN, H., and LEPORE, E. (forthcoming), 'Radical and Moderate Pragmatics: Does Meaning Determine Truth-Conditions?'.

CARLSON, F., and PELLETIER, F., eds., (1995), *The Generic Book* (Chicago: University of Chicago Press).

CHOMSKY, N. (1977), *Essays on Form and Interpretation* (New York: North Holland).

—— (1980), *Rules and Representations* (New York: Columbia University Press).

—— (1986), *Knowledge of Language* (New York: Praeger).

—— (1995*a*), 'Language and Nature', *Mind*, 104: 1–61.

—— (1995*b*), *The Minimalist Program* (Cambridge, Mass.: MIT Press).

—— (2000), *New Horizons in the Study of Language and Mind* (New York: Cambridge).

CRAIN, S., and PIETROSKI, P. (2000), 'Nature, Nurture, and Universal Grammar', *Linguistics and Philosophy*, 24: 139–86.

DAVIDSON, D. (1967), 'The Logical Form of Action Sentences', in Rescher (1967), 81–120.

—— (1984), *Inquiries into Truth and Interpretation* (Oxford: Oxford University Press).

—— (1986), 'A Nice Derangement of Epitaphs', in Lepore (1986), 433–46.

—— and HARMAN, G., eds. (1972), *Semantics of Natural Language* (Dordrecht: Reidel).

DWYER, S., and PIETROSKI, P. (1996), 'Believing in Language', *Philosophy of Science*, 63: 338–73.

EGAN, F. (1992), 'Individualism, Computation, and Perceptual Content', *Mind*, 100: 461–84.

—— (2003), 'Naturalistic Inquiry: Where Does Mental Representation Fit In?', in Antony and Hornstein (2003), 89–104.

EVANS, G. (1981), 'Semantic Theory and Tacit Knowledge', in Holzmann and Leich (1981), 118–37.

FARLEY, A., FARLEY, P., and MCCULLOUGH, K.-E., eds. (1986), *Papers from the Parasession on Pragmatics and Grammatical Theory* (CLS 22.2; Chicago: Chicago Linguistics Society).

FODOR, J. (1983), *The Modularity of Mind* (Cambridge, Mass.: MIT Press).

—— (1987), *Psychosemantics* (Cambridge, Mass.: MIT Press).

—— (1998), *Concepts: Where Cognitive Science Went Wrong* (Oxford: Clarendon Press).

FREGE, G. (1892), 'Über Sein und Bedeutung', *Zeitschrift für Philosophie und philosophische Kritik*, 100: 25–50, translated as 'On Sense and Reference', in P. T. Geach and M. Black (eds.), *Translations from the Philosophical Writings of Gottlob Frege* (Oxford: Blackwell, 1953), 56–78.

GEORGE, A., ed. (1989), *Reflections on Chomsky* (Oxford: Blackwell).

HARMAN, G. (1972), 'Logical Form', *Foundations of Language*, 9: 38–65.

HIGGINBOTHAM, J. (1985), 'On Semantics', *Linguistic Inquiry*, 16: 547–93.

—— (1986), 'Linguistic Theory and Davidson's Program', in Lepore (1986), 29–48.

—— (1989), 'Knowledge of Reference', in George (1989), 153–74.

—— (1993), 'Grammatical Form and Logical Form', *Philosophical Perspectives*, 7: 173–96.

—— and MAY, R. (1981), 'Questions, Quantifiers, and Crossing', *Linguistic Review*, 1: 47–79.

HOLZMAN, S., and LEICH, C., eds. (1981), *Wittgenstein: To Follow a Rule* (London: Routledge & Kegan Paul).

HORNSTEIN, N. (1984), *Logic as Grammar* (Cambridge, Mass.: MIT Press).

—— (1986), 'Pragmatics and Grammatical Theory', in Farley *et al.* (1986), 234–48.

HORWICH, P. (1990), *Truth* (Oxford: Blackwell).

—— (1998), *Meaning* (Oxford: Oxford University Press).

IRVINE, A., and WEDEKING, G., eds. (1993), *Russell and Analytic Philosophy* (Toronto: University of Toronto Press).

KAPLAN, D. (1989), 'Demonstratives', in Almog, Perry, and Wettstein (1989), 565–614.

KEEFE, R., and SMITH, P., eds. (1990), *Vagueness: A Reader* (Cambridge, Mass.: MIT Press).

KOSLICKI, K. (1999), 'Genericity and Logical Form', *Mind and Language*, 14: 441–67.

KRIPKE, S. (1980), *Naming and Necessity* (Cambridge, Mass.: Harvard University Press).

LARSON, R., and LUDLOW, P. (1993), 'Interpreted Logical Forms', *Synthese*, 93: 305–55.

—— and SEGAL, G. (1995), *Knowledge of Meaning* (Cambridge, Mass.: MIT Press).

LEPORE, E. (1983), 'What Model-Theoretic Semantics Cannot Do', *Synthese*, 54: 167–87.

—— ed. (1986), *Truth and Interpretation: Perspectives on the Philosophy of Donald Davidson* (Oxford: Blackwell).

—— and SMITH, B., eds. (forthcoming), *Handbook of Philosophy of Language* (Oxford: Oxford University Press).

LEWIS, D. (1972), 'General Semantics', in Davidson and Harman (1972), 169–218.

—— (1986), *On the Plurality of Worlds* (Oxford: Blackwell).

McGEE, V., and McLAUGHLIN, B. (1995), 'Distinctions without a Difference', *Southern Journal of Philosophy*, suppl. 33: 203–51.

McGilvray, J. (1998), 'Meanings are Syntactically Individuated and Found in the Head', *Mind and Language*, 13: 225–80.

—— (1999), *Chomsky: Language, Mind and Politics* (Cambridge: Polity Press).

—— ed. (forthcoming), *The Cambridge Companion to Chomsky* (Cambridge: Cambridge University Press).

Marr, D. (198), *Vision* (New York: W. H. Freeman).

Montague, R. (1970), 'English as a Formal Language', in B. Visentini *et al.* (eds.), *Linguaggi nella società e nella tecnica* (Milan: Edizioni di Comunità, 1970), 189–227; repr. in id., *Formal Philosophy* (New Haven: Yale University Press, 1974), 188–221 [cited from the reprint].

Neale, S. (1990), *Descriptions* (Cambridge, Mass.: MIT Press).

—— (1993), 'Grammatical Form, Logical Form, and Incomplete Symbols', in Irvine and Wedeking (1993), 97–139.

Parsons, T. (1990), *Events in the Semantics of English* (Cambridge, Mass.: MIT Press).

Pietroski, P. (1994), 'A Defence of Derangement', *Canadian Journal of Philosophy*, 24: 95–118.

—— (2000*a*), *Causing Actions* (Oxford: Oxford University Press).

—— (2000*b*), 'On Explaining That', *Journal of Philosophy*, 97: 655–62.

—— (2000*c*), 'The Undeflated Domain of Semantics', *Sats, Nordic Journal of Philosophy*, 1: 161–76.

—— (2000*d*), review of Larson and Segal (1995), in *Mind*, 109: 960–4.

—— (2002), 'Function and Concatenation', in Preyer (2002), 91–117.

—— (forthcoming), *Events and Semantic Architecture* (Oxford: Oxford University Press).

Preyer, G., ed. (2002), *Logical Form* (Oxford: Oxford University Press).

Rescher, N., ed. (1967), *The Logic of Decision and Action* (Pittsburgh: University of Pittsburgh Press).

Sainsbury, M. (1990), 'Concepts without Boundaries', in Keefe and Smith (1990), 251–64.

Schein, B. (1993), *Events and Plurals* (Cambridge, Mass.: MIT Press).

Schier, S. (1987), *Remnants of Meaning* (Cambridge, Mass.: MIT Press).

—— (1992), 'Belief Ascription', *Journal of Philosophy*, 89: 499–521.

Segal, G. (1989), 'A Preference for Sense and Reference', *Journal of Philosophy*, 89: 73–89.

Stainton, R. (forthcoming), 'Meaning and Reference: Some Chomskian Themes', in Lepore and Smith (forthcoming).

Stanley, J. (2002), 'Making it Articulated', *Mind and Language*, 17: 149–68.

STANLEY, J., and SZABO, Z., (2000), 'Quantifer Domain Restriction', *Mind and Language*, 15: 219–62.

TARSKI, A. (1944), 'The Semantic Conception of Truth', *Philosophy and Phenomenological Research*, 4: 341–75.

TRAVIS, C. (1985), 'On What is Strictly Speaking True', *Canadian Journal of Philosophy*, 15: 187–229.

WILLIAMSON, T. (1999), *Vagueness* (London: Routledge).

WITTGENSTEIN, G. (1921), *Tractatus Logico-Philosophicus*, trans. D. Pears and B. McGuinness, 2nd edn. (London: Routledge & Kegan Paul, 2001).

# CHAPTER 8

# Grasping Objects and Contents

*Reinaldo Elugardo and Robert J. Stainton*

## 1 An Example

Imagine Andrew walks into a room, holds up a cigarette, and says 'From France' to Sylvia. We think it is obvious that, in this case, Andrew could easily convey a proposition. Let us agree that Andrew communicates, about the cigarette, that it is from France. A singular proposition. He can do this because, as will be obvious to both Andrew and Sylvia, what Andrew means clearly is not the property $\lambda x$ . from-France$(x)$. How could he mean *that*? Thus, to treat him as co-operating, Sylvia must find a proposition meant, and the most obvious one is precisely this singular proposition. Supposing that what is communicated is this proposition, consider now what expression was produced. We maintain, though this is not entirely obvious, that Andrew did not utter a sentence. He did not, we maintain, utter the ordinary sentence 'This cigarette is from France'. Nor did he utter any of: 'This thing is from France', 'The item in my hand is from France',

We are grateful to the Social Sciences and Humanities Research Council of Canada for a grant held jointly by the two authors. Among other things, this grant provided support for a Research Assistant, Jennifer Schellinck. We are also grateful to the University of Oklahoma Research Council for a grant that helped in the production of this paper. Thanks also to Alex Barber, Anne Bezuidenhout, Andrew Botterell, Robyn Carston, and Zenon Pylyshyn for comments on earlier drafts, and to the participants in the Epistemology of Language Conference at the University of Sheffield in 2000, where this paper was read. We must especially single out Emma Borg, who presented a very insightful and helpful commentary at that conference, as a reuslt of which the paper has been improved in many ways. An earlier draft was presented to the Department of Philosophy at the University of Missouri (Columbia), and we are grateful for the helpful comments we received on that occasion. Finally, special thanks to Ernie Lepore for encouraging us to pursue what, to some, will seem an excessively idiosyncratic topic.

or even 'This is from France'. What he uttered was the bare prepositional phrase:[1]

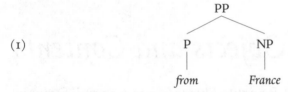

(1)

It also looks, at first glance, as if Andrew's interlocutor *recovered* a non-sentence as well. (Again, this is controversial. We return to it below.) Prima facie, what Sylvia heard was precisely what Andrew produced: a prepositional phrase. Yet she understood the singular proposition that Andrew meant.

Note too: the *meaning* of this PP is subpropositional. For instance, it clearly does not contribute a proposition as it appears in 'I brought this wine back from France'. Its meaning as it appears in this sentence is some kind of property, $\lambda x$ . from-France($x$). And it would be absurd to suppose that it and every other phrase in the language has *two* meanings, this subpropositional one (which it contributes within sentences and other larger structures) and some cluster of fully propositional meanings (one of which it exhibits when it occurs alone).[2] Now, the fact that a subpropositional expression can be employed to communicate a proposition should not be that surprising. In fact, there are lots of cases in which what the speaker communicates goes well beyond the meaning of her words. This surely occurs in conversational implicature, and many would maintain that it equally occurs in metaphor, indirect speech acts, irony, etc. We strongly suspect that it occurs when quantificational domains are contextually restricted (for example, 'Everyone got drunk on Friday' is used to mean, not that every person in the world got drunk on Friday, but that everyone in some salient group did so). It occurs when speakers refer to things using expressions that do not, even in

[1] Throughout this paper we simplify syntactic trees, using notation that will be more familiar to philosophers. For instance, in this tree we ignore the P-bar level. And we treat 'France' as an NP, not as a DP. We presume that these simplifications are only expository.

[2] Why a *cluster* of propositional meanings, rather than just a single propositional meaning? Because a given phrase can be used to communicate a proposition of subject–predicate form, of quantificational form, an identity, etc. And these cannot arise from the contextualization of a single propositional meaning. For the arguments see Stainton (1995).

the context, denote those things (for example, someone says 'Your mother is very tall', referring thereby to your much older sister). And so on. So, we think it is plausible that the same happens here: the hearer understands the proposition which the speaker meant, even though the speaker's words do not, even in context, mean that proposition.

Thus, because of pragmatics, a person (e.g. Andrew) can successfully communicate a complete proposition by uttering something subsentential, with neither the syntax nor the semantics of a sentence. (In the case at hand, Andrew uttered a prepositional phrase of semantic type $\langle e, t \rangle$.) That said, though a pragmatic process plays a part in determining the proposition, it does not seem that Andrew merely *implicated* a proposition. He asserted one. Certainly he could not later say, accused of lying about the origin of the cigarette: 'Actually, I made no statement at all. Neither about the cigarette, nor about anything else. Sylvia just drew inappropriate conclusions.' This would radically misdescribe the case.

Given that an assertion was made, it is very tempting, upon first encountering such examples, to dismiss them as 'elliptical'. But, we maintain, what Andrew did cannot be explained by appeal to the sort of thing that contemporary syntax calls 'ellipsis'. Of course Andrew 'spoke elliptically', in some pre-theoretical sense—Andrew definitely communicated more than what his words meant. What we deny, however, is that one can explain away what Andrew did by assimilating it to the previously understood phenomenon of, for example, VP ellipsis. It is, surely, an empirical issue whether we are right about this. But this is not the place to lay out the evidence in full—instead, we sketch some sample evidence in the sequel.

## 2 Background Issues in Epistemology and Philosophy of Language

Much of this paper will be dedicated to the question of how exactly a hearer of subsentential speech—e.g. a hearer of 'From France', said on its own— manages to arrive at the proposition meant. This may look like a merely psychological issue. We think it is not. To see why these sorts of example might matter to philosophy, we want briefly to remind the reader of some initially plausible philosophical views, in epistemology and philosophy of language. We shall not be exploring these views here—our aim, rather, is to gesture at the philosophical backdrop of our paper. The views are:

- Only expressions of natural language have logical form. Or anyway, anything else which is assigned a logical form gets it derivatively from a natural-language expression. Thus if there are propositions, and they have logical forms, they do so only because they are expressed by natural-language sentences that have logical forms. Similarly, if there are 'Mentalese' sentences, and they have logical forms, they too must get them derivatively.

- All effects of context, at least on what is strictly asserted, are traceable to elements of syntactic structure. Thus, once all explicitly indexical 'slots' are filled in, what is literally said by an agent is exhaustively determined by the conventional meaning of the (disambiguated) expression. Anything else which the speaker might have meant is not part of what is said.

- Issues about disambiguation and reference assignment to indexicals aside, knowledge of a language L is sufficient for interpreting utterances in L.

- The semantics/pragmatics boundary amounts to this: semantics assigns truth conditions to utterances, thereby yielding what is literally asserted, while pragmatics goes beyond this.

- Assertion is a conventional activity. What makes something an assertion is not one's intentions, but the conventions governing a certain public linguistic practice. Specifically, assertion is the act of producing a declarative sentence under conventionally specified circumstances.

- Only sentences can be used to make a move in the language game.

- Only sentences have meaning in isolation.

- Specifically, quantifier phrases (including definite descriptions) do not have meaning-relata. Instead, their meaning must be given metalinguistically, in terms of how they affect the meaning of complete sentences.

- Because sentences are the only things which have meaning fundamentally, word meanings (if such exist) must supervene on the total class of sentence meanings.

- Word meanings are underdetermined by the complete class of sentence meanings. Therefore, given the above, word meaning is indeterminate.

As we have argued elsewhere, all of these claims are prima facie in tension with the genuine existence of subsentential speech acts. We shall not rehearse the arguments here. Instead, we shall merely gesture at where the tensions might come from.

Let us start with logical form. Thoughts communicated subsententially, including the Andrew–Sylvia example above, typically have a full-blown logical form. The proposition about the cigarette can, for example, serve as a premiss in an argument. For instance, suppose Andrew had in previous days been debating with Sylvia (who is a renowned Francophobe) about whether anything really fabulous had recently been produced in France. But Sylvia knows and appreciates fine cigarettes. So, Andrew addresses his remark 'From France' to a person who, both discussants know, will recognize the inherent value in the displayed cigarette. Which cigarette is, let us agree, of quite recent vintage. In this instance, Sylvia draws inferences on the basis of the cigarette proposition, concluding that her claim, that nothing fabulous is being produced in France, is false. The crucial point is, if the thing-meant is to serve as a premiss in an inference, it must have a logical form. Yet the hearer apparently does *not* recognize this logical form derivatively—e.g. by recovering a sentence that has it. Rather, she assigns it a logical form fundamentally. If this is right, people can non-derivatively assign logical forms to things which are not expressions of natural language. (For rather more on this point, see Elugardo and Stainton 2001.)

Subsentential speech also suggests that understanding what a speaker said requires rather more than knowledge of language. It even requires more than knowing the disambiguated structure/content of the thing uttered, and the referents of any of that structure's indexicals. For, returning to the example, what Andrew said (i.e. asserted, stated, claimed) was a proposition; but the meaning of the prepositional phrase which he uttered, even after disambiguation and fixing of reference for indexicals, is a property, not a proposition. So knowing what Andrew said—knowing, for example, the conditions under which it would be true or false—requires knowing more than the structure and meaning of the thing he uttered. Knowing language, even knowing contextualized and disambiguated language, is not, therefore, sufficient for interpretation. This ties in very directly with the issue of the determinants of what is said. Some philosophers—e.g. Paul Grice in some moods, Jason Stanley in all moods—maintain that to arrive at 'what is said', it is sufficient to assign reference to all elements of the syntactic structure, and disambiguate. Anything further, which the speaker might have meant, cannot be 'said' but must instead be merely 'implicated'. (This minimalist view has recently been challenged by, among others, Carston 1988; 2002; Récanati 1989; Sperber and Wilson 1986; and Travis 1985. It is defended in Stanley 2000.) Assuming that the phrase 'what is said' is used here in the sense of what is asserted, stated, or claimed, this view seems also to be falsified by subsentential speech, as Stainton (1997a; forthcoming) argues.[3] For, as noted, agents who speak subsententially do not merely *implicate* propositions. They assert them. Yet, as was just seen, the meaning of the disambiguated reference-assigned expression, in the case of subsentential speech, is (typically) subpropositional. So the content of what speakers assert often goes well beyond the meaning of the expression used, even after reference assignment to indexicals. In the same vein, subsentential speech suggests that there are effects of context on what is said with no syntactic counterpart. (Here again, see Stainton forthcoming and Elugardo and Stainton forthcoming, which respond to Stanley 2000. See also Clapp 2001 and forthcoming for a critique of Stanley.)

This result about the determinants of what is said clearly has implications, in turn, for the analysis of assertion and for debates about where to draw the semantics/pragmatics boundary. *Pace* Dummett (1973), for example, assertion cannot be analysed as the production of a declarative sentence in conventionally specified circumstances, because one can use subsentences to assert, and to make other 'moves in the language game'.[4] Nor will it do to say, 'Semantics is about truth conditions'—so that semantics assigns truth conditions to utterances, thereby yielding what is literally asserted, while pragmatics goes beyond this. This will not do because if subsentential speech is a genuine phenomenon, pragmatic processes play a key role in determining the truth conditions of the utterance.

---

[3] This caveat is important. Some authors, most notably Kent Bach (1994a; 1994b; and elsewhere) essentially *define* 'what is said' as the result of disambiguation and reference assignment. In which case, it is of course true that 'what is said' never goes beyond this. Still, Bach allows that what is asserted/stated/claimed may go well beyond 'what is said', so defined. Indeed, what he calls 'implicitures' count as contributions to what is asserted that go beyond 'what is said' (in his sense). So any disagreement between Bach's views and the stance taken in the text is (mostly) terminological.

[4] For discussion see Stainton (1997b). An insightful reply can be found in Kenyon (1999).

Consider, finally, Frege's context principle, and its (supposed) implications. If only sentences have meaning in isolation, then subsentences do not. So, in particular, quantificational expressions cannot be assigned meaning-relata. Yet, as Stainton notes (1998a; 1998b), such phrases can be used, and understood, on their own. (See also Botterell forthcoming.) What, then, is being claimed, when it is said that they lack meaning in isolation? Must it not be the case that users *know* the meaning outside any sentence, and can employ that meaning without a sentential environment? Another implication: understood in certain ways, the context principle can be used to support word-meaning indeterminacy, on the grounds that word meaning, if it exists, must supervene on sentence meanings—this because only sentences *have* meaning non-derivatively. It is often added that, as a matter of fact, there are many possible lexical entries for each word consistent with the complete set of meaning-specifications for whole sentences. So word-meaning must be indeterminate, since it is left underdetermined by the reputed source of 'meaning facts', taken in its entirety. But if subsentences can be *used* so freely, in speech, in precisely what sense do they lack meaning in isolation?[5] And if non-sentences have meaning in isolation, why should their meaning have to supervene on sentence meanings? Why can they not have meaning non-derivatively? In sum, what the 'context principle' amounts to, what it entails, and whether it is even true, will all three have close ties with the phenomenon of non-sentence use. Or so it appears.

Granted, appearances could mislead. Not just with respect to the context principle, but with respect to all the foregoing doctrines. It is not obvious that the prima facie implications for epistemology and philosophy of language really will obtain, once all is said and done. Countermoves for explaining away the apparent tensions are certainly available. (See e.g. Barber forthcoming; Davis forthcoming; Kenyon 1999; forthcoming.) On the other hand, one equally cannot rule out a priori the relevance of subsentential speech to issues like indeterminacy, the domain of logical form, the

---

[5] Maybe it is true that to give the meaning of a word/phrase, one must say what other meanings it could combine with to yield something truth-evaluable. This certainly seems a plausible methodological precept. If so, this would maintain the centrality of truth, or Fregean Thoughts, for lexical semantics. But it would not entail that *sentences* have any special place in natural language. And it certainly would not entail that the only supervenience base for word meanings was complete sentences. (For discussion see Stainton 2000.)

determinants of what-is-said, the nature of assertion, the context principle, etc. (Philosophy of language owes debts to empirical work on language, just as philosophy of biology owes empirical debts to biology.) We think that the mere possibility that these doctrines might be in trouble ought to be sufficient motivation for philosophers to consider the issue of subsentential speech seriously.

## 3  Our Questions and Aims

We began by introducing an example of subsentential speech. We then highlighted, in the previous section, prima facie tensions between subsentential speech and a wide range of widely held views in epistemology and philosophy of language. As noted, we shall not explore those doctrines further here. Instead, our central question in this paper is

(Q1) 'How do hearers interpret subsentential speech of this sort?'

We do not give anything like a definitive answer to (Q1). What we do instead is sketch the salient options, and provide arguments—some philosophical and some more empirical—to the effect that certain of these options are implausible.

One reason for addressing (Q1) is that we find it inherently interesting. In part it is interesting because it affords a case study of the fascinating phenomenon of *cross-modal integration*, here of information got from language with information got from visual perception. This is

(Q2) 'How is perception-based information seamlessly combined with communication-based information?'

What is rather novel about the present paper is how we approach this larger question: by looking at a seldom-studied variety of linguistic communication, namely less-than-sentential speech. Another quite different motivation is this. Defenders of the above philosophical claims can respond to the prima facie tension in two ways. On the one hand, they can insist that the tension is only apparent. This will not be our concern here. On the other hand, they can deny that the phenomenon of subsentential speech is genuine. It is this latter strategy we resist here, by arguing that the options for treating the phenomenon as not genuine are implausible. In contrast, there is an empirically open option, the one we tentatively endorse, according to which the non-sentential speech phenomenon *is* genuine. This leads to our third question in this paper:

(Q3) 'In the light of the answer to (Q1), is it plausible that the phenomenon of subsentential speech is genuine, or is it more plausible that it is merely apparent?'

Having noted what our aims and questions are, let us also clarify what they are not. To repeat, for the most part, we shall not argue that apparent tensions between familiar philosophical doctrines and non-sentential speech are real; in the light of this, we equally shall not argue that these philosophical doctrines are actually false.[6] The exception to this rule is a lengthy discussion of the role of 'inner speech' in occurrent thoughts. Here we do question the truth of certain philosophical doctrines. The doctrines in question are:

- Having an occurrent thought is a matter of having a sentence of natural language pass through one's mind.
- Having a genuine thought about an external object requires that some natural-language singular term, which refers to that object, pass through the mind.

Again, we take these to be in tension with the existence of the sort of example sketched at the outset.[7] We shall argue that this tension is real. And we shall conclude that these two doctrines are false. To anticipate:

[6] As noted, we have done both things elsewhere. Some of the relevant papers include: Elugardo and Stainton (2001; forthcoming, *a*); Stainton (1995, 1997*a*; 1997*b*; 1998*a*; 1998*b*; 2000; forthcoming).

[7] We distinguish this version of the inner-speech view of thought from the weaker analogical version. According to the latter, thoughts are inner episodes that are psychologically type-individuated by their functional/conceptual roles in an internal system of representation; the roles they play are said to be formally analogous (in the appropriate ways) to the functional/conceptual roles played by sentences in public natural languages. Public natural-language sentences are also said to be conceptually prior to thoughts in the order of explanation. The idea is that the intentionality of thoughts is to be explained on the model of the semantic referential properties of natural-language sentences, which in turn get explained in terms of their conventional use in communicational contexts, rather than the other way around. Sellars (1963) is the classic defence of the analogical account of thoughts. Some recent, Sellarsian-inspired accounts of thoughts can be found

this hard-line view conflicts with the existence of genuine subsentential communication because hearers can understand complete propositions— e.g. the singular proposition about the cigarette, to the effect that it is from France—even when what passes through their mind is an expression that merely encodes a property. Thus there is more to the thought grasped than what appears in the supposed vehicle for it. Specifically, and interestingly, it seems that something *in the environment* is part of the thought grasped: in the case at hand, the cigarette itself is part of the thought meant by Andrew and understood by Sylvia. And this external object gets to be part of the thought grasped even though, or so it appears, no natural-language expression denoting this object passes through the mind of the agent who grasps the thought. Finally, continuing with what we shall *not* do, we shall not try to answer (Q1) with respect to all cases of subsentential speech. We are trying to take only the very first steps here, and our example is highly simplified as a result. Specifically, we shall be addressing only cases in which (1) the speaker produces a predicate and (2) the object talked about is visually attended to. As will emerge at the end of the paper, there are lots of cases of subsentential speech that are more complex than this. Thus, an enormous amount of work will remain to be done even if we get things right with respect to visually grasping an object and making a claim about it subsententially.

## 4 The Options

As it stands, we can conceive of only four approaches to (Q1), including especially the 'visual grasping of the object' in the environment that is being talked about. The first divide between approaches is what we call 'S-representationalist' vs. 'Non-S-representationalist' approaches. By 'non-S-representationalism', we mean the view that beliefs, thoughts, and the like do not have compositional syntactic structure. In particular, non-S-representationalists reject what William Lycan calls 'Forthright Sententialism': the view that all (occurrent) tokens of beliefs, thoughts, etc. are inner

in Gauker (1997) and Lycan (1988). None of the arguments that we raise in this paper against the 'hard line' version of the inner-speech view affects the analogical version. Considerations against the analogical theorist's conceptual-priority claim are, however, raised in Elugardo and Stainton (2001).

brain states that exhibit syntactic structure, have truth conditions in virtue of referential relations between their 'syntactic elements and things in the world', and further, 'stand in causal relations to each other of the sort that constitutes inference' (Lycan 1990: 149). In short, S-representationalists embrace some version of the 'Language of Thought' Hypothesis: the view that thinking occurs in an internal language-like system of representation; non-S-representationalists, in contrast, reject any minimally interesting version of the LOT Hypothesis.

Within S-representationalism, there are two main suboptions. On the first, the inner thought-sentences are sentences of the speaker's native language: for instance, sentences of English. Such sentences could in principle include either ordinary sentences, or special 'elliptical sentences'. We pause to stress: if either 'natural-language sentence' suboption is true, then the appearance that people understand subsentential speech without processing a complete sentence must be a mere appearance. Thus, recalling Sylvia and Andrew, this view would entail that Sylvia recovered either an ordinary sentence (e.g. 'This is from France') or some elliptical sentence. Either way, it would not be true that she understood a thought that went beyond what was encoded in the words passing through her mind.

The other suboption within S-representationalism is that, though there are internal representations with both syntactic structure and compositional semantics, this 'language' is not a spoken language. Instead, it is some kind of 'Mentalese'. Within this latter option, the question arises as to whether the items which denote external things, thereby allowing the agent to 'grasp them' mentally, are exclusively descriptive or whether they (or anyway, some of them) might be indexicals. These two 'Mentalese' suboptions, in contrast to the prior 'natural-language sentence' ones, would yield that our phenomenon is genuine. For example, the only natural-language thing which passes through Sylvia's mind is a PP, and it is not of semantic type $\langle t \rangle$ even in context. The thing which is of semantic type $\langle t \rangle$, and which purportedly passes through her mind, is not a natural-language expression— it is a Mentalese sentence (containing an indexical, or not, depending on the approach proposed).

We shall explain each of these suboptions more fully in the sequel. For now, we summarize the lay of the land in Figure 8.1.

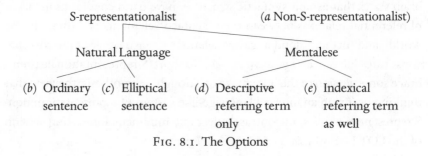

FIG. 8.1. The Options

### 4.1 *The non-S-representationalist option,* (a)

We introduce the non-S-representational view mostly to put it aside. By way of explaining it, we begin with the following rather rough-and-ready way of thinking about the original example. The hearer, goes this story, understood the prepositional phrase, and grasped the property (i.e. the propositional function) $\lambda x$ . from-France$(x)$ for which it stands; she also noticed the cigarette that Andrew was holding up. She input the cigarette into the propositional function, and came thereby to grasp a singular proposition, about the cigarette, to the effect that it is from France. It was this process, and not the recovery of a sentential representation, *either in English or Mentalese*, that actually occurred.

Now, put this baldly, the approach seems to commit a serious use–mention confusion. 'She recovered the propositional function; then she input the object into the propositional function.' What can this mean? She did not physically pick up the cigarette, and put it into some kind of grinder, which then yielded a singular proposition at the far end. All of the 'recovering' and 'applying' occurred in her head. The underlying complaint here is that whenever a mental operation occurs—grasping an object, forming a thought about it, recognizing a property—some *representing* goes on. If that is right, then, one might think, something like the following must happen in non-sentential speech situations: the hearer tokens a representation of the object (i.e. a singular term) and also a representation of the property in question (i.e. a predicate); she combines these into a sentence; and she thus arrives at the complete thought. Hence, one might suppose, option (a) is a total non-starter.

This criticism of the general approach is far too quick, however. Of course something must be happening to the agent, as she notices, considers, and so forth; and, if we are physicalists, that something must be broadly speaking material. Moreover, and equally obviously, the process of understanding non-sentential speech does not involve putting some external object into some sort of grinder. But this alone does not entail that this 'something' which happened in the head was a tokening of (a series of) quasi-linguistic symbols. Here are some reasonable alternatives. What happened to the agent was that her informational state changed—thereby altering her 'representing state', but without necessarily tokening any specific representation. Or, in a quite similar vein, what happened to the agent was that different counterfactual conditionals came to be true of her—counterfactuals about what she would do or say, for instance; again, without some sentence being 'written' anywhere in her head. Or, what happened was that her 'neural nets' got reconfigured in complex ways, once again without any tokening of a sentence-like representation. All of these are live options in the philosophy of mind. And it is at least possible that some or all of them could be used to interpret talk of 'grasping the object' and 'putting it into the function', without appealing to *internal sentence-like* things.[8]

Going 'non-S-representational' in this sort of way might be an option for explaining how less-than-sentential communication functions. But we shall not consider it further here. Suffice it to note that we have our reasons for being sceptical of any non-S-representationalist view. Our main reason is this: the central aim of our paper is to explain what might be going on in subsentential speech when we perceptually grasp an object and *then* combine this perceptual information with independently derived information, got from a different (i.e. linguistic) source, to form eventually a complete thought about the perceived object. To make sense of this, we need to be able to separate object-grasping from content-grasping, as distinct and

---

[8] It should be noted that we include, in the category of 'non-S-representationalist approaches', such philosophical views as those of Robert Stalnaker, who defends an information-theoretic account of singular thoughts; cf. Stalnaker (1990). It would equally include those connectionists who insist that neural nets are (holistic) representations. Clearly these theorists do not reject mental representations of all sorts. But they equally do not think of representing as a matter of tokening inner *sentences*. The other camp, within non-S-representational approaches, deny the existence of mental representations of any variety. Connectionists of an eliminativist stripe would fall here, as might certain philosophers inspired by Davidson or McDowell.

isolatable processes. We suspect that a theory that posits mental representations that have a constituent structure has the best chance of explaining
this type of phenomenon. By contrast, non-S-representationalist theories
explicitly deny that our mental states have any combinatorial constituent
structure. The minimal mental state they allow is, we take it, the comparatively holistic one of grasping a complete thought. Thus, by our lights,
non-S-representationalists will be unlikely to be able to give a satisfactory
account of subsentential talk. (We hope to take all of this up at length in a future paper.) That said, we do not argue in this paper that the only account of
singular thought which can handle subsentential speech is one which posits
the manipulation of internal, syntactically structured representations. That
would take us too far afield, given the number of such views that have been
defended in the literature. Rather, our strategy is to assume, for the sake of
argument, that (what we are here calling) S-representationalism is correct
and see what *kind* of S-representationalism best explains the phenomena of
non-sentential speech, given certain empirical data about perception. (To
anticipate: we shall argue that only a form of S-representationalism that
posits a language of thought that is not a natural language has the best
chance of explaining the phenomena. In which case, the phenomenon is
genuine, and not merely apparent. In which case, those who endorse the
philosophical doctrines noted at the outset have some work to do.)

## 4.2 *The natural-language-sentence options,* (b) *and* (c)

We begin our detailed discussions with options (*b*) and (*c*), within the
natural-language-sentence approach. According to this view, there is a language of thought, namely, the natural language that a speaker/hearer actually uses in writing or in speaking. According to the view we have in
mind (see note 7) all thought-tokens are internal speech-tokens of natural-
language sentences. Given this, here is what a proponent of the view
would probably say about (Q1) and (Q2). Since all thought is inner speech,
whenever a person notices an object, she must subvocally token a natural-
language singular term (e.g. 'that') which, in the context, stands for the
object noticed; and when this person considers whether the object has a
certain property, she tokens a natural-language sentence—containing both
a singular term which stands for the object, and a predicate which encodes

the property (e.g. 'That is red'). (When it is stated this baldly, one might think that no one really endorses this line, but some philosophers actually do endorse it or are at least committed to it.[9]) Adopting this approach, perceptual information must be combined with communication-based information by having all the information in question encoded in natural language. In which case, the hearer of (apparently) non-sentential speech must have somehow tokened a complete natural-language sentence, which then completely encodes what the speaker meant. Applying this to the example noted above, such a theorist would have to say something like this: Andrew's hearer must have recovered some sentence, in her native tongue, which meant (something like) *This is from France*. Maybe she recovered the ordinary sentence 'This is from France', reconstructing it on the basis of the less-than-sentential words Andrew produced. Maybe she recovered some special 'elliptical sentence', which Andrew also uttered. But she definitely recovered some natural language sentence or other.

The question is, are such views really plausible? Let us take the options in reverse order, starting with (*c*). The following considerations should at least make our claim that no 'elliptical sentence' was uttered/recovered plausible enough for present purposes. (This matter is dealt with at much greater length in Stainton 1997*a* and forthcoming. See also Barton 1990; Carston 2002; Clapp 2001; forthcoming; Elugardo and Stainton, forthcoming *a*; and Morgan 1989.) Here is the first anti-ellipsis consideration. Syntactic ellipsis is a matter of grammatically necessary syntactic material 'being left out', but such that the omission does not matter because the very material which is omitted is present elsewhere in the discourse. Classic cases of syntactic ellipsis include VP ellipsis and 'sluicing', illustrated below:

(2) Joan will buy a car but Laxmi won't [$_{VP}$].
(3) Joan will buy a car. I wonder why [$_S$].

These sentences are bona fide cases—more than that, they are paradigm cases—of the phenomenon of ellipsis. (The first is VP ellipsis. The second, in which an S is elided, is the example of 'sluicing'.) Now, if what appeared to be subsentential speech were really just like this, then one could explain what was occurring between Andrew and Sylvia, for example, without

---

[9] The inner-speech view of thought is defended in Carruthers (1996), in Devitt and Sterelny (1999), and in Ludlow (1999).

granting thoughts *sans* natural-language vehicles. On the other hand, if what one means by 'ellipsis' is *not* this, then 'ellipsis' is merely a comforting label, in lieu of an account. So, to give the hypothesis teeth, and explanatory power, we shall take it that the proponent of 'elliptical sentences' wants to assimilate the phenomenon to this already understood kind of case.

That said, notice two key features of the examples. To start with, in (2) and (3) the omitted material ('buy a car' and 'Joan will buy a car', respectively) is spoken elsewhere, just prior to the ellipsis. And this feature is shared by elliptical expressions in general.[10] Syntactic ellipsis, in short, requires prior linguistic material. But then, to anticipate, what Andrew produced was not an elliptical sentence, because in the situation described there was no (immediately) prior linguistic material.

To see *why* prior material is required, we briefly introduce one standard view of syntactic ellipsis. It is by no means the only account, but it is representative enough to give the feel of the thing. According to a theory first proposed by Edwin Williams (1977), syntactic ellipsis works as follows. Covert anaphors, which Williams dubbed 'deltas', are base-generated within elliptical sentences. That is, ellipsis is not transformationally introduced: put metaphorically, elliptical structures are present already at the level at which the sentence parts are first put together. Deltas are, then, very like the null-subject pronouns one finds in languages like Italian and Spanish, that give rise to sentences like:

(4) [pro] está.          comiendo.

pro  $be_{3rd\ pers.\ sing.,\ present}$ $eat_{present\text{-}continuous}$.

---

[10] The qualifier 'in general' is necessary because of certain special cases noted in Hankamer and Sag (1976). These are cases in which something is sufficiently salient in the environment for VP ellipsis to be comprehensible, though it still sounds awkward. For instance, while looking at a man standing on a ledge, someone could say 'He won't', meaning that he will not jump. Such an utterance is definitely interpretable. However, the use of words and phrases is neither as constrained as the Hankamer–Sag cases, nor does it sound in any way awkward. See Stainton (forthcoming) for extended discussion. We should also note special cases of 'frozen ellipsis', in which a set phrase has been created from what was originally an ellipsis construction. An example would be 'May I?', used to request a cigarette. If the aim of this paper really were to establish, once and for all, that a sentence is not used in the contested cases, a full discussion of both sorts of case would be required. Since, however, we are here trying only to make our anti-ellipsis claim plausible, we shall set both aside.

'[He/she/it] is eating.'

In such elliptical sentences, deltas occupy the places where, pre-theoretically speaking, material is 'left out'. They have no pronunciation, and no meaning *per se*, but they get linked to prior syntactic material at the point of interpretation. More concretely, Williams (1977) assigns the following sort of structure to (2):

(5) Joan will buy a car but Laxmi won't [$_{VP}$ [$_V$ $\Delta_1$][$_{NP}$ $\Delta_2$]]

In context (and roughly speaking), $\Delta_1$ is co-indexed with 'buy' and $\Delta_2$ is co-indexed with 'a car'. This structure yields the proper interpretation for the second conjunct of (2), namely that Laxmi won't *buy a car*. Moreover, the structure accounts for why (2) is not pronounced the way 'Joan will buy a car but Laxmi won't buy a car' is: precisely because deltas have no pronunciation.

Suppose that William's story is right. Now, look again at Andrew's utterance. He walks into the room, and the first thing he says is 'From France'. Clearly there is nothing for any purported covert anaphors in 'From France' to be linked to in this situation. There is lots of physical context. But there is not the requisite linguistic context. There is, therefore, no way within those countenanced by the theory for the supposed deltas to be interpreted—because there is no prior material to which the deltas are linked. The hearer in this case cannot, then, link up the 'empty slot' with these prior words, because there are no prior words. (Put another way, if what Andrew produced really were an elliptical expression, in the sense familiar to syntacticians, it ought to sound precisely as odd as 'She doesn't', produced on its own. But 'From France' is not the least bit odd in this situation.) We conclude that what Andrew did looks to be importantly unlike syntactic ellipsis, as encountered in (2) and (3).

It will help make our point if we distinguish between (1) the agent as a whole making an all-things-considered inference, in principle using all the information at her disposal, about what sentence the speaker might have had in mind and (2) an automatic, formal operation of syntactic reconstruction, performed subpersonally within an informationally encapsulated module. VP ellipsis is a process of the latter sort: the language faculty does not 'guesstimate', on the basis of all evidence in principle available to the agent;

rather, it blindly churns out a structure, based solely on the representations input into it. Being automatic and encapsulated in this way, all the syntactic material required for the grammatical operation must be available to the linguistic module: where, basically, that required material consists in, first, the fragment actually spoken plus, second, *the immediately prior discourse*. That is why prior discourse is essential. Moreover, the latter must contain an expression identical (at the level of logical form) with the element omitted, so that the ellipsis site may be linked to it. So not just any prior discourse will do. (For the arguments see Sag 1976. The point is applied to subsentential speech in Stainton forthcoming, and Elugardo and Stainton forthcoming, *a*.) In sum, it is because ellipsis of this sort is a strictly grammatical recovery process that prior *spoken* material is required for ellipsis to be grammatically licensed. Without that material, no narrowly syntactic process could recover the 'missing' elements.

Our point is that the process of subsentential comprehension is not like this. At best it is the 'whole agent'—i.e. the agent in principle using all the information available to her, both linguistic and non-linguistic—who figures out what sentence the speaker had in mind. (We discuss this latter possibility below, under the rubric of option (*b*). This is not to say that the whole agent cannot interpret a person who employs a genuinely elliptical expression without appropriate prior discourse. *Whole agents* can understand discourse-initial ellipsis constructions, using all the information at their disposal. But the things understood sound awkward indeed.)

The foregoing is a pretty theory-internal bit of reasoning. Here is an argument which is more data-driven. Accounts of ellipsis agree that, as a matter of fact, genuine syntactic ellipsis, of the sort exemplified by VP ellipsis and sluicing, involves the omission of a syntactic constituent: a VP, an S, or some such. Absolutely no account of syntactic ellipsis countenances free deletion (and with no linguistic context) of whatever material happens to be necessary to leave a free-standing phrase. Thus, for example, (6) is ill-formed, as an elliptical version of (7):

(6) John's sing.
(7) John's mother loves to sing.

This is so even if it might be perfectly plain what is being talked about. (Thus Andrew might say 'Raymond's mother loves to dance'. If a non-native speaker responded with (6), we might well understand her as meaning what (7) says. But this is not syntactic ellipsis in the requisite sense: it is the whole agent forming an all-things-considered hypothesis about what the speaker 'really meant'.) One reason why (6) is ill-formed is that 'mother loves to' simply is not a syntactic constituent of 'John's mother loves to sing'.[11] The (simplified) tree for (7) is (8), and 'mother loves to' clearly does not fall under a single node in this tree.

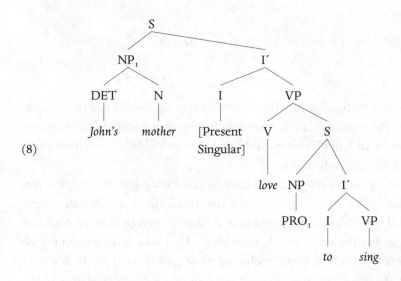

(8)

Hence it is not possible to delete this non-constituent, so as to arrive at 'John's sing'.

That said, consider what would have to be omitted to derive 'From France' from its more obvious sources. Suppose the source sentence was 'This cigarette is from France'. The (simplified) tree structure for that sentence is given in (9).

---

[11] Again, there are complications even here. Though ellipsis of the VP sort requires that a constituent be omitted, *gapping* does not. Thus 'John's mother loves to sing, Jill's to party' is reasonably good, grammatically speaking. But what is omitted is 'mother loves', clearly not a constituent. However, whereas it might be plausible to suppose that Andrew performed something akin to VP ellipsis, it is not at all plausible that he produced a gapped expression. The reason is that gapping by definition involves leaving an empty 'gap' *between two expressions*. Clearly, however, *if* Andrew left anything out, it was not material in the middle of a sentence. For more on gapping and ellipsis see Berman and Hestvik (1992); Chao (1988); and Lappin and Benmamoun (1999).

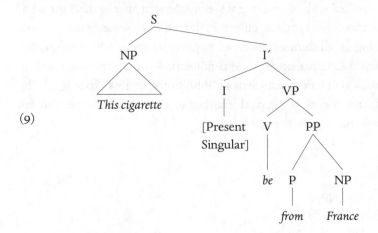

(9)

The deleted material would have to be everything but 'from France'. But, patently, this is not a syntactic constituent. That is, it does not fall under one node. So, what would have to be deleted here would be a non-constituent, violating the generalization.

This is by no means a knock-down argument against treating the Andrew case as VP-style ellipsis: on the one hand, the generalization might be mistaken—indeed, one could take Andrew's utterance to be evidence against it. On the other hand, there might be a way of diagramming an appropriate source sentence such that what gets deleted really is a constituent. However, it certainly does not look to be syntactic ellipsis of the VP ellipsis sort, as this is currently understood. And that is sufficient for present purposes, since it therefore will not do to dismiss the question of how non-sentential speech gets interpreted by saying: 'Oh, we know how that works. It's just like VP ellipsis'. And, as noted, to say 'Well, it's not that kind of ellipsis. But it is ellipsis none the less' is to put a familiar label on the phenomenon, while refusing actually to explain it. A concrete account is still required.[12]

[12] We should note some examples which seem to pull the other way, i.e. in favour of an ellipsis account. As Peter Ludlow noted in discussion, one can use expressions like 'All in the garden' (to assert, for example, that all the cousins are in the garden) or 'By John' (to assert, for example, that a salient work of art was painted by John) in isolation. But these seem to be derived via sentence-level transformations, which suggests that the things uttered must actually be remnants of transformed sentences. See Ludlow (forthcoming) for extended discussion. (A similar argument was given independently in Morgan 1973, in favour of an ellipsis approach to what he termed 'fragments'. But see Morgan 1989 for

So much for option (c), which appeals to syntactic elliptical expressions. Let us now turn to option (b). We think the idea that to understand less-than-sentential speech one must recover an *ordinary* natural-language expression that picks out the element supplied by the environment is no more plausible than the idea that whenever someone notices an object, she tokens a natural-language expression that refers to it. It is highly implausible to suppose that, when someone looks at her desk and sees the objects on it, recognizing their features, a constant flurry of English sentences runs through her head. But then why suppose that when one notices an object *being discussed*, and considers its properties, one must token a singular term in English that refers to it? Certainly if we ask the hearer, 'Which complete sentence did you understand?', she will be at a loss to answer. At least sometimes. What makes one so sure that, in every such case, there will be the precise sentence used by the hearer? We say: nothing but a priori ideology. (Compare the case where Andrew says, 'This cigarette is from France', and we ask the hearer what sentence she understood.)

The argument against option (b) just presented presupposes the following principle: a hearer (i.e. the whole agent) recovers a natural-language sentence from an utterance of a subsentential linguistic item only if the hearer knows precisely which sentence she recovered. One might reject that principle on the grounds that the hearer could conceivably recover the sentence 'off-line', i.e. unconsciously; in which case, the precise natural-language sentence is potentially unavailable to the hearer's conscious mind.

We contend that this alternative 'off-line' picture, proposed on behalf of option (b), is equally unlikely. To see why, consider two accounts of

some rethinking.) Focusing on the first example, roughly speaking, it would be treated as having been derived as follows:

[[All the cousins] are in the garden]$\rightarrow$[t$_1$ the cousins are [all$_1$ in the garden]]$\rightarrow$[all in the garden]

But if this is how 'All in the garden' was derived, then ellipsis must have been performed on the (derived) complete sentence [t$_1$ the cousins are [all$_1$ in the garden]. This seems the only way to generate this fragment. (Similarly for the case of 'By John'.) Nor will it do to say that *this* is genuinely a case of ellipsis, while 'From France' *et al.* are not, because 'All in the garden' can occur discourse-initially, and would have to be derived by deletion of a non-constituent. So if these are cases of syntactic ellipsis, the tests given in the text are not actually diagnostic. Such examples are discussed critically and in detail in Stainton (forthcoming). We ignore them here.

how the unconscious sentence would be constructed. On the first story, it is the language module which outputs the whole sentential structure. On the second, the language module outputs a subsentential string, and a complete sentence is built up using the Central System (in the sense of Fodor 1983), and all information available to the agent. Let us begin with the first, noting that the so-called 'recovered sentence' is not *completely* unavailable to consciousness.[13] In our example, the hearer *is* consciously aware of the linguistic item that was pronounced in the speaker's utterance. Specifically, she is aware of the prepositional phrase 'From France'. So, if it is the language module which is outputting the complete sentence, certain of its results are available to consciousness, but certain others are not. Hence, if the inner-speech view is true, then the hearer is consciously aware of only part of the sentence that her language module outputs. Surely it would be odd for the language module to output a whole sentence only part of which is accessible to consciousness. But that is precisely what must happen if this first inner-speech theory is correct. Consider, then, the second story. Could it be that the language module outputs a subsentential structure, here a PP, such that it is the Central System's task to use all available sources to construct a natural-language sentence, given the subsentential structure as its input? This has a certain initial plausibility. Notice, for instance, that in the case at hand there is insufficient information within the language module to output a whole natural-language sentence, precisely because there is no syntactic antecedent. So the second story has that much going for it: it allows in contextual information not in the language module. But it will not work either. The activities of the Central System are typically accessible to consciousness. Thus, if this second inner-speech view were right, then the whole recovered natural-language sentence should, barring some argument, be available to consciousness, in line with the principle stated in the preceding objection to our argument. Neither proposal, then,

---

[13] We also think that the reply goes against the spirit of the inner-speech view. One of the primary motivations for the inner-speech account is behaviourism. The idea is that thinking must be observable and public, at least in principle: it has to be either actual self-talk or dispositions to utter/accept natural-language sentences. Otherwise, we would have to relegate thoughts and the activity of thinking to the ghostly realm of covert, private, Cartesian mental objects and mental processes. Or so it was believed. Postulating a level of wholly unconscious mental processing is thus antithetical to certain aims of classical inner-speech theorists.

will account for why *part*—and *ex hypothesi*, only part—of the 'recovered sentence' is unconscious.

Although we think the above arguments are effective against the 'ordinary sentence' approach to subsentential communication, some might think otherwise. Also, some might think that the idea of having English sentences running through one's head, as one attends to an array of objects, is no more implausible than the idea of having Mentalese sentences running through one's head. (And we ourselves will endorse the latter idea.) We would like to offer, therefore, two other arguments against option (*b*).

First, it appears that a subject who clearly is cognitively deficient in natural-language understanding/processing *vis-à-vis complete sentences* can still understand non-sentential speech. Here are two considerations. First, presumably Helen Keller was already forming thoughts some time before she learnt how to sign full sentences. (Inner-speech theorists will probably deny that; in which case, they must explain how Keller was able to learn and understand sign language even though she lacked natural-language competence.) Suppose, then, that her teacher placed Keller's hand in a bowl of water when she was teaching her the sign for 'wet'. At some point during the learning process, Keller was able to understand her teacher as saying *that is wet* when the teacher made the sign 'wet'. But it is doubtful that Keller tokened a natural-language sentence in her head that meant that: she did not yet have any at her disposal. Second, if the inner-speech theory is true, then it follows that as a person loses his competence to form and understand complete sentences, he also loses (in varying degree) his ability to think and reason. But, though typically true, this conclusion is not obviously correct across the board, given recent findings about language-specific deficits. For our purposes, the issue is whether a patient could still understand non-sentential assertions/questions/commands, etc., having lost the ability to use/understand complete sentences. If she could, then it is not plausible that, in the normal circumstance, someone who understands subsentential speech is, even unconsciously, deploying a complete sentence. Here is why: if understanding an (apparently) subsentential utterance demands constructing (and then understanding) a complete sentence, then someone who cannot construct a sentence should not be able to understand subsentential speech. The two capacities should both suffer equally, across the board. On the contrary, however, empirical studies appear to show that certain pathological individuals understand non-sentential speech even when their ability to construct complete natural-language sentences is severely impaired. That is, though they have lost many of their grammatical abilities with respect to natural-language sentences, including even the ability to distinguish ungrammatical from grammatical sentences, their comprehension of isolated lexical items (or sometimes even phrases) remains comparatively good. For example, the patient discussed by Chatterjee *et al.* (1995) had flawless comprehension of single words, and, as demonstrated by his response to pictures, could still understand concepts like agent of an action, recipient of an action, etc. But he could not encode this sort of information into sentences: he lost the ability to map thematic relations onto appropriate grammatical categories. Thus his broadly conceptual powers seemed normal, as did his understanding of bare lexical items; but his sentence-construction (and comprehension) abilities were severely impaired. This exemplifies intact thought (and subsentence understanding), but impaired sentence capabilities.[14] In another case, certain patients described by Sirigu *et al.* (1998), who exhibited damage to Broca's area, could understand subsentential expressions such as 'pay', 'arrive at the news-stand', 'leave', and 'ask for the paper'. In particular, they could arrange these isolated phrases into 'scripts', choosing the appropriate temporal order. (In this example, the correct order for the script would be: 'arrive at the news-stand', 'ask for the paper', 'pay', 'leave'.) But despite understanding subsentences apparently as well as normal individuals, these Broca's aphasics were severely impaired when it came to ordering words *within a sentence*. (As the authors note, typical 'sentences' produced by these patients included 'The husband of less likeable my aunt is much than my cousin' and 'Gave a kiss to the boy the lady who it is'.) It is at least not obvious how this could be if people have to construct a complete sentence in order to understand an (apparently) subsentential utterance. (See also Varley 1998.)

Interestingly, this dissociation of thought and sentence abilities can go the other way as well. Thus DM, a patient described in Breedin and Saffran (1999), retained the ability to detect grammatical violations, and to recover

---

[14] Of course, it is possible in principle that the person could *internally* construct sentences, even though she could neither produce them, nor distinguish grammatical ones from ungrammatical ones. But 'possible in principle' does not amount to plausible as an empirical hypothesis, unless some evidence is brought forward.

syntactic information generally—including especially the ability to assign thematic roles on the basis of grammatical clues. But DM had a severely degraded lexicon, no longer knowing the meaning of concrete words. Here we have impaired lexical (and thinking) skills, but relatively intact sentence capabilities.

None of these arguments is knock-down. But they do make the inner-speech theory of subsentential communication look implausible. And that is all we hoped to show here, since showing even this goes some way to answering (Q1) through (Q3):

(Q1) How do hearers interpret subsentential speech of this sort?
(Q2) How is perception-based information seamlessly combined with communication-based information?
(Q3) In the light of the answer to (Q1), is it plausible that the phenomenon of subsentential speech is genuine, or is it more plausible that it is merely apparent?

The answers suggested by the foregoing arguments are these. First, regarding (Q1), hearers do not interpret subsentential speech by recovering a complete natural-language sentence: neither an ordinary sentence, nor an 'elliptical sentence'. Hence, regarding (Q2), it is not the case that perception-based information gets combined with communication-based information by always having the former encoded into an expression of natural language. For this is not what happens in subsentence cases of the sort described. Given this, the answer to (Q3) would seem to be that the phenomenon of subsentential speech *is not* merely apparent. For instance, our description of the 'From France' case at the beginning of the paper was accurate: Andrew produced a PP, whose meaning is a property, and Sylvia recovered that PP *and only it*. She then figured out the proposition asserted not semantically, by decoding a complete sentence, but pragmatically, by combining information got from perception with information got from her knowledge of language.

That said, to make the case for genuineness even more compelling, one needs a positive story in answer to (Q1), a way of fleshing out this rough sketch. We turn, therefore, to the two remaining initially plausible alternatives, namely (d) and (e).

### 4.3 *The Mentalese options,* (d) *and* (e)

Both remaining alternatives hold that the hearer tokens a Mentalese sentence, containing a Mentalese singular term referring to the displayed object. This is what it is to think about the object being discussed. In the Andrew example, the hearer tokens a term that stands for the cigarette, and she also tokens a Mentalese predicate which stands for that property had by all things from France. (She gets the latter by decoding the natural-language predicate produced by Andrew.) She puts these two Mentalese expressions together, and arrives at a Mentalese sentence, which encodes the aforementioned singular proposition.

In filling out this idea, the nature of Mentalese can be left open in numerous respects. For instance, whether it is mostly innate, whether it is universally shared by all humans *and* higher animals, etc. are not things we need to take a stand on. For our purposes, Mentalese is a language of thought, with compositional syntax and semantics—but no phonology. Hence, it is not a natural language. We shall also stipulate that the syntax of Mentalese is importantly different from that of spoken languages. What 'importantly different' amounts to is notoriously hard to say. It is fair to suppose that, unlike natural languages, Mentalese is disambiguated; fair also to suppose that all syntactic features in Mentalese have content effects. For instance, there will not be case markings that do not indicate grammatical function, or semantically vacuous prepositions, or verbal elements (like the copula, in some of its incarnations) whose contribution is merely grammatical. In a similar vein, Mentalese surely would not be 'multi-stratal': it would not, for instance, have analogues to Phonetic Form, D-Structure, S-Structure, and Logical Form. In contrast, natural languages are systematically ambiguous, they are riddled with grammatical features which are solely driven by surface syntax, and they are multi-stratal. (Why make this stipulation about being 'importantly different'? The reason, at bottom, is that even assuming the truth of S-representationalism, it must remain a non-trivial claim that one thinks in Mentalese. If our Mentalese were, say, just like English but with no phonology, the claim would lose most of its interest.)

We assume a picture of the mind proposed and defended in Jerry Fodor's 1983 book *Modularity of Mind*. We are not committed to the minutiae of

Fodor's views—nor, indeed, is he. But adopting this picture will help us express our speculations about subsentential communication fairly clearly. Given this picture, it seems impossible that the representation which is got by perception should remain, at every stage, in a format specific to the perceptual module in question. That is, considering the Andrew case again, the representation which stands for the cigarette in Andrew's hand cannot be one over which the visual system alone can operate, come what may. The obvious reason is that the representation must be capable of combining with another representation got by hearing and understanding a natural language phrase. Put in Fodor's terms, the two parts of the Mentalese sentence, at which the hearer eventually arrives, must be encoded in a single representational system. For, were that not the case, the representation of the cigarette could not be combined with the representation of the property $\lambda x$ . from-France($x$)—because the latter representation comes, in the first instance, from a different module, the parser. But cross-modal understanding of this sort clearly does occur, since the hearer understands a proposition. Assuming this modular picture, then, it must be that *either* the representation of the cigarette is already in a format that can be conjoined with something got from the parser, *or* it is somehow 'translated' or 'incorporated' into that format prior to being combined with the representation that comes from the parser. (More on this in the final section.) This is one reason for thinking that the representation which encodes the whole proposition about the cigarette, to the effect that it is from France, is what Fodor calls a 'Central System' representation. There is, in addition, another reason for thinking this. As Fodor (1983) describes the Central System, it is the place where general-purpose inference occurs. But, as noted above, there are cases in which the propositions communicated in non-sentential speech serve as premisses in inferences. For instance, recall the imagined Francophobic debate, about whether anything really fabulous had been recently produced in France. In this instance, Sylvia draws inferences on the basis of the cigarette proposition, concluding that her claim, i.e. that nothing fabulous is being produced in France, is false. But then, if it is to serve as a premiss in an inference, the cigarette proposition must be in a format suitable for general-purpose inference. And that format, in Fodor's picture, is a Central System representation.

Let us now specifically consider the nature of the representation of the cigarette within the Central System. The question we want to ask is: does the visual representation denote the cigarette *by description*, or is it rather an indexical whose content just is the displayed cigarette? That is, which of (*d*) or (*e*)—Descriptive Mentalese or Indexical Mentalese—in our options tree (Figure 8.1) is correct? We believe that there are broadly empirical considerations that favour the latter view. We turn to them now.

### 4.4 *Visual indexes; or,* (e) *over* (d)

This section is structured as follows. We begin by abstracting away from subsentential speech for the moment, considering how objects are 'visually grasped' in the general case. We first argue that if objects are 'visually grasped' via properties, then the only property which is at all viable is spatial location. We then appeal to recent experimental work in cognitive psychology to show that spatial location probably cannot do the job either. We conclude that, in general, objects are not visually attended to via their properties. The positive alternative, proposed by Zenon Pylyshyn in several recent writings, is that there are 'visual indexes', functionally reminiscent of natural-language demonstratives. Visually tracking an object is then a matter of tokening a visual index which refers to the object tracked. What this probably means for subsentential communication is this: it is surely plausible that, in answer to (Q1), visual indexes are among the things which are employed in understanding (certain cases of) less-than-sentential speech. That is, given how 'visual grasping' works in the general case, it seems reasonable to assume that, with respect to visual grasping in subsentential communication, it works in the same way. In which case (*e*), which posits indexicals, is the most promising option.

With respect to the more general question, abstracting away from sub-sentences, let us begin by considering whether non-locational properties would allow 'visual grasping'. The idea behind the proposal is this: what the person noticing an object does is token some kind of Mentalese definite description. The thing denoted is then the unique object which satisfies the (non-locational) properties specified in the definite description. There are some pretty obvious problems with this idea. First, there will not in general be just one thing which satisfies the description. So denotation is predicted to fail regularly, which it does not. Indeed, humans and other animals have no trouble seeing numerous examples of the same kind of thing, distinguished only by their location. Thus we can very easily count the number of 'smiley' faces in the following line:

This despite the fact that the only difference between them is locational. (It is, of course, possible in principle that whenever we perceive 'exceedingly similar' objects, like the five smiley faces, there are very complicated and fine-grained—but non-locational—differences between them, which the visual system makes use of. If the descriptive material is that fine-grained, however, it is hard to see how we manage so easily to keep track of objects as they change their properties.[15]) These intuitive considerations aside, there are experimental results that point in the same direction, namely away from visual-system 'definite descriptions'—at least where the denotation is the unique thing exhibiting certain non-locational properties. For instance, take Figure 8.2. It is very easy to tell that the various shapes are in a linear order, and that there are six elements. What is more, experiments have shown that

---

[15] There are other problems with the descriptivist approach. For one thing, the object of a singular judgement, whether perceptual or non-perceptual, figures essentially in the truth-conditions of that judgement. Suppose that what fixes the object of a thought is some descriptive condition that the object in question just happens to satisfy uniquely. Then, it is conceivable that the same thought could be true in worlds in which that particular object does not exist—as long as some other object satisfies the same condition in the world in question. In which case, the thought is not about the particular object in question (or about any particular object that happens to make its content true, for that matter). We can, of course, require that the relevant description be 'rigidified' by incorporating an 'actual' operator or some (rigid) designator of the actual world. Leaving aside the question of whether we normally think of objects in that way, the solution still does not help capture the *res* aspect of singular thoughts. To use Keith Donnellan's famous example, one can judge that Smith's actual murderer is insane and yet one's judgement fails to be about Jones, who actually murdered Smith. For it may be that one's judgement involves an attributive occurrence of the description in question (whether in some natural language or in Mentalese). Adding a causal relation to Jones (even a non-deviant one) will not help avoid that problem either, since the description may still be attributively used in that context. If it is, then the judgement would not be about Jones (strictly speaking); it would be about *whoever* murdered Smith, which in this case just happens to be Jones. For a comprehensive discussion of these and other related issues on singular thought, see Bach (1986); Burge (1977); and Lycan (1986).

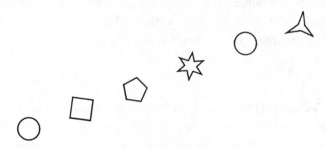

FIG. 8.2. (from Pylyshyn 1999)

subjects can determine linearity and quantity of elements more quickly than they can judge whether any two elements are of the same type. With respect to the case at hand, you can more quickly judge that there are six elements in the above figure, and that they form a line, than you can judge whether only two items are the same. These facts suggest that subjects do not need to determine which objects satisfy which non-locational descriptions before they note *where* the objects are, and *how many* there are. Indeed, the subject's speed at recognizing linear order does not even depend upon how many objects there are, whereas, as Pylyshyn notes in a 1999 paper, later published in revised form in Branquinho (2001), the time it takes to judge whether the same display consists only of identical (or duplicated) objects increases linearly with the number of objects in the display. So, whereas recognizing which objects have which properties takes more time when there are more objects, recognizing what pattern the objects fall into does not take more time. But then doing the latter—seeing patterns, or quantity—cannot require doing the former, i.e. attending to descriptive properties had by each object. This strongly suggests that subjects do not have to identify the non-locational properties of each object when they count it, or see its place in a pattern. That is, they do not have to settle on a uniquely denoting description of the object. Since one cannot count objects, or see their place in a pattern, without grasping them, it seems equally unlikely that *grasping an object* requires describing it to oneself.

Having mentioned location, let us now consider whether the visual system, when it 'grasps an object', might be using 'definite descriptions' that employ *locational* properties. Appeals to intuition here are much less helpful. So let us go straight to the experimental work. We quote at length from Pylyshyn:

In a typical experiment . . . observers are shown a screen containing anywhere from 8 to 24 simple identical objects (points, plus signs, circles, figure-eight shapes). A subset of these objects is briefly rendered distinct (usually by flashing them on and off a few times). Then all the objects (which are visually identical) move about in the display in unpredictable ways. The subject's task is to keep track of this subset of objects (called 'targets'). At some later time in the experiment (say 10 seconds into the tracking trial) one of the objects is again flashed on and off. The observer must then indicate whether or not the flashed (probe) figure was one of the targets. (In other studies the subject has to indicate *all* the targets using a mouse or other pointing device.) A large number of experiments, beginning with the studies described in Pylyshyn & Storm (1988), have shown clearly that observers can indeed track up to 5 independently moving identical simple visual objects. (Pylyshyn 1999: 13–14)

This finding is important because computer simulations of object-tracking which employed definite descriptions that denoted via locational descriptions did not come even close to human performance. The locational-/description-based simulations made many more mistakes, regularly losing track of the objects.

To get an intuitive handle on the proposal to be rejected, consider a little thought-experiment. Imagine that each object in our visual system is described via an ordered triple, using Cartesian co-ordinates. That is, each is described as 'object at co-ordinate $x, y, z$'. In Pylyshyn's experiments, we start off with about five objects tracked, plus 15 in the background. So, in the imagined visual system, that would be 20 locational triples. With each motion of each object, all the co-ordinates would have to be updated. And such a system would need a tracking function that would, at least five times over, have to note something like: '$O_{\langle 28,132,87\rangle}$ at $t_0 = O_{\langle 29,133,87\rangle}$ at $t_1$'. The complexity of such an imaginary tracking system is daunting. Now, obviously one need not suppose that the locational descriptions, if any, which humans actually use are precisely like these imagined ones. But it gives one the idea of what a locational-description view would say.

Now back to reality: Pylyshyn's simulations, using his sophisticated locational descriptions, produced lots of errors, far more than real humans, who actually do quite well at tracking objects in the visual field. Assuming that his simulations were otherwise accurate, it seems safe to conclude that we humans—who succeed so well in this task—do not in general attend to objects via a locational description. (Surprisingly too, subjects were able to keep track of up to five objects as they changed location *and their other properties*.) Pylyshyn and others have concluded that descriptions of location cannot be what humans actually use as the basis for visual tracking. But, given that, as argued above, locational descriptions were the best candidate for an identifying property, we conclude that objects are attended to without using any description of them, locational or otherwise.

To be sure, Pylyshyn's experiments do not fully justify the claim that visual indexes function as referential devices that refer non-descriptively to perceived *objects*. For instance, the results described above are also compatible with the claim that, in vision, we use *spatial locative demonstratives* ('there' rather than 'that') in the visual system. That is, for all we have said here, the visual system might refer pre-conceptually to the *locations* of objects, then 'describing' the object via such demonstratives. On this view, visual indexes are referential mechanisms that directly pick out locations in the subject's visual field, without either referring to or describing the objects that occupy those locations. Visual indexes non-descriptively encode information about the spatial locations of moving or stationary objects. As such, they function as indexical representations of spatial locations rather than as representations of spatially located objects. (In terms of the thought-experiment introduced above, the object would then be not $O_{\langle x,y,z \rangle}$ but $O_{there}$. It is clear how this would simplify the computational burden.) We therefore concede that Pylyshyn's experiments do not conclusively rule out the view that visual indexes function as spatial locatives. That is an empirical matter on which, given our immediate purposes, we need not take a particular stand.[16] But, as before, Pylyshyn's own view emerges as initially the most plausible. (It is worth recalling that if *either* option (*d*) or (*e*) ends up being true, then subsentential speech is surely genuine. So the outstanding issues at this point, when applied to subsentence cases, have to do with (Q1) and (Q2), not (Q3).)

[16] Pylyshyn's general position is not undermined if it should turn out that visual indexes function as demonstrative spatial locatives rather than as demonstratives that pick out objects. For his experiments are intended to show only that we do not perceptually track things solely by describing them.

Following Pylyshyn, then, we conclude that there are 'visual indexes'. These are representations within the visual system which refer to, without describing, objects in the environment.[17] It is worth stressing that visual indexes are representations whose contents are determined only relative to their context of occurrence. (Cf. Bach 1986; 1987; and Récanati 1993.) Two individuals may token type-identical visual indexes, in qualitatively indistinguishable perceptual environments, have qualitatively indistinguishable percepts, and yet have different perceptions because the contextually determined objects of the tokened indexes are distinct. The object of a (tokened) visual index is not thought of as the unique object of a certain sort, i.e. under a definite description (whether in Mentalese or in a natural language), but is rather thought of in some contextually sensitive way. To put the point another way, something is an object of perception not in virtue of its uniquely satisfying some descriptive condition imposed by the perceiver's representation of her environment; but rather, it is an object of perception in virtue of its standing in the appropriate causal-contextual relation to the perceiver, a relation that the person's perceptual mechanisms do not represent in thought.

We propose to treat visual indexes as representations in the visual system rather than as outputs of the visual system. Their contents, which are the perceived objects, get into the Central System by further processing. Although we do not know how the process actually works, we shall argue in the next section that the representational contents of visual indexes somehow combine with material got from the parser in the understanding of non-sentential speech—at least in the sort of case considered here. If that is right, then, to account for subsentence cases, there must be representations in the Central System that somehow link up with visual indexes in some indirect way. We shall turn now to that topic, taking for granted from here on that, because of how visually grasping seems to work in the general

---

[17] An early version of the idea that subjects mentally employ visual representations as singular referential devices can also be found in Chastain (1975). However, Chastain thinks that it is the conscious *visual experience* involved in a subject's seeing an object—and in virtue of which it is (in that context) a seeing of *that* object—that actually functions as a singular referring mechanism. Neither Pylyshyn nor we are committed to that view since all three of us hold that visual indexes function at a level of processing inaccessible to conscious experience or direct awareness.

case, option (*e*) from Figure 8.1 above is the most viable suboption for how hearers understand subsentential speech.

## 5 From Visual Indexicals to Indexicals in Mentalese

A quick review, before we proceed. We began by introducing a single example of subsentential communication: Andrew uttered the prepositional phrase 'From France', and thereby asserted, of a visually salient cigarette, that it was from France. We then noted a host of philosophical doctrines which, at least at first glance, appear to be in tension with the existence of subsentential speech acts. These included theses about: the domain of logical form, the contextual determinants of what is said, the sufficiency of knowledge of language in interpreting literal speech, the proper analysis of assertion, the location of the semantics/pragmatics boundary, the context principle and its implications, etc. Given the importance of these doctrines for philosophy of language and epistemology, two issues become pressing. First, is subsentential communication a genuine phenomenon? Second, if it is genuine, are the philosophical doctrines described genuinely in tension with it? We have skirted the latter question. But we have been trying to urge a positive answer to the former question, largely by considering five options for treating subsentential speech. One result of that investigation was that the options which treat the phenomenon as *merely* apparent face real problems. (These were options (*b*) and (*c*). Option (*a*), it will be recalled, was put aside for future research.) A striking upshot of this, with respect to at least one larger philosophical doctrine, was that thought is not inner speech. Or anyway, occurrent thought does not require that a natural-language vehicle for that (whole) thought 'pass through the mind'. This in itself is not so surprising. It has long been suggested that language learning, image manipulation, task memory, etc. do not involve inner speech. But if we are right, not even reasoning, nor argumentation, *nor even the understanding of speech* can be exhaustively explained by inner speech of this sort. The reason is, the thought which the hearer recovers and uses as a premiss, in subsentential communication, goes well beyond the meaning of the words which pass through her mind. Closer to the truth, at least if the S-representational picture is correct, is that the recovery of the thought involves the processing of sentential mental representations of a special sort, Mentalese expressions.

Having arrived at that result, we began to delve more deeply into the nature of the representations processed during subsentential comprehension. Part of the point of this, beyond its intrinsic interest in allowing us to address (Q1) and (Q2), is to support the genuineness of subsentential understanding—by telling a positive story, consistent with what is known, that shows it to be such. To develop this story, we abstracted from subsentential speech for a moment, and explained and defended the notion of a 'visual index', a device which allows the visual system to track objects indexically. The plausibility of this idea in the general case of 'visually grasping' supported option (e), an option according to which the phenomenon is genuine. We now pursue (e) even further.

The main question of this section is this: what precise bearing does our discussion of visual indexes have on the issue of non-sentential communication? In particular, how might visual indexes get employed in subsentential understanding? To answer that question, we shall borrow some helpful ideas from Joseph Levine's account of indexical thought within Mentalese (cf. Levine 1988). His account operates on the assumption that we think in Mentalese, which is also our working hypothesis. To see how his account works, let us first consider a case in which a speaker explicitly uses a demonstrative to refer to some perceived object. Suppose you see a dog a few yards away, and you say, 'That is a cocker spaniel', as you point to the dog. You thereby expressed a singular, demonstrative, thought about the dog. Levine's question is this: What is the cognitive role of the linguistic demonstrative in the expression of an indexical *thought* about the dog? In developing his answer to that question, Levine presents the following picture:

our cognitive architecture is modular at least to the extent that we have relatively autonomous perceptual systems which take impinging stimuli as inputs and deliver perceptual representations—percepts—as outputs. Percepts then serve as inputs to the more general 'CPU', the system within which belief-fixation takes place. A mental demonstration is a particular kind of causal/computational relation between an expression of mentalese and a percept. The mentalese expression standing in this relation to a percept is a pointer. We can think of a pointer as an 'internal finger' pointing at the percept, except that the ultimate object of the demonstration is not the percept 'ostended' itself, but the external object it represents . . . The main point is that some computationally significant causal relation obtains between the mental representation corresponding to the use of a demonstrative and a perceptual representation output from the perceptual module such that the former inherits its referent from the latter. (Levine 1988: 232)

Levine continues:

A pointer, then, is a mentalese demonstrative that underlies my use of demonstratives in natural language. The canonical form of a pointer can be represented as follows: $[\rightarrow(\alpha)]$, where $\alpha$ designates a percept. A pointer is really a directly referential term, its referent being the object represented by the percept $\alpha$.

Thus, with respect to the present example, the indexical thought you expressed when you reported what you saw ('That is a cocker spaniel') involves the generation of a perceptual representation of the dog. We shall use $\alpha$ to designate your percept of the dog rather than the dog itself. To facilitate discussion, we shall depart from Levine's notation by representing Mentalese indexicals—whether demonstrative or otherwise—as English indexicals in bold capitals. Thus, in the dog example, a token of $IT_{[\alpha]}$ (in your language of thought) refers to the dog you saw. Being a perceptual case, it does so in virtue of demonstrating a percept, namely $\alpha$, that itself represents the dog. The demonstrated percept, in turn, represents the dog in virtue of certain causal facts about the perceptual situation, including facts about the visual indexes that play a causal role in the tracking of the perceived dog. The indexical thought that you mentally tokened in your Belief Box, and which you expressed by means of your report, was: **COCKER SPANIEL($IT_{[\alpha]}$).**[18]

Levine's account of the cognitive role of demonstratives in natural language is quite ingenious. We would like to make two points about it. First, it is entirely neutral on the empirical question of the nature, structure, and representational properties of percepts—as it should be. In particular, his account of indexical thought is compatible with the empirical hypothesis, supported above, that we employ visual indexes when we visually perceive objects. Nothing in the account rules out the possibility that, in some perceptual contexts, and at some level of processing, vision employs visual

---

[18] We wish to remind the reader of our convention of using capitalized English expressions in bold to represent Mentalese expressions. We do not mean to suggest that Mentalese is a natural language. On the contrary, we have supplied an indirect reason in this paper to think that it is not.

indexes. Thus, the 'visual index' account can be made to fit nicely with the view we are outlining in this section.

Second, even though Levine's account is an explanation of the cognitive role of public-language demonstratives in the expression of demonstrative thought, we see no reason why it cannot also be used to explain how hearers can cognitively grasp singular thoughts that speakers often convey by way of non-sentential speech. The difference is that, in the latter case, the speaker does not actually produce a natural-language demonstrative. Nor is her utterance 'elliptical' for a natural-language sentence that contains a demonstrative (whether a pure demonstrative, a complex demonstrative, or some other indexical expression). In the dog example, you could have drawn attention to what you saw by assertively uttering the bare phrase 'Cocker spaniel' as you pointed to the dog, rather than by uttering 'That is a cocker spaniel'. And yet, your friend will have interpreted you as having said of the demonstrated dog that it is a cocker spaniel.

To explain how both things can be true, let us apply Levine's story, thereby illustrating our answer to (Q1). In interpreting your utterance, your friend employs a Mentalese indexical that designates (in that perceptual context) the dog you pointed to. However, it refers to the dog by virtue of demonstrating, via some causal and computational route, a (tokened) perceptual representation your friend formed (presumably a visual index) of the dog. This, we may suppose, is how visual indexes manage to get 'translated' into the Central System: what really happens is that a (tokened) Mentalese indexical demonstrates a percept, whose represented object is indexically fixed by a visual index, and takes over as its referent the referent of that index. Eventually, at some level of Central System processing, your friend stores a Mentalese sentence of the form:

$$\textbf{SAID(S)(COCKER SPANIEL(IT}_{[\alpha]}\textbf{))}$$

in his Belief Box, where **S** is a Mentalese expression that refers to the speaker; $\alpha$ is a percept, i.e. a representation within the visual system, specifically a visual index that (in this context) designates the dog; and $\textbf{IT}_{[\alpha]}$ is a Mentalese indexical that (in this context) refers to the dog indirectly, by virtue of demonstrating the visual index $\alpha$.

If true, this explains how a hearer can grasp, without tokening a natural-language sentence, a singular thought conveyed by a speaker who utters a subsentential expression. And, we stress, it does not follow from this story that the assertive utterance of the phrase 'Cocker spaniel' is semantically or syntactically equivalent to (or elliptical for) an utterance of the sentence 'That is a cocker spaniel', even if the same speaker reference/demonstratum is involved. Hence, in answer to (Q3), the genuineness of the phenomenon is maintained. At most, all that follows (if our extension of Levine's account to non-sentential assertions is correct) is that, in certain communicative contexts, a bare phrase and a natural-language sentence can have the same underlying cognitive role within the Central System, in speech perception and interpretation. (This is not surprising if, as seems inevitable, natural-language sentences themselves must get translated into Mentalese during interpretation.) Similar remarks apply, of course, in the case of assertive uses of prepositional phrases. Consider, once again, our example about Andrew and his cigarette. By hypothesis, the hearer interpreted Andrew's non-sentential utterance of 'From France' as meaning that *that* cigarette (the one that he demonstrated) is from France. Our proposal is that, in understanding Andrew's utterance, the hearer used a Mentalese indexical, which we shall represent as $IT_{[\beta]}$ that refers (in that context) to the visual index $\beta$, and thereby refers, via deferred demonstration, to the cigarette. Computationally, the tokening of the Mentalese indexical demonstrates, in Mentalese, the (tokened) percept of the cigarette; semantically, it refers to the cigarette.[19] It is also combined with the representation that the language module emits from the processing of Andrew's verbal input, namely, the Mentalese predicate **FROM-FRANCE.** The result is (something like) the Mentalese sentence **FROM-FRANCE($IT_{[\beta]}$).** That sentence is, in turn, encoded as part of a more complex Mentalese sentence,

**SAID(ANDREW)(FROM-FRANCE($IT_{[\beta]}$)),**

which Sylvia comes to harbour in her Belief Box. Semantically, the latter

---

[19] Relative to the context in question, the tokened Mentalese demonstrative, $IT_{[\beta]}$, does not refer to the percept $\beta$. It refers instead to Andrew's cigarette. But it does not refer to it by describing the cigarette in terms of certain properties that the cigarette uniquely possesses. Rather, it refers to the cigarette by its demonstration of a (tokened) percept that represents the cigarette. We are suggesting, then, that Mentalese indexicals, at least in these perceptual cases, function as deferred demonstratives in the language of thought. For a defence of the view that deferred demonstratives in natural language are directly referential singular terms, see Borg (2001).

sentence is true just in case, relative to the context in which he displayed the cigarette and uttered 'From France', Andrew said of the cigarette that it is from France. If Andrew said that, then it is reasonable to conclude that he asserted a singular proposition, one that (necessarily) is true if and only if that particular cigarette is from France. It is also reasonable to conclude that that is what Sylvia interpreted him as saying—even though she did not recognize any available natural-language sentence in interpreting his utterance.

## 6 Conclusions and Further Research

We can best summarize our conclusions by recalling the three guiding questions of the paper:

(Q1) How do hearers interpret subsentential speech of this sort?

(Q2) How is perception-based information seamlessly combined with communication-based information?

(Q3) In the light of the answer to (Q1), is it plausible that the phenomenon of subsentential speech is genuine, or is it more plausible that it is merely apparent?

Recalling that we were only discussing the use of predicates to talk about objects that are visually grasped, our answer to (Q1) goes like this. The hearer forms a visual index, which is locked onto the displayed object. That index, in turn, is linked up with a Mentalese indexical, where the said linking is achieved by demonstration of the visual index. As a result of this two-step process, the Mentalese indexical derivatively refers to the displayed object. The Mentalese indexical then gets combined with a Mentalese predicate, where the latter comes from the language module, having been decoded from the natural-language predicate actually spoken. It is, we conjecture, the concatenation of such a parser-derived Mentalese predicate with a Mentalese indexical, whose reference is contextually fixed by a visual index, that constitutes understanding less-than-sentential speech, at least in cases of visually grasping objects, and combining them with a predicate-meaning got from the parser. (Or anyway, it is something like that.) What this suggests about (Q2) is that at least in these cases the information is integrated by having both kinds of information converted into Mentalese—the one from visual processing, the other from linguistic decoding. What is *not* going on is the translation of all the information into natural language. Finally, what all of this suggests as an answer to (Q3) is that the phenomenon is indeed genuine—it *appears* that neither the speaker nor the hearer processes a natural-language sentence, because neither of them *does* process a natural-language sentence.

Of course there remain two questions that, as we warned above, we have not addressed here—even putting aside the fact that the issue of option (*a*) in Figure 8.1, the non-S-representationalist option, remains unresolved. The first of these is the question of whether the apparent tensions between subsentential speech and the various philosophical doctrines noted in Section 2, are real tensions. The second is equally important. We end with it.

What, one surely wants to know, is to be said about cases of non-sentential speech that are not as simple as the one described here? We have been discussing only perceptual cases—indeed, only perceptual cases involving vision. But it is quite clear that there must be more to the story than that. In addition to their *visual demonstrative* roles, Mentalese indexicals can serve other functions. For a start, in the same sense that one can 'visually demonstrate', one can 'demonstrate' an object by hearing it, or smelling it, or otherwise sensing it. And these cases too will give rise to subsentence use. Altering the Andrew case somewhat, for example, one might notice the quite distinctive scent of some cigarette smoke, and say: 'From France'. Here the cigarette being described, i.e. the one which is the source of the smell, is not linked up to the Mentalese demonstrative by a *visual* index. For the cigarette has not (yet) been seen. Or again, hearing a very loud noise, recognizable as a sonic boom, Rohit could say to Dom: 'An American jet fighter', thereby describing not the boom, but its source.

Moreover—non-visual perceptual cases aside—one can talk about an object which is not *presently* perceived at all, visually or otherwise. Thus, suppose that several days after the just-mentioned sonic boom, Dom reads that the Concorde has begun flying over their town, throttling up to Mach 1 precisely overhead. He could then say to Rohit, at their next meeting: 'That boom the other day? Not a jet fighter. The Concorde'. For such cases, one would need Mentalese indexicals whose content is not determined demonstratively. They would be multi-purpose, usable for any contextually salient thing however it is grasped. Demonstration of a percept would apply only in the specific case of presently perceived objects. For instance, Mentalese indexicals would need to serve as temporary file-names for contextually determined referents, and be maintained even when the referents are not perceptually available. Information about the object could then be appended to the symbol as a way of keeping a track history of the object. (Returning to the first example, the hearer's perception of Andrew's cigarette resulted in her acquiring and storing information about it in short-term memory, so that she can later come to wonder where Andrew bought the cigarette, even when no longer perceiving it. The reason one can do this, we conjecture, is that there is now a 'file' which stands for that object, available for later use. This would also help explain, by the way, why one is able to go from hearing Andrew's assertive utterance of 'From France', and seeing the demonstrated cigarette, to reporting things like, 'Andrew said that the cigarette he was holding in his right hand is from France', 'Andrew said that that cigarette is from France', etc., even though Andrew did not use any of these singular terms.) Indeed, Mentalese indexicals can surely be used even if the object discussed was not perceptually grasped in the first place: the object discussed could be a conjectured object. Here is an example. Two physicists could be discussing the strange behaviour of a newly postulated particle, the Fridgeon. Returning the next day, one scientist could say to the other: 'Positron-emitting'. She would thereby have asserted, about the *postulated entity*, not perceived by any of the senses ever, that it is positron-emitting.

One last complication. As has just emerged, it is emphatically not the case that subsentences can be used only to talk about visually perceived objects: one can also speak subsententially about objects perceived non-visually (the smelt cigarette, the heard jet), and even about things never perceived. That the thing talked about happened to be visually perceived is, therefore, a quite accidental feature of the original Andrew case. But, surprisingly, that it is a thing—i.e. an object—being talked about is *also* an accidental feature of that specific example. (Though it is not accidental that we selected such an example: the aim of the paper was to take the very first steps towards understanding how subsentential speech is understood. Hence we deliberately picked a very simple case.) One can perform subsentential speech acts in which 'what is salient'—seen, heard, remembered, imagined, whatever—is a property, or even a generalized quantifier. Thus, one can point at graffiti on a wall and say 'John', meaning thereby that John *did the graffiti*. (Here, a property is supplied by the environment, and an object is supplied by decoding.) Or, one could say to a person who is searching everywhere in the house, clearly in need of a cigarette, 'In the fridge', thereby asserting that *there are cigarettes* in the fridge.[20] (Here a generalized quantifier is contextually supplied, with decoding providing a missing property. For more on quantificational cases of subsentential speech, see Barber, forthcoming; Botterell, forthcoming; Stainton 1998*a*; 1998*b*.) Clearly, then, there is *much* more to be said about these matters. But that will have to wait for another day.

# REFERENCES

BACH, K. (1986), 'Thought and Object: *De Re* Representations and Relations', in Brand Harnish (1986), 187–218.

—— (1987), *Thought and Reference* (Oxford: Oxford University Press).

—— (1994*a*), 'Semantic Slack: What is Said and More', in Tsohatzidis (1994), 267–91.

—— (1994*b*), 'Conversational Impliciture', *Mind and Language*, 9: 124–62.

BARBER, A. (forthcoming), 'Co-extensive Theories and Unembedded Definite Descriptions', in Elugardo and Stainton (forthcoming, *b*).

[20] Further complicating things, Ernie Lepore drew our attention to very interesting modal cases. Thus Andrew could have said not 'From France', but 'Maybe from France'. It is not obvious what the process of interpretation of such utterances would be, given our answer to (Q1). It might seem, for instance, that the modal 'maybe' must apply to a complete sentential structure—something which, on our view, is only available *after* the complete Mentalese sentence, **FROM-FRANCE(IT$_{[a]}$)**, is constructed. But then the language module cannot be outputting a unitary meaning for the element uttered, since there isn't the right sort of thing for 'maybe' to modify: it modifies complete sentential expressions, not prepositional phrases. We remain unsure how exactly to treat this sort of example. As a first pass, however, we would note that 'maybe' and other modals can actually modify subsentential structures within sentences. For example, suppose the police suspected a six-foot-two criminal in a robbery. A witness describing the robber could disabuse them of their suspicion by saying: 'The bandit was about five foot eight, maybe six foot, but definitely not six foot two'. Here 'maybe' does not modify the complete proposition. Nor does 'definitely not' modify that proposition. Rather, the thing modified is subpropositional. Our hope, then, is that whatever story is told about modal modifiers in these less-than-propositional cases will equally apply to modals used in subsentential speech.

BARTON, E. (1990), *Nonsentential Constituents* (Philadelphia: John Benjamins).

BERMAN, S., and HESTVIK, A., eds. (1992), *Proceedings of the Stuttgart Ellipsis Workshop* (Sprachtheoretische Grundlagen für die Computerlinguistik, Bericht 29; Stuttgart: University of Stuttgart).

BORG, E. (2001), 'Deferred Demonstratives', in Campbell, O'Rourke, and Shier (2001), 214–30.

BOTTERELL, A. (forthcoming), 'Acquaintance and Isolation', in Elugardo and Stainton (forthcoming, *b*).

BRAND, M., and HARNISH, R. M., eds. (1986), *The Representation of Knowledge and Belief* (Tucson: University of Arizona Press).

BRANQUINHO, J., ed. (2001), *The Foundations of Cognitive Science* (Oxford: Clarendon Press).

BREEDIN, S. D., and SAFFRAN, E. M. (1999), 'Sentence Processing in the Face of Semantic Loss', *Journal of Experimental Psychology: General* 128: 547–62.

BURGE, TYLER (1977), 'Belief *De Re*', *Journal of Philosophy*, 74: 338–62.

CAMPBELL, J. K., O'ROURKE, M., and SHIER, D., eds., (2001), *Meaning and Truth: Investigations in Philosophical Semantics* (New York: Seven Bridges Press).

CARRUTHERS, P. (1996), *Language, Thought, and Consciousness* (Cambridge: Cambridge University Press).

—— and BOUCHER, J., eds. (1998), *Language and Thought: Interdisciplinary Themes* (Cambridge: Cambridge University Press).

CARSTON, R. (1988), 'Implicature, Explicature, and Truth-Theoretic Semantics', in Kempson (1988), 151–81.

—— (2002), *Thoughts and Utterances* (Oxford: Blackwell).

CHAO, WYNN (1988), *On Ellipsis* (New York: Garland).

CHASTAIN, C. (1975), 'Reference and Context', in Gunderson (1975), 194–269.

CHATTERJEE, A., MAHER, L. M., GONZALEZ ROTHI, L. J., and HEILMAN, K. M. (1995), 'Asyntactic Thematic Role Assignment: The Use of a Temporal-Spatial Strategy', *Brain and Language*, 49: 125–39.

CLAPP, L. (2001), 'What Unarticulated Constituents Could Not Be', in Campbell, O'Rourke, and Shier (2001), 231–56.

—— (forthcoming), 'On the Interpretation and Performance of Non-Sentential Assertions', in Elugardo and Stainton (forthcoming, *b*).

DAVIS, S. (forthcoming), 'Quinean Interpretation and Anti-Vernacularism', in Elugardo and Stainton (forthcoming, *b*).

DEVITT, M., and STERELNY, K. (1999), *Language and Reality*, 2nd edn. (Cambridge, Mass.: Bradford Books/MIT Press).

DUMMETT, M. (1973), *Frege: Philosophy of Language* (Cambridge, Mass.: Harvard University Press).

ELUGARDO, R., and STAINTON, R. J. (2001), 'Logical Form and the Vernacular', *Mind and Language*, 16: 393–424.

———— (forthcoming, *a*), 'Shorthand, Syntactic Ellipsis, and the Pragmatic Determinants of What is Said', *Mind and Language*.

———— eds. (forthcoming, *b*), *Ellipsis and Non-Sentential Speech* (Dordrecht: Kluwer).

FODOR, J. A. (1983), *Modularity of Mind* (Cambridge, Mass.: MIT Press).

GAUKER, C. (1997), *Thinking Out Loud: An Essay on the Relation between Thought and Language* (Princeton: Princeton University Press).

GUNDERSON, K., ed. (1975), *Language, Mind, and Knowledge* (Minnesota Studies in the Philosophy of Science, 7; Minneapolis: University of Minnesota Press).

HANKAMER, J., and SAG, I. (1976), 'Deep and Surface Anaphora', *Linguistic Inquiry*, 7: 391–426.

KACHRU, B. B., LEES, R. B., MALKIEL, Y., PIETRANGELI, A., and SAPORTA, S., eds. (1973), *Issues in Linguistics: Papers in Honor of Henry and Renée Kahane* (Urbana, Ill.: University of Illinois Press).

KEMPSON, R. M., ed. (1988), *Mental Representations* (Cambridge: Cambridge University Press).

KENYON, T. (1999), 'Non-Sentential Assertions and the Dependence Thesis of Word Meaning', *Mind and Language*, 14: 424–40.

—— (forthcoming), 'Non-Sentences, Implicature, and Success in Communication', in Elugardo and Stainton (forthcoming, *b*).

LAPPIN, S., and BENMAMOUN, E. (1999), *Fragments: Studies in Ellipsis and Gapping* (Oxford: Oxford University Press).

LEVINE, J. (1988), 'Demonstrating in Mentalese', *Pacific Philosophical Quarterly*, 69: 222–40.

LUDLOW, P. (1999), *Semantics, Tense and Time*, Cambridge, Mass.: MIT Press).

—— (forthcoming), 'A Note on Alleged Cases of Nonsentential Assertion', in Elugardo and Stainton (forthcoming, *b*).

LYCAN, WILLIAM G. (1986), 'Thoughts about Things', in Brand and Harnish (1986), 160–86.

—— (1988), *Judgment and Justification* (Cambridge: Cambridge University Press).

—— (1990), 'Mental Content in Linguistic Form', *Philosophical Studies*, 58: 147–54.

MORGAN, J. (1973), 'Sentence Fragments and the Notion "Sentence"', in Kachru *et al.* (1973), 719–51.

—— (1989), 'Sentence Fragments Revisited', *Chicago Linguistics Society: Papers from the Parasession on Language in Context*, 25: 228–41.

PYLYSHYN, Z. (1999), 'Connecting Vision with the World: Evidence for a Preconceptual Mechanism that Individuates and Keeps Track of Objects' (draft manuscript, Rutgers University).

—— and STORM, R. W. (1988), 'Tracking of Multiple Independent Targets', *Spatial Vision*, 3: 1–19.

RÉCANATI, F. (1989), 'The Pragmatics of What is Said', *Mind and Language*, 4: 294–328.

—— (1993), *Direct Reference: From Language to Thought* (Oxford: Blackwell).

SAG, I. (1976), 'Deletion and Logical Form' (diss. Ph.D., Massachusetts Institute of Technology).

SELLARS, W. (1963), *Science, Perception, and Reality* (London: Routledge and Kegan Paul).

SIRIGU, A. (1998), 'Distinct Frontal Regions for Processing Sentence Syntax and Story Grammar', *Cortex*, 34: 771–8.

SPERBER, D., and WILSON, D. (1986), *Relevance: Communication and Cognition* (Cambridge, Mass.: Harvard University Press).

STAINTON, R. J. (1995), 'Non-Sentential Assertions and Semantic Ellipsis', *Linguistics and Philosophy*, 18: 281–96.

—— (1997a), 'Utterance Meaning and Syntactic Ellipsis', *Pragmatics and Cognition*, 5: 49–76.

—— (1997b), 'What Assertion is Not', *Philosophical Studies*, 85: 57–73.

—— (1998a), 'Quantifier Phrases, Meaningfulness "in Isolation", and Ellipsis', *Linguistics and Philosophy*, 21: 311–40.

—— (1998b), 'Unembedded Definite Descriptions and Relevance'. *Revista alicantina de estudios ingleses* (special issue on Relevance Theory), 11: 231–9.

—— (2000), 'The Meaning of "Sentences"', *Noûs*, 34: 441–54.

—— (forthcoming), 'In Defense of Non-Sentential Assertion', in Szabo (forthcoming).

STALNAKER, R. (1990), 'Mental Content and Linguistic Form', *Philosophical Studies*, 58: 129–46.

STANLEY, J. (2000), 'Context and Logical Form', *Linguistics and Philosophy*, 23: 391–433.

SZABO, Z., ed. (forthcoming), *Semantics vs. Pragmatics* (Oxford: Oxford University Press).

TRAVIS, C. (1985), 'On What is Strictly Speaking True', *Canadian Journal of Philosophy*, 15: 187–229.

Tsohatzidis, S. L., ed. (1994), *Foundations of Speech Act Theory* (London: Routledge).

Varley, R. (1998), 'Aphasic Language, Aphasic Thought: An Investigation of Propositional Thinking in A-Propositional Aphasic', in Carruthers and Boucher (1998), 128–45.

Williams, E. (1977), 'Discourse and Logical Form', *Linguistic Inquiry*, 8: 101–39.

# CHAPTER 9

# *Knowledge of Meaning*

*Stephen Schiffer*

Every speaker knows what numerous expressions mean. In what does such knowledge consist? What is it to know what an expression means? In asking this question, I am using 'know' and 'means' in ordinary, non-technical ways. There may be legitimate technical senses of 'know' or 'means' that would yield a different question and have a different answer, and later I shall touch on this, but in this paper my question is the non-technical one. The question interests me because I believe its answer has important implications both for the nature of meaning and for foundational questions about language understanding. The question needs refinement, but some progress can be made with it even before it is recast.

## 1 An Easy Answer?

For a lot of theorists, the question ought (at least initially) to be perceived as having an easy answer—namely (where '*e*' ranges over meaningful expressions and ambiguity is ignored) that

(1)  To know what *e* means is to know that *e* means *m*, for suitable way *m* of identifying *e*'s meaning.

The reference to a suitable way of identifying a meaning should be understood on analogy with, for example, knowing to whom Jane is married. You do not have that knowledge just by virtue of knowing that Jane is married to her husband, but you do if you know that she is married to Bill Bloggs in

I am indebted to Alex Barber, Ned Block, Paul Boghossian, and Chris Peacocke for their comments on an earlier draft. A much different paper bearing the same title as this one was read at the conference on the Epistemology of Language at Sheffield University, July 2000, and Adam Morton was its illuminating commentator.

the History department. To know to whom $x$ is married is to know that $x$ is married to $m$, for suitable way $m$ of identifying $x$'s spouse.

To be married is to stand in the marriage relation to someone, and if $x$ stands in that relation to $y$, then $y$, by that very fact, is $x$'s spouse. Likewise—it is tempting to suppose—to have meaning is to stand in the meaning relation to something, and if $x$ stands in the meaning relation to $y$, then $y$, by that very fact, is $x$'s meaning. This conception of meaning is implied both by a face-value reading of our use of 'means' as a transitive verb, as displayed in

'Existence precedes essence' *means something*,

and by a face-value reading of our use of 'meaning' as a sortal noun, as displayed in

'Bank' has *two meanings*.
What's *the meaning of* 'hermeneutics'?
'Il pleut' means *the same thing* as 'It's raining'.

The many theorists who accept the relational conception of meaning are those who ought to be disposed to accept (I); for (I) is the direct conclusion of the following two assumptions:

(*a*) If *e* has meaning, then $\exists y(e$ means $y)$.
(*b*) If (*a*), then (I).

The prima facie case for (*a*) was just glossed, and the case for (*b*) is even more straightforward; it is simply an instance of a platitude about all relations expressed by transitive verbs—namely, that if *a* Rs *b*, then to know what *a* Rs is just to know that *a* Rs *m*, for suitable way *m* of identifying *b* (that is, a way of thinking of *b* which enables one to satisfy contextually appropriate standards for knowing what *a* Rs). For example, if Henry believes *that there was a hailstorm yesterday*, then even if the proposition that there was a hailstorm yesterday = the first proposition Jane asserted today, you do not *ipso facto* know what Henry believes by knowing that he believes the first proposition Jane asserted today. But you would know what he believes by knowing that he believes that there was a hailstorm yesterday.

## 2 Not So Easy

It is doubtful that (I) holds for *every* meaningful expression. There are numerous expressions *e* such that one's knowing what *e* means seems not to consist in one's knowing that *e* means *m*, where *m* identifies that which *e* means. Sally, a normal speaker of English, knows what 'Stop singing!', 'It's raining', 'Is she there yet?', 'of', 'spells badly', 'run', and a 'a lonely cyclist' mean, but when any of these expressions is taken to be the value of '*e*' in

Sally knows that *e* means *m*,

it is doubtful that anyone can go on to replace '*m*' with a singular term that both refers to the expression's meaning and yields a knowledge ascription that would secure Sally's knowing what the expression in question means. Where, for example, is the singular term that would turn

(1) Sally knows that 'Is she there yet?' means *m*

into such a true statement? Theorists who hold that meaning is a relation between an expression and its meaning have adopted various conventions for forming names of an expression's meaning. A currently popular convention is to form a name of the meaning of an expression by writing the expression in capital letters.[1] Clearly, however, we no more answer our question about (1) by writing

Sally knows that 'Is she there yet?' means IS SHE THERE YET?

than we do by writing

Sally knows that 'Is she there yet?' means the meaning of 'Is she there yet?'

Notice that it does no good to suggest that Sally's propositional knowledge of the meaning of 'Is she there yet?' is merely 'implicit' or 'tacit', for what seems impossible is to say what it is that she knows implicitly or tacitly. If a theorist is to insist that (I) is not refuted by Sally's knowledge of what 'Is she there yet?' means, then he must hold either (*a*) that there is a relevant substituend for '*m*' in (1) even though we cannot now say what it

---

[1] See e.g. Fodor (1997) and Horwich (1998).

is, or (b) that although there is no relevant substituend for 'm' in (1), this is because the value of 'm'—that way of thinking of the meaning of 'Is she there yet?'—that makes (1) true is ineffable. I see nothing further to discuss on this score until the proponent of (a) gives some reasonable account of why we cannot say what 'Is she there yet?' means, or the proponent of (b) gives some reasonable account of why the canonical way of identifying the meaning of the sentence resists effability.

Given that (I) does not hold for *every* meaningful expression, one should expect it not to hold for *any* expression. It is implausible that our ordinary notion of expression meaning should encompass two disparate notions, one on which knowing what an expression means consists in a suitable identification of the thing that is the expression's meaning, the other requiring no such identification. We should therefore expect there not to be any relevant substitution instance of '*e* means *m*' which expresses a truth knowledge of which suffices for knowing what the expression it concerns means. This is borne out, I hazard, by a search for counter-examples. Is there a single substitution instance that would do the trick? If we knew that there was something that was the meaning of, say, 'dog', then we could utilize the capital-letter convention and write

'Dog' means DOG.

But, in the first place, we cannot be assured that there is anything that 'DOG' names; if there were, would there not be a more revealing way of referring to it than by a made-up technical convention, and would we not then have no need for the made-up convention? I shall return to this thought later. And, in the second place, even if the displayed meaning ascription expressed a truth and one knew that truth, it still would not follow that one knew what 'dog' meant. Given the nature of the capital-letter naming convention, there is nothing to guarantee that one's knowledge of the meaning of 'dog' is under a suitably revealing mode of presentation; the cash value of what one knew, we have already noticed, might be nothing more than that 'dog' means the meaning of 'dog'.

Nor would (I) find support in examples like

'Vixen' means 'female fox',

for the truth it conveys is merely that 'vixen' means the same as 'female fox' and implies nothing about any *thing* being the meaning of either expression. The best support for (I) comes from an example like

(2) 'Snow is white' means that snow is white.

For 'means' here expresses a dyadic relation, 'that snow is white' refers to a proposition in the range of that relation, and knowledge of the truth expressed by (2) would provide knowledge of what

(3) Snow is white

means. Nevertheless, I do not think (2) shows that (I) is true of any expression. I do not think (2) provides a *relevant* substitution instance of the schema '*e* means *m*', because the sense of 'means' in (2) is not the sense of 'means' applicable to any sentence. The reading of (2) on which it is true involves not the sense of 'means' strictly applicable to sentences in their own right, i.e. the sense of 'means' on display in, say,

'It's raining' and 'Is it raining?' both mean something,

but is rather the sense of 'means' applicable to *speaker meaning*, which *is* a relation between a person and a proposition. What is actually conveyed by (2) is that in uttering (3) the *speaker*, if speaking literally, would mean that snow is white. That is to say, 'that snow is white' in (2) refers to the proposition that the speaker would mean and not to anything the sentence (3) means in its own right, in the sense of 'means' at issue when we ask what it is to know what any sentence means. For consider the sentence

(4) Is snow white?

A literal utterance of either (3) or (4) requires a speech act whose propositional content is, or involves, the proposition that snow is white.[2] With what right, then, would that proposition be the meaning of (3) but not (4)?

If there are such things as sentence meanings, then those things should have something in them that marks the difference in meaning between (3) and (4). Better candidates for those meanings would be something along the lines of

---

[2] I am here ignoring my view that no that-clause has a wholly context-independent reference. See Schiffer (2001) and (forthcoming).

(5) ⟨asserting, the proposition that snow is white⟩
(6) ⟨asking-whether, the proposition that snow is white⟩

respectively. At the same time, there does not seem to be any ordinary, non-technical sense of 'means' according to which it is true to say that

(7) 'Snow is white' means ⟨asserting, the proposition that snow is white⟩.
(8) 'Is snow white?' means ⟨asking-whether, the proposition that snow is white⟩.

If we could say that, one would think, then we could also say that Sally knows the truths expressed by (7) and (8), since she certainly knows what (3) and (4) mean; but I do not think there is anything that warrants ascribing to Sally the knowledge that, for instance, 'Is snow white?' means ⟨asking-whether, the proposition that snow is white⟩.

Does this mean, as it certainly seems to imply, that there are no such *things* as the meanings of linguistic expressions, since (I) would be true if there were such things as expression meanings, and (I) is not true? I think that on balance it probably does mean that, but the situation is complicated by there being abstract entities that do much of what meanings would do if there were meanings. This question will be addressed in the final section, after I have tried to resolve the question about knowledge of meaning.

## 3 Knowledge of Meaning as Knowledge How

Our question—What is it to know what an expression means?—needs to be refined before considering further attempts to answer it. I have been asking what it is to know what an expression means, as though that question could be answered in those terms. It cannot, of course, since an expression has its meaning only relative to a language, a person, or a group of persons. Our question should not be 'What is it to know what *e* means?', but rather 'What is it to know what *e* means in language *L*, or for person *x*, or for group of persons *G*?' Nor is that enough. Meaning something is one thing when it is a matter of the kind of meaning an expression has when it is used in interpersonal communication, but it is something else when it is a matter of the kind of meaning an expression has when it is used in a *lingua mentis*, an inner system of mental representation. Meaning in a public language is a matter of how the expression is used, or apt to be used, in communication, while meaning in a system of mental representation is a matter of how the expression is used, or apt to be used, in thought. Moreover, use in communication is a matter of *intentional action*, of intentionally performed speech acts, whereas there is nothing intentional about the kind of processing role that defines use in thought. If ordinary people think in a language of thought, they are ignorant of that fact, and thus ignorant of what expressions belong to that language and of what they mean in it.

The question I mean to ask is, 'What is it to know what an expression means in the public language of a given group?' By 'the public language of a given group' I have in mind natural languages and dialects of them, used in the familiar interpersonal way. A lot could be said in explication and refinement of these notions, but I do not think doing so is necessary for my purposes. If my question demands further refinement, those demands should be met as they arise in my attempt to answer the question. Henceforth I shall take the restriction to shared public languages to go without saying.

The first attempt to answer our question construed knowledge of meaning as a kind of *propositional* knowledge, a matter of knowing that such-and-such is the case. The next attempt construes it as a kind of knowing how, a kind of ability or skill.[3] The idea is familiar and even has long-standing slogans. In the later Wittgenstein, we are advised not to ask for an expression's meaning, but for its use (Wittgenstein 1953). His thought, no doubt, was that knowing what an expression means is knowing how to use it. But use it to do what? As money is used to buy things, so words are used to . . .? 'Perform *speech acts* of certain kinds' was J. L. Austin's famous way of making Wittgenstein's idea more precise. A simplification of Austin's idea

---

[3] Knowing how to X may not entail having the ability to do X. A former ballerina, thirty years older and thirty pounds heavier, may still know how to do jumps she is now unable to do. What is crucial to the proposal about knowledge of meaning presently under consideration is having the ability to use language and to know what others are saying when they use language. Recently, Jason Stanley and Timothy Williamson (2001) have argued that knowing how is a kind of knowing that, and this would affect the proposal in question, since if one is able to understand utterances, then, presumably, one knows how to understand them. But, as I try to show in Schiffer (2002), the claim for which Stanley and Williamson argue is implausible, notwithstanding their ingenious arguments for it.

is that to know what an expression means is to know how to use it to say things (Austin 1962).

At best, Austin's slogan merely provides a sufficient condition for knowing what an expression means, since one can know what an expression means in a language one does not speak. A revision of Austin's slogan—that to know what an expression means is to know how to use it to perform speech acts—points to a way of putting the knowledge-of-meaning-as-knowledge-how idea which helpfully loosens the connection between knowing what an expression means and being able to say something with it. One knows what an expression means if one is able to use it to say things that are consonant with the expression's meaning.[4] One also knows what the expression means if one is able to *understand* what others are saying when they use it. In fact, understanding trumps saying in that one can understand utterances containing an expression without being able oneself to say things with it, but if one is able to say things with an expression, then one is able to understand utterances containing it. The knowledge-how idea, then, may be put in terms of a certain understanding ability. But first we need a narrowing of our question.

We cannot simply ask what it is to know what an expression *e* means in a language *L*, since we cannot assume that knowledge of meaning will be the same for every kind of expression. For example, we should expect that knowing the meaning of a word is significantly different from knowing the meaning of a sentence. I propose to begin with the question

(9) What is it to know what sentence *s* means in language *L*?

where a sentence is taken to be something that occurs on its own, not contained in a larger expression. I allude to the contrast between, for example, 'Snow is white.' and 'snow is white'. The former cannot occur as part of another sentence, but the latter can, as in 'Either snow is white or grass is green'.

---

[4] This may need qualification. I have enough mastery of the word 'titanium' to enable me to say that my new spectacles have titanium frames, but I do not know much more about titanium than that it is a strong light metal called 'titanium'. Do I know what 'titanium' means? The question may not have a determinate answer, although there is some temptation to say that I do not fully know what 'titanium' means. There are interesting and important things to be said on this issue, but in this paper I shall ignore them and the potential need for a qualification of Austin's thesis.

As a first approximation, the idea is that

(II) To know what $s$ means in $L$ is to have the ability to know what speakers of $L$ are saying when they utter $s$.

This is very much a first approximation, since, among other things, we need to know what 'saying' is meant to involve, and since it is clearly not a requirement on one's knowing what $s$ means in $L$ that one be able to understand *any* utterance of $s$ by *any* speaker of $L$. At the same time, the problems confronted by (II) make it doubtful that there is enough here to be worth trying to fix.

Knowledge of meaning plays an important explanatory role in language understanding, and thereby in language production, and it is hard to see why we should care much about it if it did not. One problem with the knowing-how account, (II), is that it precludes knowledge of meaning from playing that role. Sally, facing Al, utters 'He refuses to take it', and Al immediately knows that Sally is telling him that their son Ludwig refuses to take his medicine. Al's information-processing transition manifests his understanding of Sally's utterance, his knowledge of what she said in it. How was Al able to move from his perception of Sally's utterance to his knowledge of what she said? We may not yet know the complete answer, but it is reasonable to suppose that part of it is that Al knew what the sentence type 'He refuses to take it' meant. This could hardly be part of the explanation of Al's ability to know what Sally said in uttering the sentence if that ability simply was Al's knowledge of what the sentence meant.

A second problem with (II) is that it fails to state a sufficient condition for knowing what $s$ means in $L$. Leona does not know what any Hungarian sentence means but she is able to understand what Hungarians are saying. This is because her Siamese twin, Fiona, knows Hungarian and tells her what is said whenever anyone speaks Hungarian to them, which is often, as they live in Budapest. Thus, although Leona has the ability to know what a speaker of Hungarian is saying when he utters a particular Hungarian sentence, she still does not know what the sentence means.

A third problem with (II) is that it fails to state a necessary condition for knowing what $s$ means in $L$. I might know what a certain spoken Japanese sentence means because I was told its English synonym but yet not be able to recognize the sentence in normal Japanese speech (I cannot make any kind of meaningful division in any stream of Japanese speech). In this case I know what the sentence means in Japanese but I do not have the ability to know what Japanese speakers are saying when they utter it.

Is there some other version of the knowledge-of-meaning-as-knowledge-how idea that would not be subject to such quick collapse? Paul Horwich has proposed that a word's having a certain meaning is constituted by its having a certain non-intentional 'use' property and that one qualifies as knowing what the word means if one's deployment of the word results from that use property.[5] If this proposal worked for words, it would not be hard to make it the basis for an account of one's knowing what an expression of any kind means. The proposal would help with the first problem raised against (II)—viz. that it precludes knowledge of meaning from playing a role in understanding utterances—if we could take the categorical use property to be a property that plays the knowledge-of-meaning role in the processing that results in one's knowing what was said in the utterance of a sentence containing the word. That would have to be spelt out in some detail. If we understand Horwich's use properties to apply to expressions that one does not deploy, perhaps because they belong to a language one does not speak but which one understands, then a Horwichean revision of (II) yields

(II′)   $x$ knows what $s$ means in $L$ iff $\exists\Phi$ ($\Phi$ is that non-intentional 'use' property such that $\Phi(x, s)$ both constitutes $s$'s having the meaning it has for $x$ and 'grounds' $x$'s ability to know what speakers of $L$ are saying when they utter $s$).

Although this improves on (II) in at least one respect, it has problems of its own. One problem is that one may reasonably doubt that public-language meaning is constituted by Horwichean use properties (see Schiffer 2000). A more serious problem is that Horwichean use properties are not well suited to play a role in the processing that takes one from the perception of an utterance of a sentence to the knowledge of what was said in that utterance. As I shall later emphasize, in order for a property of a sentence

---

[5] Horwich (1998), 16–18. Horwich combines this knowledge-how idea with the just-rejected (I), to which he is evidently committed by virtue of his holding that having meaning is a matter of being related to a meaning. He says that 'although understanding is indeed a practical ability, it may none the less be characterized as an instance of "knowing that"—providing we recognize that the knowledge is *implicit*' (p. 18). This attachment stands vulnerable to the objections raised against proposal (I).

to enable one to know what was said in the utterance of the sentence, the property must somehow serve to connect the sentence both with the kind of speech act performed in the utterance and with the kind of propositional content that speech act enjoys. Horwich's use properties, however, can make no such connection; they are non-relational and have nothing about them to connect sentences bearing them with any particular kind of speech act or with any particular kind of propositional content. In any case, the deep moral as regards knowledge of meaning as knowing how to do things with words is that nothing can come of it unless it is somehow made to incorporate something categorical that can play the knowledge-of-meaning role in language processing. More on this presently.

## 4 'Characters*' and Knowledge of Meaning as a Different Kind of Propositional Knowledge

To know what an expression means is not to know that it has the property of meaning such-and-such; but maybe it is to know that it has a different property. We can help to motivate this idea by considering these three sentences:

(10) You sing it.
(11) Do you sing it?
(12) You, sing it!

These sentences differ in meaning, but they also share a common meaning feature. They differ in meaning in that each sentence is associated with a different kind of speech act—a speech act that a person must be performing if she utters the sentence in conformity with its meaning. Thus, a literal utterance of (10) requires the speaker to be performing a speech act of *stating*, or *saying that*; a literal utterance of (11) requires the speaker to be performing a speech act of *asking whether*; and a literal utterance of (12) requires the speaker to be performing a speech act of *ordering*, or *telling someone what to do* (or something along those lines). The meaning feature the three sentences share is that they impose the same constraint on the propositional contents of the speech acts they require—the content of each speech act must be a proposition of the form $m$ sings $m'$, where $m$ identifies the speaker's audience and $m'$ the thing to which the speaker's utterance of 'it' refers. Two sentences will differ in meaning just in case they differ in the kind of speech act they require or in the kind of propositional content they require the speech act to have. These two constraints characterize what a sentence means. This suggests that to know what a sentence means in a language is to know what kind of speech act, with what kind of propositional content, a speaker of that language must perform in a literal utterance of the sentence.

In other words, we reach the following account of what it is to know what a sentence *s* means:

(IIIs) *x* knows what *s* means in *L* iff ∃*A,P* (*x* knows that in a literal utterance of *s* the speaker performs a speech act of kind *A* with a propositional content of kind *P*).

For example, to know what 'Is it raining?' means is to know that in a literal utterance of the sentence the speaker is asking her audience whether it is raining at some contextually determined place. A literal utterance of a sentence is one in which what the speaker means in uttering the sentence is in conformity with what the sentence means, as when 'It's raining' is uttered to say that it is raining, as opposed to when it is uttered to test one's voice, make a joke, or speak metaphorically. Even if an ordinary person lacks the vocabulary to mark the distinction between literal and non-literal utterances, he has at least implicit knowledge of the distinction. It will be convenient to speak of the propositional content of a literal utterance of a sentence, where that is the content of the speech act performed in conformity with the sentence's meaning.

As a first approximation, word meaning may be characterized in terms of its contribution to the propositional constraints imposed by the sentences containing the word. This contribution will itself be a kind of proposition: corresponding to a word *w* is a kind of proposition *P* such that the propositional content of a literal utterance of *any* sentence containing *w* must be a proposition of kind *P*. The same goes for all subsentential expressions, and we reach the following first approximation of an account of what it is to know the meaning of any subsentential expression *e*:

(IIIe) *x* knows what *e* means in *L* iff ∃*P*(*x* knows that the propositional

> content of a literal utterance in $L$ of a sentence containing $e$ is a
> proposition of kind $P$).

(IIIe) is a first approximation because it cannot be assumed that an unambiguous expression imposes the same constraint in every sentential context. Whether the account is worth correcting in this regard will be determined after a brief digression.

Different utterances of the word 'she' make different contributions to the propositional contents of the utterances containing them, but there is a meaning factor shared by all tokens of 'she', *qua* English pronoun. In recent years it has become customary to follow David Kaplan (1989) in calling this common factor *character*. But Kaplan's 'character' also stands for a particular conception of what these common meaning factors are, and while it is eminently reasonable to suppose there are common meaning factors, it is considerably less reasonable to suppose that Kaplan was right about their nature. In order to forestall confusion on this score, let me dub the shared meaning factors *characters**.

I propose that we represent the character* of a sentence by an ordered pair $\langle A, P \rangle$, where $A$ is the kind of speech act that must be performed in a literal utterance of the sentence, and $P$ is the kind of propositional content that speech act must have. The character* of a subsentential expression will be a kind of propositional content, and we should expect the character* of a complex expression to be determined by its syntax and the characters* of its component expressions.

In the final section I shall ask whether, or to what extent, we can say that an expression's character* is its meaning. In the meantime we can at least take note of the fact that there seems not to be anything in our common-sense concept of meaning that would enable us to *discover* that, say,

(13) 'Is it raining?' means ⟨asking-whether, a proposition of the form *it is raining at place m at time m′*, where *m* identifies a place implicitly referred to by the speaker and *m′* identifies the time of the utterance⟩.

At the same time, it is not *unreasonable* to suppose that your understanding an utterance of 'Is it raining?' is in part enabled by your knowing that someone uttering that sentence literally is asking you whether it is raining at the time of the utterance at a place implicitly referred to by the speaker. Given this, we are still motivated to ask whether (III)—i.e. the conjunction of (IIIs) and (IIIe)—is the correct account of knowledge of meaning.

Well, it does seem to supply a sufficient condition for knowing what a sentence means, and it satisfies the important requirement of supplying something that is capable of playing the 'knowledge-of-meaning' role in language processing. The reasonable worry is whether (III) yields a necessary condition for knowledge of meaning. One worry is whether ordinary people—say, your Uncle Clyde in Cleveland—really can be said to have the propositional knowledge (III) implies they have. It is not clear that they do; it is also not *entirely* clear that they do not. We have lots of knowledge we cannot easily articulate, and perhaps we can be relaxed as to how exactly Uncle Clyde conceptualizes the notion of a 'literal utterance' and related matters. Still, things look worse for Uncle Clyde's knowing when we consider that getting a sentence's propositional constraint right can require some real analytical skill (think of debates about the logical form of belief reports). In any case, a more serious worry is whether anything like the propositional knowledge (IIIs) ascribes *actually* plays, or is needed to play, the knowledge-of-meaning role in language processing. If something else plays that role in the processing that takes you from your perception of an utterance of 'Is it raining?' to your knowledge that the speaker was asking you whether it was raining in your locale, then should it not be what constitutes knowledge of meaning? This leads me to a final proposal about knowledge of meaning.

## 5 Knowledge of Meaning as a Role in Language Processing

Sally utters:

(14) Eating clams is morally permissible,

and says thereby that eating clams is morally permissible. Now consider three people who understood her utterance, i.e. three people who knew that in uttering (14) Sally said that eating clams was morally permissible. The first is Mao, a monolingual speaker of Mandarin Chinese who knew, as a result of having been told, that the English sentence (14) was such that in a literal utterance of it a speaker of English would be saying that eating clams was morally permissible. This propositional knowledge of Mao's, propositional knowledge of the kind implied by (IIIs), is part of what enabled Mao to move from his perception of Sally's utterance of (14) to his knowledge of what she said in uttering it. In this bit of information processing, Mao's type-(III) propositional knowledge about (14) played the knowledge-of-meaning role. The second person who understood Sally's utterance is Al, who is one of us, and it is an empirical question as to what played the knowledge-of-meaning role in him, though it seems clear that something did. There is something he brought to the utterance without which he would not have been in a position to know what Sally said in uttering (14), something of a type he brings to every English utterance he understands and which, by virtue of the role it plays in his language understanding, constitutes his knowledge, on each occasion, of the meaning of the sentence uttered. The third person to understand Sally's utterance of (14) is clever Pierre. Nothing plays the knowledge-of-meaning role in the information processing that took him from his perception of Sally's utterance to his knowledge of what she said in uttering (14). Pierre correctly inferred what Sally said just on the basis of contextual clues. Having correctly inferred what Sally said, he may still not know what (14) means, since several English sentences, all differing in meaning—e.g. 'That's morally permissible', 'Eating clams is OK', etc.— may have literal utterances in which the speaker says that eating clams is morally permissible. In any event, Pierre did not know what (14) meant when he correctly inferred what Sally said in uttering it.

Intuitively, we want to say that Al and Mao, but not Pierre, knew what (14) meant when they encountered Sally's utterance of it. The basis of this intuition is that in the case of Al and Mao, there was something, though not necessarily the same thing, playing the knowledge-of-meaning role in the information processing that resulted in the knowledge of what Sally said in uttering (14). Nothing played that role in Pierre, and that is why we are unwilling to say he knew what (14) meant. What this suggests is that *knowledge of meaning need not be any one kind of state but is rather any state that plays the 'knowledge-of-meaning' processing role.* I shall try to be a little more specific.

Many different kinds of information processing can take one from the perception of the utterance of a sentence to the knowledge of what was said in that utterance. For example, typically when in conversation we hear an English sentence, we instantaneously know, without any conscious thought, what the speaker said; that is, we instantaneously know what primary speech act she was performing and what propositional content that speech act had (of course, we do not have any conscious thoughts about what the speaker said; we do not, for example, say to ourselves *sotto voce*, 'She just asked me whether it's raining'; but we know what the speaker said all the same). On other occasions, we may have to do some conscious reasoning to figure out what, if anything, the speaker was saying; even more is this so when we struggle to know what someone said in a foreign language in which we are somewhat less than fluent. It might also be that utterances of different kinds of sentence are processed in interestingly different ways, or that not everyone processes utterances in quite the same way. Moreover, there is no one kind of process that must subserve the normal case where we hear the utterance immediately as the performance of a certain speech act with a certain content. Perhaps the unconscious part of the process involves a state that pairs the uttered sentence with its character*, or perhaps it pairs it with a Mentalese synonym. Thus, whatever is meant by 'the knowledge-of-meaning processing role', it must be a role that can be played in very different kinds of information processing. What I mean by the knowledge-of-meaning processing role may be put in the following way.

Consider any instance of an information-processing sequence that begins with an agent $x$'s perception of the utterance of a sentence $s$ of a language $L$ and ends with $x$'s knowing what was said in that utterance, and where it is clear to us that this information processing was owed in part to $x$'s knowing what $s$ means in $L$. In saying that $x$ knows what was said in the utterance of $s$, what I mean, more specifically, is that (a) there is a kind of speech act $A$ and a kind of proposition $P$ such that $\langle A, P \rangle$ is the character* of $s$; (b) in uttering $s$, the speaker $\Psi$'ed $q$, where $\Psi$ing is a speech act of kind $A$ and $q$ is a proposition of kind $P$; and (c) $x$ knows that in uttering $s$ the speaker $\Psi$'ed $q$. Now, whatever the specific details of how this information processing is effected—and they may be extremely various—the explanation of how $x$ came to know that the speaker $\Psi$'ed $q$ will entail that the information processing that resulted in $x$'s knowledge included a token of a state-type that represents $s$ as directly or indirectly linked with its character*, $\langle A, P \rangle$. *Whatever state represents that linkage is the one that plays the knowledge-of-meaning role.*

The linkage need not be of any one sort. Perhaps the state that represents it represents $\langle A, P \rangle$ as the value of a certain function which utilizes semantic information about the parts and structure of $s$; perhaps the state is a token of the belief that a literal utterance of $s$ in $L$ requires the speaker to be performing a speech act of kind $A$ with a content of kind $P$; perhaps the state is simply a representation of the ordered pair $\langle s, \langle A, P \rangle \rangle$; perhaps it links $s$ with its character* only indirectly, either by representing it as paired with a synonymous sentence of $x$'s idiolect or of $x$'s neural system of mental representation, perhaps à la Harvey of Schiffer (1987), ch. 7, whose language-understanding ability is, by construction, explicable without recourse to any kind of compositional semantics for the language he understands. But even where the linkage is indirect, the complete explanation of how $x$ came to know that the speaker Ψ'ed $q$ will advert to the state's effecting a linkage with the kind of speech act and kind of content that comprise $s$'s character*. In the typical case, where $s$ is a sentence of the public-language dialect $x$ shares with the speaker, the state that represents $s$ as linked with its character* will itself be determined by other states in the information-processing sequence, which states effect linkages of the words in $s$ with their characters*; but, as previous examples illustrated, someone can know what a sentence (e.g. of a foreign language) means without even knowing how to parse it into its component words. Presently I shall formulate a speculation about the kind of state that might in fact play the knowledge-of-meaning role in us.

My final proposal, then, for knowing what a sentence means is that

> (IVs) $x$ knows what $s$ means in $L$ iff $x$ is in (or disposed readily to be in) a token of a state-type capable of occupying the knowledge-of-meaning role in $x$'s understanding of a literal $L$ utterance of $s$.

This can be mimicked to produce a corresponding account of what it is to know what a subsentential expression means:

> (IV$e$) $x$ knows what $e$ means in $L$ iff $x$ is in (or disposed readily to be in) a token of a state-type capable of occupying the knowledge-of-meaning role in $x$'s understanding of a literal $L$ utterance of $e$.

But what constitutes the knowledge-of-meaning role for words and other subsentential expressions?

Let '$\Sigma(sLx)$' designate the state-type that plays the knowledge-of-meaning role with respect to $x$'s knowing what sentence $s$ means in $L$. In the normal case, where $x$ knows what $s$ means by virtue of knowing the language to which $s$ belongs, the information-processing sequence in which $\Sigma(sLx)$ is tokened will see that token produced via an algorithm that starts with state tokens that represent the words composing $s$ as directly or indirectly linked with their characters*, yields state tokens that represent larger subsentential expressions contained in $s$ with their characters*, and so on, until one gets to $\Sigma(sLx)$. The algorithm, or algorithms, utilized in the processing will be based, *inter alia*, on functions that map sequences of word-size characters* onto sentence-size characters*. Roughly speaking, we may expect the same state to play the knowledge-of-meaning role for a word whenever one understands the utterance of a sentence containing that word, and this will be a state that directly or indirectly links the word with its character*.

It may be helpful to illustrate this account of knowledge of meaning with a speculation about the kind of states that in fact play the knowledge-of-meaning role in our normal understanding of public-language utterances. A *compositional character\* theory for a language L* is a finitely axiomatized theory of $L$ that assigns characters* to the words of $L$ and associates recursive functions with basic syntactical structures in such a way that the theory entails, for each meaningful expression of $L$, a theorem that pairs the expression with its character* in $L$. If such a theory is internally represented, understanding the utterance of a novel sentence might work in the following way. Al hears Sally's utterance of $s$, a sentence he has never before encountered but which is composed of familiar words in familiar ways. Al's perception of the utterance of $s$ combines with other stuff to form a representation of the uttered sentence, which representation serves as input to Al's internally represented compositional character* theory for his English dialect, which theory in turn yields as output a representation of $s$ as paired with its character*, $\langle A, P \rangle$. This representation is fed into certain higher, more consciously accessible, information processing to enable Al defeasibly to believe that Sally is performing a speech act of kind $A$ whose propositional content is of kind $P$. Still further consciously accessible, but not necessarily conscious, information processing results in the knowledge that Sally, in uttering *s*, was *A*-ing that such-and-such. It is the state that pairs *s* with its character* ⟨*A*, *P*⟩ which plays the knowledge-of-meaning processing role.[6]

The foregoing raises several questions, such as: What relation must obtain between two things in order for the first to be the character* of the second? How does the answer to that question bear on issues about the supervenience of the intentional on the non-intentional? How are my characters* related to David Kaplan's characters, and to other uses of so-called two-dimensional semantics? Can characters* be construed as meanings, contrary to what the discussion in Section 2 may seem to imply? The next section considers the question about characters* as meanings; for the other questions just touched on, I invite the reader to consult Schiffer (2003).

## 6 Are Characters* Meanings?

On the one hand, characters* seem primed to be meanings. On the other hand, we seemed at the end of Section 2 to have a good argument to show that there are no such *things* as the meanings of expressions.

Characters* are primed to be meanings because an expression has mean-

---

[6] In other writings—e.g., Schiffer (1987) and (1994)—I have argued that natural languages neither have nor need compositional semantics, neither compositional meaning theories nor compositional truth theories. Is my speculation about compositional *character** theories an apostasy of my scepticism? No. The root of my scepticism is my claim that there can be no compositional theory of the propositions we believe and assert (see e.g. Schiffer 2001 and 2003). That is to say, we cannot see those propositions as recursively constructed from antecedently given propositional building blocks. If there were such building blocks, they would have to be (I am prepared to argue) concepts, or modes of presentation, of the objects and properties our beliefs and assertions are about, and these concepts would have to be identifiable apart from the propositions they are supposed to build. The propositions in the ranges of our various propositional-attitude relations are, I claim, fine-grained but unstructured. We can in a Pickwickian way speak of them as being composed of concepts of the objects and properties our propositional attitudes are about, but those concepts are really just epiphenomenal abstractions from propositions that are individuated without reliance on the concepts that may be abstracted from them and which can be identified only in terms of the propositions from which they are abstracted. Characters*, however—or the part of them that constrains propositional contents—are simply properties of propositions, and it is consistent with there being a compositional (i.e. finitely axiomatized) theory of them that there is no compositional (i.e. finitely axiomatized) theory of the propositions that have those properties.

ing just in case it has a character*, and two expressions have the same meaning just in case they have the same character*. The good argument implied by Section 2 is that it is a platitude that if *a* Rs *b*, then knowing what *a* Rs requires knowing that *a* Rs *m*, for a contextually suitable way *m* of identifying *b*, and we seem not to have such knowledge for any expression, which shows that for no expression is there some thing which that expression means. Certainly the suggestion that characters* are meanings gives no support to the rejected thesis

> (I)  To know what *e* means is to know that *e* means *m*, for suitable way *m* of identifying *e*'s meaning.

For it seems, as already remarked, that knowing what, say, 'Is it raining?' means does not require knowing that it means ⟨asking-whether, a proposition of the form *it is raining at place m at time m′*, where *m* identifies a place implicitly referred to by the speaker and *m′* identifies the time of the utterance⟩.

So we have a choice. We could say that we have in the case of meaning an exception to the just-mentioned platitude about knowing what *a* Rs. Characters* are meanings and (I) is false. It is both *true* that

> 'Is it raining?' means ⟨asking-whether, a proposition of the form *it is raining at place m at time m′*, where *m* identifies a place implicitly referred to by the speaker and *m′* identifies the time of the utterance⟩

and *false* that

> Knowing what 'Is it raining?' means = knowing that it means ⟨asking-whether, a proposition of the form *it is raining at place m at time m′*, where *m* identifies a place implicitly referred to by the speaker and *m′* identifies the time of the utterance⟩.

It is precisely the *meaning relation* that *x* must bear to *y* in order for *y* to be a character* of *x*; the character* relation = the meaning relation.

Alternatively, we could say that the failure of characters* to satisfy (I) shows they are not meanings, that the relation that *x* must bear to *y* in order for *y* to be a character* of *x* is not the meaning relation; there is no meaning *relation* for the character* relation to be identical with. This is supported by the fact that, while knowing what, say, 'Is it raining?' means is not the same as knowing that it means ⟨asking-whether, a proposition of the form *it is raining at place m at time m'*, where *m* identifies a place implicitly referred to by the speaker and *m'* identifies the time of the utterance⟩, knowing what the character* of 'Is it raining?' is *is* the same as knowing that its character* is ⟨asking-whether, a proposition of the form *it is raining at place m at time m'*, where *m* identifies a place implicitly referred to by the speaker and *m'* identifies the time of the utterance⟩.

If I *had* to choose, I would choose the second thing to say: notwithstanding their role in meaning, characters* are not meanings. But why should we care about saying whether or not characters* are meanings once all the facts are in? As far as I can see, all that matters is that we know that having meaning consists in having a character* and that knowledge of meaning consists not in any sort of propositional knowledge but rather in occupation of the processing role described in the preceding section.

# REFERENCES

ALMOG, J., PERRY, J., and WETTSTEIN, H., eds. (1989), *Themes from Kaplan* (Oxford: Oxford University Press).

AUSTIN, J. L. (1962), *How to Do Things with Words* (Oxford: Oxford University Press).

CAMPBELL, J. K., O'ROURKE, M., and SHIER, D., eds., (2001), *Meaning and Truth: Investigations in Philosophical Semantics* (New York: Seven Bridges Press).

FODOR, J. (1997), *Concepts: Where Cognitive Science Went Wrong* (Oxford: Oxford University Press).

HORWICH, P. (1998), *Meaning* (Oxford: Oxford University Press).

KAPLAN, D. (1989), 'Demonstratives: An Essay on the Semantics, Logic, Metaphysics, and Epistemology of Demonstratives and Other Indexicals', in Almog, Perry, and Wettstein (1989), 481–563.

SCHIFFER, S. (1987). *Remnants of Meaning* (Cambridge, Mass.: MIT Press).

—— (1994), 'A Paradox of Meaning', *Noûs*, 28: 279–324.

—— (2000), 'Horwich on Meaning: Critical Study of Paul Horwich's *Meaning*', *Philosophical Quarterly*, 50: 527–36.

—— (2001), 'Meanings', in Campbell, O'Rourke, and Shier (2001), 79–102.

—— (2002), 'Amazing Knowledge', *Journal of Philosophy*, 99: 200–2.

SCHIFFER, S. (2003), *The Things We Mean* (Oxford: Oxford University Press).

STANLEY, J., and WILLIAMSON, T. (2001), 'Knowing How', *Journal of Philosophy*, 98: 411–44.

WITTGENSTEIN, L. (1953), *Philosophical Investigations*, trans. G. E. M. Anscombe (Oxford: Blackwell).

# CHAPTER 10

# Understanding and Knowledge of What is Said

*Elizabeth Fricker*

## 1 Introduction

When a human speaker-hearer of a language hears and understands an utterance by another speaker of a sentence of their shared language, she typically comes to know, or comes to be in a position to know, what speech act was effected in the utterance. But her forming of a knowledgeable belief about what was said is not the most immediate psychological upshot of her auditing of the utterance. In fact she may not, as it were, bother to form a belief about what was said at all. The most immediate personal-level psychological effect of her auditing of the utterance is that she enjoys a representation of a distinctive kind special to language understanding: a conscious representation of the content and force of the utterance. She hears the utterance not merely as sound, but as the speech act that it is. This representation of meaning is not phenomenologically distinct from her hearing of the sounds. She hears its meaning in the utterance itself, experiences it as a semantically laden event. It is for her as if, in perceiving the utterance, she perceives not just the sounds, but equally perceives their meaning. It is a fact of phenomenology that we enjoy such understanding-experiences, quasi-perceptions of meaning.

The psychological core of the competence that distinguishes a normal

An earlier version of this paper was presented at the conference in Sheffield in July 2000. I am grateful for comments from many participants, especially my commentator, Sandy Goldberg. Sect. 3 was added in response to those comments. I am also much indebted to Robert Audi, Alex Barber, Ernie Lepore, and Stephen Schiffer for very useful sets of comments on my early draft.

speaker-hearer of a language is her capacity to enjoy these experiential states of understanding of heard utterances of its sentences. Someone who has this core capacity with respect to a language is a fluent speaker and understander of it, able to 'think in' the language itself. For her, understanding a heard utterance is typically a matter of effortlessly and instantaneously hearing it as meaning what it does—enjoying one of these understanding-experiences.[1] In contrast, one's understanding of an utterance of a sentence of a language in which one is not fluent will not be experiential and direct, but will be effected by translating into one's native language, or some other language in which one can think. One's native language is indeed the language in which one thinks (or one of them), the phenomenal vehicle of much of one's occurrent thought.

These understanding-experiences are conscious representational states characteristic of language use, distinct from belief.[2] They involve representation not only of the syntactic properties of utterances, but also of their semantic properties, including the content and force of the speech act effected in the utterance. They are analogous in various ways to visual experiences.[3] For instance, their category difference from belief is shown in the fact that they exhibit the independence of belief also exhibited by visual experiences. Thus, there can be illusions of meaning—illusory understanding-experiences which persist despite the subject's knowledge that they are illusory—analogously to *trompe l'œil* paintings and other visual illusions.

[1] An effortless enjoyment of an understanding-experience is what occurs consciously to the thinking subject. Of course, very complex processing must take place subpersonally to enable this. My remarks in this paper all describe the conscious, personal-level nature of linguistic understanding, and are intended to be neutral on the nature of the psychological and neurological processing mechanisms which underlie this. Cases where understanding is not, at the personal level, effortless, and conscious attention is needed to work out, for instance, which item is the referent of a demonstrative, are discussed in sect. 3.2. I argue that these cases are secondary.

[2] However, as I emphasize in sect. 4, similar 'inner' representations—mental hearings of sentences—often serve as the vehicle of occurrent belief and judgement, as well as occurrent conjectures, fears, etc. Understanding-experience occurs and is essential both in language perception and in thinking.

[3] Strawson (1994) emphasizes the existence of such states, and the fact that it is meaning, not just syntax, which is experienced. The label 'understanding-experience' is taken from him.

This paper has two interlocking themes. I address an epistemological project: to offer an account of how, in normal everyday language use, a hearer's beliefs about what speech act has been made amount to knowledge.[4] In doing this, I develop a characterization of the process of understanding, as the means by which this knowledge is normally achieved. The characterization of linguistic understanding is a second theme of interest in its own right. I assert the existence of understanding-experience and its centrality to human language use. I offer two arguments for its centrality. First (Section 2), I argue that we must acknowledge the occurrence, in normal language use, of understanding-experiences, to explain how, in such fluent language use, a hearer's beliefs about what is said constitute knowledge. In this normal case, I argue, a speaker-hearer's understanding-experience, aptly derived from the utterance in its context, is the ground of her belief about what has been said in that utterance, an essential ingredient in its status as knowledge. Second (Section 4), I argue that even though there are some cases where a hearer comes to know what is said in an utterance without enjoying an understanding-experience of it, these cases are secondary, since a capacity to enjoy correctly derived understanding-experiences is essential to any human thinker's use of her first language. In the light of this, I argue, a theoretically well-motivated characterization of what it is to understand a natural language L (or some fragment of L) has, as its main component, the core psychological capacity just sketched—to enjoy correct understanding-experiences of the meanings of heard utterances of L.

The proposed account of understanding is arrived at via critique of a minimal conception of what understanding is, of the kind proposed in Schiffer (1987). According to this minimal conception, all that is needed for understanding a natural language is that one somehow or other embodies a function which takes heard acoustic strings as inputs, and yields correct beliefs about what speech act has been made as outputs. I argue (Section 2.3) that this minimal conception of understanding is too thin, since it fails to explain how beliefs about what is said are knowledge. I propose a thicker characterization of what it is to understand a natural language, whose main

---

[4] This links with my interest in how knowledge about the world is gained through others' testimony. One can learn that $p$ through someone's telling one that $p$ only if one knows, or is in a position to know, that one has been told that $p$. See Fricker (1994; 1995; forthcoming).

component is the capacity to enjoy correct understanding-experiences of the meaning of heard utterances. In Section 3 I consider the significance for my account of the role of context in determining reference, and discuss cases where a hearer comes to know what is said without enjoying an understanding-experience, or where she enjoys one only after some effort—conscious working out of what the correct assignment of reference is. We see that the epistemology of these unusual cases is somewhat different. In Section 4 my second argument is deployed against the minimal conception. It is incoherent, or radically incomplete,[5] as a characterization of one's understanding of one's first language. In humans at least, understanding of one's first language necessarily involves a capacity to enjoy understanding-experiences, quasi-perceptions of meaning. This being so, the cases discussed in Section 3 are secondary, and our definition of understanding as involving a capacity to enjoy quasi-perceptions of meaning is well motivated despite them.

An *utterance* is a dated event, the production by a speaker of a particular token of a well-formed sentence type, in a communicative context. For the purposes of this paper I define *an utterance's meaning* to be its truth-evaluable content, the proposition expressed by it, plus its force.[6] What I

---

[5] Incoherent, if we read it as excluding understanding-experiences from the psychology of language understanding; radically incomplete, if we read it as merely failing to mention them.

[6] Propositions include reference, and so are truth-evaluable, but cut more finely than possible worlds. '$H_2O$ is wet' expresses a different proposition from 'water is wet'. Cognitively synonymous sentences express the same proposition. Delicate issues as to whether two a priori equivalent sentences with different structure may express the same proposition I leave open. By 'force' of an utterance I mean here merely whether it is a saying, a question, or a command/request. There are further fine points of detail regarding exactly which of the semantic and other properties of an utterance may on occasion feature in the content of an understanding-experience. A saying may or may not be an assertion, and it may, in the right context, be a warning, a promise, an insult, a hint, a joke, and so forth. Moreover, even for utterances whose primary content and force is their literal meaning—viz. a speech act which the utterance type is conventionally apt to convey— the information intentionally communicated by a speaker by means of her utterance very often exceeds its literal meaning; cf. conversational implicature. Determining which of these properties of an utterance may feature in the content of an understanding-experience, and which are merely instantaneously inferred from it, is no less, and with luck no more, difficult than determining the line between what is present in the content of a visual perception and what is merely instantaneously inferred from it: for instance,

have so far called understanding-experiences I shall also sometimes refer to as *quasi-perceptions of meaning* of heard utterances. These are, I maintain, conscious mental states distinct from belief with three key perception-like properties: (1) phenomenologically they have the nature of experiences, perceptions of meaning; (2) where the hearer forms a belief about what is said, her understanding-experience will be the proximate (perhaps simultaneous) cause of this, and feature in the causal explanation of her belief; (3) alongside (2), in fluent language use understanding-experiences also play a key epistemic role in grounding a hearer's knowledge of what is said. This is analogous to the role which visual perceptual experiences play in grounding perceptual beliefs. On the proposed account of how knowledge of what has been said is such, a hearer's understanding-experience of the meaning of an utterance she hears grounds her belief about what has been said, in a way exactly parallel to that in which visual experience, with its objective content, grounds visual perceptual beliefs.[7]

This paper deliberately puts to one side the question whether our quasi-perceptions of the meanings of heard utterances are properly regarded as full-blown *perceptions* of meaning—whether, that is, these understanding-experiences are the core conscious event in a genuine relation of perception to an objective, perceptible property of heard utterances, their content and force. Some may be happy to discern perceptual relations unstintingly, holding that any case of quasi-perception is *ipso facto* a case of perception.[8] But there are problematic metaphysical and epistemological issues to be addressed, before we can conclude that we literally perceive the content and force of heard utterances. These issues cannot be settled in this paper, and I here confine myself to the claim that human language-users enjoy quasi-perceptions of meaning, experience-like states which play a crucial epistemic role in grounding beliefs about what is said. The term 'quasi-

does one literally see that it is going to rain shortly in perceiving a threatening grey sky and immediately forming the belief that it will rain shortly? Here I shall not investigate what principles determine this boundary. I do insist that the full truth-evaluable content of an utterance, not just the semantic character of the sentence type, typically features in understanding-experience. In this paper I do not attempt to extend my investigation to consider what happens—neither the phenomenology, nor the epistemology, nor any precise description of what occurs—in the production and understanding of non-literal uses of language (sarcasm, metaphor, etc.).

[7] See Brewer (1999).                    [8] See e.g. McDowell (1980).

perception' is introduced to be neutral on this metaphysical issue. It applies equally to genuine perceptions of meaning, if there be such, and to mere quasi-perceptions of meaning, supposing these to be all we enjoy.

My concern in this paper is with how a hearer gains knowledge of what speech act has been made, in paradigmatic occasions of everyday natural-language use. As a spin-off I offer a characterization of understanding, as the process by which this is effected. I approach these two interlocking issues by considering whether understanding can be defined in terms of knowledge of what is said.

## 2  Can Understanding be Defined in Terms of Knowledge of What is Said?

### 2.1  *No simple equivalence*

It is an indispensable commonplace that competent speaker-hearers of a language $L$ will usually know, or be in a position to know, what has been said[9] in an utterance which they hear (or read) of a sentence of $L$.[10] In contrast, non-speakers of $L$ will not usually know what has been said in an utterance which they hear of a sentence of $L$. Inspired by this commonplace contrast, and by the thought that an ability to understand utterances of a language is

---

[9]  More accurately: said, or queried, or commanded. To avoid cumbersome repetition, I shall talk throughout of what is said, but the thesis is, strictly, that speaker-hearers will usually know both the full propositional content and the force of the speech act which has been effected in an utterance—whether it be a saying, command/request, or question. A competent speaker-hearer will not always be in a position to know what is said. Context dependence in determination of reference means that a speaker's dispositional ability regarding the sentence types of a language (labelled $U_{disp}$ below) does not guarantee full referential understanding of particular utterances of them, since the deployment of purely semantic knowledge regarding sentence types is not sufficient for this.

[10]  In treating the commonplace as indispensable I dismiss any scepticism which challenges common sense in this respect, and with it meaning-scepticisms which entail that utterances do not objectively possess determinate meanings, candidates for being known. My argument in this paper can be seen as an investigation of what it takes to provide an epistemological account which systematizes and underwrites common sense in this matter. My own stance is that this is what positive epistemology should be doing. I also hold that an account of how knowledge is gained in some particular way (perception, testimony, etc.) must mesh with a general conception of knowledge which it instantiates. See Fricker (forthcoming).

what differentiates its speakers from non-speakers, we might seek to define understanding in terms of knowledge of what is said, perhaps as an ability to generate this. We need first to distinguish two kinds of understanding. The first kind is by a person, a language-user, of a particular utterance $U(S)$ of a sentence $S$. It is an occurrence, a dated event in the person's mental life. Call this kind of understanding *occurrent understanding* ($U_{occ}$). The second kind is by a person, of a sentence-type $S$. It is a disposition possessed by that person, one which is usually stably possessed by her over an extended period of time: the capacity to attain occurrent understanding of particular heard utterances of $S$.[11] Call this *dispositional understanding* ($U_{disp}$). An individual who speaks a certain natural language $L$ possesses dispositional understanding for a large fragment of the possible sentences of $L$.

We can begin our endeavour by seeing why the simplest proposal for defining occurrent understanding in terms of knowledge of what is said does not work. We shall then move on to more refined attempts. So let us try:

> *Naive $U_{occ}$*: To understand occurrently an utterance of a sentence $S$ just is to know what was said in that utterance of $S$.

If understanding an utterance just is knowing what is said in it, then these two conditions are equivalent. Are they? One might think that, at any rate, understanding an utterance is sufficient for knowing what is said in it. In fact this is not so, for a reason we shall be able to grasp better later on in the paper. It is not so, because one might understand an utterance—that is, correctly quasi-perceive its content and force—as the exercise of a general capacity one possesses to do so, yet fail to know what that is, owing to misleading background beliefs which defeat what would otherwise be one's knowledgeable belief in this.

But in any case, there are clear counter-examples to the thesis that under-

---

[11] There is certainly some holism in understanding. If I understand a sentence '$F\hat{\ }a$', where $F$ is an atomic predicate, and $a$ a name, I must understand some other sentences containing $F$, and some others containing $a$. Otherwise there would be no reason to interpret the sentence as understood by me to be structured. See Fricker (1982). Moreover, most terms of natural languages denote concepts which are theoretical in the sense that they are defined by their place in a network of beliefs. This engenders further holism. But there is no reason to deny the evident empirical fact that one can understand part of a language without understanding all of it.

standing an utterance is necessary for knowledge of what is said in it. My multi-lingual companion and I are in Moscow. We both audit the sayings of the hotel receptionist. She understands them and tells me what was said. Through her testimony I come to know this. But only she understood the receptionist's sayings. They were uninterpretable gobbledegook, mere complex unfathomable noise, to me. Here I know what was said, not through understanding the utterance myself, but through reliance on the testimony of another person who can get that knowledge for herself, because she does understand it. (Notice that knowledge of what is said, like other objective knowledge, is not route-dependent: even if there is a canonical, most direct way of coming to obtain it, it can also be obtained via other less direct routes. What is known is logically distinct from how it is known.)

So our first, simplest attempt to characterize occurrent understanding in terms of knowledge of what is said, *Naive* $U_{occ}$, fails. Understanding an utterance cannot be equated with knowledge of what is said in it, since it is neither necessary nor sufficient for this. In fact, as we shall see, understanding cannot be equated with possession of any set of items of objective knowledge at all. Neither what it is to understand an utterance occurrently, nor what it is to understand some of the sentences of a language dispositionally, admits of characterization solely in terms of what is known by an understander. This is because understanding is not just a matter of what is known, but also of how it has come to be known—namely, through the capacity to get into psychological states of a special kind, to enjoy appropriate understanding-experiences in response to heard utterances in their context.

## 2.2 *Reliabilism about understanding*

Intuitively, it seems that someone who understands an utterance both knows what is said in it, and has come to know this in a particular way, by means of a certain characteristic process—one which someone who is told the meaning of a sentence of an unknown foreign language by a translator does not instantiate. What exactly is this characteristic process, then? If it can only be picked out as 'by understanding the utterance', then we have no non-circular account here—although we have some progress in elucidating the nature of understanding, since we have picked it out as a process with a particular characteristic upshot, something it enables one to do.

Can the process of understanding be captured non-circularly, in other terms? Perhaps a more sophisticated, oblique means than *Naive U*$_{occ}$ of characterizing understanding in terms of knowledge of what is said could work to do this. Perhaps to understand an utterance $U(S)$ of $S$ occurrently just is to have a correct belief about was said by $U(S)$, which is the outcome of a general capacity to generate such correct beliefs. These beliefs will thereby be knowledge, on this conception. Let us formulate such a simple reliabilist conception of both kinds of understanding, *Reliabilist U*:

> *Reliabilist U*$_{disp}$:  To understand a sentence $S$ of a language $L$ disposition-ally is stably to possess a reliable capacity (of whatever kind) to form correct beliefs about what is said on particular occasions by heard utterances of $S$.[12] These beliefs will be knowledge.

> *Reliabilist U*$_{occ}$:  To understand a particular utterance $U(S)$ of a sentence $S$ of $L$ occurrently is to know what was said in $U(S)$, as the result of one's dispositional understanding of $S$—that is, through the exercise of a stably possessed reliable capacity to achieve such knowledge with respect to utterances of $S$.

If this two-clause definition works, we have characterized understanding (both kinds) in terms of the notions of knowing what is said and of a reliable process for generating such knowledge.[13] Will this simple reliabilist conception of understanding do?

---

[12]  Given the role of context in fixing the reference of some expressions, and in resolving syntactic and semantic ambiguities, two points follow. First: $U_{disp}$ as thus defined will include the possession of general interpretative skills, as well as specific knowledge of the semantic 'character' of the expressions occurring in $S$. This seems fair enough. Narrowly semantic knowledge in the absence of those further skills is virtually useless. Second: even so, $U_{disp}$ will not guarantee occurrent understanding on every occasion.

[13]  Notice that in *Reliabilist U* the notion of $U_{disp}$ is prior to that of $U_{occ}$. Occurrent understanding consists in knowing what is said through an exercise of $U_{disp}$—that is, a stable capacity for generating bits of knowledge of this kind. In contrast, the definition eventually proposed in sect. 2.4 is a no-priority account. Occurrent understanding involves the occurrence of a *sui generis* kind of event, an understanding-experience. But this must be aptly derived from a stable capacity for this.

We need to distinguish two questions: Does *Reliabilist U* capture the extension of our ordinary concept of understanding? Is *Reliabilist U* well motivated theoretically? Regarding our first question, one possible finding is that our intuitions about what kinds of reliable process count as understanding may be vague, or indeterminate. Even if they are firm, our ordinary concept may have rather arbitrary boundaries. The philosophically more interesting question is our second. Is there a motivated way of delimiting what sorts of process-for-generating-knowledge-of-utterance-meaning count as understanding, hence a theoretical reason for rejecting or endorsing *Reliabilist U*?

I shall take our first question first. What is the verdict of ordinary language on *Reliabilist U*? Does intuition furnish counter-examples? It does. Suppose I have never learnt Russian, and utterances by Russian speakers sound like mere complex noise to me. But—for some diplomatic or political reason—I have a reliable translator always by my side. Whenever a sentence of Russian is uttered in my earshot, my translator whispers the English equivalent in my ear. He is always there, and I do not even notice him any more, most of the time. I just absorb what he says, and form a belief about what was said by the Russian speaker he is accurately translating. My belief is knowledge, however, since I know that he is there, and is correctly translating.[14] In these circumstances I satisfy *Reliabilist U* with respect to sentences of Russian. But, I maintain, I do not understand Russian in virtue of having the translator always with me, though I would not know what was said without him. On the contrary, I need him precisely because I do not understand the Russian sentences myself. They sound like so much jumbled noise to me. Moreover, this translational mechanism for getting knowledge of what is said only works because I do understand English—directly, not through being given, or myself effecting, a translation of it. (We shall return to the significance of this point in Section 4.) A reliable process which goes through a human translator does not count as understanding, so *Reliabilist U* is false. More significant than this verdict of ordinary language is the fact that, even supposing we did coin a relaxed notion of 'understanding' on which this does count as one way of understanding Russian, it would be

---

[14] This background knowledge is available to justify my belief, and to provide the material for an epistemically rationalizing explanation of it—what I propose in sect. 2.3 to be needed for knowledge.

a derivative, secondary way. A person's ability to 'understand' Russian via a translator-into-English depends on the translator's ability to understand Russian directly, and her own ability to understand English directly.

What about a reliable process which goes through a translation mechanism outside my body, which is not another person? Suppose instead of the human translator I have permanently secured to me an electronic device which registers the acoustic event and (embodying a syntactic and semantic analyser) delivers into my ear, microseconds later, an audible rendition of the English translation of what has been said.[15] This is still not understanding, since it remains true that I come to know what has been said only through perceiving the English translation of the original Russian sentence, and this is needed only because I do not understand Russian, and works only because I do understand English. My ability to 'understand' Russian through this non-human translating device is a derivative phenomenon, parasitic on my ability to understand my own language directly, not on its translation into some other medium.[16]

Suppose now that the reliable language processor is internal. It is not a box attached to me with a strap, which feeds renditions of English sentences into my aural perception system, but an encapsulated module internal to my brain which yields—what? Its output, we must suppose, to be consistent with the minimal reliabilist conception of understanding, is correct occurrent beliefs about what has just been said, somehow generated in my mind/brain by this module. Note that any internal module which somehow generates these correct beliefs counts as an understanding-generating process, according to the minimal conception. Its minimalism consists in the view that what the intermediate stages are does not matter, so long as

---

[15] This is in fact virtually impossible for any actual natural language, since determination of the reference of indexicals and other semantic features will not supervene on the acoustic profile given stable facts about expression meanings which a machine could be built to embody, but will turn on contextual factors in ways whose resolution depends on background knowledge and current perception, and which are highly resistant to systematic specification. See sect. 3.

[16] Translation from one natural language into another is in any case always an unsatisfying compromise to get the least bad approximation. Different languages have different expressive resources, and learning a new language literally extends one's range of thought. This point reinforces my overall drift, especially the argument of sect. 4.

the correct beliefs are generated.[17] The restriction to internal processing gives us the most plausible two-part reliabilist definition of understanding, *I-reliabilist U*:

> *I-reliabilist* $U_{disp}$: To understand a sentence $S$ of a language $L$ disposition-ally is stably to possess an internally constituted reliable capacity to form correct beliefs about what is said on particular occasions by heard utterances of $S$. These beliefs will be knowledge.
>
> *I-reliabilist* $U_{occ}$: To understand a particular heard utterance $U(S)$ of $S$ occurrently is to know what was said in $U(S)$, as the result of one's dispositional understanding of $S$—that is, through the exercise of a stably possessed, internally constituted reliable capacity to achieve such knowledge with respect to utterances of $S$.

Will this internalized reliabilism do as a definition of both kinds of under-standing?

According to *I-reliabilist U*, one understands a sentence $S$ dispositionally just if one has an internal mechanism which is such that, almost whenever one hears an utterance of $S$, this generates in one a correct belief about what has been said. (This belief will, according to *I-reliabilist U*, be knowledge.) This is what Lepore (1997) calls the minimal 'template' view of understand-ing, as proposed in Schiffer (1987). One understands the sentences of a language so long as one somehow embodies the right function, the right 'template' mapping from heard acoustic strings to beliefs about the content and force of a speech act.[18]

Is instantiating the correct mapping from acoustic strings to beliefs about

---

[17] Correct beliefs were equally the ultimate, needed result with our external reliable processes. Empirical plausibility engendered the supposition that these were produced via the recipient's hearing of English translations of the sentences to be understood. We can construct a science-fiction case where correct beliefs about what was said are produced in me by an external mechanism, but directly, i.e. not via my perception of utterances in any language: a benevolent scientist or God, or a machine of her creation, which directly manipulates the individual's brain to produce occurrent beliefs about what has just been said directly, not via her hearing of English sentences. These correct beliefs would fail to be knowledge, and this is not understanding. See sect. 2.3 on the requirements for knowledge.

[18] Schiffer (1987) puts forward this view, in the course of denying that an understander

what is said sufficient for dispositional understanding? (I shall assume without further argument that something approaching this is necessary for it.) And is having a correct belief generated by such a mechanism all that occurrent understanding consists in? Consider the following possible individual Ida. When Ida hears a sentence of Russian, it sounds like meaningless noise to her. Yet after hearing it, she finds herself with a strong inclination to believe that a certain speech act has been effected by that—to her—meaningless burst of noise. Ida instantiates the correct 'template'. Her beliefs about what is said in Russian utterances are due to a language-processing, belief-generating module in her, and are reliably true. (High-tech surgical intervention or brain damage might bring about Ida's condition.) Ida satisfies the *I-reliabilist U* conception of both dispositional and occurrent understanding. But, intuitively, she does not understand Russian at all—on the contrary, it sounds like meaningless noise to her. This is surely the ordinary-language verdict. If so, then *I-reliabilist U* is broader than our ordinary concept of understanding, and does not capture it.

There are three points to be made about Ida. First, normal understanding, as we have already seen, is not like Ida's case. It has a distinctive phenomenology. In normal everyday language use a hearer does not hear a burst of apparently meaningless sound, and then suddenly find herself with an inclination to believe something. No, the uttered sentence itself 'has life' for her. She hears it as bearing a structured proposition, put forward with a certain force. It seems to her that she perceives its meaning in the utterance, an intrinsic property of it. She enjoys an understanding-experience. (Think of how we see a figure in a line drawing, or how, when one can read fluently, the words spring out at one from the printed page.) Compare vision. Mature visual experience does not present one with an intrinsically meaningless colour mosaic, from which one works out what might be in the world out there in front of one. Visual experience presents a range of fine-grained perceptible properties of space-occupying objects, in certain spatial relations to oneself. Similarly, when one understands an utterance

must have knowledge, tacit or otherwise, of semantic properties of subsentential expressions. Schiffer takes it for granted that the minimal-template view of understanding is correct, and then argues that for it to be causally possible for someone to instantiate it does not require that they have any semantic knowledge. See n. 12 above for the significance of 'almost'.

of a sentence, the immediate object of one's aural experience is not a mere burst of sound, nor merely a syntactic entity. The phenomenal given in normal language perception is an utterance perceived as syntactically structured and semantically loaded. One hears the words, and one hears what they mean—one hears them as expressing a certain proposition.

*Ex hypothesi*, sentences of Russian do not bear this phenomenally immediate semantic significance, this 'life', for Ida. (Nor do they for me, when I am told a translation. Notice that this remains so even if I am told a word-by-word rendition, not just a sentential equivalent. The fact that some words have life for me is not a matter of my having a knowledgeable belief about what they mean.) So—our first point—Ida's way of gaining correct beliefs about what is said is *ex hypothesi* phenomenally different, phenomenally lacking, in comparison with normal understanding. (It is comparable in this respect to the phenomenon of 'blind sight'. As with blind sight, brain lesions in the relevant area might bring about just such a phenomenon.)

The second point about Ida is that, I suggest, our ordinary concept does not count her situation as a case of understanding. The characteristic phenomenology of understanding is essential to our concept of what it is to understand occurrently the sentences of a language, and hence of what it is to have dispositional understanding of a range of sentences, this being a stable capacity to achieve occurrent understanding of them. Our third, most important point about Ida brings in considerations from epistemology, and merits a new section.

## 2.3 *Reliabilism rejected: the epistemic role of understanding-experience*

Swapping of intuitions about ordinary language can be a tedious and fruitless pursuit. Let us turn to our second question about understanding. Suppose this ordinary-language restriction in force, on what occurrent understanding is. There must be understanding-experience. If so, *I-reliabilist U* is too thin, since it does not require this. Is this ordinary-language restriction on what counts as understanding an utterance, or a sentence, well motivated? Perhaps, on the contrary, it can be argued that any mechanism which reliably produces correct beliefs about what has been said is equally valid, so that *I-reliabilist U* should be accepted as a theoretically motivated, revisionary conception of understanding.[19]

I shall not take this reliabilist line. I think there is a powerful motivation from epistemology for rejecting *I-reliabilist U* as insufficiently restrictive. We have neglected so far the fact that understanding is a process which provides not merely correct beliefs, but knowledgeable ones, about what speech act is effected in an utterance. Reflecting on the present case underlines once again the inadequacy of reliabilism as an account of what constitutes knowledge for reflective human agents.

On a pure reliabilist conception of knowledge,[20] Ida's beliefs about what has been said are knowledge, since they are generated by a mechanism which reliably generates true beliefs, and only true ones, about what is said in utterances she hears. But Ida's beliefs about what has been said— suppose she yields to her inclination to form them—are absurd to her. She finds herself with a strong inclination to believe that such-and-such has been said to her. But, *ex hypothesi*, nothing within her own cognitive perspective connects that inclination to believe that such-and-such has been said with such-and-such indeed having been said. She hears some noise made by another person, and she finds herself thinking that he said some specific thing. But she did not hear him doing so. So she lacks any internal rationale for forming a belief. She has no reason to think that what she finds herself inclined to believe is likely to be true.[21] Of course, if she acquires an inductively based empirical belief that these inclinations of hers in fact correlate with truth, this changes the situation. In her new situation she would now have a reason to accede to her inclinations to form beliefs about what is said, one which would provide a justifying ground for those beliefs. She would possess a general belief endorsing as reliable the process which, in itself, yields her only brute inclinations lacking any intrinsically apparent

[19] The issue is reminiscent of discussions of deviant and standard causal routes in the analysis of our ordinary concepts of memory, and of perception. In these cases the question equally arises whether there is any deeper issue at stake than the whims of ordinary language. It may be that considerations about conditions for knowledge analogous to those raised in my next paragraph can be applied in these cases too.

[20] Goldman (1986) gives a detailed articulation of a reliabilist conception of knowledge.

[21] See the discussion in BonJour (1985), ch. 1. I accept this internalist constraint on rational-belief formation, and regard rationality, so construed, as a necessary condition for knowledge.

connection with truth. This is a possible route to knowledge of what is said, an alternative justifying basis for it, which a wised-up Ida could enjoy. It is not the sort of basis which knowledgeable beliefs about what is said have, in normal language use.

In the absence of an empirically based 'top–down' endorsing belief—a general belief to the effect that her inclinations on this topic are reliable—Ida lacks any sense of how she has been in touch with the fact she finds herself inclined to believe in. So her belief is absurd to her.[22] Such beliefs, even if carelessly formed, cannot survive reflective scrutiny, in a rational agent. But knowledge should be stable under some scrutiny conducted within the agent's own perspective. Lacking any internal rationale, any reason available to Ida herself to think it likely to be true, Ida's belief is not stable, and is not knowledge. Reliability alone is not enough, because it does not ensure the satisfaction of the internal rationality condition without which a belief will not possess stability under common-sense reflective scrutiny. This is my third, epistemological, point about Ida. It is the main moral to be drawn from consideration of her case.

We can capture the apt-scrutinizability requirement[23] with the following necessary condition. For an agent's belief to be knowledge, she must be in a position to construct an epistemically rationalizing explanation of it: an explanation of how she has come to believe it, which reveals it as likely to be true. An explanation will do this if it reveals the fact of her believing what she does as appropriately linked to the fact believed in, if it shows how the agent has had epistemic access to the believed fact.[24] I think this requirement is a necessary condition for knowledge by reflective agents, for the reasons just given.[25] A consequence is that knowing entails being epistemically equipped

---

[22] Other examples of a *de facto* reliable source of beliefs, whose reliability is brutely external to the subject's own epistemic perspective, abound in the literature, offered as further counter-examples to reliabilism. See BonJour (1985), ch. 3. These examples underline the general point that, if I just find myself with an inclination to believe something, in the absence of an empirical voucher for its connection with the truth of what is believed, the potential belief is absurd to me, and it is irrational to yield to it.

[23] The kind of reflective scrutiny a knowledgeable belief must be able to withstand needs to be carefully circumscribed. A clever sceptic could undermine many of an ordinary thinker's beliefs that are in fact knowledge.

[24] Jones (1999) develops the idea of an epistemically rationalizing explanation of belief, and its role in making sense of her belief to a subject.

[25] There is perhaps a worthwhile purely reliabilist notion of knowledge—a property

to know that one knows, since it entails being epistemically equipped to know *how* it is that one knows.

How is this condition which Ida fails—that she has epistemic means available to her to see how her belief is appropriately linked to the fact putatively believed in—satisfied in normal language use? The main proposal of this paper is that it is satisfied in part in virtue of the phenomenology of understanding. In normal language use a hearer does not, like Ida, hear—as it seems to her—a meaningless burst of sound, and then find herself with a brute inclination to form a belief about what has been said, whose aetiology is a mystery to her. As already emphasized, we do not hear meaningless bursts of sound, but meaningful speech acts. We enjoy understanding-experiences, a special type of conscious representational state distinct from belief. I shall now argue that this quasi-perception of the heard utterance as a meaningful speech act both provides the hearer with a ground, a justifying basis, for her belief about what has been said, which renders it knowledgeable, and equally constitutes the core of what makes available to her an epistemically rationalizing explanation of her belief as to what has been said, enabling her to know how she knows.

Why does a quasi-perception of someone saying that $p$ to one provide a ground for belief in this, while a mere inclination to form a belief does not? An inclination to believe that $p$ does not present itself intrinsically to its subject as a confrontation with the fact that $p$. But a quasi-perception of a speech act, analogously to a visual experience with objective content, appears as just such a confrontation with the fact of that speech act's being made. When a hearer quasi-perceives that someone is saying that $p$ to her, this is how things seem to her objectively to be, no less. So far as her aural experience represents things, this is what currently is happening. Taking her aural experience at face value, that is what she would judge to be the case. (This fact of the phenomenology of language use the reader will verify by reference to her own experience.) Thus a quasi-perception of the content and force of a heard utterance is, by its intrinsic nature, a prima facie though defeasible ground for belief. The default epistemic response to one's experience—both naturally and normatively—is to take it at face value: to

of beliefs of central importance—applicable to simpler, non-reflective creatures. But for those capable of reflection the twin requirements of stability and non-absurdity seem to me too crucial as desirable features of belief for the simpler notion to be of much interest.

take it that what appears to be, is. This holds equally for quasi-perceptions of speech acts and, more familiarly, for our objectively contentful visual experience of the visually perceptible world.

Thus the characteristic phenomenology of understanding is crucial to the epistemology of a hearer's knowledge of what is said, in these normal cases. A hearer's quasi-perception of a speech act provides a prima facie, albeit defeasible, ground for belief, in the same manner that objectively contentful visual experience grounds visual perceptual belief. Ida lacks understanding-experience, and so her inclinations to believe are, in the absence of empirically based supporting beliefs providing an explanatory link to the facts in which she finds herself inclined to believe, epistemically opaque and absurd to her. An experience as of $p$ is not epistemically opaque. By its nature it is, as it were, self-warranting, though defeasibly so. The very manner of its presentation of its content means that it is, unlike a mere yen to believe, intrinsically a ground for belief.[26]

Thus knowledge based on experience, including understanding-experience, though it is subject to defeat by ancillary information showing the experience should not, on this occasion, be taken at face value, is not inferential. Empirical supporting beliefs are not needed as first-level support for belief based on experience. (They will be involved in supporting second-level knowledge, knowledge of how one knows.) Quasi-perception-based knowledge of what is said, the normal case, contrasts in its epistemology, as well as its phenomenology, with translational knowledge of what is said— knowledge gained through recourse to a translational mechanism of some kind, whether another person, or a dictionary. Translational knowledge of what is said is inferential, based on premisses about word meanings, or about the reliability of a translator.

A hearer's quasi-perception of the content and force of a heard utterance provides, in normal cases of language use, the necessary 'internal' ground for her knowledgeable belief as to what was said, its justifying basis. Equally, it constitutes the core of what enables satisfaction of the proposed stability

[26] Here I share the approach to empirical justification taken in Peacocke (1999). Peacocke maintains that various kinds of occurrent conscious representational states, including experiences, but also memory impressions, provide a rational prima facie ground for belief. The present emphasis is that this list also includes understanding-experience. See also Fricker (2002).

requirement on knowledge held by reflective creatures: the need to provide an epistemically rationalizing explanation of one's belief, thus knowing how one knows. The experience or quasi-perception is the ground of one's first-level belief, needed for it to be knowledge. Knowing how one knows requires both this first-level ground and some background theory. Our common-sense theory of ourselves and the world we find ourselves in includes a basic conception of our own nature as embodied thinker-agents, and of the nature of the extended, solid objects and other things we encounter in our environment. Equally, and crucially for our ability to make sense of our own epistemic position in the world, it includes a conception of various ways we have of finding out how things are in our environment: a range of epistemic links which we from time to time, under certain conditions, enjoy, which give us access to objective, independent states of affairs of various kinds. These links include the various modes of perception: seeing, touching, hearing, smelling, and tasting; memory, and also testimony. In the case of knowing what is said, the needed conception is of our ability to hear-say—that is, to hear the content and force of what is said or told to one. Thus conceptually equipped, someone, say Ella, who hears an assertion that $p$ by Petra, and hears it as such a speech act, is able to answer the question 'How do you know that Petra said that $p$?' with the reply 'Because I heard her do so.'[27] This reply is short because compressed. It is powerful and effective. Packed into it is the ordinary concept of hearing as an epistemic link which affords access to such states of affairs. Also packed into it is the fact, obliquely cited, that Ella enjoyed a quasi-perception of the content and force of Petra's utterance. Her quasi-perception, this phenomenally given understanding-experience, is the conscious core of her being the subject of the epistemic link of hearing-say. Because being a subject of this link is something Ella is consciously aware of, when she is, she can know that she is, when she is. The fact that she has been a subject of this epistemic link is what she cites

---

[27] The substantiality of this reply is shown up by its contrast with another situation, and possible reply: 'Well, I could hear that she was talking, but I did not hear what she said'; or: '. . . but I could not understand what she said—she was talking a foreign language'. When someone answers the challenge 'How do you know she said that?' with 'Because I heard her do so', she invokes the fact that she has enjoyed a quasi-perception of the content and force of the utterance. Hearing what is said is not just hearing the sounds; it is additionally enjoying a conscious quasi-perpetual representation of certain syntactic and semantic properties of the utterance.

in explaining—to another, or equally to herself—how she has had access to the fact of Petra's making this assertion. This reply to the challenge 'How do you know?'—which we may think of as posed by another, or reflectively to oneself—exemplifies the general style of common-sense epistemically rationalizing explanations of one's belief. One shows how one knows by citing the fact that one has been the subject of a known epistemic link, one which gives access to the kind of state of affairs one is claiming to know about. 'I saw it', 'I can remember doing it', 'I was told by a reliable person' are other examples of such common-sense justifying explanations of belief, explanations that show how one knows about the matter in question.

My labelling of our quasi-perceptions of the content and force of heard utterances as states of understanding is apt. Even with a language one is completely fluent in, there is a noteworthy phenomenal and functional difference between hearing an uttered sentence with and without 'uptake'. Like me, you must sometimes read a sentence or hear an utterance without 'taking it in', and have to read it again, or ask for a repeat. No doubt the ultimately neural basis for this is a difference in whether one's language-processing equipment has done its stuff on the acoustic input. Consciously, it is natural to describe the difference as residing in whether one has understood the token which one has heard or read. What one gets, when one has understood and not otherwise, is precisely a conscious representation, a quasi-perception, of not just the phonology or syntax, but also the meaning of what one hears. Moreover, the characteristic cognitive-functional consequences of understanding will generally go with this phenomenology.

By applying some general epistemological theory to the question how it is that understanding an utterance yields not just correct beliefs, but knowledge, of what is said, we have found a theoretical motivation to endorse the verdict of ordinary language that the normal phenomenology of understanding is essential to it. Both *Reliabilist U* and *I-reliabilist U* are to be rejected as being insufficiently restrictive. Not just any reliable mechanism for going from acoustic input to beliefs about what is said, even an internally constituted one, constitutes understanding. It must be one which does so via the generation of phenomenal states of a distinctive kind, understanding-experiences. This is so since it is only through our enjoyment of these quasi-perceptions of the content and force of utterances that we possess knowledge of what is said—that is to say, they are the ground for such knowledge, in normal language use. Of course, alternative routes to the same piece of knowledge are possible. A wised-up Ida could attain knowledge, but her knowledge will have a different basis. It will be inferential, grounded in other beliefs, not in understanding-experience, as our beliefs about what is said normally are.

*I-reliabilist* $U_{occ}$ also errs in the other direction, ruling out some cases of understanding. This is so since, as mentioned earlier in our rejection of *Naive U*, one can understand an utterance—that is to say, enjoy a correct, aptly derived, quasi-perception of its force and content—yet not be in a position to know what was said in it, if one does not form belief in what one seems to hear said, owing to misleading defeaters. This can happen because states of understanding, like visual experiences, exhibit belief-independence. That is to say, a hearer's quasi-perception of content and force may persist, despite her lack of belief that what she apprehends as being said is indeed being said. (Suppose one thinks one is hearing the non-intentional productions of a speech synthesizer, but in fact it was the experimenter talking. Or suppose one hears what sounds like an assertion in English, but falsely believes it to be an utterance of a sentence in another language, with a coincidental similarity to the English sentence. 'See!' my Italian friend says to me, enjoining me to look. I hear it this way, but then falsely conclude that he is uttering 'Sì', the Italian for 'Yes'.[28])

## 2.4 *What understanding really is*

Considerations from epistemology have led us to conclude that the minimal reliabilist conception of understanding, as embodying the correct function from acoustic intake to beliefs about what has been said, is too thin. The phenomenology of understanding is essential to how knowledge of what is said is gained, in normal language use. But our discussion suggests that another two-part definition of both kinds of understanding, on which their essence is still functional, may be correct, *Adequate U*:

> *Adequate* $U_{disp}$: To understand a sentence $S$ of a language $L$ dispositionally is stably to possess an internally constituted reliable ca-

---

[28] I myself have experienced this kind of case, and also the related phenomenon of aspect switching: hearing the same sound sequence first as a sentence of one language, then of another.

> pacity to enjoy correct quasi-perceptual representations of the content and force of heard utterances of S.
>
> *Adequate U*$_{occ}$: To understand a particular heard utterance of S, U(S), occurrently is to enjoy a correct quasi-perceptual representation of the content and force of U(S), and to do so in part as the result of one's dispositional understanding of S—that is, through the exercise of a stably possessed, internally constituted reliable capacity to enjoy such representations with respect to utterances of S.

An individual will instantiate *Adequate U* with respect to the sentences of a language (utterances of which are realized in acoustic strings) so long as she somehow or other embodies a mechanism which takes these acoustic strings as inputs, and whose output is correct quasi-perceptual representations of the content and force of the utterance, the speech act, which that acoustic string realized. Since context dependence in determination of reference is a pervasive feature of everyday use of natural languages, possession of dispositional understanding of a sentence S as defined in *Adequate U*$_{disp}$ will include general interpretative skills, as well as embodied knowledge of the conventional semantic character of the expressions that occur in S. None the less, a hearer's possession of *Adequate U*$_{disp}$ with respect to S will still not guarantee that she is in a position to achieve full occurrent understanding of every utterance of a token of S—if, for instance, she cannot see who is being indicated by the speaker in her use of a pronoun which occurs in S.

It seems plausible that the essence of understanding is functional. Any internal mechanism which embodies the function specified in *Adequate U* will do—no further restrictions on how it works are essential to the concept, so long as the right quasi-perceptual states are generated.[29] *Adequate U* thus preserves something of reliabilism about understanding, although the reliabilist thesis that any means of producing reliably correct beliefs about

---

[29] The issues we raised in connection with *Reliabilist U* rearise. Suppose a benevolent God, or scientist, manipulates someone so as to induce reliably the right final quasi-perceptual states. Does this external mechanism constitute understanding? It certainly cannot yield knowledge, unless it counts as a means of hearing, according with the subject's own conception of her epistemic link, since her own epistemically rationalizing explanation of her belief 'I heard him say so' must be correct. See Peacocke (1999), sect. 2.5, for a discussion of presuppositions and operational conditions on an epistemic link yielding perceptual representations which ground knowledge.

what has been said constitutes dispositional understanding was shown to be incorrect. For this reason *Adequate U* is also controversial. To accept *Adequate U* is to accept that the details of how one's language-processing mechanism works are inessential to whether one understands, so long as the right final states are generated. There is a familiar debate over whether representations of particular syntactic and semantic properties of subsentential expressions, representations which are deployed in arriving at states of understanding of whole sentences, are essential to language mastery. This debate survives, in a new guise, on the alternative conception of occurrent and dispositional understanding that has been argued for here. My hope is to stay clear of these issues. However, I had better say that, in my view, anyone who satisfies the function specified in *Adequate U* is thereby, trivially, to be credited with embodied knowledge of the semantic properties of primitive expressions of the language. Whether, and if so how, these are explicitly represented in her mind or brain is a further, empirical question.

I call this theory *Adequate U* rather than *Correct U* because I do not claim that *Adequate U* covers absolutely all cases of a hearer's or reader's understanding an utterance, including all the unusual possibilities which do or might occur. The next section will discuss some of these cases, which arguably furnish counter-examples. My claim is that *Adequate U* captures the essence of understanding, in the following sense. First, it describes the overwhelming preponderance of instances of utterance comprehension in everyday language use, and it includes only what is essential to how understanding yields belief whose aetiology is intelligible to its subject, and constitutes knowledge, in these instances. Second, the instances of understanding it describes are basic—others can occur only for a person most of whose occurrent understanding is as described by *Adequate U*. My argument backing this second claim is given in Section 4.

We noticed earlier that *I-reliabilist* $U_{occ}$ wrongly rules out cases where someone understands an utterance $U(S)$, i.e. enjoys a correct quasi-perception generated in part through her general capacity for this with respect to $S$, but fails to form a belief in what she quasi-perceives. I mentioned the case where misleading defeaters block belief. But the phenomenon of understanding without belief is arguably much more pervasive than this. Criteria for attribution of belief are hazy, to say the least, but it seems plausible that very often, when someone effortlessly understands an utterance, but is not actively reflecting about her communicative situation, she simply takes on board the content of what is said to her, and carries on with the conversation. She is certainly in a position to form knowledgeable belief about what has been said to her. But she may not in fact devote cognitive resources to forming that belief, unless some feature of the situation draws her attention to the matter. While it is essential to understanding that it equips the hearer to form knowledgeable belief about what has been said, it is a strength of *Adequate U* that it squares with this fact. *Adequate U* does so by recognizing and giving centre place to the fact we began this investigation by noting: the immediate psychological upshot in a hearer of auditing an utterance is not belief, as the proposals we criticized had it, but her correctly formed quasi-perception of the utterance's meaning. I have argued that occurrent understanding of an utterance $U(S)$ of a sentence $S$ consists in enjoyment of a correct quasi-perception of $U(S)$'s meaning, and that a stably possessed capacity with respect to $S$ to enjoy such correct quasi-perceptions of the meaning of utterances of it constitutes dispositional understanding of $S$.[30]

I have argued that the typical phenomenology of understanding is essential to how knowledge of what is said is gained, in normal language use. This furnished one major argument for *Adequate U*. In my discussion proposing necessary conditions for knowledge, I sought to develop a concept of it on which having knowledge is not a recherché theoretical matter, but is something of importance for ordinary language users themselves. Thus I hope this first argument will weigh with all those interested in the description of everyday language use, even those who are not primarily concerned with

---

[30] To what extent does the proposed account of understanding contradict the extensive exploration in Wittgenstein (1958)? Wittgenstein argues vehemently (see sects. 138–243) against the idea that there is a phenomenal state whose occurrence is constitutive of understanding. However, he also emphasizes later on the distinctive phenomenology of understanding. I think Wittgenstein's main target is the view that there is some phenomenal event distinct from the hearing of the sentence itself, such as the occurrence of a mental image, which is the essence of understanding, and the present proposal agrees with this. However, I hold that occurrent understanding of a particular utterance is a real, conscious event with a causal role, and this is certainly in tension with the behaviouristic leanings of much of Wittgenstein's discussion. My discussion has not touched on Wittgenstein's central concern with the normative consequences of understanding. I agree with his contention that no phenomenal occurrence can in itself have such consequences, and that these accrue only when the conscious events are embedded within the right sort of context of rule-governed regularities in thought and action.

epistemological matters. But in case some anti-epistemologists are not convinced, in Section 4 I shall put a second, independent argument which also purports to show, from a different route, that the phenomenology of understanding is essential, not incidental, to human language mastery, and hence that *I-reliabilist U* is too thin, and *Adequate U* should be accepted instead. This second argument does not appeal to considerations from epistemology, but to the intrinsic nature of human thought. In the next section I first examine further the significance of context dependence, and some unusual cases of linguistic comprehension, for my proposed account of understanding, and of how a hearer gains knowledge of what is said.

## 3 Context Dependence and Unusual Cases

### 3.1 *Implications of context dependence*

Many sentences of English and other natural languages exhibit syntactic or semantic ambiguity. For such sentences $S$ a specific meaning for an utterance $U(S)$ is fixed only in and by the context in which $U(S)$ is made. In addition, natural languages contain many indexical expressions—pronouns, demonstratives, etc. These are expressions whose conventional semantic property is a rule for determining a referent from the context of utterance. For example, '"Now" refers to the time of utterance.'[31] Moreover, it is argued by some that context sensitivity in determination of the precise extension of apparently non-indexical expressions pervades natural language. It is certainly true that many uses of definite descriptions exhibit contextual determination of reference.

What are the implications of this for our proposed account of understanding, and our account of how knowledge of what is said is gained? I shall make three points.

(i) We observed earlier that where there is context dependence, of whatever kind, in determination of an utterance $U(S)$'s meaning, general interpretative skills are needed, in addition to embodied knowledge of the

---

[31] The full Lewisian analysis of convention, found in Lewis (1969), may be too strong, but the semantic properties associated with expression types of a language are certainly conventional, in some apt explication of that notion. They are antecedently arbitrary facts, supervenient on self-perpetuating regularities of use in a linguistic community. Of course some slippage in usage, hence evolution of meanings, occurs.

conventional semantic properties of expressions occurring in $S$, to confer successfully exercisable dispositional understanding of $S$. And we observed that dispositional understanding of $S$, even thus broadly construed, still does not guarantee a hearer's occurrent understanding of each and every audited utterance of $S$. This should not make us lose sight of the primary fact about language use, that dispositional understanding incorporating specific semantic knowledge is the core of natural-language mastery. Specifically, it is what differentiates the speakers of a certain natural language $L$ from others who speak not $L$, but some other natural language. A hearer's dispositional understanding of $S$ is an essential component in how she arrives unaided at correct interpretation of an utterance $U(S)$, in all or virtually all cases. In Section 3.4 I briefly consider whether occurrent understanding must in all cases result from the exercise of a stable capacity, as *Adequate U* insists.

(ii) Our definition of understanding, *Adequate U*, makes enjoying the correct phenomenology, a correct quasi-perception of the full propositional content and force of $U(S)$, derived in part from the exercise of a stable capacity for this, both necessary and sufficient for occurrent understanding of $U(S)$. Is this definition consistent with the fact of pervasive context dependence?

In itself, context dependence is entirely consistent with *Adequate U*. There is no reason why a hearer may not enjoy what is, from her subjective standpoint, an immediate and effortless quasi-perception of the full meaning of $U(S)$, equally when $S$ includes expressions whose reference is determined in part by the context of utterance. Of course, where there is context dependence in the determination of reference, the correct interpretation of an utterance does not supervene on its acoustic profile. Specifically, it does not supervene on the acoustic profile relative to a fixed set of facts about the semantic character of expression types—non-contextual facts which a language processor might be built to embody. This being so, the correct interpretation of an utterance containing context-dependent expressions will always involve an exercise of something like inference to the most likely explanation. But this could all be done subpersonally, and the first conscious result be a subjectively effortless and immediate, albeit highly cooked, quasi-perception of the utterance's full meaning. My own casual reflection confirms that understanding of, for instance, utterances including demonstrative pronouns is often thus. Further support comes from the fact that this is the situation with visual perception, all the time. Our highly cooked visual experiences exceed in content anything which could conceivably supervene on the raw sensory input. Subpersonal hypothesis formation within the visual processing system, involving inference to the best explanation, is the rule, in the aetiology of our objectively contentful visual experiences. This is so when one seems to see a red cube; much more so when one seems to see a friend, or a mobile phone.

I conclude that the mere fact of context dependence in fixation of reference does not show *Adequate U* to be empirically false. However, it is true that context dependence of reference in an utterance makes it more likely that a hearer will not understand it immediately and effortlessly. She may need to devote conscious attention to the question what the sense is here of an ambiguous expression, or the referent of a definite description or demonstrative. But a hearer's having consciously to work out what the correct interpretation is can arise without context dependence. The presence of context-dependent elements, and non-immediate phenomenology, the hearer needing to work out the full utterance meaning consciously, are cross-cutting phenomena. In Section 3.2 I shall consider three different cases of non-immediate phenomenology in language comprehension, discussing their bearing on *Adequate U*. I shall argue that they do not detract from its validity.

(iii) The reader may object that *Adequate U* was motivated by the epistemological thesis that a hearer's correct and aptly derived understanding-experience is the ground of her knowledgeable belief in what was said. And that context dependence may affect this motivation. Whether and how context dependence affects the epistemology of knowledge of what is said, and thereby bears on the motivation for *Adequate U*, will be discussed below (Section 3.3). We shall see that in the unusual cases of absent understanding-experience, or non-immediate understanding-experience, the epistemology is, inevitably, different; and that even where understanding-experience is immediate and effortless (all the cooking being subpersonal), the epistemology is somewhat different where there is context dependence in determination of meaning. However, as we shall see, the differences are not such as to undermine the motivation for *Adequate U*. Nor do they falsify, but merely constitute footnotes to, the basic proposal of this paper about how, in normal language use, a hearer's correct belief about what is said constitutes knowledge.

## 3.2 Three types of case where understanding-experience is not effortlessly enjoyed

In this section I describe these cases and assess their bearing on *Adequate U*, which emerges unscathed. In Section 3.3 I consider their somewhat different epistemology.

> Case 1: I do not immediately enjoy a full understanding-experience of U(S). I first have to attend consciously, to determine the referent of some expression in U(S). After this, I then enjoy a full understanding-experience of U(S)'s meaning.

We remarked above that, while context dependence of reference of an expression in S makes this more likely, it can happen without it—e.g. in grasping the meaning of a syntactically very complex sentence. One understands, in such cases, when one achieves the full understanding-experience. These cases are entirely in harmony with *Adequate U*.

> Case 2: I hear an utterance of a context-dependent sentence S, but while I possess dispositional understanding of S, I am not so placed as to be able to come to know the full referential meaning of U(S). For instance, I cannot see who or what the speaker is talking to, or demonstrating. In this case I do not fully understand the utterance. Since I do not understand it—I was unable on this occasion fully to exercise my dispositional understanding—there is no counter-example to *Adequate U*. However, in such cases there is something it is like for me, when I hear U(S); and the content of this subjective conscious state exceeds mere phonology or syntax.

Case 2 shows us that we need to acknowledge that the semantic character of expressions, as well as their full reference, is something which is sometimes consciously represented, quasi-perceived. There is a distinctive kind of understanding-experience of expression types, as well as of interpreted utterances of them. If I have dispositional understanding of S, I shall enjoy this, even where I am not placed to grasp the full referential meaning of U(S).

*Case 3*: I do not immediately enjoy a full understanding-experience of
U(S). I have to attend consciously, to determine the referent of
some expression in U(S). Through this I come to know what the
full meaning of U(S) is, but I still do not enjoy a full understanding-
experience of U(S).

Is this possible? It is crucial to appreciate that there are strict limits to how
Case 3 can occur. The reason why will be explored fully in Section 4, but here
I shall briefly anticipate what is argued there. If I am to know what is said in
U(S), I must in some manner think, entertain that content. The normal way
is by enjoying an understanding-experience of U(S)—by hearing its content
in U(S) itself. *Ex hypothesi*, this does not occur in Case 3. But, it is supposed,
I know what is said in U(S). So—human occurrent thought requiring a
phenomenal vehicle—there must be some other mental vehicle of the
content of U(S), through entertaining which I think that content. For many
types of thought, this can only be another sentence which serves roughly
to express the same proposition. So, though I do not enjoy phenomenal
understanding of U(S), there must be some other sentence S′ such that a
mental hearing-with-understanding of S′ is the vehicle of my thought of
U(S)'s meaning. This being so, Case 3 describes an essentially secondary,
parasitic way of knowing what is said in an utterance. It occurs when
knowledge of what is said in U(S) is effected by translating into a language
in which one is fluent. It may occur when one as it were decodes a sentence
which is syntactically unmanageable—for instance, one with many stacked
propositional attitude operators—into a simpler equivalent which one can
grasp. (These hardware limits on human processing capacity mean that
introducing new notation can literally extend one's powers of thought.)

Does this way of knowing what is said in U(S) without enjoying a full
understanding-experience of U(S) threaten *Adequate U*? It does not. In line
with my discussion in Section 2, I would describe this as a case of knowing
what is said in an utterance, without fully understanding it. I shall not
labour this point further. Even if Case 3 is a case of understanding, it is—as
claimed above, and to be further argued in Section 4—a secondary, parasitic
form of it. *Adequate U* describes the primary form of understanding, a kind
there must be if there is to be any at all. It is strongly primary: every case

of understanding of an utterance U(S) involves understanding-experience—either directly of U(S), or of an equivalent, mentally heard sentence S'.

### 3.3 The epistemology of these unusual cases, and of context-dependent utterances

We observed in Section 3.1 that context dependence in determination of the reference of some elements in U(S) is consistent with a hearer's understanding of U(S) being entirely effortless, inference to the correct interpretation being effected subpersonally. In these cases the basic epistemology of the hearer's knowledge of what is said is as previously proposed: the hearer's understanding-experience affords her a prima facie ground for belief. However, the need for inference to the most likely explanation in the aetiology of this understanding-experience affects the epistemic situation, in that this prima facie ground for belief is in these cases more open to challenge, and defeat.

When a hearer believes that the speaker has said that p, because that is what she heard him say, she is taking her understanding-experience at face value: taking it that what seemed to be said is what was in fact said. Similarly, I take my visual experience at face value when I judge that my friend is walking towards me in the street, because I seem to see him doing so—that is, I see someone, whom I seem to recognize as him. I attempted to say something about why taking experience at face value is the default response to it, both naturally and epistemically-normatively, in Section 2.3. The matter is too large to be defended fully here.[32] But particular experiences are more or less open to challenge, and potential defeat, according to the richness of their content and to the circumstances. I am epistemically more daring when I judge on the basis of my experience that my friend is walking towards me than when I merely judge that someone is doing so. Someone doubtful of my eyesight or familiarity with him might ask, 'How are you sure it is him?' I may reply, 'Because I know

---

[32] I hold that the content of experience is partly externally determined, and this is a crucial element in defence of this view. Externalist-causal determination of experience content engenders general reliability of certain basic features of experiential content, and this necessary reliability underwrites the epistemic entitlement to take such experiences at face value.

very well what he looks like'—asserting my right to take my experience at face value, on this occasion.

When I take my quasi-perception of what is said in $U(S)$ at face value, my doing so is more open to challenge, and admits of more interesting circumstantial defence, when $U(S)$ contains context-dependent elements. Where $S$ is a sentence of English free of all contextual determination of reference, there is no answer to be given other than 'I heard the speaker clearly, and he was speaking English, and I can speak English.' Where there is context dependence, there is scope, and correspondingly there may be need, for a more substantial answer, citing features of the current situation: 'How do you know she was talking about Peter?' 'She pointed at him.' etc. The subpersonally formed quasi-perception is more open to challenge. This is the footnote necessitated by context dependence to my account of how knowledge of what is said is gained in normal language use.

The same sort of ancillary circumstantial defence that may be offered to defend taking a context-dependence-infected quasi-perception at face value will be invoked to defend the hearer's interpretation of a context-dependent utterance in our unusual cases, when understanding-experience is not immediate, or is lacking entirely. The phenomenological difference between the cases is that the inferences which are in the basic case effected subpersonally, are in the unusual cases effected consciously, by the person rather than by her language-processing faculty. The corresponding epistemological difference is that the conclusions of these inferences will be, as it were, up front, in the epistemic support of her belief.

At the other extreme from effortless understanding of a sentence, what we might call Case 4, we have the case of wholly translational knowledge of what is said, obtained through using a dictionary, for an utterance of a sentence of a language of which one has no knowledge. For instance, I may know that 'colonus domum festinat' means 'the farmer hurries home', in this manner. I argued in Section 2 that this is knowledge of what is said, without understanding. Whether or not this is so, we have here a case of knowledge of what is said which is inferentially based, in metalinguistic beliefs about word meanings—such as 'festinat' means 'hurries'. But metalinguistic beliefs about the semantic properties of sentences or their component words are not my ground for my knowledge of what is said, in normal natural-language use. A strength of my proposed account is that it shows how a hearer can gain knowledge of what is said without the sophistication of metalinguistic beliefs of any kind.

There are no principled limits on how one may gain knowledge of what is said in a particular utterance; all kinds of inferential routes may be possible, in different circumstances. My argument has been that when someone effortlessly understands an utterance, as is normal in everyday language use, her knowledge of what is said is not inferentially based, but has a quasi-perceptual ground, in her understanding-experience. Thus in a case like Ida's, where this quasi-perceptual ground is absent, and there are, as we supposed, no supporting beliefs which provide an alternative ground, a belief of hers about what was said would not be knowledge.

Where a hearer enjoys an effortless quasi-perception of the full meaning of $U(S)$, her belief is grounded in that quasi-perception, and the common-sense explanation of how she knows, which she is able to give either to another or to herself, is: 'I know he said that $p$, because I heard him do so.' We saw that this prima facie ground for belief is more open to challenge when $U(S)$ has context-dependent elements. When the hearer does not enjoy an effortless quasi-perception, but works out some of the referential features of $U(S)$, her belief is based instead in a quasi-perception of the semantic character of $U(S)$, plus beliefs about its reference. Acknowledging the possibility of such alternative, inferential knowledge of the meaning of an utterance is entirely consistent with my claim that in normal, fluent language use a hearer's knowledge of what is said is grounded in her understanding-experience, not in other beliefs.

### 3.4 Occurrent understanding without dispositional understanding?

I finish this section by discussing another case, call it Case 5, which may seem to threaten *Adequate U*. A hearer or reader may sometimes successfully interpret an utterance $U(S)$ despite lack of any prior knowledge of the semantic character of some or all the expressions in $S$, through clever inference to the best explanation.[33] If this counts as understanding, it is a counter-example to the claim embodied in *Adequate U*, that occurrent

---

[33] Alex Barber tells me he is able to read Tintin in French this way. Thanks to him for pointing out this case. A similar case occurs when a hearer successfully interprets a speaker who uses inappropriate words to express her intended meaning. I have omitted

understanding must be the upshot of dispositional understanding. We have not yet specified the phenomenology of Case 5. If it is like Case 3, a case of translational understanding, then we need say no more about it. But suppose that, once the meaning of the previously unknown expression is successfully guessed at, it then as it were springs to life for one, and one enjoys a full understanding-experience of the sentence itself. This is a counter-example to *Adequate U*.

Such cases are the exception, as emphasized in Section 3.1, and I would not mind admitting this occasional possibility, it being agreed that occurrent understanding is inevitably going to be achieved only by means of prior dispositional understanding in the overwhelming majority of cases. But a more aggressive response may be available. There is no space here to argue it fully, but I shall indicate how it might go. First: to have a full understanding-experience of $U(S)$, I must apprehend $S$ as having the semantic structure that it has. This already suggests that one could not achieve understanding of $U(S)$ unless all but one or two of its constituent expressions were already familiar to one. (Maybe I can do it for Tintin in French, in which my vocabulary is limited, but I have a working knowledge of grammar and basic vocabulary. I could not do it for Tintin in Chinese, even if I could sometimes guess what the utterance must mean. I could not even parse it.) This makes the phenomenon very limited. But suppose I read an utterance of a sentence of French $U(S_F)$ in which there is one unfamiliar word $e$. It is evident from the syntactic context that $e$ must be an adjective, and I successfully infer its meaning. A full understanding-experience is generated in me. Then, I suggest, *ipso facto* I have now acquired dispositional understanding of $e$. That is, I have acquired a capacity with respect to $e$ which is in principle general in its application, going beyond my understanding of the current utterance. Even if I very quickly forget it, at the moment at which I enjoy understanding-experience of $U(S_F)$, I possess it. If this aggressive response to Case 5 is maintained, then it provides a counter-example to *Adequate U* only of a very weak kind. We have occurrent understanding without prior dispositional understanding of one constituent expression, but even here

discussion of such cases, along with my omission of non-literal uses of language generally. This would be bad methodology if the literal use of language were not its basic use. I think it is, since I think understanding of the non-literal uses to which a sentence may be put exploits grasp of its literal meaning.

there is simultaneous dispositional understanding. Further, I make this conjecture. Understanding-experience is necessarily of the sentence as bearing the structured content it does, hence involves apprehending the sentence itself as semantically structured. But such structured apprehension can only occur, barring magical interventions, as the exercise of a general grasp of the semantic properties of its semantically primitive constituents.[34]

## 4 The Incoherence of Translationalism

I turn finally to my second argument against *I-reliabilist U*, and in favour of *Adequate U*. Its conclusion is that fluent understanding, involving immediate and effortless understanding-experience, as characterized by *Adequate U*, is necessarily the preponderant and basic form of language understanding, at least in humans. I further conjecture, though do not try conclusively to prove, that this is true of all possible language users, not only of humans.

In arguing against *Reliabilist U*, we considered two counter-examples in which there was an externally constituted mechanism whereby, ultimately, the subject gained correct beliefs about what is said by utterances of Russian sentences through this external mechanism's supplying her with an English translation of them. (In the first case the translator was human, in the second it was a machine.) I commented that, even if this translationally mediated 'understanding' of Russian counted as understanding, it was a secondary phenomenon—since it exploits the subject's non-translational understanding of her own language.

I start my argument by observing that it is a necessary truth that not all understanding is translational. If one understands any language at all, there must be some language that one understands directly—that is, not in virtue of translating it into another language which one understands. This point is most obvious where the translations in question are supplied to me perceptually, from an external source. If I am able to 'understand', in a loose sense, Russian utterances in virtue of being constantly supplied with utterances of their English translations, the regress of translations must stop eventually if I am to understand anything: there must be some language whose utterances I can understand without being supplied from an external source with translations into a further language. But the point

---

[34] See Fricker (1982).

holds equally, as a matter of logic, if the translations are supplied, or effected, by me: understanding a language $L_1$ by translating it into another $L_2$ is only a way of understanding $L_1$ if one understands $L_2$, and how does one satisfy that condition? So it is a logically necessary truth that anyone who understands any language understands at least one language directly.

For any human language user, there is at least one language which is her home public language, as I shall call it. That is, it is a language she speaks fluently, and which is for her a primary vehicle of everyday communication, and of expression in speech or writing of her own thought. For most individuals, her home public language is the public language she learnt first in her life, though this is not always the case—if, for instance, her family emigrates while she is a small child. Now, our logical truth—that anyone who understands any language understands at least one language directly— does not entail that one's understanding of one's home public language is not translational. It could be, consistently with this logical necessity, that understanding one's home public language consists in 'translating' it, in some sense, into a private language of one's own—one's own idiosyncratic 'language of thought'. Nor have I yet given any positive description of what direct, i.e. non-translational, understanding of a language does or must consist in.

I shall first elaborate a thesis about what a human's understanding of her home public language is in fact like. It is, in a subjective and cognitive-functional sense, direct and not translational. This human direct understanding involves understanding-experience. So human home-language use is as described by *Adequate U*. I shall then make some brief comments on whether this descriptive thesis about human language use can be elevated into a necessary thesis about human language use, and even about all possible home-language use. First, the thesis about what human language is in fact like.

Not all thought is occurrent. (True ascription to someone of a thought does not entail the occurrence of an episode in consciousness.) But there is much occurrent thought, and in humans it typically has a phenomenal vehicle. Occurrent thoughts are conscious episodes with a phenomenal character. The conscious vehicles of thought, the bearers of the structured content which is the thought itself, must themselves be structured (how else could they perform that role?).[35] What are they? In humans, they are very often mentally heard utterances of sentences of one's home public language—that, or any language one is fluent in.[36] (In fact, it is plausible to see the capacity for silent, private thought as derivative from a developmentally prior capacity for communicative linguistic expression of thought. Talking is not thinking out loud; rather, thinking is talking while repressing the physical output.)

Now: if a certain phenomenal episode, a mental hearing of an utterance of a sentence, is the vehicle of a certain thought, this entails that it has the cognitive role characteristic of that thought—that is, it implies a complex set of dispositional linkages of that episode. Phenomenal vehicle type and cognitive role must hang together for there to be episodes in consciousness which constitute the occurrence of particular thoughts, one thought rather than another.[37] When one understands a language fluently, utterances of sentences of that language are such phenomenal-cum-cognitive vehicles of thought for one. Thus when one hears, with uptake—either literally, or in one's mind's ear, as it were—an utterance of a sentence of a language one is fluent in, this constitutes, cognitive-functionally speaking, an occurrence of the thought which is the meaning of that utterance, the proposition represented by it. (Of course, there are crucial cognitive-functional differences between hearing someone assert that $p$, and oneself judging that $p$; and between judging that $p$, and wondering whether $p$, etc. These differences will need to be addressed in a fuller account.)

So, when one hears someone assert that $p$, in a language in which one

[35] The thought itself, in Frege's sense, is an abstract object, a structured content or proposition. A thinker stands in the relation of entertaining or grasping, vis-à-vis such an abstract object, in virtue of enjoying a conscious state which is a phenomenal vehicle of it. As emphasized shortly, this episode in consciousness is the occurrence of that particular thought in virtue of having the right cognitive role. Such roles will not be purely 'internal', but will involve relations to the thinker's environment.

[36] To accommodate context dependence, we need to extend the idea of an utterance of a sentence to include a particular use of the sentence in thought on some occasion, to express a specific meaning.

[37] This remark can and should be interpreted so as to be consistent with externalist determination of the content of thought. The thesis is not that a given phenomenal type and role are associated across different environments, but that relative to a particular environment, they are correlated. I do not want to use up more space, and the reader's patience, getting into fiddly detail on this here.

is fluent, there is no need, in order to grasp the content $p$ that is asserted, to convert, 'translate' the heard utterance $U(S)$ into some other medium of representation. On the contrary, the hearing of $U(S)$ itself, when it is heard with 'uptake', constitutes a thought of the proposition which is the meaning of $U(S)$. $U(S)$ itself is the vehicle in consciousness through entertaining which the subject thinks of that proposition. This is the subjective state which we have labelled understanding-experience of $U(S)$. Fluent understanding of a language $L$ is, from the point of view of the conscious subject, precisely not translational understanding, but is direct: she enjoys understanding-experience of utterances of sentences of $L$. It is equally cognitive-functionally direct. As already remarked, phenomenology and cognitive role must run together for there to be phenomenal vehicles of thought. When one is fluent in a language, it is enough that one hears with uptake an utterance of a sentence of it for one both to enjoy an understanding-experience and to go into the cognitive-functional state characteristic of understanding (the state which, on a broadly Wittgensteinian view of what understanding is, should be regarded as constitutive of having understood the sentence in question). When one has understood, one will thereby possess a complex bunch of dispositions to actions and further thoughts apt in the light of what was said.

So far we have two theses:

(T1) Human thoughts typically have syntactically structured phenomenal vehicles, bearers of the cognitive-functional role of that thought. That is, human thinking mostly occurs in episodes of conscious entertaining of utterances of sentences of a language of thought, and consists in understanding-experiences of those mentally heard utterances.

(T2) In a human, utterances of sentences of her home public language HPL serve as vehicles of thought, for her.

T1 and T2 together imply:

Human home-public-language use involves understanding-experience, i.e. conforms to *Adequate U*.

By T1, human occurrent thought involves understanding-experience of utterances in a language of thought; by T2, HPL is this language of thought for a human thinker; it follows that understanding-experience of utterances of HPL is enjoyed by her.

En route, we have equated fluency of someone's understanding of a language with utterances of its sentences playing this role as bearers of thoughts, in her cognitive life. And we described what human direct understanding of a language is like. Since human thinking involves phenomenal vehicles of thought, and understanding an utterance requires thinking of the proposition it expresses, direct human understanding of any utterance $U(S)$ consists in enjoying correct understanding-experience of $U(S)$. Translational understanding of $U(S)$ would consist in translating it into some other uttered sentence, $U(S')$, of which one enjoyed understanding-experience.

We could establish the necessity of *Adequate U* if we could establish the necessity of both T1 and T2—either that they are necessary features of human language use or, most strongly, that they hold for all possible language users. These are large questions, which I cannot hope to demonstrate here. But I shall suggest the line an argument might take. First the necessity of T1.

Is there any reason to think that thinking, episodes in which thought-contents are entertained, must be effected by means of conscious vehicles of thinking which are syntactically structured and have a distinctive phenomenal character? I think this is plausible, for thought of any degree of complexity, because I do not see how complex episodes of thought can be individuated, how they can be pinned down in a particular person's cognitive economy, as it were, without canonical syntactic vehicles to pick them out by. If we can argue further that true thought must be a property of a conscious being, and that her thoughts must themselves sometimes be conscious occurrences, then we can show that conscious entertainings of syntactic vehicles of thought, i.e. mental hearings of sentences of a language of thought, are required for thought. Whether or not this claim about thought in general can be demonstrated, we can be sure that, whatever might in principle be possible for noumenal intelligences, humans do not and cannot manage to entertain complicated thoughts other than through the means of consciously entertaining a syntactic vehicle of that thought. We can get our minds around a complex thought only by getting our minds around a sentence which expresses it. The conclusion is: human thinking, perhaps all possible thinking, requires a language of thought, supplying syntactic vehicles for it, whose content is entertained in episodes of understanding-experience of utterances of its sentences.

We could show the necessity of T2—that one's home public language is understood directly, being one's language of thought (perhaps along with other learnt public languages)—if one could show that the idea of an idiosyncratic private language of thought, such that one understands one's home public language indirectly, via translation into it, is impossible. I think this is true since—to give just one reason—I think that norms governing the correct application of terms of a language cannot get a grip privately. But I shall not retread this much-disputed territory here.

I must head off a likely misunderstanding. The argument above makes no claims about the subpersonal, ultimately neural, cognitive machinery which underlies our understanding of language and our power of thought. My claims have been about what language use is like at the conscious, personal level. I have claimed that our understanding of our home public language is direct, not translational, at this level, in the phenomenal-functional sense explained. This is entirely consistent with there being a private neural 'language of thought' in the sense advocated by Fodor (1975). Fodor's language of thought is broadly analogous to the machine language of a computer. For all I have said, what goes on in the subpersonal works which underlie conscious thought may involve translation—one might say compiling—into such a neural language. For all I have said, there could be identities between a person's understanding-experience of utterances of sentences of her home public language, and tokenings of sentences of the machine code of the brain.

It is worth returning briefly to the case of Ida, in the light of the discussion of this section. Ida, we supposed, hears utterances of sentences of Russian as meaningless noise, and yet finds herself inclined to form beliefs as to what is said in them. We must raise the question: what is the medium, the vehicle of these occurrent beliefs of hers? Since human thought needs a conscious syntactic medium, there must be one if she is indeed to entertain these thoughts, as supposed. *Ex hypothesi*, utterances of sentences of Russian are not vehicles of thought for her: they sound like meaningless noise. But then she must be a fluent speaker of some language other than Russian, which serves as the vehicle of the beliefs she entertains about what has been said in utterances of Russian sentences. For humans at least, there is no just having of beliefs without any medium for this. One entertains a content, whether of a belief or other attitude, through the medium of some language in which that content is expressed. So we can draw the same conclusion about the case of Ida that we drew concerning our counter-examples to *Reliabilist U*: even if Ida's situation were to be counted as a way of 'understanding' Russian, by some generous concept thereof, it is necessarily a secondary phenomenon. Laws of human psychology entail that it is only possible for Ida to 'understand' Russian in this deviant way if there is some other language which she understands in the normal way—that is, fluently, by enjoying understanding-experience of the meanings of heard utterances of sentences of it.

The arguments of this section have shown that we can, at the very least, be confident that it is a psychological law about humans that their under-standing of their home public language is direct, and is as characterized by *Adequate U*. Instances of human understanding of an utterance $U(S)$ which do not involve understanding-experience of $U(S)$ must be translational, and as such are necessarily secondary and derivative. The hypothesis that the hearer knows what is said by $U(S)$, since it requires that the proposition expressed by $U(S)$ is grasped by her, entails that understanding-experience of some equivalent sentence $U(S')$ is enjoyed. This result provides us with a further motivation, additional to the argument from epistemology devel-oped in Section 2, for accepting *Adequate U* as a good theoretical charac-terization of human language-understanding, and for rejecting all weaker characterizations, such as *I-reliabilist U* and its variants, as too thin.

## 5 Summary of Conclusions

I have argued that the capacity to enjoy understanding-experience—a spe-cial kind of conscious representational state, involved in language use, in which the meaning of a heard utterance is directly present to one—is the psychological core of the ability to speak a particular natural language. Its occurrence is essential to how knowledge of what is said is gained, in normal fluent language use. A hearer's understanding-experience is, in this normal case, the ground of her belief about what is said. It is because she enjoyed such an experience that she knows how she had access to the believed fact: her belief has an intelligible aetiology, one which connects it with its subject matter in such a way that she has reason to think it likely to be true. Its occurrence is cited when she describes how she knows that so-and-so said that *p* with the explanation 'I heard him do so'. This everyday explanation reports not just her auditing of his words, but her enjoyment of a conscious representation of their meaning. Of course, knowledge of what is said can have a different, inferential basis—for example, in metalinguistic beliefs about word meanings. However, in this basic case a hearer's knowledge of what is said is not inferential, but is grounded in her understanding-experience.

Moreover, it is necessary that we enjoy such understanding-experience in relation to our home public language. Human direct understanding of an utterance must involve understanding experience, and our coming to know what is said in an utterance of which we do not enjoy such understanding-experience is secondary, relying on our enjoyment of understanding-experience of some other utterance for us to grasp the proposition expressed. These considerations motivated a definition of understanding of a natural language as the capacity to enjoy correct understanding-experiences (quasi-perceptions) of the meanings of utterances of its sentences. All definitions which merely mention reliable formation of correct beliefs about what is said were rejected as too thin. There can be cases where knowledge of what is said is gained without understanding-experience, but these are secondary. Our definition describes the overwhelmingly preponderant and basic case.

# REFERENCES

BonJour, L. (1985), *The Structure of Empirical Knowledge* (Cambridge, Mass.: Harvard University Press).

Brewer, W. (1999), *Perception and Reason* (Oxford: Clarendon Press).

Fodor, J. A. (1975), *The Language of Thought* (New York: Crowell).

Fricker, E. M. (1982), 'Semantic Structure and Speakers' Understanding', *Proceedings of the Aristotelian Society*, 83: 31–48.

—— (1994), 'Against Gullibility', in Matilal and Chakrabarti (1994), 125–61.

—— (1995), 'Telling and Trusting: Reductionism and Anti-Reductionism in the Epistemology of Testimony', *Mind*, 104: 393–411.

—— (2002), 'From Concepts to Knowledge: Critical Notice of Peacocke: *Being Known*', *International Journal of Philosophical Studies*, 10: 75–91.

FRICKER, E. M. (forthcoming), 'Testimony: Knowing through Being Told' in Niiniluoto, Sintonen, and Wolenski (forthcoming).

GOLDMAN, A. I. (1986), *Epistemology and Cognition* (Cambridge, Mass.: Harvard University Press).

JONES, W. (1999), 'The View from Here: a First-Person Constraint on Believing' (diss. D.Phil., Oxford).

LEPORE, E. (1997), 'Conditions on Understanding Language', *Proceedings of the Aristotelian Society*, 97: 41–60.

LEWIS, D. K. (1969), *Convention: A Philosophical Study* (Cambridge, Mass.: Harvard University Press).

McDOWELL, J. (1980), 'Meaning, Communication and Knowledge', in Van Straaten (1980), 117–39.

MATILAL, B. K., and CHAKRABARTI, A., eds. (1994) *Knowing from Words* (Synthese Library Series; Dordrecht: Kluwer).

NIINILUOTO, I., SINTONEN, M., and WOLENSKI, J., eds. (forthcoming), *The Handbook of Epistemology* (Dordrecht: Kluwer).

PEACOCKE, C. A. B. (1999), *Being Known* (Oxford: Clarendon Press).

SCHIFFER, S. (1987), *Remnants of Meaning* (Cambridge, Mass.: MIT Press).

STRAWSON, G. (1994), *Mental Reality* (Cambridge, Mass.: MIT Press).

VAN STRAATEN, Z., ed. (1980), *Philosophical Subjects* (Oxford: Clarendon Press).

WITTGENSTEIN, L. W. (1958), *Philosophical Investigations*, trans. G. E. M. Anscombe, 2nd edn. (Oxford: Blackwell).

# CHAPTER 11

# Truth Conditions and their Recognition

*Alex Barber*

This paper is concerned with the relation between two attractive perspectives on meaning and truth conditions. The first perspective takes the central goal of semantic theorizing to be the explicit statement of individual language users' tacit knowledge of the clauses of a semantic theory.[1] The second takes meaning to be inherited from the intentions that give rise to utterances.[2] I hold that the two perspectives need each other more than is often acknowledged, for reasons that have not been recognized, and in a way that has consequences for both. Semantic knowledge is possible only if we have semantic intentions of a surprisingly strong kind, and these semantic intentions can be formed only by an agent with the appropriate semantic knowledge.

Semantic knowledge is instrumental in guiding us towards the produc-

Thanks to Stephen Barker, Ben Caplan, David Davies, Dominic Gregory, Rosanna Keefe, Stephen Laurence, Betty-Ann Muir, Stephen Schiffer, audiences at the Open University, McGill University, and the University of Sheffield Epistemology of Language conference, and Jenny Saul in particular for her commentary on that occasion.

[1] This is the 'psychologized Davidson'/'extensionalized Chomsky' perspective referred to in the Introduction to this volume, p. 14. See Larson and Segal (1995).

[2] See Grice (1989) and Searle (1969; 1979). Others who have examined and developed their work include Avramides (1989), Bach (1994), Bach and Harnish (1979), Récanati (1987), and Schiffer (1972; 1982). As will become evident, I am attracted to the intention-based account of utterance meaning, but not to its standard partner, convention-based semantics (Lewis 1975). One aspiration of this paper is to show how intention-based accounts of utterance meaning need make no appeal to external conventions, since the meaning of expressions can be treated as an abstraction from the utterer's semantic knowledge.

tion of appropriate utterances, as well as in enabling us to understand the utterances of others successfully. Semantic knowledge can play this dual role only if it is suitably objective. Such objectivity requires that *utterances have their truth conditions constitutively determined by the intentions with which they are performed*. (The argument for this, summarized in Section 1, is developed at greater length in Barber 2001.)

But conversely, semantic intentions of this kind are possible only if we have semantic knowledge. Human psychology is such that an intention cannot even be formed unless the agent expects that the resulting action will yield the intended outcome. Without semantic knowledge, the expectations that normally allow the relevant semantic intentions to be formed would be unsustainable.

The tricky part of all this is coming up with an acceptable statement of the constitutive relation holding between the truth condition of an utterance and the intention of its performer. That is my main concern in this paper. But the picture that results of the connection between semantic knowledge and semantic intentions is attractively simple. On the production side, semantic knowledge will typically inform the intention and so indirectly shape the truth condition of the resulting utterance. On the interpretation side, semantic knowledge will typically be needed for recognition of the content of the intention from which the truth condition of the utterance is inherited.

In Section 1 I elaborate on the general prospects and motivations for an intention-based account of the truth conditions of utterances. The rest of the paper is given over to providing one. I reject an account implied by Grice's work on meaning (Section 2). This account is incompatible with the phenomenon of *anti-lying*: performing a true utterance with the intention that one's audience believe it to be false. I opt for the simpler proposal according to which an utterance has some particular truth condition just in case it is performed with the intention that its intended audience recognize it as having that truth condition.

This proposal is elucidated in Section 3 and defended in Sections 4–5. Considerable delicacy is called for in the interpretation of 'recognition'. Moreover, since truth conditions are extensional and intentions intensional, this statement of the view requires qualification. On top of this, methodological attention is needed to see off the charge of analytical circularity (with the analysans containing the analysandum). And finally, I reject the view that the truth conditions of utterances are in any interesting sense inherited from the semantics of expressions, where these can float free of the psychological states of particular utterers.

## 1 Utterances: Actions with Truth Conditions

Utterances are actions with a unique and interesting feature: they are, some at least, true. An action is performed truly when it has a truth condition that is met. But what is responsible for an action's having the truth condition it does (if it does)?

A common view is that the complex expressions appearing in utterances have semantics, which utterances inherit. On most versions of this view the agent's intentions will play at most an important supporting role in the determination of the truth condition of the utterance. Perhaps it will be allowed that specifically indexical or conventionally ambiguous expressions can be assigned a semantic value only by appealing to the intentions of the utterer; and perhaps the utterer must intend the expression to belong to a particular (meaningful) language for the utterance to have a truth condition at all. Griceans may seem to go further in treating ('timeless') expression meaning as somehow derivative from a more basic, intention-ally determined meaning. But what Grice and others fail to provide is an acceptable account of the determination of *truth conditions* by intentions, focusing instead on what is often called *speaker's meaning* and at other times the *total signification* of an utterance, incorporating any implicature.

Reluctance to award a more central and direct role in the determination of truth conditions to the intentions of the utterer often springs from an exaggerated assessment of the dangers of Humpty-Dumptyism: that what we mean will, implausibly, end up being entirely up to us. A convincing response to this worry has been available for a long time. It has not received the currency it deserves, and so bears repeating.[3]

Humpty was indeed wrong: we cannot use expressions with whatever meaning we wish. But this fact flows easily *from* the view that intentions determine truth conditions. Humpty's wishes are frustrated because it is

---

[3] The argument is found in e.g. Grice (1989); Donnellan (1968) (in reply to Mackay 1968); and Schiffer (1972).

often impossible to satisfy a wish to intend something. Suppose one wished to use 'to curtain' as a verb that is correctly predicated of, and only of, those who laugh daily. In normal circumstances one could not so use it because in normal circumstances one would find it impossible to form the intention to be interpreted in that way. One could not form this intention because, presumably for obvious evolutionary reasons, intention formation requires some expectation of success. (Try forming the intention to leap the English Channel.) And for equally obvious evolutionary reasons, one cannot form expectations merely because one wishes to do so. (Try forming the expectation that there is a human-sized pigeon behind you, taking as the mark of success a willingness to bet that there is a human-sized pigeon behind you.) Fear of being like Humpty, arrogantly presuming to mean what we wish, should not lead us to reject an intention-based account of truth conditions.

A weaker form of the 'Humpty' charge is untouched by this response. Imagine a Humpty who is able to form abnormal communicative intentions because he is ignorant rather than arrogant. Unaware of the peculiarity of the use to which he is putting 'curtain', his utterance would be so severely out of keeping with standard practice that many would wish to disregard his intentions as irrelevant to meaning when set against community-held norms. Having, I hope, seen off the more virulent form of the Humpty-Dumptyism charge, I defer to Section 5 consideration of this 'communitarian' judgement that intentions can be trumped by the norms governing the meaning of expressions *qua* components of a salient social language.

Treating intention as the source of truth conditions calls for the recognition and avoidance of at least two traps. The first turns on the fact that 'is true iff . . .' generates an extensional context, whereas 'intends that . . .' generates an intensional one. A simple biconditional of the form 'An utterance is true iff $p$ just in case it is performed with the intention that . . . $p$ . . .' will for this reason be susceptible to Frege-style counter-examples. This was not a concern for Grice, whose aim was to analyse the intensional 'means that . . .' rather than 'is true iff . . .'. But the danger can be avoided even when the task is to provide an intention-based account of truth conditions or other extensional notions. The details are in Section 4, and depend on the specifics of the account I offer of the relevant intention.

The second trap I have in mind is less obvious. A plausible generalization about actions is that the condition on an action's being a successful $X$-ing must extend beyond its being performed out of an intention to X. This generalization would be violated if we were to characterize the relevant intention exhaustively as, say, the intention that our utterance have some particular truth condition. The account of the relevant intention defended in Sections 3–5 avoids reducing success in acting on the intention to the very mental act of forming the intention.[4]

But why should we want an intention-based account of truth conditions? Neo-Gricean reasons for seeking an intention-based account of meaning are reductionist: reduce the linguistic to the mental (specifically, to intentions), perhaps with the aim of subsequently reducing the mental to the physical.[5] My own reasons spring, not out of any commitment to this reductionist enterprise, but out of a wish to understand the role of semantic knowledge in linguistic practice given the requirement that this knowledge be properly objective.

It is appealing to suppose that our productive and receptive linguistic capacities are underpinned by, and so partially explicable by reference to, semantic knowledge. A number of traditional objections to attributions of semantic knowledge turn on the supposition that such knowledge would need to be unconscious, non-conceptual, inferentially non-promiscuous, and so forth (see the Introduction above, pp. 7–9). I think these objections can be and have been met, but objectivity is a requirement of knowledge that has been less extensively discussed in this context.

Suppose that such knowledge is a form of belief (or, if not belief, then some

---

[4] Stephen Barker spotted a potential if baroque difficulty for my account of the relevant semantic intention (already summarized in the opening section). $A$'s intending that $p$ and $q$ plausibly requires $A$'s intending that $p$. Moreover, if an utterer intends that a designated audience *recognize* that $p$, then this can be taken to imply that the utterer intends it to be the case both that $p$ and that the audience $\varphi$s that $p$ (where $\varphi$-ing is the attitude of recognizing, stripped of its factivity—comparable to judging as opposed to knowing). Combining this with my account of what it is for an utterance to have a particular truth condition, I am committed to holding that an utterer *will* have to intend that the utterance have the particular truth condition it does if ever she is to intend her audience to recognize her action as having that truth condition. It is because of this that I have included the qualification 'exhaustively' in the statement of the principle that needs to be respected (see the preceding sentence in the main text).

[5] See Schiffer (1972). Avramides (1989) and Rumfitt (1995) question any attribution to Grice of such reductionist motives, and they are noticeably absent from Grice (1989).

other state that is, at a minimum, representational).[6] Representational states like that of belief must have correctness conditions, and semantic beliefs should be no exception. Normally, whether the correctness condition of a representational state is satisfied will turn on something other than whether the subject is in that representational state. This is what the objectivity requirement on semantic knowledge amounts to. It turns out that for semantic beliefs to have correctness conditions requires an intention-based account of the truth conditions of utterances.[7]

One could, of course, try to insist that semantic beliefs do not have objective, independent correctness conditions. But this sits uneasily with their apparent utility in facilitating mutual understanding. How could a purely subjective representational state have the leverage needed for us to come to know what others are saying?

A first impulse is to suppose that semantic beliefs are evaluable as correct or incorrect relative to a language. But reflection renders implausible the thought that the semantic beliefs most directly informing the intentions with which an utterance is performed are beliefs about what the rules are of a salient social language; still less could they be beliefs about idiolectal languages. (Idiolectal languages are ill suited because a belief about one's own idiolect would be *ipso facto* correct, making its correctness conditions over-dependent on the fact that it is held. Social languages are no help, but for a different reason. The intentions that give rise to communicative acts are *directly* informed by how we believe these acts will be interpreted; where this belief fails to accord with the dictates of a belief about some social language, a speaker who stuck by these dictates would more resemble a soliloquist than an ordinary speaker.[8]) Semantic beliefs that are not about either social or idiolectal languages are not to be evaluated relative to such entities either.

More plausibly, the semantic beliefs that directly form linguistic intentions

---

[6] If it is belief, then it will be deeply tacit belief. But the argument that follows would go through no matter what kind of cognitive relation it is that one bears to the content of the clauses of semantic theories, so long as states of that kind are representational, and so evaluable as correctly or incorrectly representing. See Rey (this volume) and Barber (2001), § 4, for related discussion of the notion 'representation' in this context.

[7] A less truncated version of the argument that follows is in Barber (2001).

[8] Burge (1975) also calls into question, for this reason, the appeal to conventional languages within the content of communicative intentions.

are beliefs about how projected utterances are likely to be interpreted by the target audience; we need to understand how they could be evaluable as such. The utterer's semantic beliefs represent the potential audience as liable to judge in some way as to the truth condition of the projected utterance. For these latter judgements to have correctness conditions in their own right—and so for the correctness conditions of the original utterer's semantic beliefs to be properly earthed—there must be something it is for the utterance to have a truth condition. But where could this truth condition spring from? Having ruled out the language to which the expressions used belong as the source, assigning a constitutive role in the determination of the truth condition of an utterance to the communicative intentions out of which it is performed is an obvious move.[9] The audience's judgement will be correct just in case it accurately represents some aspect of the content of the utterer's intention; the utterer's semantic belief will be correct just in case it anticipates such judgements accurately.

## 2 Gricean Intention-Based Views and the Problem of Anti-Lying

Granting a need to treat intentions as the constitutive source of the truth conditions of utterances raises the question of what form the relevant intentions could have. A positive answer to this question grows out of recognition of the failure of a different view. This different view is a consequence of a familiar claim about meaning:[10]

[9] Stephen Schiffer put it to me that the source of an utterance's truth condition may be *neither* the intentions of the utterer *nor* the expressions whose meaning can float free of these intentions; rather, it could be the proposition or thought *expressed by* the action that is the primary bearer of a truth condition. This in my view is not really a separate option, just an alternative way of talking. Asking after the source of an utterance's truth condition and asking what makes it the case that it expresses the proposition that it does come to the same thing (subject to certain qualifications to be taken account of in sect. 4, having to do with the non-extensionality of propositions—see n. 29 below). Nothing more than terminological redundancy distinguishes an utterance's expressing the proposition that $p$ from that utterance's being true iff $p$ (again subject to the qualifications).

[10] This formulation is not identical to any Grice himself put forward, but it is similar in its essentials to that found in Grice (1957). Other than Grice (1989), see Schiffer (1972; 1982); Bennett (1976); Loar (1981); and Avramides (1989). Neale (1992) presents an integrated view of the work on intentions, on truth conditions, and on implicature.

Where *A* is an agent and *U* is an utterance performed by *A*, *A* means that *p* by *U* ⇔ *U* is performed with the intention that its intended audience:

(1) come to believe that *p*;
(2) recognize the performer's intention that they come to believe that *p*;
(3) come to believe that *p* *through* recognition of the performer's intention that they come to believe that *p*.

Grice and others have offered modifications to this, for a multiplicity of reasons. Though the resulting versions often constitute genuine improvements, I shall treat this original version as expressive of the basic idea and look at variants only in so far as the improvements they contain bear on the current agenda. Two alterations are clearly called for immediately in this regard. On the left-hand side of the biconditional, in what Grice would call the analysandum, he is talking about what he calls *speaker's* meaning, whereas I am talking about utterances; and he is talking not about truth conditions but about meaning.

Grice would be perfectly happy to treat 'what the speaker means (in performing the utterance)' as longhand for 'what the utterance means'.[11] The label is not important, so long as the species of meaning being characterized is rooted in the intentions that give rise to an action rather than tied constitutively to the independent meaning of the expression used in that action. Whether such meaning is predicated of the agent of the action *qua* agent of the action ('speaker meaning'), of the expression as it occurs in the context of the action ('occurrent-expression meaning'), or of the action itself ('utterance meaning') is of little consequence. Of all these options, predicating it of the action strikes me as the most straightforward.[12]

On the other hand, Grice would certainly quarrel with any attempt to treat the *truth condition* of an utterance (as opposed to the utterer's meaning) as governed by intentions. For him truth conditions are tied instead to the 'timeless' significance of expressions. This is something that can come apart from the total signification of the utterance, most impressively when

---

[11] Grice does indeed talk this way occasionally, e.g. (1957), 381 (p. 217 in the 1989 reprint).

[12] In particular, there is no need to add the otherwise necessary qualifications '*qua* agent of the action' for speaker's meaning or 'as it occurs in the context of the action' for occurrent-expression meaning.

implicature carries total signification beyond anything extractable from expression meaning.[13]

Still, suppose we were to co-opt Grice's analysis for our own purposes. Doing so would give us:

An action $U$ is true-iff-$p \Leftrightarrow U$ is performed with the intention that its intended audience:

(1) come to believe that $p$;
(2) recognize the performer's intention that they come to believe that $p$;
(3) come to believe that $p$ *out of* a recognition of the performer's intention that they come to believe that $p$.

Although Grice quite rightly never proposed anything like this biconditional, he would seem to be committed to its holding for utterances that meet three conditions: first, there is no implicature to force a discrepancy between what is said and the total signification; second, there is no deviance from ordinary usage to force a discrepancy between what is said and the total signification; and third, any Fregean slippage between truth condition and what is said is disregarded. After all, these seem to be the only three factors that stand in the way of expecting truth conditions to chime in harmony with total signification (or utterer's meaning).[14]

An examination of this proposal is a good place to start our enquiry. If the biconditional holds whenever implicature, semantic deviance, and Fregean considerations are held in abeyance, we shall have made interesting progress. If it fails for any such case, we may be able to garner clues as to how to conceive of the relevant intentions; we may also have found a shortcoming of Grice's overall position.

As it happens, the biconditional can fail, for reasons having nothing to do with implicature, unorthodox use of language, or semantic opacity. The problem resides in the first clause on the right-hand side. Cases of what I call *anti-lying* show that if an intention-based account of the truth conditions of utterances is to succeed, this first clause must go. That the first clause is too strong is not in itself a new claim; but the type of example used to

[13] Grice, 'Logic and Conversation' (1989: 22–40).

[14] The view that what is said and implicature exhaust speaker meaning is attributed to Grice by Stephen Neale (1992).

show it is, and the replies Griceans have offered in the face of other alleged counter-examples are implausible as a way of dealing with anti-lying.

Lying is performing an action you believe to be false, typically with a view to getting one's intended audience to believe the falsehood expressed. Anti-lying is saying something you believe to be true with a view to getting one's intended audience to disbelieve that truth. Here is a case of anti-lying:

> At 3 o'clock this morning, Lillian was helping herself to the contents of the safe in the bank on the corner. She is now being interviewed by a police officer. This police officer falsely suspects not only that Lillian is innocent, but also that she is being blackmailed into acting as a patsy by a vicious local criminal outfit. Lillian is aware of the officer's suspicion and is keen to exploit it. So when the officer asks Lillian where she was last night, Lillian replies: 'I was in the bank on the corner.'

(To forestall the objection that there is a kind of implicature going on, let me stress that Lillian is not deploying insinuation, and is wary of being too obvious in the execution of her strategy of deception.) Lillian's utterance has a truth condition that is met just in case she was in the bank last night, so in fact her utterance is true. But the first component of the complex intention in the 'Gricean' biconditional is not met: Lillian does not wish her audience to believe that what she said is true. That biconditional is therefore too strong.

Other cases have been put forward to demonstrate that the first clause is unnecessary, and modifications have been offered in response. These modifications are mostly of no help with anti-lying. Of some relevance are cases of *counter-suggestion* ('reverse psychology') and of *confession*, discussed by Grice himself and by Stephen Schiffer.[15] A typical example of counter-suggestion is where a parent, in speaking to a recalcitrant teenager, says exactly the opposite of what it is hoped the teenager will believe or do. In a case of confession the utterance expresses a proposition that may already be believed by the audience. Anti-lying seems to be what results if the counter-suggested proposition is the contrary of a truth, or if it is intended that the confession be disbelieved. The most promising response prompted by these cases is due to Schiffer.

[15] Grice (1989), 107; Schiffer (1972), 33.

He suggests we insert a harmless extra clause at a suitable point in the right-hand side of the biconditional (underlined), thus:[16]

An action $U$ is true-iff-$p \Leftrightarrow U$ is performed with the intention that the intended audience believe that $U$ is performed with the intention that the intended audience

(1) come to believe that $p$;
(2) recognize the performer's intention that they come to believe that $p$;
(3) come to believe that $p$ out of a recognition of the performer's intention that they come to believe that $p$.

This emendation deals nicely with the Lillian case of anti-lying. Our intuition is that Lillian's utterance is true iff Lillian was in the bank last night; with Schiffer's clause in place, all the alleged conditions for this being the case are met. Moreover, Schiffer seems to be right that the insertion is harmless in so far as it does not create an opportunity for new and unforeseen counter-examples of a standard (i.e. not of an anti-lying) sort.

There are, however, *other cases of anti-lying* available to show that Schiffer's amendment fails to correct the problem they pose. We can adapt the Lillian case to this end. The new scenario is complex, reflecting the complexity of the proposal it is meant to undermine:

As before, Lillian is trying to get the police officer to believe, falsely, that she, Lillian, was not in the bank. But her strategy is more complex. Without insinuation, she utters 'I was in the bank'. In so doing she intends the officer to think that she is attempting to use the strategy deployed in the old scenario (that is, the strategy of exploiting the officer's prior suspicion that Lillian is being blackmailed). The officer is then expected by Lillian to reason still further as follows: *The only way Lillian could know about my suspicion is if she overheard something I said in a nightclub at 3 o'clock this morning (seriously violating her parole conditions, which must be why she is not simply using the truth as an alibi). In which case, she could not have been in the bank.*

Although we would still describe Lillian's utterance as true iff Lillian was

[16] Schiffer (1972), 72. Schiffer's many other amendments to the basic biconditional have been left out here, not because they are not genuine improvements but because they are not relevant in this context.

in the bank, Lillian is intending the officer to think that the utterance was intended to bring about the belief, not that Lillian was in the bank, but that she was not. This is contrary to the supposed necessity of the first clause of the biconditional, even allowing for Schiffer's amendment.

## 3 A Non-Gricean Intention-Based View

The phenomenon of anti-lying calls out for the following intention-based view of the truth conditions of utterances:[17]

> An action U is true-iff-$p$ ⇔ U is performed with the intention that its intended audience recognize it as true-iff-$p$.

This gets the truth condition right for Lillian's utterance, in both the original and the modified scenarios. In both circumstances, Lillian is intending the police officer to treat her utterance as true iff she was in the bank the night before; and our intuitions tell us that these are the conditions under which Lillian's utterance would be true.

A further advantage is simplicity. Even after a qualification needed to cope with Fregean cases, this biconditional lacks the complexity of traditional Gricean theories.[18] Still, it is worth peering at some of the subtleties behind its simple façade before turning to objections in the next section.

Donald Davidson has proposed the following as a necessary condition:[19]

---

[17] Many others have recognized the value of abandoning perlocutionary effects as the object of the content-determining intention, including but not only Searle (1969); Dummett (1989), 300; Bach and Harnish (1979); Récanati (1987); Davidson (1992); and Bach (1994). Grice (1989), 351–2 (the 'Retrospective Epilogue'), is unpersuaded.

[18] Strawson (1964); Ziff (1967); Schiffer (1972); Grice (1989); Avramides (1989; 1995); Neale (1992).

[19] See Davidson (1990), sect. III; and (1986)—his definition of 'first meaning'. Davidson (1992), 258, comes closest to what I have here: 'an interpreter (correctly) interprets an utterance of a speaker only if he knows that the speaker intends the interpreter to assign a certain truth condition to his (the speaker's) utterance'. I have taken this to imply the conditional in the main text, charitably eliminating the error of assuming that only an intended audience can successfully interpret an utterance. Also, Davidson is explicitly non-committal (p. 258) about what is meant by 'assigning truth conditions'. So I have felt free to think of it for now as 'judging to be true iff . . .'. The discussion of judgement vs. recognition, below, can be treated as an attempt to spell out what assignation is.

An action $U$ is true-iff-$p$ $\Rightarrow$ $U$ is performed with the intention that its intended audience judge it to be true-iff-$p$.

Though I am indebted to Davidson's discussion, there are two important differences between his conditional and my biconditional: his is merely a conditional; and he talks of the intended audience as *judging* rather than as *recognizing* the action to be true-iff-$p$. Take these differences in turn.

Davidson claims that his characterization of the relevant intention cannot be advanced as a sufficient condition. At the very least, he says, the utterer must also intend (i) that her intended audience judge her to have the first intention, and (ii) that it is on the basis of this latter judgement that the audience forms its judgement about the truth condition of the utterance.[20] In other words, he claims that if sufficiency is the goal, we should perhaps adopt Grice's original version (or one of its more complex descendants), albeit with talk of an audience's believing 'that $p$' displaced throughout by talk of their judging 'that the utterance is true-iff-$p$'.

But conditions (i) and (ii) will be met whenever the original condition is in operation, so they are not extra conditions at all. The argument to this effect for condition (i) runs as follows (the argument for (ii) is omitted but follows a similar pattern):

*Premise 1*: In general, you can form the intention to perform an action (e.g. leaping the English Channel) only if you have some expectation of success.

*Subconclusion 1*: You can form the intention to perform an action that will be judged by your intended audience to be true-iff-$p$ only if you have some expectation that it will indeed do so. (*Instance of P1*)

*Premise 2*: You expect your intended audience to appreciate the truth of Davidson's conditional.

*Subconclusion 2*: You expect that your intended audience will judge your action to be true-iff-$p$ only if it also judges you to have acted with the intention that it judge your action to be true-iff-$p$. (*From P2*)

*Conclusion*: You can form the intention to perform an action that will be judged by an intended audience to be true-iff-$p$ only

[20] Davidson (1992), 258 n. 5, and the text it accompanies.

if you expect to be judged by your intended audience to
have acted with the intention that it judge your action
to be true-iff-*p*. (*From subconclusions*)[21]

The conclusion is not *quite* what I am after, since expecting something to
be an effect of one's actions could be argued not to entail one's intending
that effect. Appeals to the doctrine of double effect in debates over the
conditions under which abortion is morally permissible presuppose just
such a distinction, contentiously so in that context.[22] But it is hard to
imagine what objection or counter-example could trade on the possibility
of a discrepancy. So, for all that Davidson has said, his condition may be
taken to be sufficient and not merely necessary.

My biconditional also differs from Davidson's conditional in that where he
has 'judges that' I have 'recognizes that'. The significance of this difference
is complex but important. Consider three versions of the biconditional:
version one with 'judges that', version two with 'judges correctly that',
and version three with 'recognizes that'. Someone could insist that the
replacement of 'judges' by 'recognizes' is a trivial one that brings nothing extra. After all, version one on its own entails version two,[23] and

---

[21] I have left implicit the limited deductive closure among your expectations that this
argument presupposes.

[22] The doctrine holds that, given an act $A$ (removing foetus from Fallopian tube) with
good effect $E_1$ (woman lives) and bad effect $E_2$ (pain to foetus), where $E_1$'s goodness is
proportionally greater than $E_2$'s badness, $A$ is morally permissible if $E_2$ is not intended. For
this decree to carry any practical benefit for pregnant women—and it is debatable that
it ever could—it must be possible not to intend the foreseeable consequences of one's
actions.

[23] (In the following proof of this claim, subscripts next to arrows are merely indices
to make the proof easier to read through.) Assume that any action $U$ is true-iff-$p \Leftrightarrow_x$
$U$ is performed with the intention that its intended audience judge it to be true-iff-$p$.
Now show that any action $U$ is true-iff-$p \Leftrightarrow_y U$ is performed with the intention that its
intended audience correctly judge it to be true-iff-$p$. For $\Leftarrow_y$, assume that some arbitrary
$U$ is performed by $S$ with the intention that $H$ correctly judge it to be true-iff-$p$. It follows
trivially that $U$ is performed with the intention that $H$ judge it to be true-iff-$p$, since to
judge correctly is to judge. Given our assumption of $\Leftarrow_x$, we get what is needed, that $U$
is true-iff-$p$. For $\Rightarrow_y$, assume that some arbitrary $U$ is true-iff-$p$. By $\Rightarrow_x$, this means $U$ is
performed with the intention that $H$ judge it to be true-iff-$p$. To establish from this that
$U$ is performed with the intention that $H$ *correctly* judge it to be true-iff-$p$, it is enough to
establish that the identity of the success conditions of these two intentions are manifest

version three could be held to differ at most locutionally from version two.

But recognition must differ from judgement, since version one fails in the sufficiency direction, though not for Davidson's reasons. Replacing 'judges' with 'recognizes' must bring something to the table. But what? The agenda for the rest of the section is, first, to outline the problem case for version one; and second, to draw appropriate morals concerning what more there must be to recognition over and above judgement. 'Recognition' (as it appears in version three) must be regarded as judgement *of a certain kind.*

The counter-example to version one is a variant of a scenario envisaged by Christopher Peacocke.[24] Prior to hearing a monologue in a personal audience with Brezhnev, you, who are unversed in Russian, are informed in English by his assistant that in the first sentence of Brezhnev's speech he will say that production doubled in 1973. Brezhnev then gives his speech, knowing perfectly well that you have no familiarity with Russian. He cannot be bothered writing out a real script so mumbles some (to you Russian-sounding) gobbledegook. It seems wrong to view Brezhnev's utterance as true iff production doubled in 1973; yet his utterance manages to satisfy the requirements of the *judges* version of the biconditional. For Brezhnev intends his utterance to be judged by its intended audience—you—as true iff production doubled in 1973.

What must recognition be, over and above judgement, if this is not to count as a counter-example to version three, the version I favour?

Clearly the gobbledegookishness of Brezhnev's utterance is a component

to $S$, i.e. to establish that $S$ can see that: $H$ judges $U$ to be true-iff-$p \Leftrightarrow_z H$ correctly judges $U$ to be true-iff-$p$. We can reason to $\Leftrightarrow_z$, without appealing to anything opaque to $S$, as follows. $\Leftarrow_z$ is trivial. For $\Rightarrow_z$, assume that $H$ judges $U$ to be true-iff-$p$. By $\Rightarrow$ x, $H$ judges that $U$ is performed with the intention that its intended audience (not necessarily known by $H$ to be $H$) judge $U$ to be true-iff-$p$. But this judgement of $H$'s is correct, since we have already established that $U$ is performed with the intention that $H$ (the intended audience, it so happens) judge it to be true-iff-$p$. And if $H$ is correctly judging that $U$ is performed with the intention that its intended audience judge $U$ to be true-iff-$p$, then by $\Leftarrow_x$, $H$ is correctly judging that $U$ is true-iff-$p$.

[24] Peacocke (1976: 170). Peacocke uses the example to argue against the claim that knowledge of the meaning of an utterance is insufficient for understanding it. The gap between the notion of understanding and the issue I am concerned with can be bridged by treating understanding as equivalent to the recognition of truth conditions. See Schiffer, above, p. 311, and Fricker, above, p. 332, for related discussion.

of the problem. Regular cases of true utterance involve proper sentences. Equally troubling is the unusual route by which he expects his audience to come to make the judgement. These two aspects of the example can be neutralized by equating recognition with coming to know the truth condition *through exploitation of your semantic knowledge*. Peacocke himself favours this view, insisting that understanding, tantamount to what I am calling recognition of truth conditions, must be *articulated*, i.e. must come about as the result of decomposition of the expression uttered into its component expressions followed by the exploitation of semantic knowledge.

This suggestion is almost right but is too strong as it stands. It is possible to perform actions with truth conditions without intending that one's audience exploit prior semantic knowledge when figuring out those truth conditions. Consider Joss, a Cumbrian apple trader. He is unaware that his present audience is unfamiliar with his Cumbrian dialect. He projects three red apples onto his presentation screen before displacing them with four green ones as he utters the sentence:

Tethera red gowks sell fer muur thun methera green gowks.

He expects his audience to treat his utterance as true iff three red apples sell for more than four green apples. They do in fact figure out his intention, though it was never a part of his plan that they should have to rely on contextual cues. After later on discovering both his error and its unimportance, Joss reasons that, since the first audience figured out how he intended to be interpreted, the second would do the same. He calculates that the authenticity of his dialect will generate increased sales without jeopardizing comprehension, and performs the same action sequence before the audience in the next town on his circuit. He is primed for their ignorance but this does not seem to matter. It seems to me that Joss's second utterance is true iff his first is, since a fuller appreciation of the audience's situation does not alter the truth condition of the respective utterances; and his first is true iff three red apples sell for more than four green apples. All this is consistent with the biconditional that an utterance is true-iff-$p$ just in case it is performed with the intention that its intended audience recognize it as true-iff-$p$. But the cost of maintaining this consistency is that recognition not be restricted to correct judgement that is based on *prior* semantic knowledge.

So mere judgement is insufficient, and exploitation of prior semantic knowledge is too strong. It is tempting at this point to suppose that the extra element distinguishing recognition from mere judgement is veridicality. Why not collapse version three of the biconditional into version two and say that what the correctness of a judgement about truth conditions turns on *is an independent fact about a salient social language*—Russian, for example, or Cumbrian? By this measure, Brezhnev's utterance is ruled out as lacking a truth condition and Joss's are ruled in, as desired.[25]

Against this, suppose Joss reads about the subliminal importance to sales of the letter X. He switches from 'tethera' and 'methera' to the new words 'texxa' and 'mexxa' without this affecting the tendency of his audience to interpret him as he intends. The truth condition of his utterance seems to me to be as before. This may be because I am in the grip of a picture, but I have already promised to say more about independent expression meaning in Section 5. For now, I want only to show that it is possible to reach an adequate notion of recognition that avoids following this communitarian path.

To count as recognition, the intended audience's judgement about the utterance must *culminate* in an articulated assignment of significance to the components of, as well as to the whole of, the utterance. They must discern the involvement in the utterance of a syntactic structure, and arrive at *or impose* an interpretation on the utterance that reflects this structure. This makes recognition more than mere judgement, more even than correct judgement, and so it rules out Brezhnev's utterance. But recognition does not have to call on prior semantic knowledge. Like Joss's original apple-purchasing audience, one can impose an articulated interpretation on an utterance without necessarily exploiting a knowledge base possessed prior to bearing witness to that utterance. In case use of the term 'recognition' seems inappropriate here, remember that visual recognition can involve the imposition of a plausible interpretation on a perceived object: knowing that you are eyeing a duck can play a critical role in your recognizing it as such.

---

[25] Searle's response (1969: ch. 2; 1986: opening pages) to his example of an American soldier captured in Italy is to require not only that the interpretation be based on antecedently known rules, but also that these rules be public rules or conventions.

## 4 Objections to This Non-Gricean Intention-Based View

The four objections I consider are, first, that truth conditions are extensional whereas intentions are intensional, leaving the biconditional open to refutation through Fregean counter-example; second, that the biconditional I have offered is circular since it uses the term it is trying to define; third, that the split-audience phenomenon is inconsistent with the biconditional; and fourth (deferred to Section 5), that expression meaning can override the intentions of the utterer in determining the truth condition of an utterance.

I choose to focus on these objections because they are peculiar to the current proposal. Other potential objections have been discussed extensively, more or less satisfactorily, elsewhere. These include objections springing out of the apparent fact that utterances are often performed either with no intended audience, or with an immediate audience that the utterer has no expectation will interpret in accordance with what we would intuitively deem to be the truth condition of the utterance (such as a dog). Such objections call for imaginative but not unrealistic interpretations of 'intended audience': the intended audience could be known under some description ('the person I imagine will pick up this bottle from a beach'); it could be the subject herself or posterity (in diary-writing or soliloquy), or a fantasy construct (a linguistically gifted dog).[26] A second set of objections takes issue with the assumption that intentions of this complexity could be processed in real time.[27] As it happens, the intentions invoked by the non-Gricean biconditional are relatively anodyne compared with the best available Gricean or Lewisean theories. But this aside, the debate over the psychological reality of intentions will more or less mimic that concerning the psychological reality of attributions of grammatical knowledge (see the Introduction and opening papers of this volume).

### 4.1 The intensionality of intentions

$\ulcorner p \urcorner$ on the right-hand side of the biconditional always occurs within an extensional context; on the left-hand side it falls within an intensional

---

[26] For more discussion see Grice (1989), 112–16, and Schiffer (1972), § 3.4.

[27] For discussion of this and related objections see Burge (1975) and Laurence (1996), both on Lewis (1975), and Schiffer (1987), ch. 9.

context. This creates space for counter-examples such as the following. Lois Lane utters the sentence 'Superman is gorgeous'. This utterance is true iff Clark Kent is gorgeous, yet it was no part of Lois's intention that her utterance be interpreted as having that truth condition. This does not challenge the sufficiency of the biconditional, but it does challenge its necessity. In fact it is a challenge to the necessity of any intention-based account of either truth conditions, including Davidson's condition discussed earlier, or reference.[28]

We can cope with this by noticing that Lois clearly does have *an* intention of the relevant form, namely the intention that her intended audience interpret her utterance as being true iff Superman is gorgeous. And Clark Kent *is* gorgeous just in case Superman is gorgeous. From this, we can generalize to give a modified version of the biconditional, in which $\ulcorner p \urcorner$ occurs extensionally on both left and right, yet where the intensionality of 'intends' and 'recognizes as' is allowed for:

An action U is true-iff-$p$ $\Leftrightarrow$ $\exists q$ [(U is performed with the intention that its intended audience recognize it as true-iff-$q$) & ($q$ iff $p$)]

('$\exists$' is a substitutionally interpreted existential quantifier ranging over sentences in the metalanguage, or as an objectual quantifier if quantification over propositions is acceptable. 'Iff' can be read at any strength at all, so long as it is read at the same strength on both occurrences.[29])

As a matter of interest, this modified biconditional is naturally viewed as having two components. One component is our original biconditional, altered to begin thus: 'An action U is a saying-that-$p$ $\Leftrightarrow$ . . .'. The truth conditions of those actions that have truth conditions would be systematically related to what they say, as follows:

An action U is true-iff-$p$ $\Leftrightarrow$ $\exists q$ ((U is a saying-that-$q$) & ($q$ iff $p$))

Taken together, these two components generate the modified biconditional of the previous paragraph.

[28] See Searle (1969; 1986) for a discussion of reference and intention.

[29] Dominic Gregory pressed me on this matter, and suggested the solution adopted here. The use of a substitutional existential quantifier in a similar context can be found in Wright (1992), 31. Stephen Laurence noticed that 'iff' can be read at one's strength of choice. If it is read strongly enough, then having the same truth condition amounts to the same as expressing the same proposition. See n. 9 above.

### 4.2 Circularity

The biconditional, which is supposed to be telling us what constitutively determines the truth condition of an utterance (if it has a truth condition), exploits in its right-hand side the notion of an utterance's having that truth condition. The analysandum appears in the analysans, making the definition useless. As Grice puts it (1989: 352), 'Circularity seems to be blatantly abroad.'

This would perhaps be objectionable if the biconditional were being offered as an exhaustive and reductive characterization of the concept expressed by the phrase on the left-hand side of the 'iff'.[30] But the use of the same expression twice over is compatible with my slightly more modest ambition, which is to isolate a core component of semantic metatheory, one that is both substantial and true. Two analogies can bring out the fact that using the term one is interested in on both sides of a biconditional is compatible with this ambition.

First, in the formulaic expression of the claim that the total energy before an event is equal to the total energy after that event, the fact that the letter $e$ occurs on each side of '$=$' would not in itself bar this claim from serving as a core component in a theory of energy.

Second, the response-dependency theory of the colour red contains the term 'red' on the right-hand side:

An object is red $\Leftrightarrow$ it seems red to normal-sighted people in normal circumstances.

One noteworthy feature of this second analogy is that, even if it is true and substantial, this claim fails to distinguish red from the other colours. There would be many other acceptable substitution instances of the response-dependency schema:

An object is $C \Leftrightarrow$ it seems $C$ to normal-sighted people in normal circumstances.

---

[30] Even then, Lloyd Humberstone (1997) argues that there is no objectionable circularity if the occurrence in the definiens is embedded within intentional operators, so long as they are not factive operators (and depending what the definition is for). Though 'recognition' as it is used here is factive, 'intention' is not. Keefe (2002) offers a helpful discussion of acceptable circularity in analysis.

The problem here is not that instances of this schema are circular. On the contrary, the second may well capture an important truth about what it is to be a colour and the first an important *part* of a theory of red. The point, rather, is just that the claim about red would benefit from supplementation with a statement of what distinguishes the colours from one another. This is noteworthy because exactly the same is true of the present claim about the truth conditions of utterances: it fails to discriminate truth conditions from the conditions on other illocutionary notions.

In *Speech Acts*, John Searle claims that Grice mistakenly treats meaning-bestowing intentions as intentions to bring about perlocutionary effects. The relevant intentions are in fact to bring about illocutionary effects, and acts performed with this intention are illocutionary acts. An illocutionary effect is an effect that is characteristic of the successful execution of an il-locutionary act; an illocutionary act is an act that is successfully performed when, and only when, a target audience recognizes the performer's inten-tion to perform an action of that type. In other words, any action $U$ is illocutionary if there is some reading of 'ℵ(. . .)' under which:

> $U$ is ℵ(. . .) $\Leftrightarrow$ $U$ is performed with the intention that its intended audience recognize it as ℵ(. . .).

The performance of an action that is true-iff-$p$ is, on the account I am advocating, an illocutionary act in this sense.[31] What is now apparent is how little we yet know about what *kind* of illocutionary act it is. There are many correct substitution instances of the schema, just as there are many response-dependent colours. What distinguishes the result of replacing 'ℵ(. . .)' with 'true-iff-. . .' from the result of replacing it with a term picking out some quite distinct type of illocutionary act—for example, 'a request to bring it about that . . .'? Or 'refers to . . .'? Or even 'false-iff-. . .'?[32]

This lacuna cannot really be described as circularity or vacuity. But it

[31] Searle (1969; 1979; 1986). Unfortunately, Searle has little systematic discussion of the truth conditions of utterances, though he does talk of reference, predication, and assertion. His 'essential condition' for assertion, the feature that one would naturally look to in the present context, is convincingly criticized by William Alston (1991). And as noted earlier, he does not seem to spot the problem of the extensionality of semantic notions like reference when discussing the speech act of referring.

[32] Crispin Wright makes just this point about truth conditions and falsity conditions in the introduction to Wright (1986).

would nevertheless be desirable if the biconditional I favour were comple-
mented with some further substantial claim about truth or truth conditions,
sufficient to distinguish truth conditions from these other semantic notions.
The suggestions below of how this could work are tentative first steps only.

One place not to look for this complement is the disquotational schema:

An utterance of '. . .' is true iff . . .

This expresses a substantial truth about truth only if substitutions into '. . .'
are restricted to pairs of sentences that share a common truth condition.
The disquotational schema itself cannot serve as an independent guide to
what truth conditions are.

One feature of truth that sets it apart from most other semantic properties
is that one ought not to perform those actions that fail to be true. This feature
is ideal as a complement to that which is expressed in the biconditional. No
one would ever claim that one ought to perform false actions. There will
be exceptions to the requirement that one tell only the truth. Some of these
can be put down to the widely acknowledged complexity of moral theory,
as when a person tells a lie in order to prevent a murder. Such exceptions
do not undermine the appeal to moral obligation as a way of distinguishing
truth from falsity, though they do perhaps call for *ceteris paribus* clauses.[33]

More demanding than moral complexity are those cases where a message
is conveyed without being stated explicitly. If the highest praise in a letter of
reference for an outstandingly gifted candidate for a philosophy job were

He has excellent handwriting,

someone would have done wrong. This shows that further work is needed to
distinguish implicating that *p*, also an illocutionary notion, from being true
iff *p*—mostly likely by fixing on a plausible refinement of the broad claim that
truth conditionality, unlike implicature, is tied compositionally to syntax.
In this exploratory paper I shall not attempt to integrate this illocutionary

---

[33] David Lewis talks of a convention to be truthful and trusting in a language (1975).
The shortcomings of this way of putting it are that it seems possible and preferable to
think of the principle as being, not truthfulness in a language, but truthfulness *Punkt*. The
biblical commandment was not 'Thou shalt not bear false-in-Hebrew witness'. Moreover,
the notion of a convention brings with it connotations—more than connotations for
Lewis—of arbitrariness, as if there were some alternative convention that would serve
just as well as the convention to speak truthfully.

account of truth conditions with an account of illocutionary notions that are, so to speak, upstream and downstream of truth conditionality (such as referring and implicating, respectively), or to deal with non-indicative utterances.

## 4.3 *Split audiences*

Suppose you utter a sentence with two distinct intended audiences in mind. Perhaps one is at the other end of a telephone line while the other is in the room. The first of these you intend to interpret your utterance as true-iff-$p$, and the second you intend to interpret your utterance as true-iff-$q$. The problem goes deeper than utterance ambiguity. For if $q$ and $p$ differ in truth value, our biconditional would appear to lead to a violation of the law of non-contradiction. Your utterance would be both true and not true.

But there is a questionable assumption implicit in the reasoning: that these cases involve just one action. The logic that leads from the biconditional to the contradiction would be sabotaged if there are in fact two distinct actions / utterances. And in fact this assumption is independently plausible. First, actions can and should be individuated not merely as bodily movements but by reference to their intentions. Second, the phenomenology of split-audience utterances is (I imagine) more like frying an egg at the same time as boiling the kettle (two actions) than killing Lincoln at the same time as pulling a trigger (one action). And finally, the two outcomes are not part of a single causal chain as is the case with ordinary utterances.

# 5 Truth Conditions and Expression Meaning

The final objection to consider turns on the claim that the truth conditions of utterances are inherited from the semantics of the expressions involved in the utterance.

The view that the truth condition of an utterance is tied to the truth condition of the sentence involved in the utterance is not in itself incompatible with the view that intentions determine the truth conditions of utterances. For one thing, there is a rump notion of expression meaning according to which an expression's semantic significance is relativized to the occasion of its utterance and then simply identified with the significance the utterer intends it to be recognized as having in the context of that action. Such a notion could not be used to generate an objection to the biconditional I have been defending.

A notion of expression meaning that is more substantial than this rump notion is needed even on the view that truth conditions are inherited from intentions. To form the intention that one's utterance be interpreted in a particular way, one must have some confidence that this is how it will be interpreted (see the discussion of Humpty in Section 1). This confidence, this expectation that one will be interpreted in a particular way, is bound to turn in some degree on assumptions about how expressions are typically interpreted. These assumptions will for the most part need to be correct if communicative intentions are to be pursued successfully. Since communicative intentions frequently are pursued successfully, it is reasonable to treat the assumptions about how expressions are typically interpreted as knowledge. Expression meaning *thought of as a projection or abstraction from this knowledge base* is thus critical to the intention-based account I have been defending. What I wish to resist is only the claim that there is a notion of expression meaning that is determinative of the truth conditions of utterances even to the extent of trumping communicative intention.[34]

We have intuitions that appear to be discordant with an intention-based view, sitting more readily with the view that the truth conditions of utterances are inherited from the community-governed semantics of expressions. Suppose Tanja were to utter 'You have beautiful fingers', intending Marco to recognize the utterance as true iff Marco has beautiful eyes. Our intuition appears to be that the salient social language trumps any intention of the utterer, or at least that some distinction between expression meaning and utterer's meaning is called for. Social language may itself be a construct from the typical intentions of typical members of the linguistic community; the point of the objection is that the truth conditions of particular utterances can float free from the intention of any particular utterer.

I propose to accommodate these awkward intuitions by offering a re-description of their content. Properly identified, the content of the intuition that 'a salient social language trumps the speaker's intention' is that one *ought to avoid* using any but some specified vehicle of expression when performing actions with such-and-such a truth condition.

[34] Laurence's criticisms (1996) of the convention-based theory of Lewis (1975) turn on something very close to the contrast I have in mind here.

The point is peculiarly transparent at the level of names rather than sentences. Marie-Louise moves from Quebec to Wisconsin, where, non-maliciously, everyone at high school calls her 'Mary Lou'. She is not fond of the new name, and when anyone calls her by it she acts as if she has not heard, insisting that (as she puts it) they cannot be referring to her since 'Mary Lou' is not her name. But in reality it is clear to all involved that they *are* referring to her. It is just her *wish* that people desist from using that particular vehicle of expression to do so. She expresses this wish in the—clearly false—claim that they are not referring to her; and she combines this expression of her wish with the coercive practice of acting *as if* they have not referred to her.

A parallel example at the level of sentences concerns President Kennedy's famous utterance of 'Ich bin ein Berliner'. Some maintain that it was true iff Kennedy was a tasty local delicacy (on the grounds that he failed to omit the indefinite article). With persuasion, most can be won round to the thought that his utterance was in fact true just in case he was a spiritual resident of Berlin, but that he used an *unlicensed vehicle of expression*, a vehicle that it would be proper to use only in the performance of actions that are true iff the utterer is a tasty local delicacy (i.e. never). From the intuition that one *ought not* to perform actions that are true-iff-*p* using sentence *S*, it in no way follows that one *cannot* perform an action that is true-iff-*p* using sentence *S*. One might do so if, for example, one expected one's audience to interpret an utterance of *S* as having that truth condition.

Returning to the earlier example, Tanja's utterance *is* true iff Marco has beautiful eyes. Our intuition that she has used an improper vehicle of expression is mischaracterized in the claim that her utterance is true iff Marco has beautiful fingers. Such an expression of the intuition should be thought of as parallel to Marie-Louise's sulky refusal to answer to the name 'Mary Lou': a kind of sanction against what we deem to be substandard linguistic behaviour.

I have encountered resistance to this reading of the intuition. Some have expressed reluctance to generalize from the name case, my description of which tends to go over quite well, to sentence cases. I have yet to hear a convincing defence of this arbitrary stance, however. Others have suggested that in addition to an intention to be interpreted in a particular way, the expectation that one will be so interpreted must be *reasonable*, not only by the utterer's own standards, which is a given, since intention formation requires some expectation of success, but also by the standards of the intended audience. This alternative strikes me as having some merit. But what is important, ultimately, is not that one makes a choice between it and my own suggestion, but that one understands what if anything turns on the choice.

The second paragraph of this paper is heavily invested in a perspective on language that treats it, like perception or rational inference, as a chapter in our epistemology. Language allows us to come to know things. But like perception or rational inference, language can go wrong. A mono-lingual English speaker may fail to realize the person they are addressing is a monolingual Hungarian speaker, or later on that their own English–Hungarian dictionary has been sabotaged. One can become tongue-tied or catch the hiccups. Lungs can implode mid-sentence. When such factors are absent and an intention to be interpreted in a particular way is acted on successfully, there will be no discrepancy between my own biconditional and the demand that interpretability be reasonable. When things do go wrong, however, we seem to be called on to make a decision on how to classify the action. Which sabotaging factors should count as sufficiently serious to undermine an action's pretensions to having the truth conditions associated with the intention that triggered the action? Imploding lungs seem extremely serious; hiccups less so. What about reasonableness for the intended audience? My claim is that the decision is not all that important, but that on balance we should not impose a reasonableness requirement.

A role model here is the convention in logic of treating an argument as a set of claims, one of which is distinguished as the conclusion. Some arguments, thus conceived, are good; others are so ludicrously deficient that their classification as arguments *at all* strikes many as misguided. The convention has won out over these reservations because the distinction between bad arguments and non-arguments is not an interesting one. What is interesting is the distinction between good arguments and the rest. It is simpler to classify all the rest as arguments than to get bogged down in deciding at what point sets of sentences gain the right to be called (bad) arguments when things go wrong. We can go as low as convenience dictates in our classification of something as an argument so long as we are clear about the factors that enter into something's being a good argument.

It would be just as much a distraction to worry over whether to disqualify an utterance from having the truth condition associated with the intention when, for one reason or other, this intention is not fulfilled. In the long run we are interested in how successful attempts at language use are possible; reasonableness of the interpretative task is bound to play a role in this. But in cases where the audience is entirely deaf and unable to lip-read, or for some other reason unable to interpret as intended, we face a choice:

> Associate the truth conditions of the utterance with the utterer's intention (adding that, of course, success in the pursuit of this intention requires certain other conditions to be met).

Or:

> Associate the truth conditions of the utterance with the utterer's intention, subject to the condition that the expectations informing the intention are reasonable (the audience will be in a position to interpret as predicted, unless they are deaf, in which case it does not matter; the utterer's lungs will not implode mid-sentence, but mild hiccups are okay; etc.).

The decision is unimportant from a perspective that takes in our overall epistemological ambitions. Still, taking the second option seems to generate unnecessary work, equivalent to trying to legislate a point at which a set of sentences becomes good *enough* to be called an argument. Intuitions may ask us to strike a compromise, but these intuitions can knowingly be set to one side, here as in the logic case.

## 6 Conclusion

I have made two claims: that there are theoretical reasons for wanting an intention-based account of utterances' truth conditions to be available; and that an intention-based account of utterances' truth conditions is available.

The first claim arises out of the fact that semantic knowledge, pivotal in everyday productive and interpretative practice, is like any representational state in that its content needs to have independent correctness conditions. The only way of understanding how this is possible requires that utterances inherit their truth conditions from the intentions of the utterer.

Showing *how* utterances inherit their truth conditions from the intentions of the utterer demands a plausible description of the form of the relevant intention. Using a slightly attenuated notion of recognition, I have sought to defend one particular account against the charge of circularity, susceptibility to Fregean counter-example, and the supposedly overriding importance to truth conditions of expression meaning.

# REFERENCES

ALSTON, W. (1991), 'Searle on Illocutionary Acts', in Lepore and Van Gulick (1991), 57–80.

AVRAMIDES, A. (1989), *Meaning and Mind: An Examination of a Gricean Account of Meaning* (Cambridge, Mass.: MIT Press).

—— (1995), 'Intention and Convention', in Wright and Hale (1995), 60–86.

BACH, K. (1994), *Thought and Reference* (New York: Oxford University Press).

—— and HARNISH, R. M. (1979), *Linguistic Communication and Speech Acts* (Cambridge, Mass.: MIT Press).

BARBER, A. (2001), 'Idiolectal Error', *Mind and Language*, 16: 263–83.

BENNETT, J. (1976), *Linguistic Behaviour* (Cambridge: Cambridge University Press).

BURGE, T. (1975), 'On Knowledge and Convention', *Philosophical Review*, 84: 249–55.

DONNELLAN, K. S. (1968), 'Putting Humpty Dumpty Together Again', *Philosophical Review*, 77: 203–15.

DAVIDSON, D. (1986), 'A Nice Derangement of Epitaphs', in Lepore (1986), 433–46.

—— (1990), 'The Structure and Content of Truth', *Journal of Philosophy*, 87: 279–328.

—— (1992), 'The Second Person', in *Midwest Studies in Philosophy*, 17: 255–67.

DUMMETT, M. A. E. (1981), *Frege: Philosophy of Language*, 2nd edn. (Cambridge, Mass.: Harvard University Press).

EVANS, G., and McDOWELL, J., eds. (1976), *Truth and Meaning* (Oxford: Clarendon Press).

GRANDY, R., and WARNER, R., eds. (1986), *Philosophical Grounds of Rationality: Intentions, Categories, Ends* (Oxford: Oxford University Press).

GRICE H. P. (1957), 'Meaning', *Philosophical Review*, 66: 377–88; repr. in Grice (1989), 213–23.

—— (1989), *Studies in the Way of Words* (Cambridge, Mass.: Harvard University Press).

GUNDERSON, K., ed. (1975), *Language, Mind and Knowledge* (Minneapolis: University of Minnesota Press).

HUMBERSTONE, L. (1997), 'Two Types of Circularity', *Philosophy and Phenomenological Research*, 57: 249–80.

KEEFE, R. (2002), 'When Does Circularity Matter?', *Proceedings of the Aristotelian Society*, 102: 253–70.

LAURENCE, S. (1996), 'A Chomskian Alternative to Convention-Based Semantics', *Mind*, 105: 269–301.

LEPORE, E, ed. (1986), *Truth and Interpretation: Perspectives on the Philosophy of Donald Davidson* (Cambridge: Blackwell).

—— and VAN GULICK, R., eds. (1991), *Searle and his Critics* (Oxford: Blackwell).

LEWIS, D. (1975), 'Language and Languages', in Gunderson (1975), 3–35.

LOAR, B. (1981), *Mind and Meaning* (Cambridge: Cambridge University Press).

MACKAY, A. F. (1968), 'Mr Donnellan and Humpty Dumpty on Referring', *Philosophical Review*, 77: 197–202.

NEALE, S. (1992), 'Paul Grice and the Philosophy of Language', *Linguistics and Philosophy*, 15: 509–59.

PEACOCKE, C. (1976), 'Truth Definitions and Actual Languages', in Evans and McDowell (1976), 162–88.

RÉCANATI, F. (1987), *Meaning and Force: The Pragmatics of Performative Utterances* (Cambridge: Cambridge University Press).

RUMFITT, I. (1995), 'Truth Conditions and Communication', *Mind*, 104: 827–62.

SCHIFFER, S. (1972), *Meaning* (Oxford: Clarendon Press).

—— (1982), 'Intention-Based Semantics', *Notre Dame Journal of Formal Logic*, 43: 119–56.

—— (1987), *Remnants of Meaning* (Cambridge: Mass.: MIT Press).

SEARLE, J. R. (1969), *Speech Acts* (Cambridge: Cambridge University Press).

—— (1979), *Expression and Meaning* (Cambridge: Cambridge University Press).

—— (1986), 'Meaning, Communication, and Representation', in Grandy and Warner (1986), 209–26.

STRAWSON, P. F. (1964), 'Intention and Convention in Speech Acts', *Philosophical Review*, 73: 439–60.

WRIGHT, C. (1986), *Realism, Meaning, and Truth* (Oxford: Oxford University Press).

—— (1992), *Truth and Objectivity* (Cambridge, Mass.: Harvard University Press).

—— and HALE, R., eds. (1995), *A Companion to the Philosophy of Language* (Oxford: Blackwell).

ZIFF, P. (1967), 'On H. P. Grice's Account of Meaning', *Analysis*, 28: 1–8.

# PART THREE

Linguistic Externalism

# CHAPTER 12

# *Externalism, Logical Form, and Linguistic Intentions*

*Peter Ludlow*

## 1 Introduction

Externalism is often characterized as the doctrine that the contents of our mental states are determined at least in part by the external environment. But why should externalists stop with psychological *contents*? Why can the *forms* of those mental states not be sensitive to environmental conditions as well? There is, of course, a standard supposition that even if the contents of our mental states are externally fixed, the forms of our mental states supervene directly on our physical microstructure, but what basis is there for this supposition? More to the point, why should thoroughgoing externalists accept the supposition? Still more, why can the externalist not go one step further and argue that the logical form of our *utterances* is also sensitive to external conditions? In this paper I explore the possibility of being an externalist about logical form in this sense, and I shall argue that the position needs to be taken seriously, and indeed, that it offers some interesting perspectives on at least one long-standing philosophical puzzle. I shall conclude, however, with some potential difficulties for the position.

Can the logical form of an utterance really be tied to properties that are partly external to the speaker? As my initial comments suggest, there are two issues here. First, does it make sense to talk about the form of a mental

An earlier draft of this paper was presented at the Epistemology of Language conference at the University of Sheffield, and to my graduate seminar at Cornell University. I am indebted to members of those audiences and to Brian McLaughlin and Barry Smith for helpful comments and discussion. I am particularly indebted to Alex Barber, Ray Elugardo, and an anonymous referee for comments on the penultimate draft.

state being environmentally determined? Second, does it make sense to talk about the logical form of an *utterance* being tied to the form of a mental state? Let us begin with the second question.

Are the logical forms of our utterances tied to the forms of our mental states? In referring to mental states we are presumably talking specifically about linguistic intentions of some type.[1] (For the time being I shall assume without argument that mental states have forms of their own—I shall return to this issue presently.) There are at least three approaches one can take here. First, one can reject any link whatsoever, in which case our linguistic intentions are causally inert with respect to the logical form of our utterances. If one chooses this path, then the route to externalism about logical form seems almost inevitable. If no fact about the agent in isolation is able to fix the logical form of an utterance, then what else but the environment *could* fix it?[2]

A second possibility moves in the opposite direction. One could maintain that talk about the logical form of an *utterance* is a mistake; we should rather

[1] An anonymous referee points out that we could also argue that the logical form of our utterances is tied to the logical form of the thoughts that we express. This would force us to a position that I discuss below under the heading of 'bald externalism about form'. The position is certainly a possibility, but here I am trying to determine if there is room to be serious about the role of linguistic intentions in fixing logical form *and* to be an externalist about form.

[2] One *could* say that there is no fact of the matter about the logical form, or one could reject the notion of logical form altogether, but this strategy is not open to all externalists. Burge, for example, has been clear in his defence of logical form: 'Radical anti-formalist positions, to the effect that judgments about validity and other semantical features can never be adequately captured by appeal to formal structures, often stem from reaction against the traditional tendency among logicians to underestimate the prevalence of such context-dependent or 'messy' phenomena as indexicality, vagueness, presupposition, implicature, metaphor, irony, malapropism, differences of idiolect or dialect, and so on. There is, however, a gulf between recognizing the complexities that these phenomena force upon theories of language and embracing the anti-formalist position. Numerous validity judgments that are widely shared generalize across arguments (and argument tokens). Many such generalizations parallel the recursive aspects of language mastery. To try to account for such phenomena 'contextually' or piecemeal (or to ignore them) would be to lose the strongest theoretical grip we now have on the semantical—and indeed, the pragmatic—aspects of language use. Worse, it flies in the face of well-established facts about grammar and its relation to logical consequence' (Burge 1986: 205). I propose that we endorse this general view that the notion of logical form cannot be dispensed with—at least for purposes of discussion.

talk about the logical form of an I-language representation (in the sense of Chomsky 1986). In this case, the link between linguistic intention and logical form is very close to being one of identity—or in any case one mediated by an internal interface component, and the link between linguistic intentions and logical form appears well secured.

Thirdly, we might suppose that when we form a linguistic intention we tacitly construct a mental representation of a linguistic form and that this representation or data structure is what determines the logical form of our utterance. In other words, in forming a linguistic intention, one of the things we do is to construct a kind of mental representation that has a logical form, and it is this 'inner' logical form which determines or fixes the logical form of our utterance. *How* is this link secured? In this case we could say that the logical form of the utterance is inherited from the form of the linguistic intention by virtue of its standing in an appropriate causal relation to the intention. Forms could thus be inherited in much the same way that contents are. And why should they not be? It is quite natural to suppose that if forms are environmentally sensitive in the same way that contents are, forms should be inheritable via the same mechanisms that contents are—paradigmatically via causal relations.[3]

One might object that we have jumped the rails at the outset by admitting talk about mental states as having forms—after all, not everyone is smitten with the Language of Thought hypothesis. However, it has to be conceded that some of our thoughts are general and some are singular, and I assume that there is *some* sense in which singular and general propositions have different forms—certainly different structures. If not—if they differ only in content (and I have trouble making sense of this idea)—then the general conclusions reached here still follow. The environmental sensitivity of content would be enough to determine whether one's linguistic intention is to

---

[3] Clearly, more needs to be said here. Just as one needs to explicate how contents can be transmitted causally, one needs eventually to tell some story about how forms can be transmitted by the same sorts of mechanism. While a full exposition would be impossible here, one thing is clear: forms individuated widely may turn out to be more fine-grained than forms that can be brought into spatial correspondence. So, for example, we may want to distinguish form $F_1$ (which an object has if it is a projection of an ellipse from one plane onto another parallel plane) from form $F_2$ (which an object has if it is a projection of a circle from one plane to another plane which lies at a $45°$ angle to the former plane). Whether something has form $F_1$ or $F_2$ will depend on what it is projected from.

express a singular or general proposition, and that in turn would be enough to determine the logical forms of the corresponding utterances. The idea is that the linguistic intention would differ in form depending upon whether the proposition one wishes to express is a singular or a general proposition (it would have a logical form containing a referring expression in the former—singular—case and a denoting expression in the latter—general—case). In turn, the linguistic expression would have the logical form that it does by virtue of its standing in an appropriate causal relation to the linguistic intention.[4]

There may be other ways of thinking about the linkage between linguistic intentions and logical forms, but the above cases cover a lot of ground. On the first approach, where we cut the link altogether, we seem driven immediately to externalism about logical form. On the second approach, talk of the logical form of I-language expressions replaces talk of the logical form of utterances, with the result that there is arguably no gap between linguistic intentions and the logical form of linguistic objects. On the third approach the link is causally mediated. But the latter two approaches both require us to address the question raised earlier: does it make sense to say that the forms of linguistic intentions are environmentally determined?

One natural response would be that it is simply implausible to suppose that the logical forms of these mental representations—these linguistic intentions—are fixed by the external environment. How *could* they be? Are the forms of our mental states not supposed to supervene on our microstructure? Are they not simply data structures in an internal computational system? And while it might make sense to say that *what* those

---

[4] Ray Elugardo notes that this move harbours some Tractarian ideas about the relation between language and the world—in particular, that it suggests the world is itself propositionally structured. I am not sure that this follows, but I am perfectly willing to accept the conclusion if it does follow. Meanwhile, an anonymous referee wonders whether I really want to say that the logical form of the utterance is inherited by standing in a causal relation to the linguistic intention. An alternative idea would be that both the form of the linguistic intention and the form of the utterances are inherited by virtue of their both standing in a causal relation to the same state of affairs. This is possible, but it arguably scuttles any attempt to account for an interesting relation between linguistic intentions and the forms of our utterances. So again, it would seem to force us to bald externalism about form. There is, of course, room to say more about how forms can be transmitted causally, but let me just note here that the problem is no more mysterious and difficult to explain than the issue of how *contents* can be transmitted causally.

data structures are representing will depend upon the environment, it cannot make sense to say that data structures themselves are environmentally sensitive, for this amounts to saying that the syntactic state of a system is environmentally sensitive. Or so goes the objection.

It has to be conceded at a minimum that this is a fairly radical thesis. This is not like the wide computationalism explored in Wilson (1994) and Clark and Chalmers (1998). The kind of wide computationalism they are interested in involves computations that incorporate the environment into the system (e.g. using your fingers or a notepad to help solve a cognitive problem). For them, the part of the computation that takes place intracranially is stable across Twin Earth scenarios. *This* story, alternatively, is one in which the intracranial computations and syntactic states *are* sensitive to Twin Earth scenarios.

The thesis may be radical, but I would suggest that the externalist has good grounds for asserting that the syntactic states of a system can be and often are determined by environmental considerations—even for systems like digital computers and mechanical adding machines.

The basic idea is simple enough: any physical system can be used to instantiate any Turing machine program, provided that it is possible to read the input and output codes. So, for example, to consider an extreme case, a simple rock lying on a desk might be used to perform computations of arbitrary complexity. Suppose that the input consists of my pushing the rock with my finger and the output consists of the final resting place of the rock. Then the syntactic states of the machine (here taken as the system including the table and the rock) supervene on those inputs and outputs and the surface friction and irregularities of the rock and the table. Hypothetically, there could be creatures for whom making the appropriate finger movements and 'reading' the final resting positions of the rock on the table would be simple.

Bontly (1998) has suggested that this standard view—that any physical system can instantiate any computation—is too liberal, but maintains that given certain constraints the general point about the environmental sensitivity of computation will hold. One such constraint would be the function of the physical system, so that in the ordinary course of affairs the rock and table could not possibly serve as a computer, and hence could not instantiate any computer program. Of course, for the creatures that we envisaged earlier, the system *would* instantiate a program. What the externalist might argue is that the external environment determines *whether* a computation is being performed by the system and also fixes the allowable inputs and outputs so that the environment also fixes *which* computation is being performed.[5] In short, whether the rock instantiates a program, and if so which program, will depend upon its embedding conditions. Extending this line of reasoning to the cases that we are interested in, the idea would be that a single physical system might have a syntactically simple representation for a name like 'Socrates' in some environments—by hypothesis those where Socrates existed—and a more complex representation in other environments—those worlds where he did not exist.

If this general position holds (and it seems a natural position for an externalist to adopt in any case), then syntactic states do not supervene exclusively on individualistic properties of the system. It would follow that this holds not just for computers, but for any system that can be ascribed syntactic states. So, for example, if there is a language of thought, then these externalist considerations would extend to the language of thought as well. Ultimately, then, an externalist can argue that the logical form of an utterance is inherited from the form of the corresponding linguistic intention and that the form of the linguistic intention is environmentally sensitive (as it is an environmentally sensitive syntactic state). The logical form of the utterance will therefore be environmentally sensitive.

## 2 A Possible Application

If we adopt externalism about logical form, we find that we are offered some new ways of approaching at least one long-standing philosophical puzzle. Since Russell (1905) the descriptive theory of names has offered a tantalizing if (to date) elusive solution to the problem of empty (non-referring) names. If empty names can be taken to be denoting expressions—expressions standing proxy for descriptions (for example, if 'Santa Claus' can be taken as a proxy for 'The fat jolly elf who lives at the North Pole etc. etc.'[6])—then we have a natural account of how a sentence like 'Santa Claus delivered the toys'

---

[5] For some criticism of externalist theories of computation, see Egan (1992).

[6] Here I am ignoring more sophisticated versions of the descriptive theory of names, such as that in Searle (1958). Nothing I say here turns on the choice between a theory like

can be meaningful (and false) even though 'Santa Claus' does not refer.[7] Unfortunately, there appear to be fatal problems for descriptive theories of names as a general thesis about names. In particular, Kripke (1980) has shown that among other limitations the descriptive theory simply cannot account for our intuition that most uses of names rigidly designate.

Kripke's positive proposal, of course, was to say that names are referring expressions. While that proposal works well for most uses of names, it at least appears that it cannot be extended to the analysis of empty names. Barring attempts to treat such names as referring to fictions or to non-existent objects, one is left with the alternative of saying that sentences with empty names fail to express a determinate proposition or that they express some sort of 'gappy' proposition or 'propositional radical'. Such strategies can certainly be carried out, but one wonders if it has to come to this.

One possible way out is to hold that some names are referring expressions and that others are descriptive. That is, one could allow that names like 'Bill Clinton' are referring expressions and names like 'Santa Claus' are descriptive. This would allow us to treat names like 'Bill Clinton' as rigid designators and at the same time allow that names like 'Santa Claus' are purely descriptive. The problem is, how do we know in general which names are referential and which are descriptive?

One possible answer is that we simply do not know. We make certain utterances and the logical forms of those utterances are what they are as fixed by the external world, completely independently of facts about our linguistic intentions. Accordingly, the logical form of an utterance of 'Santa delivered the toys' depends entirely on whether Santa exists. If Santa exists, then 'Santa' is a referring expression. If Santa does not exist, then 'Santa' is a denoting expression. This move—let us call it 'bald externalism about logical form'—arguably solves the problem, but many philosophers, myself among them, have not been prepared to sever the link between the logical form of an utterance and our linguistic intentions.

Russell's take on the matter in Russell (1910–11) was that whether a

Searle's and the classical Russellian theory of descriptive names. There may, of course, be independent reasons for favouring Searle's version.

[7] Here I am ignoring the possibility, discussed in Kripke (1980), that 'Santa Claus' might refer to some actual historical saint. For purposes of discussion let us suppose that there is no individual relevantly linked to the name 'Santa Claus'.

name was a genuine referring expression (a 'logically proper name' in Russell's terminology) or a denoting expression (and hence a description in disguise) was tied to the speaker's psychology.[8] If the speaker had knowledge by acquaintance of a particular individual, then he was able to employ a genuine referring expression to refer to that individual. If the speaker had only knowledge by description of an individual, then the speaker would have to employ a denoting expression and would have to speak about the individual under a description. The idea is that we have singular and general thoughts, and when we express those thoughts linguistically, the logical form of our linguistic expressions will depend upon the nature of the thoughts being expressed.

The problem, of course, is that some names that we take to be referential turn out to be empty, and often we may wonder whether a particular name (like 'King Arthur') is referential or not (i.e. whether there exists an individual to which the name refers). Accordingly, if there is some room for doubt about whether I am directly acquainted with some individual answering to a particular name, then the name cannot be a referring expression in my idiolect but must be a denoting expression. Problem: is there not always room for doubt about whether we have knowledge by acquaintance? Historical names, which we take to have a causal history linking them with some particular individual, may in fact be unanchored; they may turn out to be the invention of a past storyteller. Names and demonstrations that appear to refer to individuals in the perceptual environment may in fact not do so at all, given the possibility of illusions and hallucinations. One can see how Russell (1918) was driven to the extreme position that we are only acquainted with sense data and with 'egocentric particulars'. Correlatively, it is also easy to see how Russell was driven to the position that genuine referring expressions (logically proper names) are deployed only on rare occasions and that denoting expressions are rather the norm. Such are the dangers of linking logical form to the speaker's psychology.

The problem of empty names thus presents a dilemma for the philosophy of language. One can take the first horn and argue that all names are in fact descriptive, but then one is skewered by Kripkean rigidity arguments.[9] One can take the second horn, and argue that all (or most) names are

---

[8]  See Evans (1982) and Neale (1990) for discussion of this point.

[9]  One can try to follow Dummett (1973: 110–51) and hold that rigidity effects can be

referring expressions, but then one is skewered by the counterintuitive conclusion that many sentences containing empty names fail to express a determinate proposition.[10] Finally, if one attempts to escape between the horns (in the manner of Russell) by distinguishing referring expressions and denoting expressions psychologically, one gets forced back towards the first horn. Meanwhile, if we choose bald externalism about logical form, we are forced to sever the link between logical form and our linguistic intentions.

But the externalism about logical form that I explored in Section 1 provides an alternative way to escape between the horns. Suppose that Twin Earth is a world that is just like the actual world except that Socrates was an invention of Plato (here we ignore differences in the causal history between Earth and Twin Earth that are due to the agency of Socrates). On Twin Earth everyone assents to the same basic utterances involving the name 'Socrates' that we do ('Socrates taught Plato', 'Socrates drank hemlock', etc.). In the version of externalism I have in mind, my twin—a molecular duplicate of me—has thoughts that not only differ in content from mine, but also differ in form. So, for example, my thought that I express as 'Socrates was a philosopher' is a singular proposition containing Socrates as a constituent. The thought that my twin expresses as 'Socrates was a philosopher' is a general proposition. More, the linguistic expressions of our thoughts will differ in ways correlative to the ways in which the thoughts differ in form. So, for example, the logical form of my utterance of 'Socrates was a philosopher' contains a referring expression. My twin's utterance of 'Socrates was a philosopher' does not contain a referring expression but rather a denoting expression. The idea is that the logical form of an utterance is tied to the speaker's psychology, and that the wideness of the speaker's psychology allows the environment to help fix the logical form of the utterance.

If we are drawn to the idea that the formation of linguistic intentions involves forming mental representations having standard logical forms, then a similar story holds. Oscar has a mental representation containing a refer-

accounted for if we think of descriptions as taking mandatory wide scope in these cases, but see Soames (1998) for extended criticism of this strategy.

[10] Alternatively (following the Meinongian route), one can say that all (most) names are referring expressions that in the case of so-called empty names refer to non-existent objects. See Parsons (1980) and Zalta (1983; 1988) for examples of this strategy, which I pass over for reasons outlined in Russell (1905).

ring expression. Twin Oscar has a mental representation with a denoting expression in place of a referring expression. Oscar's mental representation is in effect syntactically simpler than Twin Oscar's representation.[11] The logical forms of those mental representations in turn fix the logical forms of the utterances.[12]

In effect, one can say that Russell was right. Some names are logically proper names, others are denoting expressions in disguise, and which are which depends upon the speaker's psychology. Russell's mistake was the residual Cartesianism in his psychology. Once that is discarded, we appear to make great headway in solving this puzzle about names.

The type of strategy I just outlined is not married to a Russellian theory of names; it can be extended to any theory that has two distinct kinds of names. For example, if one held that some names are genuine referring expressions and others are fictive names, one could argue that these two kinds of names are distinct in form and that the forms are environmentally sensitive in precisely the same way as I outlined above. Likewise, one could hold that some utterances contain genuine syntactic names and others do not (perhaps non-referring expressions just contain noises in the name

---

[11] See Neale (1993) for a discussion of the idea that referring expressions are syntactically simple and that quantified expressions (including denoting expressions) are syntactically complex.

[12] Alex Barber and an anonymous referee have observed that there might be issues about the treatment of names for fictional characters here. As noted by the anonymous referee, we ordinarily suppose that if there were someone who had all the properties that Sherlock Holmes is supposed to have, that individual still would not be Sherlock Holmes. It seems to me that for most of us the descriptive content of 'Sherlock Holmes' includes a property like being a fictional character. Clearly any real-world individual is going to lack that crucial property, so we are not inclined to allow that Sherlock could exist even if someone satisfied most of the description. Barber raises another case. Suppose I believe that Sherlock Holmes is a real live detective, and suppose further that, as it happens, there is a real character having all of the properties that the fictional character Sherlock Holmes is supposed to have. What is the logical form of my use of 'Sherlock Holmes' in this case? The answer, for the social externalist, is that I have deployed a common-coin descriptive name that includes the property of being a fictional character—so I have employed a denoting expression that fails to denote. If we shrink from social externalism and suppose that speakers have environmentally fixed idiolects, then it might be possible for me to have a non-standard lexical entry for 'Sherlock Holmes'—in this case one that does not contain the property of being a fiction. In this case I have employed a denoting expression that successfully denotes. If this is implausible, then it simply offers evidence for social externalism.

position) and whether they contain genuine syntactic names or not can be environmentally sensitive. The strategy can be generalized across a wide number of theories about names.

## 3 Outstanding Problems

There are obviously a number of anti-externalist arguments that can be raised against this position, but since I think it is more interesting to consider how the position holds up assuming externalism to be true, let me conclude with a couple of theory-internal worries that the externalist about logical form must face. The first problem is related to what Schiffer (1992a) has called the 'meaning-intention' problem.

### 3.1 *The meaning-intention problem*

Notice how we preserved the link between linguistic intentions and logical form. By allowing that the forms of our thoughts and intentions can co-vary according to external conditions, we can resecure the link between linguistic intentions and logical form. That is, following the usual Twin Earth considerations, Oscar might have one linguistic intention and Twin Oscar may have quite another, despite their both having the same physical microstructure. Oscar, when he utters 'Socrates taught Plato', does so with the intention of expressing a particular singular proposition. Twin Oscar (who lives in the Socrates-free world), when uttering words of the 'same form', does so with the intention of expressing a particular general proposition.

But now the meaning-intention problem rears its head. If linguistic intentions are environmentally determined, then it appears we cannot *know* our linguistic intentions without investigating the environment, and in some cases the kind of investigation necessary (say, to determine whether Socrates or King Arthur existed) may not be open to us. For example, when Oscar utters 'Socrates taught Plato', on this theory he may have the intention to express a particular singular proposition, but he cannot *know* that he has this intention without first investigating the environment to see if Socrates exists. In short, it would appear to follow that we cannot always know our linguistic intentions. Since we are rarely in a position to undertake such an investigation, it follows that we rarely have a handle on what we intend to say. Or so the objection would go.

This problem should sound familiar. It is simply a special case of the general problem of externalism and authoritative self-knowledge.[13] What the externalist can argue in response is that the contents and forms of second-order thoughts (and their corresponding expressions) are *also* fixed by the environment. Thus, the linguistic intention that Oscar reports when he utters, 'I intend to say that Socrates was snub-nosed' is an intention to express the singular proposition that Socrates was snub-nosed. The linguistic intention that Twin Oscar reports when he utters 'I intend to say that Socrates was snub-nosed' is the intention to express the general proposition that (for example) there is a unique teacher of Plato who drank hemlock etc. and that he was snub-nosed. In effect, this problem is familiar to the externalist, and the externalist will not find it a persuasive objection.

Perhaps we can retreat and go after the externalist again, this time focusing on the talk of logical form here. The strategy would be to concede that one can know that one intends to express the singular proposition that Socrates is sub-nosed, but deny that it is credible that one can know that one intends to utter something that contains a referring expression. In effect, the standard externalist strategy may work for contents, but it cannot be extended to forms.

But is it really impossible for the externalist to extend this strategy to forms? It could be argued that you do indeed intend to utter a sentence that has such-and-such a form. It does not follow that you must know that it *has* such-and-such a form, and it does not follow that you have the ability to individuate utterances on the basis of their forms.[14] The answer is analogous to what one says about knowledge of contents; you are thinking that water is wet, and you know that you are thinking that water is wet, but it does not follow that you can differentiate water thoughts from Twin Earth water thoughts (henceforth 'twater thoughts').[15] In the case of form, one can know one is intending to utter a sentence with a referring expression

---

[13] See Ludlow and Martin (1998) for a survey of the literature on this topic.

[14] Part of the misunderstanding here may stem from a failure to specify what lies within the scope of the verb 'intends'. Here is another way to put it. You intend to utter a sentence S. S has form F. You do not know that S has F.

[15] This is a point stressed by McLaughlin and Tye (1998).

without being able to distinguish utterances having referring expressions from utterances having denoting expressions. Of course, this *is* to concede that (unless we are philosophers of language) we are simply indifferent to the logical forms of what we say. And if we *are* philosophers of language— perhaps uttering a sentence with 'Santa Claus' in the subject position and (quote–unquote) *intending* to employ a referring expression—well, we are simply trying to do the impossible. Again this is exactly parallel to the discussions of content externalism and self-knowledge, where one is indifferent to the individuating conditions of a thought, yet one can still know what one is thinking. (As Davidson would put the point, one can know what one is thinking/saying, but it does not follow that one knows what one is thinking/saying under all descriptions.)

## 3.2 *The environmental sensitivity of logic?*

If the logical forms of our utterances are environmentally sensitive, then it appears that there are some strong consequences for the nature of logic. In a way this should not be surprising; it has already been observed that externalism about content has unusual consequences for logic. For example, Boghossian (1992*a*; 1992*b*) and Schiffer (1992*b*) discuss cases in which an agent unwittingly slow-switches from Earth to Twin Earth, and reasons thus:

> I fell into water at $t_0$.
> I just fell into water at $t_1$.
> ∴ I have fallen into water more than once.

The problem is that the agent is equivocating without realizing it. The first use of 'water' picks up water, and the second picks up twater. (If we say that the first use no longer invokes the water content but only the twater content, then the argument fails by virtue of the first premiss being false.)

Externalism about form raises the ante somewhat. Not only will there be cases of equivocation, but the very notion of what counts as a logical inference will come unhinged. Here is the problem. Suppose that the forms of proper names like 'Socrates' depend upon environmental embedding in the ways outlined above. If we live in a world with Socrates, then 'Socrates' is a referring expression. If we live in a Socrates-free world, then 'Socrates' is a description in disguise—perhaps something of the form 'the teacher of Plato who drank hemlock . . .'. Then in the Socrates world the following inference will be invalid, but in the Socrates-free world it will be valid:

> Socrates was a snub-nosed philosopher.
> A snub-nosed philosopher taught Plato.

Obviously the analytic/synthetic distinction also comes unglued in ways that even Quine did not anticipate. If forms are environmentally sensitive, then an utterance of 'Socrates was a philosopher' may be analytic in some worlds but synthetic in others.[16] Perhaps less urgently, this would recast recent debates about the nature of the lexicon, and in particular about whether lexical entries are simple (as Fodor and Lepore 1998 suggest) or robust (as many linguists have suggested). It may turn out that one agent could have the kind of lexicon envisaged by Fodor and Lepore, while a twin (having an identical microstructure) in a different environmental setting could have a lexicon with much more robust lexical entries.

### 3.3 *The collapse of sameness of form*

While I think that the first (and perhaps also the second) objection can be answered in a way that is consistent with basic externalist assumptions, it may be that the answers given lead directly to a third problem for the externalist about logical form. Consider the case where Oscar and Twin Oscar utter 'Socrates was snub-nosed'. We are tempted to say that in such a case Oscar and Twin Oscar use expressions *of the same form'*. But *do* they use expressions of the same form? Clearly they do not, since at a minimum the logical forms of those expressions will be quite different. Strictly speaking, we can no longer say that they make utterances of the same form. At best, Twin Oscar produces the same acoustical signal as does Oscar (he may not even do that, depending upon how acoustical signals are individuated). If the considerations raised in this paper are right, then our standard ways of reporting Twin Earth happenings may be careless. Our twins do not utter the same expressions that we do for the simple reason that the forms of our respective

---

[16] If one prefers a descriptive theory of names along the lines advocated by Searle (1958), then the example in question has to be softened to something like 'Socrates had a sufficient number of a weighted bundle of properties which included being a philosopher'.

expressions are quite different. The problem could actually be much more serious than this. If forms are sensitive to the environment, then we may also wonder if we really have the same microstructure as our twins. Microstructure is, after all, largely a matter of form. The question is: can microstructure be sensitive to local environments, or is the only environment that matters to microstructure the entire universe? This is an interesting question that is well worth investigating. Obviously if microstructure is sensitive in this way, it makes a hash out of standard Twin Earth thought-experiments and may well undermine the internal/external distinction altogether.

## 4 Conclusion

My aim in this paper has been to offer a preliminary investigation into some of the consequences of externalist theories of form. Prima facie, while there are a number of external arguments that can be levelled against the position, it is not clear that the position is internally inconsistent. Also notable is the apparent elegance with which the position can unravel the dilemma for the theory of names that is posed by the twin problems of non-referring expressions and the rigidity of names in modal environments. In sum, while the position has very strong consequences that will be unpalatable to some, I would argue that many of those consequences are interesting and surprising and that the position certainly deserves further investigation.

## REFERENCES

BOGHOSSIAN, P. (1992a). 'Externalism and Inference', *Philosophical Issues*, 2: 11–28.
—— (1992b), 'Reply to Schiffer', *Philosophical Issues*, 2: 39–42.
BONTLY, T. (1998), 'Individualism and the Nature of Syntactic States', *British Journal for the Philosophy of Science*, 49: 557–74.
BURGE, T. (1979), 'Individualism and the Mental', in French, Uehling, and Wettstein (1979), 73–121.
—— (1986), 'Individualism and Psychology', *Philosophical Review*, 95: 3–45.
CHOMSKY, N. (1986), *Knowledge of Language* (New York: Praeger).
CLARK, A., and CHALMERS, D. (1998), 'The Extended Mind', *Analysis*, 58: 7–19.
DUMMETT, M. (1973), *Frege: Philosophy of Language* (Cambridge, Mass.: Harvard University Press).

EGAN, F. (1992), 'Individualism, Computation, and Perceptual Content', *Mind*, 101: 443–59.

EVANS, G. (1982), *The Varieties of Reference* (Oxford: Oxford University Press).

FODOR, J., and LEPORE, E. (1998), 'The Emptiness of the Lexicon: Critical Reflections on J. Pustejovsky's *The Generative Lexicon*', *Linguistic Inquiry*, 29: 269–88.

FRENCH, P. A., UEHLING, T. E., and WETTSTEIN, H. K., eds. (1979), *Studies in Epistemology* (Midwest Studies in Philosophy, 5; Minneapolis: University of Minnesota Press).

KRIPKE, S. (1980), *Naming and Necessity* (Cambridge, Mass.: Harvard University Press).

LUDLOW, P., and MARTIN, N., eds. (1998), *Externalism and Self-Knowledge* (Stanford, Calif.: CSLI Publications/Cambridge University Press).

MACDONALD, C., SMITH, B., and WRIGHT, C., eds. (1998), *Knowing Our Minds: Essays on Self-Knowledge* (Oxford: Oxford University Press).

McLAUGHLIN, B. and TYE, M. (1998), 'Externalism, Twin-Earth, and Self-Knowledge', in MacDonald, Smith, and Wright (1998), 289–320.

NEALE, S. (1990), *Descriptions* (Cambridge, Mass.: MIT Press).

—— (1993), 'Terms Limits', in Tomberlin (1993), 89–123.

PARSONS, T. (1980), *Nonexistent Objects* (New Haven: Yale University Press).

RUSSELL, B. (1905), 'On Denoting', *Mind*, 14: 479–93.

—— (1910–11), 'Knowledge by Acquaintance and Knowledge by Description', *Proceedings of the Aristotelean Society*, 11: 108–28; repr. in *Mysticism and Logic* (London: George Allen and Unwin, 1917; repr. New York: Doubleday, 1957).

—— (1918), *The Philosophy of Logical Atomism*, ed. D. Pears (Chicago: Open Court Publishing, 1985).

SCHIFFER, S. (1992a), 'Belief Ascription', *Journal of Philosophy*, 89: 499–521.

—— (1992b), 'Boghossian on Externalism and Inference', *Philosophical Issues*, 2: 29–37.

SEARLE, J. (1958), 'Proper Names', *Mind*, 67: 166–73.

SOAMES, S. (1998), 'The Modal Argument: Wide Scope and Rigidified Descriptions', *Noûs* 32: 1–22.

TOMBERLIN, J., ed. (1993), *The Philosophy of Language and Logic* (Philosophical Perspectives, 7; Atascadero, Calif.: Ridgeview).

WILSON, R. (1994), 'Wide Computationalism', *Mind*, 103: 351–72.

ZALTA, E. (1983), *Abstract Objects: An Introduction to Axiomatic Metaphysics* (Dordrecht: Reidel).

—— (1988), *Intensional Logic and the Metaphysics of Intensionality* (Cambridge, Mass.: MIT Press).

# CHAPTER 13

# *Ignorance of Meaning*

*Gabriel Segal*

An argument is available to demonstrate that the cognitive content a subject associates with a term differs from the term's Burgean social content. I show that the same argumentative strategy can be used to argue that cognitive content is holistic. After defending this application of the strategy, I discuss the ramifications of this holistic conclusion for both first-personal knowledge and scientific knowledge of meaning.

## 1 An Argument for Individualism

Tyler Burge's individual, Alf, appears to have a fairly typical collection of propositional attitudes concerning arthritis (Burge 1979). He appears to believe that arthritis is a painful condition, that his grandfather had arthritis in his wrists and ankles, and that he himself has arthritis in the knees. One day, he wakes up with a pain in his thigh and fears the condition may have spread. He goes to the doctor and says, 'I fear my arthritis has spread to my thigh'. The doctor informs him that this is impossible, since, by definition, arthritis is an inflammation of the joints. Alf accepts the expert's correction and goes on to ask what is wrong with his thigh.

The way in which Alf accepts correction is important. He might express himself by saying: 'I thought I had arthritis in my thigh, but I was wrong.'

Versions of this paper were presented at the Epistemology of Language conference, Sheffield, 2000, and at colloquia at the Australian National University, Flinders University, and the University of Auckland. I am grateful to participants for discussion. Thanks also to Alex Barber, Jessica Brown, Martin Davies, Ray Elugardo, Peter Goldie, Keith Hossack, Brian Loar, Laura Schroeter, Michael Tye, Tim Williamson, Andy Woodfield, and an anonymous referee for Oxford University Press. Part of the research for this paper was supported by a Visiting Fellowship at the Research School of Social Sciences at the Australian National University. I am most grateful for their support.

In his newly informed state, he appears to attribute the concept of arthritis to his previous, somewhat ignorant self. He appears to take it that when he said 'arthritis' he used the term with the same meaning as the experts, in spite of the fact that he was ignorant of a crucial definitional truth about 'arthritis'. (Here I shall assume that the meaning of a subject's term is the concept he expresses by or associates with that term.) Alf treats his past self in the same way as most of the rest of us do: we, also, are content to say of the ignorant subject that he believed he had arthritis in his thigh.

Burge argues that the concept we attribute to the ignorant Alf is partly individuated by external, social factors. Had Alf been part of a linguistic community in which the term 'arthritis' had a meaning consistent with Alf's original beliefs, i.e. had it applied to certain conditions outside the joints, perhaps including the one in Alf's thigh, then Alf would have had a different concept and would have meant something different by his term.

I think that Burge's argument is unsound, and that it is possible to account for our intuitions about propositional-attitude reporting in a way that is consistent with individualism (Segal 2000: 76–82). However, I do not propose to go into those matters here. Rather, I want to argue that whatever one thinks about social content, content individuated partly by external, social factors, we must recognize a kind of cognitive content the individuation of which is independent of such factors. (The argument is due to Loar 1987; the formulation is mine.)

We begin with an alternative biography for Alf. Alf goes to live in France for a while and there he learns the word 'arthrite'. He becomes expert in the use of this term. He knows that, by definition, it extends over all and only inflammations of the joints. But he fails to make the right connection between 'arthrite' and 'arthritis'. He does not think that the terms are synonymous and he continues to believe that 'arthritis' might in principle apply to a condition in one's thigh.

It seems clear that, in some sense, Alf means different things by 'arthrite' and 'arthritis' and that, in some sense, he expresses different concepts by the two terms. He might, for example, think to himself: 'Evidently not all arthritis is arthrite, but perhaps all arthrite is arthritis.' Normal, roughly Fregean, criteria for the individuation of meaning dictate that attitudes of this sort show that he means different things by the two terms. Here is a rough formulation of the criterion ('FD' for 'Fregean principle of difference'):

(FD) If a subject, $S$, rationally assents to $P(t_1)$ and dissents from or abstains on the truth value of $P(t_2)$ (where $P(. . .)$ is an extensional context), then $t_1$ and $t_2$ have different meanings in $S$'s idiolect and $S$ associates different concepts with them.

It seems clear also that if either of Alf's terms has the same meaning as the experts' term 'arthritis', then it is 'arthrite'. Since the meaning of Alf's 'arthritis' differs from that of his 'arthrite', it must also differ from the expert's. Hence, contrary to Burge, when ignorant Alf says 'arthritis', he does not mean *arthritis*.

Note that I am claiming only that there is an important sense of 'mean' that renders this true. One might accept that on one perfectly good way of individuating meaning, Alf's 'arthritis' does mean the same as the experts' and, indeed, as Alf's own 'arthrite'. But that mode of individuation offers us nothing to say about Alf's linguistic behaviour when he says things like 'Not all arthritis is arthrite'. To account for that, it seems best to recognize a different kind of content, one that is independent of social factors and one that accounts for the term's role in Alf's cognitive economy. Let us call this 'cognitive content'.

The cognitive contents of Alf's 'arthrite' and 'arthritis' differ. Cognitive content is what individuates concepts and meaning under FD. So cognitive content resembles Fregean sense: differences in cognitive content are what rationalize Alf's belief that not all arthritis is arthrite. And we may assume that cognitive contents are, in some manner or other, attributed by opaque propositional-attitude attributions. If two terms are associated with different cognitive contents, then they cannot be freely intersubstituted in opaque attributions.

Cognitive contents are certainly not individuated in the way Burgean social content would be.[1] The 'arthrite' argument can easily be generalized to the words of any Burgean partially ignorant subject. Hence we

---

[1] I would claim further that they are individuated independently of all social factors. But it would take some argument to establish that.

should conclude that all terms have a cognitive content that is individuated independently of Burgean social factors.[2]

## 2 An Argument for Holism

Loar's argument for individualistically individuated cognitive content deploys a particular strategy. It uses an *intra*subjective difference of content among concepts to argue for an *inter*subjective one. Thus it moves from the premiss that Alf's 'arthrite' and 'arthritis' concepts differ in content to the conclusion that Alf's 'arthritis' and the expert's 'arthritis' concepts differ in content. The same strategy can be used to generate an argument for a certain kind of holism about cognitive content.[3] The argument is designed to show that cognitive content is holistic, in roughly the following sense: any (intra- or interpersonal) conflict between the beliefs associated with terms $t_1$ and $t_2$ entails a difference in the cognitive contents with which they are associated.[4] For example, if Thelma believes that tigers are indigenous to India, while Louise thinks they are indigenous to Africa (and they would express these beliefs using the word 'tiger'), then it follows that their 'tiger'

---

[2]  I have offered here only a crude sketch of the argument. It is spelt out and defended in detail in Segal (2000).

[3]  Ned Block has also used the same strategy in an argument to the effect that narrow content, if there is such a thing, is holistic (Block 1995). Block's argument differs from Loar's in two important respects. First, the argument relies on the narrowness of the content it concerns to derive the conclusion that such content is holistic. Secondly, it uses a different difference principle to distinguish contents within a single subject. In place of FD Block has: 'If at one time a person has substantially different beliefs associated with terms $t_1$ and $t_2$, then $t_1$ differs in narrow content from $t_2$ for that person at that time.' Block's (1995: 154) difference principle invokes *substantial* differences in the beliefs associated with two terms to argue for a difference between their contents. The formulation runs from the premiss through to the holistic conclusion, which is that any substantial difference in beliefs associated with terms $t_1$ and $t_2$ (intra- or interpersonal) entails a difference in their narrow contents.

[4]  I emphasize that this is only a rough formulation. Metalinguistic beliefs are certainly to be excluded. I believe that 'start' and 'begin' are spelt differently, but that does not entail that they express different cognitive contents in my idiolect. The case of metacognitive beliefs is more complicated: for example, Mates believes that Scheffler believes that one might start something without beginning it. For the sake of simplicity, I have formulated FD so as to exclude these too. Further, it is probably not true of all terms $t_1$ and $t_2$, but rather of terms from a very broad range (see below).

concepts differ in cognitive content. I shall introduce the argumentative strategy in relation to an example, then discuss how to generalize it.

Thelma and Louise have pretty standard concepts of tigers. However, Thelma believes they are indigenous to India, and Louise thinks they are indigenous to Africa. Fred also has a fairly typical concept of tigers, and, like Louise, believes they are indigenous to Africa. In conversation with Thelma, he learns of a large cat called 'Panthera tigris' that is indigenous to India. Curious about these panthers, he asks Thelma about them, and learns that they are yellow–black striped etc. In fact, 'Panthera tigris' is just the Latin species term for tigers, as both Thelma and Louise happen to know. But Fred fails to make the connection. He comes to believe that there are two similar-looking but different species of large cats, one indigenous to Africa, the other to India. He asserts 'Pantherae tigres are indigenous to India' and he denies 'Tigers are indigenous to India'.

FD dictates that Fred associates different concepts with 'Panthera tigris' and 'tiger' and means different things by them. Since FD individuates concepts by cognitive contents, the conclusion is that Fred associates different cognitive contents with the two terms. Thus far we have an intrasubjective difference in content. We now use this to force some intersubjective differences in content.

If Fred's 'Panthera tigris' concept has the same cognitive content as Thelma's 'Panthera tigris' concept, and Fred's 'tiger' concept has the same cognitive content as Louise's 'tiger' concept, then Thelma's 'Panthera tigris' concept differs in cognitive content from Louise's 'tiger' concept. And this is already a pretty holistic result: for the only relevant difference between Thelma and Louise is that one of them thinks that the things called 'tigers' or 'Pantherae tigres' are Indian and the other thinks that they are African.

On a non-holistic conception of 'same cognitive content', it would seem that Fred's and Thelma's 'Panthera tigris' concepts do have the same cognitive content, and likewise for him and Louise in respect of their 'tiger' concepts. For the only relevant difference between, for example, Fred and Thelma is that Fred thinks that 'tiger' differs in extension from 'Panthera tigris' and applies to similar-looking but distinct animals that come from Africa. We would not normally take that sort of difference to indicate a difference in cognitive content. For example, when I learnt the term 'ocelot', I came to believe that it has a different extension from 'domestic cat' and applies to similar-looking but biologically distinct animals. Non-holistic standards of individuating cognitive contents would not suggest that my learning about ocelots entailed a change in the cognitive content of my 'cat' concept.

These sorts of differences—the difference between Fred and Louise with respect to 'tiger' and between Fred and Thelma with respect to 'Panthera tigris'—only indicate differences of content if holism is true.

Fred's relations to Thelma and Louise are of the same ilk as Thelma's and Louise's relations to one another. There is no principled reason to allow that Thelma and Louise have the same 'tiger' concepts as each other while denying that Fred and Louise share a 'tiger' concept or that he and Thelma share a 'Panthera tigris' concept. We have to distinguish Fred's 'tiger' concept from his 'Panthera tigris' concept. This forces us to make a further distinction: we must either distinguish Fred's 'tiger' from Louise's, or his 'Panthera tigris' from Thelma's, or make a distinction between Thelma's 'tiger'/'Panthera tigris' concept and Louise's.[5] All of these options are on a par. None of them seems to sit very happily with non-holistic modes of individuating concepts. All of them invite holism. The conclusion that suggests itself is therefore that we should individuate cognitive content holistically and distinguish all three subjects' 'tiger' concepts.

The argument appears to generalise easily enough. Here is the structure: take two subjects $a$ and $b$, and terms $t_1$ and $t_2$ such that $t_1$ is in $a$'s vocabulary and $t_2$ in $b$'s. (It does not matter whether $t_1$ and $t_2$ have the same surface form or are, in some sense, the same word.) Suppose that there is a small doxastic difference between the subjects in respect of the words: there is some extensional sentential context $P(\xi)$ such that $a$ assents to $P(t_1)$ and $b$ dissents from or abstains on $P(t_2)$. Otherwise $a$'s cognitive relations to $t_1$ and $b$'s to $t_2$ are as alike as can be. There exists a possible third subject, $c$, who has terms $t_3$ and $t_4$ in his vocabulary. By non-holistic standards of individuating cognitive contents, $a$'s $t_1$ would appear to have the same cognitive content as $c$'s $t_3$, and $b$'s $t_2$ would appear to have the same cognitive content as $c$'s $t_4$. $a$'s cognitive relations to $t_1$ and $c$'s cognitive relations to $t_3$ are as alike as can be, compatibly with the stipulations of the scenario (*mutatis mutandis*

---

[5] Alternatively, we might just distinguish 'tiger' from 'Panthera tigris' concepts for all the subjects and allow those two to be shared all round. But that does not appear to be an attractive idea and I shall ignore it.

for $b$'s $t_2$ and $c$'s $t_4$). $c$ assents to $P(t_3)$ and dissents from or abstains on $P(t_4)$. By FD, $t_3$ and $t_4$ have different cognitive contents for $c$. So at least one of the following must be false:

- $a$'s $t_1$ shares a cognitive content with $b$'s $t_2$.
- $a$'s $t_1$ shares a cognitive content with $c$'s $t_3$.
- $b$'s $t_2$ shares a cognitive content with $c$'s $t_4$.

But fairness dictates that if one of them is false, then they all are. So they are all false. So holism is true: any small conflict between the beliefs associated with $t_1$ and $t_2$ indicates a difference between their cognitive contents.

The argument schema might well not apply across the board to all terms and sentential contexts. For example, it is not easy to imagine running the argument successfully for 'two', 'a pair of', and the context 'Frege had . . . uncles'. It is difficult to describe a subject, c, who would rationally adopt the required attitudes to the sentences. And if one could concoct such a subject, the argument would probably falter at the fairness step. We could probably motivate identifying one of $c$'s concepts with those of both $a$ and $b$, and distinguishing $c$'s other concept from that one.

The existence of these exceptional cases may or may not be highly significant. It could be that the concepts involved are just as subject to holism as 'tiger' and 'Panthera tigris', but that the argumentative strategy fails to show that they are. Or it could be that the concepts are not subject to the same sort of holism. Maybe (only) a specific range of $P(\xi)$s are relevant to the concepts' cognitive content; perhaps mathematical ones, in the case of 'two' and 'a pair of'.

I shall briefly consider two ways of blocking the argument. One would be to deny FD. As Jessica Brown (this volume) makes clear, an externalist might well want to deny FD. I shall not here attempt to argue for the principle in any detail. But an argument I would endorse goes along the following lines. The use of opaque propositional-attitude attributions is essential to standard psychological explanation. Such attributions attribute cognitive content. Cognitive content must respect FD, if it is to bear its explanatory burden. All of these claims, of course, require detailed defence, which I postpone to another occasion.

I shall take the time, however, to discuss a specific objection to FD that was suggested by Tim Williamson (pers. comm.). Williamson offered an apparent counter-example of the following sort. Suppose I use 'begin' and 'commence' as synonyms. Then Noam Chomsky tells me (falsely) that he has discovered a case that I shall judge to be a counter-example to

(1) For all $x$, $y$, $x$ begins $y$ iff $x$ commences $y$.

While I am waiting for Chomsky to e-mail me the example, I have time to ponder. I wrack my brains, trying to figure out what kind of example he has in mind. I fail to come up with anything. Nevertheless, since I have great faith in Chomsky's judgement, I believe him. And so, without any failure of rationality, I come to believe that (1) is false. Now it seems that I can rationally dissent from (1), while assenting to

(2) For all $x$, $y$, $x$ begins $y$ iff $x$ begins $y$.

Yet it does not seem as though 'commences' and 'begins' have different cognitive contents in my idiolect.

What is going on here? (1), even in my idiolect, expresses a simple conceptual truth. And indeed, it seems to me to do so, even as I contemplate the thought it expresses. It is just that Chomsky has given me a reason to believe that, in this particular case, things are not as they seem. So I reject the deliverances of my normally authoritative modes of access to features of my own concepts and favour Chomsky's judgement over my own.

The result is that I behave in a way that would be typical of someone who had two concepts associated with 'commence' and 'begin' and for whom (1) was not a conceptual truth. Such a person's attitude to (1) would be an accurate reflection of their concepts. But my behaviour and my attitude to (1) do not similarly reflect the structure of my conceptual repertoire.

My tentative reaction to all this is simply to add a *ceteris paribus* clause to FD. The idea is that, in typical cases, people's judgements about possible or actual divergences among the truth values of sentences are partly based on mechanisms that do reliably reflect the structure of their conceptual economy. FD is correct for those cases. There are, though, further factors that can intervene, such as Noam Chomsky. When there is such interference, *cetera non sunt paria*.[6]

Another way out of the argument for holism would be to give up on

---

[6] As I said, this is a tentative reaction. Another possibility would be to bite the bullet and hold that I would indeed associate different cognitive contents with 'commences'

using a univocal notion of sameness of cognitive content inter- and intra-subjectively. Thus, for example, Fred has 'tiger'/'Panthera tigris' concepts with different intrasubjective cognitive content, but the same intersubjective content. Hence he and his two friends can all have the same concepts in spite of their minor cognitive differences.

But that in effect would just mean that there is no useful notion of cognitive content that applies across subjects. And that would be disastrous for psychology. Psychology works with opaque attitude attributions, and generalizes over subjects. If there is no notion of intersubjectively shared cognitive content, then either we cannot use opaque generalizations in psychology, or we need some other account of how opaque generalizations might work. But we have no satisfactory way of doing psychology without opaque attributions and no satisfactory alternative account of opacity.[7] So giving up on intersubjective similarity of cognitive content would be a bad move.

I shall return to the matter of psychological generalizations in Section 4. First, I shall briefly discuss knowledge of meaning in the light of holism.

## 3 Knowledge of Meaning

As I mentioned above, the enlightened Alf seems to believe that his present 'arthritis' concept is the same as the one he had before his enlightenment. This suggests that he has undergone a conceptual and linguistic change without noticing it. It would appear to indicate that there was a change in what he, himself, meant by 'arthritis' that he failed to detect. If the argument for holism is correct, then it looks as though this sort of thing happens all the time. Every time you change your mind about something, you undergo an undetected conceptual and linguistic change. And this might seem to constitute some sort of threat to the authority of our knowledge of our own meanings.

That would be interesting. For the apparent threat looks rather like the apparent threat to first-person authority posed to externalists by the

and 'begins'. After all (one might argue), I believe that commencing is properly called 'commencing' and not 'beginning'.

[7] These claims are controversial, and stand in need of extensive defence. For a lengthy defence of an anti-Fregean approach to psychological explanation, see Braun (2001).

possibility (or actuality) of slow-switching. But the present threat applies to cognitive content, content that is, or at least might be, individuated by purely individualistic factors. It would mean that we are not in a particularly healthy epistemic position even with respect to that. Further reflection, however, suggests that holism poses no serious threat to first-personal knowledge of meaning.

Suppose that I assert:[8]

(3) It is a theorem of a correct semantic theory for my language that for all $x$, $x$ satisfies 'tiger' iff $x$ is a tiger.

Suppose also that even a small change in my 'tiger' beliefs would lead to a change of meaning. After such a change, I might again assert (3). But it would have a different meaning on this second occasion of utterance. Suppose I believe, falsely, that my two utterances of (3) said the same thing. Is my knowledge of the truth of (3) threatened?

Apparently not. After all, in saying (3) I am deploying my 'tiger' concept to express the meaning of 'tiger' in my idiolect. There is nothing wrong with my 'tiger' concept. I have a perfectly good grasp of what I am saying when I utter (3). And I have reliable mechanisms that link the concept to the word, these being the mechanisms that allow us to find the right words to express ourselves and to understand our own language. We do not know much about how these mechanisms work, but they seem to be extremely reliable. So I am in a fine position correctly to judge the truth of (3). I know that it is true. (Of course, the mechanisms can break down in cases of aphasia, or even parapraxis: 'by "worm" I mean a cluster of phonological, syntactic, and semantic features', I might incorrectly assert.[9])

If my two utterances of (3) were relatively close together, say only three minutes apart, then it might seem worrying that I think that they meant the same thing when in fact they did not. How can I really claim to know what I mean, if I cannot tell when two of my own utterances, separated by just three minutes, mean the same?

I think that if large and sudden shifts of meaning passed unnoticed,

---

[8] (3) is my way of saying 'By "tiger", I mean tiger'.

[9] Notice that I am not invoking the homophonic nature of (3). The same remarks would apply to 'It is a theorem of a correct semantic theory for one of my languages that for all $x$, $x$ satisfies "tigre" iff $x$ is a tiger.'

then that might be worrying. But this is only a very small one. The sorts of meaning shift that are, according to holism, induced by small doxastic changes are very slight indeed. (I shall say more about the measurement of the semantic distances below). The fact that I cannot distinguish very similar meanings is not a matter of grave concern.

Here is a rough analogy. I am in a paint shop with an extensive supply of colour samples. I am looking at a particular sample, called 'Just Yellow', and enjoying the colour experience. I know what colour Just Yellow is: it is that one. I look away. I am then presented with the same sample along with other closely similar shades. I am unable to reidentify Just Yellow. That does not reflect badly on my initial knowledge of the colour. I had and still have a good grasp of which colour Just Yellow is.

There is also a sense in which I do not know *exactly* which colour it is. That is the sense that comes into play when, as I am presented with the samples and asked to pick out Just Yellow, I say: 'No, I don't know which one of those colours is Just Yellow'. But I do know which colour Just Yellow is, up to a reasonably high degree of specificity. I could certainly distinguish it from shades of yellow that are not so close to it. In the context of that easier trial, I might say 'Yes, I know which colour Just Yellow is. It's that one there'.

If I were hopeless at discriminating it from other colours, that would indicate that I do not know so much about Just Yellow. I look away from the sample, and then I am presented with it again, along with green, blue, and red. Suppose I cannot pick it out. Suppose also that this failure is not due to a memory lapse or anything like that, but rather has to be put down to my initial cognitive contact with the sample. Then it looks as though that initial contact did not endow me with a decent grasp of Just Yellow. I was colour-blind.

The same seems to apply to knowledge of meaning. The fact that I may be unable to distinguish slightly different meanings when these are presented to me at different times—even if the times are only three minutes apart—does not seem threatening. Of course, if I actually thought that I meant the same thing—rather than not having a view on the matter—then I would have overestimated my cognitive skills. But so what? That just shows that not having a view on the matter is the best policy, prior to serious theorizing. (Obviously, if one becomes convinced of the truth of holism, then one should take a view on these cases for theoretical reasons).

Let us continue the parallel with the paint-shop example. If there were a sudden large shift in the meaning of a word of mine and I failed to notice it—again, supposing there is no memory lapse—that would seem to show that I had a relatively poor grasp on what I meant. But we do tend to notice such shifts: I used to think 'hiatus' meant *commotion*, now I think it means *interruption* or *gap*. This constituted a substantial and sudden shift in the cognitive content of 'hiatus' in my idiolect. But I noticed it, so everything is fine.

The 'hiatus' case differs in an important respect from the 'tiger' case. It is reasonable to classify the former as a purely linguistic change. Before the change I had the concepts of a commotion and of a gap (more or less, small shifts aside), and I still do. Only my opinion about the semantics of 'hiatus' changed. By contrast, the 'tiger' case involves a conceptual change: an ancestor 'tiger' concept evolves into a descendant 'tiger' concept with a different cognitive content.

It is not particularly easy to find conceptual changes that are both large and rapid. Perhaps they occur when someone—a child, say, or an academic—experiences an epiphany. My feeling is that such changes are indeed noticeable by the subject: 'My whole concept of the physical has changed!' a philosopher might declare, having suddenly come to believe that the brain is a thinking thing.

Burge (1988) offers a defence of the authority of first-personal knowledge of one's own concepts that seems to be insensitive to the distinction I am discussing here. He points out that certain kinds of second-order judgements, like 'I think (with this very thought) that *p*', are self-referential and self-verifying. In making the second-order judgement that one thinks that *p*, one thereby thinks that *p*, and thus renders the judgement correct. That seems right. But the sort of knowledge delivered by such judgements ('basic cases' of self-knowledge, in Burge's terminology) may still be rather limited.

Compare a judgement of the form 'I am now looking at this colour'. Such a judgement is not self-verifying. The act of making it does not make it true. Nevertheless, a colour-blind man observing a colour sample in an ordinary sort of context could still make the judgement truly and knowledgeably. For whatever colour it is that he is looking at, he is in a position to refer to it as 'this colour.' But this knowledge is still compatible with considerable ignorance about which colour he is observing. Basic cases of self-knowledge may be compatible with a similar sort of ignorance in respect of the content of their embedded first-order thoughts.

Consider a radical externalist position about singular concepts, the so-called 'neo-Fregean' view inspired by John McDowell (1977) and Gareth Evans (1982).[10] This position allows that in certain cases of delusion, where a subject apparently has an attitude to a non-existent individual, the subject may believe that he is having a thought when in fact he is not. Thus someone, call him 'Norbert', in the grip of a hallucination, saying (4) would actually be uttering something false or non-sensical:

(4) I think (with this very thought) that that little green man is staring at me.

Suppose that the hallucination is quickly replaced by a veridical perception: a real little green man is surreptitiously put in place, just as the causes of hallucination wear off. Norbert repeats (4). According to the externalist position I envisage, what he says this time is true.[11] So the second utterance of (4) expresses a basic case of self-knowledge. But surely, on the position I am envisaging, there is a good sense in which Norbert's knowledge of the contents of his own thought is limited. For he cannot distinguish a state of mind that consists in a failed attempt to think a thought from an immediately subsequent state of mind that consists in the actual thinking of a thought. This may not be a problem for externalism.[12] But it does support the unsurprising conclusion that individualism is consistent with a greater degree of first-personal self-knowledge than externalism. It need not allow that there could be any cases of sudden, large conceptual shifts that would pass unnoticed by an attentive and functioning subject.[13]

[10] Burge rejects the neo-Fregean position. See e.g. Burge (1977).

[11] I am not suggesting that neo-Fregeans would automatically want to allow that the second attempt at a thought is successful. It might not be that easy for them to disallow it, though.

[12] See Burge (1996) and Peacocke (1996) for further discussion of externalism and self-knowledge.

[13] I am indebted to an anonymous referee for Oxford University Press for bringing to my attention a serious mistake in an earlier version of this section.

## 4  Ignorance of Meaning

The problem posed by holism, as Jerry Fodor has pointed out (e.g. Fodor 1987), is to explain how, if it is true, psychological generalizations can generalize. Thelma, Louise, and Fred all believe that enraged tigers are extremely dangerous. If any of them were trapped in a cage with a tiger, they would take great pains not to enrage it, precisely because of this belief that they all share.

On the face of it, holism suggests that they do not all believe the same thing: the cognitive contents of their 'tiger' concepts are all different. So how can the same generalisation, one expressed by a referentially opaque propositional-attitude report, apply to all three of them? The natural answer is that concepts with slightly different cognitive contents can all qualify as 'tiger' concepts: that is, they can all be correctly specified by use of the term 'tiger' in opaque propositional-attitude attributions.

The problem then is to explain how this can be. Presumably—and *pace* Fodor and Lepore (1992)—it has to do with similarity. I use the term 'tiger' in

(5)  Thelma believes that enraged tigers are extremely dangerous.

My report is true because the cognitive content of 'tiger' in my idiolect is similar enough to that of Thelma's concept. A Davidson-inspired (Davidson 1968) account of propositional-attitude reporting explains this. To a first approximation, we might say, for example (borrowed from Segal 2000):

(P)  A report of the form '*a* believes that *s*' as uttered by *b*, in conversational context *c*, is true iff the content of *s* in *b*'s mouth is similar enough, by the standards of *c*, to some belief of *a*'s.

The standards of similarity vary considerably from context to context: sometimes even approximate identity of extensions is enough, at other times considerable closeness of cognitive content is required.[14]

We ordinary folk psychologists appear to be reasonably adept both at judging what standard of similarity is appropriate in a given context and at judging when two concepts meet the required standard. We tend to agree

---

[14]  (P) is supposed to account both for *de re* and *de dicto* reports. The distinction features as one between different standards of similarity of content.

on how to evaluate the truth of propositional-attitude reports, and so we must be agreeing in our judgements of similarity of cognitive content.

That is all fine. But the problem is that we do not know what it is that we are doing when we make these judgements. That is to say, we do not have a good theoretical account of the metric of similarity. It is very hard to believe that any formal account in terms of extensions, intensions, situations, characters, functions from possible worlds to intensions etc. is going to help much here. Firstly, these accounts never seem to be fine-grained enough to capture all the differences of cognitive content that we want. Secondly, it is difficult to know how we could develop a reasonable metric of similarity for them. For example, at how many possible worlds would the intensions of Thelma's and Louise's 'tiger' concepts have to coincide for them to be similar enough to count as a concept of tigers in a typical conversational context? 147 billion? 92 per cent?

I am also somewhat sceptical about the prospects of so-called 'functional-role' accounts.[15] We have been offered no workable way of saying what the functional role of a concept is, let alone one that promises to allow us to measure how similar the roles of two concepts are.

We are, indeed, nowhere close to having a proper theoretical account of cognitive content. In that sense, our ignorance of meaning remains profound.

# REFERENCES

BLOCK, N. (1995), 'An Argument for Holism', *Proceedings of the Aristotelian Society*, 95: 151–69.

BRAUN, D. (2001), 'Russellianism and Explanation'. *Philosophical Perspectives*, 15: 253–89.

BURGE, T. (1977), 'Belief De Re', *Journal of Philosophy*, 74: 338–62.

—— (1979), 'Individualism and the Mental', in French, Uehling, and Wettstein (1979), 73–121.

—— (1988), 'Individualism and Self-Knowledge', *Journal of Philosophy*, 85: 649–63.

—— (1996), 'Our Entitlement to Self-Knowledge', *Proceedings of the Aristotelian Society*, 96: 91–116.

[15] See Segal (2000), 88–104, for discussion.

DAVIDSON, D. (1968), 'On Saying That', *Synthese*, 19: 158–74.

EVANS, G. (1982), *The Varieties of Reference* (Oxford: Clarendon Press).

FODOR, J. (1987)a, *Psychosemantics* (Cambridge, Mass.: MIT Press).

—— and LEPORE, E. (1992), *Holism: A Shopper's Guide* (Cambridge, Mass.: MIT Press).

FRENCH, P. A., UEHLING, T. E., and WETTSTEIN, H. K., eds. (1979), *Studies in Epistemology* (Midwest Studies in Philosophy, 5; Minneapolis: University of Minnesota Press).

GRIMM, R., and MERRILL, D., eds. (1987), *Contents of Thought: Proceedings of the 1985 Oberlin Colloquium in Philosophy* (Tucson, Ariz.: University of Arizona Press).

LOAR, B. (1987), 'Social Content and Psychological Content', in Grimm and Merrill (1987), 99–139.

McDOWELL, J. (1977), 'On the Sense and Reference of a Proper Name', *Mind* 86: 159–85.

PEACOCKE, C. (1996), 'Our Entitlement to Self-Knowledge: Entitlement, Self-Knowledge and Conceptual Redeployment', *Proceedings of the Aristotelian Society*, 96: 117–58.

SEGAL, G. (2000), *A Slim Book about Narrow Content* (Cambridge, Mass.: MIT Press).

# CHAPTER 14

# Externalism and the Fregean Tradition

*Jessica Brown*

## 1 Introduction

Two traditions dominate philosophical discussion of thought-content and its individuation. According to the externalist tradition, associated with Putnam and Burge, a subject's thought-contents are partly individuated by her environment. By contrast, the Fregean tradition stresses that one component of thought-content is sense, or the mode of presentation of the objects or kinds thought about. Although some have assumed that these two traditions are incompatible, others have attempted to combine them in a single position.[1] This combined position may seem attractive: on the one hand, there are strong arguments for externalism, such as the Twin Earth arguments of Putnam and Burge; and on the other, Fregeans argue that their notion of cognitive content is required to make psychological sense of subjects. Here, I examine whether it is coherent to combine Fregean sense and 'social externalism'—the view, associated with Burge, that a subject's thought-contents are partly individuated in terms of the practices of her linguistic community.

I shall investigate this combination by examining Segal's recent arguments against social externalism and for an internalist notion of content (Segal 2000; and in this volume). As we shall see, Segal's arguments rely on the Fregean notion of cognitive content individuated by differences in attitude. However, I shall argue that although Burge combines social

[1] Kripke (1972), Salmon (1986), and Millikan (1993) hold that the two traditions are opposed; Evans (1982), Peacocke (1983), McDowell (1986), and Burge (1986) attempt to combine them.

externalism with this Fregean notion of content, the two are in fact incompatible. As a result, I conclude that Segal's arguments pose no threat to the social externalist, who should, and indeed must, reject the Fregean notion of cognitive content. The arguments concerning neo-Fregean externalism raise key questions about the epistemic capacities of rational subjects and, in particular, their grasp of thought-content, sameness and difference of thought-content, and the logical properties of their thoughts. In the last section I consider one particular epistemological issue—whether Segal's internalist view undermines a subject's knowledge of her thought-contents.

## 2 Segal's Arguments

In his contribution above and in his recent book, Segal argues against the externalist claim, associated with Burge, that a subject's thought-contents are partly individuated in terms of the practices of her linguistic community. For ease of reference, I shall call this view 'social externalism' and those who hold it 'social externalists', whether or not they endorse other parts of Burge's position. In the present volume, Segal describes several cases in which, he claims, we cannot give an adequate account of a subject's thoughts by using a notion of cognitive content that is individuated socially but, rather, need a notion of cognitive content which is individualist and holist. I shall briefly sketch his arguments before investigating the key assumptions on which they rely.

His first argument concerns Alf, who is stipulated to be competent with two terms which are in fact synonyms, the English term 'arthritis' and the French term 'arthrite', while deferring to the relevant experts for their correct explication. However, Alf is ignorant of the fact that 'arthritis' and 'arthrite' are synonyms. He fully understands 'arthrite', correctly holding that 'arthrite' just means inflammation of the joints. By contrast, he misunderstands 'arthritis', and incorrectly supposes that it applies to inflammations of the joints and the thigh. Thus, Alf assents to 'Arthritis is arthritis', but dissents from 'Arthrite is arthritis'. Segal then argues that Alf associates different cognitive contents with 'arthritis' and 'arthrite' by appeal to a neo-Fregean principle about the individuation of thought. As is well known, Frege held that two thoughts $p$ and $q$ are distinct in content if it is possible for a subject rationally to hold different attitudes to these thoughts, such as believing one while doubting the other.[2] Segal formulates this Fregean idea in the principle FD:

(FD) If a subject, $S$, rationally assents to $P(t_1)$ and dissents from or abstains on the truth value of $P(t_2)$ (where $P(. . .)$ is an extensional context), then $t_1$ and $t_2$ have different meanings in $S$'s idiolect and $S$ associates different concepts with them.[3]

Applying FD to Alf, who assents to 'Arthritis is arthritis' but dissents from 'Arthritis is arthrite', Segal concludes that Alf associates different concepts with the two terms.

However, Segal argues that we cannot accommodate this conclusion solely by using a notion of socially individuated content. Social externalists hold that a subject who is competent with a term and defers to the experts expresses the same concept with that term as the experts. Now, Alf is competent with the terms 'arthritis' and 'arthrite', and defers to the relevant experts. Further, Segal assumes[4] that, since 'arthritis' and 'arthrite' are synonyms, the relevant experts express the very same concept by these terms, namely <u>arthritis</u> (I use underlining to indicate concepts). If that is right, then the social externalist has only one concept to attribute to Alf. Segal concludes that, whether or not there is a type of cognitive content which is individuated socially, there is also a type of cognitive content which is individualist (above, pp. 416–17, and 2000: ch. 3, where the argument is filled out). The existence of such individualist content would be disputed by many externalists, including Burge.[5] Segal (2000) adds further considerations to the example of Alf in order to argue for the outright denial that there is a type of content which is partly individuated by social factors (p. 122). In particular, he argues against the attempt to combine externalism with a narrow, or internalist, notion of content via a two-factor theory (ch. 4). In addition, he argues that what is often taken as a central objection to

---

[2] Frege (1892; 1980: 80, 153). See also Evans (1982), 18–20; Peacocke (1983), 108; Campbell (1987–8), 281–6.

[3] Segal (2000) does not explicitly use the principle FD, but it is clearly at work (pp. 65–7).

[4] The legitimacy of this assumption, which is made explicit in Segal (2000), 67–9, is discussed below.

[5] e.g. Burge (1986), 6–24; McCulloch (1995), 199–201; Peacocke (1993).

internalism—that it lacks a principled and complete way of individuating the extensions of subjects' concepts—also applies to externalism (ch. 5).

Segal's second argument concerning Fred aims to show that there is a type of cognitive content which is not only individualist but also holist. What is important for our purposes is that the first half of this argument has the same structure as the argument concerning Alf. Thus, Fred, like Alf, is stipulated to be competent with two synonymous terms, in his case 'tiger' and 'Panthera tigris', and to defer to the experts for their explication, despite being ignorant of their synonymy. As a result, he has different attitudes to statements involving the terms. He assents to 'Pantherae tigres are indigenous to India', but denies that 'Tigers are indigenous to India', and instead assents to 'Tigers are indigenous to Africa'. Segal appeals to the principle FD to argue that Fred associates different concepts with 'tiger' and 'Panthera tigris'. On grounds analogous to those used in the Alf argument, it may be concluded that, whether or not there is a notion of cognitive content which is individuated socially, there is a type of cognitive content which is individualist. Segal adds further considerations to argue for a notion of content which is holist. Although the details of this further argument will not concern us, it is useful to sketch out its general form. The further argument involves two other subjects, Thelma and Louise, who are also competent with the terms 'tiger' and 'Panthera tigris' but, unlike Fred, know them to be synonymous. However, Thelma and Louise disagree about where the things called 'tiger' or 'Panthera tigris' are indigenous: Thelma believes that they are indigenous to India, Louise believes that they are indigenous to Africa. Segal argues that, given the earlier conclusion that Fred associates two different concepts with 'tiger' and 'Panthera tigris', we are forced to accept a holistic notion of content when we try to specify what relations obtain between the concepts possessed by Fred, Thelma, and Louise (pp. 418–21). However, he argues that a socially individuated notion of content cannot accommodate this holistic conclusion. Segal concludes that whether or not there is a notion of cognitive content which is socially individuated, there is also a notion of cognitive content which is individualist and holist. But many externalists would reject the existence of this kind of content.

We have seen that the first part of the Fred argument has the same structure as that concerning Alf. In each case, Segal appeals to FD to argue that a subject associates different concepts with two terms which are in fact synonyms. However, he argues that a social externalist cannot accommodate this conclusion since she would claim that the subject associates the same concept with the terms. For, in each case, the subject is competent with the relevant terms and defers to the experts for their correct explication. Further, Segal assumes that the experts associate the same concept with a pair of synonymous terms. It seems, then, that each of Segal's arguments rests on three key assumptions:

(1) FD is correct.
(2) Experts associate the same concept with a pair of synonymous terms.
(3) A social externalist would accept that a subject who is competent with a term and defers to the experts has the same concept as the experts associate with the term.

Of these three assumptions, the social externalist cannot reject (3). For, it is central to the social-externalist view to hold that a subject who is competent with a term and defers to the experts has the same concept as the experts associate with the term, even if she incompletely understands the term. For example, in his arthritis thought-experiment, Burge argues that the patient shares <u>arthritis</u> with the doctor despite his incomplete understanding, since he is competent with the term and defers to the relevant experts for its correct explication (Burge 1979: 94).

However, Burge would deny assumption (2), that experts associate the same concept with a pair of synonymous terms. He motivates this denial by two considerations. First, he argues that even experts can rationally doubt true statements of synonymy, such as 'arthritis is a rheumatoid ailment of the joints', whereas they cannot rationally doubt the corresponding identity judgements, such as 'arthritis is arthritis' (Burge 1986: 715). Second, he argues that even if the conventional linguistic meaning of a term such as 'arthritis' changes, subjects can be characterized both before and after the change as sharing beliefs, e.g. that arthritis is painful (Burge 1986: 715–17). Thus, we cannot identify the cognitive content of a term at any given time with the cognitive content of the expression which gives its conventional linguistic meaning at that time. So Burge would object to Segal's arguments by denying assumption (2).

However, Segal (2000) ingeniously blocks this objection. He points out that his arguments only require the possibility that two synonymous terms express the same concept, and argues that cases of this kind are created whenever an abbreviation is introduced and explicitly stipulated to be synonymous with an existent expression. 'In such cases, it is hard to see how the synonymous expressions could express different concepts, since the introduced expression has no life of its own. It simply inherits all of its cognitive properties from its older sibling' (2000: 69). Further, Segal provides several variants of his argument which do not require that experts associate the same concept with a pair of synonymous expressions. In each variant, a subject has two concepts which are deferentially linked to just one expert term and concept. In one variant Alf, as before, is acquainted with the term 'arthritis', and falsely supposes that it applies to certain inflammations of the joints and thigh. He then reads a poor photocopy of an article about arthritis, and misreads 'arthritis' as 'anthnitis', coming to believe that 'anthnitis' is a distinct condition that means inflammation of the joints only. As before, Segal can apply FD to argue that Alf associates distinct concepts with the two terms. But in this case there is only one chain of deference leading back to a single expert term and concept. Segal concludes that we need to introduce a type of cognitive content that is independent of social factors to accommodate the fact that Alf has two distinct concepts (2000: 73–4). Segal generates other variants by pointing out that a subject might mistakenly think that a single term has both a generic and a more specific meaning (p. 75).

The only remaining way for a social externalist to block Segal's arguments would be by denying assumption (1), that FD is correct. Burge is unlikely to adopt this response, for he endorses the principle FD. This is clearly apparent in his argument that experts associate different concepts with a pair of synonymous expressions. Recall that Burge holds that even experts can rationally doubt true statements of synonymy, such as 'arthritis is a rheumatoid ailment of the joints', whereas they cannot rationally doubt the corresponding identity judgements, such as 'arthritis is arthritis'. He concludes that synonymous expressions are associated with distinct concepts, and that belief content is distinct from conventional linguistic meaning.

However, although Burge himself apparently accepts FD, I shall argue that any social externalist, including Burge, should reject it.[6] For, the case of Alf which Segal combines with FD to argue for internalism could instead be used to show that social externalism is incompatible with FD. Recall that it is part of Segal's case that Alf is not only competent with 'arthrite' and defers to the experts concerning its correct explication, but also fully understands 'arthrite'. Thus, the social externalist should accept that Alf associates the same concept with 'arthrite' as the experts do. Further, Alf is in exactly the same position with respect to 'arthritis' as the patient in Burge's original thought-experiment—he is competent with 'arthritis', defers to the experts concerning its application, but mistakenly supposes it applies to certain inflammations of the joints and the thigh. Now Burge and other social externalists hold that the patient in Burge's original thought-experiment associates the same concept with 'arthritis' as the experts do. Given that Alf is in the same position as the arthritis patient, the social externalist should say the same about Alf. Thus, Alf associates the same concept with each of 'arthritis' and 'arthrite' as the experts do. On the assumption that the experts associate the same concept with each term, then so does Alf. But, then, Alf provides a counter-example to FD. For, it is part of the description of the case that Alf assents to 'Arthritis is arthritis' but dissents from 'Arthrite is arthritis'. Thus, whereas Segal applies FD to the case of Alf to argue that there is a type of cognitive content which is individualist, the social externalist should regard the case of Alf as providing reason to reject FD, and thus Segal's arguments.

Now, Burge would reject this argument since he rejects the assumption that experts associate the same concept with a pair of synonymous terms. However, we can avoid this objection by appeal to Segal's variant cases. For example, take Segal's photocopy case, in which Alf is acquainted with the term 'arthritis' and falsely supposes that it applies to certain inflammations of the joints and thigh. Alf then reads a poor photocopy of an article about arthritis, and misreads 'arthritis' as 'anthnitis', coming to believe that 'anthnitis' is a distinct condition that means inflammation of the joints only. Notice that Alf is in the same position with respect to 'arthritis' as the patient in Burge's original thought-experiment—he is competent with the term 'arthritis' and defers to the experts concerning its correct explication,

---

[6] Kimbrough (1998) provides a different argument for the conclusion that social externalism is incompatible with a principle similar to FD.

but falsely supposes that it applies to certain inflammations of the joints and thigh. So, the social externalist should accept that Alf associates the same concept with 'arthritis' as the experts do, namely <u>arthritis</u>. Further, Alf has a concept which he would express by 'anthnitis' where (i) 'anthnitis' is deferentially linked to the concept the experts associate with 'arthritis'; and, (ii) Alf understands 'anthnitis' to mean inflammation of the joints—the expert definition of 'arthritis'. So, the social externalist should accept that Alf associates the same concept with 'anthnitis' as the experts associate with 'arthritis'. Thus, Alf associates the same concept, <u>arthritis</u>, with 'arthritis' and 'anthnitis'. But then the case constitutes a counter-example to FD. For, Alf would assent to 'Arthritis is arthritis', but dissent from 'Anthnitis is arthritis'. Thus, my argument for the claim that social externalism is incompatible with FD can be made independent of the assumption, which Burge would reject, that experts associate the same concept with a pair of synonymous terms.

The above arguments have two important consequences. First, although Burge tries to combine social externalism and the Fregean notion of content, in fact the two are incompatible. Second, the arguments leave us with a dialectical stand-off between Segal and his social-externalist opponents. Segal applies the principle FD to the cases of Alf and Fred to argue for a kind of cognitive content that is individualist and holist, and against socially individuated content (Segal 2000; and in this volume). But, I have argued that the social externalist should apply social externalism to Alf's case to argue against FD, and thus reject Segal's arguments. Each side may agree with the overall shape of the issues, and how the various positions and assumptions are related. However, they disagree about the starting point of argument in this area: Segal assumes FD and uses it to argue for a cognitive content that is individualist and holist, and against social externalism; the social externalist assumes social externalism to argue against FD and Segal's arguments. In order to further his position, Segal needs to motivate his starting point, rather than the social externalist's, by providing some reason against the considerations supporting social externalism, and providing some reason for FD. I consider each issue in turn.

## 3 Motivating Social Externalism

Segal (2000) identifies two considerations supporting the social-externalist claim that Burge's arthritis patient has the same concept as the expert, arthritis, despite his incomplete understanding: the first-person evidence that, after seeing the doctor, the patient would attribute arthritis to his earlier self; and the third-person evidence that we find it natural to attribute arthritis to the patient (Segal 2000: 77–8). Segal attempts to reconcile these intuitions with internalism. According to internalism, although we regularly attribute incompletely understood concepts to subjects, these attributions are literally false. Segal suggests that we make such attributions, despite their falsity, for the pragmatic reason that we do not always know precisely what concept a subject has, and/or have a term which expresses that concept (2000: 78–83). However, although Segal holds that our third-person attributions of incompletely understood concepts are literally false, he suggests a way of understanding the patient's own first-person attributions such that they are true. Segal holds that before Alf sees the doctor, he does not have arthritis but an individualistic concept; Segal agrees, however, that after seeing the doctor and hearing the expert definition, Alf has arthritis. None the less, Segal admits that, after seeing the doctor, the patient will attribute to his past self the same concept as he then has, namely arthritis. If, in his self-ascription, the patient were using the notion of cognitive content, then, on Segal's view, the patient's self-ascription would be false. To avoid this counter-intuitive conclusion, Segal suggests that the patient is operating with a different notion of a concept as an organic unity:

I suggest that to understand Alf's view of the matter, we need to think of concepts as organic entities that can persist through changes of extension. Alf takes it that after correction he still deploys the same concept he had earlier. In a sense he is perfectly correct. It is the same concept in the sense that it is the same organic unity that has survived conversation with the doctor. However, it has undergone a change of cognitive content and even of extension conditions. (2000: 77)

Thus, Segal suggests that we can accommodate the patient's self-attribution without claiming that the patient is just wrong about his thought-contents.

However, it seems *ad hoc* for Segal to argue, without independent justification, that the patient is using a notion of a concept as an organic unity.

Further, this view fails to cohere with what Segal says elsewhere about the role of cognitive content in psychology:

... cognitive content is part of the subject matter of psychology. It is what gives psychology its explanatory and predictive power. (2000: 121)

... psychology as it is practised by the folk and by the scientists, is already, at root, internalist ... Internalism, therefore, does not need to posit any additional notion of content beyond that which is already attributed by content sentences of propositional attitude reports. (2000: 122–3)

These quotes suggest that Segal thinks that folk-psychological attributions standardly use the notion of cognitive content. Given this, it is odd to suggest that the arthritis patient's self-attributions use some other notion of a concept. Why should the patient use different notions of a concept in making self-attributions and other-attributions? Segal's problem here illustrates a more general problem for the internalist. Either the internalist makes the counter-intuitive claim that subjects such as the patient are just wrong about their own mental contents, or she attempts to find some way of understanding first-person ascriptions so that the patient's self-attribution is correct although compatible with internalism. Taking the latter option involves claiming that the patient is using some notion of content other than the internalist one in his self-ascriptions. However, internalists standardly defend their position by arguing that the internalist notion of content is central to folk-psychological explanations and predictions. But, if the internalist notion of content is central to folk psychology, it is odd to argue that first-person ascriptions use some other kind of content.

## 4 Motivating FD

There are well-known Fregean reasons for introducing a notion of cognitive content which is individuated in accordance with FD. The classic Fregean argument for such cognitive content concerns the need to account for informative true identity judgements (Frege 1892; 1980: 80). To take Frege's well-worn example, imagine that an astronomer, Celeste, has been observing the planet Venus in both the morning and evening, but does not realize that the morning and evening observations are of the same planet. Instead, she has two terms for Venus—'the Morning Star' and 'the Evening Star'—

which are appropriately connected to observations of Venus at different times. She has the beliefs that she would express by saying:

(a) 'The Morning Star is the Morning Star';
(b) 'The Evening Star is the Evening Star',

but finds neither of these informative. Now suppose that she gains new evidence that in fact the two stars are the same heavenly body. In a moment of sudden realization, she thinks the thought she would express as:

(c) 'The Morning Star is the Evening Star'.

This belief seems very informative, and allows her to bring together a host of information about the Morning Star and the Evening Star which she previously kept separate. The Fregean argues that we cannot accommodate these facts unless we introduce the notion of sense. Suppose that the semantic content of the thought-constituents corresponding to 'the Morning Star' and 'the Evening Star' were exhausted by the object referred to. In that case, the Fregean says, it is hard to see how Celeste could find the thought she would express by (c) informative. For, the two thought-constituents corresponding to 'the Morning Star' and 'the Evening Star' would have the same content; and so would the complete thoughts she expresses by (a), (b), and (c). The Fregean concludes that although the thought-constituents corresponding to 'the Morning Star' and 'the Evening Star' have the same reference, they differ in some other aspect of cognitive content, or sense.

A second and connected motivation for the Fregean notion of cognitive content individuated in accord with FD arises from the explanation of inference and action. Consider Celeste at a time before the realization she would express with 'The Morning Star is the Evening Star'. Suppose that Celeste has attitudes she would express by:

(d) 'The Evening Star is clearly visible in the evening';
(e) 'It is crucially important to make as many observations as possible of the Morning Star'.

Celeste would fail to draw the conclusion she would express by:

(f) 'It is crucially important to make observations of the Evening Star in the evening', and she might fail to make any observations of the Evening Star in the evening. A Fregean would argue that we cannot explain these failures of inference and action if we suppose that the cognitive content of the thought-constituents corresponding to 'the Evening Star' and 'the Morning Star' is identical. For, on this view, the inference from (d) and (e) to (f) is a simple valid one. She would argue that we can explain these failures only if we suppose that the cognitive content of the relevant thought-constituents is different. While Segal provides no detailed argument for endorsing FD either in his contribution above or in his recent book, he appears to endorse these standard motivations for a Fregean notion of cognitive content, saying that 'the cognitive content of a concept . . . [is] what accounts for the concept's role in psychological explanation' (2000: 85).[7]

Although these arguments for a Fregean notion of cognitive content may seem forceful, I shall argue that a social externalist should not find them persuasive. My argument exploits the relationship between social externalism and a principle which I shall call 'the opaqueness of sameness of content' (OSC):

> (OSC) A subject may have two thoughts, or thought-constituents, with the same content at a single time, although she supposes that they have different contents, and is unable to realize that they have the same content without using empirical information.

I shall argue that social externalism is committed to OSC and, as a result, that social externalists should reject the classic Fregean argument for sense.

There are well-known arguments that social externalism is committed to OSC (e.g. Boghossian 1994: 37; Falvey and Owens 1994: 110–11).[8] These arguments concern subjects in the same type of situation as Segal's Alf: the subject has two terms which are in fact synonyms, although she does not realize this. For instance, in Falvey and Owens's argument, Rudolf is competent with the terms 'cilantro' and 'coriander'. Although they are synonyms, he mistakenly supposes that they name different herbs. Since

---

[7] See also Segal, above, p. 421; Burge too endorses the idea of a notion of cognitive content—his 'cognitive value'—which is used in psychological explanation (Burge 1986: 717).

[8] These authors phrase the point by saying that social externalism is incompatible with the positive claim that whenever a subject has two thoughts with the same content she can know non-empirically that they have the same content.

Rudolf is competent with the terms and defers to the relevant experts, a social externalist would claim that Rudolph associates the same concept with 'cilantro' as the experts do; and similarly for 'coriander'. Since the terms are synonyms, Falvey and Owens conclude that Rudolf associates the same concept with the two terms. Thus, the beliefs he would express with 'Coriander should be used sparingly' and 'Cilantro should be used sparingly' have the same content. But Rudolph mistakenly supposes that these beliefs have different contents since he thinks that 'coriander' and 'cilantro' name different herbs. Further, he can realize that these beliefs have the same content only by using empirical information about how the terms are used in his linguistic community.

Now, like Segal's original argument concerning Alf, these arguments are open to the objection that Burge denies that experts associate the same concept with a pair of synonymous expressions. For example, if the experts associate different concepts with 'coriander' and 'cilantro', then the beliefs Rudolf expresses with 'Coriander should be used sparingly' and 'Cilantro should be used sparingly' differ in their content, and the case fails to show that social externalism is committed to OSC. However, we may respond to this objection using the materials with which Segal defended his Alf argument. First, it seems that the argument merely requires the possibility of a pair of synonymous terms which express the same concept. But Segal has argued that such cases exist and are created whenever an abbreviation is introduced and explicitly stipulated to be synonymous with an existent expression. Second, we can use Segal's variant cases to make the argument that social externalism is committed to OSC independent of the assumption that synonymous terms express the same concept. Recall the photocopy case: as we saw above, a social externalist should hold that Alf associates the same concept with 'arthritis' and 'anthnitis', namely <u>arthritis</u>. Importantly, this claim does not rest on the assumption that experts associate the same concept with two synonymous terms. For, Alf's 'arthritis' and 'anthnitis' lead back to only one expert term and concept. Now, consider the thoughts that Alf would express by saying 'Arthritis is arthritis', and 'Anthnitis is arthritis'. The social externalist would hold that these thoughts have the same content. However, Alf would suppose that they have different contents since he thinks that 'arthritis' applies to certain conditions of the thigh, whereas 'anthnitis' does not. Further, Alf would need to gain empirical information about the use of terms in his language in order to realize that the relevant thoughts have the same content. So, irrespective of whether experts associate the same concept with a pair of synonyms, the social externalist should accept OSC.

I shall now argue that since social externalists are committed to OSC, they should reject the classic Fregean arguments for a notion of cognitive content individuated according to FD. The Fregean argued that we cannot explain Celeste's failure to put 'Morning Star' and 'Evening Star' thoughts together in inference without assuming that the thought-constituents she associates with 'the Morning Star' and 'the Evening Star' differ in cognitive content. However, an alternative explanation of Celeste's inference failures would be available if sameness of content were opaque, i.e. if a subject may have two thoughts, or thought-constituents, with the same content at a single time, yet believe mistakenly that they have different contents, and be unable to realize that they have the same content except by using empirical information. Suppose, then, that although Celeste associates thought-constituents having the same content with 'the Morning Star' and 'the Evening Star', she supposes that they have different contents since she thinks that the two expressions refer to different planets. This would explain why she fails to put 'Morning Star' and 'Evening Star' thoughts together in inference without the need to appeal to Fregean sense.

Now consider the Fregean argument from the identity judgements. The Fregean argued that Celeste finds the judgement she would express by (c) 'The Morning Star is the Evening Star' informative and that we can explain this only by assuming that the thought-constituents associated with 'the Evening Star' and 'the Morning Star' have different cognitive contents. However, if sameness of content is opaque, then an alternative explanation is available. Suppose that the thought-constituents Celeste expresses by 'the Morning Star' and 'the Evening Star' have the same content, but she initially mistakenly believes that they have different contents since she thinks that they refer to different planets. This explains the different cognitive role[9] played by the thoughts corresponding to (c) and (a), 'The Morning Star is

---

[9] If the thought-constituents Celeste associates with 'the Morning Star' and 'the Evening Star' have the same content, then the thoughts corresponding to (c) and (a) cannot differ in their semantic information. However, someone who endorses OSC can explain the cognitive differences between the two thoughts without invoking sense.

the Morning Star'. In particular, it explains the fact that (*c*), unlike (*a*), enables Celeste to bring together items of information about Venus previously held separate. Thus, both Fregean arguments are persuasive only if OSC is false. Since social externalists are committed to OSC, they should reject both these arguments.[10]

Now let us reconsider the dialectical stand-off between Segal and the social externalist. Recall that Segal assumes FD and applies it to the cases of Alf and Fred to argue for a type of cognitive content that is individualist and holist and, in his book, against socially individuated cognitive content. However, we saw that a social externalist could respond by applying social externalism to the same cases to argue against FD and Segal's conclusions. Faced with this response, Segal needs to provide some independent reason in favour of FD and against social externalism. In the last section we examined Segal's attempt to deal with the first- and third-person evidence which apparently supports social externalism, and found it inadequate. In this section we have examined the classic Fregean arguments for a notion of cognitive content individuated according to FD. We have seen that a social externalist should reject these classic arguments given that she endorses OSC. In conclusion, Segal's arguments present no threat to the social externalist. For, Segal's arguments rely on FD. But social externalism is incompatible with FD; the social externalist should not find the classic arguments for FD compelling; and, Segal's attempts to undermine the considerations which favour social externalism are inadequate.

These arguments provide further reason to suppose that one cannot coherently combine social externalism and the Fregean notion of cognitive content. In Section 2 we used Segal's cases to show that social externalism is incompatible with the Fregean notion of cognitive content individuated by FD. In this section we have seen that the same cases can be used to show that social externalism is committed to OSC. But, since the classic arguments

---

[10] Dummett makes a related point at the level of language, arguing that 'The underlying assumption [of the Fregean argument from informative identity statements to the notion of sense] is the compelling principle that, if someone knows the senses of two words, and the two words have the same sense, he must know that they have the same sense: hence, if the sense of a name consists merely in its reference, anyone who understands two names having the same reference must know that they have the same referent' (Dummett 1973: 95).

for the Fregean notion of cognitive content depend on the assumption that OSC is false, the social externalist should reject these classic arguments.

## 5 Cognitive Content and Knowledge

Before ending, I want to return to Segal's paper and his notion of a type of cognitive content that is individualist and holist. In the last part of his paper (above) Segal raises a putative problem for his view—that it undermines a subject's knowledge of what cognitive content she associates with a term. Although Segal is not explicit about this, I take it that the kind of knowledge of cognitive content at issue is non-empirical knowledge. Many philosophers suppose that a subject's knowledge of her own thought-contents is non-empirical—that is, she can know her thought-contents without depending in a justificatory way on empirical information.[11] Such non-empirical knowledge of content may seem to be threatened by Segal's internalist account of content since, on that view, there may be a change in the cognitive content a subject associates with a term which she fails to notice. For example, on Segal's view, the arthritis patient associates a different concept with 'arthritis' after seeing the doctor, but the patient would take himself to be thinking with the same concept both before and after the visit. If Segal's internalist view (above, p. 423) does threaten a subject's non-empirical knowledge of her thought-contents, then there would be an interesting parallelism between internalism and externalism about content. As is well known, one of the most important objections to externalism is that it threatens a subject's non-empirical knowledge of her thought-contents. If internalism faces the same objection, then externalism's alleged difficulties with knowledge of content could hardly be used as a basis for preferring internalism over externalism. In what follows I first question whether Segal's notion of cognitive content in fact raises any problem about knowledge of content. Second, I query whether Segal's proposed solution would provide an adequate solution, were there a problem.

According to Segal, his internalist notion of content threatens knowledge of content since it has the result that a subject may fail to notice a change in the cognitive content she associates with a term. However, failure to notice

[11]  e.g. *inter alios*, Davidson (1987); Burge (1988); Heil (1988); Falvey and Owens (1994); Gibbons (1996); Boghossian (1997); and McLaughlin and Tye (1998).

change *per se* does not undermine knowledge. For instance, I may know by vision that my friend's hair is blonde, even though I fail to notice that her hair has changed from brown to blonde since yesterday (perhaps I am too preoccupied to notice). However, intuitively, my knowledge of her hair colour would be threatened if I could not now visually distinguish blonde and brown hair. Sometimes failure to notice change is evidence for lack of a discriminative ability, but this is not always the case. I suggest, then, that for Segal's notion of cognitive content to raise, even prima facie, an intuitive problem about non-empirical knowledge of cognitive content, it must threaten a subject's discriminative abilities. In more detail, the key question is whether Segal's notion of cognitive content shows that the cognitive content a subject associates with a term may change from $c_1$ to $c_2$ such that, after the change, the subject cannot distinguish non-empirically between the actual situation in which she associates $c_2$ with the term, and the possible situation in which she associates $c_1$ with the term.[12]

Notice that taking such a lack of discriminative ability to undermine knowledge of cognitive content does not require the implausible view that a subject knows that $p$ only if she can distinguish the actual situation in which $p$ from *every other* possible alternative, including the possibility that she is brain in a vat. In the situation in which the cognitive content a subject associates with a term has changed from $c_1$ to $c_2$, the possibility that the subject associates $c_1$ with the term is a 'relevant' or 'nearby' possibility.[13] So, for Segal to take it that lack of a discriminative ability may undermine knowledge of cognitive content only requires him to suppose that a subject's knowledge that $p$ may be undermined by her inability to distinguish $p$ and other *relevant* alternatives. Even this view is controversial,[14] though it does not immediately invite scepticism about knowledge of the external world.

[12] This diagnosis fits in with Segal's text. Segal seems to assume that if a subject does not notice that the cognitive content she associates with a term has changed, then she cannot distinguish the two cognitive contents (above, p. 424), and he attempts to solve the putative problem by arguing that, in the case of colour, a subject can have knowledge without discriminative abilities.

[13] There are different ways of explaining what it means for a possibility to be 'relevant' or 'nearby': see Goldman (1976) and Nozick (1981).

[14] Some externalists have argued that a subject can non-empirically know that she thinks that $p$ even if she cannot non-empirically distinguish the actual situation in which she thinks that $p$ and *relevant* alternative situations in which she thinks some other thought (Falvey and Owens 1994; Gibbons 1996).

However, I shall leave this issue aside, and consider merely whether Segal's notion of cognitive content shows that a subject may be unable to distinguish non-empirically between the actual situation in which she associates one cognitive content with a term, and a relevant alternative situation in which she associates a different cognitive content with the term.

Consider why it is that Segal supposes that his notion of cognitive content gives rise to the possibility that the cognitive content a subject associates with a term may change, although she fails to notice. According to Segal's individualist notion of cognitive content, Burge's arthritis patient associates different cognitive contents with 'arthritis' before and after seeing the doctor. However, Segal admits that the patient himself does not seem to notice this change. In particular, after visiting the doctor, the patient would attribute the concept he then has, namely <u>arthritis</u>, to his earlier self. For instance, he would ascribe to his earlier self the belief that he has arthritis in his thigh (Segal, above, p. 415–16). Let us use the term 'tharthritis' to refer to the concept which Alf expresses with 'arthritis' before the visit to the doctor. Now consider whether this case shows that the subject cannot distinguish non-empirically between the two concepts. Someone might answer negatively as follows. On Segal's view, the change in the patient's cognitive contents is caused by the change in his views about what kind of ailment 'arthritis' applies to. Before seeing the doctor, he thought that 'arthritis' applied to inflammations of the joints and thigh; afterwards, he thinks that 'arthritis' applies only to inflammations of the joints. But, in principle, such a change of view seems introspectively accessible. Further, if the subject accepted Segal's view of cognitive content on the basis of Segal's philosophical arguments, then he could use his non-empirical knowledge of the change in his views to come to know non-empirically that the cognitive content he associates with 'arthritis' has changed. So, it seems that the subject can non-empirically distinguish between the situation in which he associates <u>arthritis</u> with 'arthritis' and the situation in which he associates <u>tharthritis</u> with 'arthritis'. The same point can be made in response to Segal's view that cognitive content is holist. On Segal's view, every time a subject changes her views (e.g. about where the animals called 'tigers' are indigenous), she changes her cognitive contents, although she might not notice this (above, p. 423). But, again, the change in view which causes the change in cognitive content seems introspectively accessible. So, although Segal's notion of cognitive content does lead to the possibility that the cognitive content a subject associates with a term may change from $c_1$ to $c_2$ although the subject does not in fact notice, it may be said that it does not follow that the subject lacks the ability to notice the change non-empirically, or to distinguish non-empirically between the situation in which she associates $c_1$ with the term, and the situation in which she associates $c_2$ with the term.

However, in fact this response is unsatisfactory. First, it relies on the subject's having non-empirical knowledge of Segal's internalist theory on the basis of philosophical arguments. But many subjects lack such knowledge, and have never even considered the debate between internalists and externalists. So, the defence seems inapplicable to the majority of subjects. Second, the defence depends on the idea that whenever a subject's views change, and thus her concepts change, she can have introspective access to that change. But this is not obviously the case. On Segal's view, even tiny changes in belief, such as a change in belief about where the things called 'tigers' are indigenous, can change one's concepts. Although subjects are sometimes aware of such changes of belief, this is not always so. Reading a gardening book which says that carrots are indigenous to the Middle East, I may be surprised and note that I had always thought they were indigenous to Britain. But, at other times, my beliefs may change without my registering this. Furthermore, it is not clear that it is even possible for me to register introspectively all of the changes in my beliefs. Given the sheer number of beliefs a subject has, and the number of changes in them over time, keeping track of all such changes would require a huge amount of cognitive resource. In conclusion, it seems that Segal's internalist view does have the result that the cognitive content a subject associates with a term may change from $c_1$ to $c_2$ although the subject cannot non-empirically distinguish between the situation in which she associates $c_1$ with the term, and the situation in which she associates $c_2$ with the term. Prima facie, this seems to threaten the subject's non-empirical knowledge of her thought-contents.

Notice that the threat to self-knowledge raised by Segal's internalist notion of content is very similar to that raised by externalist accounts of content. According to externalism, a subject's thought-contents are partly individuated in terms of the environment. Thus, externalists accept that a subject may be 'slowly switched' between two environments in such a way that her thoughts change. Perhaps she is originally on Earth and acquires the concept of water, but is then switched to Twin Earth, where she acquires the concept of twater. It seems plausible that the subject cannot distinguish non-empirically between the actual situation in which she thinks that twater is wet, and the possible situation in which she thinks that water is wet. Everything seems phenomenally just the same, whether she is on Earth thinking that water is wet, or on Twin Earth thinking that twater is wet. The change in her thought-contents is caused by external factors of which she can have only empirical knowledge. Incompatibilists have argued that the subject's inability to distinguish non-empirically between water and twater thoughts undermines her ability to know non-empirically what she is thinking. How, they say, can she know non-empirically that she is thinking that twater is wet if she cannot non-empirically distinguish water and twater thoughts?[15]

The standard externalist response to this incompatibilist argument is to stress that a subject is always reliable about what she thinks, even if she is subject to such a slow switch. As Burge points out, second-order thoughts of the form 'I judge that I think that $p$' are self-verifying. In judging that I think that $p$, I do indeed entertain the thought-content that $p$, and thus make the second-order thought true. Segal considers a parallel defence of the compatibility of his internalist notion of content and non-empirical knowledge of content. He points out that, on this internalist notion, a subject is always reliable about what cognitive content she associates with a term. For example, consider the term 'tiger'. At any time, a subject can correctly assert the following sentence with understanding:

It is a theorem of a correct semantic theory for my language that for all $x$, $x$ satisfies 'tiger' iff $x$ is a tiger. (Segal, above, p. 424)

However, Segal denies that this point about reliability answers the worry that internalism undermines non-empirical knowledge of content. For, he argues, such reliability is compatible with considerable ignorance about cognitive content.[16] Instead, Segal attempts to answer the worry about

[15] For a discussion of the slow-switch argument and the standard externalist response, see Burge (1988) and Falvey and Owens (1994).

[16] See Segal's comments about Burge's point that second-order judgements of the form 'I think with this very thought that $p$' are self-verifying and self-referential (above, pp. 426–7).

knowledge of content by appeal to an analogy with knowledge of colours. The thrust of the argument is as follows:

(1) On his notion of cognitive content, a subject would fail to notice a change in the cognitive content she associates with a term over a short time interval only if the change were small.

(2) A subject's failure to notice a change in the cognitive content she associates with a term over a short time interval would undermine her knowledge of what cognitive content she associates with that term if and only if that change is large.[17]

However, it seems to me that the analogy to knowledge of colour that Segal uses to support (2) establishes a weaker conclusion than Segal supposes.

In Segal's example, a subject looks at a certain colour—'Just Yellow'. She looks away for a few moments, and is then presented with a set of samples, including Just Yellow. The subject cannot distinguish Just Yellow from similar colours present in the set. Given this, Segal argues that she does not 'know *exactly* which colour it [Just Yellow] is' (above, p. 425). However, she can distinguish Just Yellow from shades of yellow which are less close, and from very different colours, such as blue and green. On this basis, Segal argues that she knows which colour Just Yellow is up to a 'reasonably high degree of specificity' (above, p. 425). Let us apply this conclusion to a subject's knowledge of cognitive content. Segal allows that his notion of cognitive content gives rise to the possibility that the cognitive content a subject associates with a term may change from $c_1$ to $c_2$ although she does not notice, where $c_1$ and $c_2$ differ only slightly. The Just Yellow analogy suggests at best that, after the change, the subject knows which cognitive content she associates with the term up to a 'reasonably high degree of specificity', although she does not have non-empirical knowledge of '*exactly* which' cognitive content she associates with the term. But, this is

[17] Segal says: 'If my two utterances . . . were relatively close together, say only three minutes apart, then it might seem worrying that I think that they meant the same thing when in fact they did not. How can I really claim to know what I mean, if I cannot tell when two of my own utterances, separated by just three minutes, mean the same? I think that if large and sudden shifts of meaning passed unnoticed, then that might be worrying. But this is only a very small one. The sorts of meaning shift that are, according to holism, induced by small doxastic changes are very slight indeed . . . The fact that I cannot distinguish very similar meanings is not a matter of grave concern' (above, pp. 424–5).

a weaker conclusion than Segal makes—that a subject's inability to distinguish very similar cognitive contents does not undermine her non-empirical knowledge of the cognitive content she associates with a term:

The fact that I may be unable to distinguish slightly different meanings when these are presented to me at different times—even if the times are only three minutes apart—does not seem threatening. (Above, p. 425)

More importantly, it is not clear that the conclusion he has established provides a full solution to the original worry. The original intuition that a subject can have non-empirical knowledge of her thought-contents seems to involve the idea that she has non-empirical knowledge of the actual contents she has, not just knowledge of them up to a reasonably high degree of specificity. Further, it may be problematic for Segal to accept that a subject does not know precisely which cognitive content she has. As we saw in Section 3, Segal supposes that fine-grained cognitive contents play a key role in folk psychology. He says that 'cognitive content is part of the subject matter of psychology. It is what gives psychology its explanatory and predictive power'. Further, he holds that 'psychology as it is practised by the folk and by the scientists, is already, at root, internalist' (Segal 2000: 121–3). But, if it is fine-grained cognitive content that is central to folk psychology and our everyday explanations and predictions of action, it would be odd if subjects cannot have non-empirical knowledge of the cognitive content of their attitudes at that fine-grained level. In particular, if a subject lacks non-empirical knowledge of her cognitive contents at the fine-grained level, then this may undermine her own psychological understanding of herself. If she cannot non-empirically distinguish different cognitive contents, even if they are only slightly different, then this may affect her reasoning. So, if a subject cannot have non-empirical knowledge of the fine-grained cognitive contents of her attitudes, this would seem to undermine the role that Segal assigns to cognitive content in folk psychology.

## 6 Conclusion

I have been examining whether one can coherently combine social externalism with the Fregean notion of cognitive content, or sense, via an investigation of Segal's arguments against socially individuated content and in favour of an internalist notion of content. Segal's arguments rely without justification on the Fregean notion of cognitive content individuated by difference of attitude. Although Burge accepts this notion of cognitive content, I have argued that it is in fact incompatible with social externalism. Further, I have argued that Segal cannot successfully appeal to the classic arguments for the Fregean notion of cognitive content to persuade the social externalist to accept that notion. For, these classic arguments are persuasive only if one denies what I have called 'the opaqueness of sameness of content', the claim that a subject may have two thoughts with the same content at a single time, yet suppose that they have different contents, where she can realize that they have the same content only by using empirical information. But, I have argued, social externalism is committed to the opaqueness of sameness of content. Thus, Segal's arguments do not threaten social externalism, for those arguments depend on a Fregean notion of cognitive content which the social externalist should reject.

# REFERENCES

BOGHOSSIAN, P. (1992), 'Externalism and Inference', *Philosophical Issues*, 2: 1–28.
—— (1994), 'The Transparency of Mental Content', in Tomberlin (1994), 33–50.
—— (1997), 'What the Existentialist Can Know A Priori', *Proceedings of the Aristotelian Society*, 97: 161–75.
BURGE, T. (1976), 'Belief and Synonymy', *Journal of Philosophy*, 75: 119–38.
—— (1979), 'Individualism and the Mental', in French, Uehling, and Wettstein (1979), 73–121; repr. in Ludlow and Martin (1998), 21–83 [citations are to the first printing].
—— (1986), 'Intellectual Norms and the Foundations of Normativity', *Journal of Philosophy*, 83: 697–720.
—— (1988), 'Individualism and Self-Knowledge', *Journal of Philosophy*, 85: 649–63.
CAMPBELL, J. (1987–8), 'Is Sense Transparent?', *Proceedings of the Aristotelian Society*, 88: 273–92.
DAVIDSON, D. (1987), 'Knowing One's Own Mind', *Proceedings of the American Philosophical Association*, 60: 441–58.
—— and HARMAN, G., eds. (1972), *The Semantics of Natural Language* (Dordrecht: Reidel).

DUMMETT, M. (1973), *Frege* (London: Duckworth).

EVANS, G. (1982), *The Varieties of Reference* (Oxford: Clarendon Press).

FALVEY, K., and OWENS, J. (1994), 'Externalism, Self-Knowledge, and Scepticism', *Philosophical Review*, 103: 107–37.

FREGE, G. (1892), 'On Sense and Reference', in *Translations from the Philosophical Writings of Gottlob Frege*, ed. P. Geech and M. Black (London: Blackwell, 1970).

—— (1980), *Philosophical and Mathematical Correspondence*, ed. G. Gabriel *et al.*, abridged for the English edition by B. McGuiness, and trans. by H. Kaal (Oxford: Blackwell).

FRENCH, P. A., UEHLING, T. E., and WETTSTEIN, H. K., eds. (1979), *Studies in Epistemology* (Midwest Studies in Philosophy, 5; Minneapolis: University of Minnesota Press).

GIBBONS, J. (1996), 'Externalism and Knowledge of Content', *Philosophical Review*, 105: 287–310.

GOLDMAN, A. (1976), 'Discrimination and Perceptual Knowledge', *Journal of Philosophy*, 73: 771–91.

GUNDERSON, K., ed. (1975), *Language, Mind, and Knowledge* (Minnesota Studies in the Philosophy of Science, 2; Minneapolis: University of Minnesota Press).

HEIL, J. (1988), 'Privileged Access', *Mind*, 97: 238–51.

KIMBROUGH, S. (1998), 'Anti-Individualism and Fregeanism', *Philosophical Quarterly*, 48: 470–82.

KRIPKE, S. (1972), 'Naming and Necessity', in Davidson and Harman (1972), 253–355.

LUDLOW, P., and MARTIN, N., eds. (1998), *Externalism and Self-Knowledge* (Stanford, Calif.: CSLI Publications).

McCULLOCH, G. (1995), *The Mind and its World* (London: Routledge).

McDOWELL, J. (1986), 'Singular Thought and the Extent of Inner Space', in McDowell and Pettit (1986), 137–68.

—— and PETTIT, P., eds. (1986), *Subject, Thought, and Context* (Oxford: Oxford University Press).

McLAUGHLIN, B., TYE, M. (1998), 'Content Externalism and Privileged Access', *Philosophical Review*, 107: 349–80.

MILLIKAN, R. (1993), *White Queen Psychology and Other Essays for Alice* (Cambridge, Mass.: MIT Press).

NOZICK, R. (1981), *Philosophical Explanations* (Oxford: Oxford University Press).

PEACOCKE, C. (1983), *Sense and Content* (Oxford: Blackwell).

—— (1993), 'Externalist Explanation', *Proceedings of the Aristotelian Society*, 93: 203–30.

PUTNAM, H. (1975), 'The Meaning of "Meaning"', in Gunderson (1975), 131–95; repr. in Putnam (1979), 215–71.

—— (1979), *Philosophical Papers*, ii. *Mind, Language and Reality* (Cambridge: Cambridge University Press).

SALMON, N. (1986), *Frege's Puzzle* (Cambridge, Mass.: MIT Press/Bradford Books).

SEGAL, G. (2000), *A Slim Book about Narrow Content* (Cambridge, Mass.: MIT Press).

TOMBERLIN, J. E., ed. (1994), *Logic and Language* (Philosophical Perspectives, 8; Atascadero, Calif.: Ridgeview).

# PART FOUR

Epistemology through Language

# CHAPTER 15

# *What is the Acquisition Argument?*

*Alexander Miller*

## 1 Introduction

Semantic realism, as I shall understand it in this paper, is the combination of the views (1) that sentential understanding is constituted by grasp of truth conditions and (2) that the notion of truth which figures therein is essentially epistemically unconstrained. In a single slogan, understanding a sentence consists in some cases in grasp of potentially recognition-transcendent truth conditions. For example, a semantic realist about the past holds that our understanding of 'Caesar sneezed fifteen times on his 19th birthday' consists in grasp of its truth condition, where this is capable of obtaining even though there is no guarantee that we shall be able, even in principle, to recognize that that is so.

Semantic realism, thus characterized, has come under attack from Michael Dummett and his supporters.[1] Dummett has at least two distinct arguments against semantic realism: the *acquisition argument* and the *manifestation argument*. Briefly, these arguments go as follows. If our understanding of some sentences of a given discourse is constituted by grasp of

This paper grew out of a talk I gave at the Epistemology of Language conference in Sheffield in 2000. For useful discussion, I am grateful to the audience on that occasion, and in particular to Barry. C. Smith for a helpful and perceptive commentary. I am also grateful to the conference organizer, Alex Barber, for inviting me to speak, and for some helpful written comments on this paper.

[1] See e.g. Dummett (1978), Preface and essays 1, 10, 14, 21; Dummett (1991); Dummett (1993), essays 1–7, 11, 20; also Wright (1986), *passim*; Tennant (1997), *passim*. For an overview, see Miller (1998), ch. 9, and Miller (2001).

potentially recognition-transcendent truth conditions, how could we have *acquired* that understanding, given that our training in the use of sentences is a training to respond to situations which we are, necessarily, capable of recognizing to obtain when they obtain? And if our understanding of some sentences of a given region of discourse is constituted by grasp of potentially recognition-transcendent truth conditions, how could we *manifest* that understanding in our *use* of those sentences, given that the situations to which we respond in our uses of those sentences are, necessarily, situations which we are capable of recognizing to obtain when they obtain? In this article, my focus will be on the first of these, the acquisition argument.[2]

Before beginning the discussion of the acquisition argument, I would like to enter some caveats. Firstly, I shall not be concerned with the question whether semantic realism constitutes the *essence* of any metaphysical view worth calling realist, nor even with whether evaluating semantic realism provides an interesting way of evaluating realist/anti-realist disputes in metaphysics.[3] Secondly, I am not concerned with the relationship between semantic realism, as characterized above, and realism characterized in terms of unrestricted adherence to the *principle of bivalence*.[4] Thirdly, although I shall utilize some claims about the nature and plausibility of Dummett's manifestation argument, I shall not, apart from that, be concerned with other arguments that might be developed against semantic realism, such as Crispin Wright's arguments from *rule-following* and *normativity*.[5] Fourthly, I shall not be concerned with the plausibility or otherwise of *semantic anti-realism* conceived as a positive meaning-theoretic proposal.

I shall proceed as follows. In Section 2 I outline what I shall call the *strong acquisition argument*. In Section 3 I quickly review the response to the acquisition argument which utilizes the notion of a *truth-value link*, and also of why that response apparently fails. I then, in Section 4, outline John Mc-

---

[2] My approach to the acquisition argument here rests heavily upon a response to the manifestation argument (see especially sects. 11–12). For a full development and defence of this approach to the manifestation argument, see Miller (2002).

[3] A fuller treatment would at this point need to include some discussion of Michael Devitt's illuminating work on this issue: see e.g. Devitt (1991). But I cannot digress here: I discuss the matter more fully in Miller (forthcoming).

[4] For some excellent discussion, see McGinn (1982); Currie (1993), § II; the Introduction to Wright (1986); and Rosen (1995).

[5] For these arguments, see Wright (1986), 23–9.

Dowell's 'M-realist' response to the acquisition argument and explain why anti-realists have been untroubled by that response. In Section 5 I explain why, in the light of considerations concerning the *compositionality* of truth conditions, anti-realists more or less concede that the strong acquisition argument, as it stands, is a failure. In Section 6 I argue that given the cogency of the compositionality response, anti-realists ought also to concede that McDowell's M-realism effectively undermines the strong acquisition argument.

By the end of Section 6, then, it is clear that the strong acquisition argument, as it stands, is a failure. In the rest of the paper I investigate whether there is some other version of the acquisition argument potentially more harmful to semantic realism. In order to do this, in Sections 7–8 I look at Dummett's manifestation argument, as developed and presented by Wright. It emerges in Section 9 that this argument, which I call the *strong manifestation argument*, is, like the strong acquisition argument, apparently conceded by anti-realists to be a failure. In Section 10 I argue that this concession is only apparent: anti-realists develop what I call the *weak manifestation argument*, which, in the presence of a certain conception of implicit linguistic knowledge, has the same force as the strong manifestation argument. In Sections 11–12 I sketch a response to the weak manifestation argument. In Section 13 I investigate the prospects for a *weak acquisition argument*. I conclude that it is by no means clear whether the anti-realist can mount a weak acquisition argument, but that even if he can, the argument can be neutralized by the semantic realist.

## 2 The Strong Acquisition Argument

In this section I outline the *strong acquisition argument*. This takes off from the observation that speakers of English are not born with the ability to speak English, but rather acquire that ability through being trained by those already competent in the language. The conditions which we are trained to respond to are, of necessity, conditions which we are capable of recognizing to obtain when they obtain. So how do we extract from this training a grasp of conditions whose obtaining may outrun even our most refined recognitional capacities? Alternatively, if our understanding of sentences about the past (say) is constituted by knowledge of potentially recognition-transcendent truth conditions, it seems utterly mysterious how we could have *acquired* that understanding, given that our training in the use of such sentences is a training to respond to situations which we are, necessarily, capable of recognizing to obtain when they obtain. The challenge the realist faces is to dispel this apparent mystery.

Dummett's canonical formulation of the acquisition argument is contained in the following passage:

The general form of the argument employed by the anti-realist is a very strong one. He maintains that the process by which we came to grasp the sense of statements of the disputed class, and the use which is subsequently made of these statements, are such that we could not derive from it any notion of what it would be for such a statement to be true independently of the sort of thing we have learned to recognise as establishing the truth of such statements. What we learn to do is to accept . . . the occurrence of certain conditions which we have been trained to recognise, as conclusively justifying the assertion of a given statement of the disputed class, and the truth of certain other statements, or the occurrence of certain other conditions, as conclusively justifying its denial. In the very nature of the case, we could not possibly have come to understand what it would be for the statement to be true independently of that which we have learned to treat as establishing its truth: there simply was no means by which we could be shown this. (Dummett 1978: 362)

Wright, in expounding Dummett's argument, provides the following formulation:

How are we supposed to be able to *form* any understanding of what it is for a particular statement to be true if the kind of state of affairs which it would take to make it true is conceived, *ex hypothesi*, as something beyond our experience, something which we cannot confirm and which is insulated from any distinctive impact on our consciousness? (Wright 1986: 13)

While McDowell, who goes on to offer the realist a response to the argument, frames it thus:

All that can be imparted, by the training that results in competence with a language, is an ability to suit one's linguistic behaviour to circumstances that impinge on one's consciousness. How can the capacity so acquired involve the idea of states of affairs that may obtain even though they defeat all attempts to bring them to our awareness? How could the training have given one any conception of what it would be for such a state of affairs to obtain? (McDowell 1998: 296)

In its simplest form, then, the acquisition argument can be represented as follows. Let (1) be the statement of semantic realism: (1) Our understanding of the sentences of discourse D is constituted by our knowledge of their potentially recognition-transcendent truth conditions. Let (2) be: we acquired our understanding of the sentences of D from a course of training in their use. Then the argument against semantic realism is simply:

> If (1) then not (2).
> (2).
> ─────────────
> ∴ Not (1).

In this way the acquisition argument purports to establish the falsity of semantic realism. Call any such version of the acquisition argument— which aims to establish that semantic realism is false or unacceptable—a *strong* version of the acquisition argument. The argument is clearly valid, so the only way for the semantic realist to mount a response is to question one or more of its premisses. Most of the responses developed in the realist literature take issue with the first premiss: they attempt to show that even given the assumption that our understanding is constituted by knowledge of potentially recognition-transcendent truth conditions, we can still hold on to the claim that that understanding was acquired from ordinary, everyday training in their use. I shall now consider a number of realist responses of this type.

## 3 Responses to the Strong Acquisition Argument

Consider two types of sentence where a dispute between semantic realism and anti-realism can arise: statements about other minds and statements about the past. In both cases we can form sentences which are not effectively decidable. Take 'Jane has toothache' and 'Julius Caesar was the victim of a sneezing attack on his 19th birthday'. In neither case do we know a procedure the correct implementation of which is guaranteed to issue in a correct verdict about the truth value of the sentence. Suppose, however, that *first-person* ascriptions of mental states, and sentences about the *present*, are otherwise unproblematic from an anti-realist point of view. The idea behind the *truth-value-link* defence of realism is that we can acquire a grasp of the truth conditions of sentences in the anti-realistically *problematic* class via our grasp of (a) the truth conditions of sentences in the anti-realistically unproblematic class and (b) a set of propositions which systematically link the truth values of other-ascriptions and first-person ascriptions of mental states and the truth-values of sentences in the past tense and sentences in the present tense. Examples of (b) would be:

(A) 'Jane has toothache', as uttered by me, is true iff 'I have toothache', as uttered by Jane, is true.

(B) 'Julius Caesar was the victim of a sneezing attack on his 19th birthday', as uttered by me now, is true iff 'Julius Caesar is the victim of a sneezing attack on his 19th birthday', as uttered by a Roman in 81 BC, was true then.

Since the right-hand sides of these concern, respectively, first-person ascriptions of mental states and sentences in the present tense, the thought is that we can exploit our unproblematic grasp of the truth conditions of these, and then move from right to left to form an unproblematic grasp of the truth conditions of the sentences in dispute.

This style of response to the acquisition argument is held to be hopeless by both realists and anti-realists alike. McDowell's rejection of the truth-value-link manœuvre is perhaps canonical. Of the application of the manœuvre to the case of the past, McDowell writes:

An anti-realist finds it unintelligible that a conception of the truth-condition of a past-tensed utterance, thought of as something whose obtaining is, in itself, inaccessible, should be involved in linguistic competence. The realist's purported reply is on these lines: 'You can see how someone can know what it is for rain to be falling. Well, a sentence like "It was raining" is understood as saying that that very circumstance obtained at some past time.' Again, this does not meet the worry, but simply restates the claim that gave rise to it. The problem was precisely an inability to see how the past obtaining of that circumstance—an instance of a kind of circumstance that the realism we are considering makes inaccessible—can possibly enter into any meaning one could succeed in attaching to a sentence. (McDowell 1998: 301; see also Hale 1997: 276–77)

The truth-value-link move attempts to meet the strong acquisition argument on the anti-realist's own terms: it concedes that the only cases in which grasp of truth conditions can be held to be unproblematic are those in which the sentences concerned have truth conditions which are guaranteed to be accessible, and attempts to show that this concession, together with the truth-value links, is enough to render it possible for speakers to acquire an understanding of sentences whose truth conditions are potentially inaccessible. However, McDowell's point is that the problem with this is that the right-hand sides of the likes of (A) and (B) are not in fact anti-realistically unproblematic. What is unproblematic, according to the anti-realist, is that our understanding of present-tense sentences *as uttered now*, or my understanding of self-ascriptions of mental states *as uttered by me*, can be construed in terms of grasp of those sentences' truth conditions. But of course, these do not figure on the right-hand sides of (A) and (B): what figure there are rather present-tense sentences *as uttered in the past*, and self-ascriptions of mental states *as uttered by others*. Since the truth conditions of such sentences, considered in these contexts of use, are as inaccessible as the relevant past-tense sentences and ascriptions of mental states to others, to take them as unproblematic starting points for an acquisition of a grasp of the truth conditions of the disputed sentences is simply to beg the question against the anti-realist. Wright summarizes the point nicely:

The important projection is not that from right to left across the truth-value links; it is that involved in securing *ingress*, as it were, into the right-hand sides. The problem, after all, was to explain how it was that a trainee, familiar with what it is for it to be raining at the present time, could arrive at a conception of what it is for that very same sort of circumstance to have obtained, in a manner possibly transcending our present capacities of awareness, at a particular past time. In supposing that the biconditional in question can be of any use to him, the problem is tacitly assumed to have been solved. (Wright 1986: 91)

## 4 McDowell's Response to the Strong Acquisition Argument

McDowell develops a realist response to the acquisition argument against semantic realism about the past and other minds which, he claims, avoids the charge of question-begging to which the truth-value-link manœuvre succumbs. Wright argues that McDowell's 'M-realist' response falls prey to a worry which is very similar to that faced by truth-value-link realism. In this section I shall briefly outline the M-realist position, and Wright's objection to it. I shall argue in a later section that Wright's objection fails.

Suppose we reject the assumption—which may be implicit in some versions of truth-value-link realism—that the truth conditions of statements about the past or about the mental states of others are not *always* inaccessible. In other words, we reject the assumption that although we may have access to states of affairs which constitute *evidence* for the obtaining of such a truth condition, we never have access to the truth condition itself. That is to say, suppose that *sometimes* the obtaining of a past-tense statement's truth condition, or the truth condition of an ascription of a mental state to another, is directly accessible to us.

How could this be? Take the sentence 'I was in Cardiff yesterday'. McDowell will say that my memory affords me direct access to its truth condition: I simply remember *that I was in Cardiff yesterday*. Likewise, suppose that Jones accidentally spills some boiling tea on his hand, and howls and grimaces as a result. McDowell will say that in observing his howling and grimacing I have direct access to the truth condition of the statement 'Jones is in pain'. I simply see *that Jones is in pain*. Now the truth conditions to which, in these cases, I have direct access are instances of *kinds* of truth-condition: on the one hand, the kind of truth condition that concerns the past, on the other, the kind of truth condition that concerns the mental life of others. Now, because we can in this way embrace the truth conditions of 'I was in Cardiff yesterday' and 'Jones is in pain' in consciousness, there is no problem, from the anti-realist's point of view, with the idea that we can acquire a grasp of these truth conditions. But the truth conditions of 'Julius Caesar was the victim of a sneezing attack on his 19th birthday' and 'Smith is in pain' (as uttered in a context where Smith is relaxedly watching *Coronation Street*) are truth conditions which concern the past, and the mental life of others, respectively. They are thus of the same kind as the truth conditions of 'I was in Cardiff yesterday' and 'Jones is in pain'. Thus, a normal training in the use of past-tense statements, and ascriptions of mental states to others, allows me to grasp, in a manner unproblematic from the anti-realist perspective, truth conditions which belong to a kind, other instances of which are capable of obtaining, or failing to obtain, undetectably. Thus, McDowell suggests, we can unproblematically see ourselves as having acquired grasp of a *kind* of truth condition, some instances of which can obtain, or fail to obtain, undetectably. Thus, semantic realism can meet the acquisition argument.

Obviously, one source of difficulty with the M-realist proposal concerns the notion of direct access to truth conditions which it utilizes, and another is the distinction between kinds of truth condition all instances of which are inaccessible and kinds of truth condition only some instances of which are so (Wright 1986: 14, 95–100). But Wright claims that, even ignoring these sources of difficulty, the M-realist proposal fails for reasons broadly similar to those which scuppered the truth-value-link suggestion. The essence of Wright's objection is contained in the following passage, which deliberately mimics McDowell's own objection to the truth-value-link move:

The M-realist is saying in effect, 'You can see how a person can have the idea of what it is for someone else to be in pain—when the pain is conclusively manifested in his behaviour. Well, a sentence like "He is in pain", uttered in a context which fixes a reference for the pronoun, is just to be understood always as saying of the appropriate person that he is in that very same state, whether or not there is any behavioural manifestation of it.' But so far from solving the problem, this simply ignores it. If someone cannot see how another person's being in pain—on an interpretation of that circumstance which allows it to hide from our view—can possibly enter into the meaning which we attach to the appropriate statement, if he cannot see, that is to say, how the putative M-realist truth-conditions can intelligently be received by a trainee as anything other than a certain sort of verification-conditions, one does not allay his worry by baldly insisting that they can. (Wright 1986: 103)

Mutatis mutandis for M-realism about the past. We can restate Wright's worry as follows. The M-realist argument turns essentially on a claim about sameness of kinds of truth condition. If, as McDowell intends, the M-realist argument is to meet the acquisition argument on the anti-realist's own terms, any claims about sameness of kinds of truth conditions which it utilizes must be unproblematic from the anti-realist's point of view. If not, the argument will appear to presuppose a solution to the problem posed by the anti-realist. And this, Wright claims, is actually what happens in the M-realist argument. The claim that the truth condition of 'I was in Cardiff yesterday' belongs to the same kind as the truth condition of 'Julius Caesar was the victim of a sneezing attack on his 19th birthday' will be problematic from the perspective of the anti-realist, since although both truth conditions concern the past, one of them is apparently such that, if it can obtain, it can do so undetectably. The M-realist, in taking these two truth conditions to belong unproblematically to the same kind, in effect begs the question against the anti-realist.

A related worry might be stated as follows. The M-realist story is supposed to show us that, from materials agreed by the anti-realist to be unproblematic, we can acquire a grasp of a *kind* of truth condition. McDowell is explicit about this:

It is crucial to [the M-realist] rejection of the anti-realist argument that the conception that the realist claims the right to ascribe is a conception of a *kind* of circumstance. (McDowell 1998: 308)

And it is clear that this emphasis on kinds of truth condition is what does the work:

[The M-realist] claims the right to ascribe it on the basis of behaviour construable as a response to *some* instances of the kind, in spite of the admitted fact that *other* instances, on his view, are incapable of eliciting any response from the possessor of the conception. (McDowell 1998: 308)

But the anti-realist can now protest that it is utterly mysterious how one could acquire grasp of a *kind* of truth condition, and thereby a grasp of *all* its instances, including the evidence-transcendent instances, via acquiring a grasp only of those instances which are such that if they obtain, they do so detectably. It seems that the M-realist has done nothing to dispel this air of mystery, and as such has simply failed to engage with the anti-realist challenge.

## 5 Compositionality and the Strong Acquisition Argument

M-realism thus appears to fail as a response to the strong acquisition argument. However, Wright, and following him Bob Hale, have more or less conceded that the force of the strong version of the acquisition argument can be blunted by invoking considerations to do with the *compositionality* of meaning and understanding. For example, Wright says:

the realist seems to have a very simple answer. Given that the understanding of statements in general is to be viewed as consisting in possession of a concept of their truth-conditions, acquiring a concept of an evidence-transcendent state of affairs is simply a matter of acquiring an understanding of a statement for which that state of affairs would constitute the truth-condition. And such an understanding is acquired, like the understanding of any previously unheard sentence in the language, by understanding the constituent words and the significance of their mode of combination. (Wright 1986: 16)

In addition, Hale presents the thought very succinctly:

a very simple response is available: we come by a grasp of realist truth-conditions by coming to understand sentences having those truth-conditions, and we come to understand such sentences in just the way in which we come to understand the vast majority of sentences in our language, by understanding their words and semantically significant syntax. (Hale 1997: 279)[6]

For example, the anti-realist asks how I can acquire a grasp of the truth condition of 'Julius Caesar was the victim of a sneezing attack on his 19th birthday' despite the fact that the relevant state of affairs is not one to which I have some guaranteead means of access. The realist will reply that the anti-realist raises no objection to the idea that we understand the constituents of the sentence (all of which after all appear in a range of anti-realistically unproblematic sentences), nor to the idea that we grasp its semantically relevant syntax (which is after all shared by a host of anti-realistically unproblematic sentences). Given this, we can acquire a grasp of the relevant truth condition by acquiring, via a compositional route, an understanding of 'Julius Caesar was the victim of a sneezing attack on his 19th birthday'.

Of course, the anti-realist may then respond that this begs the question: it only works as a response to the acquisition argument if we presuppose that our understanding of the constituents is as the realist would describe it. The anti-realist will reply that *of course* we learn the meanings of sentences such as 'All even numbers are the sum of two primes' by learning the meanings of their constituents and grasping their mode of combination. That much is not at issue. What is at issue is whether the understanding thereby achieved can plausibly be construed as grasp of a potentially evidence-transcendent

---

[6]  I shall follow Hale and sometimes abbreviate 'potentially recognition-transcendent truth condition' to 'realist truth condition'.

truth condition. And—barring the question-begging assumption that the realist is right about what constitutes our understanding of e.g. the universal quantifier—nothing in the compositional reply implies that it has to be.

However, this anti-realist rejoinder depends on a misconstrual of the strong acquisition argument. Recall that the argument can be formalized as follows:

If (1), then not (2).
(2).
———————————
∴ Not (1),

with (1) and (2) as before. In effect, the compositionality response to the argument proceeds by undermining the first premiss, and it does so by arguing that (1) and (2) can in fact be true simultaneously. The strong acquisition argument grants the assumption (1) that our understanding of the relevant sentences is constituted by our knowledge of their potentially recognition-transcendent truth conditions, and argues that this assumption rules out the idea that this understanding is acquired via an ordinary training in their use. So in responding to this, via the compositionality argument, the realist is *allowed* to presuppose that our understanding of the relevant sentences is constituted by our knowledge of their potentially recognition-transcendent truth conditions, since that much is *granted* by the anti-realist at the outset, if only for the sake of argument. (Imagine someone responding to a *reductio ad absurdum*, by assuming the premisses that allegedly give rise to the contradiction, and showing that in fact they do not. He can hardly be accused of begging the question for assuming the premisses.) Again, the essential point is nicely made by Hale:

The realist may, and should, concede that the proposed response does not *prove* that we understand the problematic sentences as having realist truth-conditions. But she can point out that it is not intended to do so; the aim was rather to explain, on the *assumption* that our understanding has that character, how we may have acquired it. In the absence of an argument showing that a grasp of realist truth-conditions cannot emerge, via composition, from agreed unproblematic starting points, or an independent argument—perhaps based on manifestation—for the bankruptcy of the distinctive realist conception of truth-conditions (of which it would be a corollary that we cannot have acquired it), it seems that this is enough to neutralise the acquisition challenge. (Hale 1997: 279–80)

I shall investigate—after considering the manifestation argument—whether there is a version of the acquisition argument which the compositionality response leaves untouched. Before considering the manifestation argument, however, it is worth pausing to note that, *contra* Wright, Hale, and the arguments sketched above, the M-realist argument *does* constitute a valid response to the strong acquisition argument, for essentially the same reasons that the compositionality response does not fall prey to the anti-realist rejoinder just considered.

## 6 M-Realism Revisited

Thus, the semantic realist's aim in responding to the strong acquisition argument ought to be to show, on the *assumption* that our understanding of the problematic sentences consists in grasp of realist truth conditions, that that understanding could have been acquired from an everyday training in their use. This follows directly from the character of the strong acquisition argument, which argues that that assumption rules out the idea that our understanding might have been acquired via a normal training. Wright and Hale do not appear to realize that this—which after all they concede to undermine the obvious objection to the compositionality response— disables their own central objection to the M-realist response.

Recall that their objection to McDowell's M-realist response to the acquisition argument turned on the claim that it is simply question-begging to assume, as the M-realist does, that the truth conditions of 'It rained in Cardiff in April 2000' and 'Julius Caesar was the victim of a sneezing attack on his 19th birthday' belong unproblematically to the same kind. But we can now see that the M-realist's assumption here is not question-begging, since it is actually licensed by the assumption which the anti-realist grants him in order to get the strong acquisition argument underway: namely, that the truth conditions of both 'It rained in Cardiff in April 2000' and 'Julius Caesar was the victim of a sneezing attack on his 19th birthday' are *realist* truth conditions. The anti-realist thus grants the assumption that the truth conditions of 'It rained in Cardiff in April 2000', and 'Julius Caesar was the victim of a sneezing attack on his 19th birthday', belong to the same kind at the outset of the acquisition argument. So the M-realist can hardly be accused of begging the question for making use of an assumption which the anti-realist grants him.

Likewise with the related difficulty we raised for the M-realist. The anti-realist concedes that we grasp certain instances of truth conditions of the past, such as the truth condition of 'It rained in Cardiff in April 2000', and he also concedes that these instances are *realist* truth conditions. So are the truth conditions of 'Julius Caesar was the victim of a sneezing attack on his 19th birthday'. So there should be no mystery about how our confrontations with truth conditions like the former can lead to our grasping truth conditions such as the latter, and thence to a grasp of the *kind* of truth condition to which they both belong. Of course, there may be problems about how, in general, confrontation with instances of a kind can lead to grasp of the kind itself, but these are not problems specifically concerning grasp of kinds of truth condition. Waiving such general problems, the difficulty for the M-realist story seems to fade away.

Thus, *both* the M-realist and compositionality rejoinders constitute effective responses to the strong acquisition argument. I submit, therefore, that the strong acquisition argument fails. It is a very interesting question whether there is any other version of the acquisition argument to which these rejoinders provide no convincing response. I shall return to this question in Section 13. In the next section I shall look at the second of the anti-realist arguments developed by Dummett and his followers, the *manifestation argument*.[7]

## 7 The Strong Manifestation Argument

What is the manifestation argument, and what exactly is it supposed to establish? According to Wright, the argument is better viewed as a 'challenge', where 'A philosophical challenge consists in an argument that a number of beliefs, which are held individually to be attractive, are, if not outright inconsistent, at any rate in tension with each other' (Wright 1989: 53). In the

---

[7] It is an interesting question whether the sort of defence of M-realism and the compositionality response which we have considered can be used to defend even the truth-value-link response to the strong acquisition argument. If it can, it starts to look as if the strong acquisition argument might be *completely* toothless.

case at hand, the beliefs in question are three in number. The first two are the two components in our characterization of semantic realism:

(1) Understanding a declarative sentence is a matter of grasping its truth conditions.
(2) Truth is essentially epistemically unconstrained: the truth of a sentence is a potentially recognition-transcendent matter.

The third ingredient needed to set up the tension is what Wright terms the *Manifestability Principle*:

(3) Understanding a sentence is a complex of practical abilities to use that sentence.

This idea has obtained such wide currency in the philosophy of language since the publication of Wittgenstein's *Philosophical Investigations* that it is apt, as Wright notes, 'to strike most people now as a harmless platitude'(Wright 1989: 53). This notwithstanding, according to Wright the idea has at least two important consequences. The first is that we must repudiate the idea of understanding 'as a kind of *interior informational state*, the source and explanation of correct use' (ibid.). The second is that

[Since] the performance abilities that constitute an understanding of an expression do not count unless associated with the ability to *evaluate* one's own and others' performance with that expression [it follows that] understanding, if it is to be viewed as a practical ability at all, has to be seen as a complex of *discriminatory* capacities: an overall ability to suit one's use of the expression to the obtaining of factors which can be appreciated by oneself and others to render one's use apt. (Wright 1989: 54)

With the Manifestability Principle, thus understood, in place, the tension with the combination of the two ingredients in semantic realism is spelt out as follows:

If truth in general is evidentially unconstrained, then—depending on its subject matter—knowing the truth-conditions of a sentence may require an understanding of how it could be undetectably true. And how could that knowledge consist—as the Manifestability Principle requires it must—in any ability whose proper exercise is tied to *appreciable* situations? How can knowing what it is for an unappreciable situation to obtain be constituted by capacities of discrimination exercised in response to appreciable ones? (Wright 1989: 54–5)

If these questions do not admit of satisfactory answers, we will have established the resources necessary to mount the following argument against semantic realism:

If (1) and (2), then not (3).

(3).
_____

∴ Not ((1) and (2)).

It would follow that we would have to give up at least one of the two components which together make up our characterization of semantic realism. We would be forced to reject the idea that linguistic understanding is a matter of grasping truth conditions, or hold on to that idea subject to the proviso that the notion of truth in play is epistemically constrained and not potentially recognition-transcendent. The former course was that originally adopted by Dummett, who took the argument to 'dethrone truth and falsity from their central place in the theory of meaning' (Dummett 1978: 19); the latter is that which Dummett subsequently favoured, and which Wright has attempted to develop by modelling truth on superassertibility.[8]

Either way, the argument, if cogent, provides us with a reason to reject semantic realism, and to seek some form of semantic anti-realist alternative. Call an application of the Manifestability Principle which seeks in this way to establish the falsity of semantic realism a *strong version* of the manifestation argument. Dummett himself clearly sees his manifestation argument as having this strong form. He writes, of semantic realism:

It is, in fact, plain that the knowledge which is being ascribed to one who is said to understand the sentence is knowledge which transcends the capacity to manifest that knowledge by the way in which the sentence is used. The [semantic realist] theory of meaning cannot be a theory in which meaning is fully determined by use. (Dummett 1978: 224–5)

Given that meaning cannot transcend use, it follows that semantic realism presents a false picture of what linguistic understanding consists in. In Section 9 I shall show that in response to some well-known objections to

---

[8] See the Preface to Dummett (1978); Wright (1992), ch. 2; Wright (1986), essay 14.

the strong version, semantic anti-realists have in fact silently switched to a version of the manifestation argument with much more modest pretensions. Before doing so, I shall spend some more time clarifying how the strong version of the argument is supposed to work.

## 8 More on the Strong Manifestation Argument

Wright asks us to consider the example of a simple language consisting only of simple taste predicates like 'is bitter', 'is sweet', 'is salty', and so on, and a range of demonstrative terms. Consider a competent speaker of this language fragment, and suppose that the application of the taste predicates is restricted to a range of demonstrated items within easy reach of the speaker. It is a feature of this language fragment that any sentence constructible within it is *effectively decidable*: for any sentence, we know of a procedure which, if correctly implemented, is guaranteed to issue, in finitely many steps, in a correct verdict about the truth value of the sentence. For example, we can decide the truth value of 'This is sweet' by correctly implementing the procedure: put the demonstrated object in your mouth and taste it.

What can we say about the competent speakers' understanding of the sentences of this language? Even in this case we have to do some work to show that

(1) Understanding a declarative sentence is a matter of grasping its truth conditions

can mesh with the Manifestability Principle:

(3) Understanding a sentence is a complex of practical abilities to use that sentence.

As Wright notes:

The Manifestability Principle bids us to view the understanding of a declarative sentence as a complex of abilities, and the Truth-Conditional Conception seems to superimpose a unifying frame, to postulate a thread which runs through the evidence-sifting, inferential, and other abilities involved in understanding the sentence and somehow binds them together. Knowing the truth-conditions of the sentence has to be a state which somehow guarantees possession of these abilities, and the question must therefore arise how the guarantee is sustained. (Wright 1989: 54)

The 'evidence-sifting, inferential, and other abilities'—the 'neighbourhood abilities'[9]—which Wright refers to are as follows. For a sentence such as 'This is bitter' the competent speaker of our language fragment will typically (*a*) be able to evaluate whatever evidence there is for or against it or recognize that no evidence within his reach bears on it; (*b*) be able to recognize some of the inferences which it licenses and recognize which other sets of sentences entail it; (*c*) be able to tell which conditions do and do not render it appropriate to ascribe beliefs to the effect that the demonstrated object is bitter, which do and do not render it appropriate to ascribe desires for bitter foodstuffs, and so on; (*d*) know how to use the sentence to explain certain things (for example, why Jones grimaced when he accidentally dropped the substance in his tea).

These, and probably many other sorts of ability, will be germane to our competent speaker's understanding of the sentences of our language fragment. This certainly speaks to (3), but what of (1) and the Truth-Conditional Conception? What we need to find is some *core ability*, justifiably describable as grasp of truth conditions, which constitutes understanding, and which ensures, more often than not, that the speaker possesses the other 'neighbourhood' abilities in our list. In the case at hand, Wright thinks that such a core ability is easily identifiable: the ability to recognize the taste of a sample by placing it in one's mouth, and to report such recognition by using 'This is bitter', 'This is sweet', and so on. Moreover, recognizing the taste of a sample of Guinness by imbibing it *is* to recognize that in virtue of which the description 'This is bitter' is true. So the ability is plausibly describable as knowledge of truth conditions, and is also plausibly fundamental in so far as one who lacked it but possessed all of the neighbourhood abilities would not be uncontentiously describable as understanding the sentence.[10]

In this case, then, (1) and (3) can be seen to mesh relatively easily:

[9] The phrase is Simon Blackburn's: see Blackburn (1989).

[10] Wright also suggests, as he surely has to, that someone who possesses the 'core' ability but lacks all of the neighbourhood abilities can still be described as fully understanding the sentence. This strikes me as implausible, but here I am willing to concede the point for the sake of argument.

'grasp of such judgements [e.g. "This is sweet"] will be a manifestable, recognitional skill, and there will be a case for regarding it as constitutive of an understanding of them' (Wright 1989: 57).

In contrast, consider the case of regions of discourse which permit the formation of sentences which are not effectively decidable. For our purposes, we shall say that a sentence is not effectively decidable if we do not know a procedure which, if carried out properly, will guarantee a correct verdict on its truth value.[11] The regions of discourse over which semantic realists and anti-realists disagree are, of course, of this nature. 'Julius Caesar sneezed fifteen times on his 19th birthday' is, in this sense, not effectively decidable. How, in cases like this, can we mesh (1) and (3) together? The problem is that we can find no ability to play a role analogous to that played by the ability to recognize the taste of samples by placing them in one's mouth, so no ability emerges as a candidate for grasp of truth conditions in the kind of case over which semantic realists and anti-realists disagree. As Wright puts it,

To grasp the truth-conditions of such judgements could not be identified merely with the ability to recognise that they were satisfied in the favourable kind of case; it would be necessary, in addition, to understand what it would be for them to be satisfied unrecognisably. And the problem would then be to construe that understanding as the Manifestability Principle requires. (Wright 1989: 57)

What we require is an account of 'A practical ability which stands to understanding an evidence-transcendent truth-condition as recognitional skills stand to decidable truth-conditions' (Wright 1986: 23). If no such account can be given, we are again left with the strong version of the manifestation argument:

> If (1) and (2), then not (3).
>
> (3).
> _____
> ∴ Not ((1) and (2)).

As before, we appear to have been presented with an argument which, if cogent, forces us to give up at least one of the essential features of semantic realism.

[11] For an excellent explanation of the notion of 'undecidability', as it figures in Dummett's arguments against semantic realism, see Shieh (1998).

## 9 Realist Responses to the Strong Manifestation Argument

Faced with an argument to the effect that there is a tension or inconsistency between (1), (2), and (3), the natural course of action for a semantic realist to take would be to argue that there is no tension or inconsistency: that is, to argue that there is an ability, or abilities, which can be viewed as constituting our understanding of sentences from the disputed areas, in such a way that neither (1) nor (2) is ruled out. This is in fact how a number of philosophers responded to early expositions of the manifestation challenge. For example, Colin McGinn writes:

One's knowledge of meaning is manifestable in one's capacity to interpret—with all that that involves—the speech behaviour of others. A central component of this ability is correctly ascribing beliefs to the speaker, where these will figure— in combination with suitable desires—in explanations of his behaviour. These beliefs may, or may not, be of realist persuasion. (McGinn 1980: 30)[12]

And Peter Strawson writes:

It *is* obvious that, as Wright puts it, 'grasp of the sense of a sentence cannot be displayed in *response* to unrecognisable conditions'. No truth-theorist needs to dispute this tautology. It is enough for the truth-theorist that the grasp of the sense of a sentence can be displayed in response to recognisable conditions—of various sorts: there are those which conclusively establish the truth or falsity of the sentence; there are those which (given our general theory of the world) constitute evidence, more or less good, for or against the truth of the sentence; there are even those which point to the unavoidable absence of evidence either way. (Strawson 1977: 16)

Strawson's suggestion is that understanding can—alongside (1) and (2)—be construed as an ability to respond appropriately to the sorts of recognizable conditions mentioned.

The responses proffered by and on behalf of anti-realists to this type of realist reply have a common structure. They *concede* that the abilities mentioned in the reply are consistent with the essential features of semantic realism. But they claim that nevertheless, the suggested abilities do not

[12] Of course, by 'beliefs of realist persuasion', McGinn means not beliefs *in* realism, but rather beliefs with the sort of content which semantic realism would call for.

*require* to be described as 'grasp of potentially recognition-transcendent truth-conditions'. This is clear in the replies which Hale makes, on behalf of the anti-realist, to McGinn and Strawson. Of McGinn's suggestion, Hale writes:

There is an obvious difficulty with this kind of response. Evidently there is no reason why an anti-realist should not go in for interpretations of linguistic behaviour, or explanations of behaviour in general, in terms of beliefs. It is therefore essential to show, if the proposed reply is to make headway, that such interpretations and explanations must sometimes proceed in terms of specifically realist beliefs. That is, it needs to be indicated what specific aspects of behaviour, or the capacities to which they bear witness, call for explanation in terms of the hypothesis that the subjects of ascription hold beliefs, the content of which demands characterisation in terms of realist truth-conditions rather than conditions of warranted assertibility, say; otherwise the ascription of realist beliefs will merely incorporate so much theoretical slack. (Hale 1997: 280)

And of Strawson's suggestion:

Here it is crucial to remember that the truth-theorist to whose defence Strawson is (or ought to be) contributing is a realist, who holds that grasp of the sense of a sentence consists, in the case where the sentence is not effectively decidable, in knowledge of its possibly evidence-transcendent truth-condition. The responses Strawson mentions, however, are entirely consistent with the anti-realist view that, in such cases, understanding the sentence consists in knowing the conditions for its warranted assertion. That is, such responses do not distinctively display grasp of *realist* truth-conditions for the sentence. (Hale 1997: 281)

It is important to note what has happened here. The manifestation argument was originally presented as ruling out semantic realism. In response to the claim that if semantic realism were true, sentential understanding could not be construed as a practical capacity, realists have responded that we *can* construe understanding as a practical ability without jeopardizing either the claim that understanding consists in grasp of truth conditions or the claim that truth is potentially recognition-transcendent. In response, defenders of anti-realism have pointed out that no features of the abilities cited provide us with a warrant to describe those abilities as grasp of potentially recognition-transcendent truth conditions. The conclusion now is not that we have reason to *reject* semantic realism, but rather that in so far as considerations pertaining to the manifestation of understanding are concerned, we have *no reason to accept* semantic realism in preference to semantic anti-realism. Thus, a *strong version* of the manifestation argument seeks to establish the falsity of semantic realism; a *weak version*, by contrast, seeks to establish the much more modest conclusion that we cannot justify accepting semantic realism *solely* on the basis of considering the practical abilities which constitute linguistic understanding. So it seems that anti-realists have implicitly conceded that the strong version of the manifestation argument is a failure.[13]

## 10  Manifestation and Implicit Knowledge

A strong version of the manifestation argument purports to establish that semantic realism is unacceptable, whereas a weak version of the argument purports to establish only that, so far as the practical abilities constitutive of linguistic understanding are concerned, there is no reason to accept semantic realism. In the previous section I argued that anti-realists have conceded that the strong version fails. One way for anti-realists to avoid weakening their position in this way would be to argue that there are considerations— so far undiscussed—which would take us from the conclusion of the weak manifestation argument to the conclusion of the strong manifestation argument. One such argument might start with the observation that in the characterization of semantic realism as the claim that

(A)  Understanding a declarative sentence is constituted by knowledge of its realist (i.e. potentially recognition-transcendent) truth condition

the notion of knowledge in play has to be, in the general case, that of *implicit knowledge*. Time and time again, Dummett stresses that in general, we cannot take a speaker's understanding of a declarative sentence to be constituted by explicit knowledge of its realist truth condition, by the ability to state the truth condition in other words: this can hold only for a fragment of the speaker's language, and could not hold for his understanding of every sentence in his language on pain of infinite regress. Dummett writes:

A theory of meaning which takes truth as its central notion has to supply an

[13]  For an investigation into the consequences of this, see Miller (2002).

explanation of what it is to ascribe to someone a knowledge of the condition which must obtain for a sentence to be true. If the sentence is of a form which a speaker can come to understand by means of a verbal explanation, then there is no problem: his knowledge of the truth-condition of the sentence is explicit knowledge, knowledge which is manifested by his ability to state that condition. An explanation of this form obviously presupposes that the speaker already knows a fairly extensive fragment of the language, by means of which he can state the condition for the truth of the given sentence, and in terms of which he came to understand it. It follows that, however large the range of sentences of the language his understanding of which can be explained in this way, this form of explanation will not suffice generally. . . . His understanding of the most primitive part of the language, its lower levels, cannot be explained in this way: if that understanding consists in a knowledge of the truth-conditions of sentences, such knowledge must be implicit knowledge, and hence the theory of meaning must supply us with an account of how that knowledge is manifested. (1993: 44–5)

Thus, semantic realism should be characterized as

> (A) Understanding a declarative sentence is constituted by *implicit* knowledge of its realist (i.e. potentially recognition-transcendent) truth condition

and the thought would be that the move from the conclusion of the weak version of the manifestation argument to the conclusion of the strong manifestation argument is mediated by constraints on the ascription of implicit knowledge. How might this thought be developed? One way might be as follows. Suppose we held that any ascription of implicit linguistic knowledge to a speaker had to be explained in terms of specific linguistic abilities the exercise of which would manifest that knowledge. Dummett clearly has something along these lines in mind, at least in some of his discussions of this topic:

In fact, whenever the condition for the truth of a sentence is one that we have no way of bringing ourselves to recognise as obtaining whenever it obtains, it seems plain that there is no content to an ascription of an *implicit* knowledge of what that condition is, *since there is no practical ability by means of which such knowledge may be manifested*. (Dummett 1993: 46, latter emphasis added)

This suggests that Dummett is working with a conception of implicit knowledge which is such that we are warranted in denying its possession by a speaker unless the claim that the speaker possesses it flows from the description of the linguistic abilities which the speaker has: ascriptions of implicit knowledge have no content over and above ascriptions of practical abilities.[14] Thus, if we take

(B) Speaker S's understanding a sentence is a complex of *practical abilities* to use that sentence

and

(A) Speaker S's understanding a declarative sentence is constituted by *implicit* knowledge of its realist truth condition,

what this construal of implicit knowledge entails is that unless (A) flows from (B), unless a full description of S's linguistic abilities contains some ingredient which requires to be described as grasp of a realist truth-condition, we are warranted in denying (A). Schematically,

(C) $\neg((B) \to (A)) \to \neg(A)$.

We are now in a position to see how this conception of implicit knowledge would take us from the conclusion of the weak manifestation argument to the conclusion of the strong manifestation argument. The conclusion of the weak manifestation argument was that a consideration of the abilities possessed by speakers provides no reason to attribute to them implicit knowledge of realist truth conditions. We can represent this schematically as:

(D) $\neg((B) \to (A))$.

Now assume that semantic realism is true: namely, (A). We get a straightforward contradiction, since (C) and (D) give us, by Modus Ponens, $\neg(A)$.

Thus, the constraint on the ascription of implicit knowledge, the conclusion of the weak manifestation argument, and the assumption that semantic realism is true generate a contradiction. Assuming the correctness of the account of implicit knowledge, and the cogency of the weak manifestation argument, we can thus conclude that semantic realism is false. So we reach the conclusion of the strong manifestation argument after all, and

[14] For a good exposition of this conception of implicit knowledge, see Kirkham (1989), 211–16.

the gap between strong and weak versions of the manifestation argument accordingly closes.

How plausible is the conception of 'implicit knowledge' in play in this suggestion? The notion has received a great deal of attention in the literature, and there is no space to add substantially to that literature here. But some brief comments are in order. The notion described certainly does correspond to some key passages:

Our problem is, therefore: What is it that a speaker knows when he knows a language, and what, in particular, does he thereby know about any given sentence of the language? Of course, what he has when he knows the language is practical knowledge, knowledge how to speak the language: but this is no objection to its representation as propositional knowledge; mastery of a procedure, of a conventional practice, can always be so represented, and, whenever the practice is complex, such a representation often provides the only convenient mode of analysis of it. Thus what we seek is a theoretical representation of a practical ability. (Dummett 1993: 36)

Or, as Richard Kirkham puts it:

Language competence, according to Dummett, is a practical ability, so a theory of meaning must *model* (or *represent*, Dummett uses the two words interchangeably) this practical ability. The model is a set of propositions which *represent* what a competent speaker of the language knows. This does not mean that a competent speaker of the language has propositional knowledge of these propositions. Knowing a language is a knowing-how not a knowing-that. It is ability knowledge, not propositional knowledge. . . . But ability knowledge can be *represented* by propositions. (Kirkham 1989: 212)

Kirkham gives a nice example to illustrate the idea that knowledge-how can be represented by knowledge-that. Jones knows how to touch-type: he can type accurately without looking at the keyboard. But he does not have propositional knowledge of the layout of the keyboard: he does not know *that the 'R' is immediately to the left of the 'T'* and so on. This is shown by the fact that Jones cannot draw a map of the keyboard without looking at it (and we might add, would not be able to identify the correct map if presented with it alongside a group of inaccurate maps). However, even though he does not know, for example, that the 'R' is immediately to the left of the 'T', this piece of propositional knowledge *represents* Jones's ability in so far as he acts *as if* he had it: he acts *as though* he knew that the 'R' is immediately to the left of the 'T'. And the same goes for implicit knowledge of truth conditions:

Dummett would label the sort of epistemic relationship I have with these propositions as 'implicit knowledge', meaning I do not really know *them* at all, but it is as though I did. So, too, according to Dummett, linguistic competence is *implicit* knowledge. But . . . he means only that one could *represent* a competent speaker's linguistic behaviour with a list of this set of propositions. He does *not* mean that the speaker *really* knows these propositions. (Kirkham 1989: 212)

This clearly meshes with the notion of implicit knowledge which I suggested might mediate the move from the weak to the strong version of the manifestation argument: if an ascription of implicit knowledge has content only in so far as it represents some practical ability, then if nothing in a speaker's linguistic abilities requires to be described as implicit knowledge of a realist truth condition, the ascription of such implicit knowledge is not acceptable.[15]

Note, too, that this would explain why the anti-realist has no weak version of the acquisition argument. It is a striking fact that Wright and Hale both react to the compositionality response to the strong acquisition argument by conceding that it disables that argument, and by suggesting that the anti-realist must turn to the manifestation argument (which they suggest is the more fundamental of the two). But suppose someone tried to respond to the manifestation argument by invoking compositionality considerations: the complex ability constitutive of our understanding of 'Every

[15] This probably needs some sharpening up. A semantic realist might reply that we act *as if* we had propositional knowledge to the effect that a particular sentence has a realist truth condition (even if it is also true that we act *as if* we had knowledge of its assertibility conditions). Dummett clearly needs something like: to have implicit knowledge of the proposition that X is to have an ability which can be represented—*without residue*—with the proposition that X. The weak manifestation argument would establish that the ascription of a realist truth condition did, in virtue of its realistic aspect, contain residue, and the conception of implicit knowledge would then kick in to establish that the competent speaker did not have implicit knowledge of a realist truth condition (i.e. to give us the conclusion of the strong manifestation argument). Now Dummett may face some problems in spelling out the relevant notion of 'residue', and so on, but I shall not pursue this further here, since I go on to argue that Dummett's argument fails even if we waive these further problems.

even number is the sum of two primes' is constituted by the abilities which constitute our understanding of its subsentential components. Wright and Hale would reply that *of course* we learn the meanings of sentences such as 'Every even number is the sum of two primes' by learning the meanings of their constituents and grasping their mode of combination. But they will say that that much is not in dispute. What is in dispute is whether the understanding thereby manifested requires to be construed as grasp of a potentially recognition-transcendent truth condition. And—barring the question-begging assumption that the semantic realist is right about what constitutes our understanding of the constituents of the sentence—nothing in the compositionality reply implies that it must be. In effect, this represents a move to the weak version of the manifestation argument: nothing in our understanding of the problematic sentences *requires* to be described as grasp of a realist truth condition. So in reply to the compositionality response to the strong manifestation argument, the anti-realist would reply that nothing in the abilities constitutive of our linguistic understanding provides us with a reason to accept semantic realism, and thereby moves to a weak version of the manifestation argument. The ruminations above on implicit knowledge would explain this asymmetry. The connection between the weak and strong versions of the manifestation argument is forged by the intimate tie between the notion of implicit knowledge and the practical linguistic abilities which it models, and by the fact that the manifestation argument concerns *precisely* the semantic realist account of those practical abilities. Since the acquisition argument does *not* concern the practical abilities constitutive of understanding, but rather the *training* required to impart that understanding, there is no scope for a similar connection between a weak and a strong version of that argument. The ability–implicit knowledge link ensures that in response to replies to the strong manifestation argument the anti-realist can fall back on a 'weak' version of the argument with just as much bite as the stronger: since the acquisition argument does not concern the constitutive abilities, there is no scope for such a move. Thus, the anti-realist, in response to the compositionality reply to the strong acquisition argument, has to concede that the argument fails and turn to the manifestation argument.

However, despite explaining how the weak and strong versions of the manifestation argument are connected, and explaining the asymmetry between the anti-realist's use of the acquisition and manifestation arguments, the notion of implicit knowledge invoked here appears not to sit well with the *explanatory* aspirations which Dummett sometimes seems to harbour when discussing theories of meaning. For example,

It is one of the merits of a theory of meaning which represents mastery of a language as the knowledge not of isolated, but of deductively interconnected propositions, that it makes due acknowledgement of the undoubted fact that a process of derivation of some kind is involved in the understanding of a sentence. (Dummett 1993: 13)

A competent speaker of the language under consideration hears a sentence he has never heard before. He derives his understanding of the sentence from his understanding of its constituents and their mode of combination. If we could view the speaker as knowing the propositions expressed by the axioms of a theory of meaning for his language, we could explain this fact about comprehension: he derives his understanding of the novel utterance from his understanding of its constituents just as the theorem for the sentence in the theory of meaning is derived from its axioms. But this explanation will only work if the speaker *really does know* the propositions expressed by the theory's axioms. As Wright puts it:

For Dummett, the explanatory ambitions of a theory of meaning would seem to be entirely dependent upon the permissibility of thinking of speakers of its object language as knowing the propositions which its axioms codify and of their deriving their understanding of (novel) sentences in a manner mirrored by the derivation, in the theory, of the appropriate theorems. (Wright 1986: 207)

Thus, the notion of implicit knowledge needed to mediate the move from the weak to the strong version of the manifestation argument seems at odds with the notion Dummett needs in order to underwrite his explanatory aspirations.[16]

Another problem is that the notion of implicit knowledge which mediates the connection between the weak and strong versions of the manifestation argument is explicitly rejected by Dummett in his recent writings on the

[16] For more on the problems Dummett faces in squaring his explanatory aspirations with his official notion of implicit knowledge, see Antony (1997). For an overview of the various conceptions of implicit semantic knowledge, see Miller (1997).

topic. According to that suggestion, when we say that a speaker has implicit knowledge of e.g. a sentence's truth condition, we are not saying that the speaker *really* knows the truth condition, but rather giving a theoretical *representation* or *model* of the practical capacity in which the speaker's understanding of that sentence consists. In the Preface to *The Seas of Language*, Dummett records that he soon became unhappy with this idea:

I now think that knowledge of a language has a substantial theoretical component; better expressed, that the classification of knowledge into theoretical and practical (knowledge-that and knowledge-how) is far too crude to allow knowledge of a language to be located within it. (Dummett 1993: x)

We cannot view linguistic understanding as a pure practical ability which can only be represented by theoretical knowledge, because we need a more robust attribution of knowledge to speakers if we are to pay sufficient heed to the fact that 'linguistic utterances are (usually) rational acts, concerning which we may ask after the motives and intentions underlying them' (ibid.). In addition:

the classic examples of pure practical abilities, like the ability to swim, are those in which it is possible, before acquiring the ability, to have a fully adequate conception of what it is an ability to do. By contrast, there is a clear sense in which it is only by learning a language that one can come by a knowledge of what it is to speak that language, just as it is only by learning how to play chess that one can come by a knowledge of what it is to play chess. (ibid.)

So linguistic understanding is not an example of a pure practical ability: it is not something that can only be *modelled* on theoretical knowledge; it really does, at least in part, *consist in* theoretical knowledge.[17]

The notion of implicit knowledge which seems required to mediate the transition from the weak to the strong version of the manifestation argument is thus at odds with Dummett's explanatory aspirations, and sits uncomfortably with his most recent remarks on the notion. This leaves us with a question: is there a workable notion of implicit knowledge, congenial to Dummett, which will take us from the weak to the strong version of the manifestation argument and explain the asymmetry between the anti-realist's treatment of the acquisition and manifestation arguments? I shall

[17]  For a useful exposition and discussion of some of the issues here, see Bar-On (1996), esp. section 3.

not pursue this question here. Rather, I shall assume that Dummett can answer it satisfactorily, but argue that even *given* that concession, Dummett's arguments against semantic realism fail.

## 11 Assertoric Content and Truth Conditions

In order to do this I shall begin by considering another instance of the switch from a strong to a weak version of the argument, exemplified by Hale's responses to McGinn and Strawson. John McDowell has pointed out that there is a platitudinous connection between the notion of the content of an assertion and the notion of truth conditions:

To specify what would be asserted, in the assertoric utterance of a sentence apt for such use, is to specify a condition under which the sentence (as thus uttered) would be true. (McDowell 1998: 88)

And:

There is a truistic connection between the notion of the content of an assertion and a familiar notion of truth . . . the connection guarantees, as the merest platitude, that a correct specification of what can be asserted, by the assertoric utterance of a sentence, cannot but be a specification of a condition under which the sentence is true. (McDowell 1998: 319)[18]

Wright has no disagreement with this. He speaks of the claim that 'asserting a proposition—a Fregean thought—is claiming that it is true' as displaying a 'basic, platitudinous connection of assertion and truth' and as 'partially constitutive of the concepts of assertion and truth' (Wright 1992: 23–4). The platitude ensures that linguistic understanding can always be described as 'grasp of truth conditions'. Take any declarative sentence 'P' and competent speaker S assumed to understand 'P'. Then, trivially, S knows what 'P' says. What 'P' says is that a certain state of affairs, P, obtains. By the

---

[18] Akeel Bilgrami, in Bilgrami (1986), objects to McDowell's claim on the grounds that 'one may make virtually any assertion with the assertoric use of a given sentence, given a special enough context' (p. 120). But this is beside the point. What McDowell requires is that *if* I assert, by the assertoric utterance of 'Snow is white', *that snow is white*, then I thereby specify a condition under which 'Snow is white' (as thus uttered) would be true. This plainly does not require or imply that in *every* assertoric utterance of 'Snow is white' I assert that snow is white.

platitude, the obtaining of state of affairs P is necessary and sufficient for the truth of 'P'. Thus S understands the assertoric content of 'P' to be that a certain state of affairs, necessary and sufficient for its truth, obtains. So S 'grasps the truth conditions' of 'P', regardless of what abilities constitute his understanding of it.

Wright has no problems with the derivation of a truth-conditional conception of meaning from the platitude connecting assertion and truth.[19] But he denies that this derivation can be put to work in favour of semantic realism. Although the derivation speaks against the anti-realist who would seek to replace the notion of truth as the central concept in a theory of meaning with some other epistemically constrained notion, it does nothing to undermine the anti-realist who would retain the truth-conditional conception of meaning while insisting on an epistemically constrained notion of truth. Consider again the example of 'Julius Caesar sneezed fifteen times on his 19th birthday'. When we look for abilities constitutive of our understanding of such sentences, all we can find are the sorts of 'neighbourhood abilities' mentioned earlier: the ability to appraise evidence for or against them, or to recognize that no evidence in one's possession bears either way, the ability to explain agents' behaviour by embedding them in propositional attitudes, the ability to recognize their logical consequences and ancestors, and so on. But these are all 'appreciable, recognitional abilities', abilities to respond appropriately to conditions whose obtaining, if they obtain, we are at least in principle capable of recognizing. So although appealing to the platitudinous connection between assertion and truth allows us to mesh (1) and (3) from our original trio, we have as yet no justification for including (2) and the absence of any epistemic constraints on truth:

The staring fact is that the line of thought does absolutely nothing to dissipate the tension to which this anti-realist [who holds to an evidentially constrained notion of 'truth' in his truth-conditional theory of understanding] is responding. Identifying grasp of a statement's truth-conditions with possession of a network of practical, discriminatory abilities—the 'neighbourhood abilities'—simply makes it the more puzzling how, in grasping those truth-conditions, we are somehow guaranteed to understand the possibility, in the case of a suitable example,

---

[19] Indeed, Wright himself makes the derivation explicitly. See Wright (1986),18; (1989), 58.

that those conditions be satisfied undetectably. There is absolutely no progress. (Wright 1989: 58; also 1986: 18)

Note again the move to the weaker version of the manifestation argument. The conclusion is no longer that semantic realism is inconsistent with the construal of linguistic understanding as a practical capacity, from which it would follow, given the correctness of that construal, that semantic realism should be rejected, but rather the more modest conclusion that considerations pertaining to the practical capacities which constitute understanding *by themselves* provide no warrant for the acceptance of semantic realism in preference to semantic anti-realism.

## 12 A Response to the Weak Manifestation Argument

I shall now argue that the semantic realist can convincingly respond to even the *weak* version of the manifestation argument.[20] The key ingredients in this rebuttal will be the platitudinous connection between assertion and truth adverted to in the previous section and the presence, within disputed areas, of sentences agreed on all sides to be not effectively decidable. The insight that such a response to the weak version of the manifestation argument is possible is due to McDowell:

If a sentence lacks an effective decision procedure, then the condition which any competent speaker knows he would be asserting to obtain if he used the sentence in order to make an assertion—which is in fact a condition under which the sentence would be true, whether or not the theory of meaning explicitly calls it that—is ex hypothesi not a condition whose obtaining, if it does obtain, a competent speaker can be sure of being able to put himself in a position to recognise. Thus, without lapsing into psychologism, we seem to have equipped ourselves with a kind of realism. (McDowell 1998: 322)

Although McDowell does not spell out this thought in detail, it is relatively easy to do so. Take one of the sentences over which the realist and antirealist dispute: 'Julius Caesar sneezed fifteen times on his 19th birthday.' This sentence is not effectively decidable. Thus, in the presence of the platitude

---

[20] I do not have space here to do anything more than give a bald presentation of the argument. For a full defence of the argument, and responses to many objections raised by semantic anti-realists, see Miller (2002).

connecting assertion and truth, we can mount the following argument in favour of semantic realism:

(a) We understand the assertoric content of 'Julius Caesar sneezed fifteen times on his 19th birthday' to be that conditions obtain which are necessary and sufficient for its truth; our understanding of 'Julius Caesar sneezed fifteen times on his 19th birthday' consists in our grasp of these truth conditions. [From the assertion–truth platitude]

(b) 'Julius Caesar sneezed fifteen times on his 19th birthday' is not effectively decidable; we do not know a procedure the correct implementation of which will guarantee us with an adequate case either for or against the sentence. [Agreed on all sides]

(c) Our understanding of 'Julius Caesar sneezed fifteen times on his 19th birthday' consists in our grasp of truth conditions which have the following property: we do not know a procedure the correct implementation of which will guarantee us with an adequate case either for or against their obtaining. [From (a) and (b)]

(d) Our understanding of 'Julius Caesar sneezed fifteen times on his 19th birthday' consists in our grasp of truth conditions which, if they obtain, we may be incapable, even in principle, of detecting. [From (c)]

And (d) is simply a statement of semantic realism about the past. Note that if this argument is cogent, it constitutes a rebuttal of even the weak version of the manifestation argument. Understanding a sentence such as 'Julius Caesar sneezed fifteen times on his 19th birthday' is identified with the complex of associated neighbourhood abilities. From the platitude connecting understanding, assertion, and truth, and the agreed fact that the sentence is not decidable, we have done something to justify the idea that the notion of truth involved is potentially recognition-transcendent. This speaks directly to the demand to provide a reason for describing the competent speaker's grasp of truth conditions as grasp of potentially *recognition-transcendent* truth conditions. Which is exactly what the weak version of the manifestation argument demanded.

## 13  A Response to the Weak Acquisition Argument

So far, I have argued that the strong acquisition argument fails and also that the semantic realist has an effective response to the weak (and strong) versions of the manifestation argument. But is there any scope for Dummett's anti-realist to mount a weak acquisition argument? It appears that any such argument simply could not have the intended force of the weak manifestation argument. As we saw in Section 10, Dummett's 'thin' notion of implicit knowledge ensures that the conclusion of the weak manifestation argument gives rise to the conclusion of the strong manifestation argument, namely, that semantic realism is unacceptable; and we also saw that there is no scope for a similar transition from a weak acquisition argument to the strong acquisition argument. The 'thin' notion of implicit knowledge will not take us from the claim (i) that nothing in the acquisitional route we traverse with regard to sentences in a contested area requires our understanding of those sentences to be construed as implicit knowledge of realist truth conditions, to the conclusion (ii) that construing our understanding of those sentences as consisting of knowledge of realist truth conditions is unacceptable. This explains the anti-realist's lack of interest in the weak acquisition argument. However, we saw that Dummett's commitment to the 'thin' notion of implicit knowledge is at best equivocal and unstable. So semantic realists would do well to consider the following possibility: that Dummett can come up with a notion of implicit knowledge which will mediate both the transition from the weak to the strong manifestation argument and the transition from the weak to the strong acquisition argument. If this were the case, Dummett's anti-realist could live with the fact that M-realism and the compositionality response disable the original strong acquisition argument, as well as the fact that the various manifestation arguments fail, and fall back on the weak acquisition argument to show the unacceptability of semantic realism. Neither M-realism nor the compositionality response will be effective against the weak acquisition argument. Hale writes, concerning the latter response:

The anti-realist must indeed accept that our understanding of sentences of the various kinds central to the dispute . . . is, in general, acquired along compositional lines. But he will likely object that the further claim—that that understanding involves the association with those sentences of realist truth-conditions, rather than, say, conditions of justified assertion—is entirely gratuitous. The realist may, and should, concede that the proposed response does not *prove* that we understand the sentences as having realist truth-conditions. (Hale 1997: 279)

Thus, compositionality considerations would provide no response to the weak acquisition argument. And it is clear that M-realism would not do so either. We saw that M-realism avoids the charge of begging the question against the strong acquisition argument since the relevant assumption— that e.g. the truth-conditions of 'It rained in Cardiff in April 2000' and 'Julius Caesar was the victim of a sneezing attack on his 19th birthday' belong to the same kind—is actually *licensed* by the strong acquisition argument. But no such licence is afforded by the weak acquisition argument: the challenge would no longer be to show, on the *assumption* that our understanding of both consisted in grasp of realist truth conditions, how that understanding could have been acquired, but rather to show what, in the route whereby we acquired an understanding of 'Julius Caesar was the victim of a sneezing attack on his 19th birthday', *requires* us to view that understanding as consisting in knowledge of realist truth conditions. So the M-realist response could in that case be justifiably accused of begging the question.

So, although the strong acquisition argument fails, as do the weak and strong versions of the manifestation argument, and although we have shown that there is no straightforward way in which Dummett can mount a weak acquisition argument with the same potential significance as the weak manifestation argument, we have not shown that he *cannot* do so. In defending semantic realism, therefore, we would do well to show that even if Dummett could mount a weak acquisition argument with the same potential significance as the weak manifestation argument, the semantic realist has an effective response. This would show that semantic realism is untouched by *all* forms of the acquisition and manifestation arguments.

In fact, the semantic realist has a ready response to the weak acquisition argument. This follows straightforwardly from the response to the weak manifestation argument outlined in the previous section. We acquire our understanding of the sentences in the contested areas by being taught the various neighbourhood abilities in which that understanding consists. Since the anti-realist, too, thinks that we possess the neighbourhood abilities, he can have no objection to the thought that we acquire those abilities in the normal way, by training and exposure. But by our reply to the weak manifestation argument, these abilities require to be described as consisting in grasp of realist truth conditions. So, the acquisitional route we traverse in coming to understand e.g. 'Julius Caesar was the victim of a sneezing attack on his 19th birthday', since it ends in our acquiring the neighbourhood abilities, requires us to describe that understanding in terms of knowledge of realist truth conditions. And this is all that the semantic realist requires in order to respond to the weak acquisition argument.

Thus, it is by no means clear that Dummett can mount a weak acquisition argument with the same potential significance as the weak manifestation argument. But if he could, the semantic realist, via the response to the weak manifestation argument, can neutralize even this weak version of the acquisition argument.

# REFERENCES

ANTONY, L. (1997), 'Meaning and Semantic Knowledge', *Proceedings of the Aristotelian Society*, 71: 177–208.

BAR-ON, D. (1996), 'Anti-Realism and Speaker Knowledge', *Synthese*, 106: 139–69.

BILGRAMI, A. (1986), 'Meaning, Holism, and Use', in Lepore (1986), 101–22.

BLACKBURN, S. (1989), 'Manifesting Realism', in French, Uehling, and Wettstein (1989), 29–47.

CURRIE, G. (1993), 'On the Road to Anti-Realism', *Inquiry*, 36: 465–83.

DEVITT, M. (1991), *Realism and Truth*, 2nd edn. (Princeton: Princeton University Press).

DUMMETT, M. (1978), *Truth and Other Enigmas* (London: Duckworth).

—— (1991), *The Logical Basis of Metaphysics* (Cambridge, Mass.: Harvard University Press).

—— (1993), *The Seas of Language* (Oxford: Clarendon Press).

FRENCH, P. A., UEHLING, T. E., and WETTSTEIN, H. K., eds. (1989), *Contemporary Perspectives in the Philosophy of Language, II* (Midwest Studies in Philosophy, 14: Notre Dame, Ind.: University of Notre Dame Press).

HALE, B. (1997), 'Realism and its Oppositions', in Hale and Wright (1997), 271–308.

—— and WRIGHT, C., eds. (1997), *A Companion to the Philosophy of Language* (Oxford: Blackwell).

KIRKHAM, R. (1989), 'What Dummett Says about Truth and Linguistic Competence', *Mind*, 98: 207–24.

LEPORE, E., ed. (1986), *Truth and Interpretation* (Oxford: Blackwell).

McDOWELL, J. (1998), *Meaning, Knowledge and Reality* (Cambridge, Mass.: Harvard University Press).

McGINN, C. (1980), 'Truth and Use', in Platts (1980), 19–40.

—— (1982), 'Two Notions of Realism', *Philosophical Topics*, 13: 123–34.

MARTINICH, A., and SOSA, D., eds. (2001), *A Companion to Analytic Philosophy* (Oxford: Blackwell).

MILLER, A. (1997), 'Tacit Knowledge', in Hale and Wright (1997), 146–74.

—— (1998), *Philosophy of Language* (London: UCL Press).

—— (2001), 'Michael Dummett', in Martinich and Sosa (2001), 378–92.

—— (2002), 'What is the Manifestation Argument?', *Pacific Philosophical Quarterly*, 83: 353–83.

—— (forthcoming), 'The Significance of Semantic Realism', *Synthese*.

PLATTS, M., ed. (1980), *Reference, Truth and Reality* (London: Routledge).

ROSEN, G. (1995), 'The Shoals of Language' [critical notice of Dummett (1993)], *Mind*, 104: 599–609.

SHIEH, S. (1998), 'Undecidability in Anti-Realism', *Philosophia Mathematica*, 3: 324–33.

STRAWSON, P. (1977), 'Scruton and Wright on Anti-Realism', *Proceedings of the Aristotelian Society*, 77: 15–22.

TENNANT, N. (1997), *The Taming of the True* (Oxford: Clarendon Press).

WRIGHT, C. (1986), *Realism, Meaning and Truth* (Oxford: Blackwell).

—— (1989), 'Manifesting Realism', in French, Uehling, and Wettstein (1989), 48–67.

—— (1992), *Truth and Objectivity* (Cambridge, Mass.: Harvard University Press).

CHAPTER 16

# Remembering, Imagining, and the First Person

*James Higginbotham*

## 1 Introduction

It is widely supposed that certain uses of anaphoric forms (pronouns, reflexives, and others to be discussed below) give rise to peculiarly 'first-personal' interpretations, and it has become customary following David Lewis (1979) to call these interpretations *de se*. Assuming that *de se* interpretations do indeed contrast with interpretations along the familiar, if not necessarily pellucid, *de dicto–de re* axis, there are then four questions about the *de se*, the first two more philosophical, and the latter two more linguistic:

(i) What is the nature of *de se* interpretations?
(ii) What relation do they bear to ordinary uses of the first-person pronoun?

A first draft of this paper was presented at the Sheffield conference Epistemology of Language, July 2000, Michael Martin commenting. That draft was itself based upon earlier presentations at the University of Oxford, the University of Michigan, and the tenth conference on Semantics and Linguistic Theory, Cornell University, March 2000. Presentations subsequent to the Sheffield draft include talks at the University of Siena, the University of London, and the University of California, Davis. I am grateful to my various audiences for their comments, and especially to Carl Ginet, Allen Gibbard, Alessandra Giorgi, Stephen Parkinson, Christopher Peacocke, Philippe Schlenker, Gabriel Segal, and Orsolya Schreiner. Alex Barber and Christopher Peacocke provided very useful comments on earlier drafts; and discussion with Philippe Schlenker and members of the audience at the European Summer School for Logic, Language, and Information in Trento in 2002 helped me to draw the connections between my discussion and certain revisionist movements in intensional logic.

(iii)  Why are they triggered by the particular linguistic items that trigger them?

(iv)  Are they universal in human language, and what relation, if any, do they bear to logophoric phenomena in languages having special logophoric forms?[1]

Here I consider almost exclusively the first question, hazarding only a few remarks about the second and third; and I omit the fourth, most properly linguistic, question entirely. I believe that questions (iii) and (iv) in particular are more deserving of philosophical attention than it might at first seem; but that discussion will have to await another occasion.

Constructions such as those in (1)–(3) below, stretching back to the original work of Castañeda (1966) and (1967), have been discussed at length over the years:

(1)  John/Each man expects (that) he will win.
(2)  John/Each man expects (that) he himself will win.
(3)  John/Each man expects himself to win.

To these constructions must be added the case where the subject of the infinitival complement is understood, as in *John/Each man expects to win*. Throughout this article, I represent the understood subject by the element PRO, as in Chomsky (1981). PRO is an expression having an interpretation (in fact, necessarily anaphoric to the main-clause subject), but no phonetic realization. Alternative views of the understood subject are possible. My choice may not ultimately affect the semantic question (i) above, but it will have consequences for (ii)–(iv).[2] Given PRO as the understood subject, to the examples (1)–(3) we may add:

(4)  John/Each man expects PRO to win.

The datum to be considered, then, is that there is something first-personal about the contents of the complements in (2)–(4) that need not obtain in

---

[1]  The logophors are special anaphors, said to refer to 'centres of consciousness'. The term has been extended to cases including some English reflexives. For discussion of the syntax and semantics of logophoric forms, see Huang (2000), Schlenker (1999) and (forthcoming), and references cited there.

[2]  For recent critical discussion, see Landau (2000), esp. ch. 5.

(1); that is, that there are contexts in which the assertion (1) is true (with *he* anaphoric to the subject, *John* or *each man*) that are not first-personal, but no such contexts for the assertion of any of (2)–(4). I need not give a preliminary rehearsal of the familiar scenarios given in support of this view; see below for discussion of examples.[3]

The contrast to be considered is between the ways in which (2)–(4) must be understood, and (1) need not be understood, so that (1) possesses an ambiguity that (2)–(4) lack.[4] There would appear to be three, and only three, modes of explanation of the observed contrast.

First (as in Higginbotham 1989 and 1991, for example) it may be suggested that the contexts in which (1) is not first-personal are concealed *de dicto* contexts, where some Fregean 'mode of presentation' attends the bound pronoun *he*. Consider Castañeda's example of the amnesiac war hero who is reading about himself and his heroic exploits, all unaware, indeed disbelieving, that it is he himself that he is reading about. We are licensed to say truly:

(5) The war hero thinks that he is a hero,

but not:

(6) The war hero thinks that he himself is a hero.

How can these be distinguished? According to the first method, they are distinguished in that, while the pronoun in (5) need not be taken as a mere variable, having for its antecedent the expression *the war hero*, the emphatic reflexive must be so taken. Suppose that we understand the

---

[3] The scenarios are of two basic kinds: (*a*) those in which a subject knows (or believes etc.) something about herself that it is questionable whether others know, as when I know in the ordinary way that I am standing; and (*b*) those where a subject knows something about himself, but does not have the knowledge that would be required in order to justify the use of locutions with reflexive, emphatic reflexive, or PRO (understood subject) arguments, as when he knows (as we say) that he was elected, because he knows that the candidate with the largest war chest was elected, but does not know that he himself was elected, having failed to realize that he himself was the candidate with the largest war chest. Again, see Castañeda for persuasive examples.

[4] The case of (4) was already observed in Fodor (1975), as noted below. Chierchia (1990) provided a more systematic taxonomy, concentrating, however, on propositional attitudes.

ordinary pronoun as if, while referring to the war hero, it presented him as, say, *the person that he (the war hero) is reading about*. Then we have a sense in which (5) can be true although (6), being for whatever reason strictly *de re*, is false. So the interpretations of (2)–(4) must be, and that of (1) can be, first-personal simply because *de re*.

The above view is rejected in Lewis (1979) for substantially theoretical reasons. It may also be questioned on the ground that it does not reveal what is peculiarly first-personal about, say, John's or each man's expectations in (3). The latter point will chiefly occupy us here.

Second, following the path taken by Lewis, and in a simplified form by Chierchia (1990), it may be proposed that the complements of the *de se* constructions are of a higher logical type, properties instead of propositions. Thus, according to Chierchia, (2) has it that, for John or each man $=x$, $x$ expects the property of being a thing $y$ such that $y$ wins; or, to put it perhaps more naturally, $x$ expects of $x$ that property. If $x$'s expectations come to pass, then $x$ has the property, and so $x$ wins. Likewise, when the war hero thinks he is a hero, but not that he himself is a hero, then for him $=x$, $x$ thinks that $x$ is a hero, but it is not the case that for him $=x$, $x$ thinks, or ascribes to $x$, the property of being a thing $y$ such that $y$ is a hero.

I shall elaborate somewhat upon this second proposal, and what I shall argue is its chief shortcoming. For the moment, I note that Stalnaker (1981) responded to Lewis in such a way as to defend a variant of the first view above, albeit from a different angle. For Stalnaker, the modes of presentation relevant to (5) do not figure in the logical form of the examples, but rather in setting up the possible worlds in which John has expectations about himself, but does not realize that it is himself he has expectations about. I discuss this view in Section 7 below.

Third, there is a possibility, sympathetically elucidated in Perry (1983) (but leading in the end to a sceptical conclusion), and notoriously having roots in Frege's (1918) discussion of the first person, as well as in Castañeda's work: it may be that there is a *special*, first-personal interpretation of the emphatic reflexive as in (2), of the reflexive as in (3), and of PRO as in (4), contributing its meaning to the propositional complement; and perhaps this special interpretation is also involved in the first-person forms themselves. The special interpretation would be available for (1), but not obligatory. The problem then is to elucidate what this interpretation is.

In this article I shall argue that the third view is correct, and I shall offer a particular way of understanding it. If it is correct, then *de se* interpretations of embedded clauses, obligatory in (4) and (6), optional in (1) and (5) above, are not the result of suppressing a conceptualized constituent in favour of the bare object, as in the first view, nor do they call for a reconstrual of clauses as expressions of properties, as in the second, but rather they have their own conceptualized constituents (analogous to Fregean senses, but only analogous, since they may, and in the view I advance will, contain objects that are not senses), whose properties explain why they are different from *de re* contexts.

One approach to what is special about first-person contexts is already illustrated in Peacocke (1981) as well as Perry (1983), cited above. I use Peacocke's exposition: suppose that there is a special mode of presentation *self* that a thinker $x$ can employ in thinking about himself, and no one else, and others cannot therefore employ in thinking about $x$. A particular first-person thought will employ a token $[self_x]$, indexed by $x$. The problem will now be to elucidate the empirical as well as the formal content of *self* and $[self_x]$.

The view that I advance in Section 6 below will not be Peacocke's, for reasons having to do with some empirical peculiarities of first-personal embedded constructions that I outline in earlier sections. Like his, however, it may be thought of as sympathetic to a latter-day Fregean perspective; and there are some direct points of contact, as well as room for differences. My remarks will in any case cash out some promissory notes in Higginbotham (1995) and (forthcoming).

## 2 Gerundive Complements

I have outlined a general view, that there is something distinctive in the beliefs or expectations about oneself that are alleged in assertions of examples such as (2)–(4), or (6). The phenomena may be illustrated with other types of examples, where the anaphors having distinctive interpretations appear within complement clauses, and so on a classical view occur as constituents of linguistic elements referring to propositions. The linguistic contexts hosting these examples would include predicates expressing epistemic states, as in knowing oneself to be so-and-so; indirect discourse; and other predicates involving states, conditions, or activities, such as dreaming, fantasizing, or pretending. Here, however, I turn to a different domain, that of the contexts of remembering, imagining, and the like, where the anaphor is the subject of a verbal gerundive complement, as in:

(7) John/Each man remembered/imagined [his going to the movies].
(8) John/Each man remembered/imagined [him, himself going to the movies].
(9) John/Each man remembered/imagined [himself going to the movies]
(10) John/Each man remembered/imagined [PRO going to the movies]

The above examples are parallel, or as parallel as can be, to (1)–(4) above.[5] I call particular attention to (10).

The first-personal character of such reports as (10) is foreshadowed in the notorious example (11), which arose some years ago in discussion between Jerry Fodor and Judith Thomson:

(11) Only Churchill remembers giving the speech (about blood, toil, tears, and sweat).

As Fodor (1975: 133 ff.) remarks, (11) is true provided that (a) only Churchill gave the speech, and (b) he remembers doing so. Thus (12) is a valid argument (with PRO explicit in the premisses and conclusion):

(12) Only Churchill gave the speech.
Churchill remembers [PRO giving the speech].
∴ Only Churchill remembers [PRO giving the speech].[6]

---

[5] In English, the ordinary pronominal *him* as in 'John remembered/imagined [him going to the movies]' cannot be anaphoric to *John*, just as it cannot be anaphoric in simple clauses such as *John remembered him*. Hence I use the possessive form *his* in (7). The emphatic reflexive *him, himself* in (8) seems to me acceptable and interpretable, if unnatural in comparison, say, with (9) and (10).

[6] Fodor used the validity of (12), in conjunction with the Katz–Postal hypothesis, that optional grammatical transformations did not change meaning, to argue against 'pronominalization': that is, against the view that the understood subject represents deletion of an anaphoric pronominal or reflexive element in the course of the syntactic derivation of (11). His thesis translates into the present syntactic system as: PRO is not semantically equivalent to any anaphoric pronominal or reflexive form. I shall argue below that the thesis is correct.

Compare the conclusion of (12) with:

(13) Only Churchill remembers his giving the speech.

The latter is, at first sight, obviously false, and is therefore not implied by the premises of (12). Indeed, it appears that, for the simple reason that those people who listened to Churchill's speech (in person, or on the radio) at the time he gave it, were aware in the ordinary way of what was going on, and subsequently remembered it, are all of them counter-examples to the truth of (13). If so, (13) is not true on any interpretation.

Now, Fodor's observation does not, and should not, show that what Churchill remembers when he remembers giving the speech is different from what he or others remember when they remember his giving it. We shall, however, accumulate evidence that there is indeed something special about Churchill's memorial state.

Before returning to Fodor's and similar cases, I endeavour in the next two sections to establish two points: first, that the gerundive complements in (7)–(10) have an event-like (in a sense to be explained) rather than a proposition-like reference; and second, that those with PRO subjects exhibit the phenomenon of 'immunity to error through misidentification' in the sense of Shoemaker (1968), and as refined in Pryor (1999).

## 3 The Interpretation of (Certain) Gerundive Complements

It is obvious that we remember events, and that we can speak of ourselves as engaged in remembering them. Furthermore, to remember an event— the Vietnam War, for example, or a birthday party—one must have had appropriate perceptual and other experience of it. The memory of an event may 'fade', as we say, and in particular one may know that one used to remember something one no longer remembers. Using these facts, we can swiftly show that the verbal gerundive complements to *remember* fall on the event side of things, and in this way are sharply to be distinguished from the finite complements *that so and so.*

(i) My father's father died before I was born. I remember that he was called 'Rufus'. But I do not remember his being called 'Rufus', because I was not alive when he was called that. Thus the complement

>   my grandfather's being called 'Rufus'

does not refer to the proposition (or fact) that he was called 'Rufus'; for if it did, then (14) and (15) would be true or false together, whereas in fact (14) is true, and (15) false:

>   (14) I remember that my grandfather was called 'Rufus'.

>   (15) I remember my grandfather's being called 'Rufus'.

(ii) Expressions involving propositional attitude or epistemic states resist the English progressive. Thus the examples in (16) are simply ungrammatical:

>   (16) I am believing/knowing/remembering that I walked to school in the fifth grade.

However, if someone comes across me looking pensive, and I am asked, 'What are you doing?' I can well respond with:

>   (17) I am remembering walking to school in the fifth grade,

as indeed I could respond with, 'I am remembering the birthday party', where the direct object of *remember* obviously refers to an event. We conclude that the complement in (17) so refers.[7]

(iii) Finite complements contrast with the gerundive in that, whereas (18) is reminiscent of the 'Moore Paradox', the anomaly of asserting that one does not believe something that one has just asserted, (19) may be an ordinary truth:

>   (18) I used to remember that I walked to school in the fifth grade, but I no longer remember it.

---

[7] The 'success verbs', as Ryle called them, do not generally admit the progressive: thus I cannot say that I am seeing my watch. When the same verbs are used without a 'success' connotation, however, the progressive becomes possible, as when I say that I am seeing spots before my eyes. Individual dialects diverge here: thus Christopher Peacocke finds the progressive of *see* acceptable where it involves making something out, or discernment, as in *I am not seeing the third letter*, said during an eye test. In my speech, however, this is a far fetch. It is useful, though not of itself enlightening, to put the divergence down to a distinction between expressions ranging over processes and those ranging over momentary transitions, or *achievements* in a common terminology, with my dialect admitting only the latter for epistemic or 'success' expressions, including *see*.

(19) I used to remember walking to school in the fifth grade, but I no longer remember it.

The above diagnostics show that the gerundive complements to *remember* speak of memory of events, rather than remembering facts, or remembering, or remembering-true, propositions.

Throughout the above, I have assumed that *remember*, in all uses, is factive: one can only remember true propositions; and when one speaks of remembering, say, walking to school, then there was indeed an event of one's walking to school. Whether factivity can be safely assumed or not, *remember* conspicuously contrasts with the non-factive *imagine*, and indeed with most other contexts in which the analogues of the above diagnostics can be carried out. There must, then, be a general perspective, abstracting away from factivity, from which gerundive and finite complements are put into semantic contrast. Our task in bringing it out is somewhat complicated by the fact that gerundive complements do not always contrast with finite or other complements in the stark way we have just illustrated, using *remember*. Passing over the complexities of the linguistic taxonomy, I outline a way that I would favour of making the semantic contrast where it obtains.

I shall assume, as in the familiar story derived from Davidson, and exploited by myself and many others, that the basic argument structure of a natural-language predicate *P* will have, besides some number *n* of slots for the overt arguments that appear with it, a slot for a variable *e* that ranges over events, thus:

$$P(x_1, \ldots, x_n, e)$$

(We abstract as usual from considerations of time and tense, as well as from the details of English morphology.) Supposing the arguments apart from the position marked by *e* filled in, we derive a predicate $\varphi(e)$ true only of events, as it might be *love(John, Mary, e)*.[8] An assertion of the sentence *John loves Mary* is an assertion:

$$(\exists e)\ \text{love}(\text{John, Mary, } e)$$

to the effect that there is at least one event of (as we may say) John loving

---

[8] In these last sentences and in what follows I suppress some distinctions between use and mention. I use italics for mentioned English words throughout, but do not further mark elements already italicized.

Mary. Any sentence that may be asserted may occur also as a finite complement (hosted by a complementizer such as *that*), in which case it will refer to a proposition. Following Richard Montague's (1969) notation, and for the purposes of this article his interpretation as well, the reference of the finite complement is:

$$\hat{}\,(\exists e)\ \text{love}(\text{John, Mary, } e)$$

where the circumflex ' $\hat{}$ ' represents $\lambda$-abstraction over possible worlds. If $\psi(p)$ is a factive predicate with respect to a propositional argument $p$, then its factivity is expressed by adopting the postulate:

$$\psi(p) \to {}^{\vee}p$$

where ${}^{\vee}p$ refers to the extension, in this case the truth value, of $p$ in the actual world. If $\psi(p)$ is so to speak anti-factive, implying the falsehood of its propositional argument (as is plausibly the case, for instance, with the propositional argument in *He fancies that p*), then the postulate to be adopted is

$$\psi(p) \to {}^{\vee}\neg p$$

The above familiar apparatus may now be modified so as to apply to the case of event-like reference, as in the gerundive complements. Consider a predicate $\varphi(e)$ of events. This predicate yields a term $(\lambda e)\varphi(e)$ by $\lambda$-abstraction, hence a term $\hat{}\,(\lambda e)\varphi(e)$ referring (in Montague's terminology) to properties of events. We propose that a predicate $\Gamma$ with respect to an event-like argument (as established through the above diagnostics) takes arguments $\alpha$ of the type of $\hat{}\,(\lambda e)\varphi(e)$: thus *John remembers/imagines Mary singing the song* would be

$$(\exists e')\ [\text{remembers/imagines}(\text{John, } \hat{}\,\lambda e\ \text{sing}(\text{Mary, the song, } e), e')]$$

If $\Gamma(\alpha)$ is a factive predicate with respect to arguments $\alpha$, then we adopt the postulate

$$\Gamma(\alpha) \to (\exists e^{\star})\ [({}^{\vee}\alpha)\ e^{\star}],$$

and if $\Gamma(\alpha)$ is anti-factive (as is plausibly the case for the gerundive complement in *He feigned taking offence at that remark*), then the postulate to be adopted is

$$\Gamma(\alpha) \rightarrow \neg (\exists e^\star) [(\check{\ }\alpha)\, e].$$

An easy calculation now confirms that *John remembers Mary singing the song*, together with its factive postulate, implies

$$(\exists e^\star)\ \text{sing}(\text{Mary, the song, } e^\star).$$

We have thus, following in effect Montague's strategy of ascending to the worst-case scenario, found a uniform way to give the semantics of gerundive complements in our target contexts, while accommodating, via postulates, the intuitions governing the factive and anti-factive cases.

Suppose now that in place of gerundive complements we have ordinary nominal objects:

(20)  Mary remembered / imagined the party for her 33rd birthday / a tree.

We can suppose that the remembered objects are ordinary things: birthday parties, trees. But Mary may imagine the party that (as we say) she will never have, and she may imagine a tree without imagining any particular tree. Evidently, we can bring these cases under our wing by supposing that when Mary imagines, or remembers, the party for her 33rd birthday, she imagines, or remembers $\check{\ }(\lambda e)e=$ the party for her 33rd birthday, and that when she imagines a tree (but no particular tree), she imagines $\check{\ }(\lambda x)(\exists y)\text{tree}(y)\ \&\ y= x$; that is, the property of being a thing $x$ that is identical to some tree. It does not seem possible to remember a tree without there being a tree that one remembers (even if one does not remember what tree it was). But the factive postulate, applied to this case, has only the consequence that if Mary remembers a tree, then there are trees, and not also the consequence that there is a tree of which her memory is a memory. But I leave this further matter aside for the present discussion.

## 4 Immunity to Error through Misidentification: A Characteristic of PRO

The phenomenon of immunity to error through misidentification is widely appreciated, following Shoemaker (1968) and subsequent work. Recent discussions to which I will advert include Pryor (1999) and Campbell (1999).

In this section I shall sketch the phenomenon, and show that it applies to the contexts that we have been considering, of memory, imagination, and others, with respect to the positions marked by the understood subject PRO; but also, and more tendentiously, I shall show that it does *not* apply to other subjects, including the reflexive, the emphatic reflexive, and even the first-person pronoun itself. A closer examination of the phenomenon follows in Section 5.

Put in terms of language, the phenomenon of immunity to error through misidentification arises for certain circumstantial reports of experience in which one cannot sensibly wonder whether it is oneself that plays a given role in what is reported. Suppose (to use an example of John Campbell's) it seems to me, on the basis of present perceptual experience, that I hear trumpets. I might be mistaken. It may not be trumpets that I hear. If I am mistaken, I have made an error due to misidentification: misidentification, that is, of the object that is the source of my experience. I might ask myself whether I am so mistaken. But I cannot sensibly ask myself whether I am mistaken *just* in thinking that it is *I* who hear trumpets. In this sense, there is immunity to error through misidentification.

Similarly, as in a famous discussion of Wittgenstein's, if I feel that I am in pain, although I might conceivably ask whether it is really pain that I am in (perhaps others would consider it merely mild discomfort), I cannot ask whether it is *I* who am in pain if anybody is, or think correctly that somebody is in pain, and wonder whether it is me.

What I have just put in terms of language may also be put in terms of the properties of occurrent thoughts; indeed there would seem to be nothing to distinguish these descriptions of the phenomenon except for the manner of presentation; or so I shall assume in what follows.

What is the reason for immunity to error through misidentification in the case of thinking, on the basis of a present perception, 'I hear trumpets'? I shall assume it is this: that when I am in the relevant perceptual state, what I think is *that the subject of that state hears trumpets*. Hence, there can be no question of my *identifying* myself as the subject of the state. I enlarge upon this thesis below.

There are, as Pryor notes, two distinguishable cases of error through misidentification, and correlatively of immunity to error. In the first, or as I shall call it the simple, case of immunity, one is immune from the following error in believing $F(a)$: that, knowing that $F(b)$ and believing, mistakenly, that $a = b$, one believes on those grounds that $F(a)$. In the second, or as I shall call it the generalized, case, one is immune from the following error in believing $F(a)$: that, knowing that something is $F$, and believing, mistakenly, that it is $a$'s being $F$ that is responsible for it being the case that something is $F$, one therefore believes that $F(a)$.

Illustration of the simple case: John sees a woman at some distance, and sees that she is smoking a cigarette. Identifying the woman as Mary, he comes to believe that Mary is smoking a cigarette. The identification is mistaken, and so there is an error due to misidentification, even if, unbeknownst to John, Mary is indeed off somewhere smoking a cigarette. Illustration of the generalized case (from Pryor): John smells the smell of skunk in his back yard. Going outside, he sees a skunk, and concludes that it is that skunk that is (wholly or partly) responsible for the smell; but in fact the source is (entirely) another skunk.

The above characterizations of errors of identification, and of immunity to error, are rough in various ways. For one thing, they leave the notion of identification itself obscure. We often pass from the knowledge that $F(b)$ to the belief that $F(a)$ on the basis of the just-acquired belief that $a = b$; but only some such cases are cases of identifying $b$ as $a$. Knowing as I do that Fischer played the best move in position **P**, and having on the basis of my own analysis concluded that P–K6 is the best move, I come to believe that Fischer played P–K6 in **P**; but I do not thereby identify P–K6 as Fischer's move. Not all occasions on which one comes to believe an identity are identificatory of anything. Furthermore, although it is natural, as in the core cases of perceptual identification, to think of identification as identification of objects pure and simple, and therefore of the belief $F(b)$ that one has prior to identification as being *de re*, as a general rule this is too restrictive, I think: when, looking out of the aeroplane window, I identify yonder snowy expanse as Mont Blanc, no doubt I have beliefs about Mont Blanc itself; but it is also crucial to my so identifying it that it was presented to me as a snowy expanse glimpsed from an aeroplane window.

Passing over the further subtleties that would be required precisely to delimit errors due to misidentification, and even with the limited apparatus sketched to this point, we can now ask, as Shoemaker (1970) asked, whether immunity to error through misidentification arises in the case of ordinary memory, as it does in perception. That memory of events is subject to errors of misidentification is evident. Suppose that it seems to me that I remember Mary walking through the streets of Oxford. I describe the scene: certain buildings, cobblestones, etc., and Mary walking along. You observe, however, that the buildings and streets I am remembering are obviously in Cambridge, not Oxford, and from my description you recognize that it is Alice I am talking about, not Mary. I stand corrected. As you might say to me: you remember something all right, but it is not Mary walking through the streets of Oxford, but Alice walking through the streets of Cambridge that you remember. I have made a (double) error of misidentification: everything is in place for knowledge by memory of past events, except that certain objects have been misidentified.

Suppose I seem to remember walking through the streets of some city or another. I might again be corrected about which city I am remembering walking through, or informed that the city I am remembering walking through is in fact Cambridge, not Oxford: but can I be mistaken just in thinking that it is *my* walking through the streets of Cambridge that I remember, or remember someone's walking through the streets of Cambridge, and wonder whether it was me?

Such errors do not at first appear credible: but Shoemaker considers the possibility that some sort of 'false memory' has been implanted in me, so that it seems to me that I remember walking through the streets of Oxford, whereas the experience that is responsible for the memory is either non-existent, or the experience of someone else, functional bits of whose brain have been somehow transplanted into mine. In my state, I experience what Shoemaker calls 'quasi-memories': that is, what appear to me to be genuine memories of mine (and might actually have originated in the memories of someone else) but which are not memories of mine anyway, even if they could by a stretch be called memories, deriving as they did from someone else's experience.

Putting quasi-memories (and quasi-imaginings as well) aside, we appear to have immunity to error through misidentification in the case described, of seeming to remember walking through the streets of Oxford. But I am now going to observe that, when it comes to the gerundive complements that we have been considering, the problem of their first-personal character shows up when we contrast PRO subjects with the first person itself.

## 5 Ways of Remembering and Imagining

Suppose that we form a small party, agreeing that we shall call on John and encourage him to finish his thesis by July. Having cornered John, we explain how he should really be prudent, given his scholastic and financial circumstances, and so forth. After the session, I try to remember whether we merely hinted around the subject, or whether it was explicitly said to John that he should finish his thesis by July. After a time, I might remember someone saying to John that he should finish his thesis by July; but I do not remember whether it was I who said it. Your memory for the occasion is better than mine, and you do remember my saying it; and you tell me so. I draw an inference as follows:

(21) I remember someone saying John should finish his thesis by July.
In fact, as I am now assured, it was I who said it.
∴ I remember my saying John should finish his thesis by July.

The reasoning seems to me impeccable. But (22) does not follow from the premisses of (21), and is indeed obviously false:

(22) I remember saying John should finish his thesis by July.

However, the only difference between (22) and the true conclusion of (21) is that the first-person pronoun has been replaced by PRO.

A certain intuition about this case seems clear enough. When I remember (what turns out to be) my saying that John should finish his thesis by July, I remember this through my recollection of the words in the air, which turn out to have been put there by me, though I do not remember that. When I fail to remember saying that John should finish his thesis by July, that is a failure that would be remedied if I remembered my saying that as an act of mine.

But suppose I do come to remember saying that John should finish his thesis by July. It cannot (and should not) be inferred that the event that I then remember is different from the event that I remembered earlier, through remembering hearing the words in the air. There is just one event in question, namely my saying John should finish his thesis by July. I might remember this event (as indeed I remember people, cities, and other things) in any of various ways; but these different ways do not translate into different remembered events in the complements of the conclusion of (21), on the one hand, and (22), on the other.

And, finally, there is this case: I remember a certain person's (my) saying that John should finish his thesis by July, but not saying it: that is, I remember hearing the words that, given that I recognize my own voice, I know could only have come from me, but I do not remember their having done so. Again there is just one event. But it can be remembered in either of two ways, namely as an action that I performed, or as an event that I witnessed. The latter sits well with pronouns, but the former is required of PRO.

Imagination goes along with memory here. Thus (an example modelled on Peacocke 1998: 212), I can imagine my playing *Three Blind Mice* on the piano, but (since I do not play the piano) I cannot imagine playing *Three Blind Mice*; and that is because I cannot imagine it as an action that I myself perform.

As Michael Martin pointed out at the Sheffield conference, the above characteristic of PRO shows up in many contexts. There is, for instance, a difference in the intentions I may have when I intend to stop smoking (i.e. PRO to stop smoking), and when I intend merely that I should stop smoking. The latter intention might be fulfilled, say, by paying someone forcibly to remove cigarettes from my person whenever I am caught with them; but that is not fulfilment of an intention to stop smoking, which can only be done through wilful refusal to put a cigarette to my lips and light up.

I have concentrated on remembering and imagining actions, or events that could be actions; but the peculiarities of PRO appear in matters that befall one, as well as what one does. Thus for me to remember falling downstairs, or crying, is to remember those events as processes that I underwent; whereas I might remember my falling downstairs by remembering how I felt as I picked myself up, or remember my crying by remembering how the tears felt rolling down my cheeks.

Pryor (1999) alludes to remembering things 'from the inside', as he puts it, setting aside other ways of remembering. This is a useful label to put on the problem, which might be translated into the present setting by saying that if in reports of remembering events, as indicated by gerundive complements, there is no semantic difference between the first-person pronoun and the understood subject PRO, then there can be no semantic difference between (22) and the conclusion of (21), contrary to fact. Indeed, there is more: the conclusion of (21) seems to be subject to errors of misidentification, at least given the right context. Remembering as I do someone saying John should finish his thesis by July, I might, in virtue of remembering the tone of voice that I heard, ascribe authorship of this event to you by mistake, or to myself by mistake; but that scenario seems impossible with (22).

In the connection with immunity to error through misidentification, I have spoken thus far of memory; but examples with imagination come to mind as well. There is an intuitive difference between (23) and (24):

(23) Mary imagined herself flying through space (although she did not realize it was she herself who was flying through space).

(24) Mary imagined [PRO flying through space] (although she did not realize it was she herself who was flying through space).

(23) is possibly true; (24) is contradictory, or so it would appear.

If the above is correct, then we have isolated a case wherein PRO is, so to speak, more first-personal than the reflexive forms, and even more first-personal than the first-person pronoun itself. It is more first-personal in two respects: (i) unlike the first-personal forms, it is immune from error through misidentification; and (ii) the use of PRO always brings in an 'internal' dimension to the way what is remembered or imagined is apprehended. These phenomena point up the reality of the *de se* phenomenon more radically than the ordinary contexts of propositional attitude, or epistemic states. In the next section I offer a way of understanding them.

## 6 The Semantic Contribution of PRO

A solution to the problems posed thus far in our discussion should have the following properties:

(a) It should state what is peculiar about the semantic contribution of the understood subject PRO.

(b) This contribution should be such as immediately to characterize the distinction between *de se* and *de re* interpretations.

(c) It should likewise imply immunity to error through misidentification.

(d) It should do this in such a way that immunity to error through misidentification in the classification of ordinary perceptual experience follows along as a special case.

(*e*) It should explain the distinction between the 'internal' dimension signalled by PRO, and the possibly only 'external' dimension expressed by ordinary pronouns and reflexive forms.

In short, as I see it, the problems of the *de se*, immunity to error through misidentification, and the rest, call for a solution in terms of logical form. The solution, moreover, should explain the *grounds* upon which *de se* interpretation, and immunity to error through misidentification, arise.

Now, it is obvious that immunity to error through misidentification must arise, not because identification is infallible, but because there is no question of identification at all. If we ask what it is for a position, call it $\pi$, in a construction

$$\ldots \pi \ldots$$

not to require identification within that construction, there is a case that at once presents itself, namely the case where $\pi$ is a variable, free within the context $\ldots \pi \ldots$, but bound from outside it; and more generally where $\pi$ is a functional context $f(\pi')$, $\pi'$ a variable free inside but bound outside the context, and $f$ interpreted by a function that is given once the context surrounding $\ldots \pi \ldots$ is given.

In Higginbotham (1995) I argued that contexts of the above shape were crucially involved in locating events with respect to one's own position in time. So in saying (or thinking), as in A. N. Prior's famous example, 'Well, *that's* over', the event of which one is thinking that it is over is thought of as coming before one's thinking that. Thoughts of this type were called *reflexive*, the general form being

$$\varphi(e) \ \& \ R(e, e'),$$

where $\varphi$ is some condition on $e$, and $R$ expresses a temporal relation between $e$ and the episode $e'$ of thinking or saying. Suppose, for instance, I think, or say on the basis of perception, that a dog just barked. The logical form is then:

(25) $(\exists e')$ think/say[I, $e'$, $\hat{}\ (\exists e)(\exists x)$ (dog$(x)$ & bark$(x, e)$ & $e$ just before $e')$].

I cannot then ask whether I am right in having located in the near past any barking that would make my belief or utterance true; for it is given in the thought itself that it belongs to *my* near past, i.e. just before my thinking or saying.[9]

Perhaps my last statement is somewhat too strong. Perhaps, even with the alleged barking still ringing in my ears, I have misestimated the lapse of time between my perception and my thought; and how much before is 'just before' anyway? However this may be, I cannot ask myself whether I am mistaken just in thinking that it was in *my* past that a dog barked.

Following the analogy of reflexive thoughts with respect to time, suppose that we identify as the peculiar semantic contribution of PRO that it presents the subject as *the subject (or experiencer) of the event or state e* as given in the higher clause, or $\sigma(e)$ for short. This conjecture immediately gives for (4), repeated here, the logical form (26):

(4) John/Each man expects PRO to win.
(26) (For John/each man $=x$) $(\exists e)$ expect$[x, e, \char`^(\exists e')$ win$(\sigma(e), e')]$.

The intended contrast is with:

(27) (For John/each man $=x$) $(\exists e)$ expect$[x, e, \char`^(\exists e')$ win$(x, e')]$.

The complement of the latter is one interpretation of (1), repeated here:

(1) John/Each man expects (that) he will win,

an interpretation that, on the hypothesis under consideration, is not available for (4). But this complement is not immune to error through misidentification. For suppose that I expect, indeed know, that the contestant who trained hardest will win the competition I have entered; but I do not know, and I know that I do not know, whether I myself am that contestant. Then, for all I know, it is I myself whom I expect to win. But I also know that it is not true that I expect to win. Later, but still before the competition, I come on the basis of certain evidence to identify myself as the person who trained

---

[9] Thus the experience $e'$ has been 'loaded' into the proposition expressed. But is the truth of the proposition not independent of that connection, and indeed of whether there was any experience at all? An analogous problem is discussed in Higginbotham (1995), inconclusively; however, I would maintain that the interpretation of the speaker's word, or thought-constituent, marked by *just* does carry the temporal anchoring expressed in (25).

hardest. Holding fast to my previous knowledge, I now come to believe that I myself shall win, and therefore to expect that I shall win, and to expect to win. My first expectation, that I shall win, is subject to error through misidentification: if the person who trained hardest turns out, despite my evidence, to be other than me, then I have made such an error. But my second expectation, namely my expectation of winning, is not subject to such an error, despite the fact that I have this expectation only because I expect that I shall win, an expectation that involves the possibility of error.

The informal considerations just given are decisive against construing (4) as merely having the logical form (27), provided indeed that we take it that the reflexive pronoun *myself* can only be taken up as a bound variable, which is precisely what the proposal that there will be an intervening mode of presentation denies. However, the premiss that the complement of (1) on some construal is not immune to error through misidentification still stands. The situation as I conceive it is the following. When I expect that I, or I myself, will be F, my expectation is subject to error through misidentification if my grounds for it are the possibly mistaken belief that I am the G, and the knowledge merely that the G will be F. Thus the complement of (1) is subject to such error, where taken up as shown in (27). Knowing as I do that I am the experiencer of the state e of that expectation, when I expect that I myself shall be F, I also expect to be F; hence anything that supports or undermines the first expectation will support or undermine the second. However, whereas I can sensibly ask myself whether, after all, I have identified myself correctly in expecting that I shall win, I cannot ask myself whether I have identified myself correctly in expecting to win.

The considerations just given are intuitive. Indeed, so long as we hold to the thesis that the subject or experiencer $\sigma(e)$ of a state e cannot fail to be known as the thing x that is that subject or experiencer, the link between, for instance, (28) and (29) cannot be broken:

(28) I expect that I (myself) shall win.
(29) I expect to win.

There is, nevertheless, a difference between them. The thought

$$\hat{}\,(\exists e')\,\mathrm{win}(\sigma(e), e')$$

is distinct from

$$\hat{}\,(\exists e')\,\text{win}(x, e')$$

(for given values of $x$ and $e$), even if they are not intensionally different; or so I would submit. The peculiar contribution of PRO, an optional contribution of pronouns and (depending upon the context) perhaps of reflexive forms as well, is that it picks up the subject, the 'controller' in familiar linguistic terminology, through the role that it plays with respect to the superordinate or matrix predicate, in this case *expect*.

Consider the application of the above view to the classic case, Castañeda's amnesiac war hero, where the data are that (5) but not (6) may be said truly:

(5) The war hero thinks that he is a hero.
(6) The war hero thinks that he himself is a hero.

Suppose we allow that (5) is true, with the logical form:

(30) (For the war hero $=x$) $(\exists e)$ think$[x, e, \hat{}\,(\exists e')\,\text{hero}(x, e')]$,

but take (6) as false, with the logical form:

(31) (For the war hero $=x$) $(\exists e)$ think$[x, e, \hat{}\,(\exists e')\,\text{hero}(\sigma(e), e')]$.

Are the thoughts attributed in the two cases intensionally different? In other words, could anyone other than the war hero have been the subject or experiencer of that war hero's individual state? This is not a trivial question; but I shall proceed here on the assumption that the answer is negative.[10] If that is so, then there are no grounds upon which the intensionally individuated contents of (30) and (31) may be distinguished: they will coincide in truth value in any actual or counterfactual situation. Even if they do coincide, it does not follow that they are the same thought (but for a construal that would make them intensionally different, see Section 8 below).

Thus far I have concentrated upon one aspect of PRO, namely its immunity to error through misidentification. But there is also the 'internal' aspect of PRO to be considered, an aspect that is not brought out on the view given thus far.

[10] Plainly, however, a full treatment must take a view on the very general question, what properties of events (taken as objects of some sort, following Davidson) are contingent, and what necessary. (In Higginbotham 1995 I suggested that the spatio-temporal location of at least some events was a contingent matter.)

In the picture that we have been using throughout this discussion, the bare predicates of a language are to be thought of as classifiers of events, and their arguments are selected as participants in the events so classified. The relation of a given participant to an event—agent, or patient, or whatever it is exactly—is, to use a terminology that is common to a variety of perspectives, and even conceptions of semantics, the *thematic role* that the participant bears to that event. Now, without delving into the variety of linguistic and metaphysical questions that have been raised about thematic roles, we may distinguish: (i) the case where an object $\alpha$ in a predication $\varphi(e, \alpha)$ is given through some description external to its participation in $e$; and (ii) the case where $\alpha$ is given simply as $\theta(e)$, where $\theta$ expresses the thematic role that $\alpha$ bears to $e$.

I suggest that the 'internal' aspect of PRO results from that element's being considered, either exclusively or in conjunction with its value as given by its antecedent, as the bearer of some thematic role that its syntactic position selects for the bare predicate with which it is in construction. On this hypothesis, for example, the interpretation of the subject in

$$\text{PRO falling downstairs}$$

is as in

$$\text{falling downstairs}(\theta(e), e),$$

where $\theta(e)$ expresses the relation, something like *undergoer*, that a thing falling downstairs bears to an event of so falling.

The above suggestion accords with Michael Martin's observation. When I intend to stop smoking, I intend that I am the agent of my stopping smoking; but when I merely intend that I stop smoking, there is no implication of my agency in the stopping, any more than there would be on the part of the automobile in *the car stopped moving*.

In Martin's case and others, it will be a primitive property of PRO that it is construed as the bearer of one or other relation to events as classified by the predicate it appears with. Supposing this property given, we can express the difference between (22), repeated here, and the conclusion of (21), here given as (32):

(22) I remember saying that John should finish his thesis by July.

(32) I remember my saying that John should finish his thesis by July.

For (22) to be true I must remember the event in question *as* something of which I was the agent; that is, the property of events that I remember puts me in the picture as *agent of e*. That requirement does not obtain in (32).[11] Likewise we can distinguish, I believe, minimal pairs such as those in:

(33) I remember/imagine [PRO/myself falling downstairs].
(34) I remember/imagine [PRO/myself crying].

We can now join Martin's observation together with the suggested explanation for immunity to error through misidentification, as follows. When one remembers or imagines *PRO being F*, then the linguistic element PRO is distinguished in two ways: (i) by being understood as the thing $\sigma(e)$ that is in the state $e$ of remembering or imagining itself; and (ii) by being at the same time understood as the bearer of the thematic role $\theta(e')$ as determined through the selection for the subject of the predicate $F(e')$ (so in general that $\sigma(e) = \theta(e')$ is presupposed). I shall abbreviate this dual role of PRO as '$\sigma(e)$ & $\theta(e')$'. With PRO so understood, (22) for instance comes out as:

(35) $(\exists e)$ Remember$\{I, e, \char`^ \lambda(e')$ [say$(\sigma(e)$ & $\theta(e')$,that John should finish his thesis by July, $e')]\}$.

We thus bring out both the fact that, if (22) is true, then the subject cannot make an error of misidentification, and the fact that what is remembered is remembered *as* an action performed.

---

[11] As Stephen Parkinson has made me aware, there is at least one case where contexts such as (22) and (32) are not to be discriminated, namely the case where the question is not merely what one remembers, but more stringently what one remembers out of one's own memory, or of one's own knowledge. Thus suppose I am to testify as to what was said to John. I remember someone saying that he should finish his thesis, but not that it was me who said it. In that case, even if I have become convinced on other grounds that it must have been me who spoke, I cannot agree with an inquisitor's assertion that I do after all remember my saying it; for in the setting of testimony I am supposed to state what I remember without reliance upon external evidence. Cases of this sort are of course not confined to memory of oneself: if I remember the blue Ford at the scene of the crime, and have only since become convinced (rightly) that it was the getaway car, I still cannot respond 'Yes' to the question put at the trial whether I remember the getaway car at the scene of the crime.

In concluding this section, I show how the Fodor–Thomson example comes out on the view advanced here. We are given the premises:

(36) Only Churchill gave the speech.

(37) Churchill remembers PRO giving the speech.

And we aim to derive:

(38) Only Churchill remembers PRO giving the speech.

The proper name *Churchill* may be rendered as a quantifier, *for x = Churchill*, with obvious semantics, and the subject *only Churchill* of (36) and (38) is understood as quantificational as well, where in general, where *Only x such that A are B* is true if and only if all *B* are *A*. We need also to assume, perhaps as a matter of presupposition, that *Only Churchill is F* licenses *Churchill is F*.

With these assumptions, (36) will have a logical form equivalent to:

(39) $(\exists e)$ give(Churchill, the speech, $e$) & $(\forall x \neq \text{Churchill})\ \neg(\exists e')$ give($x$, the speech, $e'$).

For (37), taking PRO as merely a bound variable, we have:

(40) (For $x = \text{Churchill}$)$(\exists e)$ Remember[$x, e,\ \hat{}\ (\lambda e')$ give($x$, the speech, $e'$)];

and it will be sufficient to derive:

(41) $(\forall x \neq \text{Churchill})\ \neg(\exists e)$ Remember[$x, e,\ \hat{}\ (\lambda e')$ give($x$, the speech, $e'$)].

Supposing on the contrary

$x \neq \text{Churchill}$ & Remember[$x, e,\ \hat{}\ (\lambda e')$ give($x$, the speech, $e'$)],

we have, by the factivity of *remember*, the consequence

$x \neq \text{Churchill}$ & $(\exists e')$ give($x$, the speech, $e'$),

contradicting (39).

The assumption crucial to the above derivation of (38) is that PRO be 'captured' by the quasi-quantifier *only Churchill*. Because, as remarked above, it is not true that the premises (36)–(37) lead to the conclusion (42), we must say something about the interpretation of the pronoun *his*, even where it is anaphoric to *Churchill*:

(42) Only Churchill remembers his [Churchill's] giving the speech.

It is sufficient to suggest that the pronoun, unlike PRO, can simply go proxy for the name, that being enough to block the implication.

The simple treatment of PRO as obligatorily a bound variable is sufficient to explain the Fodor–Thomson observation. On the more complex treatment suggested in this section, the premiss (39) is replaced by (43), and the desired conclusion (41) by (44):

(43) (For $x =$ Churchill)($\exists e$) Remember[$x$, $e$, ˆ($\lambda e'$) give($\sigma(e)$ & $\theta(e')$, the speech, $e'$)].

(44) ($\forall x \neq$ Churchill) $\neg$ ($\exists e$) Remember[$x$, $e$, ˆ($\lambda e'$) give($\sigma(e)$ & $\theta(e')$, the speech, $e'$)].

The derivation of this conclusion is only marginally more complex, requiring as it does just the added point that, where $e$ is a state of Churchill's remembering, and $e'$ is any event of giving the speech, Churchill himself is indeed $\sigma(e)$ and $\theta(e')$.

But could a person $x$ be in a state $e$ of imagining being $F$ without *recognizing* that $x = \sigma(e)$, the subject of the property of events being imagined? If this can happen, then perhaps, as tentatively suggested in Campbell (1999), that person would have thoughts of which he did not seem to himself to be the author. In any case, it seems safe to assume that any such condition would be pathological.

This concludes my discussion of the contribution of PRO, and the perspective that the account given here affords upon the semantic data that suggest it. If the account is correct, then PRO, and I shall assume at least some reflexive and emphatic reflexive elements, are distinguished by having special interpretations, as in the third of the three options that I presented in Section 1 above. In the next section I take up the question of the other options directly.

## 7 Alternatives Explored

As we know from the story surrounding (5), repeated here, in any situation in which the war hero's beliefs are true, he is not reading about himself:

(5) The war hero thinks that he is a hero.

In the world according to the war hero, as we might say, there is on the one hand him, and on the other the person whose exploits he is reading about. It is this reflection that encourages the idea, expressed in the first hypothesis of Section 1 above, that the apparent existence of contexts that are simply and strictly *de re*, but not first-personal, is after all an illusion: in all such cases, there is an intervening 'mode of presentation', which would in the present instance be brought out in the logical form:

(45) (For the war hero $=x$) ($\exists e$) think[$x$, $e$, $^\wedge$($\exists e'$) hero(the person $x$ is reading about, $e'$)].

This mode of presentation contains the war hero himself as the value of $x$, and in that sense is *de re*. But if all that is going on in the example is that the thought attributed in the complement of *He thinks he is a hero* has a structure that is not revealed in the linguistic material alone, then it would seem that the first-personal or *de se* thought has no peculiar status to be explained, being simply the *de re* case unadorned.

As I understand it, Stalnaker's (1981) discussion of indexical belief could lead to a similar conclusion, transposed, as it were, into a different key. For Stalnaker, the background story (and its presuppositions, including the presupposition, if it is present, that the war hero is in fact reading about himself) serves, not to fix a mode of presentation, but rather to determine which alternative situations of utterance of *He (the war hero) is a hero* are to be taken into account. So consider all of those situations $w$ such that the war hero is in $w$ reading about a person other than himself. In those situations, the speaker's embedded subject *he* refers, not to the war hero, but to that other person. Moreover, only such situations are consistent with what the war hero believes (assuming that the speaker's presuppositions are satisfied, as they would be if the war hero thinks that the person he is reading about is not himself). The content that the speaker attributes to the war hero's beliefs is then just the content

$\hat{}(\exists e')$ hero(the person $x$ is reading about,$e'$)]

for the war hero as the value of $x$, with the presuppositions mentioned. This content is constructed, not by first filling in a mode of presentation, and then taking the expression so filled in around the counterfactual situations $w$, but rather by taking what Stalnaker calls the *diagonal* proposition, obtained by determining, for each $w$, what the truth value of *He (the war hero) is a hero* would be as said by the speaker in $w$.

It is pretty clear that, for any *particular* way of filling in the notion of a situation consistent with what the war hero believes, we can construct a mode of presentation that will, when supplanted for $x$ in the complement clause, deliver along the horizontal just what the diagonal proposition delivers along the diagonal. In the case under consideration, we supplant $x$ with *the person $x$ is reading about*, for instance. We can also proceed in the other direction, supplanting *the person $x$ is reading about* with the simple variable, but taking along the diagonal the worlds $w$ and the utterances 'He is a hero', where the pronoun refers to whoever it is would have been meant by its utterance in $w$. There are perhaps differences between these approaches, centring on the point that in the method of supplementation we ascribe a mode of presentation for which, in effect, we regard what is said as elliptical, whereas in Stalnaker's diagonal method we supply instead a conception of what is merely implicated by the speaker; but I shall not dwell on these differences here. In either case, we are taking those *de re* attributions that are not *de se* (that is, those that would sustain a use of the bare pronoun, but not of the emphatic reflexive, or of PRO) as not meant literally. And indeed, how could they be? For, after all, we know that the amnesiac war hero believes he is not the person whom he is reading about, and that he is ready to say as much, and in the first person. Yet his beliefs cannot be internally faulted, or rectified by mere cogitation. So if we are to have a conception of how the world would be if his beliefs were true, we cannot found it upon a combination of the literal interpretation of what he is reported to believe, on the one hand, and his own avowals, on the other.

I suggest that the considerations just rehearsed do show, either through Stalnaker's route or through that suggested by invoking modes of presentation, that so long as we wish to have a conception of 'how the world would be' if a believer's beliefs were true (assuming of course that there *is* such a way)—or, to put it only slightly differently, but to the same effect, so long as we need to have a conception of what the notation we use to ascribe thoughts to ourselves or to others is a notation *for*—we should regard the true report in (5), as it might be called a report of a true belief in the absence of proper identification (in this case of the person the war hero is reading about with himself), as expressing something other than just what is given on its face (taking the proposition expressed in the usual way, and not 'on the diagonal').

The tempting conclusion is that (6), repeated here, is the true *de re* report:

(6) The war hero believes that he himself is a hero.

The difference between (5) and (6) cannot be left just at that, however; for we need also to explain why (6) cannot be asserted under the same circumstances as (5), or why PRO should contrast even with the emphatic reflexive in the contexts of imagining, for example.[12]

For these reasons also in part, the construction of Lewis (1979) and Chierchia (1990) does not appear to satisfy the demands of the case. Recall that on Chierchia's view the positions critical for *de se* interpretation are abstracted over, so that the object of the thought that one is oneself a hero is: $^\wedge (\lambda x)$ hero$(x)$. There is no evident reason why immunity to error through misidentification should be associated with the abstracted position, or why, to use Pryor's term, true reports of imagining and remembering with understood, PRO subjects should always indicate imagining and remembering 'from the inside'. Furthermore, as suggested by David Kaplan in his Bielefeld lecture (1995), and subsequently in a Gareth Evans Memorial Lecture at Oxford the same year, Lewis's strategy would generalize, implausibly, to other embedded indexicals, words like *now*, *here*, *today*, and the like. Finally, as noted

---

[12] There are important comparative-linguistic questions here. To take one example, note that in English *believe*, unlike *expect*, does not take controlled complements, so that we do not have *John believes [PRO to be a hero]*. The corresponding construction in Italian, namely *Gianni crede [PRO di essere un eroe]* is, however, fully grammatical, and (I am informed) unambiguously *de se*. Corresponding to English *John believes that he himself is a hero* Italian has the construction *Gianni crede che egli stesso è un eroe*; but this, as again I am told, is not necessarily *de se*. From these facts we might draw the cross-linguistic conclusion that it is the understood subject (which, as pointed out for instance in Chierchia 1990, must for languages like Italian be distinguished from the null subject pronoun of a finite clause) that is crucially involved in the *de se* phenomena. Schlenker (forthcoming) carries these questions much further, in ways I shall not consider here.

in Landau (2000: ch. 2), the account faces difficulties in accounting for the phenomenon he calls *partial control*, where the understood subject is plural, but its antecedent is singular; I give one example of this phenomenon below.

Granting that the understood subject must be a real subject in the logical form, it may be asked whether the unadorned *de re* already exhibits the property of immunity to error through misidentification: that is, whether the recourse to $\sigma(e)$ exploited above is really necessary. The question arises because the apparent cases of *de re* that were not *de se* all seem upon closer examination, either through the invocation of hidden modes of presentation or through Stalnaker's suggestion, to be understandable as carrying more semantic baggage than the simple *de re* would suggest. This diagnosis applies even to cases of the embedded first person, as we saw above: when I remembered (what, from my point of view, turned out to be) my saying that John should finish his thesis by July, I remembered it through a conception of the subject of that action *as* some producer of words in the air, the bearer of a certain tone of voice, or something similar. Thus when the *de se* is missing, there is always, so to speak, a fall-back to some underlying content that is not strictly *de re*.

Now, this last reflection, assuming it correct, of course does not show that the *de re* thought is not there, but only that, if it is there, it is there in virtue of something else, something that is not purely *de re*. But this phenomenon holds quite generally for embedded indexicals. If I wonder, now, quite out of the blue, whether it was sunny yesterday in Los Angeles, there is no question of my misidentifying yesterday, that day being given as *the day before my wondering this*. But if I wonder whether it was sunny yesterday in Los Angeles because I wonder whether it was sunny on 27 May, believing, mistakenly, that the 27th was two days ago rather than yesterday, then I make an error due to misidentification (I have not properly grasped what I am wondering about). That fact alone does not show that I am not wondering about yesterday, the day itself. Likewise, in the setting due to Castañeda, the war hero's belief that he is a hero can be a belief about himself, purely *de re*, despite his misidentification or lack of identification. That attribution need not be withdrawn just because another stands behind it. Our question therefore remains.

For the purposes of this article, I shall leave that question unanswered. In any case, it seems to me that immunity to error through misidentification calls for a thing's being given through material supplied from a higher context, as in the example just presented of wondering whether yesterday was sunny in Los Angeles. But I must leave this matter for another occasion.

## 8 Links to Formalization

Much of the recent literature on the *de se* has taken as its point of departure the account of demonstrative and indexical expressions developed origin-ally in Kaplan (1977). Schlenker (forthcoming) proposes a modification of Kaplan's Logic of Demonstratives that is designed to incorporate the *de se* by admitting context sensitivities of the type that Kaplan dubs 'monsters'. Assuming the account of the *de se* advanced above, I examine the extent to which it can be seen, within the formal perspective of that modification, as a further specification of it.

Recall that in Kaplan (1977), truth in a model is defined relative to pairs $(c, w)$, where $c$ is a context, and $w$ a possible world, and that the content of a sentence in a context $c$ is the set of possible worlds in which it is true. Contexts, whatever they are, are anyway such that one can pull from them a speaker, a time, and a world of the context, namely the world in which the speaker is conceived of as saying the sentence at the time in question. The system thus involves double-indexing with respect to the possible worlds, as in two-dimensional modal logic, and it therefore permits, in principle, operators that generalize over context worlds as well as worlds of evaluation. Such operators are 'monsters', and Kaplan urged that, although they are definable, they could not exist in our language (or, presumably, human languages generally).

Schlenker (forthcoming) develops a formal account of the *de se* that allows manipulation of the context parameter, specifically the agent of the context (a suggestion to similar effect is found in Israel and Perry 1996). This allows Schlenker to distinguish, for example, the content of the complement in *x hopes x is elected*, namely the one true in those worlds in which $x$ is elected (independently of the agent), from that of *x hopes [PRO to be elected]*, which comprises those $(a, w)$ in which $a$ is the agent of the context, and $a$ is elected. Assuming as Schlenker does the modal account of the propositional attitudes, *x hopes that p* will be true in a context $c$ in a world $w$ just in case every *context* (not: possible world) compatible with what $x$ hopes is one in which $p$, where the context comes with a world of evaluation, and also an agent. Thus a context is compatible with what $x$ hopes in hoping that $x$ is elected if and only if it is one in which $x$ is elected; but it is compatible with what $x$ hopes in hoping to be elected if and only if it is one in which the agent of that context is elected, independently of whether that agent is $x$.[13]

Assuming the account developed in this article, we can see it as a further specification of Schlenker's method. Supposing as above that the content of the complement subject position in $x$ hopes [PRO to be elected] is $\sigma(e)$ & $\theta(e)$, where $e$ is the situation of $x$'s hoping, we may suppose that, although the individual situation $e$ belongs essentially to $x$, the kind of situation that $e$ is could belong to anybody. If, therefore, we allow the instance $e$ of that kind to vary independently, and make it part of the context, we arrive at an account that specifies more precisely, but in the same manner as the parameter of the agent of the context, what it will be for a context to be compatible with what $x$ hopes. Thus, whatever the advantages and uses, or the disadvantages and abuses, of the modal theory of the attitudes, the empirical material given here, if I am right, will supplement the purely formal move that Schlenker suggests.

## 9 Concluding Examples and Extensions

The above discussion of PRO has developed a point of view according to which two rather sophisticated concepts are involved in its correct employ-ment: (a) the concept of being an agent that thinks thoughts, expressed by '$\sigma(e)$', and (b) the concept of being an undergoer or agent of experience, expressed by '$\theta(e)$'. It follows that those who use this form, or the relevant constructions, correctly, or have thoughts that are properly reported using them, must be able to deploy both concepts. But is that really essential to first-person thoughts?

I leave aside the question of reports of the thoughts of creatures for which the question how to take our very expression of the thoughts that we attribute to them, or in what sense they have thoughts, is itself an issue. The problem is whether there are notions of the self, more primitive or anyway different from those that I have recruited, namely of oneself as a thinker of

---

[13] Schlenker's formal theory involves an extensionalization of Kaplan's Logic of De-monstratives, in which the relevant parameters occupy quantifiable places.

thoughts and undergoer of experiences, that, whether or not they answer to English PRO or anything else, deserve to be brought into the realm of first-person thoughts. Recall the general suggestion of Peacocke (1981), that first-person thoughts by $x$ contain a constituent [$self_x$], a token of a type $self$ available to all. I am proposing, to use Peacocke's terminology, that one such type is $\sigma(e)$ & $\theta(e)$, where $e$ is some particular event, so that the tokens are instantiations of $e$, where $x = \sigma(e) = \theta(e)$. That does not exclude the existence of other types. At the same time, the phenomena of memory 'from the inside', and of complements necessarily interpreted as denoting particular ways of remembering and imagining things, appear to show that these types are not included in our most basic system of speech: unsurprisingly, since we all do conceive of ourselves in the ways required for the account.

In concluding, I consider three points, the first two of which have appeared in the literature, and the third of which will probably have occurred to the reader in passing. The first point is the problem of like belief, due to Lewis, and the second concerns a question raised early on for Castañeda, whether or to what extent first-personal knowledge can be shared. The third point addresses briefly the peculiarities of the distribution of the understood subject, whose semantics has chiefly occupied us.

We owe to Lewis (1979) the case of crazy Heimson, who believes that he—he himself—is David Hume. He is ready to say, 'I am David Hume', 'I wrote the *Treatise*', 'I served my king in France, and was denied a chair in Edinburgh', and so forth, and to behave accordingly, whatever that may come to exactly. In Lewis's view, there should be a sense in which Heimson and Hume believe alike: that is, a sense in which it is not merely true that each conceives himself to be an $x$ such that $x$ is David Hume (for this would give them different beliefs, a false one for $x =$ Heimson, and a true one for $x =$ Hume), but rather, or anyway also, that each has numerically the same belief as the other. Lewis presented several considerations in favour of this view. Abstracting from these, and from the critical discussion in Stalnaker (1981) and Higginbotham (1991), I consider the question, on the view of beliefs about oneself advanced here, to what extent Lewis's view can be sustained.

It cannot, if I am right, be literally sustained. For the anaphoric possibilities for an element in a complement structure, whether (in the terminology developed here) event-like or proposition-like, are limited to these:

(i) The anaphoric element inherits the reference of its antecedent, giving for

Heimson believes that he (himself) is Hume

the logical form

For Heimson $=x$, $(\exists e)$ believes$[x, e, \hat{\ }(\exists e')$ identical$(x, \text{Hume}, e')]$.

(ii) The anaphoric element takes on the same reference, but now given as $\sigma(e)$, expressing the relation of the subject to the state that it is in, giving

For Heimson $=x$, $(\exists e)$ believes$[x, e, \hat{\ }(\exists e')$ identical$(\sigma(e), \text{Hume}, e')]$.

(iii) Besides taking on the reference as $\sigma(e)$, the anaphoric element expresses the thematic relation $\theta(e')$ determined by the events classified by the subordinate predicate, in this case identity. Then we have

For Heimson $=x$, $(\exists e)$ believes$[x, e, \hat{\ }(\exists e')$ identical$(\sigma(e)\ \&\ \theta(e'),\text{Hume}, e')]$.

In none of these cases will Heimson and Hume believe numerically alike.

On the other hand, I suggest, there is a sense in (ii), and therefore in (iii), in which Heimson and Hume do believe alike. Let $\alpha$ and $\beta$ be two belief states satisfying

$\hat{\ }(\exists e')$ identical$(\sigma(e), \text{Hume}, e')$.

Does $\alpha = \beta$? Well, we know that $\alpha = \beta$ if and only if $\sigma(\alpha) = \sigma(\beta)$; but there is as it were nothing *within* $\alpha$ and $\beta$ to distinguish them: they are states of believing that one is David Hume, possibly the same, possibly different, depending upon whether the bearers $\sigma(\alpha)$ and $\sigma(\beta)$ of those states are the same or different. In this sense, they are alike.

For an analogy, consider two collapses of bridges. Are they the same collapse, or different collapses? Ignoring time, we may say that they are the same if the bridges are the same, otherwise different. But in so far as they are given merely as collapses of bridges, there is nothing to tell them apart. It is not just a matter of one-to-one correspondences. It is true that two squares of natural numbers are identical just in case the numbers of which they are the squares are identical; but the numbers are already given as the same or different independently of this consideration. With events and states, I am suggesting, this is not so (and perhaps this counts in some degree against thinking of events as objects). Events of the same kind are discriminated through their participants, rather than intrinsically. I conclude, then, that we have a strong sense in which Heimson and Hume believe alike.

In this contribution I have been defending a version of Castañeda's original view, that there is something special about first-personal reports of thoughts. An issue for this view that was raised early on, in Kretzmann (1966), was: could anyone other than $x$ know what $x$ knows when $x$ knows something first-personal about $x$? Could even God know it? Reviewing the discussion, Perry (1983) cites Castañeda's response (Castañeda 1968), which I paraphrase as follows.

Suppose that John is in the hospital, and he knows in the ordinary way that he himself is in the hospital. What he knows is a fact or true proposition, $p$ say. Evidently, many others may know, and God in particular is bound to know, that John knows $p$. But $p$ itself is a consequence, and a pretty trivial one at that, of what they then know. We would be, to put it mildly, surprised to learn that whereas $x$ knows that John knows $p$, $x$ does not know $p$; and such incapacity is out of the question where God is concerned. So we may assume that $x$ knows $p$, and it follows in particular that God knows $p$.

The above reasoning is all very well; but it does not apply to the construction of first-person knowledge given here. Suppose we had taken up *John knows that he is in the hospital* merely as the proposition expressed by:

(46) For John $=x$ $(\exists e)$ knows$[x, e, \, \hat{}\, (\exists e')$ in-hospital$(x, e')]$.

From (46) there follows, knowledge being knowledge of truth, (47), where $\alpha$ is the person John:

(47) $(\exists e')$ in-hospital$(\alpha, e')$.

Thus Castañeda's response to Kretzmann would be vindicated. But we are supposing that the peculiarly first-personal reading of our target sentence is given by:

(48) For John $=x$ $(\exists e)$ knows$[x, e, \, \hat{}\, (\exists e')$ in-hospital$(\sigma(e) \, \& \, \theta(e'), e')]$,

and from knowledge of what (48) expresses we would have to be able to infer:

(49)  $(\exists e')$ in-hospital$(\sigma(\beta), e')$,

where $\beta$ is the state of knowledge that John is in. But this is too much to ask: from the fact that I know that there is some state $e$ or other such that John knows that its subject (him, John) is in the hospital, I cannot derive the knowledge, with respect to any state $\beta$ at all, that the subject of that state is in the hospital; to suppose otherwise would be as wrong as to suppose that merely by knowing that someone or other knows that he is in the hospital I could come to know, with respect to a particular person, that that person is in the hospital.[14]

I suppose we should concede that it would be different with God. For (49) expresses one of the things that there is to be known; and God knows everything. That case apart, we have a further dividend of the account suggested here: for John, being himself *in* the state $\beta$, can be expected to know what (49) expresses; but others in general will not, even if they know what is expressed by (48).

Of course, it does not follow that no one other than John and God can know what is expressed by (49). On the contrary, there is at least so far no intrinsic reason to suppose that one cannot have knowledge of John's state of knowledge as one has knowledge of other events and states. Events and states, I have suggested, have their participants essentially, so that no one other than John can *be* in the state $\beta$; but nothing about knowledge of $\beta$ follows from that.

We have at this point bumped up against some familiar philosophical questions of privacy, even perhaps 'privileged access', and so forth, which I shall not consider here. However, it may be observed that the construction lends credibility both to the thesis that there is a special way in which one is given to oneself when one knows in a first-personal way that one is in the hospital (or driving a car, or looking around the room, etc.), *and* that this special way is, *mutatis mutandis*, available to all.

A final example. In this discussion I have concentrated upon the properties of understood subjects, construed here as PRO. It happens that this particular element occurs only in one place in English and other languages, namely as the subject of a clausal or nominal complex lacking a tense.[15]

---

[14] Compare the discussion in Perry (1983), 88.

[15] There has been a lengthy debate in the linguistics literature about whether PRO

However, we can, so to speak, tease the effects of PRO into another position by taking it as the antecedent of a reciprocal construction, as in:

(50)  $a$ and $b$ remembered/imagined [PRO kissing each other],

where we are interested in the interpretation according to which each remembered or imagined the reciprocal kissing (and not the one where each merely remembered or imagined kissing the other).[16] Even if the events remembered by $a$ and $b$ are the same, they are given to them in different ways. For, on the account suggested here, $a$'s memory is given to $a$ as of concurrent events $e'$ and $e''$, and through a memorial state $e$ such that

$$\text{kiss}(\sigma(e) \,\&\, \theta_1(e'), b, e') \,\&\, \text{kiss}(b, \sigma(e) \,\&\, \theta_2(e''), e''),$$

where $\theta_1$ expresses agency, and $\theta_2$, say, the 'undergoing' relation, whereas not only is $b$'s memorial state different, but also the roles are reversed, as in

$$\text{kiss}(\sigma(e) \,\&\, \theta_1(e'), a, e') \,\&\, \text{kiss}(a, \sigma(e) \,\&\, \theta_2(e''), e'').$$

I believe that these consequences are in accord with intuition. If so, then we can, so to speak, push the properties of PRO into the direct-object position, as we can in verbal passives, such as *a remembers PRO being kissed by b*. That language, or English anyway, provides us with only a small window for the direct expression of the peculiarities of certain first-person thoughts is not, therefore, of itself a reason to doubt their existence.

# REFERENCES

ALMOG, J., *et al.*, eds. (1989), *Themes From Kaplan* (Oxford: Oxford University Press).

BARTSCH, R., *et al.*, eds. (1990), *Language in Action* (Dordrecht: Foris Publications).

occurs as the subject of nominals as well as clauses, a matter I do not consider in the present discussion.

[16] The example is a case of 'partial control' in the sense of Landau (2000), ch. 2, in the sense that the subject position of what each remembers includes the other as well as herself. As remarked briefly above, partial control, which brings the *de se* in its wake, threatens the Lewis–Chierchia picture of the subject as disappearing under abstraction.

CAMPBELL, J. (1999), 'Immunity to Error Through Misidentification and the Meaning of a Referring Term', *Philosophical Topics*, 26: 89–104.

CASTAÑEDA, H.-N. (1966), "He*: A Study in the Logic of Self-Consciousness', *Ratio*, 8: 130–57.

—— (1967), 'Indicators and Quasi-Indicators', *American Philosophical Quarterly*, 4: 85–100.

—— (1968), 'On the Logic of Attributions of Self-Knowledge to Others', *Journal of Philosophy*, 65: 439–56.

CHIERCHIA, G. (1990), 'Anaphora and Attitudes *De Se*', in Bartsch *et al.* (1990), 1–31.

CHOMSKY, N. (1981), *Lectures on Government and Binding* (Dordrecht: Foris Publications).

FODOR, J. A. (1975), *The Language of Thought* (New York: Crowell).

FREGE, G. (1918), 'The Thought: A Logical Inquiry', trans. A. M. and M. Quinton, in Strawson (1967), 17–38.

HIGGINBOTHAM, J. (1989), 'Reference and Control', *Rivista di linguistica*, 1: 301–26; repr. with minor revisions in Larson *et al.* (1989), 79–108 [cited from the reprint].

—— (1991), 'Belief and Logical Form', *Mind and Language*, 6: 344–69.

—— (1995), 'Tensed Thoughts', *Mind and Language*, 10: 226–49; repr. in Kühne, Newen, and Anduschus (1997), 21–48 [cited from the reprint].

—— (forthcoming), 'Tensed Second Thoughts: Comments on Richard', in A. Jokič, ed., *Time, Tense, and Reference* (Cambridge, Mass.: MIT Press).

HUANG, Y. (2000), *Anaphora: A Cross-Linguistic Study* (Oxford: Oxford University Press).

ISRAEL, D., and PERRY, J. (1996), 'Where Monsters Dwell', in Seligman and Westerståhl (1996), 1–14.

KAPLAN, D. (1977), 'Demonstratives', published with Afterthoughts in Almog *et al.* (1989), 481–614.

—— (1995), 'Meaning as Use' (Gareth Evans Memorial Lecture, University of Oxford, 1995; unpublished).

KRETZMANN, N. (1966), 'Omniscience and Immutability', *Journal of Philosophy*, 63: 409–21.

KÜNNE, W., NEWEN, A., and ANDUSCHUS, M., eds. (1997), *Direct Reference, Indexicality, and Propositional Attitudes* (Stanford, Calif.: CSLI Publications).

LANDAU, I. (2000), *Elements of Control: Structure and Meaning in Infinitival Constructions* (Dordrecht: Kluwer).

LARSON, R., IATRIDOU, S., LAHIRI, U., and HIGGINBOTHAM, J., eds. (1989), *Control and Grammar* (Dordrecht: Kluwer, 1990).

LEWIS, D. (1979), 'Attitudes *De Dicto* and *De Se*', *Philosophical Review*, 88: 513–43.

MONTAGUE, R. (1969), 'On the Nature of Certain Philosophical Entities', *Monist*, 53: 159–94; repr. in Montague (1974), 148–87 [cited from the reprint].

—— (1974), *Formal Philosophy*, ed. R. Thomason (New Haven: Yale University Press).

PEACOCKE, C. (1981), 'Demonstrative Thought and Psychological Explanation', *Synthèse*, 49: 187–217.

—— (1998), *Being Known* (Oxford: Oxford University Press).

PERRY, J. (1983), 'Castañeda on *He* and *I*', in Tomberlin (198), 15–39; repr. in Perry (2000), 77–100 [cited from the reprint].

—— (2000), *The Problem of the Essential Indexical and Other Essays*, expanded edn. (Stanford, Calif.: CSLI Publications).

PRYOR, J. (1999), 'Immunity to Error through Misidentification', *Philosophical Topics*, 26: 271–304.

SCHLENKER, P. (1999), 'Propositional Attitudes and Indexicality: A Cross-Categorial Approach' (Ph.D. diss., MIT).

—— (forthcoming), 'A Plea for Monsters', *Linguistics and Philosophy*.

SELIGMAN, J., and WESTERSTÅHL, D., eds. (1996), *Logic, Language, and Computation*, vol. i (Stanford, Calif.: CSLI Publications).

SHOEMAKER, S. (1968), 'Self-Reference and Self-Awareness', *Journal of Philosophy*, 65: 555–67.

—— (1970), 'Persons and their Pasts', *American Philosophical Quarterly*, 7: 269–85.

STALNAKER, R. C. (1981), 'Indexical Belief', *Synthèse*, 49:; 129–51; repr. in Stalnaker (1999), 130–49 [cited from the reprint].

—— (1999), *Context and Content* (Oxford: Oxford University Press).

STRAWSON, P. F., ed. (1967), *Philosophical Logic* (Oxford: Oxford University Press).

TOMBERLIN, J. E., ed. (1983), *Agent, Language, and the Structure of the World: Essays Presented to Hector-Neri Castañeda, with his Replies* (Indianapolis: Hackett).

# Index

## DATE DUE

RET'D FEB 01 2010